THE COMPLETE BOOK OF

MONEY
SECRETS

THE COMPLETE BOOK OF

MONEY SECRETS

Reader's Digest

The Reader's Digest Association, Inc.,
Pleasantville, New York / Montreal

STAFF

Project Editor
Audrey M. Peterson

Designer
Wendy Wong

Associate Editor
Linda Ingroia

Production Artist
William McGuire

Senior Production Supervisor
Michael Gallo

Special thanks
Carolyn T. Chubet
Edmund H. Harvey, Jr.
Jenny Mann
Suzanne Weiss

CONTRIBUTORS

Editor
Barbara Bedway

Consultants
Barbara Weltman (Tax law)
Edward F. Mrkvicka, Jr. (Banking)

Illustrator
Dennis Dittrich

Copy Editor
Gina Grant

Indexer
Sydney Wolfe Cohen

READER'S DIGEST COOKING, HOME, CONSUMER BOOKS

Group Editorial Director
Carol A. Guasti

READER'S DIGEST GENERAL BOOKS

Vice President, Editor-in-Chief
Christopher Cavanaugh

Art Director
Joan Mazzeo

Operations Manager
William Cassidy

Published by the Reader's Digest Association, Inc.,1999, by arrangement with Boardroom Books.

Reader's Digest and the Pegasus logo are registered trademarks of The Reader's Digest Association, Inc.

Printed in the United States of America

Reader's Digest publishes the advice of expert authorities in many fields. But the use of a book is not a substitute for legal, accounting, or other professional services. Consult a competent professional for answers to your specific questions.

Address comments about *The Complete Book of Money Secrets* to Editor, U.S. General Books, c/o Customer Service, Reader's Digest, Pleasantville, NY 10570.

To order additional copies of *The Complete Book of Money Secrets*, call 1-800-846-2100.

You can also visit us on the World Wide Web at http://www.readersdigest.com

Library of Congress Cataloging in Publication Data

The Complete Book of Moneys Secrets / Reader's Digest.

        p.   cm.

      Money secrets.

      Includes bibliographical references and index.

      ISBN 0-7621-0131-8

      1. Finance, Personal. I. Reader's Digest Association. II.

      Title: Money Secrets.

HG179.C6635 1999

332'.024—dc21   98-49625

ABOUT THIS BOOK

Do you ever get the feeling that other people know how to handle their money better than you do? That there's information to help you manage your money, but you don't know how to get it?

Help is here. *The Complete Book of Money Secrets* provides all the practical information you need to help you handle medical costs, deal with banks, plan for retirement, pay for an education, buy or sell your home, start or run a business, grow your money, and more.

At your fingertips are14 clearly-organized chapters containing more than 700 easy-to-read entries of financial advice from top experts in every money-related field— advice you can use every day.

The Complete Book of Money Secrets also helps you keep your hard-earned money by avoiding extra bank fees, unnecessary medical charges, and excessive insurance.

Concise, easy-to-understand articles take the mystery out of shrewd investing and the mishaps out of retirement planning. Straightforward language eases the doubts of financial decision-making. You'll learn how to make your money work harder, go further, and grow faster.

With top-notch advice at your fingertips, this book can help you get a sharper financial edge, and give you the peace of mind you deserve.

-The Editors

CONTENTS

4 For Businesspeople Only

5 Dealing With Banks, Credit & Debt

6 Holding the Line On Medical Costs

7 Friends, Family & Your Money

Health Insurance

Disability Insurance

Home Insurance

Auto Insurance

Insurance Traps

11 Estate Planning

12 Investing to Win

Investment Advice

Stocks

14 Buying & Selling a House, Condo or Co-op

Smart Money Management

1

The Most Common Mistakes In Personal Financial Planning

More families should note Ben Franklin's observation that "in this world nothing is certain but death and taxes." Many intelligent people don't know how to achieve their life goals, provide for their families or prepare for the death of the main income earner.

Take full control of your life—before you begin to invest. Of the many errors families make in money management, 12 are repeated constantly:

● **Only one family member is involved in financial affairs.** One spouse should have ultimate responsibility for decision making, but both should be involved in financial planning and in meetings with accountants and lawyers.

Bonus: Goals are more easily met if both partners pull in the same direction.

● **Life goals are not on paper.** Write down your goals, attach a dollar amount to them and weigh their relative importance.

● **There is no family budget.** Budget carefully, so you know what you're spending. It's easier to change what you spend than what you earn.

● **The family has no excess liability (umbrella) insurance.** Acquiring this type of insurance could be one of the wisest investments you ever make.

● **The contents of your home are not insured up to their replacement value.** To maintain your standard of living, buy replacement-cost coverage. Discuss exceptions with your insurance agent.

● **There is insufficient liquidity to handle emergencies or opportunities.** Create a war chest. Have emergency funds available equal to three to six months of spending money. Use your budget to arrive at an exact figure.

● **Tax reduction is used as a goal.** People devote too much attention to reducing taxes when they should be concentrating on accumulating wealth.

● **Employee benefits are poorly understood.** Maximize your contributions to payroll savings and 401(k) plans with corporate matching. They are the best tax-deferral mechanisms among voluntary retirement programs.

> **" Mistake: Tax reduction is used as a goal. People devote too much attention to reducing taxes when they should be concentrating on accumulating wealth."**

Also, make sure your group disability plan is adequate. Check for inflation protection, partial disability coverage, lifetime benefits and "own occupation" definition of disability—all of which most plans exclude. You can purchase a residual wrap policy that fills in some of the holes.

● **Investments are not diversified.** Buy non-specialty mutual funds, such as index funds. They are a relatively inexpensive way to play the market while making your first significant investment step a diversified one.

● **A general-practice attorney drafts the family's wills,** trusts and durable powers-of-attorney. Consult an estate-planning specialist, especially if your life insurance and death benefits equal $625,000 or more.

● **No tax projections are made.** Know the tax weather so you can better decide which "investment clothes" to wear. Read the financial pages regularly and consult with professionals.

● **Income earners do not have disability insurance.** Know your disability coverage needs and seek adequate protection. It is well worth your time and effort to do so. Most agents do not push this type of policy (because it's hard to explain the importance of it or because the commissions are lower than those on whole life insurance).

Generally, you should get as much disability coverage as the insurance company will let you have. Disability differs from life insurance in that companies are reluctant to sell you so much coverage that you would have no incentive to return to work.

Source: Charles Haines, president, Haines Financial Advisors, 302 Ash Place, 2100 16 Ave. S, Birmingham, AL 35205. The fee-only firm specializes in financial planning for families, professionals and small-business owners.

How to Apply Sophisticated Financial Techniques to Personal Finances

When finances become complicated, they often become clouded as well. When you're dealing with a variety of assets, investments, and income sources, it can be hard to focus clearly on how well things are really going for you financially.

The wizards who run the financial affairs of large corporations have developed analytical tools to deal with this problem by providing clear answers in crucial areas. These tools are just as useful for diagnosing your personal financial health.

In order to get valid and useful figures, you must begin with accurate data. A net worth statement, a cash-flow analysis and a taxable income statement should contain all the numbers you need. Simply plug the appropriate figures into the formulas below.

These tools should help you put your personal financial picture in perspective, but keep in mind that, unlike a business, there are no "objective" guidelines to follow in shaping your personal financial future. Only you can accurately assess the weight you give to factors of personal circumstance.

For example, a married couple with a taxable income in 1998 of $110,000 would have had a federal marginal tax rate of 31%. This is the percent of each investment dollar they are paying in federal taxes. At present, they have $100,000 in a taxable money-market account earning 5% ($5,000 annual income). Their after-tax return is 3.45%

$$\frac{[\$7,000 \times (1 - .31)] + 0}{\$100,000}$$

They then use this figure and compare it with tax-free money-market yields to determine which has a better after-tax return.

The same couple has monthly expenses of $6,000 and their Expense Coverage Ratio is:

$$\frac{\$100,000}{\$6,000} = 16.7 \text{ months}$$

This should highlight to them that they are being overly conservative and can invest the funds (within their risk tolerance) at a higher return. *Note:* Many financial advisers use a rule of thumb of keeping enough liquid funds to cover six months' expenses. Since many factors, including your disability coverage and your attitude, must be taken into account, be careful of rules of thumb.

Source: Joyce A. Streithorst, CFP, is manager of personal financing for Joel Isaacson & Co., a nationally known financial-planning firm based in New York, NY.

TOOL	FORMULA	WHAT IT SHOWS
Liquidity Ratio	$\dfrac{\text{LIQUID ASSETS}}{\text{CURRENT LIABILITIES}}$	Are liquid assets sufficient to meet short-term obligations?
Expense Coverage Ratio	$\dfrac{\text{LIQUID ASSETS}}{\text{MONTHLY EXPENSES}}$	How many months' expenses will your liquid assets cover?
Debt Ratio	$\dfrac{\text{TOTAL ASSETS}}{\text{TOTAL DEBT}}$	How aggressive is your balance sheet?
Working Assets Ratio	$\dfrac{\text{INVESTMENT ASSETS}}{\text{TOTAL ASSETS}}$	How much of your net worth is working for you?
Marginal Tax Rate	$\dfrac{\text{TAX RATE (FEDERAL) PAID ON}}{\text{YOUR LAST EARNED DOLLAR}}$	What percentage of each additional dollar will go for taxes?
Work ratio	$\dfrac{\text{EARNED INCOME}}{\text{TOTAL INCOME}}$	How dependent are you on your job to meet income needs?
Fixed Expenses as Percentage of Total Income	$\dfrac{\text{FIXED EXPENSES}}{\text{TOTAL INCOME}}$	How much of your income goes to cover expenses over which you have no control?

After-tax Return on Investment Assets (see formula below).

$$\frac{[\text{Taxable Investment Income} \times (1 - \text{Marginal Tax Rate})] + \text{Nontaxable Income}}{\text{Total Investment Assets}}$$

A Net Worth Calculation

Calculating your net worth is the basic method of determining if you're getting ahead or falling behind in the struggle for financial health. Those who like to keep close tabs on their progress may want to do this frequently; most ought to do it annually. January is a convenient time, since you receive year-end statements and have to do much of this work for your taxes anyway. Hopefully, each year will show you are closer to financial independence—whatever that dollar amount is for you.

Assets

Item 1: **Cash.** Total the contents of your checking and savings accounts, money-market funds, and certificates of deposit.

Item 2: **Nonincome-producing assets.** These include the value of your home (tax assessments or local real estate ads should help you determine this if you're in doubt), vacation home (if you have one and don't rent it out for part of the year), jewelry, automobiles, home furnishings, art and the like.

Item 3: **Insurance.** Determine the cash value of all insurance policies. If you haven't checked recently, it is definitely a good idea to write to your insurers and find out.

Item 4: **Investments.** Check the current value of your stocks and bonds, any rental properties, real estate partnerships, oil and gas partnerships (which may have no current value), gold and silver (and other personal commodities), company stock options, personal collections (stamps, coins, antiques, etc.), notes receivable, and the book value of your business.

Item 5: **Retirement assets.** Add in IRA, Keogh, pension and profit-sharing plans, 401(k), any deferred compensation, and company savings plans.

Be sure to count only the amount you could take from your company if you left tomorrow.

Liabilities

Liabilities include mortgages, bank loans, credit card and any other trade debit balances, and notes due.

Total up the assets. Total up the liabilities. Subtract the liabilities from the assets. That's your net worth—the figure that can help you estimate when to retire or the progress you are making each year to increase your wealth.

Source: Alexandra Armstrong, CFP, president of the independent financial-planning firm Armstrong, Welch and MacIntyre, Inc., 1155 Connecticut Ave. NW, Washington, DC 20036.

HOW MUCH OF YOUR WEALTH SHOULD BE KEPT LIQUID?

Determining the best size of liquid monetary reserves (checking account, savings account, money-market funds) is largely a matter of psychology: What do you feel comfortable with?

Remember that the purpose of keeping liquid assets is to avoid having to disturb your long-term investments in the event you need money. In fact, cash reserves are seen by many people as an emergency hedge. What fewer people see is that you can hold a larger amount as an opportunity reserve, making it easy to take advantage of investment opportunities that come along.

With this in mind, figure that adequate liquid reserves should be a minimum of three months' expenses—not income. When adding up your liquid assets, you may want to include your certificates of deposit, which could be liquidated prior to maturity with the loss of only part of the interest. The possibility of borrowing against the value of your life insurance is another plus.

Source: Alexandra Armstrong, CFP, president of the independent financial-planning firm Armstrong, Welch and MacIntyre, Inc., 1155 Connecticut Ave. NW, Washington, DC 20036.

Cash Flow

Positive cash flow is what counts. You can be getting rich on paper and still not be able to meet your bills—unless you have a positive cash flow. Fortunately, it is not difficult to make a reasonably accurate annual projection of where you stand.

Step 1

Itemize every source of income you have. This will include base salary, any bonuses, commissions, self-employment income, Social Security and pension or other retirement income (if any). Add to that any capital gains you anticipate for the year. Add any interest, dividend, trust fund or other investment income.

Step 2

Figure your yearly expenses. The following spending schedule should cover all of most people's categories of expenditure. If you have others, you can add more headings. The schedule includes this year and next so you can record the past and plan for the future. This way you can avoid the emergency expense—because you will have planned for it. Total your expenses and subtract from income. If you come up with a positive number, congratulations—you are accumulating wealth. If the bottom line comes up negative, it's time to trim some of your voluntary (nonfixed) expenditures. *Suggestion:* Consider your retirement contributions and annual investments as expenses to include.

Annual Spending Schedule

These annual figures are for the current year. If you expect next year's expenditures or deductions to vary greatly, indicate them in the second column.

Source: Alexandra Armstrong, CFP, president of the independent financial-planning firm Armstrong, Welch and MacIntyre, Inc., 1155 Connecticut Ave. NW, Washington, DC 20036.

	THIS YEAR	NEXT YEAR
Food/Groceries		
Clothing		
Mortgage Payment(s)		
Utilities		
Telephone		
Dry Cleaner, Drugstore, Hairdresser		
New Household Purchases		
Real Estate Taxes		
Auto Maintenance (gas, repairs, etc.)		
Transportation (cabs, bus, etc.)		
Car Payments		
Entertainment		
Club Dues		
Vacation Trips, Camp		
Domestic Help		
Child Care (deductible)		
Home Maintenance		
Yard/Pool Maintenance		
Subscriptions/Books		
Gifts/Birthdays, Etc.		
Medical Expenses (not reimbursed)		
Insurance Premiums		
—Life		
—Disability		
—Medical		
—Auto		
—Personal Liability		
Alimony		
Child Support		
Regular Allotments to Savings		
Retirement Contributions		
Stock Purchase Plans		
Personal Property Taxes		
Charitable Contributions		
Unreimbursed Business Expenses		
Tax Preparation Fees		
Education		
Legal Fees		
Federal Estimated Tax Payments		
State/Local Estimated Tax Payments		
Other—Source:		

A Plan to Double Your Wealth

The concept of doubling your wealth has little meaning without a specific time frame. If you have any income-producing investments, they will eventually double your wealth without your having to do anything. But doubling your wealth within a target time period calls for some planning.

If invested capital remains constant, the return on investment needed to accomplish your goal can be figured by the "rule of 72": Divide the number 72 by the number of years within which you aim to double your worth. The resulting number is the percentage you must earn on invested capital. Doubling in 10 years will require investments to yield 7.2%; in five years, 14.4%; in two years, 36%.

To find out if your current investment portfolio is producing up to your expectations, do a careful review. Consider liquidating poorly performing investments and reinvesting the capital. A good rule of thumb in deciding whether to keep or sell an investment is: "If I had the cash, would I make this investment now?"

A good wealth-building portfolio is diversified and balanced. A good balance would be about one-third in stocks, one-third in income-producing real estate, one-third in "other" (which includes municipals, annuities and precious metals).

Regardless of how well balanced your portfolio is, your wealth will grow far more rapidly if you augment it with a regular and ongoing program of new investment. This will require some self-education in investment matters to help you work more effectively with your financial adviser. Careful investigation of each new asset prior to purchase reduces your risk. Emphasize updates, too: Regular review of your portfolio on at least an annual basis will give you a better picture of how well your plan is working.

Source: *Alexandra Armstrong, CFP, president of the independent financial-planning firm Armstrong, Welch and MacIntyre, Inc., 1155 Connecticut Ave. NW, Washington, DC 20036.*

Finding a Financial Planner

Most successful people are too busy being successful to spend any serious time analyzing their financial situation, establishing goals and structuring and executing a financial plan that will enable them to achieve these goals. That is what a good financial planner should be able to do—alleviate the time burden on the very people who have the least amount of time to spare.

What to Expect

Financial-planning firms assume responsibility for coordinating your financial affairs—balance your investments, manage your taxes, plan for retirement, plan your estate and, above all, protect your assets. What they will require of you is that you take an inventory of your assets and gather every conceivable kind of financial paper. Once you've provided the necessary information, a planner will analyze your financial profile and issue a comprehensive plan for achieving your major financial objectives. The plan will make recommendations and organize follow-through.

You should receive periodic reports of your financial condition to help you adjust your decisions over time. With a good financial planner, there is no such thing as "one size fits all." A quality planning firm will help you develop the perspective needed to make intelligent financial choices.

What to Look for

Over the past several years, it seems everyone has become a "financial planner." That can make your search a little tricky, but looking for the following characteristics should provide some help.

Professional expertise: Credentials are important. The best credentials in the field are the Chartered Financial Consultant (ChFC) and the Certified Financial Planner (CFP) designations. Some attorneys and accountants also specialize in financial planning.

Resources: Financial planners should work closely with other professionals—attorneys, accountants, tax experts, investment specialists—to cover all of the important financial-planning areas for the client. State-of-the-art computer facilities are almost essential to the firm's ability to work out the tax and other consequences of various planning proposals. Also, a reliable network of contacts throughout major financial circles is an important asset.

Range of offerings: A financial-planning firm should be licensed to offer securities, limited partnerships and insurance—a full range of products to support the plans and strategies of all its clients.

Affiliation with a major institution: Many financial institutions, including banks and investment houses, are now offering financial planning in the same manner that life insurance companies have been doing for many years. A company with a strong long-term reputation can be your best guarantee of superior service.

Source: Randy Breidbart, J.D., former regional director, Mutual Benefit Financial Service Co., 633 Third Ave., New York, NY 10017.

Choosing the Best Financial Planner

A sound professional relationship with a financial planner is vital in today's increasingly complex financial world. A financial planner will help you analyze your current financial situation, define your financial goals, develop a specific plan to achieve those goals and implement the plan.

The first step in choosing a financial planner is familiarizing yourself with the field in general. Read. Talk to knowledgeable friends and professionals. Financial planning is a partnership, and the more knowledgeable the client-partner, the more effective the partnership will be. Furthermore, you will be better able to evaluate the quality of service you are receiving.

The next step is to begin interviewing planners. If you need help in getting names, obtain references from friends or other financial advisers whom you trust. Other possible sources: *The Better Business Bureau's Consumer Resource Book*, the International Association for Financial Planning (IAFP) and the Institute of Certified Financial Planners (ICFP).

Interview a number of practitioners over the telephone. You will soon get a feel for the ones who are likely to be suitable for you. Plan to narrow your choices to three or four and schedule an interview with each. In the interview, you will want to inquire about professional credentials, scope of services, areas of specialization and compensation (fees and/or commissions).

Checklist: Interviewing Financial Planners

When interviewing a prospective financial planner, make sure to cover these vital points:

✔ **Experience.** Three years' track record as a professional financial planner should be considered a minimum. A related background in brokerage, accounting, insurance, etc., is a plus.

✔ **Credentials.** CFP (Certified Financial Planner) and ChFC (Chartered Financial Consultant) credentials indicate extensive education. Admission to the Registry of Practicing Financial Planning Practitioners (maintained by the International Association for Financial Planning) indicates experience as well as expertise.

✔ **Support.** Make sure your planner has full computer services and adequate support staff. A solo practitioner is at a distinct disadvantage today. Many planners are teaming up to offer broader, better service.

✔ **Clients.** How many and what type? Favor a planner who has clients like you. A planner with more than 150 clients is spread too thin, unless he or she has adequate staff to service them. Also find out how many of them renew each year. A 75% client-renewal rate is minimum.

✔ **Reviews.** Are ongoing reviews provided to make the plan current? How does the planner keep clients up-to-date? A regular newsletter and periodic seminars are customary.

✔ **Fees.** Don't expect a personalized plan for less than about $1,500. Fees can go up to many times this figure, consistent with the complexity of your particular situation. Ask beforehand.

✔ **Trust.** Be sure you are comfortable with this person. Trust is an essential factor in producing meaningful results.

Source: Alexandra Armstrong, CFP, president of the independent financial-planning firm Armstrong, Welch and MacIntyre, Inc., 1155 Connecticut Ave. NW, Washington, DC 20036.

Credentials

Two types of certification are available to financial-planning professionals, and they indicate rigorous courses of professional training. The Certified Financial Planner (CFP) designation is awarded to those who successfully complete the comprehensive six-part curriculum of the College for Financial Planning in Denver, Colorado. The Chartered Financial Consultant (ChFC) designation is awarded by the American College, Bryn Mawr, Pennsylvania, following successful completion of its 10-course program.

Both certifications include adherence to a strict code of ethics. The CFP also indicates commitment to a plan of continuing education due to the changing nature of many areas of finance, including investments, insurance and taxes. Planners who offer investment advice must be registered with the Securities and Exchange Commission (SEC).

Continuing educational activities should be on the roster of interview questions. Three organizations sponsor major continuing-education programs in financial planning: The College for Financial Planning, the ICFP and the IAFP, mentioned on p. 23. All three issue certificates of completion for programs attended.

Scope of Services

Does this planner develop a plan that is reviewed and updated periodically? Is there continual contact as investment opportunities arise? How specific is the advice offered? Does your planner suggest investments that may be appropriate for you? What is the planner's role in actually purchasing investments?

Different levels of service may be appropriate to your needs, depending on the size and the activity of your portfolio, your degree of personal involvement, your work situation, etc. For example, many people have done a fine basic job of structuring their investments and may simply need some overall strategic advice or merely the peace of mind that comes from confirmation of the value of their efforts.

Areas of Specialization

Look for a planner who serves clients whose needs are similar to yours. A financial planner who claims to be an expert in many fields should be regarded with some skepticism. A competent planner should have working relationships with other financial-services professionals and be willing to work with the financial advisers you are already using.

Compensation

Find out how much the services are going to cost. On what basis is the planner compensated? Hourly fee? Commissions on financial products sold? Or a combination of the two? The advice of a fee-only planner is generally free from any conflict of interest. When working with a commission-compensated planner, make sure that a variety of financial instruments and products is being offered, not just the ones on which the planner stands to make the largest commission. Investigate the fee-and-commission alternative—it may provide a flexible solution for both parties.

A final qualification is personal compatibility. Your financial planner should be someone whose philosophy and background you respect and with whom you feel comfortable. Clients who have selected carefully can be rewarded with a financial-planning partnership well suited to meeting their personal goals.

Source: *Jan Walsh, MBA, academic associate at the College for Financial Planning, 9725 E. Hampden Ave., Denver, CO 80231. A Certified Financial Planner, she is a member of the ICFP and IAFP and is on the board of directors of the Rocky Mountain Chapter of the IAFP.*

Make an Asset Inventory

If something should happen to you, would your family know where your important papers and assets are? Here's an inventory form that will make this job easier. Give copies to your spouse, perhaps another relative outside your home, any outside executor and your attorney. It will make their jobs easier—and you might locate some neglected assets. Keep blank copies of the form on hand and update your inventory when significant changes take place.

If you have a fireproof lockbox at home that holds your important (nonnegotiable) papers, it is a good place to store your asset inventory. Your spouse (or whomever you designate) should know where this box is and should have access to it. You could also put the inventory in your safe-deposit box, assuming your state does not seal this box upon your death.

Source: *Alexandra Armstrong, CFP, president of the independent financial-planning firm Armstrong, Welch and MacIntyre, Inc., 1155 Connecticut Ave. NW, Washington, DC 20036.*

ASSET INVENTORY

For _____

Social Security number _____

Employer _____

IMPORTANT NAMES, ADDRESSES AND PHONE NUMBERS

Lawyer _____

Accountant _____

Stockbroker _____

Insurance agent _____

Date prepared _____

Copies given to _____

MY VALUABLE PAPERS AND ASSETS ARE STORED IN THESE LOCATIONS:

A. Residence (address and where to look)

B. Safe-deposit box (bank and address)

C. Office (address)

D.

E.

F.

ITEM	LOCATION	A	B	C	D	E	F
1. Estate Planning							
My will (original)							
My will (copy)							
Powers of attorney							
My burial instructions							
Cemetery plot deed							
Spouse's will (original)							
Spouse's will (copy)							
Spouse's burial instructions							
Document appointing children's guardian							
Handwritten list of special bequests							
Safe combination, business							
Safe combination, home							
Trust agreements							
Life insurance, group							
Life insurance, individual							
2. Insurance							
Other death benefits							
Property and casualty insurance							
Health insurance policy							
Home owners insurance policy							
Car insurance policy							
3. Business							
Employment contracts							
Partnership agreements							

ITEM	LOCATION	A	B	C	D	E	F
4. Financial							
List of checking and savings account							
Bank statements, canceled checks							
List of credit cards							
Certificates of deposit							
Checkbooks							
Savings passbooks							
Record of investment securities							
Brokerage account record							
Stock certificates							
Mutual fund shares							
Bonds							
Other securities							
Corporate retirement plan							
Keogh or IRA plan							
Annuity contracts							
Stock option plan							
Stock purchase plan							
Profit-sharing plan							
Income and gift tax returns							
5. Real Estate							
Titles and deeds to real estate and land							
Title insurance							
Rental property records							
Notes & other loan agreements including mortgages							
6. Possessions							
List of stored and loaned valuable possessions							
Auto ownership records							
Boat ownership records							
7. Personal Records							
Birth certificates							
Citizenship papers							
My adoption papers							
Military discharge papers							
Marriage certificates							
Children's birth certificates							
Children's adoption papers							
Divorce/separation records							
Names and addresses of relatives and friends							
Listing of professional memberships							
Listing of fraternal organization memberships							
Other:							

How to Handle Financial Paperwork

Here's a quick quiz to give yourself. Do you honestly know...

- **Where all your important financial papers are?**
- **How long to keep those papers?**
- **Which papers should be stored where?**

Most people would answer "no" to all three questions. Any "no" answer should indicate that it is time to go through all your important papers and records and get them organized.

Start by dedicating a file drawer or small file cabinet to your financial record keeping. Anything less than that will prove to be inadequate over time.

Keep one section of the file cabinet or drawer for files that you will have to handle often during the year. Keep another section for files that will hold permanent information.

Getting Started

Next, go through the records you currently keep...file by file, envelope by envelope, paper stack by paper stack. Follow these rules on what to keep and where to keep it:

Current records: Files you may have to update regularly. Keep these files at home in your file drawer or cabinet.

- **Auto insurance.** Policy, claim forms, records of claims filed and paid.
- **Bank statements.** Use separate files for checking, savings, certificates of deposit.
- **Charge accounts.** Have one file for each creditor. File bills and records of payments.
- **Credit cards.** File statements and records of payment. Also keep a readily available list of credit card numbers and the phone number to call if a card is lost or stolen.
- **Health insurance.** Policies, benefits explanations, claim forms, records of claims filed and claims paid.

- **Home insurance.** Home or apartment insurance, fire insurance, umbrella liability policies.
- **Mortgage statements.** Keep records of statements and evidence of payment.
- **Personal loan agreements.** Keep records of payments on all loans you owe to others...and of all loans others owe to you.
- **Retirement accounts.** Keep separate files for IRAs, Keoghs, 401(k)s, profit-sharing and stock-option plans and pension statements.
- **Stockbroker statements.** Keep records of all purchases and sales.

Long-term records: Files you have to handle rarely. Keep these at home or, when indicated, in a safe-deposit box at the bank.

Caution: Keep valuables and vital papers in a safe-deposit box, but don't overdo it. The box may be sealed when you die, so wills, cemetery deeds and life insurance policies kept there may be inaccessible just when they are needed the most.

Be sure someone you trust knows where the box is located, where the key is and what you keep in the box.

- **Life insurance.** Current policies and copies of the summary statements highlighting the terms of the policy. *Also useful:* List each policy by name of insurance company and policy number. It is usually possible to make a claim with only this information, without the policy itself. Throw out policies you have canceled.
- **Will.** File copies of the current will. Keep a copy at home in an accessible location. You can keep originals in your safe-deposit box and/or with your lawyer.
- **Living will.** Give copies to family members or close friends, your attorney and others who should know your wishes. Keep one copy accessible at home.
- **Power of attorney.** Copies of power of attorney forms giving you power over others' accounts or giving others power over your own accounts. Whoever holds your power of attorney should have a copy. So should your attorney.

> **"Long-term records:** Keep a separate folder for each year. By law you should keep all tax records for at least three years—tax returns and all backup. Be safe...keep them for seven years. In fact, keep copies of your actual returns indefinitely.**"**

● **Durable power of attorney** for health care or health care proxy. Same as above.

● **Social Security cards.** Make a photocopy of each family member's Social Security card. Originals can be stored in a safe-deposit box.

● **Birth certificates.** Make copies for each family member. Keep the originals in your safe-deposit box.

● **Marriage,** separation, divorce and prenuptial agreements, adoption papers. Keep in your safe-deposit box.

● **Military discharge papers.** Keep in your safe-deposit box.

● **Real estate.** Keep deeds and title insurance in your safe-deposit box.

● **Trust agreements.** For trusts you set up or of which you are the beneficiary. Originals should be kept in a safe-deposit box. Leave copies with your lawyer and trustees.

● **Partnership agreements.** Keep in your safe-deposit box.

● **Burial arrangements.** Include cemetery deeds and instructions. Give copies to family members or friends who will have to make arrangements.

Tax Records

This is such an important area, it should be treated separately. First of all:

Current records: Mark a file folder "1999" for all tax-related information for the year.

When your checks are returned with your bank statement, segregate checks that are important in the preparation of your taxes. Make photocopies of them and file them in the folder for the current year's taxes. Keep the originals together with each bank statement.

Long-term records: Keep a separate folder for each year. By law you should keep all tax records for at least three years—tax returns and all backup. Be safe and keep them for seven years. In fact, keep copies of your actual returns indefinitely. Just throw out the

Keeping on Top

At the end of each year, go through each current file. Save annual summary statements… all current insurance policies and outstanding loans…all claims and other matters that are still pending…all documents necessary for your taxes and for establishing the value of the assets you own.

Source: Alexandra Armstrong, CFP, president of the independent financial-planning firm Armstrong, Welch and MacIntyre, Inc., 1155 Connecticut Ave. NW, Washington, DC 20036.

backup after seven years.

For any year in which you buy or sell real estate, keep the tax returns and backup to the transaction. Keep the returns and backup, too, for any major renovations to the property. You will need this information in order to establish the cost basis, on which any capital gain will be figured.

Assets That You Own

● **Stocks and other securities.** Keep confirmation statements from your stockbroker when you purchase any stock until seven years after you sell it. You need this to establish your cost and selling price for tax purposes.

● **Mutual funds.** The monthly statement summarizes all transactions—shares purchased and sold—during that period. Subsequent monthly statements may recapitulate this data from the beginning of the year. If so, throw out the previous months' statements and keep only the most current one.

Keep each annual statement from the fund that summarizes the year's activities…basically forever. You will need the information to figure out your cost basis when you sell shares.

Source: Alexandra Armstrong, CFP, president of the independent financial-planning firm Armstrong, Welch and MacIntyre, Inc., 1155 Connecticut Ave. NW, Washington, DC 20036.

Protect Your Assets From Personal Financial Crisis

These days, most professionals and businesspeople can easily and unexpectedly find themselves embroiled in a financial conflict that could cost them most of their assets: Doctors, lawyers and other professionals sued for malpractice or misconduct; business owners who must fight liability suits; anyone dealing with whopping medical bills to cover a long-term illness; people who can't get enough insurance or can't afford to pay for the coverage they need.

In this escalating crisis, the best self-defense is to get assets out of your name far in advance of any trouble with creditors. Although judges don't look kindly on people who transfer their assets in order to defraud creditors, the longer the time between a transfer and a court judgment, the less likely the transfer will be deemed fraudulent. (Once you're involved in a suit or have been dunned by creditors, all transfers—no matter what the purpose—are considered fraudulent and can be reversed.)

Caution: Don't overdo it. If you impoverish yourself, the transfers won't stand up in court as estate and tax-planning measures, and you'll run into serious financial difficulties even if you're never sued.

Effective Strategies

● **Setting up a "family personal holding company" lets you keep control** of your assets while transferring ownership of most of them out of your name. *How it works:* You establish a corporation, giving yourself a relative majority of the stock and dividing the rest among family members. *Example:* You issue 100 shares: 30 for you, 25 for your spouse, and 15 for each of your three children. You then give your assets to the corporation as a gift, managing them yourself as chairman of the board. If you're sued, creditors can only take your 30 shares, a minority interest in a private company, which isn't very useful. In many cases, creditors will be willing to settle for much less than originally demanded if it's in a more liquid form (cash, publicly traded stocks, bonds, etc.).

Drawback: You must pay gift tax on transfers of more than $10,000 (adjusted annually for inflation after 1998) to family members other than your spouse. (You're allowed to give away up to $650,000 in your

> "Umbrella liability... which protects... above and beyond the limits of your home owners and automobile insurance...is the best...bargain there is, costing only about $200 a year for coverage of up to $5 million."

lifetime—increasing to $1 million in 2006 and after.) You should also be concerned about the tax consequences of placing assets in a corporation.

Since this type of asset transfer is a legitimate estate-planning tool (it helps lower inheritance taxes), a judge is unlikely to invalidate the transfer as long as it's done in advance of creditor troubles.

● **Spendthrift trusts are an effective way to protect inheritances** and other windfalls from ending up in your creditor's hands. *How it works:* A trust is set up with you as beneficiary and another party—spouse, lawyer, close friend—as trustee. Wording in the trust states that its assets can't be used to pay creditors. People who intend to will or to give you money—for example, your parents—then give it to the trust instead.

Drawback: You lose control of your money to the trustee, although you can have the trustee removed if he or she violates the rules of the trust.

● **Giving away assets to family members is effective,** as long as the giveaways aren't used to defraud someone. *Guidelines:* A gift must be given well in advance of credit difficulties, and the receiver has to exercise control over the gift—and be able to prove it—not merely serve as a front.

Drawbacks: Possible gift tax and complete loss of control over the assets you give away. In the event of a falling-out with the receiver (such as a divorce), you may regret the gift.

Alternative: Transferring assets into either an irrevocable or a reversionary trust, of which your heirs are the beneficiaries and a trusted third party is named trustee.

Advantages: With both types of trusts, you can give assets to family members even if you can't trust them to manage the assets wisely. With a reversionary trust, the assets are returned to you at a prearranged date in the future.

Trap: Once back in your name, the assets are again fair game for creditors.

● **Company pension plans are one of the easiest ways to sequester funds from creditors.** If you don't have access to the funds, neither does anyone else. However, creditors can attach distributions from the plan. Unprotected are retirement plans in which you do have access to the money, such as an IRA (but not a Keogh).

● **Gift-leasebacks can be used to give property to an individual,** trust or corporation, which then leases it back to you for your use, but not for your control.

● **Life insurance policy cash values can't be touched by creditors.**

Trap: Investment-advantaged insurances, such as single premium annuities, may not be protected.

Less Effective Strategies

● **Joint ownership.** In most states, judges will trace assets held jointly to see which party contributed to them and then determine the portion that can be attached by creditors. Avoid moving your assets into a joint bank or brokerage account with someone who contributes little or nothing. You might, however, be slightly better off with assets in joint ownership than in your own name because getting assets from a joint account requires extra legal proceedings that might encourage creditors to settle for a lesser amount.

● **Power-of-attorney accounts.** Transferring your assets to an account in a relative's name—while retaining control yourself—is better than leaving them in your own name, but it's certainly not safe. A judge will probably rule that the account is de facto yours. The earlier you set up such an arrangement, the more likely it will survive a court test.

● **Home ownership.** Your family's residence is protected from creditors by state law, but in most states, only up to a relatively small size or value.

After the Fact

Once you've been sued by a creditor, there's little you can do to protect your assets. *Bad idea:* To liquidate your assets for cash, gold coins or precious gems and hide them in a cookie jar or foreign bank. Such schemes are illegal and dangerous.

What can happen: The court can dig into your financial records—as far back as it wants to go. If the records show that you once had $1 million and now have nothing, you'll be asked, under oath, what happened to it. Refuse to tell, and you're on your way to jail for contempt of court. Lie and get caught, and you've perjured yourself into jail.

Strong defense: You might be able to substantially limit damage to your finances by setting up a variation on the family personal holding company

described on p. 29. Set up the corporation, but give all of its stock to family members. The corporation then issues shares of preferred stock equal in value to your assets, and you exchange your assets for that preferred stock, tax-free. The preferred stock pays, say, 6% interest a year. *Result:* The holding company now owns your assets, and the transfer is unlikely to be considered fraudulent because you didn't really give away your assets—you exchanged them for something of equal fair market value (the preferred stock). And that's all creditors can get from you. That might be all it takes to convince the creditors to settle for less.

....

Source: *Attorneys Mark N. Kaplan, partner, Skadden, Arps, Slate, Meagher & Flom, New York, NY, and Peter J. Strauss, senior partner, Strauss & Wolf, New York, NY.*

More on Protecting Your Hard-Earned Assets

Insurance

● **Mistake:** *Having no umbrella liability policy,* which protects you against liability above and beyond the limits of your home owners and automobile insurance policies (usually $100,000). This is the best insurance bargain there is, costing only about $200 a year for coverage of up to $5 million. Yet an amazing number of people don't have it.

● **Mistake:** *Having no disability insurance coverage.* At any given age, there's a much greater chance of becoming disabled than of dying. *Example:* At age 42, you're four times as likely to be disabled as to die before age 65. If you have no disability coverage and do lose the ability to earn a living, you and your family will have no choice but to live off of your assets—as long as they last.

Trap: In selecting a disability policy, be careful about the definition of disability. You want to be covered if you can't do your regular job.

A good noncancelable, guaranteed renewable policy will be expensive—about $1,980 a year for a 35-year-old lawyer to replace 60% of a $100,000 annual income for life—somewhat less so if you elect a longer waiting period than the standard 90 days. The insurance proceeds are generally nontaxable.

● **Mistake:** *Inadequate malpractice insurance.*

SAVINGS ARE COMING BACK INTO STYLE

The United States has one of the lowest savings rates in the world, placing us at the bottom of the list of industrialized nations. We save less than 5% of our income each year, compared with 12% in Germany and 20% in Japan.

In the short run, our penchant to spend rather than save isn't all negative. High consumer spending ultimately translates into a growing economy. However, over time, a low savings rate means less money is available for businesses to borrow and to invest in new plants and equipment. That means a decrease in the amount of capital goods made each year. When a nation's capital creation declines, so does its standard of living.

Who's to blame? The baby boomers—those in their thirties and forties, who make up the largest component of our population. They are spending like crazy and saving next to nothing. With their rising salaries and easy credit, most are spending beyond their means and digging into debt.

Problem: Many baby boomers are not planning for the future. Most don't even know what it will take to achieve their most basic goals: buying a home, sending their kids to college, retiring without depending on other people or the government for assistance.

Typical Example

Bob and Helen have a combined salary of $50,000 and two children ages seven and 10. They have no savings and no debt, and they want to send their children to $10,000-per-year colleges. Bob and Helen figure that if they save 5% of their income, they will have plenty for retirement.

Harsh reality: When retirement time rolls around, Bob and Helen will be $31,000 in debt.

The situation is far from hopeless. By making some small adjustments, Bob and Helen can get themselves back on sound financial footing.

● **First, they must take steps to reduce the educational expenses for their children.** By choosing less expensive schools, taking out student loans, and sending the children to work during the summer, Bob and Helen can scale back anticipated college costs from $10,000 per year to $3,000. If they save the difference and invest it at a modest tax-deferred rate of 3% (after inflation), they will have accumulated a net worth of $70,000 by retirement time.

● **Simply by selling a rarely used boat and trailer** (nonearning assets) for $10,000 and investing the money, they can boost their retirement nest egg to $94,000.

● **If they can manage to save 10% of their income rather than only 5%,** their net worth will go up to $207,000.

● **If they put some of their passbook-account savings into safe stocks,** increasing their real overall return from 3% to 5%, their net worth at retirement will increase to $293,000.

Although these steps are small, it takes planning and discipline to execute them effectively.

The Sooner, the Better

The earlier you start, the easier it is to save what you need for retirement.

The magic of compound interest makes smaller savings grow faster over long periods of time.

Example: Let's say your goal is to have $500,000 by the time you retire. If you start saving at age 20, you will have to put away only $650 a year at a 10% average return to reach your goal by age 65. If you don't start until you are 35, you will need to put away $2,750 per year. At age 50, you will have to save $14,000 per year. And at age 55, you will need to save a whopping $27,500 per year.

Prediction

In the next five to 10 years, many people will realize that they're going to come up short at retirement. They will then change their habits dramatically.

For the past two decades, we have been enjoying the present by sacrificing the future. The time has come to start sacrificing in the present so we can enjoy the future. This is what Japan did after World War II, and it's one of the major reasons that country became the world's second-largest economy.

Source: John Rutledge, Ph.D., chairman and president, Rutledge & Company, Inc., Greenwich, CT.

If you're in a business or profession with a high risk of malpractice liability, be sure to have adequate malpractice protection.

Caution: Home owners and umbrella liability policies do not cover malpractice, so separate insurance is needed.

Important: Read fine print carefully. Legal costs of malpractice defense can be huge. Some policies include legal costs in the maximum amount they will pay. Others don't limit payment for legal costs, so they will actually cover much more.

For best protection with all types of insurance, remember: Higher deductibles usually go along with higher limits of insurance protection to keep the costs in perspective. Your aim should be to protect your assets on the high end. Pick a high-deductible, high-limit policy over a lower deductible with a lower limit. *Example:* $500 deductible with a limit of $1 million, rather than a $100 deductible with a limit of $300,000.

Business Complications

● **Mistake:** *Not putting major assets in the name of the spouse who's at less risk.* It's best to do it now, before a claim arises. The Uniform Fraudulent Conveyance Act, a form of which has been adopted by many states, makes it illegal to protect assets by transferring them for the purpose of defrauding your creditors. Courts can simply set the transfer aside if it was made after the cause of action.

Singles trap: Nonmarried couples may face substantial gift taxes on a transfer of assets, while husbands and wives are allowed to make transfers freely without tax costs.

Divorce trap: In a divorce, most states now mandate equitable distribution of assets, so, in theory, title to assets doesn't matter. Tactically, however, before a judge finally rules, the person who owns the assets has control, can pay lawyers, and generally has the upper hand.

Important: Don't operate as a general partnership

> "Singles trap: Nonmarried couples may face substantial gift taxes on a transfer of assets, while husbands and wives are allowed to make transfers freely without tax costs."

when it can be avoided. Use a limited partnership or a professional corporation (which provides some protection for each shareholder in the event another shareholder does something wrong). Since many complainants name all shareholders when suing, this is not foolproof, but it can help if the complainant is not able to prove that you had any personal involvement or responsibility.

The safest way to protect your home is to transfer title to the lower-risk spouse. Owning the house together as tenants-by-the-entirety (a special form of joint ownership for husbands and wives) provides some measure of protection because creditors can't force the noncreditor spouse out. But they can still get a lien on the house, which would make it difficult to sell.

Caution: The rules differ in every state, so check with a local lawyer.

● **Use different legal entities for different projects.** If your business operates in a building that you also own, for example, put the building in a separate S corporation or a limited partnership properly formed under state law (not a general partnership). If you own several rental properties, put each in a separate legal entity so that if one has a legal problem, the others won't be lost.

Trap: If you're held personally liable, all properties in which you own stock/partnership interests may be at risk. To minimize your liability, avoid signing anything personally—that is, in your own name. Always sign in the corporate name, as an officer of the corporation (XYZ Corporation, by John Doe, president) and be sure to follow all corporate formalities in tax filings, minutes of board meetings, etc., or the courts may not respect the corporation as a legal entity and the limited liability it offers.

● **Separate assets from liabilities in arranging business entities.** *Example:* A manufacturing plant (which entails all kinds of risk) should be separated from other assets. *Helpful:* A limited partnership could own the real estate and lease it to the manufacturing corporation. Another person—such as a trustee for your child—could own the trade name and license it to the manufacturing company. Thus, an injury or a lawsuit filed against the manufacturer might not reach the real estate or trade name assets, which would be insulated from creditors.

Source: *Martin M. Shenkman, MBA, CPA, and attorney-at-law, Teaneck, NJ. He is the author of 14 books on tax and financial matters, the latest of which is* The Estate Planning Guide, *John Wiley & Sons.*

Keep Your Wealth Safe From a Lawsuit

In today's litigious society anyone can be sued. And once sued, anyone can get hit with a judgment that strips away assets.

But with foresight and nimble footwork, you can shield your assets from predators, including the IRS, former spouses, creditors and legal opportunists.

If you think you're at risk of being sued, consult an attorney who specializes in asset protection. Each state's laws are different, and what is legal and advisable depends on individual facts and circumstances. But here are a half dozen successful judgment-proofing techniques to discuss with your attorney:

● **Go abroad**. The surest protection is to move your assets out of reach of U.S. courts. Look for banks or financial institutions in countries that offer a combination of secrecy, low or no taxes for foreigners, financial asset protection trust laws and political stability.

Current favorites: Nevis; the Cook Islands, near New Zealand; Gibraltar; the Turks and Caicos in the Caribbean; and the Isle of Man, near England.

● **Buy insurance and annuities.** Every state offers significant protection of insurance policies from creditors. Protection might also extend to annuities. Therefore, moving money from bank and brokerage accounts into insurance and annuities will often lawsuit-proof those assets. Swiss annuities are fully protected from creditor claims after one year's ownership pursuant to Swiss law.

Even when states offer total insurance protection, the exemption does not extend to claims from the IRS. But you may be able to protect your holdings from the IRS by having an irrevocable life insurance trust own the insurance policies.

● **Set up a family limited partnership.** A limited partnership is a legal entity to which you can transfer assets. A husband and wife can serve as general partners and control the assets. The assets can be owned by trusts to provide an additional layer of protection.

Family limited partnerships give you control over your assets while offering strong creditor protection and an opportunity for creative estate planning and reduced estate taxes.

● **Use irrevocable trusts.** Irrevocable trusts offer asset protection because the trust owns the assets—not you. Among the types of trusts your attorney may recommend are charitable remainder trusts, spendthrift trusts, insurance trusts, and foreign-based trusts. *Tip:* Set up an irrevocable trust only when it serves a purpose other than asset protection.

The very nature of an irrevocable trust is that it cannot be rescinded or modified and that you lose control of the assets, so be 100% sure of what you are doing before you act.

Living trusts, while an excellent way to avoid probate, are generally revocable and useless for asset protection.

● **Know your state exemptions.** Every state specifically exempts certain assets from creditors. For example, Texas and Florida give 100% homestead protection, meaning that a home of any value is safe.

If you live in those states, paying off a mortgage can be a good asset-protection strategy. But in some states, such as New York, only up to $10,000 of a home's value is protected, and in Kentucky it's $5,000.

Thirty-one states, including Florida, allow married couples to protect property by holding it as "tenants-by-the-entirety," so that a creditor of one spouse cannot seize it. IRA and Keogh protection varies from state to state also. Indeed, the list of protected assets in each state is long and often complex. By studying it, you can structure holdings appropriately. ERISA-qualified pensions are generally protected from anyone but the IRS and federal agencies.

The IRS can take assets protected by state law. That is why going offshore or using more complex arrangements is the best protection from the IRS. The harder it is for the IRS to go after your assets, the less likely it is to try.

Source: *Dr. Arnold S. Goldstein, president, The Garrett Group, 384 Military Trail, Deerfield Beach, FL 33442.*

WHAT GOES ON SALE WHEN
Here is a month-by-month schedule for dedicated bargain hunters.

January

- After-Christmas sales
- Appliances
- Baby carriages
- Books
- Carpets and rugs
- China and glassware
- Christmas cards
- Costume jewelry
- Furniture
- Furs
- Lingerie
- Men's overcoats
- Pocketbooks
- Preinventory sales
- Shoes
- Toys
- White goods (sheets, towels, etc.)

February

- Air conditioners
- Art supplies
- Bedding
- Cars (used)
- Curtains
- Furniture
- Glassware and china
- Housewares
- Lamps
- Men's apparel
- Radios, TV sets and stereos
- Silverware
- Sportswear and equipment
- Storm windows
- Toys

March

- Boys' and girls' shoes
- Garden supplies
- Housewares

- Ice skates
- Infants' clothing
- Laundry equipment
- Luggage
- Ski equipment

April

- Fabrics
- Hosiery
- Lingerie
- Painting supplies
- Women's shoes

May

- Handbags
- Housecoats
- Household linens
- Jewelry
- Luggage
- Mother's Day specials
- Outdoor furniture
- Rugs
- Shoes
- Sportswear
- Tires and auto accessories
- TV sets

June

- Bathing suits
- Bedding
- Boys' clothing
- Fabrics
- Father's Day specials
- Floor coverings
- Lingerie, sleepwear and hosiery
- Men's clothing
- Women's shoes

July

- Air conditioners and other appliances
- Bathing suits
- Children's clothes

- Electronic equipment
- Fuel
- Furniture
- Handbags
- Lingerie and sleepwear
- Luggage
- Men's shirts
- Men's shoes
- Rugs
- Sportswear
- Summer clothes
- Summer sports equipment

August

- Back-to-school specials
- Carpeting
- Cosmetics
- Curtains and drapes
- Electric fans and air conditioners
- Furniture
- Furs
- Men's coats
- Silver
- Tires
- White goods
- Women's coats

September

- Bicycles
- Cars (outgoing models)
- China and glassware
- Fabrics
- Fall fashions
- Garden equipment
- Hardware
- Lamps
- Paints

October

- Cars (outgoing models)
- China and glassware
- Fall/winter clothing
- Fishing equipment
- Furniture
- Lingerie and hosiery
- Major appliances
- School supplies
- Silver
- Storewide clearances
- Women's coats

November

- Blankets and quilts
- Boys' suits and coats
- Cars (used)
- Lingerie
- Major appliances
- Men's suits and coats
- Shoes
- White goods
- Winter clothing

December

- Blankets and quilts
- Cards, gifts, toys (after Christmas)
- Cars (used)
- Children's clothes
- Christmas promotions
- Coats and hats
- Men's furnishings
- Resort and cruise wear
- Shoes

A Shopper's Guide To Bargaining

The biggest problem most shoppers have with bargaining is a feeling that nice people don't do it. Before you can negotiate, you have to get over this attitude.

Bargaining will not turn you into a social outcast. All shopkeepers see when you walk in is dollar signs. If you are willing to spend, they will probably be willing to make a deal. They know that everybody is trying to save money.

Bargaining is a business transaction. You are not trying to cheat the merchant or get something for nothing. You are trying to agree on a fair price. You expect to negotiate for a house or a car—why not for a refrigerator or a winter coat?

You have a right to bargain, particularly in small stores that don't discount. *Reason:* Department stores, which won't bargain as a rule, mark up prices 100%–150% to cover high overhead costs. Small stores should charge lower prices because their costs are less.

The Savvy Approach

Set yourself a price limit for a particular item before you approach the storekeepers. Be prepared to walk out if they don't meet your limit. (You can always change your mind later.) Make them believe you really won't buy unless they come down.

Be discreet in your negotiations. If other customers can overhear your dickering, the shop owner must stay firm.

Be respectful of the merchandise and the storekeeper. Don't manhandle the goods that you inspect. Address salespeople in a polite, friendly manner. Assume that they will want to do their best for you.

Shop at off hours. You will have more luck if business is slow.

Look for unmarked merchandise. If there is no price tag, you are invited to bargain.

Tactics That Work

● **Negotiate with cash.** In a store that takes credit cards, request a discount for paying in cash. (Charging entails overhead costs that the store must absorb.)

● **Buy in quantity.** A customer who is committed to a number of purchases has more bargaining power. When everything is picked out, approach the owner and suggest a total price about 20% less than the actual total. Or, if you are buying more than one of an item, offer to pay full price on the first one if the owner will give you a break on the others. Storekeeper's alternative: You spent $500 on clothing and asked for a better price. The owner couldn't charge you less but threw in a belt priced at $35 as a bonus.

● **Look for flawed merchandise.** This is the only acceptable bargaining point in department stores, but it also can save you money in small shops. If there's a spot, a split seam, or a missing button, estimate what it would cost to have the garment fixed commercially, and ask for a discount based on that figure. *Variation:* You find a chipped hair dryer. When you ask for a discount, the manager says he or she will return it to the manufacturer and find you an undamaged one. Your reply: "Sell it to me for a little less and save yourself the trouble."

WHAT SUPERMARKETS DON'T TELL YOU

Supermarkets usually place the most expensive items at eye level, where they are more likely to be selected on impulse. *Suggestion:* Take a look at the entire group of products before deciding on a purchase, unless you have a strong preference for a specific brand. Generic items can offer real savings, but quality varies widely.

Best bets: Products like household bleach, which, by law, must contain specific ingredients common to all brands.

Trap: National brands may be cheaper than generic brands when on sale, so comparison shop.

● **Adapt your haggling to the realities of the situation.** A true discount house has a low profit margin and depends on volume to make its money. Don't ask for more than 5% off in such a store. A boutique that charges what the traffic will bear has more leeway. Start by asking for 25% off, and dicker from there.

● **Buy at the end of the season,** when new stock is being put out. Offer to buy older goods at a discount. *In neighborhood stores:* Push the local television or appliance dealer to give you a break so you can keep your business in the community.

Source: *Sharon Dunn Greene, coauthor of* The Lower East Side Shopping Guide, *Brooklyn, NY.*

Get Out Your Scissors

When is the best time to hunt for coupons in newspapers, magazines, store circulars, etc.? Coupon clipping is most profitable in the months of June and October. Next best: May, September and November. Poorest months: July and December. (But even then, you can still save.)

Source: The Frugal Shopper *by Marion Joyce, Perigee Books.*

Catch-22 for Consumers

A new big-ticket appliance doesn't work, and no one will be home to wait for the serviceman. Nor (in most states) is the retailer obligated to take it back (because the manufacturer must be given a chance to make repairs). *What to do:* At the time of the sale, get the seller to accept a carefully worded statement, written on the receipt, that if for any reason the buyer is not satisfied, the appliance may be returned or exchanged. This will be done at

the seller's (or buyer's) expense, within a certain number of days and/or on a weekend (or whatever time is convenient for the buyer). The statement becomes part of a binding contract.

Source: *Dan Brecher, Esq., 230 Park Ave., New York, NY 10017.*

Telephone Company Secrets

A network interface is a special telephone jack that allows you to determine which wires are faulty when your phone goes dead—outside wires, which the phone company must repair at no cost, or inside, which the phone company may charge to repair. If you want to install your own interface, buy

WHAT AUTOMAKERS WON'T TELL YOU

A well-kept secret of the automobile industry is the existence of "informal" warranties. *How they work:* When a significant number of new-model cars are reported to have the same mechanical problem, the manufacturer may inform sales offices and car dealers that it will cover the cost of repair beyond the standard warranty.

Problem: Neither manufacturers nor dealers publicize these warranties.

Solution: If your car has a malfunction that may be covered under one of these warranties, write to the

Center for Auto Safety, an auto-complaint clearinghouse that tracks corporate memoranda, bulletins to sales offices and dealers, and car-owner complaints to deduce which components are likely to fall under informal warranties. Tell the Center the automobile's year, model and problem, and it will send you pertinent information. If the malfunctioning part is covered, speak with the dealer's service manager; if he or she won't fix the problem, contact the factory's regional office and ask a representative to mediate.

Last resort: Take the dealer to small-claims court or seek arbitration through the Better Business Bureau. You'll have a good chance of winning if you're armed with documentation.

Source: *Robert Dewey of the vehicle safety division, Center for Auto Safety.*

the materials at a phone-supply store such as Radio Shack. If your phone repairman installs it, you must purchase the materials from him. *Tip:* To avoid charges for the visit, have the repairman install the interface when he is at your house doing other phone work.

You can repair an internal problem yourself or have an electrician do the job, which is often cheaper than the phone company's work.

Source: *Carl Oppedahl, New York City lawyer and author of* The Telephone Book, *Weber Systems, Inc.*

> "Take particular note of a common price-padding tactic: A prep fee of $100 or more (whatever the dealership thinks it can get away with). The cost of preparing your car for delivery is already included in the manufacturer's sticker price."

How to Buy A Car Without Getting Taken For a Ride

Just Any Dealership Won't Do

There's more to buying a car than price. Where you buy it counts, too. Take the time to evaluate different dealerships. Go to a few and walk around. When a salesperson comes up to you—and one will—say, "I'm just looking around. I'll come to you when I'm ready." Don't let any of them intimidate you.

Walk through the service area and sit down. Stay for about a half hour. *Observe:*

- **Is it orderly and run efficiently?**
- **Is the manager there and working?**
- **Are the customers treated with respect?**

Proceed into the service lot and look at the license plate frames. In a good dealership, you'll see frames from competing dealerships, too.

Don't choose a dealership that's out of the way. The salespeople know that they have just one chance to make a sale, and they lean hard on you. Also avoid multifranchise dealerships. Too many people run different parts of the operation, causing confusion in service.

Choose your salespeople, don't let them choose you. Speak with several. *Ask:*

- **How long have you been at this dealership?** (The longer, the better.)
- **Where else have you worked? For how long?**

- **May I have the name and number of a recent customer?** (Follow up with a phone call.) If there's a lot of turnover, the dealership is unstable.

Trap: Looking for a salesperson who's a member of your ethnic group because you think you'll get special treatment. You won't, and you'll be letting your guard down.

Knowledge is Power

Educate yourself. Get as much information as possible about a car before you sit down with the salesperson. Collect brochures (dealers don't usually keep them on display, because they want you to approach the salespeople), and read consumer magazines that rate autos.

Don't let salespeople woo you into trusting them with their "impressive" knowledge of a car. That's how they try to establish authority and take control of the sale.

Know the competition, too. If you say that you're considering a competing brand, the salesperson will knock it and be very convincing if you're uninformed.

Know What You Want

If you're not firm about what you want, you could easily end up with what the salesperson wants to sell you—the most expensive model, with the most extravagant options, at the highest price.

Once you show serious intentions of buying, the salesperson will offer you a test drive, during which he or she will talk glowingly about the car to get you to take mental ownership of it. He or she is seducing you. Resist.

Trap: Negotiating to buy when you're tired of shopping. Salespeople are attracted to this kind of customer like bees to honey. They know that if they promise you what you've been looking for— whether they have it or not —you'll probably buy on the spot. Buy only in an energetic mood.

Few salespeople ask idle questions. Seemingly irrelevant questions are actually attempts to find out about your lifestyle, income, driving habits, etc. Avoid answering these questions.

Unscrupulous Tricks

Options are where dealers make their money.

Common tactic: The dealer says, "Sorry, but all the cars arrive with power windows. If you don't want them, I'll have to make a special order. It could take months." *Result:* You may pay for an option that you don't want. If you stand firm, the dealer will work something out—he or she wants the sale.

Another trick: Cars for the lot are ordered without carpeting, and customers are told that carpeting is extra, when it's really standard. Read the dealer's brochure carefully. It lists every standard option and every extra.

Also make sure every option has the car's name on it: That means the dealership is responsible for it if it breaks. For example, Honda uses Alpine brand radios, but Honda's name is on the faceplate—which means Honda is responsible.

To get the best price, get a range of prices from several different dealerships, and write them down. When you're at the first one, don't let the salesperson know it. When he or she asks what other dealers have quoted, say, "Why don't you give me your best deal and we'll take it from there."

Read the sticker carefully. DAP stands for Dealer Added Profit. Locator Cost means the dealer located the car. Procurement Cost means the dealer procured the car. All these charges are negotiable.

Take particular note of a common price-padding tactic: A prep fee of $100 or more (whatever the dealership thinks it can get away with). The cost of preparing your car for delivery is already included in the manufacturer's sticker price.

Salespersons' trick: Constantly consulting with the manager and pretending that they're really on your side. They aren't—they work on commission.

Don't shop for a price by phone, because salespeople will quote anything just to get you into the dealership. Shop for financing in advance so you'll know a good deal when you hear one. Don't believe salespeople who claim that they can get you good insurance rates—they can't.

Trap: Accepting a trade-in price for your old car that you know is too high. The dealership will make up the difference on the price of the new car.

Being "Turned Over"

Don't let yourself get "turned over." If a salesperson feels that he is not in control of the sale, he'll say that he's going on a coffee break and will "turn you over" to another salesperson. In a high-pressure operation, this could happen three or four times, until they wear you down. *How to resist:* Go out for a walk, have a cup of coffee at a nearby diner, say that you need to think about it. Get away from the salespeople so you can think clearly.

> "Don't let yourself get 'turned over.' If a salesperson feels that he is not in control of the sale, he'll say that he's going on a coffee break and will 'turn you over' to another salesperson. In a high-pressure operation, this could happen three or four times, until they wear you down."

Now You Own it

When the deed is done, inspect your new car thoroughly before you leave the dealership. Make sure everything works correctly.

Final dirty trick: The car was dented in transport, so the dealer parks it close to a wall to hide the damage—which greets you when you arrive home.

Source: *Two veteran car salesmen who asked to remain anonymous.*

Cheaper, Better, Faster Flying

Over 80% of all airline tickets are currently purchased at discounted fares, but because the fare system is so confusing, most travelers are still paying too much for air travel. The fare maze causes most companies to channel their travel planning through a professional travel agent.

Common problem: Many of the agencies are too ill-equipped or too ill-staffed to find you the lowest fare.

Trap: While many of the travel agencies use computerized systems to book clients at the lowest fare available at the time of making a reservation, the airlines' computers are programmed to sell the greatest number of seats at the highest fares. They release cheap seats close to flight time if they haven't sold them at higher fares.

Recommendation: Use only travel agents that contract with one of the preticketing audit services. These services monitor travel agency bookings and check fares once every 12 or 24 hours. As cheaper seats become available, they automatically change your reservation to reflect the lower rate.

Even computerized, pre-assigned seating and issuing of boarding passes don't eliminate the problem of overbooking. Although the airlines are accurate in predicting the percentage of no-shows, all flights are routinely overbooked. *Most likely people to be bumped from a flight:* Late arrivals.

Source: *Harold Seligman, president, Management Alternatives, Inc., a travel consulting firm to major American companies, Box 8119, Stamford, CT 06905.*

How to Travel Free

There are hundreds of budget guides that tell you how to cut costs on trips. Many of these books contain low-cost travel tips, but they don't give you the ultimate scoop on no-cost travel. Instead of traveling cheap, you could be traveling free—from transportation by air—or sea—to lodging, meals and entertainment. Most free travel requires no special skills, credentials or contacts. And it can be just as luxurious—and often more pleasurable—than the most expensive paid vacation.

Vacation With Tax-Free Income

Pay for your vacation with tax-free income by renting out your home while you're away. If you rent it out for less than 15 days a year, the rental income is tax-exempt. If you rent it out for a longer period, the rental income isn't tax-free, but you can deduct a pro rata share of household expenses (which are not deductible if you rent for less than 15 days a year).

Source: *Archie M. Richards, Jr., CFP, president, Archie Richards Associates, financial planners, 40 Mall Rd., Burlington, MA 01803.*

Complimentary Cruises

Cruise lines generally offer a free passage to anyone who recruits 10 to 15 paying passengers. (Many airlines offer similar deals.) If you can't lure that many customers, you can get a prorated reduction on your fare.

You can also cruise free as an expert in a pertinent subject. Historians, anthropologists, naturalists, and ornithologists are in especially high demand. Your job on the cruise would be to present a series of lectures and to be available for informal questioning. It helps to have a Ph.D. (or at least a Master's degree) and to have published articles on the subject, but an affable personality and a willingness to share your knowledge with others can stretch your credentials. After your first cruise in this capacity, a good reference will ease the way at other lines.

Free cruises are available to doctors and nurses who are willing to be on 24-hour call (a salary is an added inducement), to athletic directors who can organize recreational activities, to musicians and entertainers willing to perform and to cosmetologists who can barter their services.

There is also a strong demand for "hosts"—distinguished single gentlemen who are usually 55 years old and up. They serve by dining and dancing with the many unattached older women taking these vacation cruises. "Hosts" are required to fill out an application and be interviewed for the job. One of the prerequisites is to be an expert in social ballroom dancing.

Free Foreign Tours

Enlist enough people and get a whole trip—long or short—free. Some travel agencies recruit teachers, who receive a free trip if they bring six students. With 12 students, the teacher's spouse also travels free.

The same deal is available to anyone willing to organize a special-interest tour. An auto-racing fan might lead a group to Le Mans; an opera aficionado might arrange a trip to Milan and La Scala. Similar trips focus on photography, architecture, theater, music, golf, or wine-tasting. The group leader sets the itinerary, chooses lodgings, and arranges for side trips. Travel experience and linguistic skills are usually helpful, but not essential.

Source: *Robert William Kirk, author of* You Can Travel Free, *Pelican Publishing Co.*

Ticket Savvy

Some supersaver fares are low enough that even if you can't stay as long as their requirements (usually seven days), you will save by buying two round-trip tickets—one from your home to your destination for the day you want to leave and one from your destination to your home for the day you want to return. The total may be less than the regular round-trip fare.

Source: Your Money and Your Life *by Robert Z. Aliber, Basic Books.*

Win Bigger And Cut Your Losses

There are two kinds of odds you've got to beat to have a successful day at the casinos. Numerical odds for each game are set by the casinos, and you have little chance of controlling them. All you can do is play the games and bet the combinations that offer the best odds.

Behavioral odds, however, are what really give the casinos the winning edge. Few casino visitors are practiced or skilled enough to make the best bets every time. The casinos count on most players making the same dumb mistakes over and over. When the house holds, say, a 2% edge in a particular game, that's the numerical edge and tells only part of the story. The behavioral edge is much, much greater.

Players can turn the behavioral edge to their advantage. Professional gamblers know how, and so do casino insiders.

Biggest edge: All casinos aren't alike in the odds they offer, and there can even be important differences among neighboring tables in the same house. Nevada casinos vary widely from one another—more than do houses in Atlantic City.

Test for Loaded Dice

Fill a tall glass with water, drop each die in gently. Repeat several times, with a different number on top each time. If the die turns when sinking so that the same two or three numbers always show up, it's loaded. *Less obvious test:* Hold die loosely between thumb and forefinger at diagonally opposite corners. Loaded dice will pivot when the weighted side is on top. The movement is unmistakable.

Las Vegas

In Vegas, the best deals are usually found in the smaller casinos in the Fremont Street downtown area, away from the fabled Strip.

In Vegas craps, steer clear of the "Big 6" and "Big 8" sucker bets. The odds might look attractive, but an identical wager of place bets on the 6 or 8 gives a higher payoff. *Better:* Look for craps tables that offer triple odds bets after the come-out roll. This shaves the casino edge to well under 1%.

On the Vegas Strip, the best place to play blackjack allows you to double down on a 9, as well as on 10 and 11. All Strip casinos stymie card counters, however, by dealing players' cards face down. The less you can see, the less you can count.

Downtown Vegas rules are less strict than those on the Strip. Some houses allow for six-card Charlies, where the player wins by taking six cards totaling 21 or less.

If you can count cards: Look for a two-deck game with player cards dealt faceup. The rules in any given casino can—and do—change frequently. You're allowed to ask about the details before you sit down.

Variations to avoid: "Double exposure," in which player and dealer cards are dealt faceup. *Trade-off:* House wins all ties, instead of having to push the bet to the next hand. Overall, the odds are worse than in conventional blackjack.

Another Nevada variation is minibaccarat, played

at conventional blackjack tables. It attracts many players because of the low $2 minimum bet.

Drawback: Some casinos take out a minimum 25¢ commission on bets on the banker. On a $2 wager, that is a 12.5% built-in loss, as compared to the traditional house edge of 5%. If you like the game, find a Vegas casino that plays it with four, rather than eight, decks. The fewer the decks, the better the odds when betting the player position. In Nevada poker games, you're playing against the house.

Problem: High-stakes poker attracts pros, hustlers and cheats.

Safest: Stick to $5-limit games.

Playing slots: Vegas rules are most chaotic for slot machines. In Atlantic City, all machines must return at least 83% of the amount wagered, and a few return even more than 83%. But in Nevada, one machine might pay back 99% while the one right next to it pays back only 60%. The bettor's problem is that it's impossible to identify the hot machines. Their placement is the casino's most private and closely guarded secret.

Atlantic City

Among Atlantic City's casinos, the variations are narrower than in Vegas, but they can still be worked for or against you.

Look for a single-zero roulette game instead of one that uses a wheel with two zeros. Since the house always wins when the roulette ball lands on 0 or 00, a single-zero game halves the house edge.

In blackjack or baccarat, seek games with the lowest minimum bets.

If you are a slot player, stick to the so-called progressive slot machines, because the jackpots can build indefinitely. The best casino for slots in Atlantic City offers both liberal payoffs and coupons to exchange for prizes or hotel discounts.

Source: *Lee Pantano, a professional gambler, teacher and consultant.*

How to Spot a Card Cheat

One gambling survey indicates that cheating takes place in 10% of card games. *To protect yourself:*

● **When shuffling cards,** never take them entirely off the table, either for the riffle or for squaring the deck.

● **Get into the habit of cutting the cards** at least once during the shuffle by pulling out the bottom half and slapping it onto the top.

● **Sit with your back against the wall.**

● **If you suspect marked cards, riffle the deck and watch the design on the back.** If the cards are marked, some lines in the design will move like an animated cartoon. In an honest deck, the design will stand absolutely still. The player to suspect: the one who keeps his eyes glued to the backs of the cards—especially the hole card in stud poker and the top card of the deck in gin rummy.

Source: *John Scarne's* Newsletter.

Enjoy a Day at the Races Without Going Broke

The aim of a day at the track should be to enjoy every race while controlling your losses.

● **When betting,** begin with the choices of the "morning line." The "morning line"—the prediction of the odds that each horse will go off at and of likely winners—is done by a track official who assigns odds to the horses in the morning. Handicapping is also done by bettors in the course of the day (which causes the odds to change). One-third of the favorites chosen by handicappers win their races.

● **Decide on the amount of money you are willing to lose.** Set aside one-fifth of it for entertainment betting. The rest should be spent on serious betting.

● **Avoid the temptation to increase bets when losing in order to catch up.** Also avoid the trap of betting more when winning to try to make a killing.

● **To control spending,** bet just 20% of your remaining capital each time you bet, whether your capital goes up or down.

● **For fun betting,** choose horses by name, jockey, appearance or any means you wish. You may get lucky and win one out of 10 bets this way.

● **For serious betting,** pick the appropriate races to bet on. Always eliminate maiden races, two-year-old races and races where it's indicated that the horses chosen won no race but their maiden race.

● **To pick the two or three likeliest winners in the race,** check handicappers' choices in local newspapers, tip sheets sold at the track or the *Daily*

Racing Form, a publication most handicappers use. Look especially for handicappers who predict in great detail how the race will be run, and those who tell you the front-runners and the come-from-behind horse as well as the outcome.

● **Late scratches** (the elimination of contenders) can very much change the projected script of a race. If one of the two predicted front-runners is scratched, the remaining front-runner's chance is increased.

● **Rain.** The *Daily Racing Form* lists "mudders" (horses that have a history of doing well in the rain) with each horse's lifetime wet-track record. As the track is progressively softened by rain, the chances of mudders improve.

● **Shifts in odds.** Lengthening (higher) odds on a horse increase your chance of a good return. Observe the physical condition of your horse during the viewing ritual, when the horses are paraded at the rear of the track before each race.

You can place several types of bets:

● **To win:** Pays only if the horse comes in first.

● **To place:** Pays if the horse comes in first or second.

● **To show:** Pays if the horse comes in first, second or third. A combination of bets, such as a win and a place or a win and a show, increases your chances of a payoff. But the return will be smaller.

Source: *The late Peter Shaw, cultural critic, historian and college professor.*

Picking Harness Winners

Harness racing is far easier to handicap than Thoroughbred ("flat") racing: The bettor has fewer variables to take into consideration.

Harness races are almost always at a mile and on the dirt. The fields are more manageable, with rarely more than nine entries. And, since the horses carry no weight on their backs, there are no weight differences for which to compensate. (Thanks to the laws of physics, the sulky pulled by the horse actually adds momentum, rather than drag.)

Standardbred harness horses are calmer, tougher and more dependable than Thoroughbreds. The favorites win more often than Thoroughbred favorites—about 36% of the time. Still, most bettors are chronic losers, in part because they ignore the most important betting factors.

Post Position

Most decisive of all is post position, especially on short half-mile or five-eighths-mile tracks. The nearer the rail, the less distance the horse must travel, both at the start and around a turn. The horse in the number one post (at the far inside) has a tremendous advantage. Since he's already at the rail, he doesn't need to spend energy to get there. Even if he doesn't make the lead, he will likely be close enough to make a move in the stretch.

Conversely, if a horse draws an outside post (number six or higher), the driver will have to either "park" outside other horses while contending for the lead or take back to the rear. Later on, he may be boxed in with no racing room. To mount a stretch drive, he will have to return outside, losing at least one and a half lengths around the final turn. And given the width of the other sulkies, there may be no convenient holes to burst through. All in all, it's tough to catch the leader.

Post positions are also a key to interpreting past performances. *Example:* In his last outing, your pick raced from the eight post and finished a distant sixth. But in the race before that, starting from the one post, he led the way and won handily. If he's returning to an inside post, you can expect the horse to improve, perhaps at good odds.

> "Even the best driver can't help a slow starter from an outside post. Check each race (carefully consult the track program) for horses with good early speed. There are no Silky Sullivans in harness racing—no champions who consistently come from last place to take the purse. You'll find that the winner is usually among the first four horses at the half mile."

SAVING MONEY WITH COUPONS

Most of us pay more than we should for groceries, household products and other goods and services. The biggest mistake we make is failing to take full advantage of cents-off coupons, refund offers, two-for-one deals and other money-saving offers. With more than 300 billion coupons issued annually, fewer than 8 billion are redeemed each year. *Reasons:* Many shoppers are too embarrassed to present coupons to checkout clerks. Others are not aware, or uninterested in the available deals, or feel that clipping coupons is too time-consuming.

Today, however, more consumers are looking to cut weekly costs and stay on a budget. There are several ways to clip coupons and save up to 25% on your supermarket bill. *Helpful suggestions:*

● **Set up a system.** Spend a few minutes each week looking over newspaper inserts and other likely sources of coupons. Clip the ones you think you might use and toss them into a shoe box, then separate them by category. Mark each grouping of coupons with its own labeled note card. Be as general or as specific as you like with your categories.

Just prior to each trip to the grocery store, review your shopping list. Transfer the coupons you plan to use from the storage box to an envelope labeled unused. Take this envelope and a second, empty one (labeled

used) along to the store. As you toss each item on your list into your shopping cart, transfer its coupon from the first envelope to the second.

● **Be choosy.** Coupons should be used to buy only two types of products—those you use regularly and those you'd like to try. Don't let coupons entice you to buy products you neither need nor truly want. Don't be trapped

by brand loyalty. Buy whatever brand for which you have coupons.

● **Accumulate as many coupons as possible.** Today coupons are available from a wide variety of sources, including product labels and cartons, supermarket ads, inserts in your Sunday newspaper and displays placed along supermarket shelves. Coupons are also distributed directly through the mail, on airline flights and at movie theaters.

● **Save unused coupons.** Take them along to the supermarket. *Reason:* Some markets maintain informal coupon-exchange bins where customers can exchange coupons they don't want for those they do.

● **Join a coupon-exchange club.** There are several large clubs to choose from, all offering the same basic ser-

vice. *How they work:* Upon joining, members fill out a form specifying which products they use. Periodically, members mail in coupons they don't need and the club mails back coupons they do.

● **Shop at "coupon-friendly" supermarkets.** Some markets accept coupons only grudgingly. Others not only accept them, but will give you twice their face value.

● **Use coupons in conjunction with other savings offers.** When reading through your local newspaper's supermarket ads, watch for "double plays"—items discounted by both coupons and special sale prices. *Even better:* Triple plays. These occur when prices are reduced not only by coupons and specials, but also by a mail-in refund offer.

To keep track of the thousands of refunds being offered at any given time, there are now refunding newsletters. They not only list all the offers, but also detail the often byzantine regulations governing how to obtain the refunds.

● **Bank your savings.** Because coupons net you only a few dollars each time you shop, it's easy to squander the money you saved by using them.

Solution: Put your coupon savings in a savings account. Decide on a particular item to save for. Don't dip into the account until you've accumulated enough to make the purchase.

Source: Linda Bowman, devoted coupon clipper and the author of six books on money-saving hints, including **Free Food…& More,** Probus Publishing Corp.

The Driver

The other underrated factor: The driver's ability. Every track has a few leading drivers; check their names in your program and remember them. Steer clear of any drivers who fail to win at least 10% of their starts. And you should never bet on a novice or provisional driver.

Positive sign: A switch from a trainer-driver to a leading full-time driver. This often means the trainer believes the horse is now at his best, ready to win.

But even the best driver can't help a slow starter from an outside post. Check each race (carefully consult the track program) for horses with good early speed.

There are no Silky Sullivans in harness racing—no champions who consistently come from last place to take the purse. You'll find that the winner is usually among the first four horses at the half mile.

Pluses and Minuses

In weighing past performances, the horse's time in the final quarter-mile is more revealing than his overall time. *Most promising:* A fast final quarter (under 31 seconds) following a fast first half mile.

It's also positive if the horse:

- **Won his last race** (unless he won by a small margin that was less than the last time).
- **Is going off at lower odds than in his last race.**
- **Raced steadily last time while parked** (indicated by a small "o" in the program) for one or more calls. ("Parked" means outside one or more other horses.)

But don't bet heavily if the horse:

- **Is moving up steeply in class** (signified by purse money or claiming price).
- **Hasn't been in a race for more than two weeks.**

- **Seems clearly superior in the program** but is going off at odds of 5–2 or greater. (The horse's handlers don't think he can win.)
- **Broke stride in his last race** (check in your track program).
- **Has pinned ears** (ears are back flat against his head) or is nervous or sweating in prerace warmups.

Source: Don Valliere, manager of the Ontario Jockey Club's track in Fort Erie, and author of Betting Winners: A Guide for the Harness Fan, Gambling Book Club Press.

State Lottery Winning Strategy

When playing a state lottery, it's a good idea to choose at least one number higher than 31.

Reason: Many lottery players use number combinations based on birthdays, anniversaries and other dates. Since this group concentrates on numbers of 31 or lower, a winning combination with one or more higher numbers will likely be shared by fewer people.

Source: Dr. Jim Maxwell, American Mathematics Society.

The Truth About State Lotteries

State lotteries are one of the worst bets around. They claim that about 50% of the money wagered is returned as prizes. In fact, considering the lotteries' deferred-payment schedules (a $1 million prize is awarded as $50,000 a year for 20 years), the payout actually comes to less than 25%. Comparison: In Nevada or Atlantic City, the payout in roulette is about 94%.

Source: The Wall Street Journal.

Contest Winner's Secrets of Success

Cash, vacations, houses, cars, electronic equipment, cameras and much, much more are the dream prizes that keep millions of Americans doggedly filling out entry blanks for contests. More than $100 million in prize money and goods are dispensed annually through an estimated 500 promotional competitions and drawings.

Dedicated hobbyists know that there is an advantage of a planned approach to overcome the heavy odds against each entrant. *Winning strategies:*

- **Use your talents.** If you can write, cook or take photographs, put your energy into entering contests. They take skill, so fewer people are likely to compete—improving your chances. Photography contests have the fewest average entries.

● **Follow the rules precisely.** If the instructions say to print your name, don't write it in longhand. If a three-inch-by-five-inch piece of paper is called for, measure your entry exactly. The slightest variation can disqualify you.

● **Enter often.** Always be on the lookout for new contests to enter.

Sources: Magazines, newspapers, radio, television, store shelves and bulletin boards, product packaging.

● **Make multiple entries, if they are permitted.** The more entries you send in, the more you tip the odds in your favor.

● **Spread out your entries over the duration of the contest**—one a week for five weeks, for example. When the volume of entries is big enough, they will be delivered to the judges in a number of different sacks. The theory is that judges will pick from each sack, and your chances will go up if you have an entry in each of several different mailbags.

● **Stay informed.** Join a local contest club or subscribe to a contest newsletter. Either source will help you to learn contest traps, problems and solutions. They'll alert you, too, to new competitions.

● **Be selective.** You must pay taxes on items that you win, so be sure the prizes are appropriate for you. If you don't live near the water, winning an expensive boat could be a headache. (Some contests offer cash equivalents, but not all do.)

● **If you do win,** check with your CPA or tax lawyer immediately. You must report the fair market value of items that you win, whether you keep them, sell them or give them away. This can be tricky.

● **Some contests ask you to enclose some proof of purchase** or a plain piece of paper with a product name or number written on it. Many people assume that a real proof of purchase will improve

their chances of winning. *Fact:* In a survey, more than half the winners of major prizes reported that they had not bought the sponsor's product.

Source: Rich Henderson and Ann Faith, coeditors of Contest Newsletter, *Danbury, CT.*

Protect Your Home and Family

Request a security audit from your local police. Have your children fingerprinted by the local police. Keep fingerprints on file at home in case the children are ever missing. Children should be fingerprinted regularly until age seven, when their hands are completely developed. Also: Borrow a metal engraver—available at many police stations—to place a traceable identification number on valuables, in case they are ever stolen.

Source: Ladies' Home Journal, 100 Park Ave., New York, NY 10017.

Long-Distance Phone Savings

Here's yet another benefit of the Internet: you can save money on telephone calls. With Internet Protocol (IP) Telephony, phone calls are transmitted digitally via cyberspace; all you need is a phone. (Some companies may require an Internet account.) Calls are cheaper largely because IP Telephony providers don't have to contribute to a universal phone service fund.

Savings: You get the best deal on international calls—at least 50% cheaper than with traditional phone companies. For domestic long-distance calls you pay 5¢ a minute, instead of the 10¢ rate from phone companies.

Drawbacks: Voice transmission with IP Telephony is still sometimes quirky. Also, Internet phone companies may soon have to pay domestic industry access fees, which would then be passed on to customers.

IP telephony carriers: IDT (800) CALL-IDT/ www. net2phone.com; Delta Three (888) 335-8230/ www. deltathree.com; I-LINK (888)238-9465/www.i-link. net.

Note: To stay competitive, phone companies such as AT&T, MCI and Sprint plan to offer IP Telephony service, too.

Tax Tactics, Strategies & Opportunities

2

- Personal Tax Breaks You Can Use

- The IRS's Current Hot Topics

- Free Information From the IRS

- Tax-Free Income Checklist

- Joint Versus Separate Returns

- Checklist of Tax Tips for Retirees

- How the IRS Helps With Tuition Bills

- Making the Most of Medical Deductions

- Special Advice for the Self-Employed and Moonlighters

- The Home Office

- Tax Shelters You Can Use

Nine Big Loopholes

Congress is constantly trying to eliminate planning strategies that it perceives as abusive. Despite legislation action through the years, there are still a number of tax loopholes open to you. Here are nine loopholes to consider:

1. Income-shifting loophole. Shift income to young children so it will be taxed at a lower rate. In 1998 the first $700 of annual investment income of a child under age 14 is completely tax-free. The next $700 is taxed at the child's low rate. A child's investment income above $1,400 is taxed at the parent's top rate. *Strategy:* Put enough assets in your children's names to give each child at least $1,400 of investment income a year.

2. S corporation loophole. Virtually every newly formed, closely held company should be set up as an S corporation. An S corporation avoids the double tax that regular corporations pay: The income of an S corporation is taxed only when it is passed through to the shareholders on their personal tax returns. *Loophole:* When an S corporation liquidates its assets, only one tax has to be paid on gain from the sale.

3. Capital losses loophole. All capital losses are fully deductible. However, only $3,000 of ordinary income (e.g., salary) can be offset by capital losses in any one year. Unused losses can be carried over into future years.

4. Taking money out of the company. Owners of closely held corporations with accumulated retained earnings that are not needed in the corporation can pay out dividends, which are taxed at a top rate of 39.6%.

Caution: Watch out for state tax on dividends, which could boost the total tax bill.

Editor's note: Even better than dividends are tax-free fringe benefits (such as health insurance, group-term life insurance, education assistance, adoption assistance). The corporation can deduct the costs while you as an owner-employee are not taxed on these benefits.

5. Itemizers' loophole. If your total deductions are below the standard deduction, you must take it; you can't itemize. *Strategy:* Beat the limit by bunching two years' worth of deductions into one. If your deductions average $5,000 a year, arrange to pay $2,000 in one year, and $8,000 the following year. You would then get the standard deduction in year one and $8,000 of itemized deductions in year two. *Deductions susceptible to bunching:* charity, medical expenses, miscellaneous business expenses, real estate taxes, state income taxes.

6. Alimony loophole. Alimony payments continue to be deductible by the spouse who pays it and taxable to the spouse who receives it. There are no minimum or maximum payments. However, if payments in the first year are more than $15,000 and then drop in the second and third years by more than that amount, there will be "recapture" (requiring the spouse who claimed the deduction to report the recaptured amount as income).

7. Rental property loophole. All rentals are treated as "passive" activity under the rule that makes passive losses deductible only against passive income. But there's an important exception to the rule for taxpayers whose Adjusted Gross Income is under $100,000 and who actively participate in the management of rental property. They can deduct up to $25,000 of rental losses each year even if they have no passive income. (The deduction is phased out for taxpayers whose AGI is between $100,000 and $150,000.)

8. 401(k) loophole. The amount you can put into a 401(k) plan is $10,000 for 1998. *Editor's note:* The contribution limit is indexed for inflation. While you cannot deduct your contribution, it's still a valuable loophole because the contribution is made with pre-tax dollars. You're not taxed on salary reductions you make to fund your 401(k).

It's an especially important tax break for people who can't make deductible contributions to IRAs because of the restrictions. Plan to make the maximum contribution to your company's 401(k) plan this year.

9. Categories-of-income loophole. There are three kinds of income (and losses)—portfolio income, passive income and active income. A situation to avoid is involvement in an S corporation that reports taxable portfolio income and passive operating losses. This could happen, for instance, if you did not materially participate in the business. If the corporation had investment income, you would have to pay tax on it, and you would not be able to write off the corporation's operating losses unless you had passive income. *Strategy:* Either be active in the business or avoid having portfolio income.

Source: Edward Mendlowitz, partner, Mendlowitz Weitsen, LLP, 2 Penn Plaza, NY 10121.

Personal Tax Breaks You Can Use

While Congress has tinkered with the tax law over the years, certain important personal tax breaks remain intact. Here are some breaks you may be able to use.

> " Second-residence interest on one other home you own, such as a vacation home, is deductible even if you don't use that home during the year. "

● **State and local income taxes and real- and personal- property taxes** are still fully deductible on federal returns.

● **Home mortgage interest:** Fully deductible on your personal residence and one other residence to the extent that the mortgage loan does not exceed $1 million in *acquisition debt* (borrowed to purchase, build or improve the residence) plus $100,000 in *home equity debt* (borrowed for any purpose whatsoever). However, under any circumstances, the loan can't exceed the present market value of the residence.

Special break: The limitations are not applied retroactively. If you took a mortgage or refinanced your home before October 14, 1987, your interest deduction is not limited by the above. Interest on a mortgage remains deductible up to the fair market value of your home, even if you borrowed more than the dollar limits listed above, and you can borrow an additional $100,000 home equity loan and deduct the interest.

● **Second-residence interest on one other home you own,** such as a vacation home, is deductible even if you don't use that home during the year.

● **Gain on the sale of your home remains tax-free**, up to $250,000 ($500,000 on a joint return) if you owned and lived in your home for two out of five years before the date of sale.

● **Gifts and inheritances aren't taxable income to the recipient.** The estate or donor pays the tax at rates that were not changed by tax reform.

● **Property that you inherit gets a "stepped-up basis."** You can take the property at its value as of the date of death of the original owner. *Example:* You inherit your mother's diamond ring, which was originally purchased for $1,000. At the time of her death, its value has appreciated to $6,000. If you sell the ring for $8,000, you have to pay tax only on your gain of $2,000—that is, the difference between the value on the date of her death and the selling price.

● **Interest and dividends earned** by your existing Individual Retirement Accounts, Keoghs, 401(k)s, simplified employee pension plans, etc., are tax-deferred. Here are some more tax breaks:

● **Life insurance proceeds** that you receive as a result of the death of the insured.

● **Cash-value buildup of life insurance** policies and most deferred annuities.

● **Contributions to qualified retirement plans made by your employer,** plus the earnings on those contributions.

● **Employer-paid health insurance.**

● **Employer-provided group term life insurance policies up to $50,000.**

● **Vacation home rental if your property** is rented out for 14 days or less.

● **Scholarships and fellowships** if used to cover tuition and course equipment.

Tax Deductions and Credits

● **Charitable contribution deductions, if you itemize.**

● **Credit for child-care and dependent-care expenses.**

● **Moving expenses that are job-related.**

● **Gambling losses up to the amount of gambling winnings for the year.**

● **Alimony payments.**

● **Small-business operating expenses** that result from the cost of doing business (rent, salaries, postage, taxes, etc.).

● **Business gifts of up to $25 per recipient per year,** if you itemize.

● **Car expenses for the use of your personal car** for business purposes. Take the IRS standard mileage allowance or your total actual expenses, plus parking and tolls.

Source: *Sidney Kess, attorney and CPA, Suite 1465, 630 Fifth Avenue, New York, NY 10111.*

Benefit from IRS Mistakes

● **Abate interest.** The IRS has the authority to abate interest charges that are generated by its own errors or delays. For example, if it took the IRS a year to get around to issuing a deficiency notice, after efforts to resolve the tax dispute had been completed, you aren't liable for an additional year's interest. If the IRS is to blame for the delay, it can erase the extra interest charges.

Source: *George S. Alberts, former head of the Albany and Brooklyn IRS District Offices.*

New Laws That Help Taxpayers

Starting in 1998, interest and penalties must be suspended if the IRS fails to send a notice specifically stating the income tax liability within 18 months following the due date of the return or the date the return is actually filed (whichever is later). Interest and penalties resume 21 days after the notice is sent. After 2003 the IRS has only one year in which to send this notice or suspend interest and penalties.

Recover your attorney's fees from the IRS.

If the IRS has taken an unreasonable position that pushed you into spending money on legal fees to defend yourself, you may be able to recoup them. To win, you must meet all the following conditions:

● You were in the right (the IRS position was unreasonable).

● You exhausted all your administrative appeals with the IRS.

● Your net worth at the time the action began was $2 million or less.

● You apply for these fees.

Catch: The limit on attorney's fees recovered in 1998 is $120 an hour (unless a court determines that a higher rate is justified). It's slated to increase to $125 an hour some time in 1999 and will be indexed for inflation thereafter.

Collect for unauthorized collection action.

If you've been the victim of an IRS employee's reckless or intentional action that disregards the law or the Service's own regulations when assessing a tax or other collection action, you may be able to recover up to $1 million. (For unauthorized actions before July 31, 1996, the limit was only $100,000).

For actions of IRS officers and employees (occurring after July 22, 1998) that constitute negligent disregard of the law or the IRS's own regulations, you may be able to recover up to $100,000; it's $1 million for willful violations relating to automatic stays or discharges under the Bankruptcy Code.

Source: *Barbara Weltman is a tax attorney and the author of several books on business, including* The Complete Idiot's Guide to Making Money After You Retire, *Alpha Books, and* J.K. Lasser's Tax Deduction for Your Small Business, *Macmillan.*

What Do You Need From a Tax Preparer?

Aside from the first requirement—honesty—what do you look for in a tax preparer and adviser? The answer depends on your needs.

The Options

For most taxpayers, the IRS itself can supply some appropriate help. Its many instructional booklets are useful, though they may take the tax collector's side in arguable matters. The booklets cover subjects from record-keeping requirements to relocation expenses, deductions for bad debts to tax information for home owners, charitable contributions to self-employment tax. The IRS will also answer tax questions over the telephone, in person or by mail—

millions make inquiries each year. There are even volunteer programs located in public libraries each tax season. *Problem:* You can't expect to rely on volunteer advice or even advice from the IRS. If you get into trouble, you're on your own.

A step up from free tax advice are commercial tax preparers. They will use the proper forms and fill out your return based on the information you give them. It's usually all done correctly and inexpensively, but even at best the service is not very sophisticated.

You may have heard of an independent tax practitioner who has been helpful to a colleague. That's not a bad way to find tax help, if you remember that ability and experience vary greatly. Find out if the recommended tax adviser is an attorney, a certified public accountant or an "enrolled agent." In order to become an enrolled agent—and qualified to practice by the IRS—tax practitioners must pass a government examination and keep up their expertise. Anyone may prepare tax returns, but enrolled agents, like lawyers and CPAs, are professional specialists.

CPAs can usually be relied upon when they tell you they know about taxes. Like most other professional tax preparers, they are likely to use an independent computerized service bureau for the actual preparation of returns, but CPAs will do more: They can diagnose a current tax problem and advise on its cure, and assist you with tax planning.

The most sophisticated—and expensive—tax advice usually emanates from law offices. Unless you are already a valued client, it isn't likely that an attorney will welcome a simple tax preparation job from you. Seek a tax attorney's assistance only in extreme circumstances.

The Interview

Interview any tax adviser before signing on. (You will want someone with a permanent address.) Ask about credentials and experience. Feel free to inquire about fees. If a preparer asks you to sign a blank return, guarantees a refund, refuses to sign the return as preparer or won't use his or her identification number, look elsewhere.

Source: Robert A. Garber, vice president of a major investment-banking house. He writes frequently on tax matters, is the author of several books and has over 25 years experience as a tax attorney and in trusts and estates.

Working With Your Tax Preparer

Until recently, information you shared with your CPA or other preparer generally was not protected by a guarantee of confidentiality—as there is between a doctor and a patient or an attorney and a client. However, under new law, tax advice provided by anyone authorized to practice by the IRS (CPAs, enrolled agents and enrolled actuaries) is now confidential. This change applies to communications after July 22, 1998.

How to Pick the Shrewdest Tax Adviser

The shrewdest tax adviser (preparer, practitioner, etc.) is the one who can minimize your *overall expenditures for taxes* (your tax bill plus his or her bill plus any expenses connected with audits, etc.).

Finding the best tax adviser for you is a search for a marriage of true minds. The first requirement is that your tax professional offer the services you need. Then, in addition to being prompt, courteous, diligent, organized, thorough and well versed in new developments, the best tax adviser will be inquisitive, innovative and sensitive to your situation, temperament and outlook.

The relationship will be personal as well as professional, so plan to devote as much time and effort as necessary. It will pay off. The most effective procedure is to first solicit recommendations and referrals from friends and business acquaintances whose business acumen you respect, and to follow up with in-depth interviews.

Here's a checklist of points to consider.

● **Technical competence.** Is this person able to field most of your questions with ease and confidence? If he or she has to grope for answers or look everything up in a book, you can conclude that knowledge is weak in areas of importance to you. If, on the other hand, you find yourself being told about new developments in tax laws in your areas of interest, consider this person to be a strong candidate.

● **Organization and interview depth.** Does this professional provide an organized worksheet prior to the interview to help you gather your materials effectively

GETTING THE MOST FROM YOUR TAX PREPARER

Familiarize yourself with the tax law. By being knowledgeable, you won't waste anyone's time or your own money. There are many tax-preparation guides on the market, and the IRS itself provides plenty of free basic filing information. At the very least, review both the tax forms and the accompanying instructions so you'll understand the basic concepts and have an idea of the information your preparer will need to know to fill out your return.

Organize your materials. Don't show up with a briefcase full of tax-related paperwork that you expect him or her to sort out. If your preparer has to muddle through the papers, it will cut into the time that should be spent on figuring out the best tax strategy.

Bring the right information to the meeting. Once you have organized your records, bring the necessary information, such as:

● **Past tax returns.** If this is the first time you are working with this tax preparer, or if you have always prepared your own returns, it's especially important to bring old returns. It will give your new preparer valuable information about your tax history—and he or she can review your past three returns to see if you missed any tax breaks in those years (they can still be claimed). If you have worked with this preparer before, he or she should have copies of your old returns in the file.

●**Tax statements**. Bring your W-2 form and all 1099 forms, showing income and proceeds from security transactions.

● **Expense diary.** This will help your preparer determine the deductibility of your expenses. He or she will also be able to tell you if it meets the stringent record-keeping requirements of the IRS. If it's not in good enough shape for use on this year's return, your preparer should be able to advise you about making it audit-proof for next year's return.

● **Canceled checks.** Bring all your checks, even those not written for deductible items. Helpful: categorizing the checks (travel, etc.). Your accountant may find some deductions that you didn't know about. Nondeductible expenses may trigger deductions—for example, on a new car. Of course, the purchase price is nondeductible, but if you used the car for business, there may be some deductions. Had you not brought that check to the interview, the whole issue might never have come up.

● **Preparer worksheets.** Many firms send out detailed worksheets for you to fill out long before your actual appointment. Bring that worksheet with you, and be sure you have filled it out with scrupulous care.

Never jump to tax conclusions. Many taxpayers don't bother mentioning some financial matters to their accountant because they have already made a decision on its tax status. Yet taxpayers often reach the wrong conclusions and lose out on deductions. Tell your preparer everything, and let him or her make the final decision. Even if an item isn't deductible this year, you may get some good advice about how to make it deductible for next year.

Get a tax projection. Ask your preparer to look at next year's taxes while he or she is doing your return. You'll see early in the year where you stand, and you'll know what to expect.

Source: Edward Mendlowitz, Mendlowitz Weitsen, LLP, 2 Penn Plaza, New York, NY 10121.

and efficiently? Offer advice on record-keeping procedures that speeds and clarifies your work together? Go through your checkbook register, discuss your investments with you, pore through your records and receipts for overlooked deductions?

● **Comprehensive analysis.** In the initial interview, a top-notch tax adviser will do all of the following: review your financial activities for their tax impact; review your three prior years' returns, looking for tax breaks you might have missed; spend time discussing ways to cut your tax bill for the coming year. The only way to save on taxes is by year-round planning. This is what you pay a tax adviser for. If your adviser isn't inclined to probe, ask questions, and offer advice, you should consider a change. Filling in the forms is not what you are paying for.

● **Audit compatibility.** A vital point. While we would all love to pay the lowest possible tax bill and never be audited, the fact is that to save tax dollars, you must take aggressive positions on your financial dealings—which makes it much more likely your returns are going to be audited. If you want to cut your audit risk, you must take a more conservative approach. You can't have it both ways. What's important is that you and your adviser agree on your audit tolerance.

● **Audit representation.** Will this professional represent you at an audit? Will there be an extra fee for this? Will he or she be able to strongly argue the positions you took on your return, especially where the tax law isn't clear?

● **Support network.** Is the adviser in question a member of a firm that includes specialists/experts, attorneys, accountants? Such support personnel provide more comprehensive service.

● **Silent partner.** Even the shrewdest tax adviser is only as strong as his or her silent partner—the client. To get the most from your tax advice, you must take an active role—the more active the better. If you are careful to bring to your adviser's attention any potential out-of-the-way deductions, present your records in an organized way, make sure records are

complete at interview time, keep your expert informed about changes in essential personal and financial matters, and make your own tax education an ongoing concern, your relationship with any tax adviser you choose will be that much more fruitful.

Source: *Paul N. Strassels, a tax-law specialist, Money Matters, Inc., Box 195, Burke, VA 22015.*

The IRS's Current Hot Topics

The best way to head off unwanted problems with the IRS is to know in advance what areas on your return are likely to get the most scrutiny. Here's a list of the IRS's current hot topics and the steps that you can take to handle them and avoid a tax dispute before troubles arise.

> " Today the IRS claims that it successfully matches more than 90% of the 1099s it receives, so a taxpayer shouldn't assume that if something isn't reported to the IRS, the IRS will never know of it. "

● **Information returns.** The IRS has made a great effort to increase the number of Form 1099 information returns sent to the IRS by banks, brokerage houses, insurance companies, etc.) that it is able to match against taxpayer returns. Today the IRS claims that it successfully matches more than 90% of the 1099s it receives, so a taxpayer should not assume that if something isn't reported to the IRS, the IRS will never know of it. But a tremendous amount of paperwork is involved in the IRS return-matching program, and mistakes do occur. *Most common:*

● **The wrong Social Security number** on a 1099 causes somebody else's income to be matched against your return. *Editor's note:* If you don't correct your Social Security number after notification by the bank, brokerage firm, mutual fund or other payor of interest or dividends, then you may be subject to "back up" withholding on your interest and dividends at the rate of 31%.

● **Your broker reports the dividends paid to you** through your dividend account. At the same time, the individual companies that you have invested in report the dividends that they have paid in your name. *Result:* The same dividends may be double-counted.

● **Because of a clerical error,** a bank or brokerage house reports tax-exempt income as taxable or attributes income to the wrong time period.

What to do: When a discrepancy is found, you'll receive a computer-generated notice of the error from the IRS Service Center. Make a copy of the notice and mail the copy back to the service center along with your explanation of the discrepancy.

If a mistake was made in the issuance of the 1099 (by your bank, broker, etc.), include a letter from that issuer explaining the error. In most cases a straightforward explanation of an error on a 1099 will settle matters satisfactorily and quickly.

● **Understatement penalties.** The IRS is cracking down on persons who understate the tax due on their returns: The penalty on a substantial tax understatement is 20% of the understated tax.

A substantial understatement is deemed to occur when the amount of the understatement exceeds $5,000 (generally $10,000 for corporations) or 10% of your total tax bill for the year, whichever is greater. *Strategy:* The tax law contains many gray areas that are subject to uncertain interpretation by the IRS and the courts. If you claim large deductions that are grounded in one of these gray areas (and which don't involve a tax shelter), you can protect yourself from the substantial underpayment penalty by making an adequate disclosure of all the facts. File Form 8275, *Disclosure Statement Under Section 6661.*

You should also be able to cite a credible authority (such as a court decision, published IRS ruling, Treasury regulation, etc.) in support of your reading of the law. After making such a disclosure, you'll be safe from the 20% penalty even if the IRS and Tax Court finally rule against your position.

● **Retirement plan rollovers.** Individual Retirement Accounts and other retirement programs are an increasingly popular investment tool for high-tax-bracket individuals. Transfers and rollovers of funds between accounts have become common as persons change investment selections.

Trap: When funds are taken out of a retirement account, the account trustee will issue a Form 1099-R reporting the withdrawal to the IRS—even if the withdrawal is part of a tax-free transfer of funds between plans. Thus, the IRS will know about the withdrawal, and if it doesn't see a transfer of funds reported properly on your return, it may assume that

you kept the withdrawn money for personal use.

What to do: Include the amount shown on the 1099-R in your gross income, as reported in line 16a of your Form 1040 tax return. Then, on line 16b of your 1040, report zero as the amount of the distribution that was taxable, if properly rolled over.

Checklist: Before Mailing Your Return

Check to make sure you've completed everything on this list. A slip-up can cause delays and inconvenience. Moreover, every time you draw attention to your return, you increase the chance of audit.

✔ **Does your name, address and Social Security number appear on page 1?** If you used the IRS address label, be sure you have made any necessary corrections.

✔ **Have you put your Social Security number on every page,** every document and every check to be sent to the IRS?

✔ **Are all Form W-2s attached?**

✔ **Are all other necessary forms and schedules attached?**

✔ **Have you checked and rechecked your arithmetic?**

✔ **Is the form signed and dated?** Both husband and wife must sign a joint return.

✔ **If you owe money, is your check or money order attached to the return?** Have you written your Social Security number, the year and "Form 1040" on the check? (Note: You may be able to pay your taxes by credit card.)

✔ **Is the return addressed to the correct IRS office?**

✔ **Have you affixed the correct postage?** If your return is more than five pages, 32¢ postage is inadequate, and your return will not be mailed.

✔ **Have you made a copy of the return for your own records?**

And Avoid These Simple Mistakes. . .

The most common tax return filing errors are also the simplest: forgetting to sign a return, making math errors, and omitting necessary IRS forms.

If you forget to sign, the IRS will notify you and send you a form to sign and send back for attachment to your return. If you make an arithmetic mistake, the IRS will correct it and notify you, even if it's in your favor. If after mailing in your return, you discover that you left out a necessary document, such as a W-2 form, you'll do best to wait until the IRS notifies you of the omission and then send in the missing form. The omitted W-2 is much more likely to get lost if the IRS receives it in a separate mailing without having asked for it. In some cases, if a return requires a correction, an amended tax return (Form 1040X) should be filed.

Source: Charles Pomo, former IRS appeals officer, now tax principal with Ernst & Young, 277 Park Ave., New York, NY 10172.

How to Get More Time to File

If you need extra time to prepare your tax return, you can get it automatically: Just file Form 4868 with your local IRS Service Center by April 15. The deadline for filing your return will be pushed back four months to August 15. If you're self-employed, the extension gives you four more months in which to make contributions to a Keogh plan (if the plan was set up by December 31 of the preceding year).

Caution: A filing extension does not extend the time for paying your tax. The instructions on Form 4868 tell you how to estimate your tax. While you are not required to pay the tax to get an extension, not paying the tax can result in interest and penalties.

Never file a late return without getting an extension. The penalty for filing late without an extension is 5% of the unpaid tax per month, up to a maximum penalty of 25%. There is also a minimum penalty for not getting your tax return in within 60 days of its due date—$100 or 100% of the tax due, whichever is less. You'll also be penalized for paying your taxes late, and you'll be charged interest on the late-paid tax.

Second extensions: It is possible to get a second filing extension from the IRS by filing Form 2688. But the second extension isn't automatic. You must have a valid reason for requesting it, such as a death in the family or loss of your records. A second exten-sion, if granted, gives you an extra two months—until October 15—to file your return.

Big Tax Refund? You've Done Something Wrong

If you received a fat tax refund this year, don't feel too happy about it. It means you overpaid your estimated taxes or had too much withheld from your salary. In effect, you made an interest-free loan to the government, when you could have been using the money for yourself—in an interest-paying bank account.

Trap: The IRS can withhold all or part of your refund to offset a tax liability, a debt to a government agency (for instance, a student loan) or unpaid child support.

What to do: File a new Form W-4 or W-4A to reduce the amount withheld from your salary. If you pay estimated tax, reduce your quarterly payments.

Caution: Don't overdo it. You may be hit with underpayment penalties unless withholding taxes plus estimated tax payments amount to at least 90% of your total tax bill, or 100% of the prior year's liability. (*Note:* After 1998, high-income tax-payers are subject to special rules for avoiding underpayment penalties.)

Tax Refunds: The Second Time Around

It's not too late to get a cash refund for past years by filing a Form 1040X with the IRS. Take the time to review old tax returns to see if you overlooked any-thing that may lead to getting money back. The time limit for amending your original tax return is three years from the date you filed the original return or two years from the date you actually paid the tax, whichever is later. Early filers are treated as though they had filed on the actual due date of the return.

Caution: Filing an amended return may invite the IRS to take a second look at your original return. If there is anything on it that you think may not pass this additional IRS scrutiny, you should be wary about amending. On the other hand, if you will get back a significantly larger refund by amending, or you know the IRS can't challenge anything on the original return, it may be worth the risk.

What You Can Amend

The most common oversights that eventually lead to an additional refund:

● **Filing the wrong form.** Short-form filers might well have been able to file a long form and get the benefit of a lower tax bill. But you are not stuck with your original choice. Perhaps you used the short form because you were in a last-minute rush to file the return, or you thought the long form was too difficult. If you file a long form this year but filed a short form for the past two years, check your earlier returns to see if you could have used the long form.

No matter what your original reason for filing the short form, it is worth taking the time now to see how much you would save by filing the long form.

● **Overlooking deductions.** As you fill out your return this year, perhaps you will remember deductions that you should have taken in the past. If you forgot to claim an item to which you were entitled, consider amending that year's return.

● **Overlooking credits.** Taxpayers often forget about or miscalculate certain tax credits. *Carefully review the following on your past returns:*

● **Excess Social Security tax paid.**

● **Child-care credit.**

● **Earned income credit.**

● **Using the wrong filing status.** When a married couple files separately, the overall tax bill is usually larger. If you would have saved taxes by filing jointly, you are allowed to amend your return.

Editor's note: The fact that you may have filed separate estimated taxes does not commit you to that filing status on your tax return. However, once you've filed a joint return and the due date of the return has passed, you can't change the filing status to married filing separately.

● **Overlooking exemptions.** If you were supporting a parent who didn't live with you during the year, you may have forgotten to claim him or her as an exemption on your return.

● **Neglecting to do five-** or 10-year averaging on lump-sum distributions. Many taxpayers forget this special tax saver when they receive a lump sum from their retirement plan and don't expect to roll it over into another plan. If you received such a distribution, make sure you compared your tax liability with five- or 10-year averaging and without it, to see which one produced the lower tax.

● **Overpaying Social Security.** If you worked for more than one employer in a single year, you may have paid too much Social Security tax. *(Editor's note:* The maximum you must pay is 6.2% of the "wage base" ($68,400 in 1998).

● **Neglecting to check for retroactive tax changes.** Sometimes the IRS, Congress and the courts make retroactive decisions that may allow you to take a deduction for something that was disallowed in the past. Keep informed about all tax changes to see if any of them affect your past returns.

Source: John L. Withers, special consultant for IRS regulations and procedures, Deloitte & Touche, Washington Service Center, 1900 M St. NW, Washington, DC 20036.

WHAT TO DO WHEN THE IRS PLACES A LIEN ON YOUR HOME

People who owe money to the IRS often find that a tax lien has been placed on their home. The IRS files the lien to get a preferential interest in the proceeds from the sale of the house.

Catch 22: Banks usually won't lend money to homeowners while an IRS lien is outstanding. And the IRS won't release the lien until the taxes are paid.

Inside information: You can remedy this situation by taking advantage of a little-known IRS procedure. Ask for a Certificate of Discharge of Property from Federal Tax Lien. Under this procedure the IRS agrees to release the lien simultaneously with the payment of the money you owe it. The bank can then register a mortgage that takes priority over the interests of all other creditors, including the IRS. The mortgage will give you the money you need to pay the back taxes.

Free Information From the IRS

The IRS publishes a wealth of material on virtually every subject taxpayers have to grapple with. The publications are all free for the asking.

The IRS updates its general tax guides every year. They are indispensable.

Most Helpful

● Publication 17, *Your Federal Income Tax*
● Publication 334, *Tax Guide for Small Business.*
● Publication 553, *Highlights of 1997 Tax Changes.*
● Publication 910, *Guide to Free Tax Services.*

Specialized Publications

These publications contain in-depth explanations of a wide variety of tax-related subjects. Among the publications are:

● Publication 523, *Selling Your Home.*
● Publication 552, *Recordkeeping for Individuals.*
● Publication 554, *Older Americans' Tax Guide.*
● Publication 521, *Moving Expenses.*
● Publication 547, *Casualties, Disasters, and Thefts.*
● Publication 575, *Pension and Annuity Income.*
● Publication 587, *Business Use of Your Home.*
● Publication 526, *Charitable Contributions.*
● Publication 530, *Tax Information for First-Time Homeowners.*
● Publication 590, *Individual Retirement Arrangements (IRAs).*
● Publication 907, *Tax Highlights for Persons with Disabilities.*
● Publication 915, *Social Security Benefits.*
● Publication 917, *Business Use of a Car.*

To get these publications: Call the IRS toll-free number, *1-800-829-FORM*, or download them from the IRS website **www.irs.ustreas.gov.**

More Facts on Amended Returns

You can file an amended return or claim a refund on Form 1040X within three years after the original return was due or two years after you actually paid the tax, whichever is later.

The time limits are absolute. If you are even one day late, your claim must be disallowed. Use Form 1040X if you file early and discover an error before April 15. You will get faster handling.

You can use Form 1045 for claims based on carrybacks (net operating losses, certain credits). This will get you a fast refund, as the IRS must act within 90 days. But the action isn't final. The claim can be disallowed later. Time limits on these claims are figured from the year the carryback arose.

Form 1040X has space to write your income, deductions and credits as you reported them on your original return and the changes you want to make for those amounts.

Important: Include explanations for the changes you are making and the year you are amending on page 2. You must calculate the new tax on the corrected amount, just as you would on your regular return.

State all possible grounds. If the matter ever reaches court, you may be limited to the exact claim stated on the form. If, for example, you're not sure whether an item should be claimed as a business loss, a casualty loss or a bad debt, state all three grounds in the alternative. You can even assert inconsistent grounds.

Where to send it: Mail the amended return to the IRS Service Center where you now live. If you moved during the year, mail it to the service center at your new address. Be sure to complete the information on the front of the 1040X about where your original return was processed in order to expedite your return.

Caution: When you amend your federal tax return, your state tax liability from that year may be affected, too.

It's important to assess your audit risk before you amend your return. It depends on how much you will get back by amending, why you are amending and the safety of your original return.

Question: Is the amount that you are getting back worth the risk for what you might possibly lose?

Safer amendments:
● **Changes of very small dollar amounts,** especially where the amount on the original return is very small, too.

● **Mathematical changes.**

Not-so-safe amendments:

● **Any change that has huge tax consequences on your return.**

● **Losses from business activity.**

● **Reclassifying ordinary income to capital gain.**

How Long Should Tax File Documents Be Kept?

● **Normally,** tax returns and supporting documents should be kept for three years from date of filing.

● **If income has been previously underreported by 25% or more:** Six years.

● **In cases of previous failure to file or serious suspicion of criminal fraud:** Indefinitely. Put canceled checks and supporting documents into an envelope, mark it with the tax year and the discard date and put it on the top shelf of your highest closet. You'll only need this material if you are audited. Returns should be kept in an accessible file drawer.

Editor's note: You need to keep records of what you paid for stocks, mutual fund shares and other assets to determine your basis when you sell them. Keep these records for as long as you own the assets (plus at least three years after the sale).

Source: Stephanie Winston, president, The Organizing Principle, 230 E. 15 St., New York, NY 10003, and the author of The Organized Executive, *Warner Books.*

TAX-FREE INCOME CHECKLIST

The IRS isn't allowed to put the bite on every dollar that finds its way into a taxpayer's pocket. *The following is a list of what's exempt from taxation:*

● **Gain on the sale of your home.** You pay no tax on the first $250,000 of profit ($500,000 on a joint return) from the sale of your main home. The only requirement: that you owned and lived in the home for at least two out of five years before the date of sale. The exclusion is prorated if you're forced to relocate in less than two years because of a new job, bad health or some other unforeseeable circumstances.

● **Gifts you receive.** Any gift tax is payable by the person who makes the gift. The recipient gets the gift free and clear of tax.

● **Money you borrow.** Normally, borrowing is not a taxable transaction. But you'll be taxed if you borrow from your IRA, if you borrow more than $50,000 (or half your account) from your company pension fund or, in some cases, if you get an interest-free loan from your company or a family member.

● **IRA rollovers.** No tax is payable on a lump-sum distribution that is received from a company pension plan if you put it into an IRA within 60 days. You can also take money tax-free from your IRA if you roll it over within 60 days into another IRA.

Caution: To avoid withholding tax, transfer the money directly from the retirement plan to the IRA trustee.

● **Inheritances.** Beneficiaries don't pay federal income tax on an inheritance (*Editor's note:* except for regular IRAs, retirement benefits and other income items on which no income tax was paid by the person during his or her lifetime). Moreover, if you inherit property that has increased in value, you receive it at its "stepped-up" estate value. You would then use this value, rather than the original cost, to calculate your taxable gain if you sold the property.

● **Life insurance proceeds.** The beneficiary gets the full amount income-tax-free. But the estate may be liable for estate tax on the proceeds.

● **Property settlements between spouses in divorce or separation proceedings.** The recipient owes no tax at the time property is transferred. (There may be a tax later if property is sold at a gain.)

● **Child-support payments.** They are tax-free to the recipient. Alimony payments to a spouse or ex-spouse, however, are taxable to the recipient.

● **Money recovered in lawsuits for physical personal injuries.** But money recovered for nonphysical personal injuries (such as defamation), punitive damages or compensation for lost wages or other income is taxable.

● **Workers Compensation payments.**

● **Disability payments from accident and health insurance plans.** The payments are tax-free if you paid for the insurance, but taxable if your employer paid the premiums.

● **Federal income tax refunds.** Note, however, that any interest the IRS pays you on a late refund is taxable.

● **State income tax refunds,** pro-

Don't Pay More Than The Law Demands

Thirty years ago Judge Learned Hand of the U.S. Court of Appeals said: "There is nothing sinister in so arranging one's affairs as to keep taxes as low as possible. Everybody does so, rich or poor; and all do right, for nobody owes any public duty to pay more than the law demands."*

Here are the best ways I know of to keep your taxes as low as possible under the tax law we have today.

● **Be aggressive both in setting strategies that save taxes and in preparing your return.** Too many people deny themselves the full tax breaks they're entitled to because they're afraid they will be audited. They take overly conservative positions on their returns and scale back unusually large deductions that they think the IRS will disallow. In effect, these people are auditing themselves. The IRS never gets a chance to review the item. *Better way:* Take the full deduction no matter how high it is in relation to your income. Write "See substantiation attached" beside the item and attach photocopies of the bills, receipts, canceled checks, etc., that prove you paid the amount you're deducting. Don't audit yourself—let the IRS do it.

Commissioner v. *Newman, 159 F2d 848.*

● **Buy a vacation home.** The problem with renting a vacation home is that you get no tax break from it.

---

vided you didn't itemize deductions on your federal return for that year.

● **Municipal-bond interest.** Generally, it's exempt from federal income tax and sometimes from state and local tax as well. However, interest from some "private purpose" municipal bonds is subject to the Alternative Minimum Tax. And, municipal-bond interest is taken into account in figuring whether any of your Social Security benefits are taxable.

● **"Like-kind" property exchanges**—swaps of tangible property or real estate are tax-free if the properties are of similar nature.

● **Vacation home rental.** If you rent your vacation place out for 14 days or less, the income is not taxed.

● **Kids' wages.** Dependent children can earn up to the standard-deduction amount ($4,250 in 1998).

● **Kids' investment income.** Dependent children can receive up to $700 of unearned income tax-free

(dividends, interest, etc.) in 1998.

● **Scholarships and fellowships.** They are tax-free to the extent they are used to cover tuition, fees, books and course equipment. Grants for room and board, etc., are taxable.

● **Fringe benefits from your employer.** *Examples:* health insurance, pension contributions, up to $50,000 of life insurance coverage, certain child and dependent care, adoption assistance and supper money.

● **Meals and lodging,** if furnished by your employer for the employer's conve-nience—for example, to enable the employee to remain at the workplace.

● **Private annuities.** The payments are partially excludable from tax based on an interest-rate factor, the asset exchanged and the life expectancy of the person receiving the asset.

How they work: They are usually arranged by individuals who are not in the business of issuing annuities. One person makes periodic annuity payments in exchange for the other person's assets.

Example: A father owns a business worth $2 million. He wants to transfer the business to his daughter. So, he sells the business to his daughter and the daughter promises to pay a certain amount (based on IRS tables) to her father for the rest of his life, no matter how long he lives.

Loophole: On the father's death, the unpaid portion of the purchase price is not taxed.

Source: Edward Mendlowitz, partner, Mend-lowitz Weitsen, LLP, 2 Penn Plaza, New York, NY 10121.

But when you buy one, the carrying charges—mortgage interest and property taxes—are deductible. (Mortgage interest on one second home is fully deductible, as long as the loan doesn't exceed the cost of the home plus improvements.) Also, the appreciation in the property's value goes untaxed until you sell it, and you can earn tax-free income by renting out the place each year for two weeks or less. The rent is not taxable.

● **Hire the best tax preparer and planner you can find.** Don't let the fee stop you from getting sound professional advice. To save taxes, you need a specialist who can guide you through financial transactions. Most tax professionals will save you far more money than they will charge you.

● **Buy deferred annuities (SPDAs) or universal life insurance.** Interest earnings on your investment in these insurance company products accumulate tax-deferred until you cash them in. And these investments pay relatively high interest. With a deferred annuity, you have a choice of taking out the money you have invested (plus earnings) in a lump sum or in a series of payments over a number of years. If you don't cash in your universal life policy, your beneficiary will receive the proceeds income-tax-free.

Caution: Consider that all distributions from deferred annuities are taxed as ordinary income. Moreover, there may be steep transaction costs (commissions and fees) and most companies charge penalties for early withdrawal. Interest rates, fees and penalty structures vary widely, so it's important to shop around for the best deal.

● **Make the maximum contribution to your company's 401(k) plan.** Earnings on your investment are tax-deferred—and you get the equivalent of a deduction for the contribution, since you don't pay tax on the salary that goes into the plan. That's one of the biggest deductions you're going to get.

● **Keep a diary of all tax-deductible expenses.** Record the details of travel and entertainment expenses at or near the time you incurred them. Keep track of business expenses for which your company doesn't

reimburse you. Keep a list of gifts you make to charity, especially the unusual ones that you might not remember when it comes time to do your return, such as donations of old clothes and expenses of volunteer work. Also keep a list of unreimbursed medical expenses, including out-of-pocket transportation costs.

● **Create your own venture partnership.** Form a limited partnership to finance a new business that needs money up front for deductible expenses. The partnership can be structured so that income and losses are allocated differently than the individual investor's actual capital contributions. A higher share of the losses can go to the person investing the money. If the person who has the losses also has income from other types of passive investments, the partnership losses will shelter that income.

● **Invest in rental real estate, a house or small apartment building that you actively manage.** If your write-offs for depreciation, taxes, etc., exceed the rent, and your Adjusted Gross Income is under $100,000, you can deduct up to $25,000 of losses against your salary and other taxable income. If your AGI is between $100,000 and $150,000, you can deduct some of your losses against taxable income. If your AGI is above $150,000, the deduction is lost.

● **Let family members inherit assets that have appreciated in value.** If you sell the assets before you die, the full increase in value will be taxed. But if you let your beneficiaries inherit the property, they receive it at its stepped-up, date-of-death value, and income tax is forgiven on the appreciation. If you need cash before your death, borrow against the assets, rather than sell them.

● **Minimize your AMT liability.** Find out now whether you are going to be subject to the Alternative Minimum Tax (AMT) this year. If you are, plan to take advantage of the AMT. *Instead of deferring income and accelerating deductions, do the exact opposite:* Accelerate income and defer deductions. Income brought into an AMT year is taxed at a considerably lower rate than the top regular tax rate. Deductions should be shifted into next year, where, assuming it's a non-AMT year,

> "If you let your beneficiaries inherit [assets that have appreciated in value], they receive it at its stepped-up, date-of-death value, and income tax is forgiven on the appreciation."

they will give you greater tax benefits. But don't go over-board. Accelerate only enough income so that you are at your "AMT break-even point"—just short of the level at which you must pay regular tax.

Source: Edward Mendlowitz, partner, Mendlowitz Weitsen, LLP, 2 Penn Plaza, New York, NY 10121.

Frequently Overlooked Deductions

● **"Points" paid for mortgage on purchase or improvement of principal residence.**

● **State unemployment and disability taxes withheld.**

● **Expenses related to seminars attended for business purposes.** Deductible items include registration fees, travel, lodging and 50% of the cost of meals.

● **Travel expenses** to check on income-producing property.

● **Cost of telephone, postage,** office supplies and automobile operation (trips to and from broker) to monitor investments.

● **Books, magazines and newsletters** on investment, financial or tax matters, including appropriate daily papers (e.g., *Wall Street Journal).*

● **Insurance and storage charges** for merchandise held as a speculative investment.

● **Out-of-pocket expenses incurred in providing charitable services.** May deduct actual cost of auto usage, tolls and parking.

● **Out-of-pocket expenses incurred in changing jobs.** Include the cost of printing résumés or traveling to an interview.

● **A portion of health insurance for the self-employed.**

● **Charitable contributions made through payroll withholdings** (e.g., United Way).

● **Deductible items on December credit card statement,** even if paid in the following year, include medical expenses, charitable contributions, and miscellaneous business expenses.

Source: Barry Salzberg, CPA, partner in charge of Executive Financing Counseling Services with the firm of Deloitte & Touche, LLP, 2 World Trade Center, New York, NY 10181.

Easy Tests for Dependency

To be claimed as a dependent for the purposes of the income tax exemption, a person must meet certain criteria.

1. The dependent must be related to you or be a member of your household. *The individual must fall within one of the following categories:*

> Child, grandchild, adopted child, stepchild, etc.
> Brother, sister, half brother, stepbrother, etc.
> Parent, grandparent, but not foster parent.
> Stepfather, stepmother.
> Brother or sister of your father or mother.
> Son or daughter of your brother or sister.
> Father-in-law, mother-in-law, etc.

Persons you claim as dependents who are unrelated to you must live with you the entire year as members of your household. Temporary absences, such as hospital stays or vacations, are allowed.

Can a foster child be claimed as a dependent? Only if your home is the child's principal home and the child is a member of your household for the entire year. However, if you are receiving payments from a child placement agency or a state agency, the payments are considered reimbursements for expenses incurred and you are not allowed to claim the exemption.

In a divorce situation, the dependency exemption for a child normally goes to the parent who has custody.

There are instances in which a noncustodial parent can claim a child as an exemption: when there is a multiple support agreement that allows the child to be claimed by a taxpayer other than the custodial parent; when a signed release from the custodial parent gives the right to someone else; when a pre-1985 divorce decree grants the exemption to the noncustodial parent, who provides at least $600 support in the year the exemption is claimed.

2. The dependent must meet the gross income test. The person you claim as a dependent in any year must earn less than the exemption amount ($2,700 in 1998). However, the earned income test does not apply if the dependent is your child and is either under 19 or a full-time student under 24.

3. The individual must meet the support test. You must provide more than one-half of the dependent's support for the calendar year in which you take the exemption. Total support includes money spent on food, clothing, education, medical and dental care, recreation, transportation, and similar items.

There are two exceptions to the one-half support rule. The first—support is provided by several taxpayers, as in the case of caring for an aging parent. Under these circumstances, all taxpayers who contribute 10% or more to that parent's support must sign a multiple support agreement. Then, one of those taxpayers is entitled to the exemption. The second exception to the support rule applies to children whose parents are divorced or separated, as discussed above.

4. The individual must be a citizen of the United States. Only persons who are U.S. citizens, residents, or nationals, or are residents of Canada or Mexico for some part of the calendar year, are eligible to be claimed as dependents.

5. The dependent cannot file a joint return. You cannot claim as an exemption a person who has filed a joint return with a spouse. The only exception is when the joint return was filed merely to claim a refund and no tax was due.

Editor's note: In addition, you cannot claim an exemption for someone unless that person has a Social Security number. If you are in the process of a legal adoption, you can obtain a temporary taxpayer identification number from the IRS for a child placed with you by filing Form W-7A (use Form W-7 for a foreign adoption).

Source: *David L. Nelson, tax partner in charge of personal financial planning, Ernst & Young, 333 Clay St., Suite 3100, Houston, TX 77002.*

The Tricky Alternative Minimum Tax

A hidden danger that may unexpectedly increase the tax bills owed by many high-income individuals is the expanded and toughened Alternative Minimum Tax. Originally, the AMT applied primarily to people with large tax-shelter losses or unusually large capital gains. Now, however, most upper-income individuals, when devising year-ahead tax-planning strategies, will have to think about how to avoid falling into the AMT trap.

Dangers:

● **Due to recent tax law changes, many more people will be liable for the tax.** Claiming the child tax credit, education credits or other credits triggers the AMT.

● **While tax reform reduced normal tax rates,** it increased the bite of the AMT by both increasing the AMT tax rate and adding to the list of items that can produce AMT liability.

● **Many high-income executives have entered into income-deferral programs** (through salary-deferral agreements and the like). But for a person who is subject to the AMT, income deferral may be the worst strategy.

If, however, you are subject to the AMT, smart tax planning can cut your liability, and maybe even make the AMT work for you.

How the Tax Works

The AMT must be worked out—in addition to your regular tax bill. If it produces a tax liability that's larger than that derived under the regular rules, you must pay this increased amount instead of your regular tax bill.

Income that's subject to the AMT is taxed at a rate that is less than the normal top tax rate, but when computing the amount of income that's subject to the AMT, you lose the benefit of many deductions and credits that serve to cut your regular tax bill.

When figuring the amount of income subject to the AMT, you start with your adjusted gross income as reported on your normal return. *To this amount you must add certain "tax preference items," namely:*

● **Profits received from the exercise of incentive stock options.** That is the difference between the value of the stock you acquire and the price paid for it.

● **Accelerated depreciation that you claim on property or equipment.** This is depreciation that exceeds the amount you're entitled to claim for AMT purposes.

● **Excess intangible drilling costs,** such as those attributable to an investment in an oil or gas tax shelter.

● **Interest paid on certain tax-exempt bonds,** defined as private activity bonds, which are issued by local governments on behalf of private companies. Ask your broker about the status of the bonds in your portfolio.

After you total up your AMT income, you subtract your deductions. However, under AMT rules, many deductions that are allowed under normal rules are prohibited, while other deductions are limited.

No AMT deductions are allowed for:

- **State and local taxes.**
- **Tax-shelter losses.**
- **Miscellaneous deductions,** such as unreimbursed employee business expenses, tax-preparation fees, investment advisory fees, membership dues paid to professional organizations and the like.

Limited AMT deductions are allowed for:

- **Medical expenses.** Under normal rules, these are deductible to the extent that they're in excess of 7½% of your AGI. But to be deductible for the AMT, medical expenses must exceed 10% of AGI.
- **Home financings.** Under a complicated set of rules, the AMT deduction for interest expense may be limited when a house has been refinanced. Check with your tax adviser for details.

After your net AMT income (AGI, plus preference items, minus deductions) is figured out, you're entitled to claim a personal exemption. This exemption is $45,000 on a joint return and $33,750 on a single return.

After subtracting your personal exemption from your net AMT income, multiply the resulting figure by the AMT tax rate of 26% on the first $175,000 of income over the exemption amount, and 28% on excess income. This is your AMT liability. It's what you owe the IRS for the year if it's larger than your regular tax bill as computed under normal rules.

Editor's note: You can't reduce your AMT liability by tax credits (other than a limited foreign tax credit).

Looking Ahead

It's essential that you determine your potential AMT liability early in the year. Conventional tax-planning strategies that are used to reduce the normal tax bill may increase your AMT liability. Therefore, it's imperative to adopt the right strategies as soon as possible. Also, individuals are required to pay their estimated tax liabilities through quarterly estimated tax payments. If the AMT liability isn't discovered until year-end, underpayment penalties may arise.

To figure out your potential AMT liability for next year, start by looking at the tax return you've just prepared. Adjust it by estimating the amount of income you expect to earn and by factoring in the deductions you plan to take and the tax-cutting strategies you intend to use. Come to an estimate of AGI, then apply the AMT rules. Get a copy of IRS Form 6251, *Computation of Alternative Minimum Tax,* to help you with the figuring. You'll get a good picture of whether you will owe the AMT.

Cutting the Tax

When you're planning to face the AMT, the key is that the AMT tax rate is lower than the top regular tax rate. The goal is to make this fact work for you. *Strategies:*

- **Accelerate the receipt of income.** Conventional wisdom calls for taxpayers to defer the receipt of income to postpone tax. But if you know that you'll be subject to the AMT this year but not next year, it makes sense to take as much income as possible now. Consider exchanging tax-exempt bonds for taxable bonds that pay interest at a higher rate, cashing in savings bonds and paying tax on their appreciation or arranging to receive bonuses and other forms of taxable income before year-end.

- **Be selective with your deductions.** Again, because of the AMT's low tax rate, you may want to save your deductions for a later year when they'll be more valuable. But if you are going to take deductions, take those that provide you with some benefit under the AMT (such as charitable deductions). Do not incur expenses that are deductible under normal rules but not under AMT rules. Thus, you will want to postpone

AMT Avoidance Tactics

Strategies that can keep you out of the AMT:

- **Exercise incentive stock options with care.** Exercise only a limited amount or postpone your exercise of options to avoid AMT liability.
- **Avoid prepaying state and local income tax,** if paying it early throws you into the AMT.
- **Unload "private activity" municipal bonds** if the interest income makes you liable for the AMT. See your broker.

TAX SHELTERING A WINDFALL

Want to bet on a sure thing? It's certain that we all want to keep as much as we can of any windfall we get. Another sure bet is that taxes can devour a large chunk. But you may be able to substantially reduce your tax liability with a little planning. After all, a windfall usually isn't as unexpected as it appears to be: You buy a lottery ticket, or bet on a horse, or take legal action—you believe you will win or at least have a chance to win.

At one time, windfalls often did not get taxed—not so much because of active cheating, but because no effective reporting system existed and the lucky recipients didn't know, or care, that their new wealth might be taxable. Now the IRS and many state tax agencies have improved reporting systems, and tax awareness is definitely on the upswing. Most windfalls are subject to income taxes, sharing a windfall with friends and family can generate gift taxes and what you don't spend may be hit with estate taxes when you die.

The next time you enter a sweepstakes that gives a choice between a lump-sum payment or annuity payments, consider the following points.

● **A lump sum draws the higher income tax rate.** Giving some of it away can result in gift taxes. Any portion you still have when you die is includable in your estate. On the other hand, you may be able to invest a lump sum at earnings comparable to the annuity payments and keep the after-tax principal intact.

● **An annuity is subject to income tax each year,** as payments are received by you or your heirs, with generally fewer worries about gift taxes (since gifts would be smaller). The present value of future payments on the date of your death is includable in your estate. Of course, an annuity also provides some protection from spend-thrift tendencies.

Gambling Winnings

All gambling winnings are taxable. In fact, federal income tax is withheld at a rate of 28% from some types of winnings—for example, a state lottery win of $5,000 or more or a jai alai win of $600 or more. To soften the tax blow, you can deduct your losses, limited to the winnings reported on your tax return, but only as an itemized deduction unless you are in the business of gambling. Deductions for losses are not subject to the 2% limitation placed on deductions for miscellaneous expenses.

Records that document your losses are essential. The IRS does not take kindly to estimates of gambling losses or to records showing lots of losses and no wins but the big one. So, keep written records (an accurate diary is recommended), and receipts when available (wagering tickets,

the payment of items such as local property taxes until after year-end, whenever possible.

● **Time your tax moves carefully.** You may be able to maximize the benefit you receive from certain tax moves by careful timing. For example, if you own valuable incentive stock options, you may be able to avoid AMT liability by simply postponing your exercise of them or by exercising only a limited amount.

The only way to find out if the AMT poses a problem for you is to work through the figures. Ask your tax adviser to help you do this while there's still plenty of time to adopt the appropriate strategies for the upcoming year.

Sources: Howard A. Rabinowitz, tax partner, and Lawrence W. Goldstein, tax manager, Ernst & Young, 277 Park Ave., New York, NY 10172.

Tax Breaks on U.S. Securities

U.S. government securities offer tax-saving opportunities that are perfectly safe and legal. They are exempt from state and local income tax—a big saving for individuals in high-tax states. Some kinds of U.S. securities offer federal tax advantages as well.

● **Treasury bills** are issued at a discount for periods of up to one year. You pay less than the bill's face value when you buy it, then redeem the bill for its full face value when it matures. Your gain isn't taxed until you cash in the bill. This means you can defer taxes to next year by buying a Treasury bill that matures after year-end. By contrast, if you invested the same money in a bank account or corporate bond, you would owe

canceled checks, credit records, bank withdrawal statements and credit receipts), of every dollar you spend and of all of your wins and losses. All kinds of gambling fall into the same pot, from bingo to bets on races and athletic events, to a state lottery.

As another tax saver, you might consider sharing the chance for wealth with family or friends. Sharing ownership of a chance to win will cut the tax bite. Sharing your winnings won't. For example, if you win $1 million and give part of it to friends and relatives, you still pay the income tax on the full amount, and maybe some gift taxes as well. But if you can list yourself and one or more buddies on a chance to win, each winner will be taxed on his or her share of the winnings, generally resulting in a lower total tax.

Insurance or Damages Awards

Are damages taxable? Damages to compensate you for physical personal injuries are tax-free (although you cannot deduct any compensation you receive for medical expenses). Damages to compensate you for nonphysical personal injuries (such as libel and slander), on the other hand, are fully taxable. Punitive damages are also fully taxable regardless of whether they relate to otherwise tax-free or taxable injuries. Similarly, damages to compensate you for lost wages or breach of contract are fully taxable.

An award for property damages is taxable only to the extent it exceeds your basis in the property.

In any legal action, to avoid unnecessary taxes, insist that the injury be called by its correct name.

You can claim an itemized deduction for expenses, such as legal fees and court costs, to obtain a taxable award. Expenses related to a partly taxable award are partly deductible. Legal fees and court costs to obtain a taxable award must be combined with investment expenses, unreimbursed employment expenses and other miscellaneous expenses. The total of these expenses, reduced by 2% of your Adjusted Gross Income, is then deductible as an itemized deduction.

Source: Nancy A. Anderson, tax research and training specialist, H&R Block, Inc., 4410 Main St., Kansas City, MO 64111, and writer-editor of H&R Block/Macmillan Publishing Company tax publications.

tax this year on the interest earned before year-end.

● **Series EE savings bonds** let you choose how you'll be taxed. You can pay tax on your income from the bonds each year. Or you can defer paying tax on the bonds until some date between now and the time the bonds mature—an option that makes sense if you expect to have offsetting deductions or to be in a lower tax bracket in the future.

When Series EE bonds mature, you can elect to further defer tax on them by converting them into Series HH bonds. *Planning option:* Supplement your retirement income by buying EE bonds until you retire, deferring the tax on them, then convert them into HH bonds to collect extra cash income after you retire, all without paying tax on the increase in the bonds' value.

● **New I bonds.** First sold on September 1, 1998, these bonds provide both a fixed rate of interest and a variable rate adjusted for inflation. Both types of interest are taxable, but like EE bonds, you can choose to defer tax until the bonds mature or are redeemed.

Editor's note: If you redeem I bonds or EE bonds bought after 1989 in your name (or joint name with your spouse) to pay for higher-education costs for yourself, your spouse, or your dependent, the interest can become tax-free (depending on your income in the year of redemption).

Tax-Deferred Income Checklist

Deferring taxation of a portion of your income until a year in which your income will be lower can save you a bundle on your tax bill. Here's a list of the kinds of income eligible for deferral—starting with the one that no one should overlook.

✔ **Income from a regular IRA account,** Keogh or qualified corporate pension, SEP (simplified employee pension), SIMPLE (savings incentive match plan for employees) or profit-sharing plan is tax-deferred until time of withdrawal.

✔ **Interest on deferred annuities** is tax-deferred until you "annuitize" (start to receive annuity payments).

✔ **Income from U.S. Series EE or I savings bonds** is tax-deferred if you do not elect to be taxed on it annually.

✔ **Income from the exercise of incentive stock option** plans is tax-deferred until the stock is sold. (But it may trigger the Alternative Minimum Tax.)

✔ **Income is deferred under a section 401(k) plan.**

✔ **Income earned pursuant to an** "unfunded deferred compensation" plan (i.e., deferred pay) is tax-deferred until actually received.

✔ **Receipts from the sale of stock options,** typically, are not taxable until the options are exercised or expire.

✔ **Capital appreciation is tax-deferred** up to the point when you sell.

Source: Edward Mendlowitz, partner, Mendlowitz Weitsen, LLP, 2 Penn Plaza, New York, NY 10121.

Sales Tax Can Add Up— To Savings

Sales taxes are not deductible. They are absolutely off limits—but, there are ways to use the sales tax to reduce your tax bill.

If you buy a big-ticket item, you cannot claim an itemized deduction for the state or local levy on the new purchase. But don't throw away the receipt—add the sales tax to your cost basis.

For property used in your trade or business, you can increase your depreciation deductions. For other assets, adding the sales tax to your cost will reduce any eventual gain you might have to report on a subsequent sale.

For example, suppose you buy a delivery truck to be used exclusively in your business. The purchase price is $25,000 plus an additional $1,500 in state sales taxes. The whole $26,500 is depreciable. Suppose, further, that you buy a painting for $25,000 plus $1,500 for the sales levy. When, after the artist has passed on, you sell the work for $30,000, your taxable gain will not be $5,000 but only $3,500. *Keep records:* They'll save you money.

Source: Special report, New Tax Loopholes for Investors, *written for Boardroom Classics by Robert A. Garber, tax attorney and vice president of a major investment-banking house. He writes frequently on tax matters and is the author of several books.*

Loopholes for Working Families

Very few working families take advantage of all the tax breaks they're entitled to. It seems the harder they work, the more taxes they pay. But the loopholes are there—for spouses who have separate jobs or separate businesses, and for those who work together in a family business.

Separate Corporations

When a husband and a wife own separate corporations, great care must be taken that one spouse is not a shareholder, officer, director, employee or check signer of the other spouse's corporation.

Trap: Such involvement by one spouse in the other's corporation will cause the loss of the full tax benefits that separate corporations are entitled to.

Tax Tactics, Strategies & Opportunities

For one thing, the corporations will be required to split the benefit of graduated income tax rates. For instance, instead of each corporation having its first $50,000 of taxable income taxed at 15%, the two companies will have to divide that amount—only $25,000 of each company's taxable income will be taxed at 15%. The other brackets will also have to be split. *(Editor's note:* Another trap is that involvement in a spouse's corporation can require the retirement plan of that corporation to cover the employees of the other spouse's corporation.) These are very important planning items. Don't be a shareholder, employee, officer, etc., of your spouse's corporation if you, too, own a corporation.

One Business

● **Tax advantages of operating the business as a sole proprietorship,** rather than a partnership or a corporation. You can hire your spouse as an employee, and your spouse's salary, which is deductible by the business, reduces the amount of self-employment income on which you have to pay Social Security tax.

Trap: If you set up the business as a partnership with your spouse, you will both be subject to self-employment tax on your income from the business.

● **Why pay your spouse a salary.** One reason is to increase the family's deductible pension-plan contributions. You may be contributing the maximum deductible amount to a Keogh or simplified employee pension plan. But your spouse's salary can be the basis of additional deductible retirement-plan contributions.

Paying your spouse a salary also may actually reduce the total amount of state tax the family pays. You may be able to split your income on state income tax returns, thus reducing the tax. Some states allow a husband and wife to file separate returns for state taxes, even though they file a joint federal income tax return.

● **Write off working vacations with your spouse.** The extra cost of taking your spouse along on a business trip isn't ordinarily deductible. But when the spouse is an employee of the business, it's much easier to make the case that his or her services are essential to the overall business purpose of the trip.

● **Hire your children.** Instead of giving them allowances, find real work for them to do in your business. Pay them reasonable salaries and deduct the salaries as a business expense. *Tax savings:* If your business is unincorporated, you don't pay Social Security tax on wages paid to a child who is under 18. Also, in 1998 a child can earn $4,250 totally tax-free—an additional $2,000 of a child's salary would escape tax if it was put into a deductible Individual Retirement Account.

Loophole: Pay the children a salary while they are going to college. Give them jobs doing market research for your business, product testing, sales, etc.

● **Medical insurance.** If your business is incorporated as a C corporation, the full amount you pay for medical insurance for you and your family is deductible. (But then you are subject to the extra costs of being a corporation—accounting, legal fees, FICA, unemployment insurance, additional bookkeeping costs, etc.)

For sole proprietors: Self-employed taxpayers can deduct 45% of their medical insurance premiums in 1998. The remaining 55% of premium payments are included in medical expenses (subject to the floor of 7.5% of Adjusted Gross Income).

● **Avoiding probate.** You can avoid the hassle of probate by setting up a revocable living trust and having the trust own the business, rather than yourself, under terms that pass ownership to your spouse when you die. This has no tax effect, but it facilitates transferring ownership of the business to your spouse—who won't have to wait until the probate process is completed to assume ownership.

Working Couples

You may be eligible for the child-care credit even if your spouse doesn't work. The tax law's definition of a working spouse includes a spouse who is a full-time student for at least five months during the year. So if you hire someone to look after the children while your spouse goes to school and you work, that person's wages qualify for the credit.

> " *Trap:* If you set up the business as a partnership with your spouse, you will both be subject to self-employment tax on your income from the business. "

Trap: If you hire baby-sitters, you must pay Social Security taxes for them, and in some states you must pay for their unemployment insurance. This could negate part of the benefit of the child-care credit.

Underwithholding trap: When both spouses work, it is easy to have too little tax withheld by your employer. You could end up paying the IRS a penalty for being underwithheld. To avoid this, fill out your W-4 forms very carefully and completely. Keep in mind that the form is designed to figure tax withholding from the beginning of the year. (You may want to take fewer withholding allowances than you're entitled to.)

Source: Edward Mendlowitz, partner, Mendlowitz Weitsen, LLP, 2 Penn Plaza, New York, NY 10121.

JOINT VERSUS SEPARATE RETURNS

Married couples can file a joint return or separate returns. Usually, a joint return works out better, especially if one spouse has appreciably higher income than the other. Nevertheless, filing separately can be advantageous in some situations:

● **Deductions for casualty losses must be reduced by 10% of Adjusted Gross Income.** On a joint return, the casualty loss is reduced by 10% of the combined Adjusted Gross Income (AGI), even if only one spouse suffered the loss. If separate returns are filed, the loss is reduced only by 10% of that spouse's income. *Example:* A husband has an AGI of $70,000; his wife, $20,000. The wife's jewelry, worth $25,000, is stolen. On a joint return, the loss must be reduced by $9,000 (10% of combined income); on a separate return, by only $2,000 (10% of the wife's income).

● **The same considerations apply if only one spouse has heavy medical or miscellaneous expenses,** since only expenses in excess of 7½% of AGI or miscellaneous expenses in excess of 2% of AGI are deductible.

Caution: The only way to tell for sure whether it's better to file jointly or separately is to take pencil and paper and figure the tax both ways.

Source: Herbert M. Paul, tax attorney with the firm of Herbert Paul, P.C., 805 Third Ave., New York, NY 10022.

Divorce Is Never Easy

Tax issues may be the last thing on a couple's mind when they experience marital difficulties. But ignoring them can cause serious repercussions. It is important for couples involved in a matrimonial dispute to seek the advice of a knowledgeable tax professional. *Here are some points to consider:*

● **Alimony.** Payments by a husband to a wife (or former wife), or vice versa, generally are deductible by the husband and taxable to the wife. They must be paid in cash, and the obligation to make payments must end on the death of the wife.

● **Child support.** Payments are not deductible by the parent who pays them, nor are they taxable to the parent who receives them.

● **Exemptions for dependents**. The parent who has custody of the children is the one entitled to claim the dependency exemption ($2,700 in 1998), regardless of which parent pays the greater amount of support. However, the exemption can be shifted to the noncustodial parent. The custodial parent simply signs Form 8332, waiving the exemption. The waiver can be made annually or on a permanent basis. *Planning point:* Decide from year to year which parent would receive a greater tax benefit from claiming the exemption. Generally the parent in the higher tax bracket will get the greater benefit. But a high-income taxpayer (for example, a single taxpayer with an Adjusted Gross Income [AGI] over $124,500 in 1998) loses the benefit from the exemption, so the lower-bracket parent would get the greater benefit in this case.

● **Family home.** Under a property settlement, a spouse who receives title to the marital residence that had been in the other spouse's name can sell the home immediately and claim the home sale exclusion ($250,000, or $500,000 on a joint return). The new owner can treat the former owner's period of ownership as his or her own to satisfy the two-year ownership requirement for claiming the exclusion. Also, where a couple continues to own the home jointly (typically while the children are in school), the spouse who has moved out can treat the period of use by the other spouse as his or her own to satisfy the two-year use requirement for claiming the exclusion.

● Legal fees. The portion of a divorce lawyer's fee that is for tax advice or obtaining taxable alimony is deductible (if separately stated on the bill) as a miscellaneous itemized deduction. Miscellaneous expenses are deductible only to the extent they exceed 2% of the AGI.

Source: *Barbara Weltman is a tax attorney and the author of several books on business, including* The Complete Idiot's Guide to Making Money After You Retire, *Alpha Books, and* J.K. Lasser's Tax Deduction for Your Small Business, *Macmillan.*

Alimony and the IRS

Basic tax principles to keep in mind:

A property settlement made after a divorce is not tax deductible, but alimony payments are fully deductible. If you're paying alimony, know the rules:

1. Payments must be required by a decree of divorce, separation or support, or by a written separation agreement. They cannot be voluntary payments.

2. Payments must be made in cash.

3. Payments must stop at the death of the recipient-spouse. If the obligation to make payments (to the recipient-spouse's estate) continues, then even the payments before death are not treated as alimony.

● **The recapture rules** that penalize those who pay much larger amounts in the first year or years and smaller amounts in the last years have been liberalized. The first-year payment can exceed the average of the second- and third-year payments by up to $15,000 before the recapture rules come into play. The second-year payment can exceed the third-year payment by $15,000.

If the husband deducts the alimony, the wife must declare it as income. Child support, lump-sum payments, wife's legal fees, premiums on life insurance policies owned by the husband—all these are not deductible by the spouse paying them. And they need not be reported as income by the spouse who receives the payments.

In the still common case among executives in which the husband has a large taxable income and the nonworking wife has little or none, it probably makes sense to make all the payments as alimony rather than something else. The result is to shift income from the husband's high bracket to the wife's lower bracket. It's essential to prepare carefully several alternative plans, varying the mix among alimony and other types of payments, and figuring the available income from each after taxes.

The dependency exemptions for children of divorced or separated parents are given to the custodial parent unless he or she agrees in writing to waive the exemptions.

A parent who has a child living with him or her may be able to file as a (tax-favored) head of household. Conceivably, both parents might have head-of-household status. This could happen if the younger children stayed with the mother, but an older child—away at college full-time, for example, stayed with the father when home on vacation.

Child support normally stops when the children become independent. Alimony often goes on until the wife remarries or dies.

If it's agreed that the husband will pay for the wife's divorce lawyer, estimate the fee and add this amount to the alimony that has been negotiated. Then get a deduction for the amount. But don't forget it is income to the wife in that case.

> "The portion of a divorce lawyer's fee that is for tax advice or obtaining taxable alimony is deductible (if separately stated on the bill) as a miscellaneous itemized deduction."

How to File as Head of Household—Even When You're Not

Head-of-household rates are much lower than "married filing separately" rates. If you're married and have children, but lived apart from your spouse for the last six months of the taxable year, you may file as head of household if:

● **Your home was the principal abode for your dependent children for over half the year** (the full year if the children are foster children).

● **You provided more than half the cost of supporting the household.**

● **You or your spouse can claim your children as dependents.**

If each spouse maintained a household for one or more dependent children, both are eligible for head-of-household status. If only one qualifies, the other must file as "married filing separately." There's no rule for determining whether this would result in lower taxes than a joint return; that has to be calculated for each individual case.

How Much Can Your Child Earn and Not Pay Taxes?

How much income can your minor (i.e., dependent) child have in any given year without having to pay income tax? First, the IRS makes a distinction between earned and unearned income and children under 14 and those 14 years of age and over. There are different rates for each.

● **Earned income** (wages, salaries, fees, tips, etc.). First of all, the standard deduction (which is indexed for inflation) can offset the earned income of a child who is a dependent on the parents' return. *The amount:* $4,250 in 1998. (*Editor's note:* If a child earns less than $4,250, the standard deduction is earned income, plus $250 of unearned income, but no more than a total of $4,250. For example, in 1998, if a child earns $1,200 and has investment income of $1,000, his standard deduction is $1,450—$1,200 earned income, plus $250 of unearned income.)

Second, the child may open an IRA with a maximum contribution of $2,000.

● **Unearned income** (dividends and interest). Each child gets a standard deduction that cannot exceed $700 in 1997 (or the child's earned income).

So, what is the maximum income your child can make without being subject to income tax? In 1998, a child of any age can earn income of up to $6,250 and pay no tax:

Wages	$ 6,250
Deductible IRA contribution	(2,000)
Standard deduction	(4,250)
Taxable income	$ –0–

A child under 14 years of age with only unearned income is entitled to a standard deduction of $700 in 1998. In addition, the next $700 of unearned income is taxed at the child's rate of 15%. Any amount of unearned income in excess of $1,400 is taxed at the parents' rate. To avoid taxation of the income of a child who is under 14 years of age at the parents' rate, the child's principal should be invested in income-deferral investments such as Series EE bonds or growth securities.

The major difference between children 14 years of age and over and those under 14 is that the older children pay tax on their unearned income in excess of $700 at their own bracket, which begins at 15%. If the child is under 14, the child gets a $700 standard deduction and the next $700 is taxable at 15%. After this $1,400, the under-14-year-old child pays tax at the higher of his own or his parents' rate.

Source: Lester A. Marks, tax partner in Ernst & Young, 787 Seventh Ave., New York, NY 10019, who has an extensive practice related to taxation. He is a frequent contributor to professional journals and is often quoted in business publications.

Checklist of Tax Tips for Retirees

● **Check applicability of credit for the elderly.**

● **Check for special state credits. There are many.**

● **Make sure to use any state exclusions available for pension payments.** States may not tax pensions earned in their states that are payable to out-of-state residents. So, for example, if you spent your working years in New York and retire to Florida, New York cannot tax the New York–earned pension paid to you in Florida.

● **Move to a low-tax state** such as Florida, Texas and Nevada, or possibly Connecticut, New Jersey or New Hampshire, depending upon individual circumstances.

- **Downsize your home.** You can exclude gain from the sale of your principal residence up to $250,000 ($500,000 on a joint return). The only requirement is that you owned and used the home as your main residence for two out of five years before the date of sale. You don't have to be age 55 or older. You don't have to buy another home to get this benefit.

- **Check on how much of your Social Security benefits will be taxed.** As much as 85% of your benefits are subject to tax if your income is over a certain amount.

- **Take advantage of tax benefits for tax-free rollovers of pension-plan distributions.**

- **Use five-year averaging for lump-sum distributions from pension/profit-sharing plans.** A person who was born before 1936 can elect to use 10-year averaging if it is more beneficial. *(Editor's note: Five-year averaging no longer applies after 1999.)*

- **Make gifts to children of income-producing property if the children are 14 or older.**

- **Establish irrevocable trusts to shift income to grandchildren,** to other lower-bracket individuals or to a lower-bracket trust.

- **Make charitable gifts of appreciated property.**

Source: Lester A. Marks, tax partner in Ernst & Young, 787 Seventh Ave., New York, NY 10019, who has an extensive practice related to taxation. He is a frequent contributor to professional journals and is often quoted in business publications.

Use Your In-Laws to Cut Your Tax Bill

If you have suffered a loss on an investment property, you can't deduct it while keeping the property in the family by selling it to your spouse, brother, sister, parent, grandparent, child or grandchild. It doesn't matter if the sale is perfectly legitimate.

A Wedding Gift From the IRS

A parent who provides over half of a child's support can claim a dependency exemption if the child is under 19 or a full-time student. The cost of a child's wedding is considered support. So even if the child lives with a spouse after marriage, the wedding may push the parent's support cost over the 50% mark and entitle the parent to the exemption.

Drawback: The newlyweds cannot file a joint return for the year, nor can the child claim the personal exemption.

Source: Revenue Ruling 76-184.

The Tax Code prohibits any loss deduction from a sale to one of these relatives.

Loophole: The Tax Code does *not* consider in-laws to be relatives under this rule. So don't sell to your son or daughter—sell instead to your son-in-law or daughter-in-law (or some other in-law). You'll keep the property in the family and get a deduction too.

Beat Tax on Social Security Benefits

A married couple, both age 65 or over, will pay more tax on a joint return than the combined tax they would pay if they were single. *Another consideration:* If income (including tax-exempt income) plus one-half Social Security benefits exceeds certain levels, the Social Security benefits are taxable. Combining incomes on a joint return may force taxation of Social Security benefits that would completely escape taxation if the couple did not marry.

Caution: If you're married, filing separately won't prevent tax on Social Security benefits, since 85% of benefits are automatically included in the tax return of a married person filing a separate return, regardless of other income.

Paying Your Child a Tax-Deductible Allowance

Paying your children to work in your business is a good way of providing tax-deductible allowances. A child with no other income can earn up to $4,250 in 1998 tax-free.

Bonus: If your business is unincorporated, your children's wages are exempt from Social Security and unemployment taxes until they turn 18.

Caution: Keep very good records of the type of work they do and the hours they put in. The mere

MORE IRS HELP FOR TUITION BILLS

Use new tax incentives to pay for or save for college. New tax breaks starting in 1998 can be used to defray the costs of higher education.

- **Tax credits for higher education.** A HOPE scholarship credit allows you to reduce your taxes dollar for dollar by up to $1,500 (100% of the first $1,000 and 50% of the next $1,000) for tuition and fees paid during the first two years of college for yourself, your spouse or your children. You claim this credit for every student who is eligible. There's also a lifetime learning credit of up to $1,000 (20% of the up to $5,000 of tuition and fees) paid after June 30, 1998. This credit applies for all years of higher education.

- **Education IRAs.** You can save for a child's education on a tax-advantaged basis by contributing up to $500 annually to an education IRA for the benefit of a child under age 18. Contributions are not deductible, but income earned on the funds accumulates on a tax-deferred basis. To make contributions, your income cannot be more than a threshold amount.

- **Deduct interest on student loans.** You may be able to deduct a limited amount of interest on student loans (up to $1,000 in 1998, increasing to $2,500 by 2001), whether or not you itemize your other deductions. The write-off is limited to interest paid on a loan during the first 60 months in which interest payments are required. To take this deduction, your income cannot be more than a threshold amount.

Source: Pamela J. Pecarich, partner, and tax manager Steven M. Woolf, Coopers & Lybrand, LLP, National Tax Services, 1800 M St. NW, Washington, DC 20036.

fact that you pay wages to your children won't trigger an audit. Their pay is lumped in with wages of other employees on your return. But if you are audited for some other reason, the IRS is likely to question this expense. Be prepared to show the pay was reasonable.

Student Exemption Trap

A taxpayer can claim an exemption for a dependent child over 19, even if the child earns over the exemption amount, provided the child is under 24 and a full-time student for at least five calendar months during the year.

Trap: The five-month rule is interpreted strictly. The IRS has denied an exemption for a child who was a full-time student for four months but then left school when she fell ill and was hospitalized for the rest of the year.

Source: IRS Letter Ruling 8623050.

How the IRS Helps With Tuition Bills

Some expenses incurred for sending your children to school are tax-deductible. Other ordinary nondeductible expenses may be turned into tax deductions or credits with the right planning.

- **Nursery school and day-care expenses.** Married couples can take the child-care credit if the children go to nursery school or day care or are cared for at home by household help and both spouses work. The credit can be taken when only one spouse works, in the following situations:

- **When the spouse is a full-time student for five months out of the year,** *or*

- **When the spouse is physically or mentally unable to care for himself or herself.**

Amount of the credit: The calculations are based on your qualifying child-care expenses and your Adjusted Gross Income (AGI). Generally, the higher your AGI, the lower the credit will be.

- **Special institutions.** The cost of sending your child to a special school because he or she is mentally or physically handicapped can be deductible as a medical expense if the school has the resources to relieve the handicap. In addition to tuition, you can deduct related expenses such as transportation to and from the school, meals and lodging if the child lives there.

● **Combined child-care credit plus special school expenses.** The expenses for special schooling may sometimes qualify for both a medical expense and the child-care credit. The same expense can't be used to take both, but if you use only part of your expenses to get the maximum child-care credit, you can apply the unused expenses for the medical deduction. Or, you may apply the whole expense toward your medical deduction. In most cases, if you have low medical expenses, applying the expenses to your child-care credit first will give you the lowest tax bill. Otherwise, figure out your taxes both ways to see what is most beneficial to you.

● **Tax-free dependent care.** If your employer has a qualified dependent care assistance program, you may be able to exclude from income up to $5,000 of dependent-care expenses paid by your employer on your behalf.

● **Purchase an off-campus house or apartment for your college-age child to live in.** *There are two ways of handling this:*

1) Treating the house as your second home. The tax law allows you to fully deduct the interest on mortgages to acquire your principal home plus one second home. If you don't already own a second home, this purchase will provide your child with a free place to live and provide you with mortgage and property tax deductions. When your child finishes school, the house will have most likely appreciated in value and you will have a profit.

2) Treating the house as rental property. The rules are more complex, and you should consider this strategy only after discussing it with your tax adviser.

2a) You must charge your child and any room-mates a fair market rent.

2b) If you don't actively manage the house, you can't use any losses to offset your salary, dividend, interest or capital gain income. You can only use losses to offset other "passive activity" income such as income from tax shelters.

2c) If you do actively manage the house, you are allowed to deduct maintenance, utilities, depreciation, property taxes, etc., from the rental income, and if you end up with a net loss, you can use it to offset your salary and other income. But you are allowed to deduct only up to $25,000 of loss if your AGI is $100,000 or less. The $25,000 maximum deduction is phased out if your AGI is between $100,001 and $150,000.

Shifting Taxable Income to Children

The ability of a family to shift income—and taxes on that income—from high-bracket family members to those in lower tax brackets is limited.

● **Kiddie tax.** Investment income earned by a child under 14 in excess of $1,400 in 1998 is taxed to the child at the parent's highest tax rate. So large gifts of income-producing assets to children under age 14 won't cut the family's tax bill.

But opportunities do still exist for parents to transfer taxable income to children in a low bracket. If you want to give income-producing property to a minor, make sure the income is deferred until the child reaches 14. *Suggestions:*

● **Shelter the first $1,400 of income.** The first $700 of unearned income in 1998 is tax-free; the next $700 is taxed at the 15% bracket. So, if a parent gives a child $20,000 and the child earns 7% interest, tax would only be $105 ($700 tax-free; $700 taxed at 15%). If the parent were in the 31% bracket and did not make the transfer, the tax would be $434 ($1,400 x 31%).

● **U.S. Series EE savings bonds are tax-smart investments for children.** Interest can be free from tax until the bonds are cashed in at maturity. However, children over 13 can elect to report the interest and pay little or no tax on it.

● **Growth stocks or real estate that doesn't produce current income but increases in value as time goes by.** After the child reaches 14, the property can be sold if cash is needed.

Tax Advantages of Filing for Personal Bankruptcy

Tax considerations are hardly ever the main reason an individual files for bankruptcy. But the tax aspects of personal bankruptcy can be very favorable, especially for taxpayers who are heavily in debt to their employers or to their own closely held corporations. *Main benefits:*

● **Cancellation of indebtedness.** As a general rule, when a debt is forgiven, the debtor must report the amount forgiven as income. But a debt canceled in bankruptcy is not treated as income. *Example:* Among other debts, a financially troubled taxpayer owes his employer $25,000. If the debt is simply forgiven by the employer, the employee must report the $25,000 as income. If, however, the employee files for bankruptcy and the debt is canceled, he does not have to treat it as income. *Example:* An individual had credit card charges of $10,000 last year. This year the credit card debt is discharged in bankruptcy. If any of the credit card charges were previously deducted (e.g., as a business-entertainment deduction), they would have to be reported as income. But the other part of the discharged debt wouldn't have to be reported. *Example:* Five years ago, an individual borrowed heavily from his closely held corporation. For other reasons business is now so bad that the corporation must file for bankruptcy. If the individual also declares bankruptcy and the loan is discharged, he has a big tax windfall. He will not have to pick up the money he borrowed from the company as income.

● **Cancellation of back taxes.** Unpaid federal income taxes are canceled in bankruptcy if they become due more than three years before the bankruptcy filing.

● **Deductible expenses.** Fees paid to an accountant to prepare an individual's personal records for Bankruptcy Court are tax-deductible (subject to the 2% of AGI limit on miscellaneous deductions). So are legal fees, to the extent they involve the tax aspects of bankruptcy.

● **Carryovers.** Some carryovers are retained by the individual after bankruptcy. *Included:* Net operating loss carryovers (business losses), capital loss carryovers, tax credit carryovers and charitable contribution carryovers.

Limit: Net operating loss carryovers must be adjusted downward to the extent that the debt giving rise to

the carryovers is canceled in bankruptcy. The negative tax consequences of personal bankruptcy:

● **Payroll taxes.** Individuals who are personally responsible for payroll taxes (e.g., officers of a company) cannot cancel their liability for those taxes in bankruptcy.

● **Tax refunds are payable to the trustee in bankruptcy,** not to the individual who files for bankruptcy. *Loophole:* Taxpayers who expect to file for bankruptcy next year should arrange payroll withholding this year so that no tax refunds will be coming from the government.

Alternative: If large refunds are expected, file for bankruptcy prior to December 31, before the refund becomes an asset payable to the bankruptcy trustee.

Source: Edward Mendlowitz, partner, Mendlowitz Weitsen, LLP, 2 Penn Plaza, New York, NY 10121.

Appreciated Securities: Shifting Capital Gains

Give appreciated securities to your parents instead of cash if you are supporting them. They can cash in the securities and pay tax at 10% if they are in the 15% tax bracket on their other income. You'll avoid paying tax at 20%.

Caution: A large gain could push your parents into a higher bracket, which would mean the same 20% tax rate on the gain that you would have paid.

Buying Relatives' Investment Losses

If you are a high-bracket taxpayer and have a relative with little or no taxable income, consider taking advantage of a tax law provision that allows you, in effect, to acquire your immediate relatives' deductible losses. *How it works:* If a member of your immediate family sells property to you at a loss, that loss can't be deducted. But, when you turn around and sell that property, you don't have to pay tax on any gain unless the gain is more than your family member's loss. Even then, only the portion of the gain that exceeds the previous loss is taxable. *Example:* John White's mother is very ill. She has some income from dividends and a modest pension. But her deductible medical expenses are so high that her taxable income is zero. Her portfolio includes 100 shares of Consolidated Conglomerate that she bought at $35 a share. The current price is $11. If Mrs. White sells on the open market, she'll have a $2,400 loss that won't save a penny in taxes. If John buys the stock from her, he can hold on to it until the price recovers. And although he bought the shares at $11, he won't have a taxable gain until the stock hits $35 again.

In addition, John can give his mother a note for the purchase price of the stock with a reasonable interest rate. The money can help defray Mrs. White's medical costs, while John gets an interest deduction.

This special rule applies on any transaction between you and your parents, grandparents, children, grandchildren, brother, sister or any corporation in which you own more than 50% (by value) of the shares.

Charitable Giving: Good News

Smart giving strategies can let a top-bracket individual cut income taxes and estate taxes while retaining economic benefits from an appreciated investment.

Opportunities

The typical estate tax deduction results from a gift to charity made through a will. If you're planning to make such a gift, it may be better to make a deferred gift to charity now.

You can do this by establishing a trust and donating to it property that will pass to a named charity when you die. Until then, the trust will pay cash income to you. *Two kinds of trust:*

● **Charitable remainder annuity trust.** The property that you place in the trust is used to buy an annuity that will provide you with specified annual cash payments for the rest of your life, regardless of how the trust performs.

● **Charitable remainder unitrust.** This kind of trust pays you a percentage of its total value each

year. Thus, if the trust remains invested in the stock market and the market booms, the payment you receive from the trust will increase each year.

Benefits from trusts:

● **You get an income tax deduction now** for the present value of your gift to charity.

● **If you make your gift with appreciated securities,** you avoid paying tax on your capital gains.

● **Because the amount of the property you place in trust is removed from your estate,** your heirs get the benefit of an estate tax deduction without having to claim one. Thus, you preserve your estate tax exclusion amount ($625,000 in 1998, increasing to $1 million by 2006) to shelter your other property.

Low-cost alternative: If the size of your gift doesn't justify the cost of setting up your own trust, you can make your gift to a pooled income fund. These funds are trusts that are run by major charities. You make a donation to the fund, get an income tax deduction now and receive annual payments for the rest of your life.

Whether you contribute to a charitable remainder annuity trust, charitable remainder unitrust or pooled income fund, the result is the same. The charity in the end receives the same gift that you would have made through your will, but you receive benefits that are much greater.

Big-Dollar Deductions

A shareowner in a profitable privately held corporation has a unique opportunity to claim a deduction on his or her personal return for a charitable gift that's paid for by the company. The device to use is called a charitable bailout.

Here, the owner donates some of his or her shares in the company to a charity, claiming a deduction for their full value. The company then redeems the shares for cash. As long as the charity is not legally bound to tender the shares for redemption, the following benefits result:

● **The owner pays nothing out of pocket to get the deduction,** since the cash payout is made by the company.

> " **[With a] pooled income fund...run by major charities...you make a donation to the fund, get an income tax deduction now and receive annual payments for the rest of your life.** "

● **The owner avoids ever having to pay capital gains tax on the shares,** while getting a deduction for their full appreciated value.

● **The current owners retain full control over the business,** because the donated shares, once redeemed, return to the company.

Another idea for an individual who wishes to make a large contribution that will provide lasting benefits is to set up a private foundation.

A private foundation is a corporation that's required to operate for charitable purposes. While a private foundation can't be run to benefit its creator directly, a person who sets up a foundation can retain influence over its operation by naming its directors and serving as a director.

Of course, the foundation may bear the donor's name, so it may generate favorable publicity and goodwill for its creator, in addition to providing an opportunity for a large tax deduction. Again, when the foundation is funded with appreciated securities, the donor gets a deduction for their full value while avoiding capital gains tax. *(Editor's note:* Donations of appreciated publicly traded shares had been deductible at their full appreciated value until June 30, 1998, when this tax break expired. Thereafter, deductions are limited to your cost for the shares unless Congress extends this tax break, as it has done several times in the past.)

Inexpensive variation: While administration costs and reporting requirements may make the creation of a private foundation impractical for the average taxpayer, similar benefits can be obtained from a contribution to a local community trust.

Community trusts are organizations that solicit contributions from the public. And while a contributor has no legal right to direct how a donation is spent, a community trust usually will make an expenditure according to a donor's request and in the donor's name. A gift to a community trust makes particular sense when a person wants to get a deduction for a large gift now, while retaining some say over how the gift will be spent in future years.

Grandchild's Tax

The generation-skipping transfer tax has a trap. It applies to any large gift (exceeding certain exemptions) that is made to a grandchild or great-grandchild. The tax is a steep one—55%—and it applies in addition to any regular gift or estate tax. But it's possible to beat the tax with smart strategies. *Example:* You want to pass a large amount of money along to your grandchild. You don't want to pay heavy estate or gift taxes when you pass the money to the child by will or gift several years from now.

What to do: Give a charity the right to receive an annuity earned from funds that you wish to pass to the grandchild until the transfer takes place. The present value of your gift to charity will reduce the value that will be assigned to your future gift to your grandchild, according to IRS valuation tables. By having your tax adviser carefully structure your arrangement, you can eliminate both estate tax and generation-skipping tax on your future gift to your grandchild. The amount after taxes that's left to pass to your grandchild won't be increased, but money that would have gone to the IRS will go to your favorite charity instead, and you'll get a charitable gift tax deduction now.

Final Word

The technical rules involved with charitable giving are more complicated than ever before. Gifts of appreciated property may make the donor subject to the Alternative Minimum Tax. Although this provision should affect only people making very large gifts, it should be considered by your adviser when planning contributions. Also, all arrangements involving trusts or private foundations should be examined by an expert, to be sure that they meet both tax rules and the requirements of local law.

Source: David S. Rhine, partner and national director of family wealth planning, BDO Seidman, 330 Madison Ave., New York 10017.

Giving Doesn't Have to Hurt

The easiest way to make a charitable donation is by a check. But other kinds of gifts to public charities may accomplish the same objectives at less cost.

● **Donate appreciated assets** (stocks, bonds, real estate) rather than cash. If you've held the property for more than a year, you're entitled to a double tax benefit. You can deduct the full market value of the property as a charitable contribution, and you avoid paying capital gains tax on the appreciation.

Deduction limit: 30% of your Adjusted Gross Income. Any excess is deductible in the five succeeding tax years.

● **Set up a charitable remainder trust,** preferably with securities that have gone up in value. Usually, this kind of trust pays you a fixed amount of income each year until your death and then distributes the remaining assets to charity. You get a tax deduction now for a gift the charity won't receive until some time in the future. In the meantime, you continue to have the use of the money. *Example:* A man of 55 sets up a charitable remainder annuity trust with securities that cost him $25,000 but that are now worth $50,000. He reserves an income of $3,000 a year for life. *Tax benefits:* an immediate charitable deduction for the present value of the charity's remainder interest. And even though this deduction is based on the stock's current value, no regular income tax has to be paid on the appreciation.

Fund the trust with municipal bonds and you will also avoid paying tax on the income you receive from the trust. If you set up the trust with very long-term municipal bonds, your yield might well exceed current money-market rates. And it's completely tax-free.

● **Contribute to a pooled income fund.** Many charities have investment funds called pooled income funds. The fund pools the contributions of individual donors, each of whom has retained the right to receive an income for life from his or her contributions.

Tax loopholes: Similar to those of a charitable remainder trust. The investment benefits are that funds are diversified. You get the benefit of professional management without having to pay for establishing and administering a trust. *Drawback:* Pooled income funds are not permitted to invest in municipal bonds or other tax-exempt securities.

● **Charitable lead trusts are the reverse of charitable remainder trusts.** Instead of providing you with an income, the charity gets the income from the trust assets for a number of years, often eight to 10. When the trust's term is over, the assets are returned to family members. The income tax deduction for the charitable interest is seldom a consideration, since estate and financial considerations are paramount. The main advantage is the ability to shift appreciated assets to your children at reduced transfer tax cost. Lead trusts also make a lot of sense for high-earning taxpayers who intend to retire in a few years. The trust lets them continue to provide for their favorite charity, and gives them the security of knowing that the trust assets will be available for their use in retirement.

● **Community trusts.** Another way to get maximum tax benefits from your charitable donations is to set up a fund in your own name through a recognized public charity that will serve as a conduit to other charities that you recommend. You get a deduction when you set up the fund without the pressure of having to name specific charities at that time. Set up the fund and get big tax deductions in high-income years—for example, the years just before retirement. After retirement, the fund will make donations in your name to the various charities that you suggest.

Problem: You can only suggest the beneficiaries. But the administering charities usually do follow a donor's suggestions.

● **Gifts of life insurance.** The mere naming of a charity as the beneficiary of a policy on your life will not provide you with an income tax deduction. To guarantee a deduction, you must give up all ownership rights in the policy. *Loophole:* Have the charity own the policy. Make annual contributions to the charity. The charity will use its own money to pay the premiums. You will get a current income tax deduction for your annual gifts and you will have given the charity a very large gift—the proceeds payable on your death.

Source: Edward Mendlowitz, partner, Mendlowitz Weitsen, LLP, 2 Penn Plaza, New York, NY 10121.

Making the Most of Medical Deductions

You can only deduct medical expenses that exceed $7\frac{1}{2}$% of your Adjusted Gross Income, but the IRS and court decisions have expanded the definition of deductible medical costs. Plan ahead to take advantage of as many medical expenses as possible.

Medical deductions can be taken for the costs of diagnosis, for the treatment or prevention of a disease or for affecting any structure or function of the body.

Limitation: Treatment must be specific and not just for general health improvement. And the cost of unnecessary cosmetic surgery is not deductible.

Weight-Control Programs

The IRS successfully denied taxpayers deductions for the cost of weight-control and stop-smoking classes that were designed to improve general health, not to treat a specific ailment or disease. On the other hand, a person with a health problem specifically related to being overweight, such as high blood pressure, might be allowed the deduction.

If an employer tells an overweight employee to lose weight or leave, and the boss has previously enforced such a rule, the employee can deduct the cost of a weight-loss program, because money spent to help keep a taxpayer's job is deductible. The IRS says it will allow a deduction if a physician prescribes a weight-reduction program for treatment of hypertension or obesity. The same could apply for a person whose doctor certifies that a stop to cigarette smoking is an immediate medical requirement.

Other Deductions

● **Because medical costs are deductible only after they exceed 7½% of a taxpayer's AGI,** it is tempting to declare them as business expenses. The IRS rarely allows those business deductions, but there is a sizable gray area. A professional singer was once not allowed to deduct the cost of throat treatments as a business expense, but an IRS agent did allow a deduction for a dancer who found it necessary to her career to have silicone breast implants.

● **Medically unproven treatment is generally deductible,** since the IRS has taken the position that it cannot make judgments in the medical field.

● **Over a two-year period,** an ailing taxpayer and his wife consumed $2,700 worth of vitamins under their doctor's prescription. The IRS said that the vitamins were not deductible medical expenses. *Tax Court:* The IRS was wrong. When a doctor prescribes vitamins to treat specific ailments, those vitamins fall within the definition of medical expenses.

● **Deductions for nondependents are sometimes possible.** *How it works:* The daughter of a highly paid executive ran up medical bills of more than $5,000. She married later that year and filed a joint return with her husband. Nevertheless, her father was allowed to deduct the cost of treatment on his return for the year, even though the daughter didn't qualify as a dependent.

Education

The IRS draws a hard line on deductibility of special schooling for children with medical problems. *Not deductible:* the cost of attending a school with smaller classes, even for a child with hearing or sight problems. The school would have to offer special programs for the children with specific disabilities for parents to be able to take a deduction. *Deductible:* the full cost of sending a child to a boarding school equipped to handle deaf children with emotional problems. *Not deductible:* extra costs, including travel, claimed by a parent who sent his deaf child to a distant public school that was better equipped than the local public school.

Special care for the handicapped may be deductible, however. An eight-year-old child was blind, retarded, and asthmatic, and required constant care and attention. The child lived with an attendant who was paid $400 a week, plus $60 for the child's food and clothing. *IRS ruling:* The entire amount was deductible, except for the clothing costs not related to medical care.

Source: Sidney Kess, attorney and CPA, Suite 1465, 630 Fifth Ave., New York, NY 10111.

Neglected Medical Deductions

● **You can deduct medical bills paid for another person,** provided that you paid more than half that person's support in either the year the bills were run up or the year they were paid. A similar rule applies to married couples. You can deduct bills paid now for a former spouse, so long as you were married when the bills were incurred. You can deduct medical expenses you pay for your child even though the other parent is entitled to claim the dependency exemption for the child.

● **A transplant donor can deduct surgical,** hospital and laboratory costs and transportation expenses.

So can a prospective donor, even if found to be unacceptable. If the recipient pays the expenses, the recipient gets the deduction.

- **Removing lead-based paint and covering areas within a child's reach with wallboard,** to help prevent further lead poisoning, are deductible expenses. But paint removal and wallboard for areas beyond the reach of the child are not—nor is the cost of repainting.

- **A clarinet and lessons are deductible** medical expenses when prescribed to cure teeth defects.

- **A hypoglycemia patient was put on a special diet requiring six to eight small,** high-protein meals daily. The Tax Court allowed a deduction of 30% of her grocery bills—the amount spent in excess of the cost of her normal diet.

- **A taxpayer who was given power of attorney** over his mother's bank account had all of her funds deposited into his own account. He used the funds for her support and claimed her medical expenses on his return. The IRS and the Tax Court claimed that he shouldn't be allowed the deduction because the money belonged to his mother. *Court of Appeals:* For the son. His mother had made a gift under state law, and the money belonged to him.

- **Other deductibles:** Birth-control pills and other prescription drugs, vasectomies, legal abortions.

The Best Tax Shelter

The best tax shelter you'll ever have may be your own home. The major costs of carrying a house as an investment—mortgage interest and property taxes—are tax-deductible. And the appreciation in the property's value continues to qualify for a number of very special tax breaks:

- **Exclude gain on the sale of your home.** Regardless of your age or whether you buy another home, you are not taxed on up to $250,000 ($500,000 on a joint return) of gain on the sale of your main

Tax Breaks for the Handicapped

Small businesses that furnish special parking spaces for the physically handicapped (ramps, wider doorways, enlarged bathroom spaces, etc.) can take the credit. The credit is 50% of the amount of eligible access expenditures for the year that do not exceed $10,250.

Structural changes that physically handicapped individuals make to their houses automatically qualify as a deductible medical expense. And since the kinds of changes handicapped persons would make to houses do not normally increase their value, the cost is usually fully deductible as a medical expense. There is no increase in the property's value to be subtracted from the cost of the home improvement.

home. *Requirement:* You must have owned and used it as your principal residence for two out of five years before the date of sale.

- **The entire appreciation in value escapes income tax if you own the house when you die** (although it may be subject to estate tax). For income tax purposes your beneficiaries inherit the place at what is called its "stepped-up basis." They inherit the property at its value on the date of your death, and income tax on the appreciation is forgiven. If your beneficiaries later sell the house, only the difference between the selling price and the date-of-death value is taxed.

To make the most of homeowners' tax breaks:

- **Let your beneficiaries inherit the house.** Many elderly people sell their houses to their children for $1 to keep the property out of their estate.

Trap: The IRS treats these deals as gifts of property rather than sales. Because it is a gift, the children assume the tax cost the parents had in the house. When the children sell the house, they have to pay income tax on the full appreciation in value. *Better way:* Let the children inherit the house. That gives them a stepped-up, date-of-death basis, and income tax is forgiven on the appreciation.

Another problem with $1 sales to children: Depreciation deductions are severely limited if the children decide to rent the house back to the parents. The depreciation is not based on the property's current value but on the parents' tax basis in it.

- **Buy your parents' home and rent it back to**

MEDICAL DEDUCTIONS FOR HOME OWNERS

You may be able to deduct at least part of the cost of capital improvements you make to your home for medical reasons. Of course, you must be able to prove that you have a medical reason for making the improvement.

Your deduction will be limited to the cost of the improvement minus any increase in the value of your property that may result from it. To determine the value, have the property assessed before and after the improvement. (The appraisal fees are deductible.) Moreover, you can only deduct that portion of your total medical expenses for the year that exceeds 7½% of your Adjusted Gross Income.

Examples of deductible medical home improvements:

● **Central air-conditioning installed** when a member of the family suffers from a respiratory ailment.

● **A swimming pool installed** after a doctor advises swimming as therapy for an illness or handicap and public swimming facilities are not accessible.

them. This transaction will convert payments that you make toward your parents' support into a perfectly legal tax shelter. *How it works:* Buy the house from your parents on the installment method, making monthly payments on the purchase price, then rent it back to them at fair market rent. Make the installment payments equal to the rent plus the amount you had been giving for support.

The rent you receive from your parents is sheltered from tax by depreciation deductions, property taxes, upkeep, etc. And if the write-offs exceed the rent—and your Adjusted Gross Income is under $100,000—you may deduct up to $25,000 of losses against your salary and other taxable income. (If your AGI is between $100,000 and $150,000, you may deduct some of your losses against taxable income.) *Additional benefit:* Your parents' gain on the sale may be tax-free because of the home sale exclusion.

● **Buy a house or an apartment for a college-age child who is living in another city while attending school.** Charge the child a fair rent and rent extra space to other students. Now you own rental property and you get all the tax-shelter benefits it produces—you can write off up to $25,000 of losses on the property if your AGI is under $100,000. *Bonus:* You will have an attractive investment that will appreciate in value while your child is going to school.

● **Take back a note or a mortgage if you sell the house at a gain exceeding the house sale exclusion.** This will defer tax on a portion of your gain in excess of the exclusion. You only pay tax on the excess gain as you collect principal payments under the mortgage. (A 10-year mortgage would spread the tax on your gain over 10 years.)

Bonus: You collect interest on the full mortgage principal.

● **Take out your own mortgage on the house, rent it out and move into a rented apartment.**

You might do this to keep the appreciation value of the house. (You can use the mortgage proceeds for investment.) The rent income you receive will be offset by mortgage interest and depreciation deductions. If your AGI is less than $100,000, you can write off losses of up to $25,000. You don't have to pay any tax on the gain—since you haven't sold the house.

You can still qualify for the home sale exclusion if you sell the house within three years. *(Editor's note:* When the home is sold, any depreciation taken on it after May 6, 1997 is subject to tax at 25%.)

● **Convert nondeductible interest payments into deductible interest.** *Aim:* To increase mortgage interest, which is deductible, and decrease other interest that is not deductible. The interest paid on personal loans, car loans, credit card balances and interest paid to the IRS on tax underpayments is not deductible. *Editor's note:* Starting in 1998, a limited amount of interest on student loans may be deductible.

Deductions for investment interest to the amount of investment income you earn during the year are limited. But the law permits full deductions for mortgage interest on your house and on a second home.

Limit: The mortgage can't exceed $1 million in acquisition debt (borrowed to buy, build or improve the residence) plus $100,000 in home equity debt (borrowed for any purpose).

The dollar limits don't apply to mortgages taken out before October 14, 1987, provided the mortgage doesn't exceed the current market value of the home.

Source: Edward Mendlowitz, partner, Mendlowitz Weitsen, LLP, 2 Penn Plaza, New York, NY 10121.

Homeowners' Tax Breaks

For the alert taxpayer, the family home can be a major source of tax savings. Federal tax law is studded with provisions that encourage and enhance home ownership, as opposed to other forms of investment.

● **Mortgage points.** For borrowers other than home owners, mortgage points (a prepayment of interest represented by a percentage of the loan) have to be capitalized and deducted over the life of the loan. But points charged on money borrowed to buy or improve a principal residence are fully deductible by homeowners in the year they are paid.

● **The glories of giving.** Homeowners who take advantage of a technique known as deferred giving can get a large immediate income tax deduction that will produce cash flow now without giving up their right to live in the house. *How it works:* The owners give what is called remainder interest in their house to charity. This is the right the charity has to take over the house on the owners' death. But the owners reserve the right to live in the house until the survivor of them dies. The owners get a current charitable deduction for the value of the charity's interest. This is computed from IRS tables and depends on how long the charity is expected to wait before taking over the house.

● **Joint property ownership.** The tax law encourages couples to own the family home in the name of

the spouse most likely to die first. Statistically, that's the husband.

The unlimited marital deduction means that the first spouse to die can leave the house to the surviving spouse without incurring any tax at all on his or her death. Yet the property will get a stepped-up tax basis (its cost for tax purposes) to the fair market value at the date of death. No estate tax will have to be paid on the house's appreciated value.

When the surviving spouse sells, since he or she inherited the house at the increased value, any gains tax that has to be paid will be reduced. If the house remains in joint ownership, the surviving spouse would receive a stepped-up cost basis on only half of the home. The survivor's sale of the home could then trigger capital gains taxes. The Taxpayer Relief Act of 1997 allows the first $250,000 of gain ($500,000 for married couples) on the sale of a residence to be tax-free, provided that the owner(s) have lived in the home for at least two years.

Editor's note: For property acquired by a couple before 1977, it is not necessary that the title be held in the name of the first spouse to die for the surviving spouse to get a full stepped-up basis. Several courts have concluded that when the spouse who dies first paid for the property, the surviving spouse can claim a stepped-up basis for the entire property.

Source: Ivan Faggen, tax partner, Arthur Andersen & Co., in charge of the Tax Division for the South Florida offices, 1 Biscayne Tower, Suite 2100, Miami, FL 33131. Mr. Faggen is coauthor with Mathew Bender of Federal Taxes Affecting Real Estate.

Home Improvements That Provide Big Tax Savings

It has always been important to keep careful records of home improvements. The cost of capital improvements—even small ones—increases your tax basis in the house so that when you eventually sell the place, your taxable gain (over and above the exclusion you may be entitled to) is lower.

Caution: Keep invoices and contracts that specify the work done—canceled checks may not be enough to convince the IRS that the money was spent on legitimate improvements.

Improvements Versus Repairs

As a general rule, additions and improvements will be

included in your tax basis if they are intended to be permanent. Repairs and maintenance, on the other hand (repainting, replastering, fixing leaks and the like), are not included in basis. *Fine line:* The distinction between an improvement and a repair is not always clear. For example, the cost of painting a room for the first time would be an improvement, but the cost of repainting that room would be a repair.

Often the deciding factor for including an item in basis is whether it can be removed if the home is sold. For example, a bookcase unit that is built into a wall would be included in basis. But a freestanding bookcase that could be taken with you if you moved could not be included.

Checklist of costs that will generally be included in your tax basis, by category:

● **Appliances, major household:** Clothes dryer, freezer, room air conditioner, stove, washing machine—provided they will be sold with the house and not removed.

● **Bathrooms:** Bathtub sliding doors, faucets, medicine cabinets, mirrors, shower controls, toilets, towel racks, etc.

● **Building improvements:** New siding, deck, fireplace, mantel, garage, gutters, drainpipes, porch, screen and storm doors, tool shed, new roof or extensive improvements, termite inspection, waterproofing.

● **Communications:** Call bells, chimes, fire or burglar alarms, intercoms, cable installation, permanent telephone outlets.

● **Electricity and lighting:** Replacement of fuses with circuit breakers, floodlights, lighting fixtures, rooftop TV antenna and wiring.

● **Flooring:** Wall-to-wall carpeting, tiles, linoleum, wood floors.

● **Furniture and fixtures:** Built-in bookcases, built-in cabinets, closet shelves, curtains and drapes (which are not removed when the house is sold).

● **Garden, grounds, outdoor additions:** Barbecue pit, birdbath, fences and gates, greenhouse, landscaping, mailbox, swimming pool, terraces and patios, trees and shrubs, underground sprinkler system.

● **Kitchen:** Built-in dishwasher, garbage disposal, range hood, countertops, etc.

● **Laundry:** Laundry tub, laundry chute, ventilator.

● **Mechanical equipment:** Attic fan, central air conditioner, furnace, hot-water heater, radiators.

● **Paving:** Blacktop or gravel driveway, cement walks and steps.

● **Plumbing and sanitation:** Copper tubing, sump pump, water pipes, water supply system, septic system.

● **Renovation:** Conversion of unfinished basement or attic.

● **Walls and ceilings:** Insulation, wallpapering (first time only), paneling.

● **Windows and doors:** Screens, storm windows and doors, weather stripping.

Source: *Lawrence M. Axelrod, partner, and Richard A. Bockman, supervisor, in the Washington office, Deloitte & Touche, Washington Service Center, 1900 M St. NW, Washington, DC 20036.*

> **"As a general rule, additions and improvements will be included in your tax basis if they are intended to be permanent."**

Your Vacation Home

Owning a vacation home may no longer be considered one of the best investment strategies around. Advantageous tax write-offs may be limited in their application by the passive activity rules. But the news isn't all bad.

A choice needs to be made as to whether the vacation home is to be treated either as rental real estate or as a second residence. For the taxpayer to classify the vacation home as a second residence, the extent of personal usage must be greater than the greater of 14 days or 10% of the number of days actually rented. Losses in excess of rental income are never deductible. Disallowed losses cannot be carried over to succeeding taxable years. However, mortgage interest and real estate taxes are deductible without limit. Real property that is neither rented nor occupied by the owner during a year may be claimed as a second residence.

To be considered rental real estate, the taxpayer must own 10% or more interest in such property, actively participate in its operation, and the amount of personal usage must be less than the greater of 14 days or 10% of days actually rented. Active participation requires the taxpayer or spouse to participate in a bona fide sense. For example, management decisions that involve approving tenants, lease terms and repairs would be sufficient to satisfy the active participation requirement.

Passive-activity loss limitations apply to the vacation home rental. Losses (including interest expense) incurred through such rental property are added to other passive losses and are only deductible against passive income from that or another passive activity. Any losses not allowed in one tax year may be carried over indefinitely to succeeding tax years, subject to the income limitation. When you sell a passive activity you can take any carried-over losses from that activity in the year of sale without regard to the passive-income limit. In a case in which net passive income exists, passive

activity credits may be applied exclusively to the amount of tax attributable to such passive income.

An individual who actively participates in rental real estate activity may be eligible for a special break. The taxpayer can offset nonpassive income with up to $25,000 of losses and credits (in deductible equivalents) from "active" real estate interests. The deduction equivalent of credits is the amount that, if allowed as a deduction, would reduce tax by an amount equal to the credit. The $25,000 relief provision is phased out by 50% of Adjusted Gross Income between $100,000 and $150,000 without regard to the IRA deduction, and taxable Social Security benefits.

In making the choice between a second residence and rental real estate, the length of time the property is to be held should be a consideration. Keeping the home long-term as a second residence would entitle the taxpayer to continuous deductions for

TRAPS IN OWNING VACATION PROPERTY

Many people have invested in vacation properties that are leased out to others during the year. *Examples:* an apartment at a ski resort and a beachfront cottage. Such investors may fall into a number of traps.

Trap: Mortgage interest on such a property is no longer automatically deductible. Generally, the interest is deductible only if, after taking taxes and casualty losses into account, the rental activity results in a profit. If the property generates a loss during the year, your deduction for the loss (including interest costs) is limited to $25,000. Even this deduction is cut back for persons with an Adjusted Gross Income (AGI) exceeding $100,000, and eliminated for per-

sons with an AGI over $150,000.

Trap: If the average stay in your leased-out property is less than 30 days, transient rental rules may apply. If these rules do apply, you can claim no losses incurred by the property unless you manage it yourself and provide substantial services. Thus, if you hire someone else to manage the property for you (as is typically the case), you get no loss deduction.

Ways around these traps:

● **Consider increasing your personal use of the vacation property.** This will enable you to obtain full mortgage interest deductions that

would otherwise be limited. *Rule:* A property generally qualifies as a residence if you use it during the year for more than the greater of 14 days, or 10% of the days you've rented it to outsiders. But then depreciation, maintenance and other deductions are limited to net rental income after the interest, taxes and casualty loss deductions.

● **Lease out the property for periods that are longer than 30 days** to avoid the deduction limits that are imposed on properties used for transient lodging.

Source: Thomas P. Ochsenschlager, partner, Grant Thornton, CPAs, 1850 M St. NW, Washington, DC 20036.

mortgage interest and real estate taxes, but other expenses might never be deductible. On the other hand, if the property is kept short-term, as rental real estate, the taxpayer may suspend any losses until the time of sale, whereby all passive disallowed losses are allowed in full.

Source: *Thomas L. LoCicero, former IRS branch manager and presently senior tax manager and executive tax-planning specialist with the firm of Deloitte & Touche, 1 World Trade Center, New York, NY 10048.*

Tax Loopholes for Executives

One of the major income tax problems facing salaried executives is having to pay taxes currently on their salaries. Generally, executives will be better off financially if a portion of those taxes can be deferred until a later date. If your employer will cooperate, there are various methods available to structure compensation arrangements to minimize their tax impact. These generally involve the use of noncash compensation arrangements or unfunded deferred compensation arrangements.

Caution: Many experts are wary of deferred compensation arrangements because of uncertainty about tax rates in the future. *Result:* The compensation you defer may be taxed at a higher rate than if you received it now.

Cash must be included in income in the year received, but this is not always the rule for noncash compensation. There are two common noncash arrangements that can defer income significantly: *nonstatutory stock options* and *restricted property.*

Some corporations provide executives with compensatory nonqualified stock options, if permitted by state corporate law. These are stock options granted to an individual for services rendered. Such options differ from incentive stock options, which are a form of statutory stock options. In general, the compensatory portion of the nonqualified options is not included in income until the options are exercised. And, when income finally is recognized, the only amount that constitutes ordinary income is the excess of the fair market value of the stock at the date of exercise over the option price.

Corporations also have provided executives with noncash compensation in the form of "restricted property." Restricted property is property received for services, such as stock, which is not freely transferable and is subject to a substantial risk of forfeiture. For example, a corporation may stipulate that stock transferred to executives is subject to forfeiture if the executives choose not to serve out their terms of office and leave the corporation. Further, the sale of stock at a profit could subject an executive to suit under section 16(b) of the Securities Exchange Act of 1934. The executive's rights in that property are subject to a substantial risk of forfeiture and are not transferable.

The tax consequences associated with receiving restricted property are determined under specific rules. Assume you receive stock that, on the date of issuance, is not freely transferable and is subject to a substantial risk of forfeiture. You may elect to recognize compensation income when the stock is issued—if you do so within 30 days after the stock is issued. Otherwise, compensation income is recognized when the stock becomes transferable or free from risk of forfeiture. The amount of compensation recognized—ordinary income—is equal to the fair market value of the stock on the applicable recognition date less any amount paid for such stock.

Unfunded Deferred Compensation

Many corporations provide executives with the opportunity to defer compensation through the use of an unfunded deferred compensation arrangement. While these arrangements work in various ways, basically executives elect to defer all or part of their salaries, and the corporation agrees to pay deferred amounts in later years. Amounts deferred are not currently taxable to the executives.

For example, an executive might merely accept a reduced amount of cash now in return for the corporation's promise to pay the amount deferred (perhaps with an interest factor) at a later date. As another alternative, the executive might agree to receive a reduced amount of cash now if, in return, the corporation promises to pay a certain amount per year, starting at a set date, for as long as the executive lives. This is an annuity-type deferred compensation arrangement. The corporation generally protects itself by purchasing a commercial annuity with the corporation as beneficiary.

For these arrangements to be effective, the

deferred funds cannot be made available to the executives currently. Thus, the corporation generally should not set aside funds specifically for the executives to cover the compensation deferred. This means that, until they receive payment, the executives are unsecured creditors of the corporation. However, there are ways to further assure payment beyond merely relying upon the creditworthiness of the company.

The unfunded arrangement can be coupled with a third-party guarantee. Under such an arrangement, the corporation promises to pay the executive cash in the future. In addition, the executive may obtain a guarantee from a third party (e.g., a surety bond issued by an insurance company) to pay the executive should the company default on its payment. However, if the corporation purchases the third-party guarantee, the premiums will be taxed to the executive.

Many executives are not satisfied with merely having a bare corporate promise to pay in the future. The IRS has allowed a corporation to establish an irrevocable trust to administer the unfunded arrangement. Under the terms of the trust agreement, the trustee will make distributions of the principal and income to the executive or designated beneficiary on the executive's death, disability, retirement or termination of services, or in the event of financial hardship. But the trust's assets are the corporation's and remain subject to the claims of the corporation's creditors. Further, the executive's interest in the trust may not be assigned, pledged, attached or made subject to the executive's creditors.

The IRS has issued private-letter rulings approving the third-party guarantee and the irrevocable trust arrangements. While both of the arrangements should continue to work, the IRS may decide to contest them in the future.

Source: *David L. Nelson, tax partner in charge of personal financial planning, Ernst & Young, 333 Clay St., Suite 3100, Houston, TX 77002.*

Deductions for Executives

Many executives have been duped into believing that they are entitled to few, if any, job-related deductions. Not true! Job-related expenses are deductible as miscellaneous itemized deductions. *Note:* Under tax reform, total miscellaneous deductions must be reduced by 2% of your Adjusted Gross Income (AGI). *Here's a comprehensive list:*

- **Dues for professional organizations.**
- **Professional publications:** Periodical subscriptions, journals, books.
- **Personal equipment:** Attaché case, pens and pencils, calculators, diaries.
- **Fees for credit card accounts used strictly for business.**
- **Costs of looking for a new job in your field of work.**
- **Educational expenses,** if incurred for the purpose of maintaining or improving skills needed in your current position or occupation.

The following *unreimbursed expenses* are also deductible, or partially deductible to the extent that they are unreimbursed.

- **Cost of fixing up or decorating your office** (including perishable items such as flowers).
- **Gifts to business associates** (limited to $25 per person per year).
- **50% of the cost of entertainment of business associates,** people with whom you have business dealings.
- **50% of the cost of entertainment at home,** provided the function's primary purpose is business; e.g., if you invite business associates to your daughter's wedding, that expense is not deductible, as the primary purpose of the event is clearly not to discuss business.
- **Local transportation** (taxis, buses) used in the course of business (but *not* to and from work).
- **Use of your own automobile.** (The unreimbursed portion is deductible.)
- **Business use of pay phones and home phone,** except for the basic service charge of the first phone line to the home.
- **Unreimbursed cost of stationery,** office supplies, photocopies, photography, etc., used in connection with your work.
- **Unreimbursed business transportation** (airfares, cabs, etc.).
- **Lodging and living expenses on a business trip,** including getting your suit pressed, your shoes shined, tipping the doorman or bellhop, etc., *plus* 50% of the cost of food and drink.

Source: *Edward Mendlowitz, partner, Mendlowitz Weitsen, LLP, 2 Penn Plaza, New York, NY 10121.*

Bigger and Better Business Deductions on Personal Tax Returns

For executives who want to claim business deductions on their personal returns, it's more important than ever to seek out every deduction opportunity. That's because under tax reform, the deduction for employee business expenses is allowed only to the extent that such costs exceed 2% of Adjusted Gross Income. An executive who overlooks a deductible item and fails to reach the 2% limit will get no deduction at all.

There are many unusual and unexpected deductions available to executives. Here's a rundown of what's been allowed.

Legal Bills

Legal costs are deductible when they are job-related, even for those accused of a criminal act and convicted; in fact, business expense deductions have been allowed even when the business itself was illegal:

● **Executive was sued for an accounting by investors who accused him of misappropriating company funds.**

Source: Harold K. Hochschild, 161 F2d 817.

● **Company president was sued by a shareholder of the company for making fraudulent misrepresentations.**

Source: Bernard A. Mitchell, 408 F2d 435.

● **Company officer became involved in a dispute concerning control of a family business,** and some of the shareholders tried to remove him from his job.

Source: Stanley Waldheim, 25 TC 839.

● **President of a company was charged with criminal antitrust violations.** His legal fees were deductible even though he was sent to jail.

Source: Central Coat, Apron and Linen, 298 F Supp 1201.

● **Purchasing agent was convicted of extortion in a kickback scheme.** His bail-bond fees were deductible.

Source: Bernard G. Murphy, TC Memo 1980-25.

● **Government successfully held a corporate officer liable for the company's income tax evasion.**

Source: Revenue Ruling 68-662.

● **Electronics expert,** who was involved with organized crime, was accused of installing illegal wiretaps.

Source: Bernard B. Spindel, TC Memo 1965-164.

Deductible Damages

When an executive *loses* a case that arises from business, he may even be able to deduct the damages that he has to pay:

● **Company president who was found to have defrauded investors was allowed to deduct his payment of damages,** because he committed the fraud to further the company's interests.

Source: C.A. Ostrum, 77 TC 608.

● **When an auto accident occurred while a person was driving on the job,** the driver could deduct the resulting damages as being business-related.

Source: Harold Dancer, 73 TC 1103.

Plaintiffs—Right or Wrong

Persons who bring suits as plaintiffs may also be able to deduct legal costs:

● **Job candidate sued to be reinstated at the top of the candidate list,** which would have enabled him to fill a vacancy.

Source: Caruso, 236 F Supp 88.

● **An executive was summarily replaced,** given a desk in an isolated location and paid to do nothing. He sued his employer, claiming to be a victim of bias. The IRS ruled the executive could deduct the cost of the lawsuit as a business expense, even though he lost the case.

Source: IRS Letter Ruling 8712009.

● **Person sued to prevent publication of an article.** He was entitled to the deduction even though he lost his case and the article was ruled not libelous. The fact that he thought the article could hurt his business reputation was enough to justify the deduction.

Source: J. Raymond Dyer, 36 TC 456.

Charity and Business

It's sometimes possible to get around the charitable contribution deduction limits (50% AGI on a personal return, 10% of taxable income on a corporate return) and boost business deductions by claiming payments made to charity as a business expense:

● **Payments were made to a charity in order to secure the goodwill of a customer who was heading its fund-raising drive.**

Source: *Adeline Marcelle, 8 AFTR2d 5344.*

● **Contributions were made to a local organization that was fighting pollution.** The pollution had hurt tourism and thus hurt the donor's business.

Source: *Revenue Ruling 73-113.*

● **Travel agent made large contributions to charities that booked trips through her agency.**

Source: *Sarah Marquis, 49 TC 695.*

● **Person donated turkeys and entertainment tickets to the poor through a Lions Club,** which was not a qualified charity. The donations were intended to obtain favorable publicity for the taxpayer's business.

Source: *William H. Limerick, TC Memo 6/8/50.*

For the Unemployed

Business expense deductions have been allowed even for people who are unemployed. That's because, once you're in business, the IRS considers that you remain in business through any period of temporary unemployment. Unemployment is generally considered temporary if it lasts for less than one year, though the specific facts of the case may lead to a different conclusion. Business expense deductions were allowed when:

● **Unemployed salesman continued to entertain persons who had been customers in the past.** The salesman was looking for a new job, and it was important that he retain the customers' goodwill.

Source: *Harold Haft, 40 TC 2.*

● **Business manager quit his job and deducted the cost of taking a full-time MBA program.** On getting his degree, he took another management job with another firm.

Source: *Steven G. Sherman, TC Memo 1977-301.*

● **Unemployed person looked for a new job in the same line of work as his old one.** All the costs of the job search were deductible, including the cost of travel, printing and mailing résumés, taking out newspaper advertisements, getting career counseling and hiring executive recruiters.

Source: *Revenue Ruling 75-120.*

Home Deductions

Unique home deductions were allowed when:

● **Person who managed a family business was required to be on the premises around the clock to handle operations.** He incorporated the business and then signed an employment contract under which the company provided him with a house and paid his utility bills. Since the Tax Code says that lodging given to an employee for the benefit of an employer is tax-exempt, he was able to take the house and utility payments tax-free. And the company got to deduct the expense payments and depreciate the home.

Source: *Jim Grant Farms, TC Memo 1985-174.*

● **Executive owned vacation property on which he had a vacation home.** He further improved the property by building a separate office on it. Because the office was a separate structure, it did not fall under normal home-office rules, and the executive was able to fully depreciate it and to deduct related costs.

Source: *Ben W. Heineman, 82 TC 538.*

Travel Deductions

Employee travel deductions were upheld when:

● **Salesman had to cover the entire state of Ohio and was not reimbursed for his meals,** lodging or auto costs by his company. He had receipts, canceled checks and notes showing how much he had spent on his trips, but did not have records indicating the business purpose of specific expenditures. The trips themselves were clearly business-motivated, so the expenses incurred on them were business-related and deductible.

Source: *Michael J. Bernard, CICt, No. 205-84T.*

● **A taxpayer regularly drove between several job sites for business,** but didn't keep good records. The IRS disallowed his deduction for auto costs. *Tax Court:* It was clear that it was necessary to drive between these sites for work. Further, the cost could be estimated by measuring the distance between work sites and the number of trips he had to make. The taxpayer, therefore, was entitled to a deduction, but because he didn't have any records of his travels, the court allowed him to take only the minimum deduction that was reasonable under the circumstances.

Source: *Rudolph J. Barnes, TC Memo 1986-585.*

● **Employer had a formal policy of reimbursing workers for job-related expenses.** However, the taxpayer's boss had a personal policy of not approving reimbursements for car expenses. The taxpayer didn't want to get into trouble by going over his boss's head, so he deducted his car costs on his own return. Reimbursable expenses normally aren't deductible, but here there was a good business reason for not asking for reimbursement. Thus the car costs were ruled deductible.

Source: *George Kessler, TC Memo 1985-254.*

Personal Deductions

Business expense deductions were allowed for:

● **Office furnishings bought by an executive with his own funds,** in order to maintain his image as a successful district sales manager.

Source: *Leroy Gillis, TC Memo 1973-96.*

● **The cost of enrolling in an advanced-degree program concentrating on taxes and financial**

Better Than a Raise

Employee business expenses, along with the cost of investment advice, tax preparation fees and other miscellaneous items (such as the cost of subscribing to business or investment publications) are deductible only to the extent that their total exceeds 2% of Adjusted Gross Income. Thus a person with an Adjusted Gross Income of $50,000 can get no deduction for the first $1,000 worth of such items.

When executives have large unreimbursed business expenses, they may do better by negotiating with their employers for an increase in their reimbursements instead of a raise. If the executive gets a raise, it will be taxed, while the executive will lose at least part of the deduction for the unreimbursed expenses. On the other hand, an increase in reimbursements will be tax-free and completely cover the cost of expenses.

planning, even though the financial consultant involved was not required to take the courses for work. The education was job-related because it enhanced the skills used by the consultant in his current job.

Source: *IRS Letter Ruling 8706048.*

● **Briefcase bought for use on the job.**

Source: *Stanley Bailey, TC Memo 1971-107.*

● **Calculator used by a salesman for business.**

Source: *Robert G. Galazin, TC Memo 1979-206.*

● **Office supplies that were bought by an insurance salesman.**

Source: *George Blood Enterprises, TC Memo 1976-102.*

● **Medical checkups,** when proof of fitness was a job requirement.

Source: *Revenue Ruling 58-382.*

Deducting a Company Car And Chauffeur

The use of a company car can be a valuable fringe benefit. The expenses of the car, including depreciation, are deductible by the corporation and not taxable to the shareholder-employee if it is used exclusively for company business.

One way to get around the rules taxing employees for personal use of company-owned automobiles is to have a second car available for personal use. Agents are reporting cases of taxpayers buying small used cars to substantiate the fact that they have another car available for weekend and after-hours use.

If a shareholder-executive is given the use of two cars, and it is clear that one of them is being used by a spouse for nonbusiness purposes, the employee will be taxed on the value of the use of the car. But the tax liability will be less than the cost of renting a car, and most likely less than it would cost to buy, finance and maintain the car. If the extra car is treated as extra compensation, the attending expenses are deductible by the corporation as compensation, subject to the overall limitation of reasonableness. If treated as dividend income to the shareholder, it is not deductible by the corporation.

The cost of a chauffeur may be deductible by the corporation and not taxable to the shareholder-employee if deemed an "ordinary and necessary expense," sometimes translated as "appropriate and helpful."

Job-Hunting Expenses (Whether You Get the Job or Not)

If you change jobs, keep track of your job-hunting expenses. The costs of looking for a new job in your present line of work are tax deductible (subject to the 2% of Adjusted Gross Income limit on miscellaneous deductions), even if you don't get a new job. However, you can't deduct expenses of looking for a new job in a new trade or business even if you get the job.

Deductible job-hunting expenses include:

● **Fees paid to employment agencies and executive recruiters.**

● **Cost of typing, printing and mailing résumés to prospective employers.**

● **Career counseling** to improve your position in your present trade.

● **Advertising for a new job** in your present field.

● **Cab fares to job interviews,** car expenses and other transportation costs.

● **Phone calls to prospective employers.**

● **Newspapers and business publications** that you buy for employment ads.

● **Entertainment expenses** directly related to your job search.

● **Out-of-town travel expenses,** including lodging, local transportation and 50% of the cost of meals, if the trip is primarily to look for a new job. If the main purpose of the trip is personal, your travel costs are not deductible. But you can deduct out-of-pocket job-hunting expenses at your destination.

● **The cost of drumming up business by a taxpayer who is an employee,** but who wants to become self-employed in the same trade, has been

COMMUTING COSTS CAN BE DEDUCTIBLE

Most commuting expenses aren't deductible. But if a person works at least two jobs in the same day, the cost of traveling from the first job to the second job is deductible as a business expense to the extent that when added to all your other business expenses, they exceed 2% of your Adjusted Gross Income. You still can't deduct travel from home to your first job or from your second job back home. *(Editor's note: Commuting to a temporary place of work— one where you work on an irregular basis, or a few days or weeks—is deductible as long as the workplaces are within the metropolitan area where you work and live.)*

Similarly, customer visits made on your way to work are partially tax deductible. The deductible portion: the distance between the customer's place of business and your office (or the next customer, etc.).

held by the Tax Court to be deductible.* The court disagreed with the IRS's position that self-employment in a person's present line of work is really a new job.

Howard L. Cornutt, TC Memo 1983-24.

Deducting Vacation Costs As a Business Expense

Combining a tax-deductible business trip with a short vacation, perhaps with a spouse and family, can be quite attractive. It is important to keep expense categories straight, since different tests apply for deductibility.

You can deduct the cost of traveling in the United States for business or professional purposes. But you must be able to show that the primary purpose of the trip was business. This does not mean that you cannot combine business with pleasure, only that the primary purpose is business.

Best way to satisfy the IRS: Prove that more than half of your time at the destination was spent on business.

The all-or-nothing test for travel: Your transportation expenses are either fully deductible to the extent they exceed 2% of your Adjusted Gross Income (when added together with your other business expenses because they meet the test), or they cannot be deducted at all. On the other hand, meal and entertainment expenses at your destination are 50% deductible and should be separated into business and nonbusiness categories.

Do not count on deducting the full cost of a trip with your spouse. It is not enough for the IRS that a spouse's presence is a big help to you. Only your expenses at the meeting site are deductible, but you are not limited to half of the total costs there. You can still deduct the full amount of what it would cost you to attend alone at the single-room hotel rate, for instance. You can deduct the full cost of services where your spouse's presence does not boost the charge, say, for the taxi from the airport. If you drive to the meeting site, you can deduct almost the full transportation cost. If you fly or take the train, only your ticket is deductible.

For business-vacation combinations of seven days or less to spots outside the United States, the regular rules on business travel, explained above, apply. But if you are gone more than seven days and you spend more than 25% of your total time vacationing, you lose a deduction for the portion of your transportation costs equal to the number of nonbusiness days divided by the total number of days outside the United States. Ship travel can be an asset on a combined business-vacation trip. ***Reason:*** Days spent in transit count as business days in the allocations formula.

The rules are tighter for conventions outside the North American area. No costs can be deducted for such a business meeting unless the IRS can be convinced that the selection of the meeting site is reasonable. (In practice, it probably is better to be able to *prove* that it is more reasonable to hold the convention at the foreign site than in the United States.)

No deduction is permitted for a convention or related expenses incurred in connection with investments, financial planning or income-producing activities.

Both directly related and associated entertainment expenses are 50% deductible on a working vacation, if you follow the rules. Associated entertainment expenses cover nights on the town, box seats at a game, etc.

A specific business discussion must occur before or after the entertainment.

Business gifts are deductible, subject to a $25 limit. So if you give theater tickets worth more than $25 to a client, you can't deduct the excess. ***Suggestion:*** Go to the show with the client, and you can write off the whole evening as business entertainment.

Good records are essential to justify your deductions. Keep a diary in which you record expenses and their business purpose. You must also keep receipts for expenses of $25 or more. The diary alone is sufficient proof for smaller amounts.

Source: *Edward Mendlowitz, partner, Mendlowitz Weitsen, LLP, 2 Penn Plaza, New York, NY 10121.*

Imaginative Travel Deductions

Traveling for Education

Traveling costs to educational seminars are still deductible if you are in the trade or business that is the subject of the seminar. The cost of attending a

DEDUCTION CHECKLIST FOR BUSINESS OWNERS

More than ever, the best source of tax breaks is running your own business. *Business owners' tax advantages:*

● **Fully deductible business expenses.** For the self-employed, business expenses are deductible in full directly from gross income.

● **Full home-office expense write-off.** If you run a business from your home and meet certain requirements, you may deduct not only property taxes and mortgage interest, but also a percentage of depreciation, utilities, insurance, repairs and any other costs. Your home-office deductions may *not* exceed your net income from the business. You can't use them to show a tax loss. However, you can carry over any unused deductions and take them in future years, when you have income from the business.

● **Tax-deferred retirement savings.** Qualified retirement plans offer business owners an opportunity to save for their retirement on a tax-deductible basis. Self-employed owners can use Keogh plans, SEPs or SIMPLE plans to save for retirement.

Drawback: You must cover your employees on a nondiscriminatory basis, which can add considerably to the cost of coverage.

● **Hiring your kids.** Their wages are deductible business expenses. And you may still claim them as dependents.

Bonus: Children under 18 who work for a parent are exempt from Social Security tax. (The exemption doesn't apply if the parent's business is incorporated.)

Caution: Kids must perform actual services for reasonable compensation. Phony jobs and inflated wages don't stand up to IRS scrutiny.

● **Hiring your spouse.** Your spouse may participate in any retirement plans that you have for employees (pension, 401(k), etc.). In some cases he or she may qualify for deductible IRA contributions. Finally, if your spouse accompanies you on a business trip as an assistant or colleague, you may write off travel expenses for both of you.

● **Timing income.** If you use the cash accounting method, you can defer income from one year into the next. You just don't send out bills late in the year—you wait until January.

● **More deductible transportation expenses.** Going to work and coming home are nondeductible com-mutation expenses. But if you work out of your home, you're already at your place of business when you get up in the morning. So all travel costs are deductible. Justifying transportation deductions is also easier for business owners.

● **Fully deductible casualty losses.** Business casualty losses (from fire, theft, accident, natural disaster, etc.) may be written off in full against business income.

● **Full write-offs for bad debts.** Bad business debts may be deducted in full in the year in which they become uncollectible.

● **Operating losses.** If your business loses money—as many do at first—you may write off the loss against your other income. If the loss exceeds income, you may carry the excess up to two years into the past to get a refund for those years. (Longer carry-back periods apply in special circumstances). If there's still any excess loss, you may carry it forward for the next 20 years.

general seminar on how to improve your dealings with your broker is not deductible, even if you have many investments. But stockbrokers who attend the same seminar would be entitled to a deduction because that's their trade or business.

Caution: Teachers cannot deduct the cost of travel to a foreign country to enhance their general understanding of the culture and language of that country.

Traveling for Charity

You can deduct the cost of traveling with a charitable group if you serve as an escort or chaperone. You must have some kind of responsibility for the group, such as helping the handicapped to travel or assisting as a Scout leader where you are assigned the task of supervising a specific number of children in the group.

All the related travel costs can be taken as a charitable deduction, such as the cost of your meals (100% is deductible for charity) while away from home, lodging and other out-of-pocket costs. However, no deductions are permitted for family members who accompany you.

Traveling for Medical Reasons

If you must travel for medical reasons, you can deduct the cost of getting there (if you use your car, you can deduct your travel at 10 cents a mile).

In addition, deductions can be taken if travel expenses are incurred for a traveling companion needed for the trip. This could happen when the person getting the medical treatment is too ill or too young to travel the distance alone.

However, meals are not deductible during your medical stay. Lodging expenses are limited to $50 per night if it is absolutely essential that you stay overnight to receive the medical treatment.

Note: Medical expenses are deductible only to the extent that they exceed 7½% of your Adjusted Gross Income.

Source: David S. Rhine, partner and national director of family wealth planning, BDO Seidman, 330 Madison Ave., New York, NY 10017.

A Sideline Business: The Best Tax Shelter

The best tax shelter may be a sideline business. With it you can generate large paper losses, claim deductions for personal or hobbylike expenses and legally shift income to your low-tax-bracket minor children. *Here's how a sideline business can be used to get big tax-shelter-type deductions, along with winning examples of taxpayers who have already done it:*

Income Shifting

In 1998 investment income exceeding $1,400 of a child under age 14 is taxed at the rate paid by the child's parents. But this rule does not apply to the earned income of a child. *Result:* A child who works for a parent's sideline business can earn $4,250 in 1998 tax-free, and earnings in excess of this amount are taxed at the child's low tax rate. Since the parent deducts the salary paid to the child as a business expense, the family's tax bill is lowered by the difference between the parent's high tax rate and the low or zero rate on the child's salary.

> **"To qualify for the deduction, you must have a part of your home that's used exclusively for business and is the primary place where you conduct the sideline business."**

This income-shifting technique is also available for children over age 14 and other family members. And even greater tax benefits can be obtained when family members use the salary you pay to make deductible IRA retirement contributions, or when the business pays for deductible benefits.

The only rule that governs paying salaries to family members is that they must actually earn their salaries. *Salary deductions have been allowed when:*

● **The owner of a trailer park paid his children,** ages seven to 12, to perform cleaning chores, landscaping and office work.

Source: Walt Eller, 77 TC 934.

● **A doctor paid his four children,** ages 13 to 16, to answer telephone calls, take messages and prepare insurance forms.

Source: James Moriarity, TC Memo 1984-249.

- **The owner of a rental property hired his teenage sons to maintain and clean the building.**

Source: Charles Tschupp, TC Memo 1963-98.

- **A business owner hired his wife to act as the company's official hostess.**

Source: Clement J. Duffey, 11 AFTR2d 1317.

What Qualifies

A part-time activity can easily qualify as a business. The only requirement is that you operate your activity with the objective of making a profit. You don't actually have to make a profit, nor do you have to expect to make a profit in the near future. *Winning examples:*

- **Eugene Feistman,** a probation officer, collected and traded stamps for many years. The Tax Court initially refused to let him deduct his costs, saying his collecting was merely a hobby. So he filed a business registration certificate with the local government, opened an account that let him make sales by charge card, set up an inventory and started keeping good business records concerning purchases and sales. *New ruling:* Now Feistman could deduct his costs because he was operating in a businesslike manner. The Tax Court let him deduct $9,000 over two years.

Source: Eugene Feistman, TC Memo 1982-306.

- **Gloria Churchman,** a housewife, admitted that she painted for pleasure, but she was also able to prove that she had made a serious effort to sell her works at shows and galleries. The Tax Court let her deduct her expenses and losses, including the cost of a studio in her home.

Source: Gloria Churchman, 68 TC 696.

- **Melvin Nickerson,** an executive who lived in the city, bought a farm and began renovating it on weekends. He intended to retire to it in the future. Although Nickerson didn't expect to make a profit from the farm for another 10 years, the Court of Appeals let him deduct his renovation costs right away. It said that his expectation of future profits, combined with the real work he had put in, sufficed to justify a deduction now.

Source: Melvin Nickerson, 700 F2D 402.

- **Bernard Wagner,** an accountant, fancied himself a songwriter and music promoter. He hired a band, rehearsed it, booked it and copyrighted the songs he wrote. Although his chances of success were slight, he intended to succeed, so the Tax Court let him deduct his costs and losses.

Source: Bernard Wagner, TC Memo 1983-606.

- **J.V. Keenon bought a house,** moved into it, then rented an apartment in the house to his own daughter. The Tax Court agreed that he was not in the real estate rental business, so he could deduct depreciation on the rented apartment, along with utilities, insurance and related expenses. And this was in spite of the fact that he charged his daughter a below-market rent. The court felt that the rent was fair because it's safer to rent to a family member than to a stranger.

Source: J.V. Keenon, TC Memo 1982-144.

Home Deductions

A major benefit of running a sideline business out of your home is the possibility of claiming a home office deduction. This entitles you to deduct expenses that were formerly personal in nature, such as rent, utility, insurance and maintenance costs attributable to the office. *Even better:* If you own your home, you can depreciate the part of your home that's used as an office, getting large paper deductions that cost you nothing out-of-pocket.

To qualify for the deduction, you must have a part of your home that's used exclusively for business and is the primary place where you conduct the sideline business. *Winning examples:*

- **A doctor who owned and managed rental properties** to get extra income could deduct one bedroom in his two-bedroom apartment as an office.

Source: Edwin R. Curphey, 73 TC 766.

- **A woman who did economic consulting work out of a home office** could deduct it even though her husband, a famous newspaper editor, used the same office for nondeductible activities. The Tax Court did not reduce her deduction because her husband shared the office.

Source: Max Frankel, 82 TC 318.

Big Dollar Deductions

Taxpayers are prohibited from offsetting their salary and investment income with losses from businesses in which they participate as passive investors (as shareholders or limited partners without management duties). But if you manage your own sideline business, it's possible to claim big loss deductions.

Important: Tax losses do not always mean cash losses. Items such as depreciation on cars, equipment and real estate can result in deductible tax losses while the business is earning a cash-flow profit. A sideline business is presumed to have a profit objective if it has reported a profit in three out of five years (two out of seven years for horse breeders). But such a business may be deemed to have a profit objective even after reporting many years of continuous losses.

Winning examples:

● **A real estate operator tried to develop and market an automatic garage door opener.** He was entitled to deduct $355,000 over 11 years, because he had made a sincere effort to sell the door openers.

Source: Frederick A. Purdy, TC Memo 1967-82.

● **A horse farm incurred 20 straight years of losses totaling over $700,000.** During the next seven years it lost another $119,000, but in two of those years it had profits totaling $17,000. Since the two-out-of-seven-years test had been met, the farm was ruled to be a profit-motivated business and all of its losses were deductible.

Source: Hunter Faulconer, 748 F2d 890.

● **A corporate vice president and management expert ran a breeding farm as a sideline and lost $450,000 over 12 years.** The loss was deductible because evidence indicated that it often takes eight to 12 years to establish an acceptable bloodline for the animals involved.

Source: Lawrence Appley, TC Memo 1979-433.

> "The distinction between a hobby and a business is very fine. When you deduct losses from a business that the IRS could label as a hobby, you must be able to prove that you intended to make a profit."

Start-up Tactic

When starting a new sideline business, you can protect your deductions by electing to have the IRS postpone its examination of your business status until after you've been operating for five years (seven years in the case of a horse farm). You'll be able to treat your sideline as a business during that period, even if it earns continuous losses. But if you can't demonstrate a profit objective at the end of that period, you'll owe back taxes. Make the election by filing IRS Form 5213, *Election to Postpone Determination That Activity Is for Profit.*

How to Deduct Your Hobby

For your own bottom line, it can make a huge difference whether you operate a hobby as a hobby or a sideline business. As a hobbyist, your tax deductions are pretty much limited to the amount of income the activity generates. But if you run the hobby as a business, all your expenses are deductible to the extent that when they are added to your other business expenses, the total exceeds 2% of AGI—even if they exceed business income.

Problem: The distinction between a hobby and a business is very fine. When you deduct losses from a business that the IRS could label as a hobby, you must be able to prove that you intended to make a profit.

Hobby or Business

As far as the IRS is concerned, a business is an activity engaged in for profit. There's no law, however, that says you must actually make a profit. The only rule is that you must intend to make a profit.

Presumption of law that aids taxpayers: If you show a profit in three of any five consecutive years (two out of seven for breeding, showing, training or racing horses), it is presumed you are engaged in an activity for profit. Although the IRS can challenge the presumption, normally it will not.

Profit Motive

If you don't meet the presumption, the IRS may challenge your deductions as hobby losses. It will be necessary for you to prove your good intentions. Here is a checklist of things you should be prepared to show the IRS if your business losses are challenged:

● **You operate in a businesslike manner.** Keep accurate books and records.

● **You instituted new operating procedures** to correct past business practices that resulted in losses.

● **You act professionally.** Show that you hired or consulted with recognized experts in the field, and that you followed their advice.

● **You made a serious effort.** Show that you hired qualified people to run your day-to-day operation. Remember, no rule says you must devote 40 hours a week to your sideline business.

● **There is a profit potential.** Even if your business continually produces losses, you can still prove a profit motive by showing that assets you have acquired are expected to appreciate.

● **You have had past successes.** It may help establish a profit motive if you show that in the past you were successfully involved in your current activity.

Doing Business

The IRS will look for tangible indications that you have really embarked on a business enterprise. *Suggestions:*

● **Register your business name by filing a** "doing business as" statement with your local county clerk.

● **Use business cards and stationery.**

● **Take out a company listing** in the Yellow Pages.

● **Keep a log of the business contacts** you've seen during the year.

● **Advertise in local papers.**

● **Send promotional mailings** to prospective customers.

● **Set up a business bank account.**

● **Get a business telephone.**

● **Buy a postage meter** and a copying machine.

● **Hire at least some part-time help.**

Tougher Questions

The IRS will argue that, since you had other sources of income and could afford to lose money, you could not have had a profit motive.

Defense: Nobody goes into business expecting to lose money. Even with your tax deductions, you would have been better off had you done nothing and never started the venture in the first place.

Suppose your business occasionally generates small amounts of income. You can prove a profit motive if you can also show an opportunity to earn a substantial ultimate profit in a highly speculative business.

If the IRS can show that you derive personal pleasure from your business, it will count this against you. Businesses that involve horse racing, farming, car racing and antiques are particularly vulnerable to this kind of attack. Don't let the IRS bulldoze you. The courts have consistently held that enjoying what you do is not, by itself, proof that you lack a profit motive.

Source: *Randy Bruce Blaustein, Esq., former IRS agent now partner, Blaustein, Greenberg & Co., 155 E. 31 St., New York, NY 10016. He is the author of* How to Do Business With the IRS, *Prentice-Hall.*

Special Advice for the Self-Employed and Moonlighters

Those already in business for themselves know that the IRS is a force to be reckoned with—and those just starting out will soon learn it. The IRS is an overseer, and it cannot be ignored. Mistakes are costly. Even if your accountant makes the mistake on your return, you pay. *To avoid IRS trouble:*

● **Keep separate bank accounts for business transactions.** This will simplify record keeping. *Note:* It is inevitable that there will be some cross-flow of funds between business and personal accounts. Pay special attention to documenting this flow of funds. Without adequate documentation, the IRS will suspect, and may allege, additional taxable business income.

● **Have separate credit cards for business transactions.** This too will simplify your record keeping. At times, certain expenditures will be a mixture of business and personal expense. For example, your spouse may accompany you on a business trip.

Advice: Keep a diary keyed to your business credit card use and all cash expenditures for business.

The combination of receipts, credit card vouchers, canceled checks and a diary is usually strong enough proof to deter the most zealous IRS examiner.

● **Have separate equipment,** etc., for business use. If the nature of your business requires that you make and receive business calls at home, install a separate telephone for that purpose. If you drive a significant number of business miles, keep a separate automobile for that purpose. If your business requires that you do substantial work at home, set aside a room or area of your home as an office. Furnish the area exclusively with office furniture, equipment and business materials, and use it exclusively for business purposes.

● **Know your tax responsibilities.** Even if you leave the matter of taxes largely to your accountant and bookkeeper, take the time and trouble to educate yourself on the subject. The penalties for slipping are prohibitively high. Learn your personal responsibility for income tax, self-employment tax and estimated tax payments. Be sure to have some understanding of your responsibility in the area of employment taxes, and try to be aware of state and local tax requirements. *Helpful:* IRS Publication 15, commonly known as *Circular E (Employer's Tax Guide),* available free of charge from the IRS.

THE HOME OFFICE

Using a part of your home in your business may enable you to deduct certain expenses if you satisfy specific tests. To take this deduction, that portion of your home must be used exclusively and regularly:

● **As the principal place of business** for any trade or business in which you engage.

● **As a place to meet or deal with your trade or business;** or

● **In connection with your trade or business,** if you are using a separate structure that is not attached to your house or residence.

Exclusive use means that you must use that specific part of your home only for the purpose of carrying on your trade or business. Any personal use will prevent you from claiming the deduction. *Regular use* means that you use the exclusive business part of your home on a continuing basis, not just occasionally. (*Editor's note*: Starting in 1999, your home office is treated as a principal place of business if it is used for substantial managerial or administrative activities (such as paying bills, ordering supplies, and scheduling appointments) and there is no other fixed location for these activities.)

As an employee, you must be using your home for the convenience of your employer in addition to satisfying these three tests. Just being helpful to your work will not qualify you for a home office deduction.

To deduct the expenses for the business use of your home office, the use must be connected with a trade or business, not just a profit-seeking activity. For example, if you use part of your home to carry on personal investment activities, not as a broker or dealer, expenses cannot be deducted since you are not in that trade or business.

The allowable deductions attributable to the business use of the home are limited to the net income from the business activity. Income is reduced first by deductions from the home office business and mortgage interest and real estate taxes. Any loss *at this point* is deductible in the year it is incurred with other expenses (i.e., insurance, maintenance, utilities and depreciation) being carried forward, as a net operating loss from the home office business, to be used against future years' home office income. Net income *at this point* would then be reduced by other expenses to the extent it did not fall below zero.

An exception to the home office rule exists where an employee leases a portion of the home to the employer and subsequently collects rental income. In this case the home office deductions are disallowed. The only deductions allowable are those attributable to the home itself, such as mortgage interest, real estate taxes and casualty losses.

Source: *Thomas L. LoCicero, former IRS branch manager and presently senior tax manager and executive tax-planning specialist with the firm of Deloitte & Touche, 1 World Trade Center, New York, NY 10048.*

Caution: In the past, some employers used government trust funds (income taxes withheld from employees' wages and the employee's share of Social Security and Medicare taxes) to tide the company over periods of weak cash flow. Be advised that the IRS has little patience with such methods. It has an ever-increasing policy of cracking down fast and forcefully on employers who don't follow the letter of the law in handling withheld payroll taxes. *(Editor's note:* Even if your business is incorporated or set up as a limited liability company, as the owner you remain personally liable for unpaid "trust fund" taxes.)

If you are in a pinch, ask your accountant to locate an alternate source of funds.

● **Keep good records.** Your accountant has primary responsibility to provide you with a system that clearly and properly reflects your business income and transactions. A simple method of record keeping that works is one that is organized to reflect tax return items line by line. For example, if you are a sole proprietorship, set up your accounts according to the line items on Form 1040, Schedule C. Mark your checks, credit card receipts and diary entries with the appropriate type of expense or line number. *(Editor's note:* Computer records are acceptable as long as certain controls are in place to protect the integrity of these records.)

For more complex and/or active business enterprises, you would be wise to rely on the expertise of a reputable accountant familiar with your type of business. Expect your accountant to set up a record-keeping system, give business advice and represent you at the IRS if necessary. It will be money well spent.

Source: *George S. Alberts, former head of the Albany and Brooklyn IRS District Offices.*

Escaping the Penalties

Your estimated tax payments, plus the taxes withheld from your salary, must equal 90% of the total tax due or 100% of the prior year's liability, or you'll be hit with a penalty on the underpayment. *(Editor's note:* After 1998, if your prior year's AGI exceeded $150,000, you cannot rely on the 100%-of-prior-liability rule. As an alternative to the 90% current tax rule, you'll have to pay more than 100% of the prior year's tax to avoid penalty. The percentage required will vary between 1999 and 2003, when it becomes fixed at 110%.) Moreover, the penalty is imposed on a quarterly basis—if your first estimated tax payment is too small, you can't make up for it by bigger estimated payments later.

There are ways to avoid a penalty:

● **Increase withholding.** If it looks like your payments will fall short, file a new Form W-4, claiming fewer withholding allowances, to increase the amount withheld from your salary. Or ask your employer to withhold more. Withheld taxes are presumed to be paid equally throughout the year so larger withholding payments late in the year can be applied retroactively to wipe out any earlier underpayments.

● **Penalty exception.** You can rely on an annualization safe harbor. If most of your income is derived late in the year, you can take advantage of the "annualization" rules, but you'll probably need an accountant to make the calculations. *Basically, it works like this:* On any estimated payment date, you figure your income up to that point, "annualize" it and base your payment on the annualized figure. *Here's a simplified example of how the rules work:* Your income during the first quarter of the year is only $5,000, so your "annualized" income is $20,000. You pay only the estimated tax that would be due from a person with an income of $20,000 a year. Of course, you have to recompute the figures on each payment date and recalculate your payments accordingly.

A Great Tax Shelter That Isn't a Tax Shelter

If you own your corporation, you can take advantage of certain tax strategies to substantially improve your cash flow and the quality of your life. For example, you can have your corporation start a medical reimbursement plan for employees. *Rationale:* The only medical expenses you can deduct on your personal tax return are those that exceed 7½% of Adjusted Gross Income (AGI). So if your AGI is $40,000 and you have medical expenses of $1,000, you're $1,000 out-of-pocket—with no tax benefit whatsoever. But if your company reimburses you, it can deduct the $1,000.

This strategy cannot be used if you own an S Corporation, and it works only if the plan applies equally to all employees. If it is limited to top officers, they will be taxed as though the reimbursements were salary income.

Caution: In the case of shareholders, dividend treatment may result (see below). But even that isn't necessarily terrible. You're still better off paying the taxes than $1,000 in medical bills.

Salary Versus Dividends

The way you take money out of your company makes a difference in your taxes. Dividends are taxed twice—once to your company (because they aren't deductible) and once to you. Salaries are taxed only once. Obviously, the more of your total compensation you take in salary, the better.

There's a limit, though—your salary must be "reasonable." *Guidelines:* your education, knowledge, expertise and what top executives in similar companies make. If it appears to the IRS that the reason for the compensation is your ownership interest, it's probably a dividend. If, on the other hand, the reason appears to be the blood, sweat and tears you put into the company, it's probably salary.

S corporations are a way around the whole salary versus dividends problem. An S corporation pays no taxes itself. Instead, the owners pay taxes on their proportionate share of the company's income. For tax purposes, this is really equivalent to receiving all salary and no dividends.

Drawback: You have to pay the tax on your share of the S corporation income whether or not you take any money out of the company. If your company has loan covenants that restrict payment to owners (as many small businesses do), you could have trouble coming up with the cash for taxes.

Useful Perks

Perks are another way to use your business to improve your standard of living, and they are nontaxable if you can show they are necessary to your business. That can be tricky. For company cars, you must charge employees fair rental value for any personal use of the car. But the amount you charge can be less than what Hertz, for example, charges.

Of course, if a perk fails the necessity test, you can still take an unreimbursed business expense deduction to the extent your business expenses exceed 2% of AGI for whatever part of the expenses is attributable to business.

Source: Jack Salomon, partner in charge of state tax services at KPMG Peat Marwick, 55 E. 52 St., New York, NY 10055.

S Corporation Magic

The number of ways in which Subchapter S corporations can be used to cut business and personal taxes has been greatly expanded. *It is now possible to use S corporations:*

● **In syndications and other money-raising ventures.**

● **As a tax-cutting tool for personal investments.**

An S corporation combines the tax benefits of personally owning a business with the legal protection of the corporate form. The income and deductions of the firm flow directly to the shareholders, in proportion to their stockholdings, to be claimed on their personal tax returns.

For example, business losses can be used to cut the tax on shareholder salaries. But, at the same time, shareholders have personal protection from corporate liabilities (such as lawsuits and unsecured debts).

It is now possible for an S corporation to receive most of its income from investments in the form of rents, dividends and interest. Changes in the law also allow different shares of an S corporation's stock to bear different voting rights. These changes create many new tax-saving opportunities.

S corporation advantages: Tax benefits flow through to investors in much the same way as in a partnership, and the same shelter advantages (subject to passive loss rules) result. *But in addition:*

● **The corporation protects all the investors from personal liability.**

● **Since shareholders can be executives and managers of the firm,** they can control how their money is spent.

● **Shares of stock may be much easier to sell** or give away if the investor wants to get out.

Business opportunities: As most businesses

incur tax losses during their start-up phase, syndicators and entrepreneurs can attract investors by starting up a new business in the S corporation form. The flow-through of losses will offset income from other shelters.

Similarly, a large, established business that wishes to expand (by purchasing new equipment or real estate, for example) can have some of its executives and shareholders form an independent S corporation to acquire the new property on terms that are arranged to be advantageous to it and the new firm's shareholders.

Personal tax planning: Because an S corporation may have investment income, it's possible for a top-bracket investor to incorporate his or her personal portfolio. Shares of stock without voting rights may then be given to (or placed in trust for) other family members. At the same time, by keeping all the voting shares of the S corporation's stock, the taxpayer retains complete control over the investments. The same tactic is available to the top-tax-bracket owner of a family business.

Restrictions: There's no limit to the size of a company that elects S-corporation status. But the company can have no more than 75 shareholders (with husband and wife counting as one). Another corporation can't be a shareholder.

While an S corporation's losses flow through to its shareholders, the amount of losses a shareholder can claim is generally limited to the amount he or she paid for stock plus the amount of any loans he or she has made to the company. Excess losses can be carried forward and deducted from the company's future income.

The loss-limitation rule means that S-corporation status may not be best when company losses result from heavy interest payments on borrowings for which the shareholders aren't personally liable—for example, real estate tax shelters, when a mortgage is secured by the property alone.

Tactic: Shareholders can increase their deduction limit by substituting themselves for the company as the party primarily liable on the loan. (They're then assumed to have reloaned the borrowed amount to the company.) If the business is successful, they will never have to pay off the loan out-of-pocket. And since the owners of a closely held company are usually required to guarantee its major debts personally anyway, the substitution doesn't really increase their liability, even in the worst case.

There are other technical rules that apply to S corporations, making it necessary to consult with a tax professional to see if an S-corporation election is a good idea in your case. But don't overlook the flexible planning opportunities that result from the liberalized law.

Even an established company that's highly profitable may gain by electing S-corporation status:

● **The election eliminates corporate income tax at the federal level,** and sometimes at the state level as well.

● **The election eliminates the risk of two common IRS challenges:** the company pays unreasonably large salaries or has accumulated too much in earnings in the business.

A firm that expects to lose money can elect S-corporation status to pass its losses through to its owners. It can then return to regular corporate status when it returns to profitability. Normally, S-corporation status can't be elected more than once every five years. But a company can reelect S-corporation status within this time under certain circumstances.

Editor's note: Another advantage is that income can be split among family members. If shares are given to members in lower tax brackets (such as children or parents), it is possible to reduce the family's overall tax on S-corporation income. Special trusts (qualified Subchapter S trusts and electing small business trusts) can be used to hold shares for minors or other individuals.

> " **Shareholders can increase their deduction limit by substituting themselves for the company as the party primarily liable on the loan.** "

Source: *Barry D. Sussman and Martin Galuskin, partners, Milgrom, Sussman, Galuskin & Co., CPAs, New York.*

Tax Havens: What They Offer, What They Don't

"Tax haven" is probably one of the most misunderstood terms in investment jargon. Despite the visions it conjures up of tax-free investments and avoidance of a host of other taxes, so-called "tax havens" have relatively little potential for tax savings for U.S. residents. Nor do they offer (in any meaningful way) much-vaunted privacy or confidentiality of business records. But they do offer some real benefits to investors.

A tax haven is not a type of investment (like a "tax shelter"). *It is a political jurisdiction:* a state or nation in which the local government has elected not to levy taxes—on income, inheritance, property, etc. The tax-free status, however, exists only in that particular jurisdiction. U.S. residents with accounts, investments, trusts or other business structures in tax havens still pay income tax on all earnings derived therefrom; to the IRS it is income, period.

A tax haven is also not a means to privacy. Although it's true that your investments are confidential in most tax haven jurisdictions, you will keep evidence of those investments in personal records and files. No matter how or where they are maintained, the records effectively void any privacy to be gained from a tax haven the first time they are found. The only way to achieve total privacy would be to keep no records—in which case it wouldn't matter where your investments were located.

So, what is the advantage of an investment in a tax haven jurisdiction? *A big one:* higher earnings.

One of the highest nonrecoverable costs of business in the United States is taxes (income, property, *ad valorem* [imposed at a rate percent of value], etc.). Obviously, the more a business has to pay the government, the less there is to distribute to stockholders. In effect, private investors in U.S. business enterprises are taxed twice: once on the income to the business, once on dividends paid to them. A tax haven investment eliminates (or significantly reduces) that double taxation, and the investors reap the benefit.

Business investors may be able to defer a substantial amount of taxes by utilizing business structures in tax haven jurisdictions. By owning less than 50% of the voting stock of the foreign company, doing business in the international marketplace and meeting certain other requirements, business investors can effectively defer U.S. taxation until earnings are repatriated and thereby become reportable and taxable as ordinary income, not capital gains.

If you are inspired to become a business investor for the purpose of deferring U.S. taxes, be forewarned. Owning and operating a business in a tax haven jurisdiction requires business management skills far exceeding those needed for a domestic business. While the possibility of deferring U.S. taxes may be enticing, the costs (and almost assured losses) will more than outweigh any savings unless you are an international entrepreneur with proven skills.

Investors, then, should remember these rules when evaluating a tax haven opportunity:

● **Do not invest just because the asset is located in a tax haven;** your income is still taxable under the Internal Revenue Code.

● **Examine the opportunity**—not its location—for tax advantages.

● **Do not buy or establish a business structure in a tax haven jurisdiction,** unless you have the exceptional business skills necessary to operate it.

● **Privacy is not a sufficient reason for investing in a tax haven.**

● **If the investment wouldn't be an attractive one in the United States,** then its location in a tax haven jurisdiction holds no advantage for you.

Source: J.F. (Jim) Straw, owner of an offshore bank based in the Northern Marianas Islands (a U.S. commonwealth).

Three Ways to Beat the "Only 50% of a Business Meal Is Deductible" Rule

● **Company dining rooms,** employee cafeterias and other "eating facilities" operated by an employer for employees are not subject to the 50% rule if the facility is located on the business premises of the employer, brings in revenue that normally equals or exceeds its direct operating costs and does not discriminate in favor of highly compensated employees.

HOW TO HOLD ON TO MEAL AND ENTERTAINMENT DEDUCTIONS

Meal and entertainment deductions have been drastically altered by tax changes over the years. In most cases you can only deduct 50% of cost (rather than 100%). Also, the rules of proof are stricter. It's essential to comply with these rules or the whole deduction could be lost.

Tougher substantiation rules for business meals over $75. Substantiation requirements that used to apply only to entertainment expenses have been extended to cover meal expenses too. Under old law, as long as you had some way of proving the expense, you could deduct it. *Sufficient in the past:* proving meal expenses over $75 by a credit card receipt, canceled check or restaurant check stub *plus* some other proof such as a diary entry.

Substantiation: There is a specific checklist of information you must have for each business meal in order to deduct it. This checklist was always necessary for entertainment, but now you'll need it for both entertainment and meals. Be prepared to prove:

● **The amount of the expenditure.**
● **The time, date and place of the expenditure.**
● **The nature of the business discussion,** and the business reason for the expense or the nature of the

business benefit to be derived as a result of the expense.

● **Identification of the people who participated in the business discussion.**

Deduction requirements: The cost of a meal is deductible only if it occurs directly before, during or after a substantial business discussion. If a business meal occurs before or after a substantial business discussion, the taxpayer must show that the expense was associated with the active conduct of his or her trade or business. The cost of taking a customer to dinner for the purpose of retaining his goodwill, for example, is not tax-deductible unless business is actually discussed.

Special substantiation rules for business meals under $75. Business meal expenditures that total less than $75 are not subject to the strict rules above. While you still must have records of whom you entertained and why, you don't need a receipt to substantiate a meal less than $75. *Example:* a diary that you keep that shows the details of these meals. *Better, but not absolutely necessary:* a restaurant receipt that shows the amount, date, location and name of the restaurant. It's always best to have as much proof as you can to nail down a deduction.

Source: Lawrence W. Goldstein, tax manager, and Howard A. Rabinowitz, tax partner, Ernst & Young, 277 Park Ave., New York, NY 10172.

● **Company parties.** The 50% rule does not apply to certain traditional employer-paid social or recreational activities that are primarily for the benefit of the employees. Holiday parties and annual summer outings continue to be fully deductible.

● **Reimbursement angle.** Employees are not subject to the 50% rule if their company reimburses them for business meal and entertainment expenses. It's the company that's subject to the rule—the company must limit the amount of deduction it claims on its tax return to 50% of the amount given to the employee.

Bottom line: The tax law has no adverse effect for an employee on an expense account who is reimbursed in full for business meal and entertainment costs. It may be more desirable to have your employer reimburse you than for you to receive an expense allowance and deduct meal and entertainment expenses on your own return, where they will be limited to 50%.

Escaping IRS Limits on Investment Losses

The passive activity loss rule severely limits deductions resulting from certain investments. Although the purpose of the rule is to curtail tax-shelter abuses, it reaches far beyond those investments that are usually thought of as tax shelters.

Trap: Investors who don't fully understand the rule are almost certain to be caught in its net.

The Passive Loss Rule

The law requires you to separate your income and investment losses into two categories: One for "passive activities" and one for "nonpassive activities." It then prohibits you from offsetting income from nonpassive activities, such as salary, with losses from passive activities, such as tax-shelter investments. Passive activity losses may offset only passive activity income.

Passive activities:

● **Limited partnership interests of all kinds** (i.e., tax shelters).

● **All rental activities.**

● **Business activities in which the taxpayer does not materially participate,** including sole proprietorships, S corporations and general partnerships. "Materially" means being involved year-round on a regular, continuous and substantial basis.

Nonpassive activities:

● **Work that pays wages,** salary or commissions.

● **Investing that yields "portfolio income"** such as dividends, capital gains, interest or royalties.

● **Business activities in which there is material participation by the taxpayer.**

Who's affected: The passive loss rule applies to individuals, trusts and estates, personal-service corporations (self-incorporated doctors, dentists, lawyers, etc.) and S corporations. It does not apply to regular "C" corporations. Closely held C corporations are subject to the rule in a modified form. (See page 103.)

Carryovers

● **Unused passive losses may be carried indefinitely into future years**—when they may be used to offset future passive income. The accumulated unused losses on a property may generally be used to offset the gain when the property is sold. And if the unused losses are more than the gain, the excess may be written off against nonpassive income.

Trap: This break does not apply to property that is sold to a family member.

> " **[Passive activities would include] business activities in which the taxpayer does not materially participate, including sole proprietorships, S corporations and general partnerships.** "

Troubleshooting

Individuals who are locked into investments that throw off large passive losses must use new strategies to deal with their losses. *Recommended:*

● **Find investments that produce passive income,** which will absorb the passive losses.

Trap: Income from a mutual fund is not considered passive. Only investments that fit the law's definition of a passive activity will generate passive income—for example, income-producing limited partnerships and rental properties.

Income-producing limited partnerships:

Rental properties such as occupied apartments, office buildings, parking lots and shopping centers. You don't have to be a limited partner in these deals to get passive income, because all rental activity is considered passive under the new law, whether it's in the form of a limited partnership or not.

Caution: Income from many publicly traded limited partnerships, such as master limited partnerships (MLPs), is not considered passive income and cannot be used to offset passive losses.

● **Convert nonpassive income into passive income.** You might do this by converting a corporation that is not subject to the passive loss rules into a corporation that is subject to the rules. *Example:* Convert a regular corporation that is throwing off a great deal of taxable nonpassive income into an S corporation, and then hire a manager to run the S corporation. Income from an S corporation in which the owner does not materially participate (that is, in which he or she is not involved year-round on a regular, continuous and substantial basis) is passive income.

● **Restructure leasing arrangements with your business.** Suppose you are currently leasing a building that you own to a manufacturing company that you own. You've been renting the building to the company at a rate of only $100,000 a year. Your depreciation deductions on the leased building give you a tax loss, which you needed and could use under the old law. But under the new tax law, you can't use the loss.

What you need to have now is passive income.

What to do: Increase the rent to $300,000 a year, which is the building's fair market rent today. This will give you net income (above the depreciation deductions), and it will be passive income, because it comes from rental activity.

Break for Closely Held Corporations

Closely held corporations that are not personal service corporations are subject to the passive loss rule in a modified form.

Losses from a closely held corporation's passive activities may be used to offset the business income of the corporation. For example, a small manufacturing firm could offset net income from its operations with losses from tax-shelter investments. While the owner of a closely held corporation, as an individual taxpayer, will probably not wish to continue to invest in tax shelters, the corporation might very well want to.

Source: *Jerry Williford, partner, Grant Thornton, CPAs, 2800 Citicorp Center, Houston, TX 77002.*

How to Avoid the 2% Floor for Miscellaneous Deductions

Miscellaneous itemized deductions include expenses directly connected with the production of investment income, such as:

- **Fees for managing investment property.**
- **Legal and professional fees.**
- **Fees for tax preparation and advice,** investment advice and financial planning.

Problem: Most taxpayers are unable to deduct any investment expenses on Schedule A because their total miscellaneous expenses don't exceed 2% of their Adjusted Gross Income. ***Solution:*** Put as many expenses as possible out of reach of the 2% floor by accounting for them elsewhere on your return.

Possibilities:

- **Schedule C.** Report non-wage miscellaneous income, such as that earned from consulting, lecturing or speaking engagements, on Schedule C as business income, rather than as "other income" directly on Form 1040. The expenses you incur in producing that income are deductible on Schedule C, where they are not subject to the 2% floor.
- **Schedule E.** Expenses of earning rent, royalties

or other income that is reportable on Schedule E are deductible on Schedule E, where they are not subject to the 2% floor.

- **Adjust the cost of assets.** Deduct the expenses of acquiring a capital asset from the asset's cost. This will reduce the amount of capital gain you must report when you eventually sell. While this approach doesn't give you a current deduction for the expenses, it does reduce the tax you pay on the gain.
- **Bunch payment of expenses** so that you get two years' worth into one year and exceed the 2% floor in at least one year.

Source: *Richard Lager, national director of tax practice, Grant Thornton, CPAs, 1850 M St. NW, Washington, DC 20036.*

Best of the Legal Tax Shelters

Most of the old-style tax shelters have passed into history—but there are still safe and legal ways to avoid or defer taxes.

Real Estate

Congress has continued a *few* of the old-style tax shelters, and it has just *liberalized* the rules for claiming tax benefits from real estate. *If you're in a top tax bracket, consider these shelter strategies:*

- **Real estate.** Investments in real estate were the most popular old-style tax shelter. Their special tax benefit is *depreciation*—the annual deduction for a property's presumed loss in value over its life. This deduction has no cash cost but can generate a tax loss that can be deducted against income to shelter it from tax.

Thus, real estate investments can produce deductible tax losses and cash flow gains at the same time. ***Catch:*** A deduction for losses is sharply limited by the passive activity loss rule. A passive activity is any rental real estate activity and investments in which a taxpayer has only a passive, non-management investment interest. Passive losses can be deducted only against passive income—although they can be carried forward and deducted when a passive investment is sold.

Real estate professionals: "Professionals" in the real estate industry can deduct their real estate losses against income earned from sources other than real estate.

A professional is someone who spends more than

half of his or her working time and more than 750 hours a year actively involved in a "real property trade or business"—such as property development, management, leasing or brokering.

Opportunity: A couple filing a joint return qualifies for this if one spouse meets the definition of a real estate professional. *Example:* A husband works full-time as a doctor, and his wife works 750 hours a year managing their investments in rental properties. Tax losses generated by the properties can be deducted against the income earned by the husband in his practice.

Other Real Estate Tax Shelters

● **$25,000 deduction.** Persons with Adjusted Gross Incomes (AGIs) of less than $100,000 can deduct up to $25,000 of passive losses earned from real estate against their other income—such as salary. This deduction phases out as AGI increases from $100,000 to $150,000.

● **Rehabilitation tax credit** provides credit equal to the cost of 10% of rehabilitating nonresidential buildings constructed before 1936, and 20% of rehabilitating certified historic structures.

● **Low-income-housing credit** is allowed by Congress to support investments in low-income housing. It can be used to shelter up to $25,000 from tax, and it is possible that you will make money selling the property.

Risks: Once you are in an investment, it's hard to get out, and the quality of the real estate will impact your economic returns. Consult an investment professional for advice.

More Shelters

It's not necessary to resort to complicated or expensive shelter investments to reduce taxes. *Simpler strategies:*

● **Maximize deductible interest.** If you have investment income, shelter it from tax by incurring investment interest expense *instead* of normal consumer interest. *Examples:* If you intend to buy a car and make a stock market investment and you follow the conventional route of buying the car with an auto loan while purchasing the stock shares outright, you will get no interest deduction.

But if you buy the car in cash and borrow to buy the stock shares, you probably will get a deduction because investment interest is deductible to the extent of investment income.

If you have a business, you can borrow to meet business costs—such as equipment purchases—while maintaining the amount of cash available for personal expenditures.

Or you can finance personal expenditures with a home-equity loan that produces deductible mortgage interest. *Helpful:* If you know you are going to carry a certain amount of debt overall, have a borrowing plan that minimizes consumer debt and concentrates borrowing in areas that produce deductible interest.

● **Home-based business.** A business run from your home—even as a sideline—offers major tax breaks. A sideline activity can also pay off personally by promoting professional advancement or a career change. *How:*

● **You can try out a new line of work by freelancing through a sideline,** without risking a sudden career change.

● **Sideline consulting** can help you network to gain valuable contacts.

Tax breaks: Legitimate business expenses are deductible even if they exceed your business income. So if you incur a loss during your business start-up, you can deduct it against other income, such as salary. *You may be able to deduct:*

● **Salaries paid to family members who work for you.** Social Security tax is *not* owed on salary paid to a child under age 18, when the business is a proprietorship.

If a child receiving a salary is in a low tax bracket, the family's overall tax bill may be reduced. Children could receive up to $4,250 of salary *tax-free* in 1998. And another $2,000 may be tax-free if the child makes a deductible IRA contribution.

Caution: Be sure the amount of salary is reasonable for the work done.

● **Home office,** including the cost of utilities, insurance, maintenance and rent or depreciation.

To qualify for a deduction, the home office must be used *exclusively* for business and be the principal place where you conduct the business, or a place where you meet clients or customers regularly.

● **Keogh retirement** contributions of up to about 20% of your self-employment income are not subject to income tax.

To support business status for a home-based activity, you must demonstrate a genuine profit motive for engaging in it. You don't actually have to make a profit. The Tax Court recognizes that legitimate businesses suffer losses. But you must conduct the activity in a businesslike manner consistent with the goal of earning a profit—by keeping good books and records, a diary of business activities, a business checking account, etc.

● **Make retirement plan contributions early.** Most people think of the deduction they get for a retirement plan contribution as its major tax benefit. But over the long run, tax deferral on the plan's compound investment returns may be even more valuable.

Take advantage of this by making plan contributions as early in the year as possible instead of waiting until the last minute.

● **Make gifts to low-tax-bracket family members.** By giving income-producing properties to family members who are in low (or zero) tax brackets—such as children over age 13 or retired parents—you can shift income into their tax brackets and reduce the family's overall tax bill.

● **Oil and gas.** To encourage development of oil and gas resources, the tax law lets oil well owners claim depletion deductions that can be used to offset some of the taxable income earned from the sale of extracted oil and gas. These deductions are allowed in addition to the normal deduction for operating costs associated with the well.

Caution: Although oil exploration offers potentially high returns, it is a risky enterprise. An investor who seeks tax benefits from an oil well or a gas well must have a direct ownership interest in it. It's no longer possible to limit risk by investing through a limited partnership that fixes your maximum liability at the amount of money you initially invest. Direct ownership means you are directly liable for the well's obligations.

Important: Consult with an industry expert before investing.

Source: Laurence I. Foster, tax partner, personal financial planning practice, KPMG Peat Marwick LLP, 345 Park Ave., New York, NY 10154.

Tax Shelters You Can Use

● **Buying your parents' home and renting it back to them.** This can produce deductible tax losses. The transaction converts payments that you make toward your parents' support into a perfectly legal tax shelter. *How it works:* You buy the house from your parents on the installment method and rent it back to them for fair market rent. Make the installment payments equal to the rent plus the amount you had been giving for support. *Shelter:* The rental income is sheltered from tax by depreciation deductions, property taxes, etc. And if the write-offs exceed the rent—and your Adjusted Gross Income is under $100,000—you may deduct up to $25,000 of losses against your taxable income.

● **Offsetting properties.** Passive losses are deductible only from passive income. If you have a piece of real estate with a very low mortgage that is producing a positive cash flow, you might consider

> **"Most people think of the deduction they get for a retirement plan contribution as its major tax benefit. But over the long run, tax deferral on the plan's compound investment returns may be even more valuable."**

buying a second property with a high mortgage that causes the property to generate losses. *Shelter:* The losses on the second property will shelter the income from the first.

● **Company pension and profit-sharing plans** are great tax shelters, particularly for owners of family businesses. The amounts they put into their company's plan are deductible by the business. Tax is deferred, and neither the original amount contributed nor any earnings are taxed until actually paid out to the individual. This is a bonanza for business owners, who can put a share of the business profits aside for retirement and see the government contribute a sizable additional amount (equal to the taxes saved by deducting the contributions).

● **IRAs can still be a good tax shelter** even if the law prevents you from making tax-deductible contributions. Earnings on nondeductible IRA contributions are tax-deferred.

PENSION PAYOUT TAX TRAP

When you leave a company or retire, you have to tell the company to *directly roll* over your pension payout to the trustee of a new retirement plan or Individual Retirement Account (IRA). If you don't do this, the company must withhold 20% tax on the payout.

To avoid withholding, the payout must be transferred from the company retirement plan directly to the trustee of a new plan, or IRA.

The trustee is the fiduciary responsible for safeguarding your pension money.

Trap: If the payout check is made out to you, in your own name, your company will withhold 20% of it in tax.

Withholding doesn't mean that the payout will necessarily be taxable. You can still avoid tax on a payout made to you by rolling over the full amount of the distribution into an IRA or other plan within 60 days of receipt.

Problem: Under those rules, you won't have the full amount in your hands because the company will have withheld 20%. To avoid tax, you'll have to come up with cash to make up the amount withheld, and then roll the whole thing over. *Example:* Suppose you leave your company and are due a pension payout of $100,000. You tell the company to make the check out to you. The company will withhold $20,000 in tax. You decide you want to roll the distribution over into an IRA. You'll have to come up with $20,000 to make up the full $100,000 payout. (You'll get the $20,000 in withheld tax back when you file your tax return.)

If you don't make up the $20,000, you can still roll over the $80,000 tax-free. But the $20,000 the company withheld will be included in your income in the year of the distribution. You'll owe tax on that amount. And, if you're under age 59½, you'll pay a 10% early-distribution penalty on the $20,000 in addition to income tax.

Caution: The FDIC only insures up to $100,000 per bank. If you make a direct rollover of a large payout from your company plan to a bank IRA, be prepared to transfer amounts over $100,000 to an IRA in another bank to keep your accounts fully insured.

Transfers between IRAs: They are not subject to the 20% withholding requirement. The law applies only to payouts from qualified plans (that is, company plans).

If you have your payout directly rolled over into an IRA, you can take it out of that IRA, use it for 59 days and redeposit it in another IRA on the 60th day without any adverse tax effect.

Good news: Any distribution, no matter how small, can be rolled over, tax-free, into an IRA. The only distributions that you are not permitted to roll over are:

● A "required distribution"— that is, one made when you're over age 70½.

● **A distribution that is made over your life expectancy.**

● **A distribution that is made over a specified period of 10 or more years.**

Source: Stephen Pennachio, partner, KPMG Peat Marwick, 345 Park Ave., New York, NY 10154.

Editor's note: Roth IRAs may be the best shelter of all. While contributions are not deductible, earnings will be tax-free if they are not withdrawn until required holding periods are satisfied.

Source: *Edward Mendlowitz, partner, Mendlowitz Weitsen, LLP, 2 Penn Plaza, New York, NY 10121.*

Compensation Loopholes

The compensation package you get from your employer probably includes some form of deferred compensation whereby money is put away for you but is not available until some time in the future. This form of compensation boosts your pay and offers significant tax advantages.

Loopholes

● **Pension and profit-sharing plans.** Your employer contributes money to a retirement plan on your behalf, and the money accumulates on a tax-deferred basis. You don't pay a current tax on the contribution or on the interest the money earns. No tax is due until you receive a distribution of money from the plan. *More:*

Loophole: Take a tax-free loan from the pension or profit-sharing plan. Borrowing is not a taxable transaction. You can only do this if the plan permits borrowing—not all do. Plans that allow borrowing usually make it easy on the participant—there's no need to justify why the loan is needed.

Limits: The amount you can borrow is limited to your vested balance in the plan up to the greater of $10,000 or one-half of your vested balance, with a maximum of $50,000.

Loophole: Put some of your own money into the plan—many plans allow employees to make voluntary contributions. Such contributions are not tax-deductible, but the money accumulates on a tax-deferred basis.

Loophole: If your company's plan is inactive—no additions are being made and no benefits are accruing on your behalf—you are eligible to make deductible IRA contributions.

● **401(k) plans.** You contribute part of your salary to a company-sponsored savings program. You pay no income tax on the money you contribute until you make withdrawals. Interest, dividends and other earnings accumulate tax-deferred until you take them out.

Many companies "match" employees' contributions by putting additional money into the plan for the employee.

Loophole: The amount you can contribute each year is limited by the tax law. *Maximum 401(k) contribution for 1998: $10,000.*

● **Company-paid life insurance.** As long as the coverage doesn't exceed $50,000 worth of insurance, you are not taxed on the premiums the employer pays. But if it is more than $50,000, you are taxed on part of the premiums.

Loophole: The taxable amount is figured from IRS tables and is less than the actual premiums the employer pays. You pay some tax for the extra coverage, but it is far less than it would cost you to buy similar life insurance coverage outside the company.

● **Stock options.** When a company gives an employee an option to purchase stock that does not qualify as an incentive stock option (see more relevant information, below), the employee must pay tax when the option is exercised. The taxed amount is the difference between the option price and the fair market value of the stock at the time the option is exercised.

Loophole: There is no tax paid when the option is granted. Stock options are a form of deferred compensation. The employee benefits on a tax-deferred basis from the growth in value of the company stock.

● **Incentive stock options.** These are options that qualify under the Tax Code for special treatment. No tax is levied when the options are issued to the employee.

Loophole: No tax is levied when the options are exercised. Tax isn't payable until the options are sold.

Trap: The difference between the option price and the fair market value at the time the option is exercised is a "preference item" that is subject to the Alternative Minimum Tax (AMT). Employees should be careful not to exercise so many incentive stock options that they fall into the AMT. The exercise of these options must be carefully timed.

● **Restricted stock.** Sometimes an employer issues stock to an employee that is subject to a "substantial risk of forfeiture." *Most common situation:* The employee will have to give up the stock if he or she doesn't continue working for the company for a specified number of years. When the restriction lapses, the employee is taxed on the difference between the stock's fair market value at that time and the price paid for the stock.

Loophole: The employee can make an election under Section 83(b) of the Internal Revenue Code to pay tax on the value of the stock when it is originally issued. Then, there is no tax when the restriction lapses. (Tax on any gain is payable when the employee ultimately disposes of the stock.) Employees should make the Section 83(b) election in instances where they expect the company's stock to appreciate considerably.

● **Phantom stock,** also called stock appreciation rights, is sometimes issued to employees. No actual stock is given, but payments are made as if actual stock had been issued. If any dividends are paid to stockholders, they are also paid to the phantom stock holders. And when the employee leaves the company, he or she is compensated for his or her phantom shares. Payments to the employee are taxed as compensation, rather than tax-favored capital gains.

Loophole: The employee doesn't pay tax until there is an actual payment to him or her as a phantom stock holder. No tax is payable when the phantom stock is first received. So phantom stock is another form of deferred compensation.

Source: Edward Mendlowitz, partner, Mendlowitz Weitsen, CPAs, 2 Pennsylvania Plaza, New York, NY 10121. He is the author of New Tax Traps, New Opportunities, *Boardroom Special Reports.*

How to Pass Your IRA on to Your Children & Grandchildren

Most people leave their Individual Retirement Accounts (IRAs) to their spouses. But if your spouse is adequately provided for, you may want to leave some or all of your IRA money to your children or grandchildren. You get the greatest mileage from an IRA that you leave to your grandchildren, or other beneficiaries who are much younger than you. Benefits of leaving an IRA to a grandchild:

● **The IRA will continue for a long period of time**—50, 60 or even 70 years, depending on the grandchild's age and the payout method selected.

● **IRA earnings will accumulate on a tax-deferred basis for that period of time.** This can add hundreds of thousands of dollars to an IRA.

● **There's a substantial income tax saving in leaving money to a low-bracket grandchild,** rather than to a spouse. A spouse will pay income tax on IRA payouts at the 31% rate or more. But once a grandchild reaches age 14, income is taxed at his or her rate, not the parents'. A child is in the 15% tax bracket for just over $25,300 of income in 1998.

● **There's an estate tax saving.** The IRA assets and their growth over the years will not be included in your spouse's estate.

● **The IRA assets avoid probate.**

Caution: The most you can give to your grandchildren is $1 million. After that, gifts to grandchildren are subject to the generation-skipping tax, which is a 55% tax on gifts that pass over a generation of heirs—usually the parents' generation.

Problem: Few professionals know how to keep an IRA alive for a person's grandchildren. Some consultants may advise nonspouse beneficiaries to take all the money and pay tax on it the year after the account holder dies. *Solution:* Understand how IRA distribution rules work. Do the paperwork now.

Distribution Rules

IRA owners are required to begin taking money out of their account by April 1 of the year after they reach age 70½. But the distribution rules for beneficiaries are different.

● **If you die before reaching your required beginning date,** which is April 1 after the calendar year in which you attain age 70½, and you've named a grandchild as beneficiary, your grandchild has two options:

● **Option 1:** Take all the money in the account by the end of the year following the fifth anniversary of your death, or

● **Option 2:** Begin taking annual distributions based on his or her life expectancy in the year following your death. *Example:* Say a grandchild who was 20 at this time would have a life expectancy of 61 years. To satisfy the minimum distribution rules for IRAs, he or she would have to take only $1/61$ out of the IRA in the first year. If there was $200,000 in the IRA at the end of the year in which you died, the required distribution would be $3,278.69 ($1/61$ of $200,000). The IRA would continue for another 60 years.

To use the life expectancy method (option 2), your grandchild or his or her trustee will have to file a written election with the IRA institution by no later than

December 31 of the year after the year in which you die, saying the IRA money is to be paid out over the grandchild's life expectancy—61 years in the above example. Payments from the IRA must commence no later than December 31 of the year after you die.

If these requirements aren't met, your grandchild will default into option 1, and all the money in the IRA will have to be paid out to your grandchild five years after your death.

● **If you reach your required beginning date,** the rules are different. You must begin taking money from the IRA by April 1 of the year following the year you reach 70½. The amount you withdraw each year can be based on the joint life expectancy of you and your beneficiary.

> **"One of the advantages of having a trust is that the assets will be protected from the child's creditors, should the child have an accident or become involved in other legal problems."**

If your beneficiary is your grandchild, since he or she is more than 10 years younger than you, the withdrawals must be based on what is called the Minimum Distribution Incidental Benefit (MDIB) table that is found in IRS publication 590, *Individual Retirement Arrangements*, in Appendix E. The table calculates the withdrawals as if your beneficiary were only 10 years younger than you. This is required by the tax law.

Letter to your IRA custodian: To make this all perfectly clear, you should write a letter to your IRA custodian spelling out the distribution methods you are using:

"I hereby elect to take the money out of my IRA based on my life expectancy and my grandchild's life expectancy determined in the year I attained age 70½ (69.8 years in the above example). However, while I'm alive, the MDIB rule is operative and that table shall be used. Upon my death, payouts shall be based on the original joint life expectancy of me and my grandchild, reduced by all years that have passed since I was 70½."

Trust Required

If your grandchild is a minor, you'll need a trust for the benefit of your grandchild to handle the money being paid from the IRA. *(Editor's note:* In the past only irrevocable trusts were permitted. Now the IRS allows revocable trusts to be used for this purpose as long as certain requirements are met.) You can name a family member as trustee.

Bank accounts: On the death of the grandparent, the trustee would open up a bank account in the name of the trust. He or she would also open a custodial account for the grandchild at a bank or brokerage firm.

The trust says that money goes from the IRA to the trust, and then from the trust to the custodial account, until the grandchild reaches the age of majority—18 or 21, depending on state law. After your grandchild turns 21, the money goes directly to him or her. Under appropriate circumstances, the custodian could use the money to pay your grandchild's college expenses.

There's no tax to the trust because the money is going right out—the trust is just a conduit. The money is taxed to the grandchild, but at the grandchild's tax rates.

One of the advantages of having a trust is that the assets will be protected from the child's creditors, should the child have an accident or become involved in other legal problems—such as bankruptcy, divorce, etc.

Note: Even if the trust is irrevocable, you can change beneficiaries of the IRA if circumstances dictate a change. You can make beneficiary substitutions until you die.

Best: A separate trust for each grandchild to whom you leave IRA money. Cost: About $3,500 to set up the trust (or multiple trusts for a number of grandchildren) and an annual fee of $200 or $300 to prepare and file tax returns for the trust after you die.

Practical use: This is a good way to develop a college fund for a grandchild at low tax cost.

Source: Seymour Goldberg, professor of law and taxation at Long Island University and senior partner in the law firm of Goldberg & Ingber, 666 Old Country Rd., Garden City, NY 11530. Mr. Goldberg is the author of A Professional's Guide to the IRS Distribution Rules, *Field Services, New York State Society of Certified Public Accountants, New York.*

Fighting the IRS

3

What the IRS Already Knows About You

The IRS gets information from third parties and matches this information to you in its computers. Stay a step ahead by being careful to report on your tax return what the IRS already knows about you. (You should receive from the third parties copies of all the information that they send to the IRS.)

What the IRS knows, and how:

● **Your income.** The IRS knows, of course, if you have been paid $600 or more of miscellaneous income. The payer must report this payment to the IRS on Form 1099-MISC, Statement for Recipients of Miscellaneous Income. Included in this category:

● **Freelance income.**

● **Rent or royalty payments.**

● **Prizes and awards that are not for services.**

● **Payments made by medical and health-care insurers to a doctor or other supplier of medical services under an insurance program.**

● **Attorney's and accountant's fees for professional services.**

● **Witness or expert fees paid by a lawyer during a legal proceeding.**

● **Payments made to entertainers for their services.**

● **Your wages.** The IRS knows from your W-2 Form exactly how much you earned in regular income, bonuses, vacation allowances, severance pay, moving-expense payments and travel allowances. Your W-2 must be attached to your return.

● **Interest income.** The IRS knows if you've been paid interest of $10 or more. Banks and financial institutions must report these payments to the IRS on Form 1099-INT, Statement for Recipients of Interest Income.

Trap: Some interest income is reported to the IRS even though you haven't received it yet. It must be reported as part of your income. All that matters is that you are entitled to it.

● **Dividend income.** The IRS knows if you received more than $10 in money, stock, capital-gain distributions or property from a corporation. These payments are reported to the IRS on Form 1099-DIV, Statement for Recipients of Dividends and Distributions.

Important: Make sure the report you receive agrees with your records.

● **Tax-refund income.** The IRS knows about tax refunds you receive. State and local governments must report such payments of $10 or more on Form 1099-G, Statement for Recipients of Certain Government Payments.

Important Exception: If you didn't claim the state and local taxes that you paid as itemized deductions on your federal return, you don't have to report these refunds as income. If you receive a Form 1099-G, analyze it to see whether you must include it in income or if you qualify under the exception.

● **Gambling winnings.** The IRS knows about money you won from horse racing, dog racing, jai alai, lotteries, raffles, drawings, bingo, slot machines and keno. It's all reported to the IRS on Form W-2G, Statement for Recipients of Certain Gambling Winnings. *The general rule:* Payments of $600 or more must be reported by the payer. *Exceptions:* Bingo payments of $1,200 or more and keno payments of $1,500 or more will be reported.

Other Income the IRS Knows About:

● **Original-issue discounts.**

● **Mortgage interest received from individuals in the course of a trade or business.**

● **Money received from broker and barter exchanges.**

● **Distributions from pension and profit-sharing plans, IRAs, etc.**

● **Cash payments of $10,000 or more received in a trade or business.**

● **Cash deposits of $10,000 or more made to your bank account.**

● **Fringe benefits received from your company.**

● **Social Security benefits.**

● **Tax shelter participation.**

● **Unemployment compensation.**

Source: John L. Withers, special consultant for IRS regulations and procedures, Deloitte & Touche, Washington Service Center, 1900 M St. NW, Washington, DC 20036.

Unanswered Questions Cause Problems

Income tax returns with unanswered questions are considered "no returns." The statute of limitations never expires and you can be audited no matter how

Tax Return Completion Checklist

***In dealings with the IRS,
no news is good news. More precisely,
in this case, no mail is good news.***

Every time the IRS sends a letter to a taxpayer, it means that someone within the Service has taken another look at the return in question. Every look taken increases the chance that "problems" will come to light (if they haven't already). There are a number of simple steps you can take to minimize the risk of ongoing activity with your tax return.

✔ **Before filing, make sure your return is complete.** Check to see that all necessary forms and schedules are present and accounted for. This includes any and all attachments (e.g., if you donate common stock to a charitable organization, you must attach a statement of certain information regarding the gift). Staple your return together securely. Missing pages generate correspondence.

✔ **Make sure the return is accurate.** Check, double-check and recheck all arithmetic.

✔ **Make sure your reporting is consistent with the information the IRS receives.**
For example, if you have invested in IBM and General Motors stock through XYZ Brokerage, your return should list dividends paid to you by XYZ, not IBM or GM, because the IRS will receive a 1099 form from XYZ.

✔ **Double-check to see that the return is signed by all necessary parties.**

✔ **Finally, file your return on time.** By all means request an extension if you need one; otherwise mail your return well before the expiration date. In the event you must file at the last minute, use registered or certified mail in order to have evidence of timely filing.

Source: Ralph C. Ganswindt, partner specializing in closely held businesses, with Arthur Andersen & Company, LLP, 777 E. Wisconsin Ave., Milwaukee, WI 53201.

many years have passed. Unanswered questions can delay refunds, result in interest charges, and call attention to your return (the computer automatically spits out the return). If a question doesn't seem to apply to you (i.e., Do you have any foreign bank accounts?), just answer "no"—but answer.

When It's Safe to Ignore Your April 15 Deadline

You are legally required to file a tax return (or extension request) by April 15, whether you owe extra tax or not. But since the civil penalty for late filing is generally a percentage of the tax still owed (5% per month, up to 25%), there's no penalty unless you owe the government money. And you have two years to file for your refund. Nevertheless, it's advisable to file on time for these reasons:

● **You get your refund faster.**

● **It may turn out that you miscalculated,** and actually owe taxes instead of having a refund coming. In that case, you'll be charged penalties and interest for late filing.

● **If you want to file an amended return later,** you'll have three years to do it in, instead of two.

● **If the IRS concludes that you are willfully refusing to file a return,** you may be hit with criminal penalties.

How to Get Late-Filing Penalties Eliminated

Penalties for filing your tax return late without getting a valid extension may be forgiven by the IRS if you show that you had reasonable cause for filing late.

Although the IRS is not required to waive late-filing penalties, it may do so when convinced that the late filing was not the taxpayer's fault. Among the excuses the IRS may accept as cause for late filing:

● **Death or serious illness** of the taxpayer or a member of his or her immediate family.

● **Unavoidable absence of the taxpayer.**

● **Destruction of records** in a fire or other casualty.

● **Delay due to erroneous information** given the taxpayer by the IRS.

● **A timely request for needed tax forms** wasn't answered by the IRS.

- **The return was filed on time but was sent to the wrong IRS Service Center.**
- **The taxpayer was filing for the first time** and was ignorant of the law. *Encouraging:* Close to half the penalties assessed by the IRS are excused.

Bottom line: You have a relatively good chance of avoiding a late-filing penalty if you can convince the IRS that the delay was not your fault.

An Excuse That Worked

When the IRS tried to penalize William F. Haden for not filing a tax return, he claimed that he had filed a return at the post office on April 15. He said that the post office was so crowded that he had given the return to a postal worker stationed on the street to accept returns, and concluded that the worker must have lost the return. Both Haden's wife and a friend supported his story as witnesses. *Tax Court:* Although Haden's story was "shaky" on a few details, it was believable overall. The penalty was set aside.

Source: William F. Haden, TC Memo 1986-539.

If Your Lawyer Forgets to File

If you sign your tax return in time, give it to your lawyer, and he or she forgets to file it, who's responsible? *You are.* It's your responsibility to see that the return is filed. Even though it's your lawyer's fault, you pay the penalty.

How to Extend the Float On Tax Checks

The IRS Service Centers are quick to get your check into their bank. During tax-filing season, when thousands of envelopes are received every day, the IRS strives for what it calls "zero day deposit"—all checks are deposited within 24 hours. Computerized mail-processing machines can tell which envelopes contain checks by detecting, through the envelope, the magnetic ink on the check inside. *To extend the float:* Mail your check in an oversized envelope. The machines can only process standard, letter-sized envelopes; oversized ones must be handled individually. Human processing, especially during busy periods, can add as much as 10 days to your float.

TRACKING DOWN YOUR REFUND

If it has been at least 10 weeks since you filed your tax return and you still haven't received your refund, you can do something about it.

Step 1: Get out the copy you kept of your tax return. Be sure you know your Social Security number, your filing status, the exact amount of the refund you claimed and the service center to which you sent your return.

Step 2: Call the IRS's automated refund-information service to find out the current status of your refund check. Use the number for your area that's listed in the Form 1040 instruction booklet.

Step 3: If there's still a problem, write to the IRS Service Center where you filed your return. Include your name, address, Social Security number, the tax year involved and an explanation of your problem. Keep copies of the letters you send.

Step 4: If you've done all of the above and still haven't gotten your refund, it's time to call the IRS's Problems Resolution Office (PRO). The telephone number of the local PRO can be obtained from the governmental listings in the phone book, or from the local IRS District Office. To get help from the PRO, you must show that you first tried to resolve your problem through normal channels. Have a record of the names of IRS agents you've talked with, along with copies of all your correspondence with the IRS. Shortly after a PRO officer is assigned to your case, you'll get either your refund or a full explanation of what's holding it up.

Never Let the IRS Apply a Refund to Next Year's Tax Bill

If you file the short form, 1040A or 1040EZ, and claim a refund, the IRS will send you a check for that amount (provided you haven't made any errors on your return). But if you file the long form, 1040, you are offered an alternative to getting a check. The back of the form, down at the bottom, asks if you want to let the IRS keep your refund and apply it to next year's estimated tax bill.

Advice: Don't do it! Never, ever let the IRS hold on to your refund. Why not? Because it won't really help you in the long run—and it may end up hurting you. *Example:* You fill out your return and discover that you have a $900 refund coming. You decide to let the IRS hold on to it and apply it to next year's estimated tax bill. But what if the IRS finds a math error on your return? Or your employer made a mistake on your wage statement? Or you forgot to include in your income the interest you earned on a bank account?

These things happen all the time. And any one of them would affect your tax return.

Let's suppose that the bottom line is this: After correcting your return, the IRS sends you a bill for an additional $400. You already have $900 sitting in your estimated tax account. As far as you're concerned, the IRS can go ahead and take the $400 out of that. Right?

Wrong. You told it to credit the $900 to your estimated tax account, and you're stuck with that decision. In other words, you'll have to come up with the extra $400 on your own.

What if the IRS audits a recent return and finds that you owe additional taxes plus interest? You still can't touch your $900.

To make matters worse, the money you've left in your estimated tax account doesn't even earn any interest.

If you really want to earmark your refund for your future tax bill, let the IRS send you your check. Then deposit the money in a savings account or invest it for a year. Don't let the IRS have it for nothing.

Missing Refund

Irene Crosby thought she had filed an income tax return for 1979, but she never received her refund, and the IRS finally told her that it had never received her return. When she refiled to get the refund, the IRS said it was too late—the statute of limitations had run out. Irene protested.

District Court: Irene had a long history of filing on time. Moreover, during 1979 she was the sole support of six children, one of whom was gravely ill. It was reasonable to conclude that she had filed a return that the IRS had lost, and understandable that she hadn't noticed the IRS's failure to reply. Therefore, she was entitled to her refund.

Source: *Irene O. Crosby, ND Ca., No. C-85-20331-RPA.*

Unclaimed Refunds

The IRS is sitting on millions of dollars in unclaimed tax refunds. According to the IRS, the addresses listed under taxpayers' Social Security numbers are no good. *Those likely to be affected:* Anyone who has moved during the year; a surviving spouse who filed a joint return; unmarried taxpayers who later marry and change their names. Tax returns are identified by Social Security number; joint returns, by the first Social Security number listed. If you marry and are listed second on the return, you disappear from the IRS files. *Suggestion:* If you move, file IRS Form 8822 to report your change of address.

Taxpayer Penalizes IRS For Lateness

You file your tax return in February and get a refund check in May—but no interest. Does the government owe you interest on the money?

No. The government doesn't have to pay interest if it sends your refund within 45 days of the date the return was due—April 15—not 45 days from the date you filed it. But if it doesn't get the refund out within the 45 days, it has to pay interest all the way back to April 15, even if it's only one day late.

Best Time to File For A Refund

Suppose you discover, about a year after filing your return, that you omitted a sizable deduction. You immediately file a claim for a refund, only to find out that the refund claim triggers an audit. The good news is that your claim is allowed in full by the auditor. The bad news is that during the audit he or she probes other areas of your return where your proof is weak, and you end up owing the IRS additional tax.

Loophole: File your claim just a few days before the statute of limitations expires—three years from the due date of the return or two years from the date you actually paid the tax, whichever is later. If the last day for filing a claim is April 15, then file your claim on April 12.

Problem for the IRS: The limitation period that applies to your refund claim also applies to the IRS's ability to assess extra tax. Once April 15 has gone by, the IRS may consider other items to offset your claim but may not assess additional tax (except in some very specialized situations). What's more, because the year involved is an "old" year, in IRS jargon, unless your claim is for a very large amount, the chance of its triggering an audit is remote.

Source: George S. Alberts, former IRS Director of the Brooklyn and Albany District Offices.

How to Answer When the IRS Writes

The Internal Revenue Service sends out thousands of notices demanding money to taxpayers each year. By responding shrewdly to IRS notices, taxpayers can often reduce the amount they owe—and sometimes pay nothing.

Keys to success:

● **Never blindly pay what the notice claims you owe without first checking the facts.** Don't assume that the bill is correct just because it came from the IRS. It's imperative that you review the notice, line by line, and understand how the IRS arrived at each figure. Only after you do this will you be in a position to respond effectively.

Winning the Refund Game

A misplaced comma in the IRS computer resulted in the Bruces' getting a tax refund of over $49,000 instead of $4,900. They notified the IRS of its mistake, but were assured that they were entitled to the money. More than two years after the Bruces got the check, the IRS tried to get the money back. *District Court:* The IRS had two years from the date it made the mistake to correct its error. Since it waited so long, the Bruces were allowed to keep the money.

Source: Alice A. Bruce, SD TX, G-84-220.

● **Always ask that penalties be excused.** Negligence penalties are now automatically included in notices for unreported income—and other types of notices carry other penalties, such as those for late filing and late payment.

To get penalties dropped: You must show there was "reasonable cause" (that is, a good excuse) for your alleged misdeed (misreporting income, filing late, paying late, etc.). *Encouraging statistic:* About half the penalties assessed by the IRS are excused.

If You Receive a Notice

● **Answer promptly**—within one week of the day that you receive the notice—regardless of the deadline specified (usually 30 days out). *Reason:* The earlier you respond to the notice, the less likely is the possibility that you will receive computer-generated follow-up notices and that correspondence between you and the IRS will cross in the mail. *(Editor's note:* If you don't understand the notice, you may contact the IRS by phone. After September 20, 1998, an IRS employee's name and phone number must be listed on a personal notice.)

● **Keep your letter succinct.** Your response should be no more than three paragraphs long, and no paragraph should have more than three sentences. *Reason:* Brevity and directness increase the chances that the matter will be settled quickly and not turn into a full-scale investigation.

● **Back up your response with documentation.** For instance, if you are claiming that you already paid the amount of tax that the IRS says you owe, attach a photocopy of your canceled check (both sides) proving the tax payment.

● **Mail your response by certified mail,** return receipt requested. Keep the receipt in case the IRS "loses" your letter.

Shrewd Answers

Types of IRS notices and sample letters of response:

● **Penalty notices for filing a tax return late,** paying taxes late or failing to pay the correct amount of estimated taxes.

Sample response:

To Whom It May Concern:

I am in receipt of your letter dated April 26, a copy of which is enclosed, which reflects that a late-filing penalty has been assessed in the amount of $561. Given that reasonable cause exists, the penalty should be abated.

Although I had obtained an extension that permitted me to file my tax return up until October 15, it was impossible to obtain the information needed to complete my return until the middle of November. As soon as the information was made available to me, the tax return was completed and filed. The missing information was a K-1 form that reflects the amount of income I had earned as a partner in ABC limited partnership.

Because the late filing was caused by circumstances beyond my control, it is requested that the late-filing penalty be abated. In the event of an unfavorable determination, it is requested that this matter be forwarded to the Regional Director of Appeals for consideration.

● **You-owe-us-more-tax notices,** which indicate that you made a mathematical error on your return or that the IRS did not give you credit for tax withheld or for estimated tax payments.

Sample response:

To Whom It May Concern:

I am in receipt of your May 12 notice, a copy of which is enclosed, which indicates you have no record of my tax return.

Enclosed is a copy of my 1997 tax return, which was filed on or about April 15, 1998. Also enclosed is a copy of both sides of my canceled check for the balance of 1997 tax paid with that return.

● **Unreported-income notices that demand additional tax,** interest, and a penalty because—the IRS claims—income paid to you was not reported on your return.

Sample response:

To Whom It May Concern:

I am in receipt of your May 3 notice, a copy of which is attached. Please be advised that your notice is incorrect.

Enclosed is a copy of a corrected Form 1099 issued by XYZ bank in the amount of $3,124 taxable interest. The information previously furnished to you was incorrect.

Kindly correct your records.

● **No-return notices that indicate that the IRS has no record of a tax return,** which it claims you were required to file.

Sample response:

To Whom It May Concern:

Enclosed is a copy of your notice dated May 15, which indicates an amount due of $300.

Your notice fails to give me credit for estimated tax payments that I made during the past year. Enclosed are photocopies of both sides of my canceled checks for payment of estimated tax. Accordingly, no money is owed.

Thank you for your prompt attention to this matter.

How Not to Get a Notice

● **Report dividend and interest income in the same amounts,** and under the same payer names, as appear on your 1099 forms. If you lump several separately reported interest payments together, even if they're from the same bank, the IRS computer won't be able to find them. *Result:* You'll get a notice from the IRS claiming that you failed to report any of that income on your return.

● **Mail your return at least one full week before the due date,** even if you've gotten an extension. Returns received by the IRS after the due date, even though mailed on or before that date, are more likely to trigger an erroneous assessment for late-filing penalties than those received by the due date. Since the IRS often misplaces the envelopes in which returns were mailed, it may be impossible to prove that a return was filed on time.

Source: Randy Bruce Blaustein, Esq., former IRS agent, now partner, Blaustein, Greenberg & Co., 155 E. 31 St., New York, NY 10016. He is the author of How to Do Business With the IRS, *Prentice-Hall.*

Answering Unreported-Income Notices

The IRS mails millions of computer-generated notices to taxpayers whose returns did not show dividend or interest income as it was reported to the IRS by banks and financial institutions. Each notice shows a recalculated tax due, adds interest charges and imposes a negligence penalty.

How should taxpayers handle such notices? What can they learn from these notices that will help in preparing future returns? Here's the procedure:

First step: Study the notice carefully and define the problem. Discover precisely which item, or items, of income the IRS says you did not report. You'll find this information on a separate page of the multipage notice.

Second step: Review your copy of the return and the 1099 forms you used to fill it out. Determine whether the IRS notice is right or wrong. Never automatically write out a check for the amount the IRS says you owe. The notice could be dead wrong—many are.

Third step: Answer the notice, in writing, within the time limit given—usually 30 days. Write to the IRS Service Center at the address given in the notice.

● **If the IRS is right,** and you did accidentally fail to report an item of income: Pay the tax and interest but ask that the negligence penalty be waived.

Sample response:

IRS Service Center
City, State
        Re: John and Sally Connell
        Social Security Nos…
        Form 1040-1997
To Whom It May Concern:

In response to your notice, a copy of which is attached, you will find enclosed a check payable to the IRS in the amount of $x, consisting of tax of $y and interest of $z.

The item in question was inadvertently omitted from our return as filed under the following circumstances: (Give the reason for the accidental omission of the income). It is contended that this constitutes reasonable cause for the inadvertent omission of this item. It is respectfully requested that the negligence penalty assessed in your notice be abated.

Sincerely yours,
John & Sally Connell

● When you did report the income, or the notice is otherwise wrong: Review the notice and your return to discover the cause of the discrepancy. One of several things may have happened. The IRS may be working with an incorrect 1099. Or the 1099 may be right and you reported the income but not as you should have.

To Whom It May Concern:

In response to your notice, a copy of which is enclosed, I am submitting the following in explanation of the alleged omission. *(Examples follow.)*

1. The dividend of $1,200 reported on my return as being received from General Motors should have been reported as being received from Merrill Lynch as nominee. A copy of my Schedule B is enclosed. (Circle the item where it appears on your Schedule B to show that you reported it.)

Lesson: Report dividends from stock held in street name by your broker as dividends received from the broker as nominee and not from the company. That's the way the 1099 will show them.

2. The dividend of $400 from Dreyfus Liquid Assets Fund was reported as interest income of $400 from Dreyfus. A copy of my Schedule B is enclosed. *(Circle the item.)*

Lesson: Most money-market funds report their income as dividends and not as interest. Report the income as it is reported to the IRS on the fund's 1099.

3. Interest of $600 from Citibank was on an account owned jointly by myself and my brother. I reported only one half of the interest—$300. A copy of my Schedule B is enclosed.

Lesson: The correct way to report interest from a joint account would be: "Interest, Citibank, $600, less amount reported by others, $300. Net amount: $300."

4. Interest of $500 from Wells Fargo Bank was reported on my return as $100, per corrected Form 1099, a copy of which is enclosed.

Lesson: Review all 1099s when you receive them. Immediately request corrected copies of any that are wrong. Report the correct information on your return. If the IRS doesn't pick up the correction, you'll have it in your files should you need it.

5. Interest of $2,140 from American National Bank was nontaxable income distributed from my IRA account and immediately reinvested in another IRA. I enclose a copy of a corrected 1099 from American National showing $0 taxable interest in this account.

How to end the letter:

If there are any further questions, please contact me.

● If you get a second notice that seems to have ignored your letter:

To Whom It May Concern:

In response to your notice dated March 28, we received a similar notice dated February 23. We answered the first notice with the enclosed letter. It would appear that our response was not received in time to prevent the second request for payment from being issued. *(Enclose photocopies of both notices and a copy of your original letter.)*

Sincerely yours,
John & Sally Connell

Some Excuses That Work And Some That Don't

Taxpayers who face penalties for misfiling returns or misreporting income will do the best they can to come up with a good explanation. Some excuses work—others don't.

Excuses That Work

● **Reliance on bad IRS advice** from an IRS employee or an IRS publication. If the advice came from an employee, you must show that it was his or her job to advise taxpayers and that you provided him or her with all the facts.

● **Bad advice from a tax professional can excuse a mistake,** if you fully disclosed the facts to the adviser. You must also show that he or she was a competent professional, experienced in federal tax matters.

● **Lost or unavailable records will excuse a mistake,** if the loss wasn't the taxpayer's fault and a genuine attempt is made to recover or reconstruct the records.

● **Incapacity of a key person can be a legitimate excuse.** *Example:* Serious illness of the taxpayer or a death in his or her immediate family.

Excuses That Don't Work

● **Pleading ignorance or misunderstanding of the law generally does not excuse a mistake.** *Exception:* Where a tax expert might have made the same mistake.

● **Someone else slipped up.** You are personally responsible for filing your tax return correctly. You can't delegate that responsibility to anyone else. If your accountant or lawyer files late, for example, you pay the penalty.

● **Personal problems don't carry much weight with the IRS.** For example, don't expect to avoid a penalty by pleading severe emotional strain brought on by a divorce.

Perils of a Joint Return

Filing a joint tax return creates "joint and several liability." This simply means that each spouse is liable for the entire amount of tax, interest and penalties ever assessed by the IRS on that return.

When the IRS discovers that one spouse has understated income, it may be possible for the other spouse to avoid liability for the extra assessment by claiming protection under the "innocent spouse" rules. To qualify for this relief, the innocent spouse must generally prove that he or she didn't know of the understatement and had no reason to know of it under the circumstances. The IRS also has authority to grant equitable relief in situations where it would be inequitable to hold a spouse fully liable. *Strategy in negotiating a settlement with a revenue agent:* Convince him or her to include the innocent-spouse relief in the settlement.

How to Take Advantage Of IRS Mistakes

A few years back more than a million taxpayers benefited financially from a major IRS blunder. A computer foul-up at filing time caused unprecedented delays in mailing out refund checks. *Taxpayer advantage:* When the Service doesn't mail a refund check in the time provided by the tax law—within 45 days after April 15 in most cases—it must pay interest on the refund.

Other, less obvious tax law requirements that the Service sometimes slips up on:

Deficiency Notices

The IRS can't assess extra tax until it has sent you a statutory notice of deficiency, also known as a 90-day letter. You have 90 days to contest the amount of additional tax levied against you by filing a petition with the Tax Court. If you don't file a petition within 90 days, the Service may, without further notice, assess and begin to collect the tax.

Look for possible defects in a 90-day letter: Example: IRS notice wasn't mailed within the three-year limitation period. Ordinarily, the IRS has only three years from the return filing date to send a 90-day letter. One mailed on April 17 of the third year after you filed your return is no good, and any subsequent IRS attempts to collect tax are void. *Catch:* You're not necessarily home free if you don't receive a 90-day letter by April 15 of the third year. *Reasons:*

- **90-day letters mailed on April 15 of Year Three are good.**

- **The Service has six years to assess tax against persons** who have underreported their income by more than 25%.

- **If the Service is alleging fraud,** there is no limitation period—the extra tax can be assessed and billed at any time.

- **The 90-day letter was mailed on time** but wasn't sent to your last known address. This is the address shown on your tax return unless the Service has reason to know (or should have known) that your address has changed since the return was filed.

What often happens is that a taxpayer moves, files tax returns showing his or her new address and then is audited on an old return. The IRS sends the 90-day letter to the address on the old return. Is this notice good? Probably not. The courts are showing increasing impatience with the Service on this issue. *Developing rule:* If the filing division of the IRS is dealing with you at your new address, the 90-day letter should go to your new address. If the auditing division sends it to your old address and you don't receive it, and the Service knows that you haven't received it because it is returned to them by the Post Office, then the 90-day letter is invalid.

If the letter was mailed at the last minute, the three-year limitation period will have expired and the IRS won't be able to collect either the outstanding tax or any penalties you may have accrued. The IRS is also subject to a limitation period on collecting tax. It must start collection proceedings within six years after tax has been formally assessed, unless it gets you to sign a waiver of the limitation period.

Key: They only have to begin an action in court to collect the tax. The moment the action starts, the limitation period is put on hold.

Defects in Liens

Before the IRS can put a lien on your property, it must follow the collection procedure set down in the tax law. *Checklist of possible defects in tax liens:*

- **The original assessment of tax was made at a time prohibited by law.** Assessments can't be made during the 90-day period after the date of a deficiency notice, nor can they be made while a Tax Court proceeding is pending.

- **The Service failed to send you a notice of the assessment** and a demand for payment.

- **You received the notice and demand—**but weren't given—10 days to pay, as required by law.

- **The notice and demand weren't sent to your last known address.**

- **The IRS didn't begin collection proceedings within the six-year limitation period.**

- **The IRS failed to obtain supervisory approval before issuing a notice of lien.**

Audit Errors

Audits must be completed within the three-year limitation period. The IRS watches the time limit closely and almost always gets taxpayers to sign a waiver extending the limitation period. *Inside information:* Agents can be fired for not getting a waiver of the limitation period, so the chance of a slip-up is slim. It's most likely to happen when the taxpayer has moved out of state and the audit is transferred to another jurisdiction. Taxpayers should be aware that it's not always in their interest to play hardball with the IRS over the waiver.

Trap: If you refuse to sign a waiver, you could lose your right to appeal the agent's findings to the appeals division. *Service policy:* The IRS won't let you take your case to the appeals division unless there is at least six months left in the limitation period. Carefully weigh your chance of negotiating a favorable settlement in the appeals division before you refuse to sign a waiver. *Policy on waivers:* Don't give long-term waivers. If the agent has already begun the audit, don't give more than an extra six months.

Source: *Michael I. Saltzman, tax attorney with Saltzman & Holloran, 1 Rockefeller Plaza, New York, NY 10020. He is the author of* IRS Practice and Procedure, *Warren, Gorham & Lamont, Inc.*

Every Taxpayer's Dream: Catching the IRS in a Mistake

All in all, the IRS's accuracy rate is good. But the IRS is far from infallible. In many cases, its approach has been to shoot first and ask questions later. The burden has been generally on you, the taxpayer, to prove the government wrong. *(Editor's note:* The burden of proof can be shifted to the IRS if your case goes to court and you meet certain conditions.)

Some areas of IRS attack:

● **Unallowable items:** A legitimate deduction may be disallowed with no elaboration simply because it was screened out by the IRS's "unallowable items program." *Defense:* Immediately write to the service center, explaining in detail why the disallowed item is deductible.

● **Automatic penalties:** If your withholding and estimated-tax payments don't equal at least 90% of the tax owed, you're liable for a penalty unless you fall within one of the safe harbors that lets you avoid the underpayment penalty. The IRS won't go out of its way to see if you qualify for one of the exceptions. It will automatically assess the penalty and let you explain. *Defense:* File Form 2210, Underpayment of Estimated Tax by Individuals, showing which of the exceptions applies to you.

● **Mistaken information returns:** The reporting of interest and dividends by banks and brokerage companies is not always right. *The IRS approach:* The information return is correct and the taxpayer is wrong. If the interest and dividends you declare are less than what is reported on the information return, the IRS will invariably assess more tax. *Defense:* If you come up with figures different from those on the information returns, be prepared to defend your numbers with copies of bank and brokerage account statements.

The following are some common off-the-wall mistakes:

● **Misplaced estimated-tax checks:** You get a letter from the IRS saying your estimated payments don't show up on its computers.

Essential: Send in photocopies of both sides of canceled checks used to make estimated payments. The reverse side of the check tells the IRS in which account it deposited the checks.

● **No return filed:** Sometimes the IRS may say it has no record that you filed a return at all.

Precaution: Always send tax returns by certified mail, with a return receipt requested. This receipt is your best proof that the return was actually filed. If you have that receipt, send in a copy of it immediately. If you don't have one, send in a copy of your return.

● **Interest errors:** It's easy for the IRS to make a mistake in calculating interest on deficiencies and refunds. The question of when interest on a deficiency ends is governed by very complex rules. *Defense:* Make your own calculations before paying interest on a deficiency. Always

check to see that the IRS is paying you the right amount of interest on a refund. *(Editor's note:* The IRS is now required to explain how interest has been calculated.)

● **Ignored refund claims:** The IRS often has to be prodded into sending a refund. If you apply for a refund by filing an amended return (Form 1040X), send it by certified mail, with a return receipt requested. There's a three-year limitation period on refund claims. If you're close to the three-year limit, the government may well disallow the claim as being statute-barred. You have to prove that it was filed on time.

Getting Help

If you can't get any action from the IRS Service Center or IRS District Office, you can take the matter to the IRS's Problems Resolution Office (PRO). This section of the IRS is staffed with people whose job is to cut through IRS red tape. Problems Resolution officers are not advocates for the taxpayer. They're expediters. Their job is to unearth a problem that may be buried in the IRS archives and get the right people to act. The PRO won't fight the battle for you, but in these days of bureaucracy, contacting a PRO can help.

IRS forms and publications: Don't blindly rely on instructions given in IRS forms and publications. The tax laws are so complicated that the government itself makes mistakes in its own publications. IRS information booklets are often outdated. It takes a while for the booklets to catch up with changes in the law. On debatable issues, IRS instructions almost always take the government's side of the case.

How to Get the IRS to Solve Your Tax Problems

The safest way to play the IRS game is to stay anonymous. The less contact you have, the better. But there comes a time for almost all taxpayers when they have to confront the IRS. How to safely handle some typical predicaments:

IRS Mistakes

● **Computer matching notice.** This is the most common IRS mistake. You get a computer-generated automatic tax assessment from the IRS. It claims that you didn't list an item of income on your return and

HOW TO CUT THROUGH IRS RED TAPE

The frustration of getting a problem straightened out at the IRS is enough to make most taxpayers despair. But don't give up if you get bogged down in the IRS bureaucracy—when the regular channels of communication have broken down, there is a way of cutting through the red tape.

Where to Turn

The IRS Problems Resolution Office (PRO) was created so taxpayers would have somewhere to turn when the system failed. It is the one office at the IRS where your problem will not be overlooked.

Where to find the PRO: You can call or write to the Problem Resolution Office at your IRS District Office or your Taxpayer Service Center. Sample problems for the PRO:

- **Your tax refund is missing.**
- **The IRS 1099 matching program mismatched your income.** *Example:* Your bank account earned $300 in interest and the IRS mistakenly claims that the account earned $3,000.
- **Tax deposits or payments you made were incorrectly posted by the IRS to the wrong year or the wrong taxpayer.**
- **You can't get other paperwork or bureaucratic mix-ups straightened out.**

What you can't do: The PRO can't be used to resolve legal questions with the IRS, such as a dispute over your tax liability or interpretation of the tax law.

PRO Prerequisites

Before the PRO will take your case, you must have attempted to solve the problem through the normal IRS channels without success. Be ready to explain to the IRS what you have already done to try to solve your case. You must have allowed sufficient time for the IRS to act on your problem through its regular channels. Depending on the type of problem you have, there are different prerequisites for getting a case accepted at the PRO. (*Editor's note:* PRO prerequisites are spelled out in IRS Publication 1546 *How to Use the Problem Resolution Program of the IRS,* which you can obtain by calling 800-829-FORM or visiting *www.irs.ustreas.gov*.)

- **Refund problems:** First, you have to wait 90 days from the date you filed your refund claim. After the 90 days have passed, you have to make two inquiries at the IRS about your refund. Prior to making the sec-

ond inquiry, a taxpayer should wait at least 10 workdays for a response. When these attempts have been unsuccessful, the PRO will then accept your case and find out quickly where your refund is.

- **IRS notices:** If you have received three or more notices from the IRS, and have replied to at least one of them without results, the PRO will take your case and resolve the problem.
- **Inquiries:** If you wrote a letter to the IRS requesting information about a tax-related issue and 45 days have passed without a response, the PRO will take on your problem. *Also:* The PRO will take your case if the IRS acknowledged your letter, promised to respond by a certain date and that date has passed without a response.
- **Other:** Whenever the normal IRS channels have not been successful in resolving your complaint or inquiry, you should contact the PRO.

Speedy Results

Once your case is accepted by the PRO, it should be quickly resolved. You will be advised of the progress on your case and the expected resolution date. The average time it will take in most cases is 15 to 25 days. The majority of cases will be closed within 30 days, because any case that isn't closed in this time period is brought to the attention of IRS management. *Highest priority at the PRO:* Cases that are reopened at the PRO for a second time due to prior IRS mishandling.

Source: Charles Pomo, tax principal, Ernst & Young, LLP, 277 Park Ave., New York, NY 10172. He is a former IRS agent and appeals officer.

now you owe more taxes. It often turns out that you did list that item on your return, it's just that the IRS can't find it. This mistake happens because the IRS gets its information from the source of the income on a Form 1099, and sometimes the amount or other information doesn't exactly match what you reported. *Example:* You correctly reported the amount of dividends you received from a company, but the IRS got the 1099 information in your broker's name rather than the company name. When it looked for the dividend income from "Broker X" on your 1040, Schedule B, all it found was income from "Company Y." *Solution:* Send copies of all relevant papers with a letter of explanation to the IRS. Avoid this situation by reporting your income exactly as it appears on the 1099. If the 1099 is incorrect, be sure to get it corrected through the source.

● **The IRS loses your return.** This is no problem if you prepare in advance by keeping copies of all forms that you send to the IRS. Keep a copy of any checks sent to satisfy your tax liability. Make sure your Social Security number is on everything you send.

● **The IRS sends you a refund for your overpayment,** but you had asked them to apply the refund to your estimated taxes. *Solution:* To avoid a bureaucratic mess, just keep the check and pay your taxes separately.

Key: If the IRS's mistake will subject you to a penalty, get it straightened out. Send a copy of your return showing that you checked off the proper boxes and return the uncashed checks to the IRS. Keep copies of everything you send.

● **The IRS doesn't send your refund.** Wait at least 10 weeks from the date you filed your return. If you still haven't gotten your refund, get the IRS to check its status. Call the automated refund-information number set up by the IRS (look in your 1040 instructions to find the correct number to call in your area).

Any taxpayer who has tried knows it can be frustrating to call the IRS. The numbers are often busy. *Suggestion:* If you're having trouble getting through, write to the IRS. It may take longer, but it's likely to increase your chances of getting action.

More Problems

● **You can't pay your tax bill.** Contact the collection division at your local IRS office before April 15. It's almost always possible to work out an installment plan.

If the tax is $10,000 or less and you meet certain conditions, the IRS can't refuse your request. If the tax is more, be prepared to prove that you can't pay your taxes and need this "loan" from the IRS.

● **You are unsure of the tax law.** The IRS publishes a wealth of material on almost every tax subject. Look in your tax instructions for a list of publications and where to get them. If you are still unsure, favorable tax results can be guaranteed by asking the IRS for a private letter ruling on the subject. If the IRS decides in your favor, you can go ahead with your transaction knowing the law is on your side. Private letter rulings are only effective for the specific taxpayer who asked for the ruling. Ask your tax adviser for help if you think a private letter ruling would resolve your uncertainty about the requirements of the law. The IRS is required to charge for letter rulings.

Secrets of Getting Fast Action at the IRS

● **Making waves at the IRS is an effective way to move a case along.** Often, the hardest part of dealing with the IRS is getting an IRS employee to do his or her job. The thing to do if you suspect an employee is taking too long to complete a task is to confront the employee and, if necessary, speak to his or her supervisor. Don't be too concerned that you are alienating the employee. The threat to go over the employee's head may be enough to get action.

● **When Congress criticizes the IRS,** the IRS takes notice. Recent hearings on the subject of IRS abuses and the new legislation protecting taxpayer rights has made higher-level management personnel sensitive to irate and frustrated taxpayers. If you feel you're being treated unfairly by lower-level IRS employees, get in touch with the chief of the examination or collection division in your local IRS District Office. There's a good chance the chief will attempt to accommodate you.

● **Finding the right person at the IRS to solve your problem** is often the biggest problem. Many taxpayer difficulties occur at the regional service centers where tax returns and tax payments are processed. Fortunately, the IRS will now be including the name and telephone number of an employee you can contact on all notices sent to you.

● **Sometimes it's necessary to fight fire with fire.** There are rare situations when an IRS agent will use his or her position to intimidate a taxpayer or the taxpayer's representative. A taxpayer can be intimidated by an agent who threatens to disallow all the deductions on his or her tax return. A tax accountant or an attorney can be intimidated by an agent who threatens disciplinary action for delay or procrastination. The best defense in these situations is to take an offensive position. Immediately write to the agent's group manager setting forth all the facts and requesting that the intimidation stop. Such letters get immediate attention and are usually made part of the agent's permanent personnel file.

You can also contact the IRS employee listed on your personal notices about your problem.

Reduce Audit Risk

You may have the impression that the IRS computers are quite sophisticated and that it is virtually impossible to do anything legally to divert them from your tax return. By and large this is true, but there are at

IRS AUDIT TRIGGERS

If you know what makes the IRS decide to audit your return, you should be able to avoid audits entirely, right? Well, yes and no.

Approximately 70% of all returns audited are chosen through a top-secret grading process designed to indicate the probability that an audit will produce money for the government. Every tax return is reviewed and scored by this process, in which a number of DIF (Discriminant Income Function) points are assigned to key items listed on (or omitted from) the return. The higher the DIF score, the greater the likelihood of audit.

The DIF scoring process is a closely guarded secret, but experience indicates a number of red flags that may cause the IRS to scrutinize your return.

Most provocative:

● **Unusually large deductions in relation to income.**

● **Unusually large refunds** (which you should avoid anyway, unless you enjoy subsidizing the government with interest-free loans).

● **Missing forms or schedules.**

Always staple your return securely after making sure all required elements are present.

Discrepancies, including:

● **Reporting the sale of a dividend-paying stock,** but failing to report any dividend income.

● **Reporting the installment sale of property,** but failing to report interest income.

● **Married couples filing separately,** and claiming the same deductions.

The higher your income and the more complex your return, the greater the likelihood that you'll be audited.

Other factors that could lead to an audit:

● **A taxpayer's past history with the IRS.** Some taxpayers may be audited regularly, particularly if a tax deficiency has been found in the first audit year.

● **In any given year,** the IRS will target certain types of businesses and financial dealings for intensified audit

activity (for example, large corporations, small proprietorships, investors in abusive tax shelters, etc.).

Trap: The IRS maintains a list of unscrupulous tax return preparers and audits a much higher proportion of returns prepared by these persons.

There is *one* audit trigger that you cannot avoid. It is the Taxpayer Compliance Measurement Program (TCMP) audit, an entirely random selection process. If your return is selected by this program, every item on it is subject to scrutiny. In a normal audit only certain areas of the return are examined. (Luckily, these audits were put on hold indefinitely by the IRS in 1996.)

Source: Michael H. Frankel, partner in the international public accounting and consulting firm of KPMG Peat Marwick, LLP, and director of the firm's Washington National Tax Office, 1990 K St. NW, Washington, DC 20006. The author of many publications, he has lectured at several tax conferences and has been widely quoted in the newspapers.

least two things that may help minimize the effect of the IRS's high-tech capabilities.

First, how income is reported on the return may make a difference. Suppose you have freelance income. If it is merely reported as "Other Income" with an appropriate description as to its source, chances of having the return selected for audit may be smaller than if the same income is reported as business income on Schedule C Income from a Sole Proprietorship.

Second, you can minimize your chances of being audited by filing as late as legally permissible. A tax return filed around April 15 generally has a greater chance of being audited than one filed on October 15 (the latest possible date). This is because the IRS schedules audits more than a year in advance.

As returns are filed and scored by the computer, local IRS districts submit their forecasted requirements for returns with audit potential. The fulfillment is made from returns already on hand. If your return is filed on October 15, there is a smaller chance that it will be among the returns shipped out to the district office in the first batch. As a result of scheduling and budget problems that may develop in the two years after your return has been filed, it may never find its way into the second batch. Although the IRS is wise to this ploy and has taken steps to make sure that the selection process is fair, inequities inevitably result. Why not try to be part of the group that has the smallest chance of being audited?

The best way to reduce your chances of being audited is to avoid certain items universally thought to trigger special IRS scrutiny. There are also some commonsense considerations that should be thought about before you mail in your return. They are often overlooked by the very people who can least afford to be the subject of an audit.

Here are some items to check:

● **Choose your return preparer carefully.** When the IRS suspects return preparers of incompetence or misconduct, it can force them to produce a list of all their clients—all of whom may face further IRS examination, regardless of their personal honesty.

● **Avoid formal membership in barter clubs.** Members of these clubs trade goods and services on a cashless basis. The club keeps track of all transactions between members. Although no cash changes hands, these trades are taxable like any other prof-

itable deal. Very often, however, they are not reported to the IRS. The IRS can force such clubs to produce membership lists, so that the returns of all club members can be examined.

● **Answer all questions on the return.** IRS computers generally flag returns with unanswered questions. For example, there is a question asking if you maintain funds in a foreign bank account. Even if you do not, you should still answer "no" to the question.

● **Fill in the return carefully.** A sloppy return may indicate a careless taxpayer. The IRS may examine the return to be sure the carelessness did not lead to any mistakes.

● **Categorize each deduction.** Don't place deductions under headings such as miscellaneous or sundry. If you can't categorize a deduction, the IRS may decide you can't prove it.

● **Avoid round numbers.** A deduction that's rounded off to the nearest hundred or thousand dollars will raise IRS suspicions. It makes it look as though the taxpayer is guessing at the deduction's size, rather than determining it from accurate records.

● **Limit deductions for unreimbursed business expenses and casualty losses.** These deductions typically trigger audits. Try to have as many business expenses as possible reimbursed by your employer rather than taking them as tax deductions. It's cheaper for you and will not make your tax return stand out.

Make sure that casualty losses can be properly documented and be aware that the IRS may be able to make a case that you actually realized a gain from the receipt of insurance proceeds, even though you think you had a loss. Insist that your tax adviser check this out carefully before taking a deduction.

Source: How to Beat the IRS *by Ms. X, Esq., former IRS agent, Boardroom Books.*

IRS Hit List

Doctors and dentists are high-priority targets. *Items IRS agents look for:* dubious promotional expenses. If the same four people take turns having lunch together once a week and take turns picking up the tab, a close examination of diaries and logbooks will show this. Agents also take a close look at limited partnership investments, seeking signs of abusive tax shelters. And they take a dim view of fellowship exclusions claimed by medical residents.

Other target occupations:

● **Salespeople:** Salespeople are particular favorites. Agents look for, and often find, poorly documented travel expenses and padded promotional figures.

● **Airline pilots:** High incomes, a tendency to invest in questionable tax shelters, and commuting expenses claimed as business travel make them inviting prospects.

● **Flight attendants:** Travel expenses are usually a high percentage of their total income and often aren't well documented. Some try to deduct pantyhose, cosmetics and similar items that the courts have repeatedly ruled are personal rather than business expenses.

● **Executives:** As a group they are not usually singled out. But if the return includes a Form 2106, showing a sizable sum for unreimbursed employee business expenses, an audit is more likely. Of course, anyone whose income is over $100,000 a year is a high-priority target just because of the sums involved.

● **Teachers and college professors:** Agents pounce on returns claiming office-at-home deductions. They are also wary of educational-expense deductions because they may turn out to be vacations in disguise.

● **Clergymen:** Bona fide priests, ministers, and rabbis aren't considered a problem group. But if W-2s show income from nonchurch employers, the IRS will be on the alert for mail-order-ministry scams.

● **Waitresses, cabdrivers, etc.** Anyone in an occupation where tips are a significant factor is likely to get a closer look from the IRS nowadays. Many people, aware their profession subjects them to IRS scrutiny, use nebulous terms to describe what they do. Professionals in private practice may list themselves as simply "self-employed." Waitresses become "culinary employees," pilots list themselves as "transportation executives." Truly deceptive descriptions could trigger penalties. And if the return is chosen for audit, an unorthodox job title for a mundane profession could convince the agent you have something to hide.

Source: Ralph J. Pribble, former IRS field agent, president of Tax Corporation of California, San Francisco.

If an IRS Agent Comes to Your Door

The IRS has issued instructions to be followed by auditors making field visits to a taxpayer's home or place of business. *Rules:* Agents may enter private premises "only when invited in by the rightful occupant." The IRS is concerned about the growing number of lawsuits for violation of privacy rights.

Source: Manual Transmittal 4200-471.

You're Always Safe Taking The Standard Deduction, Right? Wrong.

Self-employed people are likely to have their returns audited if they take the standard deduction instead of itemizing personal nonbusiness deductions, especially if their business shows a high gross and a low net. The IRS will suspect that personal deductions have been charged to the business.

When It's Smart To Ask for a Tax Audit

● **When a business is closed down,** the records and key personnel who can provide tax explanations may disappear. A subsequent IRS examination could prove very costly to the business's former owners.

● **When someone dies,** the heirs can count only on sharing in the after-tax size of the estate. So the sooner the IRS examines matters to settle things, the better.

When a taxpayer requests a prompt assessment of taxes due, the IRS must act within 18 months. Otherwise, the IRS has three years to conduct an examination. Use Form 4810 to ask for the prompt assessment. You don't have to use this form, but if you don't use it, eliminate any uncertainty on the part of the IRS by having your letter mention that the request is being made under Code Section 6501(d).

Audits the IRS Forgets to Do

Asking the IRS to transfer your case to another district may be the key to avoiding an audit. Don't expect the IRS to admit it, but transferred cases often fall between the cracks and never get worked on even though the taxpayer has been notified of the examination. Delays caused in processing the case file between districts, combined with the fact that the case is likely to go to the bottom of the pile when it is assigned to a new agent, may bring help from the statute of limitations. Rather than asking the taxpayer to extend the statute of limitations, as is the usual practice, many agents are inclined to take the easy way out and close transferred cases without auditing them.

Source: *Ms. X, a former IRS agent, who is still well connected.*

Scheduling an Audit

Knowing how the system at the IRS works gives an experienced practitioner an advantage when representing a client at an audit. *Here are some of the truly "inside" things that go on:*

● **Postponing appointments:** It is possible, though not likely, that the IRS will change its mind about auditing you if you have postponed the appointment enough times. The IRS is under pressure to start and finish tax examinations. If the return chosen for an audit becomes "old" (i.e., more than two years have passed since the return was filed), the IRS may not want to start the audit. This may happen if you are notified of an audit about 15 to 16 months after filing. By the time you have canceled one or two appointments, the 24-month cut-off period may have been reached.

When is the best time to cancel? The day before the appointment. By that time, the next available appointment will probably not be for six to eight weeks.

● **Best time to schedule an audit:** It may seem ridiculous that one time of the day or month is better than another to have your tax return audited. However, a real advantage can be gained by following some simple tips. Try to schedule an audit before a three-day weekend. The auditor may be less interested in the audit and more interested in the holiday. Another excellent time to schedule an appointment is at the end of the month. If an auditor has not "closed" enough cases that month, he or she may be inclined to go easy on you to gain another closed case. As for the best time of the day, most pros like to start an audit at about 10 o'clock in the morning. By the time it comes to discussing adjustments, it will be

lunchtime. If you are persistent, the auditor may be willing to make concessions just to get rid of you so as not to interfere with lunch plans.

Source: *How to Beat the IRS by Ms. X, Esq., former IRS agent, Boardroom Books.*

When You Can Decline An Audit

Under its own rules, the IRS will not audit you if the same item was examined in the past two years and no change was made by the auditor.

Problem: Audit invitations are computer-generated. If you get an audit notice but you fall within the two-year rule, call the IRS and request a cancellation.

Source: *Louis Lieberman, former IRS agent, Great Neck, NY.*

How to Protect Yourself

Knowing what to do if you receive notification of an IRS office audit makes all the difference in whether or not you survive it. *Crucial things to remember:*

● **Read the notice thoroughly.** It tells you which items are being questioned and what you should bring to the audit. Sometimes the IRS is just questioning one or two items on your return. If you have the records and the items are allowable, simply show that proof at the audit.

● **Respond to the notice.** If you ignore it, the IRS may automatically adjust your bill—in its favor. You usually have 10 days from the date of the notice to answer it.

● **Prepare carefully.** Review the return for the year to be audited, and gather your evidence and documentation from your files.

● **Avoid a second appearance at the IRS office.** IRS auditors don't work under a quota system, but the more time they spend on your case, the harder they will try to find adjustments. Find out the office's working hours, and if the office closes at 4:30, don't make an appointment for 4:00. The audit may not be concluded in half an hour, and the last thing you want is to drag it out until the next day. *Best time for an audit:* In the morning, so the auditor can finish your case and start the next one.

● **Bring only relevant material to the audit.** If you include extra items of proof about other matters on your return, you open yourself to the danger of an expansion of the audit. Often your arrival at the IRS office coincides with the first time the auditor sees your file. He or she probably won't be interested in anything beyond the original matters unless you bring it up. Just deal with the items at hand as quickly and in the most organized way that you can. Where appropriate, provide adding-machine tapes of checks or invoices that show grand totals agreeing with the line items on your return.

● **Don't give the IRS original receipts or proofs.** The IRS is notorious for misplacing paperwork. Make a photocopy of everything you need, and give the copies to the agent.

● **Replace any lost records right away** if it's possible. Get a copy or statement from the original source verifying the deductions in question. *Example:* If your medical bills are being questioned and you've lost your receipts, ask your doctor for copies of them or a statement of what you paid for the year in question.

● **Be cooperative.** The IRS auditor is only doing his or her job. Starting the whole process with a surly attitude will work against you, making the auditor less willing to compromise. He or she may rule against you whenever a decision has to be made. Your courtesy may mean a more favorable decision.

● **Avoid arguments with an unreasonable auditor.** You may be confronted by an auditor who is discourteous or just plain unreasonable. Ask to see the auditor's supervisor if you feel you are being mistreated. You should also ask to speak to a supervisor if you and the auditor reach an impasse on proposed disallowances. Discuss the situation with the supervisor calmly.

Drawback: The auditor has no authority to broaden the scope of the audit without the permission of the supervisor. You may not want to draw the attention of the supervisor to your return.

● **Don't give in to pressure.** Get professional tax assistance if the audit is too overwhelming. If the auditor is obstinate about a deduction to which you are sure you are entitled, and you are sure there are no other questionable items on your return, don't give up. Rather, stop the action and tell the auditor you would rather wait until your tax professional can be present. Remember, however, that this will increase your exposure because of the second visit. If you have any doubts, ask your professional to go to the first interview.

● **Don't volunteer any information.** Otherwise, the auditor may introduce a whole new line of questions about another item on your return. Don't make "small talk."

TYPES OF IRS AUDITS

There are several different types of audits:

● **Office audit.** The IRS sends you a letter asking you to come in for an audit. The items in question are listed, and you are asked to bring in substantiation for these items.

● **Field audit.** The IRS conducts this audit at *your* home or office. You don't know in advance what will be questioned, and the scope of the audit is unlimited. Have everything in order before the agent arrives to conclude the audit as fast as possible.

● **Correspondence audit.** You are asked to mail information or proof, or to sign a form and mail it back if you agree with the IRS's conclusions. These audits often result from the IRS's 1099 computer-matching program. Read the letter very carefully, and make sure the IRS has matched the correct 1099 to your Social Security number. The IRS frequently makes mistakes. Don't agree to anything until you are satisfied that the IRS is correct.

● **Taxpayer compliance audit (TCMP).** This is the most dreaded of all audits. The IRS randomly selects a percentage of returns and asks each of the taxpayers involved to prove, in detail, virtually every item on the return. The IRS does this to measure the effectiveness of the system and to see if taxpayers are complying with the law. Luckily, very few returns are chosen for this scrutiny. (These audits were put on hold indefinitely by the IRS in 1996.)

● **Be truthful.** Lying or giving misleading information to the auditor is a criminal offense. If you find yourself in a sticky situation that you can't handle (that is, the auditor uses an indirect method and claims you have omitted income), terminate the audit right then and there. Bring in an experienced tax professional. Also, if the IRS auditor sees that you are a truthful person in general, he or she is more likely to accept your explanations of deductions. *Another plus for truth:* The auditor could be testing you by asking questions to which he or she already knows the answers.

● **Check to see if the IRS's policy against repetitive audits applies.** Have you been questioned in the two previous years about the same issue? If so, and there was no change in tax on that item either time, the IRS has a policy not to audit you on that item for the third year in a row. Get out your letters from the IRS stating that there was no tax change on that item. Then call the IRS office and say you want the repetitive audit procedures applied.

● **Know your appeal rights.** Although in general it's better to get your tax liability settled at the audit level, you don't have to accept an auditor's decision. You are entitled to a conference with the IRS Appeals Division if you think the auditor has made a mistake. If you can't come to an agreement with the Appeals Division, you can go to court.

Source: Walter T. Coppinger, tax partner and special consultant in tax practice and procedure, Ernst & Young, LLP, 2121 San Jacinto St., Dallas, TX 75201. He is a former IRS regional commissioner.

After the Examination

Once the examination is complete, the agent has three options: Accept the return as filed, find an overpayment, or propose additional taxes. If the agent proposes a deficiency, this is an opportunity to negotiate. On legal matters, the agent is bound by IRS rules and regulations, but factual determinations are to some extent discretionary. Since agents often have an incentive to settle as many cases as possible on the audit level, your powers of persuasion may help you arrive at a compromise proposal.

If the agent proposes an adjustment, you have the option of accepting the agent's findings or appealing the case. Before you make this decision,

consider the fact that on an appeal the IRS can dispute *any* item on a return, not just those already scrutinized. Thus, if there is an undiscovered issue that you know about but the IRS has not raised, it may be to your advantage to settle.

Source: Michael H. Frankel, partner in the international public accounting and consulting firm of KPMG Peat Marwick, LLP, and director of the firm's National Tax Office, 1990 K St. NW, Washington, DC 20006.

Preparing to Face the Auditor

Before facing the IRS auditor yourself, the most productive way to spend your time and energy is in gathering and organizing documentation of your deductions and exclusions.

The process includes preparation of schedules of the items involved. In the case of charitable contributions, for example, list dates, amounts, relevant check numbers, and make notations of receipts in your possession.

Such preparation will save time during the audit and may encourage the revenue agent to do a spot check rather than tie in all documentation to the amounts claimed on the return.

If you anticipate disputes over certain deductions and exclusions, a valuable added weapon is a memorandum from your accountant. *It should contain:*

● **A statement that shows you understand the law involved.**

● **A corroborating statement on how and why you fit the particular provision in question,** or how specific circumstances warrant the position taken on the return.

● **Citations of recent relevant court cases.**

Source: Ralph C. Ganswindt, partner specializing in closely held businesses, Arthur Andersen & Co., LLP, 777 E. Wisconsin Ave., Milwaukee, WI 53201.

Preparation Is the Key to Winning a Case

The weaker the case, the better the preparation and presentation must be. Always present your case as attractively as possible. Organize the material in a binder, complete with a cover, table of contents and index tabs. Address every negative point the IRS could raise and reach a favorable conclusion to those points whenever possible. Make your presentation to the IRS in person—literally read your material out loud, cover to cover, to the IRS agent.

What to Do If You Haven't Kept Good Records

Under the law, a taxpayer has the burden of proving his or her deductions. If you haven't kept good records, get duplicate receipts from the people to whom you paid money.

Alternatives: Sworn affidavits, copies of canceled checks from your bank. Under IRS guidelines, agents generally will give you adequate time to come up with proof if they believe you're making a good-faith effort to cooperate.

Most agents will allow only what you can substantiate under the circumstances. The balance is negotiable. Always present a plausible story to explain your lack of records. *Example:* "I realize I didn't follow the law 100%, but I couldn't because I had to do so much traveling and there was so much illness at home that I had to take care of. I'm willing to take a reasonable disallowance and prove the illnesses."

Records You Should Have

Itemized deductions are a common IRS target. Here's the information you'll need to support your numbers.

Medical expenses:
● Doctor and dentist bills.
● Copies of prescriptions.
● Doctor's letter describing the illness and treatment to justify travel costs.
● Copies of premium invoices and policies to prove medical insurance coverage.

Taxes:
● Copies of state and local returns.
● Tax bills and receipts (property tax).

When and Why You May Need Your Accountant

Call your accountant if the IRS is proposing a sizable adjustment of the monies that you owe. Ask your accountant to call the IRS and handle the audit for you.

By insulating yourself from the auditor in this way, you can't say the wrong things. Also, your accountant will gain more time to think about answers to complex questions, since he or she will have to get more information from you and then get back to the auditor. *Point:* Weigh the cost of bringing in your accountant against the amount of any potential tax assessment. If the tax is relatively small, it may not be worth it to pay for an accountant.

Source: Thomas LoCicero, senior tax manager and executive tax-planning specialist, Deloitte & Touche, LLP, New York, NY 10019.

Interest:
● Copies of promissory notes.
● Mortgage amortization tables.
Contributions:
● Letters from the organization that prove the donation. *(Editor's note:* If the donation is $250 or more, you must have written acknowledgment from the organization of your contribution; a canceled check won't do.)
● Appraisals or other proof of value.
Casualty losses:
● Police or fire department reports.
● Description of property and proof of ownership.
● Appraisals to establish value.
● Itemized list of stolen/destroyed items.
● Documented insurance recovery.
Professional fees:
● Invoices or letters itemizing services and detailing percentage of tax-deductible work.

Source: Stuart R. Josephs, retired tax partner, BDO Seidman, La Mesa, California.

Second-Best Evidence

Just because you can't prove something to the IRS auditor doesn't mean that you should pay more tax right then and there. Taxpayers often show up for audits with inadequate proof of their deductions. The auditor's initial reaction is to disallow the deduction, in the belief that the taxpayer would have brought the complete documentation if it existed. *Strategy:* Ask the auditor to tell you what he or she would accept as satisfactory documentation. If the auditor demands proof that you can't obtain, negotiate for second-best proof that you will be able to get. Suppose you can't find canceled checks, but can get an affidavit from the person to whom you paid the money. Get the auditor to agree that the affidavit will be acceptable.

Fighting a Bank Deposit Analysis

A routine audit procedure is a bank deposit analysis. Deposits in a taxpayer's accounts are added up and then compared with the amount of income reported on the tax return. What if you don't think that a particular deposit was income, but you can't remember the source? Ask your bank to supply you with a copy of the check that was deposited. Most banks keep these records for five years. The person who wrote the check can then furnish you with an affidavit explaining the reason for issuing the check.

Audit-Proof Your Cost of Living

If the IRS has a reasonable indication that there is a likelihood of unreported income, it will reconstruct a taxpayer's income by estimating his or her cost of living. The IRS does this by adding up all living expenses paid for throughout the year by check, then adding an amount it feels is reasonable for other living expenses it assumes have been paid for with cash. *Tip:* Make sure to pay for expenses such as food, medical expenses, automobile costs, mortgage payments, and credit-card payments by check. This should head off an agent's contention that you had "hidden" living expenses.

Source: Ms. X, a former IRS agent, who is still well connected.

How to Handle an IRS Auditor

Prepare meticulously for the audit. Gather all your receipts for the deductions the IRS has questioned. List each, in detail, on a sheet of paper. Also, metic-

ulously reconstruct cash expenditures for which you don't have receipts. Explain exactly how and when you made those expenditures. By presenting your case in factual detail, you establish your credibility. And credibility is everything at an audit. It will be easier for the auditor to allow nondocumented items if you can show him or her that you kept some receipts, that you made an effort to comply with IRS rules and regulations, and that you've reconstructed, as best you could, your cash outlays.

T & E Audits

Travel and entertainment is the most commonly audited deduction. *Your goal:* To limit the items the agent examines by persuading him or her to do a test check of your expenses. Let the auditor choose a three-month period for detailed examination. Or talk him or her into limiting the audit to items over, say, $100. Make sure you can document all items in the test-check period or in the amount. *Double benefit:* A test check cuts down your work in assembling backup data, and it prevents the agent from rummaging through all your travel and entertainment expenses.

Special Problems

● **Business audits.** If your business is being audited, have it done at your accountant's office, not at your home or your place of business. You don't want the auditor to see your standard of living nor run the risk that an employee will say something to the auditor that could hurt you.

● **Unreported income.** If the IRS has some basis for believing you failed to report income, an agent may ask "Have you reported all your income?" Never answer this or other potentially embarrassing questions with a lie. Deliberately failing to report all your income is a crime. So is lying to an IRS employee. To avoid incriminating yourself, deflect the question with, "Why do you want to know that?" or "I'll get back to you on that later." The question may not come up again. Another way to avoid answering this question is not to show up for the audit. Then the deductions you've been asked to prove will be automatically disallowed. But you can appeal the agent's disallowance at the appeals level of the IRS. There you may not be asked whether you've reported all your income.

- **Special agents.** Their job is to develop evidence for criminal tax cases. If they show up at your door, don't answer any of their questions, even seemingly innocuous ones. Tell them to talk with your lawyer. Then retain a lawyer who is knowledgeable in criminal tax matters.

Best: A former assistant U.S. attorney.

Source: Randy Bruce Blaustein, Esq., a former IRS agent, now partner, Blaustein, Greenberg & Co., 155 E. 31 St., New York, NY 10016. He is the author of How to Do Business With the IRS. *Prentice-Hall.*

How to Beat the IRS at Its Own Game

People at the IRS choose their words carefully when they want you to help them make a better case against you. They use words that intimidate, convince or cajole someone into doing something he or she otherwise wouldn't do.

To beat the IRS at this game, you must know what the agents mean when they talk tough. You must know what to expect if you call their bluff.

- **Game 1:** An IRS agent asks you to produce all of your books and records for a tax examination. More often than not, the agent doesn't want every single record. He or she may only be interested in your bank statements, or in one or two unusually large items you deducted on your tax return.

Respond to the agent's request for all books and records by simply asking, "Exactly which records do you want?" Or, "What items are you really interested in checking?" Chances are he or she will tell you, and it won't be every record you kept for the year.

- **Game 2:** The official line at the IRS is that agents do not negotiate proposed audit adjustments. *Real life:* Everything is subject to "discussion." Many agents will try to bulldoze their way through a case by taking a position and not budging from it. They will come right out and tell you that they don't bargain. But what they really mean is that they will not bargain unless they have to. If they feel they have a chance of closing the case on an agreed basis (you and the IRS agree on the extra tax owed), they will become more receptive to your proposals.

Lesson: Be persistent. This will give you an excellent chance of meeting the agent on some reasonable middle ground.

- **Game 3:** You're in the middle of an audit and the agent asks you to supply a copy of the tax return you filed in a prior year. Perhaps the agent wants to review it to determine if it contains anything worth looking into in greater depth, such as making comparisons of income and expense items. Technically, you don't have to supply it since the IRS already has a copy of the return in its files. The problem, which the agent generally fails to tell the taxpayer, is that it takes forever for an agent to get a copy from the IRS

How Long Should You Keep Your Tax Records?

Always keep tax records longer than the three-year limitation period that the IRS has to audit your return. *Example:* During an audit, a taxpayer's carryover losses were approved by the agent. After the audit, he continued carrying over the approved losses but threw out the proof thinking he didn't need it anymore. When the IRS audited him for the next few years, he lost the carryover deduction. He could no longer prove it.

Editor's note: The carryover period for net operating losses and unused business credits arising after 1997 is 20 years.

Source: Robert F. Neece, TC Memo 1986-121.

Service Center. If you don't supply a copy, most agents won't bother to pursue the matter. *Suggestion:* Tell the agent that you will give him or her copies of the returns, but only after the examination has been concluded and you have been presented with the items he or she feels should be adjusted. The agent will probably agree. By not giving copies of the two returns until the adjustments have been settled, you will prevent the agent from making potentially damaging comparisons.

● **Game 4:** Revenue officers who are in the final stages of preparing for a seizure of a taxpayer's home or business will generally request consent from the taxpayer. Consent allows the IRS to enter private premises for purposes of conducting the seizure. *Complications:* What the revenue officer usually neglects to say is that, if consent is not given, the IRS must go through the trouble of obtaining a court order authorizing the seizure. This can take up to six weeks. Taxpayers who refuse to give their consent can use this time to make a last effort to raise the money they need to pay the outstanding tax bill. *(Editor's note: As of July 22, 1998, the IRS may not seize a residence to satisfy an unpaid liability of $5,000 or less. And, the IRS must exhaust all other payment options before seizing a residence or business assets. Levy on the principal residence is allowed only if approved in writing by a judge or magistrate of the U.S. District Court.)*

● **Game 5:** Special agents handling criminal investigations often approach people they suspect of wrongdoing and try to solicit incriminating information from them. If the people are reluctant to cooperate,

AT THE AUDIT— WHEN TO TALK AND WHEN TO KEEP QUIET

If you've decided to handle an IRS audit yourself, the sound policy is to make as little sound as possible. You never can tell when some thoughtless remark will draw the agent's attention to something you want ignored.

The first step in keeping quiet is preparation. Prior to the audit, try to think of all the questions you might be asked. Go over them in your head until you're satisfied with your answers. Do not plan to lie.

During the audit itself, be on guard for seemingly innocent questions or other conversational gambits that pry into your family affairs or lifestyle.

For example, the "innocent" question, "How old are your children?" clearly has nothing to do with the

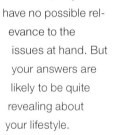

business at hand. Moreover, if you're not fully on your guard, you might find yourself responding, "Well, one is nine and the other is 11. The 11-year-old goes to private school, and boy, is that expensive!"

While questions about your upcoming vacation plans may make pleasant conversation, they can have no possible relevance to the issues at hand. But your answers are likely to be quite revealing about your lifestyle.

Also be on the lookout for trick questions. An example might be, "How many miles is your trip to work each day?" Here the agent may be looking to disallow some of your travel costs as nondeductible commuting expenses.

For questions that do legitimately relate to the audit process, take all the time you need to think through your answers. It is prudent to say no more than the minimum required to answer the question. In other words, supply only requested information. The agent can always ask for more information if you haven't provided enough.

Finally, and most important, do not, under any circumstances, answer an incriminating question. If the agent asks, "Did you report all of your income?" for example, what do you say? If you have reported all your income, you can, of course, say "yes." If you haven't and you lie (by saying "yes"), you face even more trouble. But you don't have to say either. One evasion tactic is to pose a counterquestion: "What makes you think I haven't declared all my income?" *(Editor's note: The IRS may ask this question only if there is a reasonable indication that there is a likelihood of unreported income.)*

If you can't deter the agent and you find yourself being backed into a corner, you can always terminate the audit. This is your right. You can invoke it at any time. Simply tell the agent you need the assistance of your lawyer or tax professional. Flight may go against all your instincts, but conceding the opening skirmish still gives you a chance of winning the war.

Source: Mark A. Levinson, tax manager, Edward Isaacs & Co., 380 Madison Ave., New York, NY 10017.

the special agent will usually explain that if they don't answer the questions now, he or she will have no choice but to serve a summons and the questions will have to be answered down at the office.

Editor's note: This is not 100% true—you can always claim your Fifth Amendment rights by refusing to answer any questions on the grounds that you might incriminate yourself. Taking the Fifth doesn't give a special agent any ammunition that can be used against you in court.

Source: Randy Bruce Blaustein, Esq., former IRS agent, now partner, Blaustein, Greenberg & Co., 155 E. 31 St., New York, NY 10016.

Helping Novice Auditors

One way to resolve an audit in your favor is to write up the agent's workpapers (the forms he or she prepares on the audit) yourself. Sounds ridiculous, but it can be done in some circumstances by seasoned tax professionals. Some newly hired IRS agents may not have enough experience to know how to set up audit workpapers in a way that won't be criticized by their bosses. If your adviser knows what to put in the workpapers, and what to leave out, he or she can coach the agent. Many novice agents are receptive to a helping hand.

> **"It's common practice for an IRS auditor to ask you to waive the statute of limitations to give him or her more time to work on your case.... It may be to your advantage not to."**

What Happens if You Drag An Audit On and On and On

Your odds of settling are actually *increased* if an IRS agent has been holding your case for a long time (over one year). Although tax professionals who intentionally procrastinate can be barred from practice before the IRS, the Service is basically helpless against taxpayers who procrastinate.

Source: Ms. X, a former IRS agent, who's still well-connected.

Extending the Statute Of Limitations

It is not unusual for an audit to stretch out beyond the normal three-year limitation period. When this happens, the agent will ask the taxpayer to sign Form 872 consenting to extend the period during which the IRS may propose additional tax assessments. Many times it is in the taxpayer's best interest to give his or her consent, since withholding it will only result in the agent's coming up with an arbitrary assessment in an effort to protect the government's interest. *Strategy:* Agree to extend the statute for only six months rather than the one-year period the IRS normally asks for. This will put a degree of pressure on the agent to close your case. Also, a short extension gives the agent less time to develop tax issues that you would rather not be pursued.

Editor's note: Beginning in the year 2000, if the IRS requests the taxpayer extend the statute of limitations, it must notify the taxpayer of his or her right to refuse or to limit the extension to particular issues.

Source: Ms. X, a former IRS agent, who's still well connected.

When Not to Waive

It's common practice for an auditor to ask you to waive the statute of limitations to give him or her more time to work on your case. If you refuse to sign the waiver, the examiner will often disallow the items he or she wanted to audit and issue a Notice of Deficiency. The Notice of Deficiency requires you to file a petition with the Tax Court within 90 days to avoid paying the tax until the merits of your case are considered by the court.

Important: It may be to your advantage not to sign the waiver if there are items on your return that you would rather the agent not dig into. At Tax Court, you will still have to prove your deductions. But you won't be subject to the kind of probing that can open up other items that you prefer not be opened.

When to Negotiate, When to Litigate

Unless you are prepared to cave in to the judgment of the agent on every issue, any tax audit is likely to be a negotiation. In disputes with the IRS, the outcome of the controversy depends not only upon the nature of the items at issue, but also upon the level at which settlement is reached.

Where to Negotiate

Generally, a taxpayer's chance for success at negotiating questionable items is directly proportional to the bureaucratic level at which settlement is achieved. Your chance of success is *lowest* at the lowest level—the audit. Since the function of the IRS is to raise revenue, it's no surprise that agents do not readily concede a deduction or exclude an item of income subject to debate.

The taxpayer's position and outlook improve somewhat, however, at the conference level, where the case is reviewed for technical propriety and where arguments involving precedent (such as litigation on similar issues, Treasury Department rulings, or announced policy of the Internal Revenue Service, etc.) may become the focal point of the discussion.

If the controversy is sufficiently serious, in terms of both the nature of the item and the dollar amount, litigation may be considered. Cases docketed for Tax Court generally involve a semiformal pretrial conference with a government attorney in which the Service's decision to press on is governed largely by its perceived chances of winning, a concern *not* permitted at lower levels. So there is a chance the Service may abandon the field to you at this stage.

In deciding whether to litigate in the regular Tax Court or the Tax Court for small claims, keep in mind the following: If the amount under dispute exceeds $50,000, you have no choice; the regular court is the only option. If you choose "small" Tax Court, remember that while proceedings are more informal, the rulings of this court are final. There is no further appeal.

Psychological Warfare

How do you make an IRS agent see something your way when the agent continues to hold a position that you believe is unreasonable? One technique is to try to make the agent feel guilty that if he or she doesn't budge you'll have to take the case to court and that will cause you an unreasonable amount of anxiety and cost a lot of money. By getting the agent to feel sympathetic and guilty at the same time, you may be able to work toward a negotiated settlement.

Who Should Negotiate?

We all applaud the harassed taxpayer who defends himself in court and whips the IRS. Unfortunately, such cases are few and far between. At the prelitigation stages, however, the situation is different.

Many reasonably sophisticated taxpayers can adequately represent themselves across the table from an examining agent, or even at the conference level—and do. In many instances, only the person who must eventually sign the check to pay the tax deficiency (if any) can bring to bear the requisite amount of enthusiasm to press his or her point.

On the other hand, representation by a specialist (an attorney, accountant or enrolled agent) has much to recommend it.

● **First,** the representative can be expected to have an adequate grasp of the technical aspects.

● **Second,** a specialist is generally more objective and less likely to be distracted by emotional considerations, discussing only the facts at issue, and never volunteering more than the necessary amount of information.

● **Third,** a representative acting in the absence of the taxpayer offers an additional layer of negotiating space. The representative may tentatively agree with a settlement offer but will have to confer with his or her client, thus buying additional time to evaluate the proposal.

● **Clearly,** if a situation is serious enough to litigate, it is also serious enough to justify the cost of a tax attorney.

Note: Keep in mind that a representative need not be present at the outset. A taxpayer is not obligated to agree to the IRS settlement offer at the initial meeting. A specialist may be brought in at a later time without prejudicing his or her case.

This strategy may be advisable if you detect a losing situation during or after the initial confrontation.

Source: *Richard D. Lehmbeck and Henry J. Murphy, partners, KPMG Peat Marwick, LLP, 150 JFK Pkwy., Short Hills, NJ 07078.*

How to Win the Fight After You Lose the Audit

Taxpayers who disagree with an auditor's findings can appeal the decision both within the IRS and beyond—to the courts. The end of the audit may, if you choose, just be the beginning of your fight with the IRS.

Round One

Actually, it's the IRS that really starts the fight—with what is called its 30-day letter. That contains a copy of the audit report showing the examiner's proposed adjustments to your tax bill. You have 30 days to respond or request an extension.

Important: Never ignore a 30-day letter. If you don't respond in time, you'll get a notice of deficiency (a 90-day letter) and you'll have to file a court petition to continue your fight.

Best: Try to settle the case without going to court. It's quicker that way and much cheaper.

How to get to the IRS appeals office: Send a protest letter. This will move your case from the audit division to the IRS appeals office. *Advantages:* The hearings officers at the appeals office have more authority to settle a case than the IRS auditor did. They can use their discretion to judge by the facts and circumstances of the case what the chances are of each side winning in court. *Example:* If the hear-

---

A LOOK AT TAX LITIGATION AND APPEALS PROCEDURES

Is it a good or a bad idea to appeal an IRS decision that you owe more tax? The following list of steps in the appeals process will help answer the questions you'll have when the IRS contacts you.

● **Audit.** If the IRS questions or takes exception to any portion of your tax return, you will be notified of an examination or audit, to be held either "in the field" (on your premises) or in the local IRS offices. Following the conclusion of the audit, you will receive a notification of the Service's findings and proposed adjustments. The letter of notification gives you 30 days in which to appeal an agent's decision.

● **IRS appeal.** An IRS conference at the appellate level is initiated by filing a protest ("informal," if the disputed amount is under $2,500; a brief written statement if the proposed change is $2,500 or more but not more than $10,000; "formal," if over $10,000) with

the regional director of appeals. A formal protest—a very simple document despite its name—includes the taxpayer's position on the disputed item as supported by some type of authority. The informal protest is just a short note requesting a review by the appeals division.

If the appeal decision goes against you (or if you did not appeal or otherwise respond to the "30-day letter"), you will receive a deficiency notice or "90-day letter" specifying the amount of additional tax, interest, penalties, etc., that the Service contends you owe.

● **Tax Court.** A deficiency notice allows you 90 days in which to file a petition to have your case heard in Tax Court. Within the Tax Court there is a special division for small claims (under

$50,000 for one tax year or period). Its proceedings are relatively informal, and litigating here is considerably less costly and time-consuming than in the "regular" Tax Court. However, its judgments are not subject to appeal elsewhere.

Decisions of the "regular" Tax Court can be appealed.

If you fail to *properly* file within the 90-day time limit, you forfeit the right to have your case heard in Tax Court (although alternatives remain). Then, once the 90-day period has expired, the disputed tax is due and payable, regardless of whatever alternative you choose to pursue. You can file a claim with the IRS for a refund. If that claim is disallowed, your next step is an appeal to a higher court.

Source: Mark A. Levinson, tax manager, Edward Isaacs & Co., 380 Madison Ave., New York, NY 10017.

ing officer thinks that you have a 60% chance of winning your argument about the disallowance of a certain deduction, he or she can decide to allow you to take 60% of the deduction.

If you haven't had one before, it's a good idea to get a tax professional to help you at this stage. He or she will know what the best legal arguments are in support of your case. He or she will also know what information to include in your protest letter. A protest letter should include:

- **A statement that you want to appeal the findings** of the examiner to the appeals office.
- **Your name and address.**
- **The date and reference number from the letter** transmitting the proposed adjustments and findings you are protesting.
- **The tax periods or years involved.**
- **An itemized schedule of the adjustments** with which you do not agree.
- **A statement of facts supporting your position** in any contested factual issue, declared true under penalty of perjury.
- **A statement outlining the law or other authority on which you rely.**

Appeals Conference

You will be notified by the IRS when the appeals conference will take place. You may have to wait six months to one year. While you can represent yourself at this conference, it's a better idea to be represented by a professional who is qualified to practice before the IRS. These experts have experience in presenting your side of the issue to the IRS.

There is a very high rate of settling cases at this point. Usually the cases that aren't settled involve issues upon which the IRS has decided it isn't going to compromise, such as abusive tax shelter cases. On these issues, the IRS usually wants to test the cases in court in order to set a precedent for the future. *Advantages of settling at this point:* Court proceed-

ings are costly and time consuming, and should be conducted with legal counsel.

Continuing the Fight

If you can't reach agreement with the IRS at the appeals level, you don't have to give up. You have the option of fighting it out in court. The IRS at this point will send you a notice of deficiency (also known as a 90-day letter). You have 90 days from the date of the notice to file a petition with the Tax Court.

Important: Never ignore a notice of deficiency— or fail to answer it within the 90-day period. If you do ignore it, the IRS will automatically make an assessment and bill you for what it thinks you owe. You will forever give up your right to argue your case in Tax Court.

Major disadvantage: If you lose your right to go to Tax Court, you can still sue in District Court or Claims Court. However, for either of these two courts, you must pay the tax first, and then sue. In Tax Court, you don't have to pay the tax until the trial is over.

Appealing IRS Audit Conclusions

The best forum to fight in, after the audit or examiner level, is the IRS's own Appellate Division. There, taxpayers who disagree with IRS audit conclusions and who can document their position with sound facts have a good chance of getting at least part of what they're asking for, without going to court.

An appeal to the appellate level of the IRS is handled by highly trained IRS personnel called appeals officers. It is the appeals officers' job to settle cases—to see that they don't go to court—while still getting the most they can for the government.

Unlike auditors, who are bound by the regulations and rulings of the IRS, the appeals officer is entitled to consider the hazards of litigation. That is, the

> " **[At] the IRS's own Appellate Division... taxpayers who disagree with IRS audit conclusions and who can document their position with sound facts have a good chance of getting at least part of what they're asking for, without going to court.** "

chance that the government might lose in court if it litigates a case. If the officer feels that the government has a weak position on the facts, or there are cases in the taxpayer's jurisdiction against the government, odds are that he or she will concede or agree to a settlement.

The officer has a great deal of leeway. It is possible for a taxpayer to horse-trade and negotiate on individual items with conferees. Typical is that the officer concedes half the tax bill (or a third of the bill) as being deductible. The taxpayer will have to concede the other half or two-thirds.

Some issues that are not likely to be settled at the audit level, but that taxpayers have a good chance of resolving at appeal, are:

● **Cash expenditures that the auditor has disallowed for lack of documentation,** where those expenditures are common in the taxpayer's business.

● **Travel and entertainment deductions that are disallowed because the taxpayer does not have all the support the tax law requires.** These disallowances can normally be settled on appeal if the amounts are reasonable.

● **Business use of property.** *Example:* A taxpayer uses his car in business 75% of the time. But the auditor says he hasn't supported his deduction. If the taxpayer can show that he normally uses his car in business, an appeal should be successful.

● **Charitable contributions.** Large deductions and those involving hard-to-value gifts, such as stock in a closely held business, become battles of appraisals. These often need to be settled on appeal.

● **Constructive dividends.** Are items of expense paid by a closely held company to an officer-shareholder deductible, or are they a nondeductible preferential dividend?

Despite the above, do not go up through the appeal process on a lark, hoping for the best outcome. Prepare a decent case. Get sound professional advice. The appeals officers are technically competent people. They are not likely to let anything slip by them.

Do not expect to get 100% of what you ask for. If several issues are taken to appeal, be prepared to concede some as part of the give-and-take negotiations.

Cases that involve questions of fact rather than law have the best chance of being settled because facts lend themselves to compromise. On legal issues, there's less room for negotiation. For every six cases the taxpayer can come up with in support of a legal position, the appeals officer will have six for the government. There's a standoff, which the officer will have no choice but to resolve on the principle of hazards of litigation.

The best approach in dealing with an appeals officer (or an auditor, for that matter) is to give as much factual background as possible. Point out where the auditor was wrong. Support that position with facts. What prevails is a strong factual presentation, forcefully argued.

Source: David E. Lipson, partner in charge of the tax division of the Chicago office of Arthur Andersen & Co, LLP.

If You're Out of the Country

A Tax Court petition usually has to be filed within 90 days after the taxpayer receives a notice of deficiency. However, Mrs. Mohamed was out of the country when the IRS mailed the notice. *Tax Court:* Taxpayers who are out of the country when the notice is mailed have 150 days to answer a notice of deficiency. Mr. and Mrs. Mohamed filed within 139 days, so their petition was valid.

Source: Zaid A. Muthala Mohamed, TC Memo 1987-132.

Winning in Tax Court

You've taken your case to the IRS appeals office and it has upheld the determination of the original examining agent. You still think you're right, but you don't want to go broke proving it. Does it make sense to take your fight to the next stage—the court?

If your case is strong on the facts but weak on the law, it might be advisable to pay the tax and sue for a refund in the District Court. This would give you an opportunity to be heard by a jury of fellow taxpayers. (The court of claims is an alternative, but does not provide for a jury and has no apparent advantages.)

For less subjective issues, Tax Court offers one enormous advantage: A taxpayer can dispute an IRS assessment without prior payment of the disputed tax.

Two Tax Courts

There are not one but two tax courts: the tax court for small claims ("small" Tax Court) and the tax court ("regular" Tax Court). Which you choose will depend on the arena in which you think you can win.

If you qualify, it may be to your advantage to have your case heard in "small" Tax Court. This forum is relatively informal—strict rules of evidence are not in force and the taxpayer can plead his or her own case. If the claimed deficiency plus penalties are under $50,000 for any one taxable year for income taxes, or $ 50,000 for estate or gift taxes, you can take your case to "small" Tax Court. *Advantage:* If you have a fairly simple, one-issue case, this court saves you the cost of an attorney or a tax practitioner and extensive preparation. *Disadvantage:* The decision of the court is not subject to appeal. You'll have to live with the ruling.

If the issues are complex, involving more arcane provisions of the Tax Code, and the proposed additional tax is more than $10,000, you do not qualify for "small" Tax Court. Instead, you are in for a more elaborate and expensive effort because you will have to make your case in the "regular" Tax Court. Here it's wise to retain experienced tax counsel.

How to File

Once you decide to pursue your case in one of the tax courts, you must file a petition within 90 days of receiving your deficiency notice from the IRS. Information requested in the petition includes a statement in "clear and concise" terms of the errors the IRS made in determining the tax deficiency. You are also asked to state the facts upon which you base your belief that the assessment is wrong and unfair. Your petition must be filed with the Tax Court in Washington, DC (400 Second St. NW, Washington, DC 20217). Remember, if you file anywhere else, or if you file after the 90 days are up, the petition will be held invalid, and unless you refile properly and in time, you will lose forever your right to have this case heard before the Tax Court.

Source: *Raymond Polen, attorney-at-law in private practice at 60 E. 42 St., New York, NY 10165. He specializes in estate and tax planning, and was formerly an estate tax attorney with the Internal Revenue Service, where he worked for more than 10 years.*

Tax Court vs. District Court

The two most popular courts for pursuing tax cases are Tax Court and federal District Court. *The difference:* Tax Court decisions are rendered by judges who are tax specialists. If you want a jury trial, you've got to go to District Court. *Catch:* District Courts only hear tax refund cases. So you have to pay the tax first to get your jury trial. If you win, you get your refund plus interest.

Caution: A person who had not filed a valid refund request could not have his or her tax dispute tried before a jury.

Source: *Kevin E. Krzyske, E.D. Mich., No. 81-60223.*

Getting the Government to Pay Your Legal Fees

A recent Tax Court opinion provides insight into the factors that must exist before a taxpayer can get the government to pay his or her attorney's fees under Section 7430 of the Tax Code. *(Editor's note: A taxpayer who beats the IRS in Tax Court can recover legal costs—about $125 an hour in 1999, and indexed for inflation thereafter—if he or she can establish that the IRS took an unreasonable position against him or her.)*

Factors favoring the taxpayer include: Did the IRS continue to pursue the case even though it had been aware that the case was defective? Did it send the taxpayer a long list of questions that were unrelated to the issues in the case? Did it adopt an inflexible attitude in rejecting the taxpayer's attempt to engage in settlement negotiations? Above all, the courts will not permit the IRS to wear down a taxpayer financially as a tactic to win its case.

Source: *Ms. X, a former IRS agent, who is still well connected.*

When Not to Trust a Bill You Get From the IRS

When the IRS comes up with a deficiency as the result of an audit, the taxpayer is given a waiver to sign and mail back to the Service. According to the tax law, if the IRS doesn't demand payment of the tax bill 30 days after the waiver was executed, interest on the deficiency stops running.

Problem: The IRS has been charging some taxpayers interest right up to the date of billing, which is often several months after the waiver was signed and returned. This extra interest can be several hundred dollars more than you should pay. *What to do:* Carefully check interest charges before paying the deficiency bill. Interest should be charged for the period beginning with the due date of the return and ending 30 days after you sign the waiver and mail it back to the IRS. Pay the tax you owe and the interest that you determine to be correct. Clearly explain in an accompanying letter how you arrived at your figures, including a detailed computation of the correct interest.

Note: Pay the deficiency bill within 10 days after you get it. If you don't, interest will start running again.

Source: Peter A. Weitsen, a former IRS agent, now partner, Mendlowitz Weitsen, LLP, 2 Penn Plaza, New York, NY 10121.

Stopping IRS Interest

Audited taxpayers can stop interest from building up on proposed tax liabilities (while preserving their right to contest the auditor's findings in Tax Court) by depositing the contested amount with the IRS. *Conditions:* The deposit must be made before the IRS sends a statutory notice of deficiency—a 90-day letter. The taxpayer must say in writing that the payment is "a deposit in the nature of a cash bond." *Drawback:* If the taxpayer wins in court, the IRS doesn't have to pay interest on the refunded deposit.

Source: IRS Revenue Procedure 82-51.

> "Audited taxpayers can stop interest from building up on proposed tax liabilities (while preserving their right to contest the auditor's findings in Tax Court) by depositing the contested amount with the IRS."

What Do You Do If You Can't Pay Your Taxes?

Can the IRS put you in jail because you owe it money and have failed to pay, even though the debt has been outstanding for years? The answer is no. Unless you fraudulently conceal your assets or otherwise conspire to beat the government out of its money, no crime has been committed merely because you can't afford to pay your taxes.

The best way to approach the situation of having fallen behind in the payment of taxes is to respond immediately to all notices sent you requesting payment. Make every attempt to speak to someone at the IRS and follow up the conversation with a confirming letter. If the liability is no more than $10,000 and certain conditions are met, the IRS must give you an installment agreement to pay your liability in full within three years. If the liability is more, the IRS has discretion to enter into an installment agreement for payment of the outstanding taxes. Usually, such a part-payment agreement requires a down payment, followed by monthly payments over a year or 18 months. If you fail to comply with the terms of the part-payment agreement, which also requires that all current taxes be paid on time, the agreement becomes void and your property is then subject to levy seizure.

The best time to try to get the IRS to offer you an installment agreement is at the beginning of the collection process. If you have ignored IRS attempts to work out an arrangement and it is now at your door with a Notice of Seizure, it is extremely unlikely that a part-payment agreement will be offered.

Advantage of Informal Payment Arrangements

Entering into an informal arrangement to pay your tax over a number of months may be the way to buy extra time from the IRS. Unless you're eligible for the guaranteed installment payment agreement, the Collection Division has a formal procedure whereby a taxpayer must submit a financial statement and formally request permission to pay his or her tax liability in installments over a period of time. If your financial statement shows that you own assets, the IRS will generally request that you sell them. By avoiding the formal route of an official installment plan, you may be able to gain the time you need to gather enough money together to pay the tax bill without having to sell or liquidate assets you would rather keep. *Suggestion:* Tell the revenue officer that you will pay at least 40% of the bill immediately and the balance in equal payments over two or three months. His initial reaction may be negative, but his bark may be worse than his bite. Give him the down payment anyway. He will privately be happy that your case can be closed in so short a time without extra work on his part.

> "If you have assets and no income, there is nothing the IRS can levy. [This provides] an opportunity to discuss an Offer in Compromise."

Payment Strategy

The collection division usually holds all the cards in negotiations with taxpayers who owe the IRS money. But you may be able to gain some bargaining power by using a technique that has worked well in the past. *Real case:* A client owed the IRS more than $100,000. His accountant came into the revenue officer's office with a $25,000 check made payable to the IRS. He put the check on the agent's desk and said, "It's yours—just let my client pay the rest in reasonable installments." A large up-front payment has a real impact. Most revenue officers won't want to see it slip through their fingers.

Buying Time

Just because a case has been assigned to the Collection Division, it does not necessarily mean that collection activity will begin right away. In a great many cases enforcement action will not start until after the taxpayer has failed to respond to a series of letters from the Collection Division requesting payment. Even after personal contact has been made by a revenue officer, it is still possible to squeeze out a few more months before you are in serious jeopardy of losing your house and business. The way you can really get in trouble with the IRS is to completely ignore the Collection Division. Sooner or later, time will run out.

Negotiating a Settlement When You Owe Money

The first step in negotiating a settlement of taxes owed is to provide the IRS with a current financial statement. Without a statement it can verify, the IRS will not even consider a settlement. What should you do if you don't want the IRS to know about certain assets you own? Just don't furnish the financial statement. It's better to offer no statement at all than offer one that is misleading or fraudulent.

If the IRS already knows about all of your assets, and there is no disadvantage in providing a financial statement, then go ahead and submit the statement. The IRS will be interested in knowing how much money you receive each month, how much is spent, and where. When you complete the personal living expense portion of the form, it is generally a good idea to arrange for some money to be left over each month to pay taxes. The IRS is more inclined to go along with a part-payment offer if it feels confident there is money available to make the agreement work.

If you have assets and no income, there is nothing the IRS can levy. If you are in this desperate a predicament, it does provide an opportunity to discuss an Offer in Compromise with the IRS.

An Offer in Compromise is a little-publicized procedure whereby the IRS will accept a one-time payment of as little as 10¢ for each $1 owed in settlement of your tax debt. If the IRS feels it will receive more money from you in the long run by entering into an Offer in Compromise and a collat-

NEW TRAPS IN DEALING WITH THE IRS

The IRS announced in 1996 that it was going to suspend indefinitely the full-scale Taxpayer Compliance Measurement Program audits, where information used as guidelines for ordinary audits is gathered.

Now the agency will probably elicit the same information piecemeal in its ongoing audit programs. *Result:* Taxpayers should be more careful about how they conduct themselves during audits. Becoming familiar with the various types of IRS agents and learning how to deal with them is crucial.

Revenue Agents

To qualify as a revenue agent, IRS employees must have an undergraduate degree in accounting. They typically work in the field auditing corporations, other businesses and wealthy individuals. *Contrast:* While correspondence audits (initiated by mail) are limited to the issues described in the letter, revenue agents are responsible for auditing a taxpayer's entire return.

Caution: Taxpayers can represent themselves before revenue agents if the issue is *factual,* but not when the issue is *technical. Example:* Providing documentation related to your interest expense is factual. Calculating the interest deduction arising from residential mortgage interest as well as interest on taxable and nontaxable investments is technical.

New development: Most revenue agents use the Market Segment Specialization Program (MSSP) to guide

their audits. The MSSP offers detailed guidelines for auditing various types of businesses, focusing mostly on discovering unreported income. *Example:* The MSSP instructs agents auditing self-service laundries to check the business's water bill to determine the volume of business being done. So far, more than 30 types of businesses have been completed and another 60 to 75 are in various stages of completion. *(Editor's note:* At present, 24 different audit technique guides can be purchased from the government.)

Important: Always understand what a revenue agent is requesting. This should be written down on Form IDR *(Information Document Request),* which outlines what the agent wants to see—and when. Too often, communication problems spring up between agents and taxpayers—and agents will never turn down any information that they are offered. *Strategy:* Revenue agents

work on many audits simultaneously and tend to manage them by moving from one to another. Monitor how current the agent is on your case. He or she could be tending to other, higher-priority audits. The result is that you are asked to extend the statute of limitations.

Doing so is never good. *Reasons:* Corroborating witnesses could disappear, records could get lost, and the interest you owe continues to build up until you pay the disputed tax.

At the end of the audit, you will receive a revenue agent's report that states the issues, the amount of the deduction or income in question, and the tax due. *Options:* You can sign Form 870 and be billed for the taxes. If you want to appeal the agent's decision, you can take the case to the appellate division.

Source: *Pete J. Medina, principal and tax consultant on practice and procedure before the IRS, Ernst & Young, LLP, 787 Seventh Ave., New York, NY 10019.*

eral agreement (an agreement whereby you agree to pay a certain percentage of your income for five to 10 years), it may agree to the compromise.

The best chance of successfully using the Offer in Compromise route is when the tax debt has been on the books for a number of years. The IRS must be convinced that conventional collection procedures won't work. That's why a relatively recent tax obligation will not be settled this way. But if the IRS has had a chance to collect and hasn't succeeded, it is likely to accept your compromise offer. *Here's a suggestion you should bear in mind:* Always use a tax pro to get you through the Offer in Compromise procedure.

Source: How to Beat the IRS *by Ms. X, Esq., former IRS agent, Boardroom Books, Greenwich, CT.*

Ask the IRS to Remove a Late-Filing Penalty

The IRS will assess a late-filing penalty of 5% per month (up to a maximum of 25%) of the unpaid tax if your income tax return is filed late and no extension has been granted. Many times the IRS will be willing to abate the penalty if you can establish reasonable cause for the late filing. Being physically or emotionally incapacitated at the time your tax return was due is generally considered reasonable cause. *Another approach:* Take the position that your late filing was an isolated event in an otherwise perfect record of compliance—you always file on time. And appeal to the IRS that the imposition of a late-filing penalty will cause you to suffer an unnecessary financial hardship.

Quick Way to Close an Offer With the IRS

The revenue officer who solicits an Offer in Compromise will generally never tell you how much he or she will consider acceptable. He or she wants the taxpayer to offer as much money as possible, then the agent will ask for more money. *Strategy:* Follow the IRS guidelines and offer the lowest amount possible. Then, when the revenue officer complains, volunteer to increase your offer by 10% on the condition that he or she will recommend that the offer be accepted.

Source: Ms. X, a former IRS agent, who is still well connected.

Tax Fraud: Who Gets Caught?

Executives, lawyers, doctors and other high-income professionals are accused of tax fraud more often than the general population is. Charges stem from IRS challenges that there was willful or intentional failure to file, understatement of income, or claiming of fraudulent deductions. About one out of every five charges brought by the IRS in one recent year involved a professional or business executive. The average claim for back taxes is nearly $70,000.

How the IRS Gets Inside Information

● **The IRS has the power to summon whatever information may be relevant to the audit of your tax return.** The most commonly summoned records are bank and brokerage firm records. But the courts have also ordered a department store to turn over to the IRS copies of a taxpayer's monthly statements. Presumably, these spending records would help the examiners determine whether the taxpayer was reporting all his or her income by enabling them to estimate the taxpayer's cash flow and extent of wealth.

Source: U.S. vs. Lazarus Department Stores, DCSD, Ohio.

● **The auditor can ask to see car repair bills,** even though you took the IRS allowed-per-mile deduction and didn't itemize car expenses. *Reason:* Repair bills often show the odometer reading on the car being serviced. By comparing readings at various dates, the auditor gets an idea of how far the car has been driven.

Suppose a bill in January showed an odometer reading of 10,000 miles and a December bill showed only 20,000. A taxpayer would have a hard time claiming a deduction for 50,000 miles driven during the year.

● **Some of the country's biggest data marketing firms have refused to participate** in the IRS's scheme to track down cheats by matching "lifestyle" information collected by the companies with IRS taxpayer lists. The companies say the information they gather couldn't help the IRS because it can't accurately predict a taxpayer's income.

● **Local federal attorneys have been given authority to seek search warrants** in connection with criminal tax cases without prior approval of the Justice Department in Washington.

The number of warrants is expected to rise markedly above the handful that are currently issued each year. *Reason for the policy:* The dramatic rise in the number of fraudulent tax-avoidance schemes.

● **The IRS was investigating a taxpayer and ordered his bank to produce the records of his account.** The bank refused because it was a joint account, and the IRS hadn't sent notice to the account's co-owner. The District Court ruled for the bank, and the IRS appealed. *Court of Appeals:* There's no requirement that the account's co-owner be warned of the disclosure. Produce the records.

Source: First Bank, CA-2. No. 83-6350.

● **Informant danger.** If a friend, relative or employer turns on you, steals your personal financial records, and delivers them to the IRS, there's nothing you can do to keep the IRS from using them against you.

Key: The IRS didn't take the records from you illegally; the person you trusted did.

Source: Resmondo vs. U.S., DCSD Fla, No. 79-8166.

● **Pressure is on Caribbean tax havens to provide the IRS with criminal and civil tax information.** *The bait:* Liberal rules will permit business expense deductions for people attending conventions in Caribbean countries that cooperate. *Eligible islands include:* Anguilla, the Bahamas, Barbados, Cayman Islands, Grenada, Netherlands Antilles, British Virgin Islands.

Source: Interest and Dividend Tax Compliance Act.

Badges of Fraud

If your bank deposits far exceed your income, that is a sign, or badge, of fraud to an IRS agent. Or someone reports only $15,000 in income but drives

Negligence or Tax Fraud?

Failure to report income deposited in a bank could be considered careless. That is punishable, at most, by a 5% negligence penalty. But when the omitted income represented deposits made in a bank in a different state, one court regarded the omission as a fraudulent, willful attempt to conceal income.

Source: Candella et al. vs. United States, USDC, E. Dist. WI.

a new Mercedes and wears pure silk suits. They are driving and wearing badges of fraud. Anything indicating a lifestyle beyond apparent means, or any sudden, substantial increase in net worth (assets less liabilities) is a badge of fraud. Frequently, there are honest reasons for these conditions. Included are inheritance, borrowing, successful investments, appreciation of assets, and nontaxable windfalls, such as an award of damages in a lawsuit. *More:* There is a constant flow of information from IRS informants. *(Editor's note:* The IRS cannot conduct a "financial status audit" just because your lifestyle doesn't jibe with your income unless there is a reasonable indication of unreported income.)

Best defense: Think like the IRS. Anticipate questions. Keep good records. Prepare cost of living statements and net worth statements periodically and compare them with those of prior years. Be sure you can explain large bank deposits and sudden increases in your net worth.

Warning: If you ever find yourself being questioned by an IRS special agent (criminal investigator), hire a qualified accountant and/or tax attorney for professional assistance. This is a sign that the IRS is serious about possible fraud.

Source: George S. Alberts, former director of the Albany and Brooklyn IRS districts.

What the IRS Is Really Looking for

All IRS enforcement personnel—auditors, revenue agents, special agents, revenue officers and estate tax attorneys—are trained to detect possible fraud by taxpayers. The prize they're all looking for is *substantial unreported income.* If they find it, they will refer the case to the IRS's Criminal Investigation Division.

For Businesspeople Only

4

What Should Be in Your Employment Contract?

Movement from job to job has become today's prevailing career strategy. One result of this change has been the development of increasingly complex employment contracts aimed at helping companies hold on to and motivate managers, and at protecting executives' benefits and even their jobs.

Who Benefits From a Contract?

Employment contracts offer advantages and disadvantages to both employer and executive, but overall, a well-rounded agreement favors the interests of the employee. Here are the pros and cons.

Disadvantages to employer:

● **Generally, employers don't like employment contracts for managers,** since they limit the freedom to fire employees at will. The cost to an employer of terminating the contractual relationship can be steep, measured in terms of severance payments.

● **Employers resent broad use of employment contracts** because they establish precedents.

● **Employers fear that executives protected** by contracts may not show the desired amount of drive.

Advantages to employer:

● **A contract locks in the executive for the life** of the agreement at the terms specified.

● **Annual bargaining and divisiveness over salary** and bonuses are eliminated.

● **Contracts may protect the employer** and contain a covenant that the employee will not compete for a specified period after leaving the organization.

● **The employee's use of confidential or secret information** (important in certain industries: fashion, high technology, etc.) may be barred.

Disadvantages to employee:

● **The employee is tied to the company for the life of the contract** (although if another company wants the employee badly enough, it will offer compensation for the loss in the form of up-front bonuses, enhanced benefits, accelerated vesting in the pension plan, etc.).

> " **Employers resent broad use of employment contracts because they establish precedents, [and they fear] that executives protected by contracts may not show the desired amount of drive.** "

● **Noncompete clauses may be enforced,** although courts tend to look askance at these provisions if they are too restrictive of the employee's ability to earn his or her livelihood.

Typical Contract Elements

● **Term.** This clause spells out when the contract is to begin and end. Most employment agreements run three to five years.

● **Duties.** Description of the job and status. This clause is important, as it would be the basis of any employer's claim of termination "for cause." It is often very general, but it should be specific.

● **Compensation.** The focal point of most agreements. Usually spells out minimum salary without limitation on the upside amount, and includes bonuses, stock options, etc.

● **Vacation.** How long each year, whether it can be accrued and the availability of payment in lieu of vacation.

● **Benefits.** Life and health insurance, retirement plans, etc. Can include one-time relocation expenses; can call for an up-front bonus for signing the contract, for example.

● **Place of performance.** Spells out where the employee will be performing his or her duties (corporate headquarters, subsidiary or field offices, city, state and country).

● **Termination.** Under what circumstances parties can discontinue the agreement.

● **Severance.** What compensation is due an executive upon firing. May include special provisions (e.g., "golden parachute" package, triggered automatically in the event of a change of ownership).

● **In event of death.** Can provide that the "fruits of the agreement" are assured for the employee's heirs if he or she dies and for those persons entitled to receive them if the employee is incapacitated.

● **Disability provision.** Can specify that disability of the employee does not constitute breach of the contract.

● **Options of perks.** For example, an expense

Your Perk Shopping List

The following is a list of perks commonly offered to valued executives by American corporations.

Perks are special by nature, and you might think of one or two more you'd like—and that are appropriate to your situation. Remember, when negotiating for perks, that the most important ones permit the accumulation of wealth. They allow you to build for the future rather than just live off your paycheck.

✔ Signing bonuses (usually 10% to 15% of base salary).
✔ Deferred compensation plans.
✔ Discounts on products or services.
✔ Educational programs.
✔ Employment contracts.
✔ Large expense account.
✔ Health club membership.
✔ Entertainment allowances.
✔ Incentive stock options.
✔ Group life insurance.
✔ Added life, health and disability benefits.
✔ Loans or mortgages at low or no interest.
✔ Luncheon club memberships.
✔ Medical expense reimbursement.
✔ Lavish offices.
✔ Special parking privileges.
✔ Personal computers.
✔ Personal financial, legal and tax services.
✔ Preretirement counseling.
✔ Private secretaries.
✔ Resort or convention accommodations.
✔ Supplemental retirement plans.
✔ Severance payment plans.
✔ Tickets to theater or sports events.
✔ First-class travel.
✔ Extra vacation time.
✔ Use of company aircraft.
✔ Executive apartments and suites.
✔ Company-provided cars (with or without chauffeurs).
✔ Country club memberships.

Source: Andrew Sherwood, founder, chairman and CEO of the nation's largest full-service human resources management consulting firm, Goodrich & Sherwood Company, 521 Fifth Ave., New York, NY 10017.

account (standard), limousine, club membership, financial counseling, consulting provisions, noncompete provision, arbitration clause, purchase of old and/or new residence.

● **Amendments.** Provide for continuing the agreement unchanged for an additional period.

● **Mutual assent.** The best practice is for both parties of the employment contract to sign the document.

Source: Sandra E. Rapoport, attorney and managing consultant with William M. Mercer-Meidinger, Inc., 1211 Avenue of the Americas, New York, NY 10036. Her specialty is consulting to management on labor and employment relations, including reductions-in-force, communications strategy during labor negotiations, executive compensation, employment contracts and equal employment planning.

Salary Negotiating Tactics

Negotiating salary with a prospective employer is, and probably always will be, the most awkward phase of the hiring process. Keep in mind, however, that you will probably never again have as good an opportunity to get what you want from your employer. As in any negotiation, you cannot hope to succeed unless you know what you want and what you can realistically hope to get.

Proven Strategies

The single most important bargaining tactic is to hold off the salary discussion until you know you have the job. This swings considerable weight in your direction. *Explanation:* Once you are offered the job, it usually means that other candidates have been disregarded. Most companies don't pursue runner-up applicants if their primary choice turns them down. Further, a company knows that if it must start over to fill a position, it will probably find less-qualified people on the second pass through the marketplace. The company wants *you,* and that gives you an advantage when the question of money comes up.

If the prospective employer raises the salary question early in the interview process, do your best to evade the issue. A good way to handle this is to mention your current salary, then add, "I'm really more interested in the career opportunities for me here."

Once you've been offered the job (and assuming you've been able to delay the salary question), present your salary demands with confidence. After all, you're the one they've chosen.

Trap: Don't blow your new job by asking for the moon. There has to be some give and take on both sides of the desk. Going for every last nickel can only create resentment and an adversarial atmosphere, which is not what you want when starting a new position.

If you and your new employer reach a true standoff on the salary question, and you're unemployed, try this novel approach: Make your employer an offer he or she can't refuse. Offer to work for a month at the minimum wage. At the end of the month, your boss has the option either to fire you or to give you the salary you are asking for. Chances are the firm won't take you up on your offer to work at the minimum wage, and may agree to your initial salary demands.

Source: *Robert Half, founder of Robert Half International, Inc., and Accountemps (Box 3000, Menlo Park, CA 94025), employment specialists in the financial, accounting and information-systems fields. His most recent book is* Finding, Hiring and Keeping the Best Employees, *John Wiley & Sons.*

Raising the Odds in Salary Negotiations

Most executives pride themselves on their negotiating skills in complex, high-pressure bargaining sessions. Yet it is not unusual for normally polished performers to falter badly when the issue being negotiated is as basic and personal as pay or status.

The temptation to hire a proxy to represent you in raise negotiations can be almost overwhelming. Unfortunately, this is one situation in which no one can do the job as effectively as you can. In fact, the mere presence of a third-party representative will usually create an adversarial situation.

Basic Strategies

If you dread salary discussions, you'll find that by applying business strategies to raise negotiations, you can turn a negative prospect into a positive outcome. The basics of these strategies never change.

● **Be fully informed in advance on the details of your own desired result** and on the nuances of the situation of the other party.

● **Ensure the strength of your position before you enter the arena;** you cannot negotiate from weakness.

● **Apply the same rules you would use in a business situation:** Both parties must perceive and achieve benefits; avoid cornering the other party or being cornered—ultimatums are a mistake; and begin by being sure the needs of the other party are understood.

Two Realities

Getting the raise or title you want involves taking a very close look at two realities. First, you. What do you do best? What do you enjoy doing most? What do you want to learn to do? Under what conditions do you wish to work? What are you aiming for in the company—or outside of it?

Second, the reality of your company and the position you hold in it. How is your company positioned in the market? What is its need for new products? How important is service to the buyer? Is the company in a field with growth opportunity?

What is the importance of your present function to the profitability of the company? (In the case of a not-for-profit, what is your role in the value of its service?) How is your boss positioned politically in the organization?

When there's a good match between the needs and wants of both parties, the probability of raises and promotions rises dramatically. Successful negotiations therefore rest on informing yourself of these two realities in advance.

Swing Into Action

Make the first move. Rarely do people get the best opportunities by waiting to be asked—initiate an appraisal discussion. Propose a new product or service, with an appropriate raise and change in title for you incorporated in the proposal. Volunteer your services if you can help meet a need expressed by the company.

Present your proposal with company politics in mind. Know who is politically disposed to accept or reject you and your ideas. Peers who may feel threatened, or superiors who may be displaced, should be sidestepped. The party with whom you negotiate must be able to see the overall benefit of your actions.

Always begin negotiations orally, rather than with written communiqués. This enables you to test reactions, modify your proposal, if necessary, and follow it up in writing. Since timing is very important, a conversation will aid your judgment. Then persevere. One turndown doesn't mean a permanent no.

Alternative Rewards

Consider a performance-based raise or bonus. If resources for an early monetary reward seem scarce, don't overlook the long-term monetary value of a more elevated title should you choose to leave the company. At least get that. You can also arrange for other rewards, such as time off, a better working space, etc. If you know in advance what you want, you'll be able to present your case as to how these rewards are appropriate to your responsibilities.

Be wary of asking your superior for more than the situation warrants, however. It may be tempting or even easy to do this if you appear indispensable to a project, but ultimately you will suffer for it.

Finally, be willing and prepared to move out of your present organization if your needs aren't met over time. If you don't see yourself as able to move, you can't negotiate as a free agent.

Source: *Nella G. Barkley, president and founding member, Crystal-Barkley Corporation, 152 Madison Ave., New York, NY 10016. She was formerly a private consultant to industry and nonprofit organizations on management planning and start-up projects. She has completed the Advanced Management Program at Harvard University's School of Business Administration.*

Alternatives to a Straight Salary

Tax-favored fringe benefits can reduce the after-tax cost of compensation to both the company and its employees. Review the company's compensation program to make sure it is making the best use of fringe benefits.

No Special-Break Perks

The first thing to realize is that even perks that don't receive favorable treatment under the Tax Code often can be provided to employees in a manner that provides tax benefits for both the employees and the company.

That's because even when an item provided by the company is *taxable* to an employee, the cost of the tax may be *much less* than the expense the employee would incur to buy the same item using his or her own money.

Also, the company may be able to *deduct* the cost

of the benefit as a compensation expense even if the item would not be deductible by the individual. The deduction reduces the item's cost, and the savings can be shared with the employee so both parties can come out ahead.

Both the company and the employee may do well by arranging a compensation package that pays less in salary and more in benefits—even if the benefits are fully taxable.

Taxable benefits that may be provided include:
- **Investment counseling.**
- **Legal counseling.**
- **Electronic equipment**—car phones, computers, fax machines, etc.
- **Entertainment.**
- **Insurance** (in addition to $50,000 of tax-free group term life).
- **Interest-free loans** are another often overlooked, but potentially advantageous, benefit. An employee who receives an interest-free loan from the business has income in the amount of the unpaid interest—but again, paying the resulting tax may be a lot less costly than paying the interest itself.

Caution: Shareholders taking loans from the business must make sure that the IRS won't view the loans as disguised taxable dividends.

Tax Benefits

Of course, even better than taxable benefits are benefits that are *tax-free* and *tax-favored. Consider the following opportunities:*

- **Adoption assistance.** Up to $5,000 ($6,000 for a child with special needs) can be provided to employees tax-free under a company program. Limit: The full exclusion applies only to those with an Adjusted Gross Income (AGI) below $75,000 (with a phase-out for income up to $115,000).
- **Child care.** Up to $5,000 of child-care expenses can be provided to employees tax-free, through company-provided child-care facilities or a company program that pays for child-care costs.
- **Discounts.** The company may provide its products or services to employees at a discounted cost.

Limits to these benefits:

● **When products are sold to employees,** the discount may not exceed the company's "gross profit percentage" on the product—meaning, in general, that the product cannot be sold at less than cost.

● **When a service is provided to employees,** the discount may not exceed 20% of the normal sale price.

Also, no tax is due in certain situations where a service can be provided to employees at no additional cost to the company.

● **Education assistance.** Company-provided education assistance may be tax-favored in two different ways: 1) Education costs that are job-related remain deductible by the company that pays them, and tax-free to the employee who utilizes them. 2) Up to $5,250 of company-paid education expenses per employee annually, even when the education is *not* job-related. Costs must be paid under terms of a written company plan. This break expires on May 31, 2000, unless Congress extends it.

● **Commuting subsidies.** Employers can help employees reduce the cost of traveling to work.

Editor's note: Employers can offer a choice between cash and the commuting subsidies. *Employees choosing the subsidies are not taxed as follows:*

● **Free parking,** with a value of up to $175 per month in 1999, can be provided to employees completely tax-free, even if it is provided only to selected employees.

● **Transit passes** and subsidies worth up to $65 per month in 1999 may be provided to employees to help cover the cost of commuting on public transportation.

● **Van pools,** set up to provide transportation to and from work, are tax-free up to a value of $65 per employee per month in 1999.

● **A company-provided vehicle that is used to drive to and from work may be valued at only $3 per day,** provided that certain rules are met, including that employees are not allowed to use the vehicle for personal purposes other than commuting.

Deferred-Compensation Rule

Deferred-compensation agreements make sense for executives, because interest on the deferred compensation accumulates tax-free until finally paid.

Rule of thumb: An arrangement is attractive if your company credits you with interest equal to at least the going rate on Treasury bills. **Drawback:** You have to rely on the company's staying solvent.

● **Insurance.** Up to $50,000 of group term life insurance per employee can be provided tax-free under a nondiscriminatory plan. And additional insurance may be a bargain because employees are taxed only on its value as set under IRS tables.

Another popular tax-favored insurance arrangement is *split-dollar* insurance. *How it works:*

The company buys a cash value insurance policy for an executive, retaining the right to recover premiums paid out of insurance proceeds. Thus, if the executive dies after the company has paid $60,000 of premiums on a $1 million policy, the executive's heirs would receive $940,000 and the company $60,000.

After a few years, the policy's cash value grows to the point where the cash value equals the amount of premiums paid to date by the company —and the policy dividends are sufficient to cover future premiums.

The executive can then *borrow out* funds to repay the company for the premiums it has paid. Thereafter an executive retains ownership of the policy at no further cash cost.

● **Working condition fringes.** The company can deduct expenses paid on behalf of an employee if they would have been deductible on the employee's personal return.

The company's payment of such items can save employees taxes because often employees' potential deductions for such items will be *limited* by the rule that includes employee business expenses among miscellaneous expenses, and allows their deduction only to the extent they exceed 2% of Adjusted Gross Income. And, of course, employees who do not itemize deductions get no expense deductions.

● **De minimis expenses.** Also tax-free to employees are expenses that are so small it is "unreasonable or impractical" to account for them—i.e., cab fare.

Source: David J. Kautter, partner and national director of compensation and benefits tax services, Ernst & Young, 1225 Connecticut Ave. NW, Washington, DC 20036.

Executive Pension Planning

Tax law changes have had a big impact on executive pension planning—by both increasing the cost of qualified retirement programs to the company and reducing the amount of benefits that top executives can claim through such programs.

Now is the time for the company and its executives to start considering alternatives to conventional pension programs that may provide greater benefits at less cost.

The Basics

There are two basic kinds of retirement programs:

● **Pension plans,** also known as defined benefit plans. With these, an employee receives a specified annual pension payment, usually equal to a percentage of his or her salary. The company is required to make whatever contributions are necessary to pay for this benefit. *Result:* An employee can be sure of what his or her pension will be, relative to final salary, at retirement age.

● **Profit-sharing plans,** also known as defined contribution plans. Here the company's plan contributions are usually based on a percentage of an employee's salary. Whether a contribution is made in a year is often up to the employer, and thus contributions can vary from year to year. *Result:* The employee can't be sure of the specific amount of benefits he or she will receive several years from now. The value of the benefits will simply equal the amount that has accrued in his or her profit-sharing account.

A company can have both kinds of retirement programs.

Limits and Restrictions

Qualified retirement plans cannot make contributions or provide benefits over limits set by law.

● **Pension plan limits.** *Editor's note:* The maximum

benefit that can be paid out under a defined-benefit pension program is limited to $130,000 in 1999. The limit when a pension is received before age 65 is reduced to the actuarial equivalent of a pension, beginning at age 65. The formula involved is complicated, but the result can be a dramatic reduction in pension benefits. *Example:* An employee retires at age 63 and 6 months when the plan's normal retirement age is 65. Assume the limit on pensions is $130,000 a year. This employee's limit is reduced by 10%, or $13,000 ($5/9$ of 1% x 18 months). Thus the annual limit is $117,000.

● **Defined contribution limits.** The maximum contribution that can be made to a money purchase plan is 25% of compensation or $30,000; to a profit-sharing plan it is 15% of compensation, or $30,000. However, no more than $160,000 of compensation in 1999 can be taken into account in figuring contributions. So, the top contribution to a profit-sharing plan in 1999 is $24,000 (15% of $160,000).

● **Income averaging.** A person who receives a lump-sum distribution from a qualified plan can cut the tax bite by forward averaging—treating the distribution as if it were received over a period of several years. *Special benefit:* A person who was over age 50 before January 1, 1986, can choose to have a distribution taxed under either the 10-year rule or the five-year rule. Usually, 10-year averaging will result in a lower tax bill. *Editor's note:* Figure the tax using both methods and use the one resulting in the lower tax.

Note: After 1999, five-year averaging will no longer apply. Only those born before 1936 will be able to use 10-year averaging.

● **Early payouts.** In recent years many executives have used their retirement programs as investment accounts. Often they'd leave the company at an early age, take a lump-sum distribution of benefits and use the benefit money to make further investments (such as the financing of a new business).

Trap: An executive who leaves the company and receives a distribution of plan benefits before age 59 ½ may find his or her benefits subject to a 10% penalty tax. *Exceptions:* Since this penalty doesn't apply to payments made as a result of formal early retirement at or after age 55, companies can amend their qualified programs to allow for this. Also, the penalty doesn't apply to annuity payments, death or disability payments, or amounts that are transferred directly or rolled over into an IRA.

Alternatives

● **Nonqualified plans.** These are arrangements under which the company agrees to provide benefits to key executives on an individual basis. Nonqualified plans are not subject to the distribution rules and limits that apply to qualified plans. And since a plan can be designed to meet an executive's specific needs, it's likely to be more valuable to him or her.

Some pitfalls:

Employee benefits aren't funded by a trust, as is the case with qualified plans. The employee's benefits are part of the company's general liability. And even seemingly secure businesses can incur sudden unexpected hardships.

The company can't deduct employee benefits until they are actually paid. Deductions may be available more quickly with a qualified plan.

The company must be careful not to provide nonqualified benefits to too many employees, or the

HOW TO GET FIRED PROFITABLY

Anyone can get fired. This risk is an integral part of work life. Like any other normal risk, it should be factored into your own long-range life and career plans and reduced to manageable proportions by intelligent planning. In combination with a little assertiveness, realistic planning allows you to turn a potential disaster into a positive opportunity.

Preparing for risk allows you to be alert to any early warning signs. And, unlikely as it may sound, reading the handwriting on the wall early gives you a substantial measure of control over the progress of events. Most important, it gives you time to make preparations to move smoothly on to another—and better—job or into your own business. (Note: Don't concentrate all your attention on finding a new job; take whatever time is necessary to familiarize yourself with company policy on termination and with your rights under the law.)

Making a Forceful Exit

You have picked up warning signs and have begun your preparations. Here's

an approach that may well turn the situation to your advantage: Preempt the decision by arranging a meeting and calmly asserting that you have read the signs and would like to make things easier for all concerned by asking for your own dismissal—under certain terms, of course—thus saving emotional wear and tear on all sides.

It does not take as much courage to do this as you might think—just hard-headed realism. In some cases, the reaction may be quite surprising. The impression you create by being very professional about the situation may stimulate your superior to revise earlier opinions of you. Once in a while this can lead to a real opening in which you can (if you wish) offer your own proposal as to how you could serve that same employer far better in a position much more to your liking. Your proposal might just be accepted—it has happened.

If, instead, your proposed self-dismissal is accepted, these are terms you should negotiate for (as needed):

● **Full severance pay.**

● **Use of corporate "outplacement."**
● **Use of your office for several months.**
● **Secretarial and other support help.**
● **A recommendation** (specific form to be mutually agreed upon).
● **Opportunities to meet other potential employers.**
● **Permanent or temporary use of your car or other perks.**

You may not win on every point, but you will probably win on a significant number. Realize that corporations will go to surprising lengths to avoid the unpleasantness associated with terminating highly placed employees—and make this work for you.

Source: The late John C. Crystal, founder of Crystal-Barkley Corporation, 152 Madison Ave., New York, NY 10016.

nondiscrimination rules of the pension law may come into play. The rules here are complicated, so expert advice is a must.

401(k) plans: These are now perhaps the most attractive company plans. They let executives take up to $10,000 of salary in 1999 on a tax-deferred basis and deposit it in a retirement account. (The maximum contribution is indexed annually for inflation.) This is even more valuable now that IRA deductions are not permitted for high-income executives.

IRAs: Fully deductible IRA contributions are available to persons not covered by qualified plans, and to persons who are covered by qualified plans but who report less than $30,000 of Adjusted Gross Income ($50,000 on a joint return). And an IRA contribution is among the best tax-sheltered investments. *Overlooked:* Persons who do not qualify for deductible IRA contributions can still make nondeductible contributions to an IRA account and accrue investment earnings in the account that will not be subject to tax until withdrawn. *(Editor's note:* Such IRA contributions, while not deductible, allow earnings to build up on a tax-free basis if certain conditions are met. Thus, IRAs can continue to serve as a tax-shelter device even for high-income individuals.

● **Annuities and life insurance products.** With an annuity, you make payments now that will be invested and used to fund annual payments to you at some future date. With life insurance, your invested funds increase the cash value of your policy. In each case, you obtain tax-shelter benefits because earnings on your investment are not taxed until you withdraw them. With many insurance products you can borrow against the earnings, thus obtaining the use of the money tax-free.

Source: David Kautter, partner, Ernst & Young LLP, National Tax Department, 1225 Connecticut Ave., NW, Washington, DC 20036.

Borrowing Against Your Retirement Plan

● **Loans limited to $50,000.** *(Editor's note:* For account balances up to $20,000, the loan limit is one-half of vested benefits. For account balances of $20,000 or more, the limit is one-half of vested benefits, but no more than a $50,000 loan.) All loans must be paid off at a level rate over a period of five years or less and bear a reasonable rate of interest. Loans with a longer term are allowed only in connection with the financing of a principal residence.

● **No interest deduction is allowed on loans extended** to the company's key employees.

● **No interest deduction is allowed on loans secured** by an employee's elective 401(k) plan account.

● **No interest deduction is allowed** in any case on loans made for personal (consumer) purposes.

Trap: While borrowing from a plan is easy to arrange, it should be used as a loan of last resort. Taking a loan costs you the opportunity to build up tax-deferred earnings.

Editor's note: You may be permitted under the terms of your retirement plan to borrow from your account for any purpose. Be aware of tax law restrictions on these loans. Failure to observe them will cause the loan to be treated as a taxable distribution (also subject to penalty if you're under age 59½).

Source: William E. Offutt III, partner, Grant Thornton, 1850 M St. NW, Washington, DC 20036.

When an Employment Agreement Goes Sour

Being one of the growing number of executives who demand that the employer "put it in writing," you have a written employment agreement. At the time the contract was signed, everything was rosy. Neither party thought the termination provisions of the contract would come into play. But now the relationship has gone sour. What do you do?

● **Review your employment contract.** Some people make the mistake of merely looking over the severance clause, which specifies what the company must pay if the employer terminates the agreement. Look instead for loopholes the employer might use to withhold severance pay or force you into a bad bargaining position. The key lies in the "for cause" provision, which describes the conditions under which you can be held in violation of the contract, making it unnecessary for the employer to pay you anything.

● **Fulfill the contract provisions meticulously.** Your job is in jeopardy. Do not give the employer any pretext for refusing your severance pay. Follow the terms of the agreement in detail. Work a full day. Make all meetings. Don't violate any company policy, major or trivial.

● **Collect proof.** Build a file that gives evidence of your service to the company: Appreciative memos, reports, documents showing you have achieved goals, etc.—whatever you can get that shows the employer has recognized your worth to the organization. Then, if told you've been doing a poor job, produce the evidence.

● **Request an evaluation of your work.** Go on record as giving your boss a chance to criticize your work. Send a memo reviewing your progress on a particular project. Add something like, "As I see it, this fulfills all the conditions of the assignment, and substantially achieves the stated goals." The worst that can happen is that your employer disagrees. If your document is accepted, actively or tacitly, you have evidence that you've been doing a reasonably good job.

None of this is calculated to keep your head from rolling. But it can help you get the full severance pay and benefits called for in your contract.

Planning for the Worst

If you're lucky enough to be reading this before the crunch and you don't have a contract, ask for one. This may be easier than you think—if the company values your work and wants to keep you around. Negotiate a good severance agreement and a tight "for cause" provision. Some such provisions are drawn so broadly as to cover almost anything: " 'For cause' shall mean failure to carry out assigned duties…"

Make this provision in your contract as narrow and specific as possible—e.g., "The company may terminate this agreement for cause in the event of gross, repeated and demonstrable failure to carry out reasonable instructions, if such failure is not remediated within a reasonable time after written notice…"

Also include a clause that submits disagreements over the contract to binding arbitration. This will keep you from being forced to negotiate your severance under the threat of a long and costly lawsuit.

An employment contract can be the best protection against being fired with minimum severance. It is much better to have a strong contract than to try to make up for weaknesses in the contract when the agreement goes sour—or to have no contract at all.

Source: *John Tarrant, 167 S. Compo Rd., Westport, CT 06880, author of more than a dozen business books, including* Perks and Parachutes— Negotiating Your Executive Employment Contract; Drucker: The Man Who Invented the Corporate Society; *and* How to Negotiate a Raise.

Do What You Really Want to Do

It's never too late to do what you want. The biggest barrier is not age, but fear. As one woman who went back to college in her 80s said, "I'm going to be 88 in five years no matter what I do—so I might as well do what I want to!"

Getting Ready: First Steps

Few of us embrace change with open arms—but we can gear ourselves up to make the most of it by taking some important preparatory steps:

● **Be willing to be a beginner.** One of the defining characteristics of change is that we don't know what's coming next or how to handle it when it happens. Instead of getting upset by this fact, *get curious.*

Let go of your preconceptions, especially those about your capabilities and limitations.

When your life is changing, you will not know exactly what to do. Let uncertainty keep you open to a variety of exciting possibilities.

● **Spend time with yourself.** Build into your life—every day, if possible—some kind of uninterrupted time to reflect, to acknowledge frustrations, to celebrate victories—and to dream. You'll need this emotional compass to steer by as you advance toward your goals.

● **Recognize the gifts of age.** Far from holding you back, age can propel you toward what you want. No matter what you've done with your life, you can't reach midlife without accumulating a great deal of knowledge, experience and understanding of the world.

This information and wisdom puts you well ahead of younger people who may have aspirations but lack perspective.

Self-Discovery Exercises

Some people have no problem getting in touch with their dreams—they easily remember their youthful fantasies of raising horses or learning to sail or playing the clarinet.

Others may have had to spend so many years doing what was expected of them that they aren't sure anymore what they'd love to be doing. If this sounds like you, try some of the following exercises:

● **What did you like to do at age five, 10, 15, etc.?** Jot down the activities you remember enjoying most at various stages of your life, using five-year intervals to focus your thoughts.

Write whatever pops into your mind, even if it seems silly or illogical, from singing in a choir to riding a bicycle to hunting for pinecones.

> **"There's something very powerful about hearing a group of people say, "What a great idea! I have a friend (or cousin or accountant) who knows something about that—why don't you talk to her? What else do you need?"**

Return to this exercise over a period of several days—new ideas will keep occurring to you.

Don't worry if your list doesn't immediately suggest a grandiose new life direction. Over time, you'll begin to spot patterns that suggest avenues for you to explore.

● **What do you like to do now?** Again, nothing is too trivial to put on your list—you can learn a lot about yourself from even the most ordinary things.

If one of your indulgences is a particular TV show, ask yourself, *What do I relate to most in this show?* Is it that you enjoy solving puzzles? Picturing yourself in a new house? Driving down the street and having all your neighbors smile and greet you?

Each one of these elements—intellectual challenge, a new addition to the house, a better relationship with your neighbors—is something you might be able to create more of in your life right now, once you recognize the need.

Figure Out How to Get There

I don't believe people have to be self-motivated to make their dreams real. What they do need is support from other people.

When we're doing what's expected of us, support is easy to come by. But when we strike out in new directions, the people who know us are more likely than not to discourage us—after all, they're afraid of change, too! Of course, it's possible to pursue a dream on your own, but most of us need encouragement and assistance to keep us from giving up.

Where to get this support:

● **Build a network.** Networking can be formal, such as joining organizations that interest you. It can also be informal—going to lectures you read about in the paper or simply making a point of meeting many different kinds of people and finding out what they're up to.

Networking has several important purposes. The people you come in contact with may be able to give you good advice or suggest resources.

On a more basic level, meeting people who share your interests assures you that you're not crazy for wanting what you want—in fact, these folks can serve as role models for success.

● **Get a telephone buddy.** Agree to call each other regularly—say, once a week—to share ideas and progress, deal with setbacks and give each other pep talks.

● **Join or start a Success Team.*** This is a group of six to eight people who meet regularly to help each other identify their dreams and make them come true. In the 20 years since I developed this model, I've seen Success Teams make an incredible difference in many, many lives.

There's something very powerful about hearing a group of people say, "What a great idea! I have a friend (or cousin or accountant) who knows something about that—why don't you talk to her? What else do you need?"

Invite people you know to start a team with you—or put up a notice in a bookstore. Then agree to meet once a week to brainstorm, encourage each other, troubleshoot and share resources, leads and ideas.

Feed Your Soul

Whether you're ready for a big change in your life or not, start now to do what you love—at least for part of every day. Life is made up of the things you do today, and you owe it to yourself and to this planet to live at least an hour a day from your spirit.

This might be as simple as taking a walk, gardening, drawing, going for a swim, reading Shakespeare or sitting quietly and listening to the birds, but be sure to allow yourself time for whatever feeds your soul.

*For a list of Success Teams in your area, send a stamped, self-addressed envelope to: Wishcraft and Success Teams, Box 20052, Park West Station, New York, NY 10025.

Source: *Barbara Sher, a New York City–based therapist and career counselor. She is coauthor of many books on personal fulfillment, including* I Could Do Anything If I Only Knew What It Was *(Delacorte Press) and* Live the Life You Love *(Dell).*

How to Change a Job or Career After 40

When you're in your twenties, changing jobs within the same field, or even changing to another field, is relatively easy. But it gets progressively more difficult after 40. The first thing that an over-40 job changer is questioned about is his or her track record at work.

Employment agencies and personnel people will tell you that your experience and credentials are not easily transferable. So, if you stay away from the conventional system, you'll have a better chance for success.

Understanding the Realities

The usual reaction of people who are trying to change careers or jobs is simply to keep trying. If 1,000 résumés don't work, they send out 3,000. By the time they realize that this isn't getting results, they're in a syndrome of rejection and depression. And once they are in that self-defeating cycle, it's extremely difficult to escape. *A better approach:*

● **Don't even think about looking for a job** through employment agencies or personnel departments, sending résumés or answering newspaper ads. Decide beforehand to forget that route.

● **Think of yourself as a product that you have to market.** If you've been in management, you've been trained and are experienced in analyzing your company's problems. This is the time to use those abilities in analyzing your own situation.

Marketing Yourself

● **Do research and development on yourself.** You must figure out who you are, what your skills are, and what you really want to do most. This should include considerations such as where you want to live and intermediate goals versus long-term goals. See yourself as a whole person with skills, interests, and goals that may have nothing to do with your past employment. Be specific. A vague goal such as "I'd like to be a teacher" is meaningless. "I want to teach music at the high-school level in San Francisco" is much better.

● **Do market research for yourself.** Find out exactly who would be interested in the product you're selling—yourself. *How to do this:* Talk with people to find out what's available in your area of interest. Don't look for a job. Simply survey the situation and find out what the needs are. This takes the pressure off, and enables you to make valuable contacts.

● **Meet with contacts.** Personal and business contacts are all-important. You'll make some contacts while surveying your interest area. But don't hesitate to survey friends, relatives or current business associates.

● **Go with your heart.** Radiate enthusiasm about your goal. A positive attitude is crucial and comes only from doing what you really want to do, not what you think you should do, or what seems sensible, or what someone else wants you to do. If your proposal turns you on, it will have the same effect on your potential buyers.

● **Go to the right person with your proposal.** Approach the person who has the power to accept or reject it. Find this person through your contacts. *Example:* A 42-year-old graphic artist was interested in getting into the television field but had no TV experience. She talked with a number of people in various aspects of television and found there was a need for artists to do on-screen computer graphics and animation. One broadcasting company was hiring artists who had taken a particular manufacturer's three-day course. She took the course and got the job. She's now making triple her previous salary.

● **Make them an offer they can't refuse.** Figure out not only what you can contribute but also the best method of reaching your potential market with a strong sales message. *Helpful:* The business proposal. Work up a proposal identifying a need in a particular area. Then outline and explain how you think it can be filled by using your services.

Source: *The late John C. Crystal, founder of Crystal-Barkley Corporation, 152 Madison Ave., New York, NY 10016.*

Own-Business Basics

Launch a new business only after you have formulated a complete business plan. The plan should include careful projections of your monthly cash needs and available income for the first three to five years. Rarely does a new enterprise produce a fluid cash flow early on.

Questions to answer first:

- **Is the money to be invested** in the new business money that you can afford to lose?
- **Will you be able to get another job** and build another career if the new venture fails?
- **Can you afford to replace the insurance** coverage you may have now as an employee?
- **Do you need a bank loan to start?** If so, would you be wise to apply for it before you quit your present job?

Source: Edward Mendlowitz, partner, Mendlowitz Weitsen, 2 Penn Plaza, New York, NY 10121.

To Start a Business on a Shoestring

Shoestring businesses aren't limited to small ventures tucked away in the dusty corner of someone's garage. Many are capitalized at hundreds of thousands of dollars. They're called "shoestring" because the owner has invested little—if any—of his or her own cash.

Shoestring businesses are more a state of mind than a modus operandi. They work only if the owner is willing to adhere to the One-tenth Principle. Starting a business with one-tenth of the required capital demands that you exert 10 times the effort.

HOW TO MAKE MONEY AS A CONSULTANT

At one time or another, most executives consider selling their expertise on their own, as consultants. The majority are at least moderately successful, but many fail. Most commonly, they overestimate the salability of their services and underestimate the effort needed to sell them.

How to find out if your service will sell: There is no fail-safe method. A talk with several potential clients will tell you if you are headed in the right direction. The big sellers: services that help companies keep up with change, whether it is in technology, marketing, personnel relations or other areas that business needs to know about.

Pitfalls for New Consultants

- **Not realizing that consultants,** especially new ones, spend more time selling their services than performing them.
- **Wasting time on unproductive prospects.**
- **Choosing too broad a field** in which to consult.
- **Not learning to talk the client's language.** This is essential because many consultants sell a highly specialized service with its own vocabulary to an equally specialized customer who uses a completely different language. *Example:* A computer expert who is hired to automate market research for a diaper manufacturer.

New consultants are also faced with the temptation to sell their services cheaply at first in order to build up a good track record. Do not underprice. Clients are reluctant to establish a good working relationship with a bargain-basement consultant. And without that, the job is likely to be a failure.

It is also unnecessary to hire a public relations firm at the outset because a PR campaign will not have a track record to promote. Using a part-time PR could be helpful, however, in planning a credentials brochure.

To sell their services, successful consultants:

- **Maintain pressure** by keeping in touch with clients and prospects.
- **Master such sales and marketing methods** as the art of writing letters, making convincing phone calls and developing presentations.
- **Start at the top,** contacting the chief executives of the Fortune 1000 companies. Send individually typed letters and follow up with phone calls.

Source: Charles Moldenhauer, vice president, Lefkowith, Inc., marketing and corporate communications consultants, New York, NY.

Planning Comes First

Don't fall into the trap of thinking that the smaller a business, the less risk involved. Starting too small is actually more of a risk than starting too big. If you're starting a service business, microscopic beginnings might work. But new retail and manufacturing ventures require some more capital to begin—and enough to generate profits.

Careful planning and well-researched start-up costs are the keys to attracting financing. *Helpful:* Get a copy of the Small Business Administration's excellent cost worksheet (1-800-827-5722). It's invaluable in pinpointing frequently overlooked cost items.

Once you've identified costs, the next crucial step is figuring out how to slash them. Don't emulate the small journal publisher who struggled in his plush $66,000-a-year offices when a $10,000 facility would have sufficed—and would have produced profits instead of red ink.

If your shoestring business does require extensive quarters, however, look for retail basement space or space in a large, older home (if zoning laws permit). Both are usually priced well below conventional commercial property.

Retail businesses must focus on location. These businesses need immediate cash flow, and that means a high-traffic, high-rent location. *Avoid:* low-rent space that will force you to plow rent savings into advertising to attract customers. *Better:* Negotiate with the landlord to pay partial rent early in the lease and a higher rent later when cash flow is likely to be more substantial. Or, negotiate to pass renovation costs on to the landlord. Remember that a landlord who pays for your carpets and air-conditioning is going to charge a higher rent. But this can save you as much as $100,000 in initial costs.

Equipment bargains are next on the shoestringer's cost-slashing list. In fact, it should be part of every entrepreneur's game plan to scour auctions, equip-ment supply houses, classified ads, bankruptcy sales, and trade journals for secondhand equipment and fixtures.

Smart Investing

Putting your money where your business plan is makes you likely to get backing for that plan. Venture capitalists look favorably on managers who make significant investments (relative to their personal wealth) in their own companies.

Source: Financing and Managing Fast-Growth Companies *by Teledyne, Inc., co-founder George Kozmetsky, Lexington Books.*

Nothing Down... The Smart Way

One-hundred-percent financing is plentiful—if you know where to look. Although banks and finance companies aren't prime lending sources for shoestring businesses, they'll usually consider full financing on bargain-priced equipment with established collateral value. And equipment sellers may be more interested in unloading unneeded equipment than in getting immediate cash.

Manufacturer financing can also be arranged. *Trade-off:* Manufacturers' lending standards are more lenient than those of banks, but you'll have to pay two or three percentage points more.

Leasing is often a wiser choice than buying, especially for motor vehicles, computers, carpets and cash registers. *Rule of thumb:* If it will last more than five years, buy. If it will wear out or become obsolete within five years, lease whenever possible. *Inside idea:* Whether buying or leasing, negotiate with the equipment manufacturer for a 30- to 60-day trial run. If you've planned well, your business should be generating enough cash flow to complete the buy or lease agreement by the end of the trial. If it isn't, you can return the equipment at no charge.

Look to suppliers for financial support. Big suppliers can usually afford to let you defer payment for a while if they see the possibility of more business from you down the road. And, if your business looks like it will do well in the future, small suppliers might offer price breaks or better terms. *Example:* A small enterprising baked-goods manufacturer convinced his flour supplier to buy $40,000 of baking equipment for him against $800,000 in flour purchases over four years. The deal amounted to nothing-down equipment and a 5% discount for the baker, and a long-term customer for the supplier.

If you can't offer good collateral to a lender, you'll

have to look to nontraditional financing sources.

Best bets: friends, relatives, high-tax-bracket investors and the SBA.

And while you're abandoning the idea of conventional sources, you might as well discard thoughts of conventional terms. Your best deal is whatever you can bargain for. Private backers generally want 24%–26% of your business, sometimes with a percentage of profits as well.

Seeking 100% financing when you have personal funds safely stashed away can cause potential lenders to back off. Suspicions arise when investors sense that you're playing only with other people's money.

The Shoestring Corporation

Incorporating your venture is essential. But don't buy shares with all of your investment funds. *Instead:* Use a small portion to buy shares and loan the balance to a friend or relative who, in turn, loans the money to the new corporation in exchange for a mortgage. In the event of a failure, your friend or relative will be a preferred creditor—when your friend gets his or her money back, so will you.

By contrast, if you lend directly to the corporation as a shareholder, repayment may be disallowed by a bankruptcy decision.

Source: Arnold S. Goldstein, partner, Meyer, Goldstein, Chyten and Kosberg, Chestnut Hill, MA.

Use Accrued Pension to Start Your Own Business

Employee Getum has "had it" working for his present boss. He wants out now, he has $100,000 coming from his employer's qualified plan and he is entitled to and qualifies for lump-sum payment. Getum finds out the tax bite on the $100,000, if distributed this year, would be $35,000; he needs $50,000 to finance his new business. What to do?

The steps would be as follows:

1. Getum forms a new corporation, Go-Getum Co.

2. Go-Getum Co. adopts a qualified profit-sharing plan.

3. The distribution—the full $100,000—from Getum's former employer's qualified plan is rolled over to the new Go-Getum plan.

4. The new plan would have a provision to allow loans to be made to participants in an amount not to exceed 50% of the participant's vested interest, or $50,000.

5. The new profit-sharing plan would loan $50,000 to Getum, to be repaid over five years at 11% interest per annum.

Note, however, that the documentation from the new plan itself, the plan administrator's minutes describing and approving the loan and the note payable by Getum to the profit-sharing trust must be impeccable in every detail.

Source: Irving L. Blackman, CPA, senior partner, Blackman, Kallick & Bartelstein, 300 S. Riverside Plaza, Chicago, IL.

The Basics of Using Other People's Money

Other than your own pockets, where do you go for business financing? Trends in the popularity of different types of financing vary from year to year, but the sources all fall into two categories: *debt* and *equity*. The following summary covers a few of these sources, along with their respective criteria.

Debt

● **Banks.** Short- or long-term, secured or unsecured, bank loans are the traditional form of financing for all types of business needs. Banks typically make lending decisions based on a company's operating history and potential cash flow. They analyze the past few years' financial statements, requesting that they be audited, reviewed or compiled, and examine projected cash flow, income statements and balance sheets for the next few years. Banks look at a number of key financial ratios, including receivables and inventory turnover, liquidity, debt/equity and profit margins. Their emphasis is on historic trends of the business and comparable industry averages.

Recent changes in the banking industry have increased competition, making new sources of financing available for small- and medium-sized businesses. These include large commercial banks, most of which have established market divisions to service smaller companies (generally, those with less than $100 million in revenues), and savings and loans, which are now permitted to make a limited amount of business loans.

● **Finance companies.** Small businesses with less stable operating histories can turn to finance companies for funding. Finance companies offer many of the same forms of asset-based lending as banks, but focus more on a company's collateral than its operating record or potential profits, and are often willing to lend to less stable businesses. The cost of these loans typically is higher than that of bank loans, because of the greater risk assumed and the cost of monitoring the collateral. However, the true differential may not be as great as it appears, once all the hidden costs of bank loans (compensating balances, commitment and other fees, prepayment penalties, etc.) are factored in.

Equity

● **Venture capital.** While venture funds are not as plentiful as they once were, venture capital firms continue to make strategic investments. Unlike sources of debt financing, venture capitalists place less emphasis on a company's stable financial track record—financial history and projects are important, but secondary to management, market and product. Venture capitalists are more inclined to look for medium-term payoff from a new venture's management-team strength, identification of a strong market need and ability to satisfy that need with a unique product.

● **Regulation D:** "Reg D" represents a change in the usual requirements of the Securities & Exchange Commission (SEC). Under Reg D, smaller businesses can issue securities without formal SEC registration. The amount of the eligible offering is generally dependent upon the number of investors. Form D, which must be filed with the SEC, is relatively straightforward to prepare.

● **R&D partnerships:** This form of financing involves investors willing to fund product research and development in return for tax and other benefits. Typically, investors look for businesses in a well-developed technological area with plans for rapid expenditure of funds to yield immediate business tax deductions and prospects for near-term revenues. As a result of the Tax Reform Act of 1986, and other recent legislation, the tax breaks from such partnerships have all but been eliminated so investors will be seeking other benefits.

Successful Financing

Here are three important rules of seeking financing, regardless of its form or source:

1. Keep your proposal presentation clear, concise yet informative and easy to absorb. A potential funding source should be able to quickly understand your business, your reason for requesting funding and the benefits of providing that funding.

2. Don't sign away too much in your effort to obtain financing. In equity financing, be cautious about the amount of control you relinquish. When taking on debt backed by personal guarantees, try to exempt certain assets, such as your home.

3. If you're turned down, find out why—in writing, if possible. Then, if feasible, rework your financing proposal to meet the objections and either resubmit it or try a new source.

Source: *Jacob Weichholz, tax partner in the entrepreneurial services group of Ernst & Young, 787 Seventh Ave., New York, NY 10019, specializing in the tax and organization needs of small- and medium-sized businesses.*

Unconventional Ways Of Raising Capital

When companies need cash to grow, the vast majority turn to proven sources: family and friends, commercial banks and venture capital funds. The choice depends on the amount of money needed, the stage in the corporate life cycle, and how fast the plan is to expand. But other capital avenues are open to the shrewd entrepreneur that may suit the company's needs better than the traditional ones. These include corporate ventures, joint ventures, R&D limited partnerships and marketing partnerships. It may even be possible to combine two or more of these sources in a total funding package.

Corporate ventures: The corporate venture, a direct equity investment by a large corporation in a smaller entrepreneurial company, is becoming a popular alternative to traditional venture capital investing. Corporate ventures are generally not entered into for the sake of profit alone. The investing business also may have an interest in identifying windows into new technology, screening potential acquisitions, leveraging available skills or enhancing a staid corporate image.

By the same token, the entrepreneurial company generally receives more than just cash: Its corporate partner may provide additional value in the form of credibility, a built-in customer-supplier relationship, or expertise in planning, marketing, R&D or distribution. Further, entrepreneurs entering into these strategic alliances generally don't need to give up as much equity as they would to a venture capitalist. Finally, corporate partners can offer deep pockets for later-stage financing.

Businesses likely to receive this type of investment are often smaller, technology-driven companies that have a logical "fit" with the sponsoring companies. However, unless you have a corporate partner experienced in this type of investment, you run a much higher risk of clashing corporate and entrepreneurial cultures.

Joint ventures: Joint ventures pair companies with complementary strengths on specific projects. For instance, a company that has designed a salable product may lack the cash to manufacture it. If the

HOW TO FIND A VENTURE CAPITALIST

Are you looking for venture capital? Don't reach for the Yellow Pages. The goal is not just to find a venture capital firm, but to identify the right one for you. After a successful funding, your company will be married to the firm—in spirit as well as in equity. Finding the perfect match takes research, contacts and patience.

Anxious about the prospect of raising capital, entrepreneurs are often tempted to use the "shotgun" approach: printing up hundreds of copies of the company's business plan and distributing them to anyone wearing a suit. Unfortunately, this method wastes time and money and can damage the reputation of the company.

A targeted approach can improve your chances. The majority of venture capital firms specialize in particular types of deals. Some look only at high tech, others won't touch it. Some prefer leveraged buyouts, others work strictly with start-ups. High- versus low-tech preferences are important to

determine, as well as discriminations on the basis of geographic area, industry, company growth stage or amount of money sought. Like other professionals, venture capitalists tend to stick with what they know best.

After you've figured out what kind of firm specializes in your kind of deal, the next step is to locate them.

It's a good idea to read articles in business or trade magazines for news of venture firms—take special note of deals in your industry or area.

Before you contact any venture firm, you should have developed a sound business plan and financial projections with your accountant, lawyer and banker. Stay in constant contact with them and remind them that you're interested in meeting venture capitalists. People whose businesses are already venture-backed can be particularly helpful. They've been through the process and may know venture capitalists looking for a deal like yours. *One steadfast rule:* A personal referral is infinitely preferable to

a blind letter—it will get you and your venture more attention.

Is there a venture capital club in your area? Over 50 clubs have been established across the country, with more added every year. They offer entrepreneurs and investors a place to meet and exchange ideas. For beginners, this is a good way to learn the rules of the game and the buzzwords. In the best situation, you can meet people who are willing to support your company—either with money or experience—or to tell you honestly that it isn't likely to take off.

Venture capital clubs can be difficult to find, because they want to attract only serious entrepreneurs and investors, not hucksters. Again, it's always best to get involved with an organization like this through a friend or business associate.

While the "whom do you know" side of the process may be frustrating to an eager entrepreneur, don't despair. The creative and managerial synergy produced by a well-matched venture capital firm and an entrepreneurial company is well worth the trouble it takes to find a mate.

Source: Michael A. Reagan, partner, Deloitte & Touche, 695 Town Center Dr., Suite 1200, Costa Mesa, CA 92626. He is a member of the firm's emerging business services practice. He specializes in the high-tech industry, working with companies seeking growth financing.

company can identify a partner with the right manufacturing capabilities, the two then can form a joint venture, divide the profits and eliminate the need for cash exchange.

Joint venture financing holds promise for the future in terms of providing emerging companies with a way of achieving the financial weight necessary to compete with larger corporate entities. There is plenty of room for imagination in setting up business arrangements of this type. One company was able to develop a software program for farmers and is now successfully marketing it through booths in feed stores.

R&D limited partnerships: Specific projects are financed and investors receive attractive tax shelter through R&D limited partnerships. The sponsoring company provides project management, while the investors provide capital in exchange for tax benefits and the rights to the technology developed. It is generally agreed that when the R&D work is successfully completed, the company will exercise its option to acquire the rights to the technology from the partnership through royalty, equity or joint venture.

Some of the benefits to the sponsoring company of an R&D partnership include:

● **The financial risks** are borne by the limited partners.

● **The sponsoring company retains full control** over product development.

● **The sponsoring company has the right to acquire** the successful technology.

IRS rules for R&D limited partnerships are changing and have become very complicated in certain situations. In addition, the Tax Reform Act of 1986 effectively eliminated the ability of individual limited partners to offset against all but certain other income losses generated by R&D partnerships. For these reasons, it's important to get expert financial counsel to sort out the details.

Marketing partnerships: In a variation on the R&D limited partnership—the marketing partnership—the limited partners put up cash to market an existing product or service. In exchange, the company gives them a percentage of each sales dollar.

The partners don't receive tax advantages in this arrangement, but if the product is successful, the return on investment can be very high.

Source: *David T. Thompson, partner, Deloitte & Touche, Crocker Center, 333 S. Grand Ave., Los Angeles, CA 90071, an international accounting and consulting firm. He is the national coordinator for venture financing in the firm's emerging business services practice.*

How to Appeal to Investors

To be a successful entrepreneur, you need more than a good idea. Among other things, you need money. One option is to raise the funds from family, friends and other personal sources (second mortgages, insurance policies, etc.). But if such funds are either unavailable or inadequate, you'll have to know where to find other avenues of financial backing.

Investment Sources

● **Informal investors.** These wealthy groups or individuals generally put up $10,000–$25,000 (but sometimes as much as $100,000) per investment. These investors can be found through the "in" accounting or law firms.

● **Early-stage venture capital funds.** These lend $50,000–$250,000 per investment. They look for young companies that have products ready for market and demand a substantial chunk (up to 50%) of the company's ownership.

● **Traditional venture capitalists.** These include private firms supported by insurance companies, pension funds or wealthy families—small business investment companies (SBICs) funded by a combination of Small Business Administration loans and private funds—and corporate venture-capital firms.

● **Investment bankers.** This group includes small local firms and the giants—Merrill Lynch, Paine Webber, etc. They aid young companies that can't get venture capital by helping them go public. Some firms have both a venture-capital and an investment-banking arm.

Your Next Move

Entrepreneurs see all the possibilities for making money and usually downplay the risks. Investors, on

> **"Investment bankers aid young companies that can't get venture capital, by helping them go public."**

the other hand, focus more on risk than on opportunity. They know there are more losers than winners among new businesses. Therefore, before approaching investors, it is critical to draft a detailed business plan. The plan should be 20–40 pages long, complete with a table of contents and summary (which includes the highlights of the plan). Without such a written plan, submitted in advance, few investment groups will grant an interview. *The plan should include:*

- **A clear description** of your business product or service.
- **Hard evidence of the marketability** of the product or service and the benefits to users.
- **Financial justification** of the chosen means of selling or distributing the product or service.
- **An explanation of product development** and the manufacturing process and their associated costs.
- **The qualifications of each member** of the management team.
- **Believable financial projections** that are not out of line with industry norms.
- **A statement of what the founders expect** to have accomplished three to seven years into the future.

The aspiring entrepreneur must also be prepared to give a concise and thorough oral presentation and to answer potential investors' questions.

What Turns Investors Off

- **Too much product orientation.** Entrepreneurs are often so obsessed with their product or technology that they talk too much about that instead of about who will be the user and what the user wants.
- **Insufficient attention to budgeting and finance.** There must be someone who is watching every penny and who is knowledgeable about matters such as what to do when the company needs a loan and whether it should go public.
- **Too much custom engineering.** When investors see that a company's product must be specially designed or altered for each customer, a red flag goes up. *Standard problems:* high costs and low profits. Investors also shy away from products that don't promise enough volume.
- **A one-man band.** Venture capitalists like to see a well-rounded management team of at least three players—encompassing marketing, finance, production and

research. You should have the team players outlined on paper, even if the slots have not yet been filled.

The least risky venture, from an investor's point of view, is a going concern with an established market. At the other end of the spectrum is a start-up venture whose single founder has an idea and whose market is assumed but not yet proved. Investors are especially leery of putting in money that will be used for unproductive research and development. And the greater the risk the investor perceives, the greater the ownership interest he or she will insist on.

Source: Stanley R. Rich, founder of MIT Enterprises Forum and coauthor of Business Plans That Win $$$, *HarperCollins. He is also an entrepreneur who has started nine ventures.*

When to Incorporate and When Not To

Enormous confusion surrounds the question of the best way to organize a business—as a proprietorship, partnership or corporation. Yet it is possible to make some sense out of the issues by examining the potential advantage and disadvantages of incorporating in light of specific tax and business considerations. Here are some basic rules.

When to Incorporate

- **If you, as owner, wish to enjoy tax-free fringe benefits.** A proprietor or partner is not an employee of a company and therefore can't participate in tax-free fringe benefit programs enjoyed by employees.
- **If you are trying to build working capital in the business.** This may be the single best reason for a profitable company in the growth stage to incorporate. You can conserve cash by saving tax dollars, since part of your total income will be taxed at corporate rates rather than personal rates.
- **If you want to divert income to dependent family members.** Gifts of business property can be made to family members in lower tax brackets through a trust—the business then can lease the property back from the trust. This type of arrangement virtually requires the use of a corporation.
- **Forming multiple corporations offers substantial tax advantages.** Income can be split among

multiple entities if the venture can truly be divided into separate businesses and the partners are not related. Check with a competent tax adviser before trying this tactic.

When Not to Incorporate

● **If both spouses are active in the business.** For the small family business in which husband and wife work, it is usually best to operate as a proprietorship for payroll tax savings.

● **If you want to take money out of a profitable business.** When you reach the stage of life where you want to draw out the maximum amount from a business in the form of salaries and retirement benefits, the corporate form becomes a disadvantage due to IRS limitations on "reasonable compensation."

● **If you want to maximize deductible retirement plan contributions.** Since it is no longer necessary to use the corporate form to obtain the maximum deductions for pension and profit-sharing plans, this should not be your sole reason for incorporating.

● **If you expect losses in early years that you can offset with other personal income.** When you operate a new business as a partnership, proprietorship or S corporation, start-up losses can be deducted from other taxable income.

Taxes Aren't Everything

There are two further considerations that may override strictly tax-oriented factors when determining whether to incorporate.

● **Overall, management and administrative considerations favor use of a corporation.** The bigger the business, the greater the administrative advantages.

● **Personal legal considerations favor the corporate form.** While these benefits are not as marked for an active owner as for a passive investor,

FOUR WAYS TO TAKE MONEY OUT OF A CLOSELY HELD BUSINESS

If you are the president and sole or part owner of an incorporated business and you want to take money out of the business, you really have only four options. The one you choose may be largely determined by the varying tax implications. Here are the possibilities:

1. Sell the business. The first and most obvious method is to sell all or part of the business to a third party. Under the new Taxpayer Relief Act passed in 1997, the gain from the sale of capital assets is taxed at varying rates depending upon how long the stock was held prior to sale. With certain exceptions, long-term capital gains are now taxed at the following rates:

● 20% if held at least 18 months;

● 28% if held at least 12 months but less than 18 months; and

● 18% if acquired after December 21, 2000, and held for at least five years.

Short-term capital gains (gains on assets held one year or less) are taxed at the taxpayer's ordinary income tax rates. The current maximum rate for ordinary income (e.g., salary) is 39.6%. Thus, the adoption of the new long-term capital gains rates makes selling a piece of the business more attractive and potentially more advantageous than straight salary for taking money out of the business. In addition, the tax laws continue to allow capital gains to be offset by capital losses.

2. Take a large salary or bonus. A simpler route – assuming you don't want to sell and the business generates the necessary cash – is to pay

incorporation will secure some protection from personal liability. The protection is greater than that in a general partnership, but about the same as in a limited partnership.

Source: Vernon K. Jacobs, CPA, CLU, tax and financial adviser, 4500 W. 72 Terrace, Prairie Village, KS 66208. He is the author of Tax Factors in Choosing a Form of Business *and has written more than 300 articles about legal methods of tax avoidance.*

The Top Home Businesses

Millions of Americans commute to work these days by staying home. Some want to stay close to growing kids. Some find that technological advances make it easier—and often cheaper—to work from home.

Here are the best home businesses to start now. We've chosen them based on income potential, ease of entry, growth rate, stress level, ability to resist a recession and low start-up costs.

Important: Some businesses do require specialized skills. But often they're the computer skills you've learned and used at the office. And some of our favorite home businesses don't require special skills—only the willingness to learn and work hard.

● **Multimedia production.** This is a play on the business world's increasing appetite for multimedia presentations, which today almost always include computer-generated art and animation. Large and small businesses are accustomed to farming out such work. This does require computer skills. And if you have them, there's enormous potential here.

Requirements: An $8,000 to $25,000 up-front investment in hardware and software. You'll need a very large hard drive, CD-ROM drive that runs at triple speed, sound board, color scanner, laser printer, graphic design software and probably an authoring system that ties it all together.

Income potential: You can make up to $100

yourself a generous salary or bonus. This money is deductible from the corporation's earnings and taxed as ordinary income to you. This is not the most tax-effective alternative, but it is a direct way to get cash with no strings attached. Beware, however, of excessive generosity: The IRS monitors closely held firms for "unreasonable compensation" and may assess excessive amounts as nondeductible dividends (see item 4 below).

3. Take advantage of perquisites, benefits and amenities. Another alternative is to let the company pay for business-related meals, parking and other executive perks. Again, caution is in order. The IRS has cracked down on all benefits and perquisites that are not: minimal or incidental (e.g., occasional and limited personal use of a copier, company car, secretarial services or holiday gifts); qualified employee dis-

counts (e.g., limited discounts on company products); or work-related fringes (e.g., business use of company car, cost of business periodicals, professional memberships).

Generally, the IRS holds that executives cannot receive company-provided amenities tax-free, especially when the perks are not available to all employees. But under IRS guidelines, a company can pay for such job-related expenses as entertaining clients and parking. These costs are deductible, at least in part, by the company and tax-free to the executive if various substantiation, discrimination and other IRS tests are met.

4. Pay dividends. The final way to get money from a closely held business is to declare and pay substantial dividends to the shareholder(s)–in this case, you. However, this is the most inefficient alternative because it

involves a double taxation. You must pay dividends after corporate income taxes have been paid and declare them as personal income at ordinary rates.

Clearly, there is no perfect way of taking money out of a business, but if you decide to do it, keep three basic rules in mind:

● Sell any portion(s) of the business that will not cause you to relinquish control of the company.

● Take "reasonable" salary and bonuses instead of dividends – it's more tax-efficient.

● Take advantage of all IRS-allowed benefits and perks.

Source: Brian D. Dunn, principal with Towers, Perrin, Forster & Crosby, 245 Park Ave., New York, NY 10167, specializing in incentive compensation and organizational design. He has been published and widely quoted in professional journals and newspapers, and has spoken before the Human Resources Planning Society, the American Society of Personnel Administrators and the New York Chamber of Commerce.

an hour—or as much as $5,000 for producing a three-minute video.

● **Video production.** There are two growing markets here. On the business side, the proliferation of TV channels is creating a huge appetite for programming. (*Consider:* 500 channels require 12,000 hours of programming per day.) As the number of channels grows, each channel attracts fewer viewers. That cuts the cost of advertising, making TV increasingly affordable for smaller advertisers.

Strategy: Watch cable TV to find businesses with poorly executed commercials. Convince them you can do a better job.

The second market is the consumer. More and more people will pay for professional, edited videos of weddings, parties and family histories.

Requirements: Video camera, computer with Intel 486 chip and editing/production software can all be acquired for as little as $6,000.

Income potential: $25 to $100 per hour.

● **Repair services.** Consumers don't really want to junk expensive purchases after warranties have expired. With even advanced-amateur skills—or aptitude and a willingness to learn—you can make money as either a jack-of-all-trades handyman or a specialist.

If you have the technical training, consider the fastest-growing area—high-tech products (computers, printers, copiers, fax machines and scanners).

Strategy: If you go into high-tech repair, consider concentrating on the home and home-business markets. They now account for 51% of all PC sales.

Requirements: Up-front equipment costs vary by field, as does training.

Income potential: $15 to $100 per hour.

● **Cleaning services.** You can do the cleaning yourself or hire employees. Both the business and the consumer markets are targets (consumers are increasingly willing to pay for convenience services). Niche markets include services to clean carpets, floors, ceilings, draperies and upholstery, venetian blinds, air ducts, swimming pools and much more.

Requirements: A little up-front investment in cleaning supplies and perhaps some training. The downside is that the work isn't easy or absorbing.

Income potential: $25,000 to $100,000 per year.

● **Mailing list service.** With a computer, this is one of the easiest businesses to start from home—and it can really take off. You can create and maintain mailing lists for customers, produce your own list and then sell names to clients, sell monthly updated lists or market, support and educate users in mailing-list software.

Requirements: Start-up costs will range from $2,500 to $6,000. You'll need a computer with a large hard drive, printer, database or special mailing-list software, business cards, letterhead, envelopes and a price list.

Income potential: $10,000 to $75,000 is typical annual gross.

● **Rubber stamps.** A surprisingly hot business. People love rubber stamps and buy them at craft shows, in specialty stores and via mail order. You can use metallic and glow-in-the-dark inks to boost sales.

Requirements: It's not difficult to make rubber stamps and you can use free public domain clip art for designs. Or you can create your own designs. You can now produce rubber stamps with a computer, laser printer and photopolymer system (*Cost:* $2,800).

Income potential: People have been known to sell $2,000 to $5,000 worth per day at arts and crafts shows.

Source: Paul and Sarah Edwards, authors of The Best Home Businesses for the '90s, Working From Home *and* Making Money with Your Computer at Home, *Jeremy P. Tarcher/Putnam.*

How to Profit From a Merger Or Acquisition

The thousands of mergers and acquisitions announced each year are only the tip of an enormous economic iceberg: For every deal we read about, several others take place more quietly. Mergers and acquisitions are almost considered routine, yet the rewards are not always worth the risks. Participants on both sides of the deal need to keep their strategies sharp.

The Buyer's Strategy

Most acquisitions don't work out because buyers outnumber sellers, giving sellers the edge, and because it's almost impossible to predict all of the problems involved in combining two companies. Also, diversification per se is not a sufficient reason to acquire. Most companies can't handle a totally new business.

To improve the odds of making an acquisition successful, make sure you first have a clear understanding of your own company first:

- What do you do well—or badly?
- Do you undermarket your products or services?
- Do you challenge your managers sufficiently?
- Has technology begun to pass you by?
- Will selling new products and services help your sales force?
- How much of your own capital can you really spare for acquisition?
- How do your shareholders feel about risk?

Self-analysis helps you decide when to acquire—you may decide that now is not the time. An acquisition will quickly put you into new products, services or markets, but is speed worth the risk and disruption? Acquisition makes the most sense when you have the resources to succeed, the opportunity to add something you're lacking and the chance that you'll suffer if you move too slowly.

Self-analysis also helps you develop general acquisition criteria: Industry, company size, location, growth history and prospects, profitability, debt leverage, management objectives and purchase price. More specific criteria can include union status, customer profile, competitive posture, technology levels and image. Combining your criteria with a weighting system saves time and further reduces the risk of a poor acquisition.

Identifying Candidates

How you apply your acquisition criteria depends on how you identify candidates. The two search strategies are the passive approach and the active approach. The former involves networking in the business community, especially among investment bankers, business brokers, lenders, accountants, and the like, with the goal of uncovering owners who have decided to sell or at least to think about it. The active approach involves identifying, screening and contacting companies whose owners don't yet plan to sell. The search can be conducted by your own staff, consultants or intermediaries. Which method you use to identify can-

didates depends on your management depth. If your management team is "thin," the active approach usually won't work unless you hire outsiders.

If the companies on your list aren't for sale yet, it's especially important that actual contacts be made discreetly, possibly by a third party. *Before you make the contacts, answer these key questions:* Who controls the stock? What are the current "hot buttons" ("clean up your estate"; "preserve company's existence"; "add to your marketing clout"; etc.)? Who should make each approach? How? How much are you willing to say about your own company? What must you learn? And, what should the next step be?

The passive approach to identifying candidates costs less, but can involve spending a great deal of time fielding calls without seeing the best targets—the ones on the market may not be right for you. The active method, on the other hand, focuses on the best corporate fits, but the principals in the companies have to be convinced to sell. This can be an emotional process.

The Seller's Strategy

Sellers obviously have a very different view of the acquisition process. As the owner of a company, you may be under no pressure to sell, and the years you've spent building up the business can keep you from pricing it rationally. If you want to sell and you've minimized taxes, rather than maximized earnings, your company may not even be an attractive target.

In at least one way, selling a business does resemble buying one: Both require preliminary self-analysis. Do your shareholders need liquidity? Is selling to outsiders the only way to get it? Does the company need more growth capital than your current owners can provide? Are there other gaps, in production, marketing or management, that can't be closed except by selling? Is the future rosy enough to attract a buyer at the right price?

One way to attract buyers is to prepare a

> " Self-analysis helps you decide when to acquire—you may decide that now is not the time. An acquisition will quickly put you into new products, services or markets, but is speed worth the risk and disruption? "

Eight Ways to Evaluate a Business Before You Buy it

Emotional and other less-than-pragmatic considerations often play major roles in deciding how much a business is worth. For buyers who want to rely on more logical techniques, there are eight basic methods for evaluating a closely held business with no publicly traded stock and owners who are near retirement:

1. **Capitalized earnings.** The value is judged according to the previous year's earnings, income over the last few years, or projected earnings.

2. **Corporate and shareholder earnings.** Both of these are capitalized. This amount is paid out over a period that is usually two to four times the capitalization period. *Example:* If earnings were capitalized for the previous two years payment could be over the next four to eight years.

3. **Percentages of future profits.** The definition of profit can include any items that management determines. Payments can be spread over a number of years and arranged in diminishing stages.

4. **Book value.** The sum of assets as they appear on the books (excluding goodwill) less liabilities.

5. **Adjusted book value.** Current values are applied to the balance sheet. *Example:* Fixed assets are valued at either their replacement or their knockdown value rather than as they appear on the books.

6. **Book value plus pensions.** Consideration is given to retirement plans in effect at similar companies and an equitable compensation program for the retiring sellers.

7. **Start-up cost.** A buyer who wants to enter an industry will often pay more than a business is actually worth. *Reason:* The price may still be less than the cost of entering the field from scratch.

8. **Industry custom.** Some types of businesses are valued on the basis of historic formulas. *Examples:* Dental practices may sell for the previous year's gross income. Insurance brokerages can sell for a price equal to the first year's retained renewals.

Source: Edward Mendlowitz, partner, Mendlowitz Weitsen, CPAs, 2 Penn Plaza, New York 10121.

---

well-organized corporate profile containing: an executive summary, a financial history, adjustments to show true asset values and earning power, an industry survey, the position of your company in the industry, your products or services, marketing methods, management résumés, your labor environment, brochures, etc. Such a profile can deflect casual buyers. Once they've read it, you can insist that their next step be a bid. (This also will reduce onsite "tire kicking" and employee rumors.)

Another way to identify potential acquirers is to consider your current customers, competitors, and suppliers. You may find you already know good contacts. Intermediaries may be useful, too.

Intermediaries and Confidentiality

Whether you are a buyer or a seller, intermediaries can be used as a buffer and to maintain secrecy. Most intermediaries charge nonrefundable retainer fees, along with commissions or "success fees," with total charges computed as a percentage of the purchase price—often 1% to 5% for smaller businesses. Check on the intermediary's charges, terms and credentials before making a commitment. Intermediaries can be paid by either party, or at closing. Most intermediaries prefer to be paid by the seller, since that symbolizes the seller's commitment to sell. Above all, keep in mind that most intermediaries are transaction-oriented and will push hard to close a deal quickly, even if you haven't made up your mind.

There are several ways an intermediary can help a seller maintain secrecy. He can provide you with background information on each potential buyer, use an anonymous fact sheet for each first approach, limit the number of potential buyers approached simultaneously, have each prospect sign and return a confidentiality letter before you send your profile, and provide you with a weekly status report. However, these steps can delay the selling process, so you may need to balance your desires for secrecy and speed.

Valuing the Target

How does each side arrive at a price? This is particularly difficult if the target is privately held or part of a larger company, but three valuation methods are generally used:

1. Asset appraisal, which assumes that a

business derives more value from assets than from earnings or cash flow.

2. Discounted cash flow, which assumes that a business's value is attributable to its cash flow.

3. Comparable-company multiples, which assumes that the best way to decide what a company is worth is to examine what investors have paid for similar companies.

The seller and buyer independently use these valuation methods to arrive at their assessments. Negotiations typically proceed from that point.

The seller's minimum price depends on the seller's alternatives. For example, if the company has shareholders' equity of $6 million and net earnings of $1 million, a buyer might bid $8 million–$10 million. But if the current owners collectively take out $1 million or more each year—while retaining control—this offer might not give the owners as much as they already have.

The buyer's maximum price depends on synergies that could improve the target's earning potential. This requires the buyer to make two calculations: How much is the target worth, on a stand-alone basis? And, how much more can the buyer offer, if necessary, to reflect the company's potential value?

The result of the negotiations will depend more on the people involved than even these calculations of maximum and minimum price. (This is why the initial contact between companies is always a challenge.) The negotiating process underscores how important people are to the acquisition process as a whole. Many times, one party will walk away from a perfectly reasonable offer because he or she simply doesn't want to deal with the other party. At times like these, or when such a problem seems likely to arise, intermediaries can be helpful in buffering the parties from one another. However, whether you are the buyer or seller, remember that any merger or acquisition involves people—no price can make up entirely for ill will.

Source: Stephen Bennett Blum, CPA, co-director of the merger and acquisition department, KPMG Peat Marwick, 345 Park Ave., New York 10145.

Something for Nothing — How A Leveraged Buyout Works

Any investor who has participated in a successful leveraged buyout (LBO) may have reason to question the age-old axiom You can't get something for nothing.

In a typical LBO, the amount of cash the investors put into the venture in the form of equity is a small percentage of the total acquisition cost. Most of the purchase price is financed through debt, secured by the company's assets and cash flow. The cash flow of the business is used to pay interest and debt amortization. Also, less profitable segments of the business are sold to pay down the debt. At the conclusion of the transaction, the investors have something—ownership of an operating company, for next to nothing—their initial investment.

Since operating management usually obtains an equity position in the ongoing venture, increased productivity and profits often result from the entrepreneurial spirit of the new owners. If everything goes well, it may be possible to return the investors' original investment in the form of fees or proceeds from the sale of new stock (often a public offering). When this happens, the investors can find themselves with an ongoing business that has cost them nothing.

Minimizing the Risks

Obviously, not every company can provide investors with a windfall. To minimize the risks, look for the following general indicators of a good LBO candidate:

● **Strong, predictable operating cash flow** that is neither cyclical nor affected by interest rates.

● **Opportunities to reduce costs** by eliminating unnecessary overheads.

● **Assets with fair market values** in excess of net book values.

● **Management with a strong entrepreneurial spirit.**

Once you've chosen an LBO venture, there are still risks involved in making it pay for itself. Since the LBO is heavily dependent on debt financing, interest rate movements can have a significant impact on the company's ability to service its debt. One way to reduce this risk is to negotiate an interest rate cap with the financing sources. Another is to arrange to have interest charges in excess of a certain percentage deferred for a period of time.

To ward against the chance that profits don't increase as quickly as originally planned, investors can keep a cash reserve available for future investment in the company. Sometimes a small additional investment is all it takes to put the company over the top.

Although LBOs involving millions of dollars of investment get most of the attention from the business press, smaller LBOs continue to be a strong investment opportunity. You may need to take some high short-term risks, but prudent analysis of cash flow and proper attention to management can help you get something for nothing.

Source: Kevin M. Smith, partner and director of entrepreneurial services for the New York metropolitan office of Ernst & Young, New York. He is responsible for providing financial accounting and consulting services to middle-market companies.

Selling an Unprofitable Business

There are four kinds of potential buyers for money-losing assets.

- **Large public companies** with a specific need for products or assets.
- **Risk-playing entrepreneurs** with expertise in the industry.
- **Foreign companies** looking for a toehold in a particular market in the United States.
- **The business's own management,** backed by venture capital.

To find a buyer: Figure out which one of these groups will most logically profit from acquiring the business. Then quietly send out feelers to candidates within that group to see if they express interest in acquiring.

If word gets out that the business is for sale, capitalize on the publicity. Use it to flush out as many potential buyers as possible, then pit them against each other.

Caution: Publicly putting a business on the block hurts employee morale. If a business is labor-intensive, it's generally best not to publicize the intended sale. Labor-intensive companies on the block get raided. The loss of their top talent depresses the business's value. *Sales strategy:* Know the strengths and weaknesses of the business. Address both of them openly when negotiating.

Important: Don't be tempted to spread false turnaround tales. When an owner tells a prospective buyer that the business is about to turn around, the buyer will only wonder why the owner wants to sell it. This casts doubt on the owner's credibility. *Pricing strategy:*

- **Price the business** at least 30% higher than the final acceptable figure.

Warning: Don't overbluff.

- **Keep marginal prospects** in the picture to foster competition with serious potential buyers.

Choices if the sale is not made:

- **Liquidate.**
- **Remove the business from the market** for the time it takes to revive it and increase its salability.

Source: The Profit Line. Durkee, Sharlit Associates.

> **"Publicly putting a business on the block hurts employee morale....Labor-intensive companies on the block get raided. The loss of their top talent depresses the business's value."**

What You May Not Know About Franchises

If you're considering the purchase of a franchise, you should understand first that franchises are not typically the bargains they once were. The costs and risks of running a franchise have increased, and the payback periods are longer than they were in the past.

You also should be aware of the trap that lies in the common business cycle of heavily franchised industries. In the initial phase of the cycle—launching the new product or service, or entering the new geographic area—competition and pricing pressure are generally quite low. Franchise fees may not seem like a burden to the operation experiencing rapid sales growth and strong cash flow.

As business lines mature and new competition enters the field, bringing increased pressures on profit margins, the franchise operation may be at a disadvantage compared with the independent competitor. With equal sales and gross profit margins, the independent business should make more money—franchise fees limit a franchisee's ability to meet price competition and still make a profit, unless the franchise provides some unique competitive advantage.

Very important here are the franchisor's experience and attitude. Some franchisors not only are conscientious about helping franchisees who are in trouble, but also have the experience to anticipate and avoid problems of this sort. Unscrupulous franchisors, on the other hand, may simply let individual franchises fail and then resell them.

Aside from larger economic questions, specific difficulties and pitfalls can arise in franchise schemes. *Here's what you should know about:*

● **Hidden costs.** Not all franchise agreements clearly spell out the full fees the operator will be called on to pay. To avoid unpleasant surprises when the franchisor assesses fees for national advertising, administration, group accounting and the like, be sure to find out about all costs ahead of time. Total fees paid to the franchisor could be as much as the net earnings of the franchisee.

● **Product exclusivity.** If you are paying for the right to sell a unique product or service, will it remain unique? Early in the game, buying a franchise may be the only way to obtain the right to sell a particular product. But in our free market system, it doesn't usually remain this way very long. Typical complaints from franchisees in this situation are that not enough is spent on advertising the franchise name; that anyone can get the product; that the franchisees pay a higher price because they are locked into buying from the franchisor; and that they cannot get the latest or enough merchandise.

● **Location.** Selection and provision of a business location are often the purview of the franchisor. Can you count on the franchisor to provide a good location? Are the best locations reserved for company ownership rather than franchise operations? Will the franchisor refrain from selling other franchises close

enough to compete with yours? These are important questions to have answered.

● **Standards.** Are standards of quality, appearance of premises, levels of service, etc. detailed in the franchise agreement? Are they enforced? A poorly run franchise in your area may reflect badly on your operation and the rest of the system. A franchisor needs to be able to identify these problems and take corrective action before other franchise locations are adversely affected.

Lawsuit Guidelines

There are many exceptions, but as a rule:

● **Don't sue for less than $25,000.** A lawsuit will cost so much that even if you win, you can only break even.

● **Keep in mind that the legal bills** may cripple or kill your company.

● **Remember that if your company is sued** by a determined one that's much bigger than yours, your company doesn't stand much of a chance. The legal help your company receives depends on the size of its bankroll—the facts of the case are only incidental.

● **Don't be the first to suggest a settlement.** The unreasonable party usually wins.

Source: *David W. Swanson, president, Daavlin Co., Box 626, Bryan, OH 43506.*

● **Business and management assistance.** Theoretically, this is part of the package with almost all franchise operations, but in practice the assistance may have little value. Good franchisors hold regular training sessions and have experienced and knowledgeable corporate personnel to assist individual franchisees. Some bring in successful franchisees to help. However, in other instances, assistance may be limited to printed manuals or forms backed up by little or no hands-on help. For a first-time business owner, this may be inadequate.

● **Stability of the franchisor.** It may not matter how successful an individual franchisee is if the franchisor fails. For example, a clothing store franchisor who had a policy to restrict franchisees from carrying other brands of merchandise failed. Most of the successful franchises failed, in turn, since they had no existing relations with other vendors.

● **Power of the lease.** Who holds the lease to the franchise location? If the franchisor owns the lease, a franchisee who gets in trouble and misses a payment may be evicted instead of getting expected help and support from the organization.

All in all, it is an excellent idea to investigate and evaluate the experience and reputation of the franchisor when considering buying a franchise system. Talk to other franchise owners and obtain a copy of the *Uniform Franchise Offering Circular* from your state's record office. For assistance in finding reputable franchisors, contact the International Franchise Association, a trade group in Washington, DC, that provides a list of established companies. An individual franchisor's registration statement can be obtained from the state. This includes information on financial history and strength, litigation history (especially with franchisees and suppliers) and amounts it receives from franchisees. All of these sources will help you to know whether you'll get what you'll be paying for.

Source: Donald Murray, partner and director of the enterprise and retail group Deloitte & Touche, 1000 Wilshire Blvd., Los Angeles, CA 90010. He has published several articles on retailing and frequently lectures at universities and to business groups.

The Many Benefits Of Franchising

Franchising can help you avoid much of the risk of going into business on your own. For an establishment fee and continuing royalties, a franchise offers benefits that are otherwise unobtainable.

HOW TO MAKE THE MOST OF RETIREMENT PLANNING

As we live longer and pension investments become more important, it is crucial that people take a more active role in their retirement planning. Thus, it is very important to become more knowledgeable about investing and, especially, about asset allocation—how to divide your money between stocks, bonds, cash and other investments to get the best and safest return.

Those who already have a stockbroker or who keep up with the financial press know that all the big brokerage houses issue asset allocation recommendations periodically, suggesting that institutions keep their money in stocks, bonds, and cash in various percentages. *Here are some points to be aware of:*

● **The brokerage houses's forecasts relate to large institutional accounts.** Individual planning does not need to be adjusted as often.

● **Blanket advice won't fit everybody.** The younger you are, the more risk you can take (that is to say, the more aggressive stocks you can own). As you grow into middle age, you will need to be more conservative and choose more bonds and balanced (between stocks and bonds) mutual funds.

● **Reallocating assets over the short term is disruptive to long-term planning** because it is essential for individuals to consider five-, 10-, or even 15-year time horizons to give investments a chance to turn a healthy profit.

See the Big Picture

View all your assets together, then plan your investment strategies. A reminder: try not to achieve only short-term results.

Some people invest too heavily in cash and Certificates of Deposits (CDs) for one-year maturities and money-market funds, which all have low, low returns. And they are too afraid of the risk associated with stocks, which historically offer the best long-term rewards.

What's Your Current Allocation?

Make a comprehensive list of your current assets, noting the current yield for each. Mark all taxable items.

● **Savings accounts.**
● **Certificates of Deposit (CDs).**
● **Stocks.** List the number of shares of each stock and the current value of your holdings.
● **Bonds.**
● **Mutual funds.**
● **Real estate.**
● **Corporate savings plans.**
● **Deferred annuities and life insurance.**
● **Pension plans usually are**

● **A franchise is your own business**—preplanned, prestructured, preestablished and pretested.

● **A franchise is based on more than "a good idea"**—it involves the previous establishment of pilot operations that have proved successful.

● **You are in business for yourself,** but not by yourself, since the franchise organization is behind you. The franchisor has extensive experience in implementing the business and can effectively guide you along the right path.

● **In-depth training is available to you at the outset,** with refresher training at subsequent periods. Workshops on management, communications and personal finances also may be offered.

● **The program is thoroughly documented**—manuals cover all aspects of the operation.

● **Selection of an effective site for your business** is based on standardized marketing procedures.

● **Economies are achieved from group advertising and purchases,** accelerating as the franchise system grows.

● **Each individual benefits from the whole.** As the network expands, the value of the individual franchise grows too.

● **The franchisor provides services that you often cannot afford,** because they require either too much time or too much money. These services include researching and developing new products, ideas and promotions, and the tools to help implement them. The franchisor's staff also can assist in problem solving.

Source: *David D. Seltz, president, Seltz Franchising Developments, Inc., 30 Ridge Rd., New Rochelle, NY 10804, an authority on the franchising and marketing fields. He has served as chairman of the International Franchise Congress, has conducted seminars and is a prolific writer.*

paid out as an annuity in fixed monthly payments. List the estimated annual income for both pension plans and Social Security.

● **A Keogh plan, which includes investments** of stock, bonds and money-market funds.

● **Liabilities.** List all your liabilities, such as a mortgage, car loan, college loan, etc.

Investment Strategies

The first step is to determine what income you need and what assets you already have (your house, valuable antiques, etc.) and then make some crucial personal decisions. How important is safety? Do you need safety of principal or safety of buying power?

If inflation persists at its recent historical rate of 5% a year, your money will lose half of its value in 14 years. That's why, even if you are 65 years old and have a net worth of $300,000, we would advise you to keep 25% to 35% of your assets in growth investments, such as stock or real estate. How important is your need for liquidity and what is your comfort zone? Most retirees don't need more than three months' living expenses in quickly available funds, but some older people don't feel comfortable without $100,000 in a savings account.

By keeping only $10,000 in the bank and investing $90,000 in a safe municipal bond fund, you could earn an extra couple of thousand dollars each year, tax-free.

The need for some reallocation of assets is usually revealed after you've looked at your overall financial picture.

We also advise clients to make their portfolios safer by weeding out any stocks that don't currently rate "1" or "2" for timeliness and safety by Value Line Reports (available in many brokers' offices and libraries) and any mutual funds that are not given four or five stars by Morningstar, Inc.

Source: *William W. Parrott, president, Creative Retirement Planning, Inc., One Hollow Lane, Suite 306B, Lake Success, NY 11042. He and his son John L. Parrott are coauthors of* You Can Afford to Retire: The No-Nonsense Guide to Pre-Retirement Financial Planning, *Simon & Schuster's New York Institute of Finance.*

Dealing With Banks, Credit & Debt

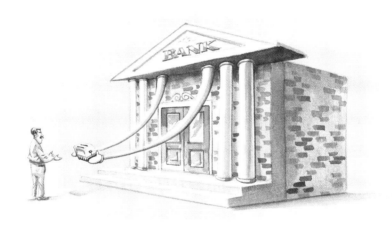

5

How Safe Is Your Bank?

Banks don't have to fail in order to hurt the customers with whom they do business. Even as financial problems are just beginning to develop, the bank's operations may begin to deteriorate, and ultimately the bank may need to rein in its growth.

When banks run into financial problems, they behave like any other troubled company. They sometimes try to hide problems and limp along the best they can. For the customer, services can quickly deteriorate. Growing companies can be especially hurt because most rely on their banks to expand credit lines. Unfortunately, a troubled bank too often will call in its loans because the bank needs the money—not because the customer is at any growth risk.

As a result, thousands of customers are hurt. Many could have avoided problems by watching for early warning signals of bank weakness. These signals can show up as early as two years before a failure.

Chances are good, of course, that your bank is among the vast majority of healthy ones in the United States. But ignoring the signs of problems may add to your future risks.

Bank problems often stem from decisions to grow aggressively. Some banks that have failed funded an ambitious growth strategy with "purchased" funds (such as large CDs), as opposed to deposits from their customers. That strategy puts them on shaky ground.

Customers who have dealt for some time with banks in this situation usually sense something is wrong:

- **There's high turnover** among the officers.
- **Paperwork and record keeping** become sloppy.
- **The bank encourages customers to extend credit** when officers know it really isn't necessary.

But even when customers suspect that a bank is going through some sort of change, they rarely take the trouble to find out if it's merely because of routine personnel problems or because of more serious financial trouble.

Essential steps: If a friendly bank officer has recently quit, invite him or her to lunch and ask tough questions about his or her former employer. If you think there's a problem, get a copy of the bank's Call Report. This document has the data on the financial conditions of a bank. (In fact, regardless of whether a customer senses trouble, he or she should routinely get Call Reports for banks with which the customer does business.)

Although Call Reports are public documents, not all banks make copies available (usually obtainable from the bank's shareholder-relations department). But if a bank balks, copies are available from the FDIC, Disclosure Section, 1776 F Street NW, Room 518, Washington, DC 20429. It will bill you for the small fee.

What to look for: By comparing figures of Call Reports over time, a customer can read the warning signals. According to Cates Consulting Analysts, Inc., the signals include:

- **Rapid expansion** as reflected in a big increase in loan yield relative to other similarly sized banks.
- **Loan recovery rate of less than 20%.** This is the percentage of written-off bad loans that a bank is ultimately able to recover. It should be well over 20% and is an excellent indication of how riskily the bank is willing to operate.
- **Low return on assets for a bank its size** (can range from 0.6% for large banks to well over 1.0% for a small bank).
- **High overhead ratio.** Failed banks had overhead expenses that amounted to nearly 80% of their income base, compared with a nationwide average of 56%. Bank failures have decreased in recent years, but that's no reason not to be diligent—it's your money.

> "If you think [a bank has] a problem, get a copy of [its] Call Report, [which contains] data on the financial conditions of a bank."

How to Protect Yourself Against Bank Failure

Banks in many areas may continue to have financial problems, but no companies or individuals should lose money if they understand how the banking system works. In order to protect against the possibility of bank failure, depositors must know how to:

- **Judge the different types** of insurance that banks can have.
- **Spread deposits legally** to maximize insurance coverage.
- **Evaluate a bank's financial data** for early warning signs of trouble.

Insurance Quality

In view of possible bank difficulties, be very cautious about doing business with financial institutions (usually thrifts) whose deposits are insured by private insurance. Even though administered by state rather than federal agencies, funds that aren't fully backed by the state's treasury run the risk of being depleted if even one bank gets into trouble.

Other problems: State insurance is often less than the $100,000 federal level, and it takes months to collect, unlike federal insurance, which normally pays depositors within days of a bank failure.

Beyond the Limit

Surprise: With careful management of accounts, it's possible to go far beyond the $100,000 insurance limit offered by the Federal Deposit Insurance Corporation (FDIC).

- **Each depositor is insured up to $100,000** at each institution, including its branches. All time, savings and checking accounts owned by the same person, with the exception of IRAs and Keoghs, are lumped together to reach the $100,000 limit.
- **Sole proprietorship business accounts** are added to the same person's individual accounts for the $100,000 insurance limit.
- **All valid joint accounts** are insured separately from individual accounts.

These rules still leave a lot of leeway. Deposits owned jointly under such conditions as joint tenancy or community property are insured separately from deposit accounts individually owned by the co-owners. *Example:* A couple can insure up to $500,000 by opening five $100,000 accounts—one in each spouse's name, one in a joint name and two retirement accounts.

Opportunity: Another simple way to expand insurance coverage at the same bank is to open revocable testamentary or trust accounts that name specific beneficiaries in case of death. *Benefit:* There's a $100,000 insurance maximum on these accounts for each beneficiary.

For a complete explanation of FDIC insurance, ask your bank for its free brochure on coverage of accounts.

Pension Strategy

Similarly, a company's pension and profit-sharing deposits are considered to be trust funds. If they meet certain conditions and record-keeping requirements, these pension and profit-sharing accounts are separately insured for up to $100,000 per participant at each depository bank. Check with bank officers to make sure the company meets FDIC regulations governing such accounts.

The most common insurance traps:

- **Believing that securities held by a bank** in IRAs and other accounts come under insurance plans. They don't.
- **Creating a corporation or other type of organization** with the sole purpose of using it to get more deposit insurance. Federal rules say that an organization must be engaged in "independent activity" in order for it to qualify for deposit insurance.
- **Using a variation of your name to open another account** in the hope of getting more insurance. Varying names or Social Security numbers on joint accounts usually isn't illegal. But it won't get you more deposit insurance.

Safety Checks

Just as a business would check the financial health of a supplier or customer, it's a sound practice to keep a running check on the viability of the company's banks. *Check on:*

- **Liquidity.** Look at the bank's cash and securities that are readily convertible into cash as a percent of total deposits. A one-to-four or one-to-five ratio is pretty good. A lower ratio could signal trouble.
- **Capital requirements.** Total primary equity at commercial banks should be $5\frac{1}{2}\% - 6\%$ of total assets.
- **Loan losses.** These shouldn't exceed 1% of a bank's total loan portfolio on an annual basis.
- **Net interest margin.** This is simply the differ-

ence between what the bank pays for funds and what it must pay out in interest.

● **Bond portfolio.** Compare current market value with the book value of bonds carried on the bank's financial statements. With many of these bonds, the actual liquidation value could be substantially less than book value.

Source: *Herbert F. Mueller, president, North Valley Bancorp, 1377 South St., Redding, CA 96001. He has been a member of the American Bankers Association's advisory panel that explains banking practices to bank customers.*

How to Question Your Banker

If you are concerned about the safety of the bank, there are things you should look for:

● **Any bank should be able to give you its financial statement.** Most banks publish them semi-annually or annually.

● **Read the statement,** looking at the net worth, the number of "workouts" (situations in which bank officers are helping troubled companies get back on their feet), and the amount of real estate owned.

What you're trying to determine is the quality of the bank's investments. This is easier if the bank is a publicly traded company. These companies must file with the Securities and Exchange Commission.

● **Look at the bank's track record over time.** If the bank has gone through extraordinary growth, it means that the institution has put out a lot of money, and it may have taken more risk.

● **If you are depositing more than $100,000,** you should be able to discuss the kind of investments the institution has made.

● **You should also look at the accountant's report (included in most shareholder's reports).** Each institution has one. Be sure to read the "exceptions" to the accountant's statement.

● **Ask about the bank's "at risk" loans or "scheduled items"** (loans that have been in default for 60–120 days).

And, of course, be sure that your bank is insured by the FDIC. *(Editor's note:* For a complete explanation of FDIC insurance, ask your bank for its free brochure on coverage of accounts.)

Source: *Franklin H. Ornstein, chairman, Central Federal Savings Bank of Long Beach, Long Beach, NY. He is the author of* Savings Banking: An Industry in Change, *Prentice-Hall.*

Can You Bank on Your Bank?

To check out the financial stability of your bank—or to find a bank in your area that's in top fiscal condition—contact VERIBANC, a banking research firm that publishes financial reports on banks, S&Ls, and credit unions.

● *Short Form Reports* provide equity, assets, their ratio, net income and projected months until equity will reach zero if the institution is unprofitable. Graphs relate these measures to the entire industry. Special factors and color classification based on capital strength and profitability are also included—"green" indicates safety; "yellow," caution; "red," danger.

● *Bank and S&L Research Reports* are much more detailed, giving data and analysis of 17–18 different financial measures.

● *Blue Bank Reports* list all the commercial banks in a particular geographic region that meet very high standards. Criteria include size, profitability, capital strength, and liquidity.

● *City Five Reports* give for the city or county of your choice, the five commercial banks or S&Ls with the most assets, that are the most profitable, that have the largest equity/assets ratio, that are the most liquid.

Note: VERIBANC develops its data from the regulatory filings of federally insured lending institutions.

> **"Any bank should be able to give you its financial statement. Most banks publish them...annually."**

Source: *VERIBANC, Box 461, Wakefield, MA 01880, 800-442-2657.*

Former Bank President Tells How Not to Be Outsmarted By Your Bank

I'm always amazed at how people go out of their way to get an extra eighth of one percent on a CD—and then pay their banks much more than that in fees they have been told are unavoidable. *Reality:* Banks don't want you to know their fees and interest rates *are* negotiable. Often all you have to do is ask.

Example: Most banks will give senior citizens, the disabled and students free checking accounts. But you have to ask. *Strategy:* Learn the chain of command at your bank. If you encounter a bank employee who won't negotiate fees, ask to speak with his or her boss. Most senior personnel would prefer you to be happy with the bank, especially if you are a good customer.

Here is how to minimize most of your bank charges, such as ATM fees, overdraft charges and the penalties for falling below minimum balance requirements:

● **Use a small bank.** Your bank should be one of the smallest in your area. A big bank often won't go the extra mile for you because it doesn't feel it needs your business. A small bank will be flexible because it needs satisfied customers in order to attract new customers and to grow.

● **Don't use ATMs**—except in emergencies. Not only can they be costly, they prevent you from establishing important personal relationships with bank officers. Those cordial relationships can help you get better rates and terms on bank loans and services.

● **Avoid overdraft charges.** Ask your bank to electronically monitor and "red flag" your checking account and telephone you if it is overdrawn. Most community banks will give you until 3 P.M. the same day to come in with a deposit before they bounce a check—saving you a $15 to $25 overdraft charge and the embarrassment of a returned check.

● **Ask for minimum balance requirements to be waived.** Many banks will waive these requirements if you insist. If your bank won't, consider a credit union, which usually is cheaper and offers better service. For more information, call the Credit Union National Association at 800-358-5710.

● **Plan before you borrow.** Go into the bank and update your personal financial statement every six months or so—even if you don't need a loan. Strike up conversations with the people who help you. *Reason:* You want at least one teller, one loan officer, and one bookkeeper to know your face. Anyone can borrow if

they have good collateral. But if you need a loan based only on collateral, you're much more likely to get it if you and your credit history are familiar to the bank's employees.

● **Refuse unnecessary products.** Banks are intimidating to average consumers, who are afraid to question what is put in front of them. *Example:* Most people are so happy to get a car loan, they're afraid to refuse the over-priced credit life and disability insurance the bank often adds to the loan. Even worse, they don't realize that because the insurance cost has been added to the loan, the premium is subject to a finance charge.

Source: *Edward F. Mrkvicka, Jr., is the author of* Your Bank Is Ripping You Off, *St. Martin's Press.*

Negotiate to Reduce Your Bank Costs

Nearly every fee charged by your bank is negotiable. It's also easy to request better terms.

Key steps:

● **Consider opening an additional savings account or investing in a CD in the future.** Some banks will negotiate only with customers who already have established different types of accounts with the institution. The promise of more business may persuade the representative to give you a better deal. Point out that a better rate will encourage you to do more business with the bank.

● **Ask about direct payment options.** Many lenders will lower car loan rates by as much as one percentage point if you agree to have payments automatically removed each month from one of your accounts. Other banks give better savings rates if you have your paycheck directly deposited.

● **Ask to have loan fees waived.** Whether the transaction is a mortgage or a home equity loan, the bank is going to make a lot of money from your business. As a result, it can afford to let several hundred

> **"Don't use ATMs—except in emergencies. Not only can they be costly, they prevent you from establishing important...relationships with bank officers [which can] help you get better rates and terms on bank loans and services."**

dollars' worth of fees slide if it thinks you'll go elsewhere for the mortgage.

● **Repeat your request if you're turned down.** In some cases, the person with whom you're speaking may deny your request because he or she does not appreciate your value to the bank. Just go over the person's head. Don't be embarrassed about being persistent. It's your money, and you're lending it to the bank. You're entitled to a good deal.

Source: Edgar Dworsky, director of consumer education at the Massachusetts Executive Office of Consumer Affairs and Business Regulation, One Ashburton Place, Boston, MA 02108.

How to Beat the Banks Before They Beat You

Since deregulation, banks vary widely in their services and in the costs of those services. In order to turn the best profit, banks depend on the fact that customers don't know what to ask for. *How you can get the most for your banking dollar:*

● **Deal with the smallest bank you can find.** After deregulation, most large banks decided to get rid of smaller depositors. They find it cheaper to serve one corporate account than 10 individual accounts. Smaller banks, on the other hand, are more responsive to individual depositors because they need this business.

● **Ask about checking accounts.**

● **What is the minimum-balance requirement?** How does the bank calculate it? Watch out for a minimum-balance calculation that uses the lowest balance for the month. A figure based on the average daily balance is best.

● **Does the balance on other accounts** count toward the checking-account minimum balance?

● **What is the overdraft charge?** Often it is outrageous. In parts of the Midwest, for example, many banks charge $25.

Free Help From the FDIC

● **FDIC insurance is carried by almost all commercial banks in the United States.** But surprisingly few depositors know just what it does—and doesn't do. *Information:* FDIC, 550 17 St. NW, Washington, DC 20429. Ask for a free copy of *Your Insured Deposit.*

● **Trouble with your bank?** The new Federal Deposit Insurance Corporation's hotline will answer questions and take complaints. It deals only with banks supervised by the FDIC, which include federal institutions but not all state-chartered banks. Call 800-934-3342. The hotline operates from 9 A.M. to 5 P.M. EST, Monday through Friday.

● **Don't buy loan insurance from a bank.** Credit life or disability insurance is often routinely included on loan forms and added to the cost of your loan. Don't sign any such policy when you take out a loan.

Caution: This insurance benefits the bank—not you. It covers the bank for the balance of your loan should you die or become disabled. You can get more coverage from an insurance agent for half (or even less) of what the bank charges.

● **Avoid installment loans.** *These loans are front-end loaded:* Even though your balance is declining, you're still paying interest on the original balance throughout the term of the loan. Ask for a single-payment note with simple interest and monthly payments, or an installment loan calculated on a simple interest basis.

If you do have an installment loan, don't pay it off early—this actually adds to its real cost.

● **Avoid ATMs.** The farther bankers can keep you from their tellers and loan officers, the more money they'll make and the less responsive they'll be to your needs. Bankers like ATMs because people can't argue with them, and they're extremely profitable.

● **Negotiate interest rates.** This sounds simple, but it means combating banks' tendencies to lump loans in categories—commercial, mortgage, retail, etc. For example, many banks offer a longtime depositor the same interest rate on a car loan as they do a complete newcomer. But often all it takes to get a better rate is to say, "I think my car loan should be 2% lower.

I've been banking here for 15 years, and I have $10,000 in my savings account."

● **Forget FDIC security.** Given the option of a higher interest rate investment with a secure major corporation that probably has more reserves than the FDIC, many people will still automatically opt for the bank investment because of FDIC insurance.

● **Ignore the banks' amortization schedule for mortgages.** When you make your monthly payment, especially in the early part of your mortgage, very little goes toward the principal. However, if you choose to pay a small amount extra every month, this will go toward the principal and save you an enormous amount of money.

● **Don't put all your money in one certificate of deposit.** Now that you can deposit as little as $1,000 for the money-market rate, split your deposits to get the same interest rate and more liquidity. If you put your money into a $10,000 or $20,000 CD and then find you need to take out $1,000 or $2,000, you will have to pay a horrendous penalty. Instead buy 10 or 20 $1,000 CDs.

Source: Edward F. Mrkvicka, Jr., is the author of Your Bank Is Ripping You Off, *St. Martin's Press.*

Picking the Right Bank for You

● **Banks are suppliers and should be evaluated as such.** Judge a bank's performance as you would that of a vital supplier—in terms of tangible factors (pricing, satisfactory performance, etc.) and intangible ones (loyalty, dependability and a willingness to be flexible).

Source: Cash Management *by business journalist John M. Kelly.*

● **Shop for a bank before deciding where to keep your personal savings.** *Check to see:* **(1)** How rush-hour traffic is handled. **(2)** If there are express lines. **(3)** If there are branches near your home and your work. **(4)** If bank officers are accessible. **(5)** If all types of services are offered.

Source: How to Invest $50–$5,000 *by financial analyst Nancy Dunnan, Harper & Row.*

> **"The average family overpays its bank more than $100,000 over the course of a 40-year relationship."**

Choosing a Bank Account

Banks offer a bewildering array of accounts and rates to choose from. In order to compare, ask:

● **Is the account tiered?** Are there different rates for higher balances?

● **What are the fees and charges if the account balance drops below a minimum?**

● **What are the monthly maintenance fees?**

● **What are the transaction fees?** How many checks can be written at no charge? What is the cost per check beyond a certain number a month? Is there a charge for using the automated teller machine?

● **Is there a penalty for closing the account early?** (At some banks you can be hit with a charge if you close a new account within the first 90 days.)

● **How is the account insured?** (FDIC insurance provides $100,000 per person, including principal and interest.)

● **Am I eligible for a low-cost "life-line" account?**

Source: Investor's Daily, *New York.*

How to Protect Yourself From Your Banker

The average family overpays its bank more than $100,000 over the course of a 40-year relationship—borrowing money for mortgages, home improvements and auto purchases, and using checking and savings accounts. But any knowledgeable customer—large or small—can easily and effectively beat the banking system.

What the banks don't want you to know:

● **Once you make a deposit,** banks cannot put excessive holds on your deposited checks. Federal law requires banks to clear your checks according to deadlines based on the type of check and its place of origin. But some banks do better than the federal requirements. *Helpful:* Ask your bank for its policy on clearing checks, and compare it with that of some others. If you run a lot of money through your account, it may pay to switch to a bank with the swiftest check-clearing policy.

• **Most loans,** whether for mortgages, property insurance or car purchases, are negotiable, and it does not matter how much or how little you've deposited with the loaning bank. You will have to push for a better deal. No bank will simply volunteer one.

• **Bank safe-deposit boxes aren't as safe as** **you've been led to believe.** Although you'll be told that the boxes are fully insured, it's difficult to collect on losses unless you can prove to the insurance company which contents you lost. If the bank is robbed or burns down, proving your loss is almost impossible

HIDE ASSETS FROM THE IRS—LEGALLY

Many people keep assets in a safe-deposit box, thinking that no one will ever find out about it. But the name of the renter of a safe-deposit box isn't kept secret.

It doesn't help to rent a box in your own name—mainly because, for a fee, the American Safe Deposit Association (317-888-1118) can run a cross-country search of member banks for an estate, family of a deceased individual, etc.

And the IRS, if it's looking for assets of yours, will do a bank search for safe-deposit boxes held in your name. (It's especially easy for the IRS to track down boxes that you pay for with a personal check—it simply goes through your canceled checks or it looks over old tax returns to see if any itemized deductions were taken for the safe deposit box rental.)

To conceal the existence of a safe-deposit box:

• **Ask your lawyer to set up a nominee corporation**—a corporation that has no other function but to stand in your place for the purposes you designate, such as to rent a safe-deposit box.

• **Rent a box in the name of the corporation and pay for it in cash.** Your name and signature will be on the bank signature card, but the corporation, not you, will be listed as the box's owner on the bank's records. And because you paid cash, there will be nothing in your records to connect the box with you.

• **You can, if you want,** name another person as signatory in addition to yourself. Then, if something happens to you, that person will be able to get into the box.

Additional protection: Having a safe-deposit box in a corporation's name permits the box to be opened by your survivors without the state's or the bank's being notified of your death and having the box sealed.

Otherwise, the survivors must get to the box before the funeral to look for a will and to find whatever else may be there.

Source: Edward Mendlowitz, partner, Mendlowitz Weitsen, CPAs, 2 Pennsylvania Plaza, New York, NY 10121.

Not Like the Good Old Days

People used to view their bank as a partner in financial dealings. Common wisdom said that if you bundled all your business at one bank, you'd have a friend for life. The loyalty of a personal relationship would be there to help when the need arose. No longer.

Today's bankers are concerned with only one thing: the bottom line. The so-called Five-C's by which banks used to determine creditworthiness—collateral, capital, condition, character, and capacity—are now referred to as the "Three C's." They no longer care about character and capacity. Even if you once starved so that you could pay off a note, your past performance will mean nothing when you apply for a new loan.

Checking and Savings Accounts

The best checking account is a NOW (negotiable order of withdrawal) account because it pays interest on outstanding balances.

Important: How interest is computed, when it accrues and at what point you can write checks against deposits.

Best: Interest should be figured on a day-of-deposit-to-day-of-withdrawal basis, compounded and paid daily.

It's almost impossible to reach a

decision by comparing the offerings of all banks in your area. *Helpful:* Ask officers at several banks, "If I put $1,000 in my account at the beginning of a quarter and write ten checks totaling $750, how much would I have—after adding interest and subtracting bank fees (charges, per-check fees, charges for deposits)—at the end?"

Overdraft: If you write a check that can't be covered by your account, the bank will usually return the check unpaid and charge you for the trouble. Some banks charge as much as $25 for an overdraft. *Real out-of-pocket cost for the bank:* About $1. To beat the overdraft system, negotiate with the bank for your own personal overdraft policy. You can often convince a bank officer to cover the check with funds from, for example, your savings account and reduce the overdraft charge to a nominal fee.

Negotiating a Loan

Research the total cost of a loan at a minimum of three banks. Let each bank know that you're investigating others at the same time. Compare every aspect of each bank's deal—interest rates, legal fees, points, etc. Then, visit the president (if it's a small bank) or manager of the one offering the best deal. Explain that in addition to opening an account, you'll also be interested in borrowing some money. Ask for an introduction to the loan officer. *Benefit:* When you're ready to take out the loan, you'll have access to the one person who can adjust the rules to your advantage.

Keep in mind that no matter how hard-nosed the bank seems, it's more profitable for the bank to knock a half a percentage point or more off the loan than to have you walk out the door, especially if it believes you'll take your other accounts with you.

● **Mortgage loans.** The bank calculates a fixed monthly figure to cover your repayment over the term of the loan. Early payments usually cover only the interest. As the loan matures, payments begin to reduce the amount of principal you owe.

Surefire way to cut your costs:
Deliberately overpay each month, even by just a few dollars. *Benefit:* Extra payments are automatically used to repay part of the principal—and the less principal outstanding, the less you'll pay in interest on it. *Example:* Paying off a $100,000, 30-year loan at 9% by adding to the monthly payment an extra $50 a month gets the loan paid in about 23 years, a net saving of almost $50,000 in interest charges.

The bank might refuse to accept the extra payments. Discuss it with the president or manager. If you get nowhere, take it up with the state or federal agency that regulates your bank. You're sure to get your way.

● **Installment loans.** You pay interest on the full amount of the standard installment loan even though you pay it off bit by bit and therefore don't have full use of the money during the life of the loan. That's costly compared with a loan you pay off all at once at the end of the term (a "single-payment note").

Not all banks are willing to provide single-payment notes—installments are much more profitable. But shopping around can save you hundreds of dollars on a typical auto loan.

Safe-Deposit Boxes

Plenty of them have been robbed, burned or otherwise compromised. Banks assure customers that with the bank's millions in insurance, the customer's valuables will be covered.

Trap: If you can't prove your loss—and most people can't—you won't collect a penny.

Self-defense: You'll have to forgo secrecy about the contents of the box. Appraise valuables and take the appraisal to the bank. A bank officer will then verify that the appraised items are in the box. Next, request from the bank a "safekeeping receipt" and list all the valuables—jewels, bearer bonds, cash, etc. Each time you open the box, take a bank officer with you to note on the receipt the removal or addition of any items. The receipt will guarantee reimbursement in the event of a loss.

It's also a good idea to insure items in your safe-deposit box through an "off-premise" rider on your home owners policy.

Source: Edward F. Mrkvicka, Jr., is the author of Your Bank Is Ripping You Off, *St. Martin's Press.*

What Banks Don't Tell You

● **Some banks say they let you draw on all checks immediately,** provided you put up another bank account as collateral. *Catch:* If a check backed by a six-month certificate of deposit bounces, the bank can break into the certificate before maturity. and you may have to pay an interest penalty.

Protection: Pick a bank that will allow you time to cover a bounced check before it takes any money from your time deposit. Be sure your bank has this policy before you decide to use a time deposit as collateral.

● **Don't bite if the bank offers you a big saving** in return for a lump-sum payoff of the old low-interest mortgage on your home. *Catch:* The discount "bonus" comes from principal, not interest, and is taxable income. You will gain a greater return on your money if you set aside the amount sought by the bank and invest it yourself.

● **Checks dated more than six months ago are usually not cashable through normal channels** no matter how much money the issuer has in the bank.

● **If the amount written on the check in words is different** from the amount written in numbers, the bank will pay the sum shown in words.

● **Be careful when endorsing checks.** To prevent loss of money, when sending checks by mail for deposit, write "For Deposit Only" above your signature on the back. That limits the endorsement. An endorsed check with nothing but a signature is the same as cash and may be used by anybody if it's lost or stolen.

Beware of Banks Bearing Gifts

"Free" gifts from banks are usually included on year-end interest statements. If the gift is generous (say, a free vacation for opening a CD), it may saddle you with considerable extra taxable income.

Source: Putting Your Money to Work *by Lana J. Chandler, Betterway Publications.*

Interest Rates Aren't Always What They Seem

One of the banker's lucrative stocks in trade is the average customer's innocent belief that 10% is always 10%. Like so many aspects of the financial business, it's not that simple.

As IRS regulations allow a business to elect from the various accounting methods available, the banking laws allow financial institutions to use varying methods of computing interest—both interest charged and interest paid.

> "The best loan deal you can get (for a given interest rate) is a single-payment, simple interest installment note, with a provision for monthly payments."

This means that in shopping for the best deal, either on a loan or on a savings account or other deposit vehicle, the customer must be aware of the method of interest computation in order to make a valid comparison and choose the best.

Savings Accounts

Banks used to advertise a complicated variety of interest-calculation methods. But the 1993 Truth in Savings Act obligates all banks to state the interest rates they pay in the same way—as the annual percentage yield, or APY. The APY represents the amount of interest your principal would earn if you left it on deposit for one year, and includes such variables as the interest rate and the bank's frequency of compounding it.

Shop for the best APY by getting quotes from at least three institutions. But be aware: In today's low-interest-rate environment, after figuring in taxes and inflation, you'll at best break even when you deposit your savings in a bank.

Loans

What about loan rates? They're even more complicated, since loan officers tend deliberately to perpetuate the mystique of borrowing. The best loan deal you can get (for a given interest rate) is a single-payment, simple interest installment note, with a provision for monthly payments.

Suppose you're shopping for a new car loan of $7,000. One bank offers it to you at 10.25 APR for 48 months on the above terms, and another bank offers you a standard installment loan at the same APR. On the second note, with exactly the same principal, the same term, and the same collateral, you would end up paying a total of $140 more in interest over the term of the loan.

SAFEGUARDS FOR SAFE-DEPOSIT BOXES

Valuables stored in bank safe-deposit boxes are not automatically protected against loss through burglary, flood or fire. To be compensated for missing valuables, depositors may have to initiate a lawsuit against the bank. The chances of winning are very, very slim.

Safeguards: Although reimbursement levels are low, buy additional, nonbank insurance for the contents of the boxes. Most negotiable items, such as securities, bank notes, gold, coins and cash, are not covered, however.

Alternative: Store stocks and bonds at the brokerage house where they were purchased. These firms have a legal and financial responsibility to guard securities stored with them.

Another option: Open a custody account with a bank. The bank holds securities and other assets in its vault. It collects and credits all dividends, but does not manage the assets. The bank will replace any asset in the vault that is lost, stolen or harmed. Charges are generally based on the size of the account and the composition of the holdings.

FDIC Insurance

Many banks advertise their Federal Deposit Insurance Corporation (FDIC) insurance as providing security for depositors at no retail cost. Customers—particularly the elderly—often will deposit only in insured accounts, reasoning that the security provided in a bank as opposed to the market justifies a lower interest rate. However, since bank depositors normally receive interest rates 2% to 3% below those available on other deposit vehicles, it's fair to say that customers do pay for FDIC insurance.

From an investment standpoint, it would be better to ignore the FDIC insurance and opt for higher market rates as long as you investigate the investment carefully. It is important to substantiate corporate reserves that would be used to repay depositors/investors in the case of default. (For example, many deposit vehicles are backed by government-issue bonds.) Corporate investment opportunities frequently have better reserves than the FDIC.

Source: Edward F. Mrkvicka, Jr., is the author of Your Bank Is Ripping You Off, *St. Martin's Press.*

More on Safe-Deposit Boxes

Can you locate all your important papers and documents quickly? Guarantee it with a safe-deposit box. Important papers will be at your fingertips and protected from fire, theft or other casualty. Of course, you can use the box to protect your jewelry and other valuable things, too.

The fee for renting a bank safe-deposit box is surprisingly low. Only two keys are made to fit the box, and you keep both of them. The box cannot be opened without your permission until you die or you don't pay your rental fee for a year.

In a nonpayment situation you will receive a certified registered letter to give you one last chance to pay the fee. If you don't, the contents of the box will be removed in the presence of a bank official, inventoried, verified, and then stored in a safe place until you eventually claim them.

Documents to keep in your safe-deposit box:
- **Birth, marriage, and death certificates.**
- **Divorce or separation agreements.**
- **Title papers to real estate, car, etc.**

- **Mortgage papers.**
- **Contracts and legal agreements.**
- **Stock certificates.**
- **Military discharge papers.**

In addition, many people keep credit cards and photographs of the inside and outside of their home in the safe-deposit box to support insurance claims.

Smart idea: Make copies of these records before you put them into the box for easy reference.

This is also important should your bank burn down—the vault may be the last thing to burn, but it will burn.

Final check: Make sure someone knows where the safe-deposit box is and where the key is, too.

Important: Safe-deposit boxes taken out in a corporate name don't get sealed upon the death of one of the principals. This might be very useful for closely held firms.

Some items should not be kept in a safe-deposit box:

- **Keep your will at your attorney's office,** with only a copy in the safe-deposit box. *Reason:* Safe-deposit boxes are sealed at death until the IRS sees what's inside. This could prevent relatives from getting into the box right away to see if a will even exists.
- **Don't hide money in a safe-deposit box to prevent taxation on it.** This is illegal, and your heirs might be taxed on the money at your death anyway.

Source: *Rudra Nath, vault custodian, Safe Deposit Department, Marine Midland Bank, NA, 140 Broadway, New York, NY 10015.*

Choosing Between Private And Bank Deposit Boxes

You can rent a safe-deposit box at either a bank or a private corporation that specializes in safety boxes. Weigh the advantages of both types before making a final decision. *What to look for:*

- **Business hours:** Private safe-deposit corporations usually have a longer business day than banks. Some are open 365 days a year. You also can make an appointment to get into your box after business hours.

> **"Don't hide money in a safe-deposit box to prevent taxation on it. This is illegal, and your heirs might be taxed on the money at your death."**

- **Insurance:** Some private corporations automatically insure the contents of your box for $10,000, with more insurance available at nominal prices. Banks provide a minimum amount of insurance with the rental, but the customer is also free to privately insure the box with an insurance company.
- **Cost:** The private safe-deposit boxes are generally more expensive than those at banks.
- **Confidentiality:** Your access to a private safe-deposit box is a numbered code, not your bank account number (as with many bank boxes). This insures the confidentiality of both your safe-deposit box and your bank account.
- **Higher security rating:** Private companies are often rated higher than banks by the Insurance Institute.
- **Sealing:** Bank safe-deposit boxes are automatically sealed at your death. To seal a private-company box, a court order, usually from the IRS, is necessary. And since in a private company your box is not tagged with your bank account number, it is much harder to trace—similar to a Swiss bank account.

Source: *Michael Butcher, general manager, Universal Safe Deposit Corp., 115 E. 57 St., New York, NY 10022.*

Hidden Costs of Automated Teller Machines

Hidden fees for using automated teller machines (ATMs): About 79% of banks charge for withdrawals and 43% for deposits at ATMs not owned by the bank. *Fees:* 6¢–$2.50. For the bank's own ATMs, only 7% charge for withdrawals and 2% for deposits. Read the fine print on the ATM agreement with your bank. If you're paying fees, shop around for a bank whose ATM use is free.

Source: *Study by Sheshunoff Information Services, Inc., a leading provider of banking-industry data, analysis and management tools.*

ATM Fees Are Rising

Almost all banks charge customers who use machines owned by other banks. Now many of those other banks are charging customers access fees as well. *Result:* The average cost of withdrawing money from an ATM anywhere other than your own bank has risen to about $3.

Self-defense: Use a bank teller...or use your own bank's machine. If you must regularly take out funds elsewhere, withdraw larger amounts less often. The average ATM user withdraws only $55. At an ATM with a $2 fee, the withdrawal cost is a very high 3.63%.

Source: Edward F. Mrkvicka, Jr., is the author of Your Bank Is Ripping You Off, St. Martin's Press.

Overseas ATM Use Alert

Notify your bank if you will be using your ATM card to make cash withdrawals overseas, especially if you are not a frequent traveler. A series of withdrawals from unexpected places might lead your bank to block your account.

Cardholders should check with their banks to be sure a primary account has been designated (checking or savings). Many banks outside the United States do not allow you to choose the account from which you make the transaction. If your primary account is not designated by the U.S. bank, the overseas bank will make the decision as to which account the transaction will affect or, in some cases, deny the request.

Caution: Many keypads of machines outside the United States only have numbers, not letters. *Good idea:* Before going overseas, know the numeric equivalent of your PIN number.

Important: If your ATM card is lost or stolen, notify the bank within four business days in order to limit your liability to no more than $50.

Source: David Keenan, vice president for operations of the Master-Card/Cirrus ATM network, Westchester, IL.

Fixing Money Machine Errors

ATM errors must be reported to your bank within 60 days of the date the problem appears on your statement. Under the Electronic Funds Transfer Act, the bank must investigate and report to you within 10 business days. If the bank needs more time, it can take another 45 days—but it must deposit the disputed amount into your account within 10 business days of the day it decides to extend the investigation.

Source: Sylvia Porter's Personal Finance.

Beware the Black-Market Foreign Exchange

Classic setup: You're in France and the official exchange rate is six francs/dollar. On the street a well-dressed gentleman offers to change your money for seven francs/dollar.

Sting: He hands you a bankroll to count—it's correct. You hand it back to get out your money. He does a quick switch, substituting a sham bankroll for the real one, hands you the roll, and disappears.

Self-defense: Exchange money only at banks and official currency-exchange locations.

Use only approved exchange locations to get currency-exchange receipts. These are often needed when you change the currency back into dollars. (Receipts are proof that currency was obtained legitimately.)

Cashing a Letter

Letters or telegrams may serve as checks. *Requirements:* The letter must be addressed to a bank. And it must state that a specific amount is to be paid on demand either to the bearer of the letter or to the order of a named person. *Point:* If any one of these requirements is not met, the letter will not be valid as a check. Of course, the bank will make its usual effort to verify that the "check" is valid.

Source: United Milk Prods. Co. *vs.* Lawndale Nat'l Bank, 392 F 2d 876, 5 UCC Rep. 143.

Checks Marked "Payment in Full"

If there's no dispute as to the amount, a check tendered for less than the amount due and marked "payment in full" (or the like) may be cashed without prejudicing the right to recover the balance.

If there's a bona fide dispute as to the amount owing, the creditor must be wary.

Alternatives: Reject the check and demand full payment. *Or:* Accept the check but risk that payment will be deemed to have settled the disputed claim for the lesser amount. It's easy for a debtor who wants to pay less than the amount he or she was billed to create a dispute on the basis of quantitative or qualitative deficiencies in the goods or services supplied.

Stamp the check with the statement "Check is accepted without prejudice and with full reservation of all rights under Section 1-207 of the Uniform Commercial Code." The effectiveness of this technique, although untested in courts, may protect a creditor's rights.

How to Spot a Forged Check

● **See if the check has perforations on one side.** (A false check often has four smooth sides, since the forger cuts them with a paper cutter after printing.)

● **The code numbers printed on a legitimate check reflect no light.** They are printed in magnetic ink, which is dull.

● **About 90% of all hot checks are drawn on accounts less than one year old.** The numbers in the upper-right-hand corner of the check indicate the age of the account. Be suspicious of those that are numbered 101–150 or 1001–1050 (the starting numbers).

Source: Frank W. Abagnale, once a master forger and now a consultant to banks and retailers, writing in Real Estate Today.

Bank Fees Self-Defense

Bank fees are on the rise. *Here are ways to reduce or avoid them altogether:*

● **Automated teller machines (ATMs).** The average cost for making a withdrawal at your own bank is now up to $1. But this fee can rise to as much as $3 when you take out cash from an ATM that is not owned by your bank.

Self-defense: Stick to your bank's ATM and find a bank that charges for ATM use only if your account balance falls below a specific amount.

You can also cut down on ATM fees by using the machines less frequently. Plan a weekly budget, and use the ATM only once each week to withdraw enough cash.

● **Minimum-balance fees.** An increasing number of banks now charge a fee if your balance dips below the minimum requirement for even a single day. Other banks still base the fee on your average daily balance over the course of a month.

In both cases, such fees can be avoided.

Self-defense: Look elsewhere for a better deal. Small banks, credit unions and savings and loans tend to have much lower balance requirements and substantially lower fees. Before giving up on your current bank, however, ask if it has a different type of account—one with fewer "bells and whistles"—that would be more cost-efficient for you.

● **Nuisance fees.** Believe it or not, some banks now charge customers $3 just for calling to find out their balances.

Self-defense: If you already have an account at such a bank, threaten to take your business elsewhere unless those charges are rescinded.

Call the bank manager and begin by saying politely that you have been a good customer for a long time.

Use It or Lose It Credit Card Alert

Credit cards are being revoked from customers with good credit standing but who do not use the cards to the issuer's satisfaction. One bank canceled 100,000 no-fee credit cards it considered unprofitable because holders did not use them often enough. Another bank threatened to close some accounts that paid no interest. It said people who want to keep the cards would have to charge $2,500 within six months…transfer a $1,000 balance and pay interest…or have their accounts closed.

Source: Ruth Susswein, executive director, Bankcard Holders of America, 524 Branch Dr., Salem, VA 24153.

Dealing with Banks, Credit & Debt

If you don't get any satisfaction from the manager, speak to the bank's vice president of operations.

Warning: This approach probably won't succeed if your account is at a large money-center bank. Generally, the smaller the bank, the more flexible it will be. If you must switch, don't sign up for a new account without reviewing the institution's full fee schedule.

● **Safe-deposit boxes.** When banks send out renewal forms for safe-deposit boxes, some ask you to pay for insurance on the box's contents. It's optional,

and, in most cases, it is best to decline the coverage.

Reason 1: Such insurance shouldn't be required to protect your valuables. The bank's vault is supposed to do that.

Reason 2: The insurance may be useless. If the boxes are robbed, the claims adjuster may not believe that the items you say you stored were actually in the box. *Better:* Insure the contents of the box through an off-premise rider to your home owners policy.

● **Inactivity/activity fees.** Some banks now have

WHAT TO DO IF YOUR CHECK BOUNCES

If you have been unlucky enough to bounce a check recently, you may well have been shocked at the size of the charge ($10, $15, $25 or more) assessed to your account for this misdemeanor. Does it seem strange that with the advent of all that cost-cutting automation in the banking industry, the expense of processing an overdraft should have risen so sharply? It should. The fact is that with deregulation, many banks have decided to transform the return of customers' checks into a profitable industry by assigning purely punitive charges, totally unrelated to the real cost of processing the transaction. (The procedure involves no monetary outlay on the bank's part—unless the bank pays your check, which is unlikely—and the in-house paperwork cost averages about $1.25 per check.)

What You Can Do

The basic precept to keep in mind is, don't allow your bank to invade your personal finances any more than you would a thief. Most people are surprisingly passive about this tres-

pass—they feel helpless, bound by the rules. But never forget, it's your money, not theirs, and they have enough ways of making your money work for them that you needn't put up with high-handed penalties for non-services.

If the overdraft was the result of a bank error (losing track of a deposit, charging other customers' checks to your account, etc.), you should demand not only to have any and all charges removed, you should also see that a letter goes out from the bank to each party to whom a check of yours has been returned, explaining that the bank was at fault.

Here are some tactics that will help you prevail:

● **Be firm.** Be persistent. Don't hesitate to go over people's heads. It is usually easier for a bank employee or officer to give in to your demands than have the matter come to the attention of his or her superior.

● **Don't forget that you have access to small claims court,** and don't be shy about making sure the

bank is aware that you know this. Small claims court is a great leveler—it makes you the equal of the bank and all its lawyers and accountants. And, again, it may cost a bank considerably more to make an appearance in court than to give in to your point of view.

● **If the threat of small claims court doesn't work,** you might mention the possibility of legal action on a grander scale. One customer of a major Chicago bank brought a class-action suit against that institution for $10 million in punitive and actual damages equal to the bank's earnings from its check-clearing policy over a 10-year period.

Of course, if your overdraft is purely a result of your own negligence or poor arithmetic, you may well have to bear the consequences as cheerfully as you can. Meanwhile, look for a new bank, one that will not charge you for this sort of "service"—or at least keeps such charges within reason.

Source: *Edward F. Mrkvicka, Jr., is the author of* Your Bank Is Ripping You Off*, St. Martin's Press.*

penalties for depositors with idle accounts. Conversely, some tack on extra fees for customers who make "too many" withdrawals and/or deposits. *Strategy:* Ask your bank about its activity-fee policy. If it doesn't make sense, write a letter to the president or bank manager politely threatening to withdraw your money.

Source: *Edward F. Mrkvicka, Jr., is the author of* Your Bank Is Ripping You Off, *St. Martin's Press.*

All About Debit Cards

Pros: Using a debit card is safer than carrying cash and handier than writing checks. Fees are comparable to using a bank Automated Teller Machine (ATM) card. If you make many purchases, you can get a card from an issuer that charges only a flat annual fee—rarely more than $24.

Cons: Many merchants do not yet accept debit cards. Some charge a fee for doing so, but since they get their money instantly, this is an extraordinary charge; be sure to ask about it before using your card. If you already have a bank ATM card that works like a debit card in stores, you won't need a VISA or MasterCard debit card unless you travel.

Editor's note: As debit card purchases are instantaneously deducted from your account, you lose the grace period you likely would have with a credit card purchase.

If your debit card is lost or stolen, you could be liable for up to $500 or more if it's used illegally. That's ten times the maximum loss potential of a credit card.

Source: *Gerri Detweiler, consumer credit consultant in Dale City, VA, and author of* The Ultimate Credit Handbook, *Good Advice Press.*

Borrow From Several Banks

Many business advisers believe it's best to bank in one place to get more influence there. But in a tight money market, that one bank can squeeze you—by recalling your loan or putting pressure on you to pay it off in a way you didn't anticipate. *Better:* Spread loans among a few banks. That way, if any one of them creates trouble for you, there's somewhere else to go immediately. This is similar to the principle of investment diversification—never put all your eggs in one basket.

Source: *Take a Chance to Be First by Warren Avis, the founder of Avis Rent-a-Car, Macmillan.*

How Fast Should Your Checks Clear?

By federal law, banks cannot place excessive holds on your deposited checks. The 1987 Expedited Funds Availability Act requires banks to clear your checks according to deadlines based on the type of check and its place of origin. Here is a guide to the maximum time limits allowed:

- **After one business day.** Federal, state and local government checks; checks drawn on the same bank; cashier's checks; certified checks; postal money orders; electronic payments (direct deposit of a regular paycheck); the first $100 of any check.
- **After two business days.** All local checks, generally meaning those drawn on banks in the same city and often the same state, deposited with a teller in the bank; all cash, cashier's checks and state and local government checks deposited into a bank's own ATM before noon.
- **After three business days.** Local checks fed into the bank's ATM machines before noon.
- **After five business days.** Nonlocal checks in the continental United States. (Banks in Hawaii, Alaska, the U.S. Virgin Islands and Puerto Rico can take an extra business day for checks from outside their borders.)
- **After seven business days.** All deposits made before noon into ATMs not owned by your bank.
- **After 30 business days.** Funds from checks deposited into a new account may not be available to you for the first 30 days after the account is opened. The same sometimes applies to checks for amounts greater than $5,000. If you are redepositing a check that has previously been returned, you may also encounter longer delays.

Source: *Reader's Digest* Know Your Rights, *1995, p. 289*

When the Bank Can't Bounce a Check

The bank may have to honor a check if it takes too long to bounce it. Uniform Commercial Code requires that the bank take some action by midnight of the business day after it receives the check.

But the bank gets more time if there's an emergency beyond its control, for example, computer breakdown.

If there is a dispute and the amount of money involved is substantial, don't take the bank's word for what the law says. Protect yourself; see a lawyer.

Line of Credit vs. Loan Commitment

A *line of credit* with a bank facilitates corporate borrowing but offers less financial security than a loan commitment. The bank can cancel the line of credit at any time. Also, the bank is not required to advance the full amount of the line. A *loan commitment*, on the other hand, cannot be canceled during its life except under special circumstances spelled out in the loan contract. Note that the company must pay a fee for this assurance of financial availability. There is no fee for the line of credit.

Source: Midlantic NB *vs.* Commonwealth General, *1980 D.C. App. (4th) 386 So. (2) 31.*

If Your Statement Is Wrong And the Bank Won't Help

When you receive a checking account statement that appears to be incorrect, your first move should be to balance the account. This means making sure that all the additions and subtractions to the opening balance do in fact produce the final balance. If you have difficulty doing this, your bank should be willing to help. Almost every branch has a bookkeeper who specializes in balancing accounts. (If this takes longer than a few minutes, the bank will charge a fee, but it's worth it.)

This process of reconciling your records and arithmetic with those of the bank should reveal the discrepancy. Most of the possible explanations will be simple to deal with. It's either your error or the bank's—a check or routine charge not recorded by you, a deposit not credited to your account, that sort of thing.

If the problem is one of those mysterious "adjustments" or "miscellaneous debits," the bank is, of course, obligated to identify and justify this to you. If it cannot do so within two or three days, insist that the disputed amount be credited to your account pending clarification.

Once you know what the bank has charged you for, you will have to pursue getting the charge dropped if you think it's unfair. For this, you will need to talk to the manager (who may be hard to locate, due to the size and organization of large banks). Discuss the dispute with him or her face to face. If you don't get satisfaction, go straight to the top—the chief executive officer. Get the CEO's name and address and write a clear letter outlining your problem. If you don't get satisfaction on this level (don't be surprised if some bank officer other than the CEO—possibly a customer relations professional—intervenes at this point), write to the nearest Federal Deposit Insurance Corporation (FDIC) office and to the local newspaper's "fix-it" column. Most banks will respond to that combination.

Then change banks.

Source: Margaret "Marty" O. Tunnell, vice president and region manager, San Francisco Regional Corporate Center, 405 Montgomery St., San Francisco, CA 94104.

> " [A bank] is...obligated to...justify [mysterious 'adjustments' or... 'debits']. If it cannot...within two or three days, insist that the disputed amount be credited to your account. "

Getting a Bank Loan After You're Refused

It's unfortunate but true that banks are not only decidedly conservative in choosing whom to entrust with their money, they are also often intimidating. Banks know that a customer who is on the defensive either will be afraid to question a refusal or will be so happy to receive an approval that he or she won't try to negotiate a better loan rate. But it doesn't have to be this way.

Preparation

The person who goes to the loan officer armed only with some vague figures entrusted to a faulty memory is not likely to be successful (unless he or she is the bank president's golf partner, in which case it won't much matter). By the same token, any potential loan customer who comprehends all the ramifications of a loan request, is on top of all the facts and figures, and has it all down on paper stands a very good chance of getting what he or she asks for. That kind of preparation impresses loan officers—it commands their respect.

If you are applying for a personal loan, bring an updated financial (net worth) statement. If the request is for a business loan, besides the financial statement, thorough documentation should include back tax returns for two to three years (if available), profit and loss projections for two or three years into the future, and a pro forma sheet describing clearly why you need to borrow, how you intend to use the money and how you intend to generate enough income to pay the tariff. A competent presentation accompanied by neat, clear documentation may make all the difference in your request, and will help lower the interest rate offered.

Persistence

If your banker turns you down, you can, of course, go elsewhere with your request, but the chances are that pursuing the matter with your original bank will eventually pay the desired dividend. Most customers, in fact, don't follow up a loan denial, possibly because they're convinced that once the bank has spoken, the answer is written in stone. This is simply not the case—these decisions are often reversed "on appeal."

Your first move after receiving a turndown is to approach the loan officer and request an in-depth explanation. Having gotten the true word, ask the loan officer what it would take to elicit a positive response. Believe it or not, this simple gambit will often be enough to turn the trick! *Explanation:* Sad but true, loan officers often turn down perfectly legitimate applications because, on some level, they can't

be bothered. Yet when a customer requests that officer's assistance, this bit of flattery often has the effect of motivating him or her to take the time that should have been taken in the first instance.

Assertiveness

If the gambit does not work and the loan officer will not help, go to his or her supervisor—or at least make it clear that you intend to do so. Bankers don't like people going over their heads and will go to great lengths to avoid that eventuality, including granting loan requests. The same principle operates with bank officers on all levels.

If you are not getting satisfaction within the bank organization and are convinced you are being discriminated against, you should consider filing suit under the Equal Credit Opportunity Act of 1961. But here again, the bank's awareness of your intention to pursue this course may decide the issue long before you get anywhere near a courtroom.

Other outside avenues to pursue include small claims court and lodging complaints with the comptroller of the currency in Washington, DC (if the bank is a national bank), the state banking authority (if it is not), and the Federal Deposit Insurance Corporation (if your bank is so insured). The point is not so much to bring these forces into play as to cause the bank to take notice. Any of these alternatives will more than likely get the bank's attention, and once your banker realizes you are serious about what you're doing, you may find your loan denial is magically turned into an approval.

> "Most customers... don't follow up a loan denial, possibly because they're convinced that once the bank has spoken, the answer is written in stone. This is simply not the case—these decisions are often reversed 'on appeal.'"

Source: *Edward F. Mrkvicka, Jr., is the author of* Your Bank Is Ripping You Off, *St. Martin's Press.*

Finding the Right Loan Officer

● **Shop for loan officers if you're seeking funding for your business.**

Key factor: Loan application approach. Before putting in your application, talk with the officer about your plans. Ask what the chances are of your loan's being granted. If the answer is something like "The committee will make that decision," try a different loan officer or another bank.

Best reply: "I've been in this business 15 years and have had only three loans turned down. I don't take an application unless I expect it to be accepted."

● **Bad credit need not prevent you from getting a bank loan.**

Key: Find a banker with clout. Junior loan officers in most banks are sternly warned never to lend to people with bad credit, no matter what explanation the applicant may offer. But a more seasoned loan officer, at the vice-president level or higher, often has the experience and authority to bend the rules.

Source: Take a Chance to Be First *by Warren Avis, the founder of Avis Rent-a-Car, Macmillan.*

Tricks Banks Play With Interest Rates

Banks teach their loan officers a number of strategies to get an extra d% or even g% from borrowers.

Recognize some of their tricks:

● **Doing the negotiating at the bank,** which is familiar territory to the banker, intimidating to the borrower.

● **Not mentioning the rate at all,** but simply filling it in on the note.

● **"Since you need the money today, let's write it up at X%.** Then we can talk later about changing it." The banker hopes you'll never bring it up again. He or she certainly won't.

● **Flat statement:** "The rate for this type of loan is X%." (Never true except for small consumer loans. There is always room to negotiate.)

● **Postponing the rate discussion as long as possible,** hoping the borrower will weaken under deadline pressure.

● **Ego building.** The bank president or manager stops by during negotiations.

● **Talking constantly about how little the mortgage interest costs after taxes,** and comparing it with finance company rates, secondary mortgage rates, or the cost of equity capital.

The banker looks at the customer's account as a package, including loans, average balances maintained and fees for service. *Borrower options:* Trade off higher average balances for a lower interest rate on borrowings, or vice versa.

The borrower is at a disadvantage because he or she negotiates a loan only once a year or less, while the banker does so full time. So prepare carefully for negotiations. *Good tactics for the borrower:*

● **Ask the interest rate question early**—in your office, not the bank. Don't volunteer suggestions.

● **Negotiate everything as a package**—rate, repayment schedule, collateral, compensating balances. The banker's strategy will be to try to nail down everything else and then negotiate the interest rate when the borrower has no more leverage and no room to maneuver.

● **React with surprise and shock** when the banker mentions the interest rate, no matter what the figure is.

Source: Lawrence T. Jilk, Jr., executive vice president, National Bank of Boyertown, PA, in The Journal of Commercial Bank Lending.

A Standard Bank Loan Rip-Off

Many loan customers are not even aware that they're paying credit life and disability insurance as part of their loan costs, but it is the standard policy of many banks to include this coverage in all personal loans.

A credit (or mortgage) life and disability policy is one that guarantees repayment to the bank of any unpaid portion of the debt concerned in the event of the customer's death or disability. It offers no benefits (other than possible peace of mind) to the customer or the customer's family. It is understandable that a bank would wish to minimize the problems that might arise in the event of such an unhappy occurrence, but asking the customer to bear the cost of this self-protection is unconscionable.

Even assuming that a loan customer is so compulsively financial-security minded as to want to cover all such eventualities, there are many more cost-effective ways to do this while securing some benefits for his or her family. A whole life policy is one such vehicle. And the chances are that such a policy, covering at least the initial debt balance, could be bought more cheaply through the family insurance agent. What makes it even more outrageous is that the coverage is often treated as part of the loan obligation, and, as such, the bank charges you hidden interest!

To top things off, the bank will also be receiving a direct cash kickback of up to 40% of the premium, just for writing the policy. Practically the only way a financially responsible adult could let such a state of affairs come about in the first place is through ignorance. Your banker will often gloss over this facet of the deal he or she is offering you.

Standard practice is to write the provision into the loan papers with nary a mention from the banker. Under these circumstances, it's easy for a customer, assuming he or she notices the provision at all, to

EARNING MONEY ABROAD

Earning income from investments or employment overseas can be profitable. What most people don't realize, however, is that nearly all of this income is subject to U.S. taxes.

Since 1962 Washington has taken successful aim at the foreign tax havens that once enticed American investors by promising to help them avoid the IRS.

● **Americans who work abroad.** If you are a resident of another country for a full year or live abroad 330 days out of a consecutive 12 months, up to $72,000 of your earned income need not be taxed by the IRS.

But depending on the foreign country, that income may be taxable there. Nevertheless, there are countries that offer tax breaks to bolster local economies. *Example:* Many countries, notably Ireland and Israel, offer a favorable tax climate for retirees, taxing only current income brought into the country.

If you must pay income taxes abroad, the United States allows you to use them against your taxes here, generally dollar for dollar. According to the IRS, you will end up paying the higher of the U.S. or foreign tax.

● **Foreign bank accounts.** Many

people assume that it is possible to avoid the IRS by opening bank accounts in, say, Switzerland. *Reality:* Americans are required to answer yes or no on their tax returns—Schedule B of Form 1040—as to whether they have any foreign bank accounts.

If someone checks no when the truth is yes, that is *tax evasion*—a serious crime punishable by interest, penalties and back taxes. In extreme cases of evasion, the IRS might even file charges of *tax fraud*, possibly punishable by imprisonment.

By checking yes, income tax is owed. As a result, putting money in Swiss banks simply to avoid taxes makes little sense, especially since Swiss income taxes are higher than U.S. taxes. *Example:* Switzerland withholds up to 35% on interest earned. Even if you are in a higher U.S. tax bracket, you will wind up paying the higher of the two taxes.

Dangerous alternatives: There are other international jurisdictions that have strict bank-secrecy laws and modern banking facilities. Unlike Switzerland, they do not withhold taxes. They are tax-haven countries that are trying to attract foreign funds and are not required to report this income to the account holder's tax authorities. *Example:* Among the alternate havens are the Channel

Islands of Jersey and Guernsey off the coast of Britain, Luxembourg, Liechtenstein, Panama, the Cayman Islands, the Bahamas and Vanuatu, a group of islands in the South Pacific. Ask your accountant about them.

Caution: Though foreign banks are not required to issue Form 1099, which reports interest and dividend income to the IRS, individual Americans must report any income. Anyone who fails to report it and is caught on an audit can expect to be prosecuted for tax evasion.

When to Send Money Abroad

So, is there any reason to deposit money overseas? Yes, but the move should be motivated by sound investment thinking rather than to shelter income from taxes. *Example:* At a time when banks in the United States are paying about 2% to 5% on savings, returns in Argentina and Brazil are as high as 15%. In Britain, returns on savings are around 8%.

But before reaching for that big interest, Americans need to assess the currency-market risks that may be involved. When sending money abroad, to earn high interest your dollars may be converted into that country's currency. You will want the value of that currency to improve in

assume it is a necessary condition (which it almost always is not) and therefore fail to question it.

All in all, it's one of the best money-grabbing scams the commercial banking system has going for it. An informed loan customer should be alert to the policy and prepared to negotiate it out of any loan agreement he makes.

Source: *Edward F. Mrkvicka, Jr., is the author of* Your Bank Is Ripping You Off, *St. Martin's Press.*

Foreign Bank Account Loopholes

If you have more than $400 of dividend and interest income, you must answer the question about whether or not you have an account in a foreign bank. The question is on Schedule B (Interest and Dividend Income).

Loopholes: Even if you do have foreign accounts,

relation to the dollar. Otherwise, your return will remain flat or may even lose ground. *The tax implications of the popular foreign investments:*

● **Foreign mutual funds.** Unlike U.S. mutual funds, many offshore funds don't pay dividends.

Instead, they reinvest all capital gains and income back into their portfolios. *Result:* The value of the fund's shares increases and investors avoid taxes until they sell shares.

When an investor receives a Form 1099 from a U.S. mutual fund reporting dividends and capital-gains distributions, he or she must pay taxes that year unless the shares are held in a tax-deferred retirement account. This is true even if the investor has the fund reinvest the distributions in more fund shares.

However, foreign funds have no such annual distributions. As a result, tax payments to the IRS can legally be avoided. *Exception:* When the appreciated shares are sold. In addition to a tax on the gains, the IRS adds an interest charge to the tax to put them on a par with gains earned by American fund shares. Alternatively, the investor can elect to pay U.S. tax on his share of the foreign mutual fund's earnings.

● **Foreign stocks or bonds.** You may want to invest in foreign securities to diversify your portfolio. In recent years markets in Europe and Latin America have performed like Wall Street.

But be prepared to pay U.S. taxes on any interest, dividends and capital gains. If another country withholds taxes—Germany, for example, withholds 15% on dividends, based on a treaty with the United States—that may be claimed as a credit, which reduces U.S. taxes, dollar for dollar.

● **Setting up a corporation abroad.** This makes sense if you are investing in an active business. The income will not be subject to U.S. tax until distributed to you as a dividend. The corporation therefore can reinvest its earnings in order to expand its business, possibly on a tax-free basis. This is because many developing countries offer tax incentives—even a tax "holiday" running for a period of years when no taxes are owed—to attract business. *Examples:* This can include a hotel in the Caribbean, a garment manufacturer in Honduras or a computer or electronics plant in Singapore, Hong Kong, Thailand or elsewhere in Southeast Asia. India is also attracting entrepreneurs.

The tax incentives, often combined with low wages, enable an entrepreneur to develop a business much faster than at home. In some developing countries, a business owner can make annual returns of 30% to 50%.

Important: There are great risks to getting those returns. The governments of some developing countries can topple in a flash, or business assets could be seized.

Source: *Solomon Packer, international tax specialist and senior tax partner, Price Waterhouse, 1177 Avenue of the Americas, New York, NY 10036.*

you can answer "no" if their combined value was $10,000 or less during the year or if your accounts were with a U.S. military banking facility.

Source: Instructions to Schedule B, Form 1040.

Offshore Scam

Beware of offshore business trusts (contractual companies) that promise to give you financial privacy and protect your assets from the IRS.

Problems: Potential for IRS litigation, high cost, extreme complexity and high profile (which defeats the purpose of a foreign trust).

Source: Jerry Schomp of INVESTigate.

Negotiating a Policy Exception Loan

The Federal Equal Credit Opportunity Act requires lending institutions to respond to your request for credit in a timely fashion and, if they turn you down, to tell you why. What you do depends on why you were turned down. *Here are the primary policy reasons for credit refusal:*

- **Bad credit history.**
- **Excessive debt-to-income ratio.**
- **Inadequate collateral.**

Normally, to get a loan once you've been turned down on a matter of policy, you will have to try to negotiate a "policy exception loan"; this is best done face-to-face with someone you know who has the authority to make such a policy exception. If the reason was bad credit history, however, you should check this out before proceeding further.

Dealing With the Reporting Agency

The bank is required to give you the name and address of the credit-reporting agency on whose records their negative decision is based. The agency is then required to give you a copy of your file on request. (Tell them you have been refused credit or you'll be charged a fee.) If the information in the file is incorrect, write to the agency and say why.

Ask the reporting agency to contact the lender who has turned you down. Also contact the company that reported you to the credit reporting agency in the first place—send them a letter and appropriate documentation, requesting an answer. Follow it up in 30 days if you don't hear from them.

Returning to the Lender

To find the person who can grant your "exceptional" loan request, start with whomever you originally dealt with and patiently work your way up the chain of command until you get to the person who answers "yes" to the question, "Do you have the authority to make exceptions to company policy?" This is the person on whom you must work all your powers of persuasion. Arrange a meeting and prepare to bring documents supporting your case.

If the turndown was for bad credit history, you will have to explain how the report was inaccurate (if it was), or make a strong case for why it will never happen again. You might also offer a cosigner with a clean payment record.

> **"[To lower your debt-to-income ratio]: Are there obligations you could pay off or credit lines you could close?"**

- **If it was a large debt-to-income ratio,** be prepared to point out additional income the lender didn't count or expenses it overcounted. Are there obligations you could pay off or credit lines you could close to reduce your potential monthly outlay? (For example, the bank may consider your fully paid up $3,000 VISA credit line as $3,000 you *owe.*)

- **If the problem was inadequate collateral,** explore flexible alternatives. Find out how big a loan your collateral will support. If it seems appropriate to you, suggest that the difference be made up in an unsecured loan of shorter term (more profitable to them, to cover the higher risk).

If after fighting the good fight they turn you down again (less likely than you may think), you can always seek a lending institution with less conservative lending policies.

Source: Margaret "Marty" O. Tunnell, vice president and region manager, San Francisco Regional Corporate Center, 405 Montgomery St., San Francisco, CA 94104.

Preemployment Credit Reports

According to the Associated Credit Bureau:

Prospective employers must indicate when their reports are to be used for employment purposes.

Credit reports will be issued only if the requester certifies that the applicant will be notified that a report is requested. Interviewers will be encouraged to reveal the reports to job applicants so any adverse information can be challenged and reexamined before a decision is made on employment.

Source: What's Ahead in Human Resources, 350 W. Hubbard St., Chicago, IL 60610.

Privacy and Credit Reports

Credit reports and credit-reporting agencies are closely regulated and monitored to assure the privacy of the information in your credit file. Who has access? No individual or company may have access to the information contained in your credit report unless there is a "permissible purpose," or a bona fide business reason for inquiring into your credit history. Any creditor who inquires into a credit bureau's database must certify a legitimate business need for the information and be a customer of the credit-reporting agency. An agency may not release information to any individual or company regarding your credit history unless the information is required by that individual or company to make a decision concerning the extension of credit to you.

Source: Thomas G. Collins, Jr., director of planning for one of the five major credit-reporting companies in the United States, The Credit Bureau, Inc., 1600 Peachtree St. NW, Atlanta, GA 30309. His responsibilities are business, marketing and strategic planning for the firm.

Dealing With Credit Unions

You can't get rich overnight by keeping your money with a credit union. But you can find a combination of old-fashioned personal attention, modern financial services, and the lowest-cost personal financial services available. The advantages are substantial. Credit unions commonly pay higher returns on passbook savings, certificates and money-market accounts than do other financial institutions.

Traditionally, credit unions have offered the lowest available rates on loans for consumer purchases, such as cars, boats and home improvements, and for student loans. Even credit life or credit disability insurance may be offered at a much lower cost than is available elsewhere. Some credit unions make loans for business purposes, generally in the form of a personal loan.

When you work for a company that has a credit union associated with it, you often can arrange to have your paycheck deposited into your transaction account for immediate access, to have loan payments automatically deducted, and to direct part of your pay into a savings or money-market account.

"Share drafts"—the credit union's version of NOW accounts—generally pay higher rates of interest than NOWs and most have no or very low minimum balances and service fees.

Credit cards from credit unions are also cheaper than cards from conventional financial institutions. Most do not charge an annual fee, and many charge substantially lower rates than other card issuers. The one drawback is that some credit unions charge interest from the date of purchase.

Your funds are generally as safe in a credit union as they are in a traditional bank. Nearly all credit union deposits are guaranteed up to $100,000 by either a federal agency (the National Credit Union Share Insurance Fund) or one of a number of private insurance funds. The federal insurance fund for credit unions is currently the strongest of the three federal insurers of financial institutions—credit unions capitalized the fund with close to $3 billion in 1998. Most of the private funds are also very well capitalized. As a result, serious credit union failures are rare.

Source: Jim R. Williams, president and CEO of Credit Union National Association, Inc., and CUNA Service Group, Inc., P.O. Box 431, Madison, WI 53701. He is also president of U.S. Central Credit Union. CUNA is a trade association serving over 90% of U.S. credit unions, while CUNA Service Group provides financial, operational and telecommunications services to the industry.

Who Can Join a Credit Union

Membership is limited to people who have so-called common bonds—working for the same employer, living in the same neighborhood, etc. If you aren't a member of a credit union but would like to be, write to the industry's trade association for a list of credit unions you may be eligible to join.

Source: *Credit Union National Association, 5710 Mineral Point Rd., Madison, WI 53705. Or visit its website at www.cuna.org.*

Establishing Consumer Credit

American businesses and consumers have come a long way from the days when credit was available only to the wealthy. Recent changes in the area of consumer credit have made it possible for almost anyone with a steady job or steady income to expect some form of credit and to keep it.

What hasn't changed are the basic criteria for getting credit. You still must have the financial capacity to pay your bills when they come due. And to build a strong credit history, you must have a consistent record of on-time payments over an extended period.

Credit for Young People

Many credit grantors will make credit available, on a limited basis, to young people just entering the labor force. The only requirement is a steady job that assures the income necessary to meet payments. As income increases and a reliable credit history develops, credit limits will usually be increased. Also, less lenient creditors that might have rejected a young person's credit application the first time around will probably make credit available.

Which Bills to Pay First

In a cash crunch, it's important to know which bills you can't put off paying without damaging your credit rating—and which you can "defer." *To pay immediately:* Bills from credit cards issued by department stores (Sears, Macy's, etc.) and banks (VISA, MasterCard, etc.). *Reason:* They submit "full-file" reports (reaching back 12–24 months) on all customers every month to credit-reporting agencies. *Less likely to file regular reports:* Oil companies and utilities. Professionals and organizations that don't have contracts with credit-rating bureaus (most physicians and hospitals) don't file at all.

Advice for young people:
Start small and build big. Certain credit grantors, such as oil companies, large department store chains and major credit card companies, employ relatively lenient evaluation policies. Most of them solicit young people while they are still in college. If there are no service charges, accept the offer. If a credit application is denied, don't be discouraged. Changing economic times can cause credit grantors to change their evaluation policies from month to month.

Credit for Women

Federal laws and regulations make it illegal for credit to be denied on the basis of race, creed, color or sex. The Equal Credit Opportunity Act, passed in the mid-1970s, assures that women will not be discriminated against when they apply for credit because of their sex or because they have been widowed or divorced or because they plan to have children.

Advice for married women:
Establish credit jointly with your husband but report to credit bureaus in your name as well as your husband's name. That way you can build up your own credit history independent of your husband's.

It is a misconception that a married woman who doesn't earn a separate income cannot obtain credit in her own name. If you would like credit entirely in your own right, simply apply in your name. Credit grantors recognize that a woman has a legal claim to half of the family's assets and income and will base their credit evaluation on that assumption.

Source: *Walter R. Kurth, president and chief executive of Associated Credit Bureaus, Inc., 16211 Park 10 Place, Houston, TX 77084, the international trade association of the credit reporting and collection services industry. He is also vice chairman of the American Society of Association Executives and a member of the board of the U.S. Chamber of Commerce.*

What Is in a Credit File?

The information contained in a credit file consists of computerized records on your payment history, how much you owe and to whom, indications as to whether payments have been received promptly or late, and information regarding legal action that may have been taken as a result of your inability or unwillingness to pay bills satisfactorily. There is also a brief section on your identification, which is used to assure that the applicable information is delivered to the inquiring creditor. This section includes your name, address, Social Security number, date of birth and other similar pieces of information regarding your identity.

Source: Thomas G. Collins, Jr., director of planning for one of the five major credit-reporting companies in the United States, The Credit Bureau, Inc., 1600 Peachtree St. NW, Atlanta, GA. 30309. His responsibilities are business, marketing and strategic planning for the firm.

About Your Credit Report

The Fair Credit Reporting Act guarantees that you can find out the contents of your credit report. If you were denied credit, insurance, employment or housing within the past 30 days, based on information in a credit report, you will be sent a notice to that effect. The creditor must provide the reason for denial as well as the name and address of the credit-reporting agency providing the information. The bureau will disclose the nature and substance of the information in the file free of charge if notified of the denial within 30 days of receipt of the creditor's letter.

If you just want to find out what is in your credit report, simply contact the credit-reporting agency by letter or telephone. The agency will charge about $8 to cover any costs associated with the disclosure. Under the Fair Credit Reporting Act, you have the right to dispute any item in your credit file. But remember that credit bureaus only store information supplied to them by others regarding your payment history. The rating you receive when applying for credit is assigned by the credit grantor, based on your payment history.

Source: Thomas G. Collins, Jr., director of planning for one of the five major credit-reporting companies in the United States, The Credit Bureau, Inc., 1600 Peachtree St. NW, Atlanta, GA. 30309. His responsibilities are business, marketing and strategic planning for the firm.

Your New Credit Rights

A recent amendment to the Fair Credit Reporting Act gives you a new set of tools for fixing credit problems created by inaccurate information in credit bureau files. The law sets a 30-day deadline for fixing mistakes, and you must be given written results within five days of the investigation's completion. Here's what the new law offers consumers:

Greater control. The credit bureaus now have to consider information from the consumer, not just creditors. *Example:* If you have a canceled check or any letter from the creditor indicating that the payment was settled, credit bureaus have to accept this as proof. (Previously, you had to pursue the creditors and convince them, then they were supposed to let the credit agencies know that the matter had been cleared up.)

More privacy. Employers may ask for credit reports on job applicants only with the applicant's written permission. Also, you can call toll-free numbers to be removed from lists used by credit card companies to solicit consumers by mail.

Greater access. Toll-free lines with employees, not just recordings, must be available to people calling credit bureaus during business hours. Credit reports—free when you've been turned down for credit, insurance or employment—are now free if you're turned down for services such as bank accounts or apartments.

Credit Card Secrets

The next time you want to switch credit cards in an attempt to get the lowest possible interest rate, *watch out.* A growing number of card issuers have been quietly adding penalties and restrictions to their applications in an effort to make up for lost revenues.

Self-defense: Forget what appears on the outside of a promotional envelope or in an advertisement. Instead, read the disclosure box that, by law, must appear on the back of all credit card applications. Unfortunately, fewer than 10% of all consumers read these boxes. Those who don't read the fine print can end up paying unexpected fees if they violate their agreements.

Disclosure-Box Red Flags

Beware: No mention of a grace period. More than 90% of credit card issuers offer a grace period of about 25 days—which means you have 25 days to pay for your purchase without being charged interest.

Self-defense: Stay away from any card whose application doesn't mention a grace period. You will pay interest on all charges—even if you pay the card's bill in full each month. That's because interest starts the day you make a purchase.

Beware: A high annual fee. It's easy today to find a no-fee credit card with a decent interest rate or a low-fee card with a very good interest rate

Key question: If the issuer charges a high annual fee, are there enough benefits you can use to justify the rate? *Example:* Airline rebate cards charge annual fees of $35 to $100. To make the deal worthwhile, you would have to charge $1,750 to $5,000 a year on the card, not carry a balance, *and* use *all* of your miles before they start to expire.

Beware: A low interest rate that is too good to be true. If the interest rate is lower than 10%, chances are it's an introductory rate—one that's offered for only a short time.

Important: The card issuer must disclose how long the rate lasts and what the new rate will be. A 7% rate that jumps to 18.9% after six months is a bad deal—unless you're sure that you'll have all charges paid off before the introductory rate expires. *Formula:* If the difference between a card's introductory rate and its long-term rate is greater than six percentage points, look for a better deal.

Beware: Any type of penalty interest rate. Some disclosure boxes may tell you that a higher interest rate goes into effect if you fail to meet the requirements of your account. Those requirements are not always spelled out clearly.

Violation of these standards usually includes making a late payment or exceeding your credit limit.

Limits are most often exceeded when staying at hotels, which charge you after you leave. *Examples:* New Citibank VISA or MasterCard applicants who fail to pay on time or exceed their credit limits may have their rates raised to 21.65%. AT&T's penalty rate is 20.65% for violation of the same rules.

In some cases, there are more obscure provisions. Your interest rate can be raised if the bank decides you've become a poor credit risk. Some banks monitor credit files semiannually.

Important: Issuers do not have to spell out in the disclosure boxes when the higher rates go into effect. Furthermore, they don't have to tell you when you will be late or over your limit. You may not even learn that your rate has increased until you get a bill that includes the new rate.

Self-defense: Call the issuer to ask about penalties before signing up.

Beware: A "two-cycle average daily balance" method. If this phrase appears in the disclosure box, throw away the application. The two-cycle method is the sum of the average daily balances for two billing cycles. *Better:* More than 85% of the industry uses a method that calculates the balance by adding all new purchases to the outstanding debt and then dividing by the number of days in the billing cycle. This is the preferred method.

Beware: Balance-transfer restrictions. Some cards limit the amount you can transfer from another card, while others cap the number of transfers you can make in a particular period.

Other issuers treat balance transfers as cash advances, hitting you with a ridiculously high interest rate and charging you interest immediately rather than waiting until after your first bill arrives.

The information provided in the disclosure box is often vague. Sometimes an issuer will say that balance transfers are just like cash advances, but they won't mention the cash-advance rate.

Beware: Bad cash-advance terms. Issuers must tell you what they charge if you use your card to borrow cash. The fee is usually 2% of the total borrowed.

Trap: They don't have to disclose the interest rate for borrowing the cash. It is often much higher

> **"If you pay off your credit card bills in full each month, you should be indifferent to creditors' interest rates ...but highly sensitive to annual fees."**

PLAYING THE BILLING-DATE GAME

If you play by the rules of the game, you can keep more of your funds earning interest while you spend someone else's money (at least temporarily). Credit cards provide opportunities to maximize your earnings at the expense of creditors.

Know Your Creditors' Policies

Credit card issuers differ in the interest rates and annual fees they charge (if any). They also differ in their payment terms and finance charge calculations. *Reason:* Most credit card companies, such as VISA, do not set national billing procedures—the bank issuing the card establishes its own policies. Consequently, billing policies vary from bank to bank.

When do banks start charging interest? Banks use one of three options in charging interest on credit cards. The first is to begin charging on the transaction date (that is, the date the customer actually makes the purchase). The second is to charge from the posting date (the date on which your bank receives notification of your purchase). The third option is for a bank to begin charging interest on the billing date (the date on which the bank actually makes up your bill and sends it out). There can be a lapse of several days or even weeks between each of these successive dates. *Helpful:* Find a bank that charges interest from the billing date; then you can save interest charges that might accrue from the transaction date to

the billing date—in some cases well over 30 days. Stay clear of card-issuing banks that charge interest beginning on the transaction date. You will start paying interest charges immediately, no matter how long the merchant takes to deliver your sales draft to his bank; or the merchant's bank takes to transmit the sales data to your bank; or your bank takes to post the transaction to your account and bill you. Effectively, you foot the open-ended bill for the system's inefficiencies.

Don't Pay Bills—Plan Disbursements

When paying credit card issuers, take advantage of interest-free grace periods and payment due dates. If you pay off your credit card bills in full every month, most creditors provide an interest-free grace period of 30 days. But some creditors provide less —25 days, 15 days or even no grace period. Because they vary, know what your creditors' rules are in advance.

When your creditor stops charging interest (or credits your payment) can make a difference too. Although creditors are required under federal regulations to credit payments on the date of receipt, there are some notable exceptions. A few creditors credit payment receipts as of the payment postmark date, which means you can mail your payment several days later than

usual and still receive timely payment credit.

Be careful of late-payment charges for "nonconforming" payments. For example, bank card issuers usually specify that payment be sent to a post office box. If that payment is received anywhere else, it is considered a nonconforming payment. Further, if you pay your VISA bill at the local branch of the bank that issued your card, your bank can legally defer crediting payment for up to five days after you hand over your check. Should this occur, you could incur finance charges or late-payment penalties on the entire balance in addition to losing use of your funds for those five days, even though you made payment to your card-issuer bank's branch on time.

Managing your credit card funds means shopping for the best overall payment terms for your particular situation. If you pay off your credit card bills in full each month, you should be indifferent to creditors' interest rates and to the timing of initiation of finance charges, but highly sensitive to annual fees and card payment terms. If, on the other hand, you incur finance charges, then interest rates and the timing of finance charge initiation would be the dominant concerns. In either case, the object of playing the billing-date game is the same—to maximize your use of your creditors' money and/or minimize your payment of finance charges.

Source: *Patricia L. McFeely, senior vice president, Littlewood Shain & Company, 175 Strafford Ave., Wayne, PA 19087, consultants to financial institutions. She is the author of* **Plastic Card Float and the Profitability of Cash Management Services,** *The Bank Administration Institute.*

Dealing with Banks, Credit & Debt

203

than the interest rate on your card's balance. For example, it's not unusual for a card with a 15% interest rate to raise that rate to 21.9% for a cash advance. *Solution:* Call the issuer's 800 number and ask about its cash-advance terms *before* you borrow money.

Cards With Favorable Terms

Here are some of my favorite credit cards. These have the lowest rates and none of the problems cited above:

● **AFBA Industrial Bank** (800-776-2265). Introductory rate for the first six months is 8.5%*. After that it increases to 11.4%. *Annual fee:* None.

● **People's Bank** (800-426-1114). This has a fixed rate of 13.9%, meaning it will always be this rate for as long as you own the card. *Annual fees:* $25/standard card, $40/gold card.

● **USAA Federal Savings** (800-922-9092). The 12.5% rate is variable. It changes every quarter and is tied to the rate on 26-week Treasury bills. *Annual fee:* None.

● **Wachovia First Year Prime** (800-842-3262). Current introductory rate is 8.5% for the first year. Then it moves to 12.4%. *Annual fees:* $18/standard card, $28/gold card.

*All rates and terms are subject to change without prior notice.

Source: *Robert McKinley, president of RAM Research, a supplier of credit card data to consumers and businesses, Box 1700, Frederick, MD 21702.*

What MasterCard and VISA Don't Tell You

One MasterCard or VISA card could be very different from another MasterCard or VISA card. What counts is the bank issuing it.

The MasterCard and VISA organizations do not issue credit cards themselves. They provide a clearing system for charges and payments on the cards and license banks to use the VISA or Master-Card name. It is the issuing bank that determines the interest rates and fees.

A bank's name on a credit card does not necessarily mean that it is the bank actually issuing the card. Seldom does a small bank issue its own.

Generally, a small bank will act as an agent for an issuing bank. The agent bank puts its name on the card, but it is the issuing bank that actually extends any credit.

Aside from costs, this can be important if the cardholder encounters an error. The correction might have to be agreed upon, not by a friendly local banker, but by an unknown, larger institution, perhaps in a different state.

No-Fee Cards for Seniors

Senior citizens may be able to get permanent no-fee cards by signing up for special package deals just for seniors. *How it works:* They open savings, money-market and checking accounts with an institution, and it provides a no-fee card. Best: Shop around.

Source: *Consumer banking expert Robert Heady, publisher,* 100 Highest Yields *and* Bank Rate Monitor.

Choosing which card to take is becoming more difficult. Individuals must be especially careful about accepting any offer that might come in the mail.

A recently discovered quirk in the federal law allows federally chartered out-of-state banks to ignore state usury laws that limit the amount of interest or fees that the issuing bank may charge on its credit cards. In Arkansas, for example, state usury laws prevent local banks from charging interest that is more than 50% over prime on credit card balances. But a federally chartered out-of-state bank, in lending to Arkansas residents, may charge whatever its home state allows. Even with individual states, the terms on credit cards can vary widely.

Aside from the actual rates and fees, individuals must carefully check the fine print of their contracts. Most banks, for example, do not charge interest on balances stemming from purchases until the customer is billed for such purposes. If the bill on which the charges first appear is paid in full by the stated due date, there is no interest charge to the holder. But some banks begin charging interest as soon as they receive the charge slip and make payment to the merchant. Thus, interest begins accu-

CREDIT CARD SELF-DEFENSE

Credit card fraud hurts everybody, not just the people whose cards are stolen or used illegally. It results in higher annual fees and finance charges, fewer free services from card issuers and higher retail prices. And rather than improving, the problem's getting worse.

Common Scams and Self-Defense

● **Telemarketing rip-offs.** These ploys succeed by preying on victims' gullibility and greed and succeed surprisingly often. *Scenario:* A phone caller informs you that you've been selected from a market survey as one of several winners of a free luxury trip, big appliance, etc. (Callers often pick numbers from the phone book at random, counting on the chance that the victim has a credit card. Or, dishonest employees at card-issuing companies sell names of new cardholders to crooks.)

All you need to do to claim your prize is verify your identity by providing the number from a major credit card. *What you've really won:* A major hassle. You won't hear from these people again until your next credit card bill, which is sure to be loaded with charges for merchandise you never ordered and cash advances from banks with whom you never did business.

Defenses: Obviously, never give your number over the phone. Inform the card issuer immediately of any potential fraud. *Liability:* Up to $50 if you don't inform the card issuer before charges are made to your account.

● **Credit card receipts.** An easy way to fall prey and you won't know anything happened until you get the bill. *Scenario:* You pay for gas by swiping your credit card through the payment slot, but you forget your receipt. The attendant throws it away. Thieves remove it from the trash and use your card number to buy items by phone.

Defense: Remember to take your receipt, and always tear up credit card receipts before you throw them away.

● **Stolen cards.** Whenever possible, keep credit cards separate from personal identification cards like your driver's license. A thief who has all your ID can easily misrepresent himself or herself as you and run up a staggering amount of charges in a single afternoon. Check your cards daily. Thieves often steal only one card, betting that you won't miss it for a few days. Always inspect monthly statements for unfamiliar charges. The sooner you inform the card issuer, the less you'll have to pay.

Source: Jack Taylor, U.S. Secret Service Special Agent.

mulating even before the cardholder receives the bill. These interest charges continue until the bank receives payment from the customer.

Source: Robert A. Bennett, banking correspondent, The New York Times.

Premium Card Traps

Don't be lulled into getting "premium" credit cards, such as Gold MasterCard or Premier VISA. The only significant "premium" is the $20–$25 extra that you pay in higher annual fees. Besides the fancy finish on the plastic, you get marginally useful benefits, such as travel insurance and protection on lost or stolen credit cards. Since by law you are liable for only up to $50 if your regular card is stolen or lost, the zero liability offered by premium cards is not worth the extra money.

Potential huge trap: Credit cards tied to home-equity lines of credit. Banks are pushing them hard. *Attraction:* Interest paid may qualify for a full tax deduction under tax reform, and the banks' risk is minimal with the credit line secured by the equity in your home.

Home-equity card rates are typically one to three percentage points above prime, and credit lines start at $10,000 and go as high as $100,000.

Cardholder risk: If you can't make the payments, you may lose your house.

Source: Consumer banking expert Robert Heady, publisher, 100 Highest Yields and Bank Rate Monitor.

Smart Alternatives To Traveler's Checks

Credit cards are now better than traveler's checks for most trips overseas. Aside from the cards' convenience, they can save as much as 6% on exchange costs.

Best bet: VISA, with a conversion markup only one-quarter of 1% above the wholesale bank currency rate. Other major cards carry a 1% markup—still far better than the 3% or more you'd pay for retail markups on traveler's checks. *Exceptions:* Poorer European countries where dollar-hungry bankers often give a break on traveler's checks or cash. *Helpful:* Check expiration dates of credit cards before you leave on your trip. An unexpected expiration would be a very troublesome surprise. (Leave unnecessary cards—such as those for local department stores or supermarkets—at home.)

Source: Forbes.

Beating the System

Credit cards have become a way of life for most Americans. However, very few people realize the unnecessary costs they incur by not utilizing their cards to their advantage or by not choosing the least expensive card to begin with.

Credit cards can be used as a bargaining chip to receive a discount from a merchant. Merchants typically pay a fee of 2% –7% of your charge when you use your credit card. With an American Express or Diners Club card, they may have to wait a while to get paid. It may be to the advantage of the merchant to go along with your suggestion of a 5% discount if you pay cash.

Another way to beat the system: Take a cash advance on your credit card and pay directly for goods and services, rather than charging them if bank-interest charges are less for cash advances. If you already are being charged interest for merchandise purchases, take a cash advance and switch the balance due to the lower rate.

If no interest charge has yet been levied, then time the cash advance to a day or two before the bill would be past due and pay off the merchandise portion of the bill. *Reason for the timing maneuver:* Cash advances are charged interest from the day that they are taken. Multiple credit cards are handy if you want to go to the limit of allowable cash advances on each without having to use your card to buy merchandise at high rates.

If you have gotten in over your head, it may be best to take out a consolidation loan to pay off a number of credit card bills. Although the consolidation loan rate may not be much cheaper than the credit card cash-advance rate, it can be significantly cheaper than the card's basic interest rate on merchandise purchases. In addition, since bank credit card payments are based on a 24-month term, one big advantage to consolidating such debt with a 36-month loan is lower monthly payments.

Source: Edward Mendlowitz, a partner with Mendlowitz Weitsen, CPAs, 2 Pennsylvania Plaza, New York, NY 10121.

Special Charge Card Trap

There are superhigh interest rates on charge accounts at a growing number of stores that offer their own cards. The biggest offenders are electronics retail chains that can charge from 21.6%–24% on outstanding balances. There's also a minimum of $100–$500 that must be charged the first time the card is used. *Alternatives:* Bank credit lines and traditional retail charge cards.

A Loan Trap to Watch Out for

A consolidation loan will do nothing but get you deeper in debt if, after paying off your credit card debt, you start charging things again.

Best: Pay off your credit card debt with a consolidation loan and then use your credit cards only for emergencies.

Source: Edward F. Mrkvicka, Jr., is the author of Your Bank Is Ripping You Off, *St. Martin's Press.*

How to Sidestep Late-Payment Penalties

Late-payment penalties on credit card accounts are becoming more common. More than one-third of the nation's banks are charging penalties of $10 or more even if payments miss the deadline by only a day or two. Some banks will waive the penalties, but the cardholder has to ask for the correction. A good payment track record and a reasonable excuse are usually sufficient grounds for having the charge lifted.

Source: U.S. News & World Report.

Advantages of Credit Card Purchases

● **Overseas purchases on a credit or charge card can be less expensive than expected.** It all depends on exchange rate fluctuations and how long it takes for the card company to process the paperwork. *Rule of thumb:* When the value of the dollar is increasing, the longer it takes to post and clear a charge, the cheaper the purchase becomes. When the dollar is falling, you want the paperwork cleared quickly. *Clearing times:* American Express/0 to 7 days, Diners Club/2 to 5 days, MasterCard/0 to 3 days, VISA/3 to 6 days. Larger retailers in big cities tend to process paperwork daily—or even immediately—electronically. Purchases made from smaller merchants and those in remote villages can take up to a week to clear.

Source: Condé Nast Traveler.

● **Pay for mail-order purchases with a credit card, rather than with a personal check.** *Reason:* If you don't receive the merchandise or it's not what you expected, you can refuse to pay (under the Fair Credit Billing Act) until the matter is resolved. But if you've paid by check and the mail-order company cashes it, you may have trouble getting a refund.

Source: Good Housekeeping.

● **Simple expense recording.** With every purchase made with your credit card, write down for whom and why on the slip when you sign it. This enables you to keep track of your business tax deductions and expenses in a single step.

BIG, BAD NEW CREDIT CARD TRAPS

B eware of complicated interest-calculation methods that can wipe out the benefits of a credit card's grace period. With the two-cycle billing method, you'll need at least two back-to-back, no-balance months to avoid interest charges. *Also:* Grace periods themselves are being shortened—some banks give only 20 days, down from 25 to 30.

Self-defense: When switching cards, avoid both traps.

Source: Gerri Detweiler, financial writer and credit card and debt-control consultant in Woodbridge, VA. She is the author of The Ultimate Credit Handbook, Plume.

Good Reason to Use Your Credit Card

Credit cards can protect you if a purchase turns out to be a lemon. Refuse to pay and demand that the amount be charged to the merchant. *What to do:* First, make an effort to settle the dispute. Then notify the credit card company, in writing, of the transaction, the amount of money involved, the name of the merchant and the attempts to settle. Act quickly. Once you've paid for the merchandise, your only recourse is to sue the merchant.

Source: Jean Noonan, credit-practice attorney, Federal Trade Commission, quoted in U.S. News & World Report.

When Tax Status Depends on Which Credit Card You Use

The general rule is that you only get a tax deduction in the year you actually pay for a deductible expense. But there's an important exception when you pay with a credit card. For tax purposes, payment is considered made on the date of the transaction, not on the date you pay the credit card company. You can sign now and deduct this year but pay next year.

Many charities accept credit card donations. You can claim a charitable contribution deduction in the year the contribution is charged. The same rule applies to payment of medical or dental expenses with a credit card.

Caution: If you charge a deductible expense on a credit card issued by the company supplying the deductible goods (or services), you can't take a deduction until the credit card bill is paid. *Example:* If you have a prescription filled at a department store pharmacy and charge it on a credit card issued by the store, you can't deduct the cost of that medication until you get the bill and pay it. But if you charge the same prescription on a credit card issued by a third party, such as MasterCard or VISA, you can deduct it right away.

American Express Card Advantage

People with duplicate credit cards from a joint American Express account don't have to worry about a stop being put on both cards if one card is lost or stolen—each card has a special identifier code. This goes for the Optima Credit Card, too. *Latest information:* Neither VISA nor MasterCard plans to institute such a coding system.

Signs That Mean You're in Trouble

Warning signs of excessive debt: You pay more than 20% of your discretionary income (after mortgage, taxes and utilities) on debt, you fail to pay all your creditors each month, you use a cash advance from one credit card to pay the bills from another, you feel nervous about how much money you're spending.

Source: National Foundation for Consumer Credit, 8701 Georgia Ave., Silver Spring, MD 20910.

Beware of Low Credit Card Rates

Bank cards with the lowest rates—11%–14%—can often cost much more than cards with traditional 18%–21% charges. *Reason:* A growing number of banks begin tacking on interest charges the minute a transaction is posted to their books. This charge accrues until the charge amount and the interest are paid in full.

Even if you pay off your charges as soon as you receive the bill each month, you'll still have to pay an interest charge.

Solution: If you pay in full whenever you use a credit card, choose a bank that charges interest only on balances that are still outstanding following the payment due date on the bill.

Source: Money magazine.

Prevent Credit Card Rip-Offs

Here's a simple trick: Pick a number and, if possible, make sure that all your credit card charges end in that number. *Example:* Say you choose the number 8 and your dinner bill comes to $20.00. Instead of adding a $3.00 tip, add $3.08. When your bill comes, check to see if all the charges have 8 as the last digit. If they don't, compare them against your receipts and report discrepancies to the card issuer.

Credit Card Protection

● **Photocopy the cards themselves** to keep track of which ones you have. It's much more convenient to have all accounts on a single sheet of paper than to rely on keeping all the original agreements together. Keep one photocopy at home where it can be used to notify card issuers if a card is lost or stolen. Put another in a safe-deposit box or other safe place.

Source: Leon Gold, Phillips Gold & Co., CPAs, 1140 Avenue of the Americas, New York, NY 10036.

● **Avoid being charged for goods or services you didn't buy by** scribbling over the shaded sections labeled "delayed charges" and "revised total" when you sign credit card slips. Often, unscrupulous merchants will add charges there, hoping the customer won't notice the discrepancy on his or her bill. By scribbling over these areas on each slip, you deter such acts of theft.

Credit Card Errors

Come January, many people find themselves in disputes over credit card charges that were mistakenly billed to them during holidays. Here are the most common problems and how to straighten them out:

● **There's a problem with the merchandise purchased with the card.**

Solution: The Fair Credit Billing Act (FCBA) gives you the legal right to withhold payment on a credit card charge if the merchandise you purchased was different from what you ordered—or it was delivered on the wrong day—or it was delivered in the wrong quantity.

Under the FCBA, you can also refuse to pay a credit card charge for merchandise you did not accept. *Example:* A new refrigerator was delivered to your home, but it was the wrong color so you refused to accept delivery and the delivery people left with the refrigerator.

How to dispute the charge: Once you notice the charge on your statement, write a letter to your credit card issuer at the address listed on your statement for billing errors and inquiries.

Don't include the letter with your payment for other items on your bill. And don't procrastinate. Under the FCBA you only have 60 days to protest the charge. (The 60-day period usually starts from the postmark date of the bill on which the charge appeared.) In your letter include your name, address, account number, the specific charge you're disputing and why.

Send your letter certified mail, return receipt requested. After the credit card company receives your letter, it has no more than 90 days to prove the

> **"You have the right to ask your credit card company to provide documentary proof of [an unknown] charge."**

charge is valid—or it must remove it from your bill.

Telephone trap: Don't just call the customer service number to complain. Telephone complaints aren't covered under the law, so you lose the clout the law gives you when you write. *The FCBA does not cover questionable charges when:*

● **You have changed your mind about a purchase.**

● **The merchant has a clearly posted "no refunds" policy.**

● **You are disputing the "quality" of merchandise or services you bought.** *Helpful:* If you're buying something valuable, such as gems, artwork or antiques, always get the seller to write on the sales slip all promises about quality and authenticity.

● **You want to dispute a charge because of the poor quality of goods or services.** These types of disputes are common.

Solution: You can dispute a credit card purchase if the quality of the goods or services was unsatisfactory as long as:

● **The amount of the charge was $50 or more.**

● **The purchase was made in your home state**—or within 100 miles of your billing address.

● **You have made an effort in good faith** to resolve the problem directly with the merchant.

There's no time limit for disputing charges because of quality. But there is one big catch—you can only dispute the amount of the charge you haven't paid off. If you've already paid the bill in full, you're out of luck.

Write it out. Although quality disputes don't have to be in writing, I strongly suggest you do so anyway. Again, send your letter return receipt requested. You can continue to withhold payment on the charge until the matter is resolved.

● **There's a charge on your bill you don't recognize.**

Solution: You have the right to ask your credit card company to provide documentary proof of the charge.

If the issuer produces proof, such as a sales slip, but you did not make the charge or authorize someone else to make the charge, the most you can be responsible for is the first $50 of the unauthorized charge—and that's only if your card was actually used in the transaction. *Example:* If someone stole your credit card number and used it without the plastic card, you are not responsible for any of the unauthorized charges.

If the issuer balks at taking the unauthorized charge off your account, tell the issuer you want to sign a "fraud affidavit" certifying you didn't make the charge. That should indicate you are serious about not paying.

Credit background: Keep all records relating to any type of credit problem—or credit report problem—for seven years. That's the length of time negative information can be reported on your account.

If your account is transferred to another financial institution, for example, you could find the same problem popping up again. Keep your records to quickly clear up misunderstandings about past accounts.

Source: Gerri Detweiler, consumer credit consultant in Woodbridge, VA, and head of public policy for the National Council of Individual Investors. She is the author of The Ultimate Credit Handbook, Plume.

Easy Way to Get Over Credit Card Addiction

People who are in debt over their heads often blame their credit cards. *Reality:* Most of those problems are related to poor money management.

Even people who are not in trouble may want to reconsider their use of credit cards, unless they always pay the entire bill each month. *Reason:* Credit card interest is not deductible.

It might be tempting to just cut up your cards and go cold turkey. But it's important to learn self-discipline and good spending habits to take advantage of the convenience of credit cards. *What to do:*

● **Limit yourself to two or three credit cards.** A bank card covers almost all purchases. Add to it a gas credit card and, perhaps, a card from your favorite department store. (Shop around for low-fee or no-fee bank cards. Don't get hooked into expensive "status cards.")

● **Record your charges in a memo book.** Because there's no written running balance, as in a checkbook, it's easy to lose track of how much you're spending.

● **Put a ceiling on your spending.** Don't let the credit card companies set a ceiling for you. They're only too happy to increase your limit each year because you're such a "good customer." You'll be tempted to spend that much more.

Warning: Sometimes applicants for a mortgage may have difficulty obtaining the mortgage if they have a high credit card ceiling—even if they don't use it. (They could, theoretically at least, get into that much debt overnight.)

● **Spend no more than 20% of your monthly take-home income on consumer debt.** (This is a general guideline. Low incomes should allow a lower percentage.) This includes car loans, credit cards, etc. If your monthly payments for debt exceed that amount, you're headed for trouble.

Solution: Stop incurring debts until all your credit cards are paid off. Then follow a budget faithfully.

If you are heavily in debt from credit cards or any kind of unsecured debt, find a nonprofit consumer credit counselor who can set up a repayment program and appeal to card companies to lower your monthly payments until the debts are paid off.

It is best to pay as much as possible as soon as possible, since interest usually continues to accrue on unpaid debt.

● **Use savings as an alternative to credit cards.** Too many people are forced to use credit in an emergency because they have no savings on which to fall back. *Change your approach:* Save to establish an emergency fund with *at least* three months' income. Use the money only in an emergency, and pay back that money as you would a bill.

> **"Once you know how much you've earned over your lifetime—net—and compare it with your current net worth now, the difference will likely convince you to make radical changes in your lifestyle and spending habits."**

● **Know your goals and budget accordingly.** Don't incur too much debt by trying to keep up with the Joneses. Know what you want out of life. *Suggestion:* Write down your goals, a time plan for achieving them and the approximate costs. Then determine which goals are important and focus your budget on the high priority items.

Source: *Cathy Pietruszewski, executive director and vice president, Consumer Credit Counselors of San Francisco and the Peninsula, 31 Geary St., San Francisco, CA 94108.*

Credit and Divorce

If a loan to one spouse is secured by property that the court awards to the other spouse in a divorce settlement, the collateral can't be claimed by the creditor to settle the debt—it must take action against the original debtor in order to recover the loan.

Even a registered lien isn't valid if it's dated after the divorce petition was filed. *Example:* A husband buys a car in his name after he and his wife petition for divorce. The wife is awarded the car as part of the settlement. The car financing company can't repossess the car if the husband stops making payments. The company's only option is to sue the husband.

Source: Hoyt *vs.* Amer. Traders, *SC Oregon, 9/3/86.*

Credit Card Debt Can Be Dangerous to Your Wealth

If you take a hard look at your credit card statements, you will probably notice that most charges are for goods and services that you really don't need. The temptation to spend money is great, but excessive spending is financially dangerous and can lead to debt.

To effectively cut back on your spending—and avoid putting off long-term dreams—you must do more than merely hide your credit cards. You must change the way you think about money. Whether you earn $10,000 or $200,000 a year, here are the steps you can use to avoid debt and save more income:

Step 1: **Look at what you already own.** Throw open your closets and drawers, and make a list of everything you see. By cataloging your possessions, either on paper or in your mind, you will be able to size up the true quality of your current life. You'll also likely discover you already own plenty of everything. By recognizing that you have enough to be comfortable, you will be more likely to stop yourself the next time you think you must have something you can't afford. *Example:* A woman I know opened her closet and counted 30 pairs of shoes. And she realized that she rarely wore most of them.

A quick and easy way to have such a revelation is to ask yourself the following penetrating questions:

● **What do I have?**
● **What does it mean?**
● **Do I still want this in my life?**
● **Do I need it in my life now?**
● **Can I give any of this stuff away?**

Step 2: **Compare your lifetime earnings with your current net worth.** This step is important, and calculating the data isn't hard. Once you know how much you've earned over your lifetime—net—and compare it with your current net worth now, the difference will likely convince you to make radical changes in your lifestyle and spending habits. *Strategy:* Start by getting a free *Statement of Earnings* from the Social Security Administration (800-772-1213). Estimate your other earnings over the years, such as gifts and capital gains from investments. Set the total aside.

To calculate your net worth, simply add up all of your assets and subtract from that number your total debt. Look at the two figures. You'll probably be shocked at the difference. *Example:* A friend of

Stretching Due Dates on Bills

Due dates on bills can be stretched—but not far—without risk. *Typical grace periods:* Telephone companies, eight days. Gas and electric utilities, 10 days. Banks and finance companies, 10 days. Even after a late charge is imposed on an unpaid bill, your credit rating should be safe for 30 days.

mine, a TV producer, found that she had made $3 million in her lifetime but had less than $100,000 in assets to show for it. She asked herself, *Where did it all go?* She realized a lot of it had been wasted on nonessential luxuries she couldn't even remember enjoying. The assessment convinced her to change her spending behavior.

Step 3: **Calculate your real wages.** When you spend money, you have to spend energy to earn it back. *Example:* If you earn $40 an hour, you must figure in all the extra expenses—such as child care, commuting and clothes. You also need to include the extra hours you spend commuting and unwinding from your job at the end of the day.

After you do those calculations, you may realize that you don't earn $40 an hour—you actually only earn $20 or $25.

The objective is to find out how much you actually get paid for your energy and to force yourself to confront the fact that you may be spending way over your head.

Step 4: **Track your daily spending pattern.** Most people ignore the fact that they are spending too much. They simply withdraw cash or use their credit cards and ignore the consequences.

Solution: Devise a system to track your daily expenses. Keep a little notepad with you, and write down every purchase you make. Then calculate how much time you must work to meet the expenses you pile up in each spending category. *Example:* Say you spent $200 last month on dining out—and your real hourly wage is $20 an hour. That translates into roughly 10 hours of energy spent. Ask yourself if you received 10 hours of fulfillment from those restaurant meals.

Lots of people keep track of every penny, but they don't evaluate whether their expenses are worthwhile.

To assess the quality of your purchases, place an up or down arrow next to each expense to indicate whether or not it was fulfilling. *Ask yourself:*

● **Did I get fulfillment?**

● **Was I happy to work that much time for each expense?**

● **Do my buying habits really reflect my values?** Chances are the answers will be all the encouragement you need to give up many unnecessary expenses.

Step 5: **Consciously lower your expenses.** Your expenses will decrease by 20% to 25% after you follow the previous steps. You'll become aware of the ways you spend your life energy. *Example:* One man recently sold the red Jaguar for which he was paying $390 a month in car payments and $140 a month in insurance. He laughed when he realized that he had gotten the car to impress people. He sold the car, paid cash for a used car and cut his high monthly car payments and insurance costs by 50%.

Source: *Vicki Robin, president of New Road Map Foundation, an organization that helps people gain greater control over their money and their lives, Box 15981, Seattle, WA 98115. The foundation offers a money-management audiocassette course. Ms. Robin is coauthor, with the late Joe Dominguez, of* Your Money or Your Life, *Viking Penguin.*

> "Most debt is manageable...[but] most people deny that they have debt problems. They refuse to admit that the problems exist or believe that they will go away."

How to Get Out of Debt And Stay Out of Debt

Many Americans are trying to reduce their credit card debt. Faced with increasing financial responsibilities, many are looking for ways to eliminate the bills and free up some of their income.

Fortunately, most debt is manageable—if it is addressed early enough. Here's what I tell people who are overburdened with debt:

● **Acknowledge the problem.** Most people deny that they have debt problems. They refuse to admit that the problems exist or believe that they will go away by themselves. The fact is that if you owe money on your credit cards and cannot pay the entire amount when the bill arrives, you have debt. If your debt grows too large, you run the risk of being unable to meet your monthly payments and seriously damaging your credit rating.

The biggest drawback to debt is that it uses up income that could have been invested or spent elsewhere. You are also paying more for something over time than if you had paid for it in full right away. Even if your debt is only temporary, immediate action must be taken to minimize interest payments.

● **Put everything in writing.** To determine how much debt you are carrying monthly, calculate how much you owe. Then determine your monthly income and expenses. If your debt is higher than your monthly income, you should take steps to reduce it. *Strategy:* Make two lists—one for expenses that are essential and the other for those that are optional. Some expenses that seem essential may have to be reclassified as optional. Hold a family meeting to plan cutbacks. While debt may be a difficult subject to discuss with your family, it is essential that all family members make sacrifices.

● **Don't slash expenses too dramatically.** Just as total-deprivation diets do not help you lose weight permanently, budgets that completely eliminate anything that hints of fun do not permanently eliminate debt. Cutting back is better than cutting out. *Example:* Maybe you can no longer dine out twice a week. But you could go out once a month for special events. Your new budget should accommodate these occasional excursions.

● **Work hard to stay on course.** Paying off debt is an incremental process. Try not to take on new debt or go on a spending binge as a reward for being frugal.

If you're having trouble making payments, don't ignore the bills. That only gets you into deeper trouble. Instead, contact all of your creditors to work out less onerous repayment plans or to assure them that you will keep making regular payments. That is what your creditors really want to hear, since regular lower payments are better than no payments at all.

Source: Alexandra Armstrong, *chairman of Armstrong, Welch & MacIntyre, Inc., a Washington, DC-based financial advisory firm. She is coauthor of* On Your Own: A Widow's Passage to Emotional and Financial Well-Being, *Dearborn Financial Publishing.*

Anyone Can Get Out of Debt

When I was young and single, I spent all of my money. When I was married with two incomes, no children and a monthly rent payment of only $95— my husband and I spent all of our money.

No matter how much money there was, there was never enough.

By the early 1980s we had two kids. I quit work, and my husband was earning $20,000 a year as a teacher. We also were $7,000 in debt.

Our First Mistake

In the beginning, we tried the conventional approach to paying off our debts. Every month, I'd pay as much as I could toward our seven different outstanding credit card bills.

But this approach was a total failure. It didn't leave us enough money to live on. We were four people living on one modest income. We could have used a good chunk of that credit card payment for food and household expenses.

As a result, a few weeks into every month, we had to use credit cards to buy things like toothpaste, soap and gas for the car. By the start of the next month, instead of our credit card bill going down, it was *higher* than the month before.

Our Solution

Finally, I discovered a plan that worked for us. The approach freed us emotionally, so we were no longer held hostage to the ridiculous concept that joy and fulfillment are only possible if you have no bills. I recognized that unpaid bills are like dirty dishes—no one likes them, everybody has them and there will always be dirty dishes if you eat. But dirty dishes and bills don't have to rule your life.

Here's how we got out of debt:

● **Don't worry if you can't pay large sums toward your balances.** The conventional wisdom is that you should pay more than the minimum required, so you can eventually extinguish your credit debt.

I began by paying only the minimum. That's because it was the only way I could start to reduce our debts and still have enough money to live on. After years of paying more than the minimum, running out of money mid-month and winding up deeper in debt the following month, I'd decided there had to be a better way. *Example:* Instead of pulling a whopping $100 out of our small checking account and sending it to our card issuer, I'd pay the suggested $22 minimum. That left us with $78 to spend on things like car repairs, laundry soap and groceries. I reveled in the freedom and the feeling of control that came with having cash.

Important: Make sure that the bank that has issued your credit card requires a minimum payment that is large enough so that it pays off some of the principal, as well as the accrued interest, on your balance. Otherwise, you'll never, ever succeed at getting out of debt. Also, make sure that the interest rate you're paying on your outstanding balance is not too high. In today's low-interest-rate environment, you should consider switching banks if you're paying much more than 6.9%. *One suggestion:* Consumers Edge Gold MasterCard, The Bank

HOW TO LIVE FEE-FREE

It's easy to save $1,000 or more by reducing or eliminating annual financial fees:

● **Banking.** Many banks charge monthly check-writing and/or ATM fees that add up to as much as $150 to $300 a year on checking accounts, and $150 to $200 on ATM fees.

Don't make the mistake of passing up a no-fee checking account just because it requires a minimum balance. It often makes sense to take money out of some investments and deposit it in the bank to meet the no-fee minimum.

● **Brokers.** If you're an active investor and you make your own investment decisions, consider a discount broker. It can drastically reduce your commissions.

But discounters aren't all the same. Traditional discounters such as Charles Schwab (800-435-4000) and Fidelity (800-544-8888) offer some services such as free investment research. They will also save you as much as 40% on commissions. Deep-discount brokers such as Wall Street Discount (800-221-4034) and Arnold Securities (800-328-4076) take a more bare-bones approach but offer even bigger commission cuts.

Potential annual savings: It depends on how many trades you make each year. The greater the number, the greater the savings.

● **Credit cards.** If you run a balance of $1,000 a year, a low-rate card could cut your interest costs in half. Good choice: Wachovia Bank VISA or MasterCard, 8.5% introductory rate, $18 annual fee* (800-842-3262). If you pay off your balance every month, choose a card without an annual fee.

Potential annual savings: $35 to $100 for a no-fee card, or $72 in interest charges if you run a balance of $1,200 and switch from a 19% card to a 13% card.

● **Mutual funds.** Many mutual funds sold by brokers carry sales charges—or "loads"—of 2% to 5%, which are used to compensate the people who sell them to investors. *Better:* Choose no-load funds, such as those sold by Vanguard, T. Rowe Price and Fidelity. On a $1,000 investment, you'll save as much as $50.

Also avoid high annual fees that some funds charge. *Ideal:* Choose

stock funds with annual fees of less than 1.25% and bond funds with annual fees of less than 1%.

Potential savings: Roughly $150 on an investment of $10,000 annually.

*All rates and terms subject to change without prior notice.

Source: Jonathan Pond, president of Financial Planning Information, Inc., in Watertown, MA. He was the host of the PBS television special "Finding Financial Freedom With Jonathan Pond."

Dealing with Banks, Credit & Debt

of New York, Box 6998, Newark, DE 19725, fixed 5.9% above the prime lending rate, no annual fee*, 800-942-1977.

● **Stop using your credit cards.** The only way to wipe the slate clean if you're paying the minimum due on your credit card bills is not to run up a higher balance. But not using credit cards is more easily said than done. If you have become dependent on your credit cards, it may take a few months of minimum payments and socking away cash before you can make it through the month without charging. *Strategy:* My new approach worked because my goal was to enjoy life with the money we already had, not to be prisoners of our bills. By making the choice to put less toward the bills and more for our independence, I felt in control. Feelings of empowerment replaced the helpless feeling of relying on our credit card to get us through the month.

● **When you completely pay off a credit card's balance,** reward yourself by setting up a special savings fund. I'll never forget how excited I was when I paid off my first credit card balance under this new system. It was a $300 department store bill that had required a fairly steep minimum payment of $60 a month.

When it was paid off, it was like getting a $60

raise. There were all sorts of things I could do with that newfound money. I decided to put $10 a month into a family-camping account, $20 a month into an account for future car repairs and to leave $30 a month in my checking account for other purchases.

The Truth About Credit Card Security Plans

Credit card security plans that protect against unauthorized charges won't save you more than $50 per card, and thus are rarely worthwhile. *Reason:* Federal law limits your liability for unauthorized charges to $50 per card. Your liability will be zero if you report your credit card as lost or stolen before any improper charges are made on it.

Self-defense: When a card is lost, notify the card issuer immediately by phone and in writing through a letter sent by certified mail. Your receipt is proof of the date on which you sent notice to the issuer. This can be valuable if a question arises over whether disputed charges were incurred before or after the card was lost.

Source: *Gerri Detweiler, consumer credit consultant and author of* The Ultimate Credit Handbook, *Good Advice Press.*

If you follow this approach, you are emotionally and financially free to make real choices about what to do with your money. It's no longer just work and bills, and bills and work.

All rates and terms subject to change without prior notice.

Source: *Carol Keeffe, who leads workshops on money, time and family management, Box 1965, Lynnwood, WA 98046. She is the author of* How to Get What You Want in Life With the Money You Already Have. *Little, Brown & Co.*

Holding the Line
On Medical Costs

6

How to Get the Best From Your Doctor

With medical care getting more complicated, and with the growing number of specialties and even sub-specialties, the field of doctoring is becoming a more impersonal industry. To the person with no medical problems, that's usually an academic point. But for the ill and the elderly, the new situation is creating additional heavy burdens. What used to be a simple doctor-patient relationship is now very complicated. For example, how do you...

● **Maintain continuity** of your medical records when you move from one specialist to another?

● **Identify the right doctor** to diagnose and treat various illnesses?

● **Evaluate the medical advice you're given—** and find the many alternative treatments that may be better for you than the conventional ones?

Taking an Active Role

Increasingly, patients are discovering they can no longer be passive in the doctor-patient relationship. They have to take an active interest to be sure they get not only the best care but, in some instances, just adequate care, as the soaring number of medical malpractice suits seems to indicate.

Here is a valuable checklist of potential problems and advice for dealing with today's doctors:

● **Checkups:** The usual procedure is that a doctor performs a checkup and lab work-ups during the examination. Then, a few days later, the doctor's nurse calls and relates an oversimplified assessment of the lab results. *Instead:* Arrange for a preliminary visit so that lab work can be done before the physical exam. That way, the doctor can go over the results of the tests in detail, answering any questions during the regular exam. If there is need for further lab work, it can be done later.

● **Medical records:** In most cases, your medical records are kept by the doctor. So if you move, decide to change doctors or subsequently see a specialist, you have to go through a long procedure to get your records.

Instead: Ask for copies of all records and keep them in your own permanent file. *Especially useful:* Electrocardiograms, blood tests and X rays. The doctor might charge you a nominal fee to make copies.

● **Selecting professionals:** It's generally very hard to find out whether a doctor treats your particular problem or uses the procedure you need until you visit the office—a waste of your time and money, since you'll probably have to wait for the appointment and pay for the visit. *Instead:* Try to get the information over the telephone.

● **Doctor-patient relations:** Doctors usually prefer to be called "Doctor." Yet they often call patients by their first names. That small difference helps to perpetuate the role of doctor as parent and patient as child—where the patient isn't expected to question the doctor's orders. This leaves the patient in a position of not sharing responsibility for his own health. *Instead:* As a symbolic gesture, settle whether the two of you are on a first- or last-name basis.

More Ways to Win

● **If the doctor always keeps you waiting,** call before you leave for your appointment. *Even better:* Ask someone else to call and explain that your professional duties make your schedule very tight.

● **If the doctor diagnoses an illness and prescribes drugs,** take notes on the name of the condition and the drugs being prescribed.

● **If you're overcome by the news of the illness** (which isn't unusual), call the doctor after you've had some time to calm down and frame any questions about the prognosis and the method of treatment. Also, arrange to bring a relative or friend with you to emotionally-charged doctor visits. That'll give you the emotional space to "collapse" or to go temporarily "deaf" to bad news, while your companion is able to listen, ask questions, and interpret what the doctor says. The period right after serious illness is disclosed is hard to handle, so make arrangements to compensate for it.

> "If you or the doctor feels that the drug you're taking may not be fully effective—but is the best currently available—consider doing some of your own research.... Check medical journals that specialize in the condition you have."

Drugs

Since even the "safest" drugs usually have some side effects, it's prudent to insist that you be included in any decisions about prescriptions. Frequently, the decision isn't only which drug to take, but whether one should be taken at all. In some cases, there are alternatives to drugs—changes in diet, lifestyle or exercise. Many doctors believe, perhaps correctly, that most patients don't feel that an office visit for an illness is complete unless a pill is prescribed. Make it clear that you don't feel that way.

● **Insist that the pharmacist include the manufacturer's fact sheet** with any prescription you're given. It's technical, but with the aid of a medical dictionary you may discover things about the drug you'll want to discuss with the doctor. It's hard, if not impossible, for doctors to know current information on all drugs. You may discover that the dose is excessive or that the drug is no longer effective for your condition.

● **If you do take a drug that has side effects** (i.e., dizziness, stomach distress), start taking it during a weekend or when you're home, so you'll be in a safer place when the side effects hit.

● **If you or the doctor feels that the drug you're taking may not be fully effective**—but is the best currently available—consider doing some of your own research. *Sources:* Check medical journals that specialize in the condition you have. Also, some brokerage firms run stock analyses of leading drug companies and include comprehensive reports on new drugs. The problem then is to find a doctor running clinical studies with the new drug. Only that doctor can legally use it if it doesn't have FDA approval. Be aware, too, that you're running a risk in using the drug. However, some new drugs have already been given full approval in other countries.

Source: Susan G. Cole, editor of The Practical Guide to Cancer Care, *Health Improvement Research Corp.*

Cost-Cutting Secret

Get free drugs simply by asking for them. Doctors are constantly visited by salespeople from drug companies who leave samples, and the samples usually sit forgotten in a desk or filing cabinet. At today's prices, they're worth asking about.

Medical Test Rip-Off

Six out of 10 medical tests are unnecessary. Doctors order them because of insecurity, pressure, hospital profit, curiosity or habit. *To hold down your medical bill:* Ask your doctor whether each test is really needed.

Source: Study at the University of California, reported in the Journal of the American Medical Association.

Generic vs. Brand-Name Drugs

Generic drugs aren't always cheaper than brand-name equivalents. Although pharmacies pay less for generics, many mark them up more than they mark up brand-name drugs. *Helpful:* Comparison shop for each drug instead of assuming that you'll always save by picking the generic.

Source: Study by the Journal of the American Medical Association (JAMA).

How to Avoid Becoming a Victim

One quarter of the surgical procedures performed in the United States each year are of very limited benefit, or entirely useless. *Part of the problem:* In the past 10 years, the number of surgeons has increased, while the demand for operations has remained constant. As the opportunities per surgeon dwindle, the pressure mounts to perform surgery that is only "marginally" indicated.

Relatively few victims of unnecessary surgery come to harm, but all are burdened with needless worry and expense. Hospital stays can be lengthy, and many insurance policies pick up only 80% of the surgical cost. *Worse:* Operations also entail some risk if they require general anesthesia.

Self-Defense

Unless you're a physician, you can't diagnose your own illnesses and decide whether or not you really need an operation. But you can and should seek a second—and third—opinion if you're considering any operative procedure.

Important: Get at least one opinion from a doctor who is not a surgeon—he or she has nothing to lose if you decide not to go under the knife. *How to get the best second opinion:* Call a teaching hospital in your area and ask to see a specialist.

Unwarranted operations are inspired not only by greedy, unethical surgeons, but also by some patients who complain so frequently that their physicians finally recommend surgery as a way to relieve the patients' subjective complaints, if not treat their disorders. Because pain is subjective, it's hard for doctors to determine through tests alone whether the conditions are serious enough to warrant surgery. Physicians must rely on patients' reports of pain.

Warning: The more you complain of pain, the more likely that your doctor will recommend surgery. *It's valuable to become familiar with the types of procedures that may be performed unnecessarily:*

● **Arthroscopy.** A surgical technique to diagnose and repair cartilage injury in the knee. The operation is performed mostly on injured athletes. A good number of orthopedists recommend it. But for many injuries, a few months of rest and rehabilitation may be just as effective a cure. Arthroscopy doesn't necessarily prevent future knee problems or pain.

● **Biopsy of the skin.** The most common surgical procedure in the United States. Several million are performed each year to remove moles and lesions—many of which may be nothing to worry about. *Potentially dangerous lesions:* Moles that change color, darken, bleed or grow rapidly may be malignant. The procedure is simple and not high-risk, but you should definitely seek a second opinion.

● **Breast biopsies.** Because of the malpractice liability crisis, doctors have become fanatical about not missing any lump and women also are scared that any lump means cancer. *Result:* Numerous unnecessary breast biopsies. These operations cost $5,000 on average (usually mostly covered by insurance), may require one to two days in the hospital and involve pain

and the normal surgical risks of doctors' errors, infection, death under anesthesia, etc.

Women under 40 may be the victims of unnecessary breast biopsies. In some cases, if the doctor and patient just wait two or three months, the lump may disappear. But waiting more than four months can be risky. *Better:* If two reputable doctors tell you that you need a breast biopsy, get one. If the surgeon asks you to sign a paper allowing him or her to perform a lumpectomy (removal of the malignant lump) in the lymph nodes of the axilla (armpit), give your consent and have it all done at one time to avoid a second anesthesia. Breast biopsies are almost never wrong, and if cancer is found, the doctor should take care of it surgically.

Caution: If the surgeon wants to perform a mastectomy (removal of the entire breast), withhold your consent until you can get second and third opinions. The need for mastectomies in some patients is controversial.

● **Carotid endarterectomy.** An operation to unclog neck arteries. *Problems:* The operation offers little relief for nearly 30% of patients, and the risk of complications may be great when performed on older people. *Helpful:* Consult a neurologist and a vascular surgeon. Neurologists may suggest more conservative forms of treatment.

● **Coronary bypass.** Very much in vogue, but about one-third of the 225,000 bypass operations performed each year are only marginally indicated. The major benefit—a longer life—doesn't occur in at least half of all cases. Quality of life usually improves after the operation, but there's no guarantee.

Danger: This is a major operation. And the weaker the patient is from his or her heart condition, the more perilous it may be.

Possible attractive alternatives: Angioplasty (cleaning out of arteries via a catheter) or control by medication.

● **Endoscopy.** About a million endoscopies are performed each year, but only 60%–65% are beneficial. The operation involves inserting a tube through the patient's mouth or anus to check for internal bleeding or tumors, costs $550–$650 and is very uncomfortable.

Risks: Possible perforation of the intestines. *Helpful:* When you go for a second opinion, consult a doctor of internal medicine who isn't an endoscopist.

● **Hysterectomy.** Be wary. Some unscrupulous physicians believe the mere presence of a uterus in a woman age 40 or older with gynecologic complaints indicates the need for a hysterectomy.

● **Lumbar laminectomy.** The removal of a disk that is pushing against the spinal cord and causing neurological impairment.

Problem: Only 20% of back-pain sufferers have a disk problem, and of these, only two-thirds benefit from this painful operation. The decision to operate sometimes depends upon the patient's report of pain.

Alternative: Live a healthier lifestyle and lose some weight. A large number of chronic back problems are caused just by excess weight and lack of exercise.

● **Tonsillectomy.** Many unnecessary tonsillectomies are performed at parents' insistence—they just can't stand their kids being sick all the time.

Problem: If recurring sore throats are caused by a virus, they may continue even after a tonsillectomy. The operation is most commonly indicated only if a child gets more than five strep throats per year. These bacterial infections travel through the blood and can cause problems in the heart and kidneys. If this is not the case, there may be little reason for an operation. Consult a reputable pediatrician.

Surgery You Don't Really Need

● **Most back-pain sufferers don't need surgery.** *Also:* Three out of 10 of the most common back operations (laminectomy and spinal fusion) are failures— and 10% make patients worse.

Source: Dr. C. Norman Shealy, founder of the Pain Rehabilitation Center, Springfield, MO.

● **Gallbladder trouble doesn't always necessitate surgery**. *Breakthrough:* Gallstones can now be dissolved by flushing the gallbladder with a form of ether known as MTBE. Recovery is faster, and there is minimal nausea and vomiting.

Source: Dr. Johnson Thistle, Mayo Clinic.

Same-Day Surgeries

You can often safely skip the cost and discomfort of an overnight hospital stay after: hernia repair, tonsillectomy and adenoidectomy, cataract extraction, some plastic surgery, removal of a tissue lesion or cyst, dilation and curettage (D&C), tubal ligation and drainage procedures for glaucoma.

Source: Whole Life Times.

Health Insurance Problems to Avoid

Insurance companies are in the business of selling security and peace of mind. But when it comes to settling claims, most insurance companies are in the business of saving money. While millions of policyholders have their claims settled with a minimum of fuss, there are many areas in which abuses by insurers are widespread. *Rule of thumb:* The higher the cost of your claim, the more likely you are to have trouble with your insurer. The most common ways insurers shortchange policyholders:

● *Unwarranted rescissions.* Attempts by an insurer to rescind—or cancel—a policy *after* a claim has been filed are common in all insurance claims and widespread in health claims. Wrongful rescissions make up 25% of the cases I handle. *How it works:* Many insurers don't investigate your insurance application until you've filed a claim. This procedure is called *post-claims underwriting.* An adjuster audits your medical records, not for the purpose of paying your claim—that's a separate department—but to see if you forgot to include something on your application.

Self-defense: Case law on this subject is clear. If you had no knowledge of a medical problem at the time of your policy application, if you failed to appreciate the significance of an omission or if the omission is immaterial or trivial to the underwriting of your policy, your coverage cannot be rescinded.

When applying for insurance: Answer all questions honestly, *yourself.* Insurance agents often paraphrase answers.

● **Failing to fully investigate claims.** According to consumer-protection laws in almost every state, it is the insurer's duty to investigate policyholders' claims *in good faith.* But insurers are sometimes adversarial when it comes to paying claims. *Result:* Insurers may deny claims without consulting the appropriate experts—doctors, appraisers, contractors—or do so only to find a reason *not* to pay.

Self-defense: If your claim is unfairly denied, enlist the help of your insurance agent and submit statements from experts who can support your claim. If your claim is for property damage, visual documentation— photographs, video- tapes—can help as well. If the insurer refuses to consider your evidence, contact a trial attorney.

● **Overturning medical opinions.** Insurers must often review medical questions—*Was this treatment really necessary? Is this person really disabled?* For this purpose, most insurers use in-house medical examiners or hire "independent" medical examiners who may not be unbiased since they have ongoing business arrangements with the insurers. *Result:* Thousands of claims are unjustly denied every year when insurers' "medical experts" override the opinions of policy-holders' doctors.

Self-defense: Most major medical policies pay for a second opinion—be sure to get one whenever possible. Choose doctors who are willing to go to bat for you if their opinions are contradicted.

● **Narrowly defining disability.** Most state laws and employers define disability as the inability to perform steadily in a job to which you are reasonably suited by education, training, experience, opportunity and physical and mental capacities.

But most disability insurance policies ignore state law and define disability as the inability to perform any job. By this definition, an executive who suffers a debilitating stroke would not be considered disabled if he or she could still wash dishes, and could be denied the benefits he or she expects based on his or her salary.

Self-defense: Look for a disability policy that cov-

ers you for your "own occupation," not just "any occupation." When filing a disability claim, describe the nature of your work to your doctor and precisely how your injuries affect your ability to work. Make sure this information is included in your doctor's report to the insurance company.

Questions to Ask a Surgeon

To protect against unnecessary surgery, ask the physician hard questions beforehand:

● What are the risks?

● What is the mortality rate for this operation?

● How long will it take to recover?

● What is the likelihood of complications? What sort?

● Are there alternative ways to treat this condition?

● How many people have you seen with similar symptoms who have chosen not to have surgery?

● How many of these operations have you done in the past year?

Once you receive answers, then get a second opinion.

● **Denying health claims that have been preapproved.** Thousands of policyholders follow their insurers' instructions. They call the insurer for "preapproval" of a medical procedure, but are turned down when they file the claim, often on the grounds that the procedure was experimental, not medically necessary or excessive treatment. *Reason:* Policyholders may have spoken with a clerk who only verified that the policy is active or that a certain procedure is covered. Clerks are not claims adjusters and do not preapprove the amount the insurer is willing to pay or whether the procedure was necessary.

Self-defense: Speak with a claims adjuster and get preapproval for the specific procedure and amount covered in writing. If you are denied approval of a formerly experimental procedure, have your doctor call the insurer and explain why you are a good candidate for such treatment. If necessary, contact an attorney.

Source: William M. Shernoff, attorney, who specializes in consumer claims against insurance companies, Claremont, CA. Mr. Shernoff is the author of How to Make Insurance Companies Pay Your Claims, Hastings House.

HMOs: Are They for You?

Do health maintenance organizations (HMOs) really save money? Typically, HMOs charge member families a set annual fee. Thereafter, visits and treatments for the family can be obtained for nominal fees. This gives the HMO an incentive to limit patient care as a way of keeping its costs down.

Most HMOs use a number of techniques to control the type and price of health care delivered to their members. Well-run HMOs can typically reduce the average health-care costs for an individual by as much as 15% to 20%. Whether such savings will be available to you depends on the local market and the benefit plans offered.

Always compare the health insurance options offered by your company. Most companies have an enrollment period once a year when you can select your insurance plan for the upcoming year.

Expect to be offered a traditional indemnity program and one or more HMO programs. Compare the costs and benefits by drafting a worksheet with the following information on each program:

- **Monthly premium.**
- **Copayments.**
- **Deductibles.**
- **Extent of coverage.**
- **Expected health-care needs** (use last year as a proxy).

HMOs make the most sense for individuals or families who expect high health-care costs or prefer to be able to accurately budget

> "[When choosing an HMO ask] how long...the health organization [has] been in business. Fifteen to 20 years is an ideal amount of time for an HMO to have established a strong staff."

health expenditures. Likely candidates are individuals with health conditions that require close medical attention or very young families whose children require frequent and unexpected visits to a physician. It is generally more economical for individuals or families with low expected health-care expenses to select insurance programs with significant copayments and deductibles.

- **Will you have to give up your current physician?** Traditionally, people thought that joining an HMO meant giving up their existing physicians. Today, many HMO programs use a large proportion, sometimes more than half, of the private-practice physicians within a local community. These HMOs, called individual practice associations (IPAs), can give you the lower cost of an HMO and allow you to keep your current physician.

Source: Eric S. Schlesinger, manager, The Boston Consulting Group, Inc., 780 Third Ave., New York, NY 10017. He has worked with insurers, HMOs and hospitals to develop strategies for the evolving health-care industry.

Key Questions to Ask About HMOs

Choosing an HMO is a big step in managing your health care. Make sure you get satisfactory answers to the following questions before making your final decision.

- **How long has the health organization been in business?** Fifteen to 20 years is an ideal amount of time for an HMO to have established a strong staff of providers.
- **What does it cost to see a doctor, and how much will you have to pay for prescriptions?**
- **Does the plan offer a wide choice of physicians?** And are these physicians accepting new patients? A good plan will have at least 90 percent of their providers with open panels (free to accept new patients).
- **What is the policy on pre-existing conditions?**
- **How easy would it be for you to see a specialist if you needed one, and does the plan offer a wide enough choice?**
- **Are the physicians happy with the HMO?** Look at the turnover rate; is it more than 10%? This may be a sign that the participating physicians are not satisfied with this particular organization.
- **Does the plan include alternative medicine or medical care?**
- **Does the plan have reciprocal care agreements with plans in other cities and countries?**
- **Who can you appeal to if you believe your doctor is wrong about a diagnosis or treatment?**

WORST TIMES FOR HOSPITAL CHECK-IN

Avoid weekend admissions for tests or elective surgery. Chances are that you will lie in bed for two days with little or no medical care at a cost of up to $1,000 a day. Because most patients are discharged by the weekend, hospitals trying to fill beds will encourage weekend admissions. As a general rule, insist that you be admitted right before a test or procedure is scheduled.

Also avoid admissions during major holiday seasons, such as Thanksgiving or Christmas. Staffing at most hospitals is particularly low during those periods, so you may end up sitting around waiting for things to be done.

Warning: If you are really sick, staff shortages may mean lower-quality care.

The worst time to be admitted to a hospital is in the month of July. Why? July is the month when residents and medical students are rotated. A major portion of day-to-day care in teaching-affiliated hospitals is performed by newly graduated resident doctors. Young residents who have just arrived or those who have just taken on greater responsibilities will not have the same level of skill as more experienced physicians.

Source: *Arthur A. Levin, MPH, director, Center for Medical Consumers, 237 Thompson St., New York, NY 10012, publishers of* **Health-Facts**, *a monthly newsletter that critiques medical practices.*

Important to note

Is the HMO accredited by the National Committee on Quality Assurance (NCQA) or any consumer groups? The NCQA bases its evaluations on measures such as whether a plan and participating HMO has high cervical and breast cancer screening rates, and high diabetic retinal testing rates (very good because the plan makes use of preventative medicine) or high heart bypass and angioplasty rates (bad because good preventative care could offset the need for surgery).

High C-section rates are also a sign of lower quality care. Each year thousands of unnecessary Cesarean sections are performed in the United States; look for a rate of 15% or lower of all births at your health-care organization.

A Tough Test For HMOs

Will the HMO you are considering hold itself to standards set by the Foundation for Accountability (FACCT)? This nonprofit group of consumer advocates and companies has tested health plans against extremely tough measures. For example, FACCT not only questions patients on whether they are satisfied with a health-care provider's technical skills, but also his or her interpersonal and communication skills.

Both the NCQA and FACCT check on preventative-care measures (What proportion of patients does the health care organization advise to quit smoking? Does the health care organization take extensive histories to uncover poor health habits and does it do anything to educate patients on improving health habits?).

They also check on issues that you may not remember to ask about—for instance, is treatment for mental health covered, and for how long? What about patient confidentiality? Other measures FACCT is planning for the future are quality of end of life, HIV/AIDS and pediatric care and treatment.

A Good Person to Talk to

More personal attention in a hospital is available through free patient-representative services. A patient representative answers your questions, acts on your concerns and intervenes between you and your doctor or you and the nursing staff if needed. A patient representative will meet you when you sign in at a small hospital. In larger hospitals, the representative's number should appear on your phone.

Source: *Ruth Ravich, director, patient representative department, Mount Sinai Medical Center, New York.*

Hospital Stays Can Be Hazardous to Your Health

Aside from keeping your hospital bills down, shorter hospital stays keep you healthier. *Fact:* The longer you stay in a hospital, the greater the risk you will end up with a problem you didn't arrive with.

Medication errors and hospital-borne infections are only two of the dangers. A research study of more than 800 consecutive hospital admissions revealed that almost 40% of the individuals checked into the hospital ended up with new doctor- or hospital-caused problems.

Source: *Arthur A. Levin, MPH, director, Center for Medical Consumers, 237 Thompson St., New York, NY 10012, publishers of HealthFacts, a monthly newsletter that critiques medical practices.*

Nonprofit Vs. For-Profit Hospitals

For-profit hospitals are much more expensive than nonprofit ones. One study shows that the average bill from profit-making hospitals is 22% higher than the bill from nonprofit institutions. The basic room cost is nearly the same at both kinds of hospitals. The cost difference comes almost entirely from ancillary services such as drugs and medical supplies.

Source: *What's Ahead in Personnel?*

Most Frequent Hospital-Bill Mistake

Ninety-seven percent of hospital bills are wrong, and less than 2% of those errors are in the patient's favor. *Average error:* $1,400.

Frequent mistake: Billing for items or services never delivered—lab work, medication, thermometers, wheelchairs, etc.

Self-defense: Insist on completely itemized bills and review them carefully.

Source: *Harvey Rosenfield, head of the watchdog group Bills Project.*

How to Protect Yourself From Hospital Billing Errors

When the mechanic hands you a bill for $500, it's unlikely that you'd pay it without a glance at the charges. But when given a hospital bill for $5,000, most people tend to do just that.

As it turns out, hospitals and doctors are far from infallible when it comes to billing. According to the New York Life Insurance Company, which has been auditing hospital bills for some years, the average hospital bill contains $600 worth of erroneous charges. This money comes not only out of the insurance company's pocket, but also out of yours. You can save money by knowing how the system works and how to spot billing errors.

When $$ Interferes With Medicine

Doctors in large private practices order 50% more chest X rays and electrocardiograms than those who work for health maintenance organizations (HMOs).

Problem: A doctor's fee structure (fee-for-service in private practice, fixed prepayment in HMOs) may determine whether or not a patient is tested.

Why Bother?

With the rising costs of health care, the current trend in the insurance industry is to have the insured employee share in the cost. Under major medical plans, employees are usually responsible for a fixed dollar amount, termed "out-of-pocket expenses," limit is $1,000. The insurance company usually pays 80% (and the patient, 20%) of all non-room-and-board charges until the $1,000 out-of-pocket expense limit is reached. After that, insurance takes over 100%. But most patients don't reach the out-of-pocket limit, since they'd have to accrue at least $5,000 worth of non-room-and-board hospital expenses or other health-care costs to do so. While your contribution to out-of-pocket is still adding up, it pays to keep costs down.

There are many billing errors for the simple reason that many hospitals have inefficient billing systems.

Problem: Hospitals are geared to make sure that patients are billed for services provided, and not to verify charges.

Typical mistake: Because of a clerical error, a $50 electrocardiogram is entered onto your bill as a $500 charge. Since you may not know the typical cost of an EKG, the error goes undetected. *Another example:* A lab technician comes in to draw blood and finds that the patient is no longer there. However, the patient is still charged. *Reason:* Billing starts from the day the charges are entered in the book, and the patient's charges are never canceled.

Similar mistakes occur with drug prescriptions. *Example:* The doctor might order 10 days' worth of penicillin and then switch to tetracycline after seven days. If the unused three days' worth of penicillin is not returned, the patient is billed for it.

The Four Major Mistake Areas

● **Respiratory therapy.** Equipment such as oxygen tanks isn't credited even though respiratory therapy was discontinued.

● **Pharmacy charges.** Credit isn't given for drugs that are returned.

● **Lab tests.** Cancellations of tests aren't noted.

● **Central supply items.** Hospital staff or nurses may run out of something and borrow it from another patient. They intend to give credit or return the item, but often they don't get around to it.

> " **[While in the hospital] keep track of the most basic things, such as how many times your blood was drawn.... If you're able, jot down what happens daily.** "

What You Can Do

● **Keep track of the most basic things,** such as how many times your blood was drawn. *Suggestion:* If you're able, jot down what happens daily.

Note: If the patient is too sick to keep track of services rendered, a family member should try to keep track of the charges. Although it may be difficult to know how many routine things such as blood counts or X rays were done, someone who visits regularly is likely to know about nonroutine services, such as barium enemas or cardiac catheterizations.

● **Ask questions.** Ask the doctor to be specific about tests. If he or she orders X rays, ask what type of X rays. If the answer is not satisfactory, ask the nurse. Always ask. It's the most important thing a health-care consumer can do. *Reassuring change:* The newer generation of doctors is more willing to involve the patient in his or her own care.

● **Insist on an itemized bill, not just a summary of charges.**

● **Check room-and-board charges.** Count the days you were in the hospital and in what kind of room. Are you being charged for a private room, even though you were in a semiprivate? Some hospitals have different semiprivate rates for two-bed and four-bed rooms. Check your rate.

● **Review the charges for TV rental and phone.**

● **Be equally careful with doctor bills**. Often these bills are made out by the doctor's assistant, who may not be sure of what was done.

Most common errors: Charges for services in the doctor's office, such as a chest X ray or an injection, that weren't actually performed, or charges for routine hospital physician visits on days that the doctors were not in attendance.

Source: Interview with Janice Spillane, manager of cost containment in the group insurance department of New York Life Insurance Co., New York, NY.

How to Prevent Overcharges

Most people pay very little attention to the actual fees and expenses charged by doctors and hospitals. The lenient medical insurance policies of the past (both private and public) gave people few incentives to scrutinize their medical bills. In the new, more competitive health-care environment, there is a growing trend by medical insurers toward greater deductibles, less complete insurance coverage and co-payment policies. The result is that Americans now have real incentives to examine their medical bills and the appropriateness of individual charges.

● **The first step in avoiding overcharges:** *Always ask, ahead of time, what a medical visit, test or procedure will cost.* Don't be shy about asking—if a doctor thinks you can pay the bill, he or she probably won't volunteer the information. Good health practitioners should present you with a financial estimate along with any plan for major medical work.

● **Next, negotiate fees or charges.** It is absolutely in your best interest to find out all fees and charges involved in your treatment and to negotiate those you feel are too high. Before visiting with a practitioner, find out what and how much your medical insurance plan will cover, and try to negotiate with your doctor any remaining amount. Some doctors will be satisfied with whatever reimbursement your insurance will provide.

● **The third step in avoiding overcharges:** *Shop around.* It goes against the traditional notion of health care, but you can look for better rates. Fees and hospital charges vary extraordinarily from one practitioner or hospital to another.

● **Finally, always find out if a test or procedure can be performed on an ambulatory (outpatient) basis.** Because traditional medical insurance reimbursement policies once favored it, many doctors still routinely admit patients to the hospital for tests or surgery that could be performed on an outpatient basis at a much lower cost.

Source: Arthur A. Levin, MPH, director, Center for Medical Consumers, 237 Thompson St., New York, NY 10012, publishers of HealthFacts, a monthly newsletter that critiques medical practices.

How to Beat The 7.5% Medical Deduction Limit

Medical expenses are one type of personal expense that you can deduct from your taxable income. How much? All of your medical expenses that exceed 7.5% of your Adjusted Gross Income (AGI).

WHAT TO DO IF YOUR DOCTOR OVERCHARGES

If you feel a medical bill you receive is out of line, the first thing to do is to make an appointment to discuss it with the practitioner. Even if you feel very angry, approaching the meeting in an open and cooperative spirit paves the way for negotiation. In today's litigious climate, being too aggressive may turn a person away from a cooperative attempt to settle differences.

If you are concerned about your ability to pay the charges, be open about your finances. It is not inappropriate to discuss a payment plan as one means of settling the bill. If you have the ability to pay all the charges, but believe them to be too high or in error, you should review them with the practitioner and try to have them corrected or reduced.

If your doctor refuses to negotiate, contact your local county, regional or state medical or dental society. Do so in writing, giving the details of your case and why you believe the charges are excessive. *Bear in mind:* There is no "official" list of acceptable charges for doctors and dentists. Most professional societies no longer conduct peer reviews of doctors' fees. Furthermore, government agencies have no blanket supervisory authority over what medical practitioners charge. Unless the charges are so excessive that they are criminal, or in cases where Medicaid or Medicare is involved, there is no sense in contacting a government agency.

Source: Arthur A. Levin, MPH, director, Center for Medical Consumers, 237 Thompson St., New York, NY 10012, publishers of HealthFacts, a monthly newsletter that critiques medical practices.

Included under medical expenses are the costs of diagnosis, cure, treatment and prevention of disease. You can deduct the cost of prescription drugs (including insulin) as well as transportation expenses to and from a doctor, dentist, hospital or pharmacy. If you use your own car, the rate is 10 cents per mile plus the cost of parking and tolls.

In addition to your own medical expenses, you can claim the medical expenses of any person who qualifies as your dependent. That includes your spouse and/or any other individual who lives with you and depends on you for his or her livelihood. *Advantage:* The definition of dependents for purposes of claiming medical expenses is much broader than for purposes of claiming them as tax exemptions. As long as you provide more than one-half of their support, you can deduct medical expenses you pay for them even if their gross income is too high to allow you to claim dependency exemptions for them. And, if you are a divorced parent, you can deduct medical expenses you pay for your child even if the other parent is entitled to claim the dependency exemption.

> **[When considering your taxes], time your use of the medical deduction wisely. Since medical deductions are a function of your Adjusted Gross Income, it is best to pay for major medical expenses in years when your AGI is relatively low.**

Timing Is Critical

Time your use of the medical deduction wisely. Since medical deductions are a function of your Adjusted Gross Income, it is best to pay for major medical expenses in years when your AGI is relatively low. For example, suppose it's close to year-end and you estimate this year's income will be $50,000 and next year's will increase to $100,000. The best time to incur major medical expenses (if you have a choice) is during the low-income year, when your 7.5% minimum only equals $3,750. If you wait until next year, you will have to incur $7,500 (7.5% of $100,000) before you can start claiming medical expenses as a deduction.

Alternatively, if you approach year-end and don't have enough medical expenses to exceed the 7.5% floor, you may want to defer as many payments as possible until next year. *You never know:* You might have more medical expenses in the following year, and/or your AGI may be lower.

If your tax bracket shifts from year to year, consider taking most of your medical deductions during years when your bracket is relatively high. A $1,000 deduction at the 31% bracket saves you $310, whereas the same deduction in a year when you're in the 28% bracket will save you only $280. The years you are in a high tax bracket and can make the most of your tax deduction can, unfortunately, also be the years you have the highest AGI and are able to deduct less of your total medical expenses. This will not always be the case.

For example, assume your AGI remains the same but your taxable income drops due to larger interest expense deductions or real estate taxes (e.g., when you buy a new home). In this situation, you should pay your medical expenses in the first of the two years, when your tax bracket is higher.

The Importance of Filing Status

For married couples in which one or the other spouse has large medical bills, it can be advantageous to file separate rather than joint returns. For example, assume a wife's and a husband's AGIs on separate returns are $50,000 and $350,000, respectively. If filed jointly, their total AGI would be $400,000 and only medical expenses in excess of $30,000 would be tax deductible. In this case, if the wife incurred $20,000 in medical expenses, none would be tax deductible. On a separate return, however, the wife could deduct $16,250 (the excess of $20,000 over 7.5% of her $50,000 AGI).

To see if this approach would work for you, calcu-

YOU CAN SHORTEN THE LENGTH OF THERAPY

You can facilitate the progress of psychotherapy, shorten its duration and save money.

1. Outside your therapy sessions, establish an internal dialogue patterned on the one you have with your therapist. Continue the process of self-exploration, introspection and honest self-confrontation.

2. Make notes on your dreams and fantasies and bring them to the sessions. They are shortcuts to the unconscious.

3. Attempt to recognize any resistance you may have to the therapy. Resistance to change is part of the process of psychotherapy and is largely unconscious—patients often spend many sessions overcoming it. Recognizing resistance and developing a therapeutic alliance with your therapist will shorten this defensive stage.

4. At regular intervals ask your therapist to join you in an evaluation of the progress of your treatment. Lengthy impasses may require a consultation with another therapist.

Source: *T. Byram Karasu, M.D., professor of psychiatry, Albert Einstein College of Medicine/Montefiore Medical Center, 2 E. 88 St., New York, NY 10128. He is also chairman of the APA Commission on Psychiatric Therapies and of the APA Task Force on Treatment of Psychiatric Disorders.*

returns, you could lose the opportunity to file in the most advantageous way.

Source: *Lawrence W. Goldstein, manager, Ernst & Young, LLP, New York, NY..*

Negotiate an Informal Contract With Your Therapist

Try to negotiate an informal contract with your therapist before you begin treatment. Your discussion should include the fee and optimum required frequency of visits. What makes therapy expensive is its open-endedness and its lack of focus—or its having too many different factors on which to focus. This makes it worthwhile to negotiate the goal of the therapy, its focus and the process.

Also ask your therapist to estimate the length of treatment. Many psychological problems are caused by narrowly definable conflicts that create corresponding defense mechanisms in the patient. These conflicts frequently lend themselves to short-term psychotherapies. Only lifelong characterologic problems and personality disorders may require long-term psychotherapy or analysis. Try to have your symptoms treated independently of your life and interpersonal problems. Although they are usually inextricable, it is quite possible to treat manifest symptoms with medication and to achieve behavior modifications quickly, while you work on life problems at a slower pace.

Source: *T. Byram Karasu, M.D., professor of psychiatry, Albert Einstein College of Medicine/Montefiore Medical Center, 2 E. 88 St., New York, NY 10128. He is also chairman of the APA Commission on Psychiatric Therapies and of the APA Task Force on Treatment of Psychiatric Disorders.*

late your tax liability on a separate basis, then see if the total is less than the tax would be if you filed jointly. If the total tax paid on separate returns is lower, file separately and take the medical deduction. Otherwise, file a joint return.

Essential: When you compare the figures for filing separately and jointly, consider your total tax burden, including state taxes.

Problem: You may find you save money by filing separately on your federal return, but that your state taxes are significantly higher filing that way. Since some states require taxpayers to file state returns the same way they file their federal

GETTING THE MOST COST-EFFECTIVE PSYCHIATRIC HELP

Psychiatric conditions that require professional help range from existential questions about oneself to disease entities such as schizophrenia, bulimia and a large variety of symptoms and syndromes such as impotence, marital conflicts, alcohol abuse and psychosomatic disorders. Many means are available for treating problems like these, but the cost-effectiveness of a particular treatment program depends almost entirely on the condition being treated.

The Correct Diagnosis

The primary rule of cost-effectiveness is to get the correct diagnosis. If you get an incorrect diagnosis in the beginning, you may become involved with a long and expensive treatment regimen that does not adequately correct your condition.

Once you start a particular program, it is usually difficult to end it. Patients have a tendency to stay with a familiar therapist even though, by all objective criteria, the therapy is not successful.

An incorrect diagnosis may be made if you select the "wrong" clinician—one competent in only a narrowly defined area, or whose treatment philosophy is not the one best suited to dealing with your particular problem. The correct diagnosis usually requires finding an eclectic psychiatrist with the training and capacity to synthesize multiple points of view.

Referrals by friends and family are always a good place to start looking for a well-qualified psychiatrist. Most good internists are also able to make recommendations. Check therapists' academic credentials—affiliations with academic institutions are a good sign. After you've narrowed the field, arrange to meet prospective therapists face-to-face.

Caution: Beware of psychiatrists who talk too much, ask the same question over and over, lecture or drop names of patients.

Even if you don't intend to be treated by a psychiatrist, consult with one before deciding on a specific treatment and therapist. Psychiatrists can determine whether a psychological disorder has a physiological basis—a possibility you should at least rule out before beginning therapy.

After the Diagnosis

Depending on the diagnosis, a variety of practitioners are available to provide treatment. Psychiatrists in private practice tend to be the most expensive of all mental health workers. However, major psychiatric disorders such as depression, anxiety and thought disorders do require a psychiatrist's involvement. Since they are also M.D.'s, psychiatrists are capable of doing comprehensive medical evaluations and can write prescriptions when pharmacological treatment is needed.

If you have no medical or organic problems (symptoms that require medical intervention), a psychologist or other mental health worker can deliver needed psychotherapy at lower cost.

For problems that are interpersonal in nature, group therapy can be very cost-effective. Although it is less confidential and less time is available for individual issues, it is possible to get around these problems by complementing group sessions with individual sessions. Couples therapy, especially when conducted in a group, can be a very cost-effective way for spouses to resolve marital difficulties.

Advantages: You and your spouse become part of a support group where you can examine your relationship, be comforted that you are not alone in your struggle, learn different styles of communication and identify with the survivors of interpersonal conflicts.

Clinics, especially those associated with medical schools, deliver good-quality, comprehensive care at a relatively low cost, even though they are largely staffed with trainees. Institutes (psychoanalytical, behavioral, etc.), also primarily staffed by trainees, specialize in more narrowly defined therapeutic approaches. However, by shopping around and choosing carefully, you can find an institute—or another of these sources—that will provide cost-effective treatment.

Source: T. Byram Karasu, M.D., professor of psychiatry, Albert Einstein College of Medicine/Montefiore Medical Center, 2 E. 88 St., New York, NY 10128. He is also chairman of the APA Commission on Psychiatric Therapies and of the APA Task Force on Treatment of Psychiatric Disorders.

The Dollars and Sense of Being Fitted With Contact Lenses

Acquiring a pair of contact lenses is quite different from buying any other consumer product. Lenses have a critical job to do and must do it without causing irritation or injury to the wearer's eyes. Of course the physical lenses themselves are a "product," but what the contact lens wearer is actually buying is a service—an effective solution to a personal health problem.

Choosing a Practitioner

Cutting corners when choosing a practitioner would obviously be foolish. Fees for a contact lens fitting can vary greatly, depending on the lens type and the complexity of your case, as well as the quality of the service rendered. But knowing up front what the charges and refund policy will be (within reasonable limits) will help you evaluate the cost-effectiveness of the care. In addition to investigating cost, then, here are several points to consider when choosing a practitioner:

> "At the conclusion of [the initial] consultation, it is a good idea to request a comprehensive... fee schedule to eliminate [any] potential surprises down the line"

- **Reputation.** Ask friends and acquaintances who wear contact lenses for their recommendations on practitioners.
- **Competency.** Inquire about the doctors' credentials and areas of expertise. Focus on practitioners who specialize in contact lenses and be sure they employ *at least* three or four various lens types from different contact lens manufacturers.
- **Compatibility.** A pleasant, comfortable relationship with the practitioner and staff will help ensure that your needs are met. It is advantageous to work with the same doctor each time you return. This will lead to a more consistent approach in satisfying your contact lens needs.
- **Personal comfort.** Pleasant surroundings are a valid consideration when selecting a practitioner, since

correct fitting requires substantial amounts of time.

The Fitting Process

A proper contact lens fitting consists of four phases. Understanding the purpose of each phase will put you in a better position to make evaluations and choices along the way.

1. In the initial consultation (the cost of which you should find out beforehand), you and your practitioner will mainly exchange information. You will be questioned about your health history and your requirements, goals and expectations concerning wearing contact lenses.

This visit is also your opportunity to question your practitioner on his or her experience, credentials and affiliations, as well as details about the further course and cost of the fitting.

It is important that you use this opportunity to eliminate many potential surprises down the line. At the conclusion of this consultation, it is a good idea to request a comprehensive and detailed fee schedule.

If, for any reason, you do not feel comfortable with the practitioner—or anything else about the situation—this is the time to terminate the relationship and look for another practitioner. You will, of course, have to pay for the consultation.

2. Assuming all went well at the initial consultation, you will return for a diagnostic evaluation (sometimes this phase and the first phase are combined in one visit). Your vision-correction needs will be determined through careful examination of your eyes and eyelids. Based on the information collected and the goals agreed upon in the consultation and the findings of this exam, a limited selection of indicated lens types will be tried out and evaluated.

Normally, this will lead to a final selection of one or more applicable lens types. If no available solution fulfills your goals, either you and your practitioner must agree on new goals or the fitting process should be terminated at this point.

3. Following a successful diagnostic, you will return for the dispensing appointment, at which the selected lenses are tried on and evaluated. Again, assuming all is well, you will be instructed in their proper use and maintenance. It is imperative that instructions pertaining to wearing and disinfection and cleaning procedures be followed scrupulously. Failure to do so is fast becoming one of the leading causes of serious eye complications.

4. The final phase of lens fitting—every bit as important as any of the preceding ones —is follow-up care. Proper follow-up to a typical dispensing of contact lenses without complication involves approximately four visits during the initial fitting period.

Patients with complex cases and those who plan to wear their lenses for extended periods and/or sleep with their lenses should plan on more frequent initial appointments. Every daily-wear contact lens wearer should return once or twice a year thereafter for regular checkups, and, in the case of overnight lens wearers, as often as four times a year.

Source: Barry Farkas, O.D., FAAO, doctor of optometry, 30 E. 60 St., New York, NY 10022. He is a diplomate of the contact lens section of the American Academy of Optometry.

Health Foods: Do You Get What You Pay for?

Since the 1960s, Americans have had a love affair with health foods. Food products labeled "healthy," "natural," "additive-free," "no preservatives" and "nothing artificial" have become not only highly marketable, but highly expensive.

While health foods are usually more expensive than other food products, they are sometimes no better or safer. Many "natural" foods have added ingredients with little nutritional value.

For example, a typical granola bar is no more nutritious than a Snickers bar and does not contain fewer calories. Furthermore, because there are many "natural" toxins in foods, the term does not even guarantee safety. It always pays to read labels carefully and be a little cynical about the claims made for any product.

A Better Value

Being healthy does not require spending extra money to eat only "health food." It is much more important to select foods that have high nutritional value and avoid those that have little.

As a general rule, avoid processed food products and opt for fresh or fresh-frozen ingredients instead. This will help you minimize your intake of

salt, fats, chemicals and empty calories.

The best advice is to maximize your intake of fresh vegetables and fruits, whole grains and sources of protein low in saturated fat. Many supermarkets are carrying some of the grains, juices and additive- or preservative-free products formerly found only at "health food" stores—and the supermarkets are doing this at lower prices.

Source: Arthur A. Levin, MPH, director, Center for Medical Consumers, 237 Thompson St., New York, NY 10012, publishers of HealthFacts, a monthly newsletter that critiques medical practices.

How to Get the Most Nutrient Value Out of the Food You Buy

● **Buy whole-grain products,** or at least enriched refined ones.

● **Buy fresh or frozen fruits and vegetables, not canned.** The best choice is freshly picked, ripe produce. Frozen produce is often more healthful than fresh, however, because it is frozen when the nutrients are largely intact.

● **Low-fat dairy products** should be fortified with vitamins A and D, which are fat-soluble.

● **Don't soak fresh produce** for long periods of time. Also, don't wash rice. This will preserve water-soluble vitamins.

● **Avoid cutting and/or cooking vegetables** until right before use.

● **Avoid boiling vegetables.** Pressure cooking and steaming preserve more nutrients.

Source: Arthur A. Levin, MPH, director, Center for Medical Consumers, 237 Thompson St., New York, NY 10012, publishers of HealthFacts, a monthly newsletter that critiques medical practices.

Health on the Internet

With so much health and medical information available on the Internet today, more and more people are educating themselves about everything from nutrition and fitness to the latest treatments for heart disease and cancer. But with this wealth of information comes an abundance of fraudulent claims and scams. *Remember:* Anyone with the right equipment can create a web page, and some of them

ARE VITAMINS WORTH THE COST?

Every year more than $2 billion worth of vitamins are sold to the American consumer. To date, however, the importance of these extra doses of vitamins to our health and nutrition is largely unknown.

The controversy rages on two fronts: How helpful are moderate supplements of vitamins in maintaining maximal health—and how helpful are large (mega) doses of vitamins in either preventing or curing certain diseases and conditions?

Regarding the second question, little evidence has been gathered to show conclusively that megadoses of vitamins cure or prevent serious medical conditions. The first question has proved easier to answer.

Are Moderate Supplements Necessary?

For some, definitely yes—for others, probably. For individuals who have clinically proven vitamin deficiencies, vitamins are clearly worth the cost. These people need extra vitamins because either their behavior results in a deficiency or their medical problem or treatment results in a deficiency. *Examples:* Heavy smokers are thought to be very deficient in vitamin C; women on birth control pills, defi-

cient in thiamin, some B vitamins and vitamin C; those taking diuretics for high blood pressure often become deficient in B_6.

Although the proof is less conclusive, most health practitioners would agree that moderate amounts of vitamin and mineral supplements are needed even by those of us who eat three square meals a day and don't have the clinical deficiencies described above. Exercise, stress, alcoholic beverages, dieting and pollution are all believed to deplete the body's reserve of vitamins and minerals.

Source: Arthur A. Levin, MPH, director, Center for Medical Consumers, 237 Thompson St., New York, NY 10012, publishers of Health-Facts, a monthly newsletter that critiques medical practices.

look extremely professional and legitimate. You could lose time, money, and worse, your health if you are duped by inaccurate or erroneous information.

Protect yourself from fraudulent and potentially dangerous health or medical advice by checking out your source of information very carefully. *Ask these questions:*

● **Whose site is it?** The most dependable sources are medical schools and universities (.uni), government agencies (.gov) and some not-for-profit health agencies (.org). Some practitioners and commercial organizations may have hidden marketing or political agendas.

● **Are the names and credentials of the people who prepared the site listed?** Can they be contacted?

● **When was the site last updated?** Frequent updates mean timely information.

● **Does the site link to other health and medical websites?** Be careful, though; anyone can link on to a legitimate source to make his or her website appear credible.

An extra caution: Be suspicious of websites that promote treatments using words such as "miracle," "revolutionary," "secret," or "breakthrough" or that are pushing you to purchase a remedy or product.

Bottom line: Any information that you gather from the Internet should be double checked with your health practitioner.

Source: Food and Drug Administration Consumer Health Information Online.

Friends, Family & Your Money

7

Financial Strategies for Working Couples

Few two-income couples take full advantage of their financial power. And they don't concentrate on making their money work for them.

Attitudes About Money

There are two types of people—savers and spenders. For better or worse, they tend to marry each other. The result is often conflicting views of money and how it should be spent and invested.

Solution: Sit down with your partner and confront your money attitudes. Then discuss how best to handle your finances. Take a close look at your overall financial picture. Ask yourselves:

● **How much of your respective incomes do you want to save?**

● **What are your savings goals** (vacation, new car, down payment on a house, college for the kids, retirement)?

● **Should you be accountable** to each other for all of your spending or should each of you have a private account?

● **How many credit cards will you use?** Or will you cut up all but one of your cards and take a weekly cash allowance?

Another way to limit the amount of damage is to set up separate accounts for a portion of your earnings. Pay your household expenses out of one joint account. *Remember:* Depending on your state of residence, you may be responsible for your spouse's debts, and your spouse's bill-paying habits could affect your credit report.

Reconcile Tax Strategies

Spouses often have different views about how to handle their income taxes and organize their records, especially if they prepare their own tax returns.

Important: If both of you sign the return, both of you are liable for any mistakes, disallowances (when the IRS disallows a deduction) or penalties.
Strategy: Seek professional tax-filing help. Find a CPA who makes both of you comfortable. It may be worth the extra expense to give you peace of mind about your taxes.

Retirement Accounts

IRAs offer a tremendous opportunity to save for your future. You may each deduct a $2,000 contribution to an IRA if neither you nor your spouse is covered by an employer-sponsored retirement plan, such as a 401(k). Even if you or your spouse is covered by a pension plan at work, the 1997 tax law allows you to make deductible IRA contributions, depending on your adjusted gross income. Another alternative is the new tax-favored Roth IRAs. They don't yield deductions when you put money in, but will result in tax-free distributions for withdrawals made after five years, if you meet certain requirements. Check with your tax adviser about which IRA is best for your situation.

Even if you do participate in such a plan, you still might be eligible to deduct some IRA contributions, depending on your income level. Even better than an IRA is a company-sponsored 401(k) plan. Try to contribute the maximum amount allowed, especially if your company matches your contributions.

Note: Some couples leave retirement planning to the highest earner. That causes two problems.

● **The couple doesn't save enough to meet their retirement needs.**

● **One of them may be at a big disadvantage if they ever divorce.**
Strategy: If you can't afford to contribute the maximum amounts to two company plans, concentrate your savings in the plan that offers the best deal.

Life Insurance Needs

If both of you are working, you might need additional life insurance to replace some of the income that would be lost if one spouse died.

That means you must figure out how much supplemental income you would need, especially to cover long-term expenses such as mortgage payments.
Helpful: Comparison shop for the least expensive term life insurance from a highly rated company.
Alternative: If you don't have a policy, consider buying a first-to-die whole-life policy. It will insure the life of the person who dies first and might be as much as 40% cheaper than buying separate policies.

Important: Make sure that the policy can be converted to cover a surviving spouse without a new physical exam.

Health Insurance

Be careful about tampering with your health insurance. Since both of you have jobs, you may be able to save some money on your coverage. For example, you might opt out of one partner's plan and let the other plan cover you both.

Warning: Such a move could leave you vulnerable if the covered spouse loses his or her job.

Compare the two plans, and figure out how much you could save by dropping one of them. If the savings are considerable, find out if you can temporarily drop one and then get back into it later—without being subject to restrictions for preexisting conditions. If not, consider keeping both plans, despite the extra cost.

One Income

Just because both of you are working now doesn't mean your family will always have two incomes.

Bottom line: Being a two-income family gives you power, leverage and maneuverability right now.

MONEY SIDE OF A COMMUTER MARRIAGE

The term "jet-setter" no longer applies exclusively to the wealthy hopping from one resort to another. Today it may more aptly describe a new generation of working couples who must travel from one home to another to maintain their two careers as well as their marriage.

Commuter marriages have increased in the past several years from approximately 700,000 to over a million. If you are faced with the possibility of entering into a commuter marriage, do not make a decision until you have given the issue careful thought and research.

A major consideration in commuting is the financial expense—it can be large, and the less obvious financial details can become very significant. Contact an accountant, who will acquaint you with the present tax laws and give you information regarding commuter marriages.

When a corporation is involved, take the time to understand the corporation's tax and legal responsibilities. You will also need to know the company's relocation procedures and schedules if you must negotiate for financial assistance.

If a home is involved, know whether your company will take responsibility if your home remains unsold: Will it absorb the cost of the sale? Will the company give rental assistance? Will it absorb the cost of your transportation from one location to another? You may need to move household goods twice in the same year—will the company pick up the tab in both cases?

A variety of options is available when it comes to arranging housing. Some couples buy homes at both ends, some rent and buy, some choose to sell their present home and buy or rent two new ones. Mobile homes and houseboats can be options as well.

If you decide to maintain two residences, be sure to budget realistically. Make up an initial budget for a two-residence arrangement, and for safety add 10%–15% to that figure. The major surprise to many couples is the cost of duplicating household items.

Items such as another set of dishes, tools, etc., can add up quickly, and many of the purchases can't be deferred. Consider renting furniture rather than buying it. In some places you can rent linens, dishes and small appliances as a package.

There are some less obvious expenses that you must also add in when budgeting for two homes:

- **Transportation costs** to and from airports, train stations or bus depots.
- **The possible need** for two or more cars.
- **Additional insurance** on rented household items.
- **Additional costs for certain services,** such as telephone and cable television.
- **Time off from work** to set up the new household and maintain your relationship.

Establishing a commuter marriage is a big step, but if it's well planned, the arrangement can be rewarding.

Source: Elaine Kay, president, Settlers Inc., 1713 Waterford Ave., Fort Collins, CO 80525, a nationwide relocation consulting firm advising corporations and real estate firms on how to better understand and assist the transferee.

Friends, Family & Your Money

Change your attitudes about spending and saving. Think of spending less now not as a penalty, but as a form of deferred consumption with a real bonus—the interest or gains you can earn on the money you save. *Remember:* If you don't see the money, you won't spend it. Start automatic monthly deductions from your paycheck or checking account into a stock or money market mutual fund. Let your money work as hard for you as you work for it.

Source: Terry Savage, the well-known personal financial expert and registered investment adviser for stocks and commodities. She is the author of Terry Savage's New Money Strategies for the '90s, Harper Business.

Premarital Agreements

Most Americans tend to remarry after a failed first marriage. A properly drafted premarital agreement can save you time, money and emotional stress should a second marriage end in divorce. Although divorced people are willing to test the matrimonial waters a second time, they do not usually want to subject assets they acquired prior to that marriage to claims of the new spouse.

The advantage of premarital agreements is that they enable you to define your rights and those of your new spouse to assets brought into the marriage, as well as what interest you and your new spouse will have in assets acquired or money earned during your marriage. If properly drafted and prepared, premarital agreements can provide for and protect you and your spouse at the end of your marriage, whether that end is the result of divorce or of death.

Basic Precautions

For a premarital agreement to be valid and provide the protection you need, several factors must be taken into account. First and foremost, the agreement should not be written in a way that appears to encourage divorce. The agreement should cover the contingency of divorce, but not encourage either you or your spouse to that end.

Any agreement should disclose the assets you or your spouse owns and the income, if any, to be received from them. The agreement should also define what interest, if any, your new spouse will have in these assets.

The agreement should appear fair. If it does not, it is unlikely to stand up to judicial scrutiny. What is considered "fair"? A fair agreement does not result from undue influence of a spouse possessing a strong economic or other advantage. Both you and your spouse should fully discuss what you want from the agreement, and each of you should be represented by an attorney. If either you or your spouse is not represented, it is more likely that the agreement will be seen as unfair by the courts.

Effects on Inheritance

Properly drafted agreements also deal with the death of either you or your spouse. In many cases, one or both of you will have children from a former marriage. You will be concerned with protecting what you previously acquired, so that your children's inheritance will remain intact.

Premarital agreements can have a significant effect on the rights granted by state law to a surviving spouse. An agreement can ensure that your spouse will be provided with financial assistance after your death and that your children will ultimately receive the underlying assets. Similarly, if you and your spouse are financial equals, an agreement can ensure that all of your estate goes directly to your children with no interest passing to your surviving spouse.

In many instances, one spouse owns a home that becomes the new family residence. In most states, by law, a surviving spouse can reside in a home after the death of the other spouse for a period of time. If

Veteran's Pension Is Not Marital Property

A veteran's pension and other benefits are not marital property subject to distribution on divorce, an Illinois court ruled. Federal law makes these benefits the sole property of the veteran, not subject to divorce orders. But this source of income to the veteran could be taken into account when deciding on an equitable division of other property.

Source: In re Marriage of Hapaniewski, Ct. App., Ill., 438 N.E. 2d 466.

this is not desired, a premarital agreement can waive the right or set forth a specific period of time that the surviving spouse can continue to use the home as a principal residence.

Premarital agreements cannot do everything. Waiving the right to receive alimony or spousal support in the event of divorce is generally impermissible, as are provisions affecting child custody and support. Provisions that attempt to define these rights will carry no weight in court. However, by agreement your spouse can waive his or her right to receive support from your estate.

Source: *Michael C. Shea, J.D., partner, Shea and Ashworth, 1855 First Ave., Suite 303, San Diego, CA 92101. He is certified by the state bar of California as a specialist in family law.*

Best Divorce Protection

Many of the controversies that develop between divorcing spouses could be avoided by making arrangements ahead of time. Prenuptial (or postnuptial) agreements are the easiest, most effective way for couples to vary the rights they would normally have under state laws.

Protecting Assets and Income

The best way to protect your income from divorce is to make a prenuptial agreement between you and your spouse regarding your present assets and income and future assets and income.

Essential: Agreements regarding income and assets must be in writing, signed by both parties, reasonable and not tainted by misrepresentations or duress. The validity of the agreement will be called into question if the financial means of the parties are unreasonably disproportionate.

Any agreement should list assets specifically. The only way to disallow your wife or husband's rights to a substantial marital asset is to prove that a contract addressed the asset specifically and established a fair method of disposing of the asset. If assets are acquired after the first agreement is drawn up, a new agreement should be made regarding those assets.

Personal Property and Gifts

Establish a fair means of dividing personal property in the event of divorce. Although usually of less value than other property, personal property often creates the largest problems for a divorcing couple. The emotion, attorney's fees and court time usually far exceed the actual value of the property.

Rights to pension plans and academic diplomas are, in many cases today, considered marital assets. These can represent particularly sticky areas in a divorce, so it's wise to cover them also.

Interspousal gifts usually are exempt from distribution. However, if a gift is of particular value, be sure to guarantee that the distribution remains equitable. Gifts from parents can give rise to disagreements. Is a gift from a parent to one or both spouses? Under most wills, substantial gifts by parents to one spouse do not present a problem, because the beneficiary is specifically named. However, substantial gifts from living parents should be written into an agreement that designates for whom the gift was intended.

Source: *Carole Mehlman Gould, attorney-at-law, 475 Fifth Ave., New York, NY 10017. Her practice is concentrated in family law, including problems of the elderly, wills, trusts, divorces and child custody. She is a member of the Pro Bono Panel of the New York Council of Law Associates and of the Battered Women's Committee.*

Best Time to Negotiate A Prenuptial Agreement

Prenuptial agreements work best when negotiated well before the wedding and when both parties avoid giving up too much in the name of love. *Legal fees:* $1,000–$10,000.

Source: *Carlyn McCaffrey, a New York lawyer.*

Agreement Trap

A prenuptial agreement provided that the wife would receive $200 a month for 10 years in case of divorce. When the agreement was signed, the husband was worth about $500,000. But his wealth later increased substantially—to about $8 million. When the wife filed for divorce, the court held that she was not bound by the premarital agreement, as changed circumstances had made it unconscionable. Such an agreement, the court said, must be fair not only at the time it is made but also at the time it is to be enforced.

Source: Gross *v.* Gross*, Ohio SupCt, 464 NE (2d) 500.*

BEWARE OF PRENUPTIAL AGREEMENTS

Adivorced woman challenged the validity of a prenuptial agreement in which she had waived her community-property rights. She had given up her interest in her husband's enormous assets.

The court held the agreement invalid. *Reason:* Although prenuptial agreements are not contrary to public policy when freely and intelligently made, the overwhelming evidence in this case demonstrated manipulation on the part of the husband. A wealthy businessman and politician, he had initiated the agreement the week before the wedding. The couple had been counseled by the husband's attorney, who neither advised the wife to seek her own legal counsel nor explained to her the effect of the agreement (to eliminate the accumulation of community property).

Source: *In re Marriage of Matson, 705 P.2d 817 (Wash. Ct. App. 1985).*

Obstetric Alternative

Birth centers offer parents more control over how their babies are born and typically charge only half as much as a hospital for a delivery. Many insurers offer reimbursement for birth center services, and most states either already have or are drafting regulations for licensing and safety.

Drawback: The centers are not as well equipped as hospitals to handle high-risk deliveries.

More Than Baby-Sitters

Trained nannies provide child care, deal with medical emergencies, even fix a blown fuse. *Training:* Child growth and development, health and safety, and interpersonal skills. Two hundred hours of classroom instruction and 50 hours of supervised child care are required of nannies trained at schools accredited by the American Council of Nanny Schools.

How to Find the Best Day-Care Services

Day-care centers often are a must for couples who both have to work to make ends meet. Yet locating high-quality care that serves a child's individual needs can be a difficult task, particularly when it comes down to making a final selection.

First thing to do: Find out the services available in your community. Check for a child-care resource and referral service (sometimes called information & referral, I&R, or R&R). R&R services typically compile data on existing programs in your area, their vacancies, fees, ages of children served and other information. R&R programs are usually listed in the telephone book. If not, contact your state's child-care licensing agency (Department of Human Services, Social Services, or Health); state or national child-care advocacy groups; your employers; or ask other parents.

If no R&R service is available to you, contact the local YM/YWCA, religious groups, local colleges, vocational schools or any of the sources listed above for information on child-care providers. In addition, local chapters of the Red Cross, the public library, and groups such as the Junior League and the League of Women Voters are good sources of information regarding programs in your community. Don't overlook newspapers and bulletin boards.

What to Expect

The most important criteria for choosing a day-care center are quality and appropriateness of care to your child's needs. The next most important are cost, location and hours of operation.

There is a broad variety of child-care centers from which to choose. Settings range from private homes to large day-care centers or facilities located within a sponsoring institution or business. To begin the screening process, look first at licensed child-care centers. Any place that takes care of a group of three to four or more unrelated children is required to be licensed by most states.

Warning: Since licensing and registration requirements vary considerably from state to state, the fact that a child-care center is licensed does not necessarily mean high quality. It doesn't hurt to contact your state's child-care licensing agency to find out exactly what the licensing requirements are.

Many family day-care providers are unaware of licensing regulations and would be willing to become licensed. Parents who rule out all unlicensed care may deprive themselves of an excellent alternative. However, be cautioned that such a care giver should be willing to become licensed.

Unannounced Visits

Before reaching a final decision, be sure to visit the prospective child-care program. You should feel free to drop in unannounced. A good child-care center expects this of parents. What do you look for in a visit?

● **Staffing.** Find out the extent of the care givers' training and experience. A good program has enough qualified adults to ensure that children receive individual attention. A good rule of thumb is one teacher and one assistant for the following groups of children:

● **Infants**—four to six children.
● **One- to two-year-olds**—six to eight children.
● **Two- to three-year-olds**—eight to 14 children.
● **Four- to five-year-olds**—11 to 20 children.

Group sizes should be set up to reflect these ratios, since children generally do better in small groups.

● **Adult/child interaction.** Check to see that children are busy, happy and absorbed in their activities. Observe the adults. Are they interested, loving, and actively involved with the children?

● **Cleanliness.** This is a high priority for young children. Cleanliness can control the spread of infectious diseases. Check to see that teachers and other adults wash their hands frequently. Do children wash before eating and after going to the toilet? Are the rooms, toys and equipment cleaned regularly?

● **Safety and emergency.** Emergency plans should be clearly posted near the telephone and include telephone numbers for a doctor, ambulance, etc. Smoke detectors should be installed and fire extinguishers readily available.

● **Play equipment.** Check to see that there is a variety of interesting play materials. Many organizations involved with child care publish guidebooks. You might want to read one before you begin your visits, but good parental judgment and monitoring are the only ways to ensure high-quality care.

Source: *Carolyn Strand, 603 First St., Hoboken, NJ 07030. She is the former deputy director, Child Care Action Campaign, New York, which is currently the only national agency concerned with all aspects of child day care. She has been a day-care teacher and instructor of vocational child-care classes.*

Summer Jobs for Kids

Friends and relatives are the best source of help in finding summer jobs. Ask them for contacts or ideas.

Two great options are:

● **Summer camps** hire students. *Usual requirements:* Camp experience, age 19 or older, and at least one year of college.

● **The National Parks Services** of the Department of the Interior provides 4,500 summer jobs each year. Applicants must be 18, high school graduates, and U.S. citizens.

Another good option: Advertise your services on local store and community-center bulletin boards. Two brothers kept busy painting houses (a very profitable enterprise) after putting up a notice in a supermarket advertising their availability.

Note: Many countries let foreign students work in temporary, seasonal jobs. The pay is usually low, but jobs can be interesting.

Work-Ethic Myth

Myth: Part-time jobs make teenagers more ambitious about education and careers. *Reality:* Typical dead-end jobs foster bad grades in school, more money for drugs and alcohol and a jaded attitude toward work in general.

Source: *Laurence Steinberg, professor of child and family studies, University of Wisconsin.*

Parent's Guide to Corporate Training Programs

What can you do to help your child land the right job?

A corporate training program may be the answer, because it permits recent graduates to earn while they learn. Such programs give in-depth training in a specific industry while also offering a practical view of the corporate world. This hands-on training is useful in whatever field the student finally picks. Best of all, most corporate training programs pay well. Starting annual salaries for trainees range from $15,000 to more than $30,000.

Competition for corporate training programs is fierce. The applicant usually has to face a number of rejections before he or she is offered a job.

How to prepare: Encourage your graduate first to learn about the industry that interests her. Then, once she understands the industry and the key players, she can zero in on particular companies. She should study their annual reports and recruitment materials, and articles written about them. (Articles can be obtained by telephoning a company's public relations department to request a press kit.)

Information interviews in advance of a job interview can also be helpful. Alumni from your son's or daughter's alma mater who are already working for that company or in that industry are often willing to take a few minutes—either over the phone or in person—to offer insights into what it's like to work there. Your own business contacts and friends may also be able to serve as informal career advisers.

Questions the job hunter should ask: What are the most satisfying aspects of your job? What are your priorities in an average workweek? What do you wish you had known about this career field before you entered it? What about this employer?

Source: *Marian Salzman, author, with Deidre Sullivan, of* Inside Management Training: The Career Guide to Training Programs for College Graduates. *This book is no longer in print.*

How to Protect Your Savings Against Catastrophic Illness

With the annual cost of nursing home care averaging $38,000 nationally and $70,000 or more in major cities, life savings can be wiped out in a very short time. Typical medical policies, including Medicare, may not cover this. However, planning can prevent this and ensure proper care.

Major medical policies and Medicare cover only the costs of acute illnesses such as heart attack and cancer. They do not cover the long-term care required for chronic illnesses such as Alzheimer's disease or arthritis. Home care for any long-term debilitating illness is also not covered.

Families that must pay for such care have three alternatives—pay cash, rely on special long-term care insurance, or become eligible for Medicaid.

Paying in cash is an option only for the very rich. Although long-term care policies tend to be more expensive if you wait until your 70s to purchase them, the cost can be reduced by co-insuring the risk—using what you can afford of your assets and income to pay some of your long-term care costs, should the need arise.

The third alternative is Medicaid—a welfare program that provides medical care for those who meet a means test.

Singles must be poor to qualify. Married persons have some protection for the spouse who does not need care—he or she may be allowed to keep some assets and income.

Transferring Assets

Assets can be protected without jeopardizing Medicaid eligibility if timely steps are taken. Assets can be given to children or others, regardless of amount, as long as the "ineligibility period" has run on the transfer. States determine the ineligibility period by a formula: the amount of funds transferred divided by the average monthly nursing home bill in the area (a figure set by Medicaid).

Caution: All gifts within 36 months (the "look-back period") of applying are examined and used in the formula. ***Example:*** Sam transfers $50,000 and 35 months later applies for Medicaid. Since the average cost of a nursing home in his area is fixed at $5,000, he is ineligible for 10 months ($50,000 divided by $5,000). If Sam had transferred $250,000 within 36 months of applying for Medicaid, he would have been ineligible for 50 months ($250,000 divided by $5,000).

ABOUT THE POWER OF ATTORNEY

Most of us are familiar with the process of planning for death by writing a will. But how would your personal and financial affairs be handled if you were disabled by illness or accident?

The power of attorney is a written document that allows you (the principal) to appoint another person (the agent) to make your financial decisions for you if you become disabled. The document is simple to create (forms are available at most stationery stores). And, in most states, you simply insert the name of the agent you've chosen and sign the document in front of a notary public for it to become valid. Once it is created, you are in no way bound by a power of attorney—the procedure is voluntary and can be revoked at any time.

The amount of control a power of attorney hands over to an agent can be either broad (your agent has the power to do anything you could have done) or limited (your agent has only the power to sell your car). The duration of the document is equally flexible. It can remain in effect even if you lose mental capacity (called the durable power of attorney). The only limitation is that its powers end automatically upon the death of either party.

Know the Risks

The greatest risk involved with creating a power of attorney is choosing the right agent. Once a power of attorney is enacted, there is very little accountability of your agent, and he or she could misuse the power. For this reason, it is important that you choose an agent in whom you place the greatest trust. The best choice is usually a close family member with a good head for finance and knowledge of your personal needs. For further protection, don't give the power of attorney to the agent. Rather, tell him or her where it is. Without the document itself, the agent can do nothing.

There is also a risk that the power of attorney might not be accepted. Most banks will question an agent to determine if the power was revoked or if the principal has died. Some banks insist that their own power of attorney form be used— some insurance companies will not honor a power of attorney if it is more than six months old.

Using the Power Of Attorney

Legislation being passed in a growing number of states would enable you to appoint an agent to make medical decisions for you when you are physically unable to do so. This arrangement would be most appropriate for situations in which you might have to undergo a serious medical procedure that would leave you unable to decide the next medical step to take. *Example:* Before undergoing serious exploratory surgery, a patient appoints a close relative to make necessary medical decisions. While the patient is under anesthesia, the doctor can consult with the agent about what has been discovered and the possible options.

Your risk? The agent might not make a sound decision. Pick an agent who is likely to know what decision you would make, and put your conclusions in writing so he or she will have guidance. Two agents can be appointed and both required to approve any decision. What is the risk of not appointing an agent? In medical situations in which there are a number of options—each with a chance of failure—lengthy, expensive legal proceedings might be necessary before the doctor or hospital is willing to act.

Special application: A great deal of public attention has been paid to situations in which medical patients not able to make decisions for themselves are kept alive by extraordinary means. Yet doctors and hospitals cannot remove life-support equipment unless they have consent from someone legally appointed by the patient. Those who are older and do not have immediate family members would be wise to create a power of attorney for this purpose.

Source: *Daniel G. Fish, partner, Freedman and Fish, attorneys at law, 233 Broadway, New York, NY 10279. He is a specialist in legal issues affecting older adults.*

Friends, Family & Your Money

Two Quick Fixes for Asset Protection

● **Strategy 1:** If there is not enough time to give all assets away, the "half a loaf" approach can still protect substantial assets. *Example:* Sam, with $100,000 in assets, transfers half his property to his daughter. Now he is ineligible for 10 months ($50,000 divided by $5,000). But Sam still has $50,000, so he can pay for his own care for those 10 months of ineligibility and then get coverage. He successfully protected $50,000.

● **Strategy 2:** Assets can be used to buy a single premium, immediate payout annuity. The income from the annuity will go to the nursing home, but if the owner dies before the end of the payout period, the heirs will receive the balance.

Caution: Annuities are a poor planning tool because Congress has authorized states to consider this type of "planning" to be a transfer of assets—even though the money goes to a nursing home! And since the annuity has to be actuarially sound, the individual could outlive the payout.

For married people, there is more flexibility. Gifts of property between spouses do not have any time requirements. So transfers to a spouse the day before entering a nursing home will not prevent Medicaid eligibility. But the law limits the assets that the non-Medicaid spouse can keep. This varies from state to state.

Caution: Assets of a married couple are viewed together. Medicaid does not care how assets are titled between spouses or how long assets have been held. Prenuptial agreements do not have any effect for Medicaid purposes.

Using Trusts

Is there a way to use a trust to protect assets? Recent changes threw the answer into doubt. Now the federal government has given its okay to shield assets in a trust if:

● **It is irrevocable** (you cannot get the property back once the trust is set up).

● **It is an "income only" trust,** one that pays the income earned on the assets in the trust to the person who set up the trust (or that person's spouse) for life.

> "Gifted property does not enjoy the stepped-up basis given to inherited property.... Capital gains can result when the recipients later sell the property."

Drawback: Under the Omnibus Budget Reconciliation Act (OBRA) of 1993, Congress allowed the states to place a lien on "income only" trusts in certain circumstances.

● **The trustee can't have any discretion** to pay out the trust's assets during the life of the person who set up the trust (or that person's spouse).

Caution: This strategy requires preplanning since a 60-month look-back period may apply to assets transferred to an "income only" trust.

Protecting Your Home

In applying for Medicaid, a house is not a countable asset. Regardless of value, it is exempt property. But, in most states, a person who becomes eligible for Medicaid will not be able to keep the house after six or nine months unless a doctor certifies that the person will be returning to the home.

A single person who gives away his or her house within 36 months of applying for Medicaid will not be eligible for assistance until the period of ineligibility has run, as determined by the ineligibility formula. (Certain house transfers are exempt, regardless of size, such as those to a disabled child or to a sibling who co-owned the house.)

A married person can transfer the home to his or her spouse at any time (before or after Medicaid qualification). *Helpful:* Make the transfer before Medicaid kicks in to prevent a lien from attaching to the property.

Retirement and Estate Plans

Sunny Florida may be a retirement goal, but this destination can prevent Medicaid coverage for some. Florida, New Jersey and others are "cap" states. They will not provide coverage if income exceeds a cap. (This figure goes up yearly.)

Asset transfers for Medicaid eligibility can throw estate plans into havoc. Reevaluation is essential.

The tax consequences of giving assets to children or others must be factored in. While there may be no federal gift tax cost in making these transfers, there may still be state gift taxes. The income tax consequences to those receiving the assets must also be considered. Gifted property does not enjoy the stepped-up basis given to inherited property so that capital gains can result when the recipients later sell the property.

Married couples must be careful to redo wills after one spouse becomes ill. If the well spouse dies first, his or her will should leave property to children or others. If property is left to the spouse in a nursing home, the funds will be spent on care that would otherwise be covered by Medicaid.

In addition to trusts and wills, there are other legal documents that can help to protect your money and see that your wishes are followed.

● **Durable power of attorney.** If you have a durable power of attorney, a written document that meets state law requirements, then someone can do your banking and make financial decisions for you even if you cannot speak or act for yourself. This power continues despite disability or competence. The failure to have made this arrangement could result in costly and time-consuming court actions to appoint and supervise a guardian or other legal representative.

Source: Harley Gordon, Esq., an elder law attorney in Boston and author of How to Protect Your Life Savings from Catastrophic Illness and Nursing Homes, *Financial Strategies Press, Inc.*

Housing Alternatives for Aging but Able Parents

Adult children often want their aging parents nearby so they can care for them. But forcing them to leave their home and community is unnecessary and unfair. Various services and housing programs throughout the United States now enable the elderly to remain safely and comfortably independent.

A Parent Who Wants to Stay Home

● **Community services for the elderly** help those who can no longer handle all the chores of daily living. Services include daily visits by social workers, telephone check-in calls, home health care, housekeeping, home repair, meal deliveries and emergency response systems (pocket-sized pagers alert an information center in case of emergency).

● **Shared-housing programs** offer companionship and the opportunity to split living costs. Two or more people occupy the home belonging to one of them. Each has private space, and the living room and kitchen are shared. Roommate matches are based on personality, interests and needs.

● **Accessory apartments** created within the elderly person's own home offer him or her rental income, the assurance that someone is nearby, and the opportunity to exchange services. *Example:* The tenant may do the yard work in exchange for transportation.

● **Home retrofitting*** involves identifying and overcoming problems such as stairs, hard-to-turn doorknobs and raised thresholds in doorways. Making changes such as these may enable an older person to remain at home longer.

Points to Remember

You and your family should take part in, but not force, decisions concerning a lifestyle change for your elderly parents. They are used to making their own decisions. Their turning 70 or 80 doesn't mean they are any less capable of or any less interested in continuing to do so.

*A free booklet on home retrofitting (including changes that can be made and how to make them) is available from AARP.

Source: Katie Sloan, senior housing specialist, American Association of Retired Persons, 1909 K St. NW, Washington, DC 20049. AARP publishes Miles Away and Still Caring, *a free booklet, and can tell you which organizations in your area handle services for the aging.*

How to Find a Good Nursing Home

Most families postpone as long as possible the decision to use a nursing home. Once the decision is reached, the process of selecting a good facility is so painful that often they move too fast. *Helpful:* Give your parent time to get used to the idea. Meanwhile, investigate every possible choice thoroughly.

How to begin: Get lists of not-for-profit, community-based homes from your church, fraternal order, state agency on aging, American Association of Homes for the Aging (Suite 500, 901 E St. NW, Washington, DC 20004), 202-783-2244 or American Health Care Association (1201 L St. NW, Washington, DC 20005), 202-842-4444.

Evaluating a Nursing Home

1. Accreditation, license and certification for Medicare and Medicaid should be current and in force.

2. It's best to arrive without an appointment. Look at everything. The building and rooms should be clean, attractive and safe, and meet fire codes. Residents should not be crowded. Visit the dining room at mealtime. Check the kitchen, too. Talk to residents to find out how they feel.

3. The staff should be professionally trained and large enough to provide adequate care for all residents.

4. If the home requires a contract, read it carefully. Show it to your lawyer before signing. Some homes reserve the right to discharge a patient whose condition has deteriorated even if a lump-sum payment was made upon admittance. The best is an agreement that allows payment by the month, or permits refunds or advance payment if plans change.

5. Find out exactly what services the home provides and which ones cost extra. Private-duty nurses are not included. Extras like shampoos or hair sets can be exorbitant. Make a list of the "extras" your parent will need for a comfortable life.

Before you decide on a home, you and your parent should have a talk with the administrator and department heads. Find out who is in charge of what, and whom to speak to if problems arise.

Source: Sheldon Goldberg, American Association of Homes for the Aging.

NURSING HOME TRAPS

Most nursing homes charge $40,000–$60,000 per year, depending on the degree of medical care provided. Even at these steep rates, private-patient waiting lists are long. Additional pressure is caused by Medicare, which often refuses to pay for hospitalization of patients awaiting nursing-home admission on the grounds that they are hospitalized inappropriately. Patients who cannot get into nursing homes are being billed by the hospital, putting tremendous pressure on the patients' families to do whatever possible to get the patients into a nursing home quickly. Many nursing homes are quick to take advantage of this pressure.

Contracts with nursing homes are often too broad. In essence, they state: You give us all your money, and we'll take care of you for the rest of your life. The federal government has outlawed such agreements because of rampant abuses. A patient who paid a home $100,000 and later wanted to move when he discovered the food was dreadful could not get his money back. Many homes demand payment of fees a year or two in advance. This practice, too, has been outlawed.

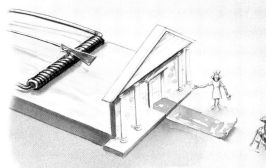

Yet another practice is sponsoring contracts to be signed with the patient's children, who guarantee that the nursing home will be paid for periods of up to two years. Often these contracts are a way to circumvent laws that forbid a home to accept more than two to three months' payment in advance.

Pursuant to the Medicare Catastrophic Coverage Act, there are unlimited options for the transfer of assets between spouses. This means that the institutionalized spouse can transfer assets to the community spouse and apply for Medicaid. However, the community spouse is subject to state spousal responsibility laws, which vary by state. This is not as bad as it seems because the court that determines support will be considering the community spouse's need to live in the community.

If there is no spouse, half the assets can be transferred to heirs, but there will be a penalty period before Medicaid will be granted. During this period, the nursing home cost can be paid by the half of the funds that was not transferred. There are always penalty periods for transferring assets, so consult with an elder law attorney.

Source: Charles Robert, partner, Robert, Lerner & Robert, 100 Merrick Rd., West Bldg., Suite 508, Rockville Centre, NY.

Lending Money to Family And Friends

Loans to friends or family members can often become a sticky business.

Number one rule: Use the same care—or more—when lending money to a friend or relative as you would when lending money to an institution.

When a friend or family member approaches you about a loan, inform him or her that this is a business deal and will be evaluated as such. By taking this approach, you help remove some of the emotional strain involved for both of you. In the long run, you will also reduce the risk of losing your money. *Analyze the situation as a banker would:* How good is your friend's credit? How will your friend use the money? How and when will your friend repay the loan?

Examine Alternatives

Always check to see that your friend or relative has examined the alternative sources for a loan. *The most obvious include:*

- **Banks.**
- **Second mortgage on house.**
- **Loan on whole life insurance policy.**
- **Company pension,** profit-sharing or savings plan.
- **Brokerage account.**
- **Small Business Administration,** if the loan is for a new or existing business.
- **Trade credit,** if the loan is for a new or existing business.

The advantage of this exercise is that it casts you in the role of financial adviser, not just friend or relative. More important, you may help the other person pinpoint a source of funds he or she overlooked.

Put It in Writing

Whether a loan is to a friend or a member of your family, any agreement should be in writing. Forms of promissory notes (also known as IOUs), which are often available in stationery stores, can be used for this purpose. What should be included in the agreement? At a minimum, it should specify the amount of the loan, its terms and the interest rate, if any.

You may want the interest on the loan to compensate you for the income forgone as a result of making the loan. For example, on a one-year loan, consider charging the going rate on one-year certificates of deposit.

Try to eliminate possibilities for future misunderstandings. *If you can, address the following questions in your agreement:* Will the loan be amortized? Will payment of principal and interest be made monthly or quarterly, or will only interest be payable at fixed intervals, with a balloon payment specified at the end? Will the loan have a fixed term, or be payable to you "on demand"?

The following is an example of a simple promissory note that covers these questions:

$5,000   Dated: _____

Promissory Note

FOR VALUE RECEIVED, I _____ ("Borrower") promise to pay to the order of _____ the sum of *Five Thousand* dollars ($5,000.00), payable commencing on _____ _____, 19____ , and each succeeding month thereafter for _____ months in equal monthly installments of principal and _____ % interest in the amount of _____ dollars ($ _____).

_____ (Borrower)

The signature of the borrower is essential to making the promissory note legally enforceable. The main purpose of a written agreement is not to frighten your friend or relative into thinking you'll haul him or her off to court, but to emphasize that borrowing money is a serious business.

Source: Karen F. Stein, Ph.D., associate professor of consumer economics at the University of Delaware, Newark, DE 19716. Author of numerous publications on consumer affairs, she is the former executive director of the American Council on Consumer Interests.

Problems With Low-Interest Loans

Be careful of low- or no-interest loans to friends or family members. Loans made with no interest or with interest that is below "market" (the applicable Federal Rate, or AFR) may result in taxable income to the lender. In such a "gift loan" situation, the lender is deemed to have made a gift to the borrower of the uncharged interest (the difference between the actual interest charged and interest that would be charged at the AFR), and then the borrower is deemed to have retransferred that amount back to the lender. Under IRS rules, the retransferred amount is taxable to the lender as interest income. *Exceptions:* Loans of $10,000 or less, at little or no interest, can be made to family or friends for any purpose other than investing. The forgone interest will not be considered income to the lender.

Warning: You can't beat this exception by making, for example, four loans of $3,000 each. They would count as one loan of more than $10,000 and therefore would result in tax liability for the lender.

Source: Karen F. Stein, Ph.D., associate professor of consumer economics at the University of Delaware, Newark, DE 19716. Author of numerous publications on consumer affairs, she is former executive director of the American Council on Consumer Interests.

Motheraid

A son paid his mother's medical expenses with money he withdrew from her bank account under a power of attorney. The IRS disallowed the son's deduction for these expenses, saying the money was really the mother's. But the Court of Appeals allowed the deduction. The money was legally his—a gift from his mother to him.

Source: John M. Ruch, CA-5, 82-4463.

Parent Supported by More Than One Child

When brothers and sisters support a parent, plan things so that one of them can deduct the parent's medical expenses. *Here's how:*

First step: File a multiple-support declaration (Form 2120). When several people contribute, this form designates the one who can take the exemption. If they pay at least 10% each, but nobody gives as much as half, any one of them can take the exemption if the others agree. Generally, the sibling with the highest tax bracket should take the exemption since this will result in the greatest tax savings. However, if that sibling is subject to a phaseout of exemptions because of being in a high tax bracket, then another sibling should claim the exemption.

Second step: The one claiming the exemption should pay doctor bills and make clear (on the check) that his or her contribution is earmarked for medical expenses. Then he or she can deduct the parent's medical expenses on the tax return. Medical expenses can be deducted only for yourself, your spouse and your dependents. You usually can't take a deduction for medical expenses paid for somebody else unless you can claim the person as a dependent.

Renting Your Own House

You can get your house out of your estate by selling it to your children and then leasing it back, paying a rent that equals your children's mortgage payments. But remember, the IRS scrutinizes intrafamily arrangements closely:

● **If you sell the house at a bargain price,** the IRS may treat the discount as a taxable gift to your children, so sell it at close to market value.

● **Mortgage interest paid by your children** will be deductible by them and taxable to you.

● **Rent payments received by your children** will be taxable to them.

● **The children will be able to depreciate the house** and claim business-expense deductions for costs they incur on it (such as insurance and maintenance). They must charge you a fair rent. But since rental real estate is considered a passive activity, they can only deduct up to $25,000 (in excess of any rental or other passive income), provided their Annual Gross Income (AGI) is under $100,000 (a partial deduction is allowed for AGI between $100,000 and $150,000). Such a rent may be 10%–20% below market rates because of the lower risk involved in renting to a relative.

● **Make sure the paperwork is in order,** and that rent and mortgage checks actually change hands each month.

● **Don't peg the rent to equal monthly mortgage payments.** Rather, fix the length of the mortgage so that the after-tax cost of the mortgage payments balances the fair rent you pay each month.

How to Give Your House Away

It's not unusual for a person to give his or her home to a spouse or children and continue to live there.

HOW TO TAKE YOUR PARENTS AS DEPENDENTS

You can claim your parent as a dependent, and qualify for an additional exemption ($2,700 for 1998). You can also obtain the benefit of medical-expense deductions that a low-tax-bracket parent cannot use.

To claim your parent as a dependent, you must satisfy the following:

● **A dependent must either be a member of your household or be related to you.** The IRS considers a father, mother, father-in-law, or mother-in-law a parental relationship.

● **A parent claimed as a dependent must make less than $2,700** (for 1998) in gross income (indexed annually for inflation) during the year he or she is claimed as a dependent.

● **You must supply more than one-half of your parent's support for the calendar year.** The IRS includes medical expenses in its definition of support, making it easier for children paying heavy medical expenses to meet the support requirement.

● **If two or more children provide support for a parent** and jointly meet the 50% support requirement, only one child can claim the parent as a dependent (provided the children meet a number of other IRS requirements).

● **Your parent must be, for some part of the year,** a U.S. citizen, resident or national, or a resident of Canada or Mexico.

● **Your parent cannot file a joint return** unless it is only for the purpose of a refund or unless no tax is due.*

Special note: Even if your parent provides you with the funds to pay for his or her medical expenses, you can

still claim the expenses on your tax return. To take the deduction, the medical expenses must exceed 7.5% of your Adjusted Gross Income (AGI), and the funds transferred by your parent cannot be earmarked for medical expenses (you should have discretion to use the funds as you wish). There is a possibility of a gift tax being applied to the funds, but the annual exclusion and lifetime credit for taxable transfers make this unlikely.

*Your parent must give you his or her Social Security number. You cannot claim a dependency exemption without it.

Sources: *Israel A. Press, CPA, tax partner, Grant Thornton, 7 Hanover Square, New York, NY 10004. Mr. Press is the author of numerous tax articles.*

Problem: The IRS may include the value of the home in the taxpayer's estate on his death, claiming an incomplete gift. *What to do:* Make a formal written conveyance of the property to your spouse or children and have the deed recorded in the proper public office. File a gift-tax return and pay the tax when the gift is made. Pay the new owner a reasonable rent for your room or apartment. Do not list the property on any financial statement or loan application. And be certain that taxes, insurance policies, maintenance bills and other documents are in the name of the new owner. *Even better:* Make a gift of the residence through a qualified personal residence trust (QPRT). You keep the right to live in the home for a set number of years (such as 10 years), after which your child owns the home outright. Since you get to subtract the value of your term interest from the overall value of the home, the gift to your child is reduced (the longer the term, the smaller the gift). At the end of the term, you can continue to live in the home by renting it from your child.

Tax Bonanza for Retired Parents and Their Children

It is legal to deduct all losses on houses rented to relatives, provided the rents are reasonable by market standards. This opens up profitable retirement loopholes. Children should buy the house their parents retire to and take the deductions for depreciation and operating expenses (subject to the $25,000 loss allowance under the passive activity loss rules) that would not be available if the parents owned the house. Parents can sell their old house and pay no tax on any profit up to $250,000 ($500,000 on joint returns), provided they owned and lived in the home for at least two out of the five years before the sale. Or they can rent out their old house, take the deductions it generates and use the income for their retirement.

Source: Tax Loopholes by Edward Mendlowitz, Boardroom Books.

How to Talk to Your Parents About Their Money

Adult children may be genuinely concerned about how their parents are managing their finances. But parents may resent that concern as an unwanted intrusion.

Guidelines for Discussion

● **Examine your motives.** Are you more interested in making sure your parents are protected against possible financial disaster—or in preserving the size of the estate you hope to inherit?

● **List the subjects to discuss.**

● **Location of financial records.**

● **Insurance**—health (Medicare and private), life, long-term care (for nursing-home expenses), mortgage, home owners.

● **Investments**—safety of principal, rate of return, goals and whether savings are sufficient to last through retirement.

● **Be diplomatic.** Don't criticize, patronize or act as though you have all the answers. *Ineffective:* "I'm worried about the way you're handling your money." *More effective:* "What financial information do you think I need in case something should happen to you? For my own peace of mind, I'd like to learn something about your financial situation. Maybe each of us has information that can be useful to the other." *Very helpful:* Financial-planning forms as a neutral way to introduce the subject. These forms are available from some company pension programs and in many of the popular financial-planning guides at your library and bookstore.

● **Prepare.** If you want to get involved, be prepared to spend a lot of time, even months, on research into insurance and investment options.

● **Respect your parents' rights.** It's their money to do with what they choose. Once you've expressed your desire to learn more about their finances, it's up to them to agree to your involvement, or refuse it. Accept their decision. When we were growing up, we expected our parents to let us live our own lives and make our own mistakes. Parents deserve the same freedom from us.

Source: Robert Atchley, Ph.D., director of the Scripps Gerontology Center at Miami University, Oxford, OH.

Transform Your Relationship With Money

I changed my views on money years ago, and today live comfortably on an annual income of $9,000. And I save as much as $3,000 a year. By understanding the basics of money, you will be able to get rid of debt, save and live happily within your means.

The Myth of More

People identify money with all sorts of wonderful things—security, pleasure, power, prestige, quality, etc. And all too often we get locked into a lifelong struggle to obtain the "more" that money is supposed to bring.

More is never enough.

If you've just bought a bigger house, there's yet a bigger house to yearn for. Happiness is always just around the corner. Turn around that old maxim "Time is money" and look at it this way: "We pay for money with our time." *Example:* Your old stereo system gives you hours of pleasure each week. Would you buy a new stereo if you were aware that you net $20 an hour after taxes and work-related expenses (clothes, transportation, etc.), and that it will cost nearly three weeks of your working life to buy the new system?

Enough—and Then Some

The constant question: "When I buy something, what am I actually getting for the hours of labor I put into earning the necessary money?" "Will I get happiness?" "What are my values?" "Does this purchase have anything to do with my values?"

As you ask the questions, the answers will lead you to become a natural saver. You will, in short, have transformed your relationship with money.

Financial independence has nothing to do with being rich. It is knowing when you have enough. Enough for you may be different from enough for your neighbor—but it will be a figure that is real for you and within your financial means.

Where Does It All Go?

The only way to learn about your spending behavior is to keep track of every cent that comes in and goes out of your life.

Only after writing this down will you become conscious of how you actually handle money, as opposed to how you think you do.

After a month you will have a wealth of specific information on how you now handle the money in your life.

Use this daily money log to set up spending categories that reflect your actual behavior. Don't oversimplify the categories in your budget log.

Instead of a broad category of food, for example, you may see there are actually several different types of foods to track—food you eat at home, in restaurants, in snacking, lunches at work, etc.

This exercise isn't just accounting. It's a process of self-discovery. And the next time you ask yourself, "Where does it all go?" you'll know the answer.

Making Money Real

Knowing these answers isn't enough. You must translate the dollars you spend into the hours of your life to reveal the trade-offs you now make for your lifestyle.

I'm not talking about being cheap, making do—or being a skinflint. I'm talking about *creative* frugality.

Ten Sure Ways to Save Money

● **Pay off your credit cards.** You pay anywhere from 8.5%–20% interest on credit card debt. That's

like working a five-day week and getting paid for four. On average, every $100 of debt costs $18.66 a year in interest. If you are in the 28% tax bracket, you have to earn $25.98 before taxes to pay for the privilege of having spent that $100.

● **Don't go shopping.** Although 70% of all adults visit a regional mall weekly, only a quarter of them are actually looking for a specific item.

● **Wait until you have the money before you buy something.** He who hesitates saves.

● **Take care of what you have.** Regular oil changes extend the life of a car. If you ignore a funny noise in your car's engine, you could burn out a water pump or otherwise incur major (and costly) damage.

● **Wear it out.** Think about how much money you would save if you decided to use things 20% longer.

● **Do it yourself.** Whenever you're about to hire an expert, ask yourself, "Can I do this myself? What would it take to learn how?"

● **Anticipate your needs.** Forethought is a huge cost saver. Blank cassettes bought at the supermarket cost less than half as much as the local convenience store charges.

● **Bargain.** Buy through mail-order discounters and discount chain stores. Ask for discounts at local stores. Haggling has become a way of life in the United States.

● **Comparison-shop by phone.** *Example:* I was able to shave $4,000 (33%) off the highest price on a car years ago by calling every dealership within a 100-mile radius and buying a deluxe demonstrator model with 3,600 miles on it.

● **Buy it used.** Clothing, furniture, kitchenware, drapes—often of high quality—can all be found in thrift stores.

Source: Vicki Robin, coauthor, with the late Joe Dominguez, of Your Money or Your Life, Viking Penguin. Ms. Robin heads the nonprofit New Road Map Foundation, an organization that helps people assume greater control over their money and their lives (Box I5981, Dept. BL, Seattle, WA 98115).

Financing
An Education

8

- Best Ways to Save for Your Child's College Education

- Biggest College-Aid Application Mistakes

- Uncle Sam Helps Pay the Way

- Obvious...and Less Obvious Ways to Get Money for College

- Nontraditional College Degrees

- More Strategies for Winning the College-Aid Game

- 10 Surprise Expenses for College Students

Calculating the Cost Of a College Education

With tuition costs rising faster than inflation, most parents face a huge expense when it comes to paying for college. This is why it is essential to plan as far ahead as possible.

Your first and most important step is to realistically assess those future costs. Use the following example to help you frame the problem.

Suppose you have an eight-year-old daughter and you want her to go to a private college that now costs $20,000 a year, including living expenses.

Assuming an inflation rate of 6%, you calculate that your costs will run $31,027, $32,888, $34,861, and $36,953.

To cover your daughter's freshman-year costs of $31,027, you would have to invest $15,521 and let it compound for nine years at an after-tax rate of 8%. Using the same assumptions, your daughter's sophomore, junior, and senior years would require investments of $15,234, $14,951, and $14,675, respectively. So the total amount that you must set aside now to cover your daughter's future college cost is $60,381.

Source: *Sheri Robinson is a CPA and CFP with The Welch Group, 3940 Montclair Road in Birmingham, AL. She is a member of the International Association for Financial Planning and has served as president of the local chapter.*

Best Ways to Save for Your Child's College Education

College costs are rising every year, causing parents and grandparents to grow ever more concerned about how to put enough money aside for their children's education.

Many families set up trusts or savings accounts in children's names to hold college funds—often hoping to cut the family tax bill as well. *But families using these strategies face costly traps:*

● **Increases in the tax rates paid by trusts reduce the tax savings they provide**—after paying administrative costs, many trusts now may be providing no savings at all.

● **Inappropriately designed savings arrange-**ments may reduce the amount of financial aid a child qualifies to receive—increasing the cost to the family for the child's education.

Here's what you need to know about college savings now.

Common Methods

The simplest and most commonly used method of saving for a child's education is to set up a savings or investment account in a child's name under the Uniform Gifts to Minors Act (UGMA) or the Uniform Transfers to Minors Act (UTMA). These accounts are actively marketed by banks and brokerage firms.

How they work: You set up a UGMA or UTMA account for your child with a bank or broker and act as the account trustee, controlling investments. Account income is taxed to the child.

● **If the child is older than age 13,** the first $25,350 of income in 1998 is taxed at the 15% rate. That income would be taxed at a higher rate if taxed to you. The benefit of the 15% bracket is that it lowers the family's tax bill overall.

● **If the child is younger than 14,** the "kiddie tax" applies, so account income over $1,400 is taxed at your tax rate.

Self-defense: You can minimize taxes by investing in tax-exempt bonds or appreciating stocks, cashing them in for income-producing assets *after* the child reaches age 14.

> " **By keeping money in your own name, you keep full control over it and avoid reducing a child's eligibility for aid that would result if the child held assets in his or her name.** "

Beware: When a college financial aid office determines how much aid a student is qualified to receive, the first thing it looks at is the child's own wealth. If you've shifted a large amount of assets into a child's name, the amount of tuition aid the child receives may be dramatically reduced, a loss that may far outweigh taxes saved through the UGMA or UTMA account.

Roth IRAs

A Roth IRA can be an ideal way to save for a child's college costs. Funds placed in the Roth IRA (the maximum is $2,000, as for a regular IRA) earn tax-free income (assuming certain holding periods are met) and can be withdrawn tax-free to pay for higher-education expenses even if you're not yet 59½. *Further advantage:* By retaining the funds in your own name, you may protect your child's eligibility for tuition assistance, which can be reduced if you put money in the child's name.

Caution: Contributions to a Roth IRA are not deductible. You must carefully weigh this drawback against the benefit of future tax-free income.

2503(c) Trusts

Because of the drawbacks of UGMA or UTMA accounts, many families have set up more restrictive 2503(c) trusts over which parents can exert more control. *The major advantages:*

● **Such trusts are not subject to the "kiddie tax"** so even children younger than 14 can benefit from lower tax rates.

● **Children have less chance to withdraw funds from such a trust.** A child must be given the opportunity to withdraw funds at the age of 21—but withdrawals may be restricted to a limited "window" of time, such as 30 or 60 days. Funds not withdrawn within that period can remain subject to trust terms indefinitely.

But these trusts have drawbacks too:

● **The problem** remains that the child has the legal right to withdraw all funds at age 21 and spend the funds in a manner that may not correspond with your wishes.

● **Funds not distributed to the child** are taxed at the trust's high tax rates (compressed tax brackets mean that taxable income over $8,350 in 1998 is taxed at the top rate of 39.6%).

Doing It Right

It is still possible to save for a child's college education while cutting the family's tax bill and maximizing eligibility for college aid. *Here's how:*

● **Maximize use of retirement accounts.** Most college financial aid formulas either do not count your retirement account funds as being available to pay tuition or include only a small portion.

Thus, by saving money in an Individual Retirement Account (IRA), Keogh plan, Simplified Employee Pension (SEP) plan, or 401(k) account—instead of a normal, taxable savings or investment account—you may increase the amount of college financial aid a child qualifies to receive.

In addition, you will receive the tax benefits of a contribution deduction and tax deferral on investment earnings that compound within the retirement account.

Opportunities: Many 401(k) plans and Keogh plans let plan participants borrow against their accounts on a tax-free basis. Thus, these accounts can serve as a tax-favored source of college funds.

When you save for college through a 401(k) or Keogh with borrowing rights, you get much larger tax benefits than from a UGMA or UTMA account or 2503(c) trust, and keep full control over the college funds. *(Editor's note:* You can withdraw funds from your traditional IRA penalty-free before age 59½ to pay qualified higher-education costs for yourself, your spouse, your child or your grandchild. However, you'll have to pay ordinary income tax on the withdrawal.)

● **Save in your own name.** After maximizing retirement plan contributions, keep any additional college savings invested in your own name. If you wish to cut taxes on investment earnings, put the money in tax-favored investments such as appreciating stocks, tax-exempt bonds, or variable annuities. *(Editor's note:* A good investment is to save for college with U.S. savings bonds. Interest on the bonds is tax-deferred. If you're over 24 when you buy them and use them to pay for higher education for yourself, your spouse, or your child, you may be eligible to exclude all the interest.)

By keeping money in your own name, you keep full control over it and avoid reducing a child's eligibility for aid that would result if the child held assets in his or her name.

Set aside funds to help a grandchild pay for college but keep the money in your own name. When the child enrolls in school, make a direct payment to the school for the child's tuition. A special provision of the Tax Code exempts such payments from gift tax.

● **"Crummey" trust.** This is a trust used to cut future estate taxes while shifting funds to a child in a way that prevents the child from obtaining premature control over them.

How: A parent or grandparent with sufficient assets to be subject to estate tax—$650,000 for an individual or $1.3 million for a married couple in 1999—makes yearly gifts to a trust set up for a child.

Use the annual $10,000 gift-tax exclusion ($20,000 when the gift is made by a married couple).

The trust allows the child to withdraw each gift within a "window" of 30 to 60 days after the gift is made. Funds not withdrawn remain subject to the trust's terms for an extended period—such as until the child reaches age 35.

Self-defense: Tell the child that if he or she prematurely withdraws a gift, there won't be another. You prevent the child from taking premature control of trust assets. Only the current year is at risk.

The trustee of a Crummey trust may be given sole authority to determine how trust funds will be spent on behalf of a child. Because a child who doesn't control trust assets may be deemed not to own them, a Crummey trust may avoid reducing a child's eligibility for financial aid even if the trustee does spend money on school costs—although the details of state law and specific aid formulas will have an impact here. But the family will be sure to benefit by reducing future estate tax bills.

Source: David S. Rhine, partner, and national director of Family Wealth Planning, LLP, BDO Seidman, CPA, 330 Madison Ave., New York, NY 10017.

New Ways to Save for School

Try using new education savings vehicles. You can contribute up to $500 annually to an education IRA for any child under age 18. Contributions are not deductible, but earnings will be tax-free if they are used to pay qualified higher-education costs. The $500 contribution limit phases out for those with an AGI between $95,000 and $110,000 ($150,000 and $160,000 on a joint return).

Your state may offer state-qualified tuition plans to cover higher-education costs (about half the states now offer such programs). Earnings in the plans build up on a tax-deferred basis. Withdrawals for education are taxed to the child (in the same manner as commercial annuities). Withdrawals for nonqualified purposes are subject to penalty.

Using a Trust to Save For College

To save for kids' college education: "Age-21 trust" (or minor's Section 2503(c) trust), which allows you to shift investment income to a child's lower tax

bracket. *Benefit:* All trust income up to $1,700 is taxed at 15% rather than your higher rate. *Catch:* Assets in a 2503(c) trust belong to the child when he or she turns 21.

Recommended 18-year plan: Set aside $2,000 a year, which would grow to $65,000 at only 6% interest, and have the student receive distributions and pay college bills to avoid having trust distributions taxed to you.

Source: Larry Rabun, director of estate planning, Deloitte & Touche, Washington, D.C.

Why You Shouldn't Stop Stashing Money in Your Child's Account

The first $700 of investment income earned by a child under 14 is tax-free, and the next $700 is taxed at the child's own low tax rate.

Thus, $1,400 of income per year is tax favored. At 7% market interest rates, it would take an investment of about $20,000 or more to earn this much interest, so a child's account could very profitably receive gifts totaling about $20,000.

Also, a child's account can receive investment income exceeding $1,400 per year without increasing the tax bill by investing in tax-exempt securities (such as municipal bonds), or appreciating assets (such as growth stocks or U.S. Series EE savings bonds).

Appreciating assets can be held until after the child reaches 14, then be cashed in with the gain being subject to the child's own low tax rate.

Biggest College-Aid Application Mistakes

Right around the fall season, high school students and their parents frantically apply for financial aid for college. While it's important to meet the application deadlines, many parents are not careful enough when filling out the forms. They also don't weigh their college options strategically when their children receive financial aid.

Here are the biggest mistakes that parents are making now when they are seeking financial aid for their college-bound children.

Mistake: **Rushing through the application**

process. Many people believe that in the case of financial aid, it's first come, first served. That is really not the case.

The reason many students are turned down for financial aid is not because their parents make too much money, but because they rushed through the aid-application process and made errors.

Take your time. I constantly tell people that it's the tortoise that wins the race, not the hare. It's better to submit a complete application the day that it is due than to hastily complete the forms and make mistakes when trying to be one of the first to submit them. You'll be rewarded for paying attention to the many minute details.

I also recommend sending all your financial aid applications and correspondence by certified mail. Some schools suggest you send it by first class, but if a piece of certified mail is lost, at least you'll have a postmarked receipt. It is better to be safe than sorry.

Mistake: **Underestimating your financial aid eligibility.** Many people assume that they make too much money to qualify—or they think that because their children's friends applied and didn't receive any aid, they won't either.

Those who underestimate their eligibility tend to limit their search to colleges they can afford even if they do not receive aid, such as state schools or community colleges, rather than those that may be best for their children.

Mistake: **Overestimating your financial aid eligibility.** Many families assume they will get tons of financial aid and, therefore, apply only to the most expensive schools. When the aid doesn't come through, they can't afford the schools to which they applied without financial help.

Solution: In addition to investigating aid options, I always recommend that families apply to one financial safety school—a college for which the child meets the admissions criteria and the family can afford to pay even if they get only a little or no aid. Usually, this will be a state-supported school in your home state.

It is also wise to apply to your child's dream school with the clear understanding that it might not be financially possible for him or her to attend that school.

Important: Some high schools limit the number of colleges to which students can apply to five or six. If this is the case, once the safety and dream schools are out of the way, I suggest applying to two pairs of schools—similar schools that attract the same types of students. Schools that look for students with similar grades and SAT scores often compete with each other for applicants. If your child is accepted at two similar schools and he or she wants to attend the school that expects you to pay more money, you can use the other college's more attractive financial aid package to bargain with the school your child prefers. Although schools often deny that they engage in such bargaining practices, it happens all the time.

Mistake: **Thinking that all state schools are inexpensive—even those in states in which you do not live.** During the past few years, the difference between tuitions at out-of-state public colleges and tuitions of private schools has narrowed.

Important: Take a really careful look at the tuition for out-of-state public colleges. You will see that they are no longer the bargains they once were. *Example:* The University of Vermont and the University of Michigan cost more than $20,000 a year each for out-of-state students, including activity fees, room and board and other expenses. This is about double what in-state students would pay.

Mistake: **Counting on the promises of relatives who say they will help pay the bills.** A while ago, a woman came to me whose child was a college freshman. The child's grandparents had promised to pay his tuition. But the grandfather died and the grandmother needed the money, so she had retracted the promise. Although the student was eligible for a lot of aid, he had not applied for it by the school's priority filing deadline, and he got less aid than he would have had he applied sooner.

Solution: Apply for financial aid even if you anticipate that you will not need it, and meet each school's priority filing deadline.

Mistake: **Waiting until your child's senior year of high school to think about financial aid for college.** Then parents and students may get nervous, and important decisions may be made emotionally and in haste.

Solution: Start thinking about financial aid eligibility when your child is in 10th or 11th grade. Try to determine how your income, assets, debts, expenses and retirement provisions will affect your eligibility. Consult one of the financial aid/college money guide-books. Make sure it contains worksheets and formulas used to determine eligibility as well as specific planning strategies. Or hire an independent aid consultant. Also, start looking into how different types of schools distribute aid. *Example:* The criteria for state schools are much different than those for private schools.

Source: *Kalman A. Chany, president, Campus Consultants, Inc., 1202 Lexington Ave., New York, NY 10028. He is the author of* Paying for College Without Going Broke, *Princeton Review/Random House.*

Tuition Tactics— It Pays to Be a Resident

Becoming a resident: Students who attend a state college or university outside their home state pay much higher tuition than do residents of that state. Also, nonresidents do not have access to statewide scholarship and student aid programs. However, the Supreme Court has ruled that although state colleges and universities can charge nonresidents higher tuition, those students must be allowed to earn residency status during the period of their enrollment.

Public institutions are subsidized by the tax dollars of the citizens of the state. Substantial tuition income is lost when out-of-state students become entitled to lower resident tuition. Therefore, the process is strictly regulated—and requirements are becoming more stringent. For instance, the University of California added to its simple requirement of a year's resi-

"Tip: Up to $5,250 of expenses paid by your employer for educational expenses do not have to be included in your taxable income."

dence in the state the stipulation that a student also must prove financial independence.

Although requirements for residency vary from state to state, most follow similar patterns. All states, for example, require continuous residence for a period of time immediately preceding application—usually one year, but as little as six months in a few states.

Some states require evidence that the student intends to become a permanent resident of the state. However, the emphasis placed on this factor varies greatly. In some states, such as New York, no such requirement exists. In others, the application forms are designed to elicit such information indirectly.

When a nonresident student enrolls, the institution assumes that he or she is there for educational purposes rather than for a permanent change of residence. Thus, the burden of proof is on the student to prove desire to become a bona fide resident.

Basic questions a residency applicant is asked:

● **Have you filed an income tax return in the state?**
● **Are you dependent on your parents for support, or are you financially independent?**
● **Have you registered and voted in the state?**
● **Do you have a driver's license or car registration in the state?**
● **Do you have a record of employment in the state?** (Students who are seeking financial aid are expected to earn some money through summer and part-time employment.)

Uncle Sam Helps Pay the Way

The government can share part of your tuition bill by allowing parents and students certain tax breaks.

Two new credits for education expenses are available for qualified individuals. You can elect a *Hope Scholarship* credit of up to $1,500 per student per year for tuition and fees for the first two years of post-secondary education. The credit equals 100 percent of the first $1,000 of qualified expenses and 50 percent of the next $1,000. Qualified students include yourself, your spouse, or your dependent as long as the student carries at least one-half the normal course load for one term during the tax year. A *Lifetime Learning* credit of 20 percent of up to $5,000 of tuition (for a maximum of $1,000) can also be elected for payments after June 20, 1998. Beginning in the year 2003, this credit will increase to $2,000. Unlike the Hope credit, it can be claimed for an unlimited number of years. It is explicitly directed for courses at an eligible institution that helps you acquire or improve job skills.

Important note: Both credits phase out ratably if your modified Adjusted Gross Income is between $80,000 and $100,000 (married, filing jointly) or $40,000 and $50,000 (other returns).

● Interest on higher-education loans.

Beginning in 1998, if you qualify you can claim an above-the-line deduction for interest on education loans used to pay tuition, room and board, and other related expenses for attending post-secondary schools, including vocational and postgraduate schools. Limited to $1,000 in 1998, the deductible amount grows to $2,500 in 2001. You can only deduct higher-education interest during the first 60 months in which payments are required. The deduction is phased out ratably for married couples filing a joint return with a modified Adjusted Gross Income between $60,000 and $75,000 ($40,000 and $55,000 for individuals). Interest on qualified home equity loans used to pay for education costs also remains deductible. And there is no prohibition against taking out two separate loans, a home equity loan producing deductible mortgage interest, and an education loan producing deductible higher-education interest.

● Individual retirement accounts can also provide tax-aided education expenses.

The 10 percent early-withdrawal penalty tax will not be imposed on amounts taken out of IRAs before age 59½ that are used to pay qualified higher-education expenses. These costs include tuition at post-secondary institutions, room and board, fees, books and supplies for you, your spouse, your child, or your grandchild. Also you can make nondeductible contributions of up to $500 per year to an education IRA for qualified higher-education expenses of a beneficiary. The $500 is phased out ratably between $150,000 and $160,000 for married couples filing jointly ($95,000 and $110,000 for individuals).

Many states have established *qualified state tuition programs*. You can prepay higher-education costs on a tax-favored basis. Amounts held in qualified state tuition program accounts are not currently taxed. When the funds are used to pay qualified higher-education expenses that now include room and board as well as tuition, fees and supplies, only the earnings are included in the income of the beneficiary of the account.

● Tax-free education.

Up to $5,250 of expenses paid by your employer for educational expenses do not have to be included in your taxable income if your employer sets up an education assistance program that meets certain requirements. As extended by the 1997 tax law, tax-free employer-provided educational assistance will be available for courses that begin before June 1, 2000, but is not available for graduate-level courses. *(Editor's note:* This tax break expires on May 31, 2000, unless Congress acts to extend the law, as it has done several times before.)

● Deduct your education costs.

You can deduct tuition, books, supplies and fees when you take courses to improve your present job skills or because they are required by your employer to keep your job. Transportation expenses, including parking and tolls, are deductible, if you commute to school directly after work.

Important limit: These expenses are categorized as miscellaneous expenses and are deductible only to the extent that they exceed 2 percent of your Adjusted Gross Income. Of course, if your employer pays your tuition bill under an employer-provided education assistance plan, you can't deduct the same items on your tax return.

● Tax-free dependent care.

Up to $5,000 paid by your employer for care of your dependents while you work needn't be included in income. Your employer must have a qualified dependent-care assistance program.

● Expenses for nursery-school tuition and day care.

The child-care credit is available when both spouses work and the children go to nursery school or day care or are cared for at home by household help. In some special cases a married couple can take the credit when only one spouse works provided…

● The nonworking spouse is a full-time student for five months of the year.

● The nonworking spouse is physically or mentally unable to care for himself or herself.

Generally, the higher your Adjusted Gross Income

(AGI), the lower your child-care credit. The calculations are based on your qualifying expenses plus AGI.

Those with an AGI over $28,000 can claim a credit of 20% on up to $2,400 worth of expenses for one child and $4,800 for two or more children. The amount of creditable expenses must be reduced by dependent-care program payments discussed above.

● **Expenses for special schooling.** Expenses of sending a physically or mentally handicapped child to a special school that has the resources to ameliorate the handicap can qualify as medical-expense deductions. *Deductible items:* Tuition, related expenses such as transportation to and from the school and meals and lodging if the child lives there.

● **Combined child-care plus special-school expenses.** Sometimes the same expenses for special schooling qualify for both a medical expense and the child-care credit. You can't use the same expenses to take both. But if you use only part of your expenses to get the maximum child-care credit, you can apply the unused expenses to your medical deduction. Or you may apply the whole expense toward your medical deduction. Generally, if you have low medical expenses, you will get the lowest tax bill by applying the expenses to your child-care credit first.

Sources: *Steven M. Woolf, director, Coopers & Lybrand National Tax Services, 1900 K St. NW, Washington, DC 20006.*

Those Tricky Tuition Tax Breaks

Tax breaks to help students and their parents deal with the expense of higher education are an important feature of the Taxpayer Relief Act.

Problem: Parents must balance the money they're entitled to receive from the government in the form of tax benefits with any scholarship money the college might provide. *Questions to ask:*

Will the tax benefits reduce the amount of financial aid available from the college? Could a student lose a scholarship because of the tax benefits? (The school may well consider the tax benefits as additional income when determining scholarship eligibility.)

Some Drawbacks to Consider:

● **HOPE Scholarship credit.** Income levels play a role: The amount of tax credit available starts to drop

once your family's income hits $80,000 ($40,000 for an individual return).

● **Lifetime Learning Credit.** It's not clear how this credit will affect aid from noncollege sources, such as companies.

● **Education IRAs.** Although called an IRA, contributions are not deductible.

Note: For any year in which a student withdraws money from an education IRA, neither a HOPE credit nor a Lifetime Learning credit can be taken.

● **IRA withdrawals.** Access to this source of funds is something else college financial officers are certain to target and label as savings for the purpose of determining eligibility for financial aid. *Result:* The very stu-

TAX TRAPS FOR SCHOLARSHIP WINNERS

Scholarships are tax-free only to the extent they're used for tuition, fees, books, course materials, supplies and other items directly connected to education. Any amounts given for room, board and personal expenses are taxable. For students who aren't candidates for college degrees, all scholarships and fellowships are fully taxable.

Record keeping: Students should keep records and receipts for all money spent on tuition, university fees, books, school supplies and the like. It's up to the student to prove how much of the scholarship went for these purposes and how much, if any, for personal living expenses.

Another trap: If the student is required to perform any services (teaching, for instance) as a condition of receiving the scholarship, some or all of the grant is regarded as taxable compensation.

Source: *Richard Shapiro, Director of Taxes, Grant Thornton, CPAs, 1 New York Plaza, New York, NY 10004.*

dent who needs help most may in fact have the most to lose. But when a student does not qualify for financial aid, the right to withdraw money from an IRA without penalty could be very helpful.

● **Tax Deductions for Student Loan Interest.** The limited deduction starts phasing out for singles with an Adjusted Gross Income above $40,000 and joint filers making more than $60,000. It disappears at $55,000 and $75,000, respectively.

Caution: You can only deduct the first five years of interest payment.

Source: David S. Rhine, partner and national director of Family Wealth Planning, LLP, BDO Seidman, CPA, 330 Madison Ave., New York, NY 10017.

Obvious...And Less Obvious Ways to Get Money for College

Most parents overlook the largest—and least-used—source of college money: their own employers and companies that operate where they live.

Other Sources

● **Athletic scholarships are an enormously overlooked source of funds.** You don't have to be a potential Big Ten halfback to be eligible. For example, 900 schools offer women's tennis scholarships, and about 5,000 students will reap the benefits. You needn't be a top player, either. Just be a good player who's academically qualified to attend a particular school. There are also about 5,000 women's volleyball scholarships available.

Helpful: Scholarships in these and less-popular sports—badminton, crew, fencing, riflery, skiing, squash and water polo—exist because of the law that requires schools with football scholarships to offer scholarships in other sports, with equal amounts of money going to both men and women.

If no one applies for a scholarship in a less-popular sport, colleges can claim the unused funds for their football programs.

> "You don't have to be a potential Big Ten halfback to be eligible [for an athletic scholarship]....You needn't be a top player, either...just...a good player who's academically qualified."

● **Private foundations can be rich sources of college funds,** but they hate to give money to people who haven't "done their homework" on the foundation, and they are known to reject applicants for what appear to be petty reasons.

● **Parents and students** can trade their creative or entrepreneurial skills for college money.

Possibilities: If you're in advertising, try donating ideas for an ad campaign that would attract more students to the school in exchange for tuition. Or work as an unpaid recruiter or interviewer.

Public relations people may be able to write press releases for the school's alumni association that would make alumni reach for their checkbooks. One golf pro sends his son to college by coaching the school's golf team.

Keys to using this strategy: Make your offer to trade your services for tuition as palatable as possible to the school. Keep in mind that schools hate that their willingness to barter might become public information. If you manage to strike a deal, keep quiet about it.

● **Armed forces:** Money is available to veterans, those who haven't yet served and those currently in the uniformed services. But you must give the military something in return—a commitment to serve full- or part-time for a specified period of time. Check for specific details with military academies, service academies, ROTC programs, the National Guard and the Reserves.

The military also offers special programs for health science specialists—doctors, nurses, medics and technicians. Army and Navy ROTC also have college money available for people enrolled in affiliated nursing schools.

For civilians with military relatives, several programs have been developed to help pay college costs without requiring a term of service.

● **Big business:** Several companies offer money to people other than employees. *Examples:* Avon, Food Fair Stores, Gannett, Gemco.

As a Last Resort

Be outrageous. There are plenty of super-rich people out there. Most are well insulated from financial requests, but every once in a while one slips through. Whether because of the creativity of the approach or the worthiness of the need, purse strings have been known to be loosened. *Cost to you:* Time, energy, a little money and perhaps some ego damage. *Resource:* The 400 richest people in America, whose names are published yearly by *Forbes* magazine.

Source: John Bear, Ph.D., and Mariah Bear, M.A., coauthors of Finding Money for College, *Ten Speed Press. He has spent more than 10 years reviewing virtually every source of scholarships and grants available in the United States.*

Quirky Scholarship Qualifications

Special scholarships have been endowed for an amazing variety of student interests and circumstances. Here are just a few samples of special grants. (Some have never been claimed, and amounts of money vary.)

- **Children of glassblowers.**
- **Students interested in the study of fungi, speleology (cave-related research), horticulture, funeral direction or wine-making.**
- **Rhode Island students studying Italian.**
- **Female helicopter pilots.**
- **Texas students who want to study and live in Sweden.**
- **Students who have roped calves in a rodeo.**
- **Children of Jewish war veterans.**
- **Former golf caddies in New Jersey.**
- **Indiana high school seniors dedicated to the ideals of Dwight D. Eisenhower.**

Special Scholarships for Being Special

If your child is a left-hander planning to attend Juniata College in Pennsylvania, or has the last name of Gatlin and is headed toward the University of North Carolina at Raleigh, a scholarship may be just an inquiry away.

Grants for students with quirky talents or particular names are numerous. They make up a sizable portion of the $25 billion in grant money logged in by scholarship search services, ranging from a flat

$500 gift to full tuition payments for four years. Funded by both private and college sources, they may or may not be limited to a particular campus. These scholarships, however, should not be a first priority in the search for college financing. The primary resource for any student should be the financial aid office of his or her school. College financial aid officers have a responsibility to help students locate and qualify for government and college loans and grants, including scholarships that might apply to that particular school.

Important: You should begin your quest for additional grants or scholarships no later than the spring of your child's junior year of high school. Successful scholarship recipients have applied for consideration by their senior year. Also, when contacting any of your child's college choices, make sure you find out what financial aid forms need to be completed, and by when.

Many colleges have athletic scholarships, for example, and some have reinstituted merit scholarships—although in a small way. *Point:* Don't limit your child's choice of colleges simply because of cost. Scholarship money is available to a wide range of students with varying talents and incomes. Some private colleges have larger endowments with which to aid students than many public universities have.

After the family has studied the college's financial aid package, it might want to try tracking down additional help through special scholarships. Your local community can be helpful. A parent's employer or social organization often sponsors scholarships, and more and more grant dollars are being awarded through high schools to college-bound seniors.

It's important to do your homework in the search for scholarships. Look at the financial aid section of college catalogs in your library. Also check the library's scholarship listings and how-to-find-financial-aid manuals. Try looking as well at the local newspaper for information about the class ahead of your child's—you'll learn about the scholarships awarded to your own high school community. *Helpful:* A website that provides detailed information on financial aid is at *www.finaid.org*. High school guidance counselors also should be able to provide materials.

Another useful tool is a scholarship search service. Most require a detailed application. Going on the information you provide, they send you a relevant listing of which scholarships you may qualify for. The listings are constantly updated, and these services provide counseling for applying. The best services do your research for you, but they make no guarantees of success. The worst ones can be a waste of your money. The two that are leaders in the field are the National Scholarship Research Service and the Scholarship Resource Network.

Since the massive federal cutbacks in aid for higher education, the trend in federal money has shifted toward loans and away from true grants. The private and business sectors are becoming the best sources of scholarships. With diligence and research, almost any college freshman can get some private-sector scholarship help.

Sources: Heather C. McDonnell, director of financial aid, Sarah Lawrence College, Bronxville, NY 10708; Dan Cassiday, National Scholarship Research Service, 2280 Airport Blvd., Santa Rosa, CA 95403.

Low-Cost, High-Performance Colleges

Having smart children has never been more expensive. Cutbacks in federal financial aid add to the problem—now few families earning over $30,000 a year are eligible for grants. Although many of the best schools devise combinations of loans and grants that make it possible for everyone they accept to attend, the payback hardships are considerable. Students may be distracted by jobs while in school, and they often graduate with debts that will burden them for years.

Solution: Inexpensive colleges with high standards. They have the prestige to attract an excellent student body, they are highly regarded by employers and their alumni turn up in *Who's Who in America* with the same frequency as graduates of more expensive schools. *Best choices:*

● **Cooper Union for the Advancement of Science**

B est Way to Find A Scholarship

Computer search services claim they match qualified students to available scholarships.

Problem: The data provided by these services are usually outdated, overly general or inadequate, according to the National College Board. *Better:* a visit to a competent high school counselor or a college financial-aid office.

and Art, New York. An extraordinary private school of art, engineering, and architecture. Its engineering programs match those of MIT and Caltech in quality of instruction and students, and because of its endowment it charges no tuition. Extremely competitive, it accepts only 7% of applicants in art and architecture and 32% in engineering.

● **Georgia Institute of Technology, Atlanta.** One of the best state-sponsored engineering schools in the country. Academic standards are very high.

● **University of California, Berkeley.** One of the toughest public universities to get into. Its social prestige ranks with that of Stanford. Of accepted applicants, 87% are in the top fifth of their high school class. Undergraduate classes are large, but the faculty is world-class, especially in business management, ethnic studies, and cinema. Unusual majors include Dutch studies and Southeast Asian studies.

● **University of Colorado, Boulder.** Unique in that it draws students almost equally from the East Coast and the West Coast. It's strong in liberal arts and sciences, and unbeatable in parks and recreation and in other outdoor subjects. Of accepted applicants, 95% are in the top half of their high school class. The setting is beautiful, and, of course, there's the skiing.

● **University of Illinois, Urbana-Champaign.** Very big and very good. The library is one of the largest on the continent, and a mind-boggling variety of majors is available. Instruction is excellent in engineering, sciences, and other professional subjects.

● **University of Michigan, Ann Arbor.** It retains old ties to the Eastern elite (its football team used to play in the Ivy League, and the faculty maintains strong Ivy League connections) but is supported by the state. UM offers more than 150 majors, most of them very strong, and some of them superb.

● **University of North Carolina, Chapel Hill.** A great old state university in a region that until recently has been overlooked by college applicants. *Especially strong:* Liberal arts and social sciences. Twelve and a half percent of nonresident applicants and 55% of resident applicants are admitted.

● **University of New Hampshire, Durham.** A beautiful small-town campus in the heart of New England, UNH is a comprehensive university, offering majors in more than 95 fields. It far outranks neighboring Bennington in terms of alumni achievement.

● **University of Texas, Austin.** One of the biggest institutions of higher learning in the country, and certainly the one with the biggest budget. If it's possible to buy academic quality, UT has done it. The facilities are lavish, and the faculty has been improved significantly in recent years, thanks to the huge endowment. Academic emphasis is prevocational.

● **University of Virginia, Charlottesville.** Stunning grounds with historic buildings designed by Thomas Jefferson, a comprehensive range of excellent academic programs and prestige that trails only those of Harvard, Yale, Princeton, and the University of Pennsylvania—at less than half the cost. In 1997 it rejected 66% of all applicants—a higher percentage from out of state.

Source: Gene Hawes, author of The College Board Guide to Going to College While Working, *College Entrance Examination Board.*

Getting the Best Education For Your Money

An alarming array of studies have shown that students are not mastering what they are supposed to learn in school. What's wrong with our education system?

While there's much talk about the need for smaller classes, better teachers, bigger budgets—the real problem is that our schools, teachers and textbooks simply don't teach the way children's minds learn.

NONTRADITIONAL COLLEGE DEGREES

Although a college degree is a valuable commodity, it does not come cheap.

Additional problem: A person in mid-career generally can't afford the years of full-time study. Alternative: Nontraditional-degree programs earned entirely off campus, at your own pace—and at less than half the cost of traditional degrees.

Many of these programs are offered by major accredited universities. Many others are unaccredited (and even cheaper) but perfectly legitimate. They are accepted by hundreds of companies as credentials for hiring, promotions or raises.

To make sure you're not dealing with a diploma mill, you can investigate an unaccredited program with the state's education department. It's unlikely that a completely phony school will have a state license. Request a list of alumni in your area, and check on their experiences. Obtain a detailed list of faculty—if most or all of them received their doctorates from the unaccredited school in question, it's a bad sign. Don't depend on unofficial reference books—one major publication listed an Arkansas "university" whose proprietor was in prison for selling fake medical degrees.

Bottom line: If it looks too good to be true (it promises a doctorate next week for $400), it probably is.

Routes to a Nontraditional Bachelor's Degree

● **Earning credit by exam—** through the College Level Examination Program (CLEP) or the Proficiency Examination Program (PEP). Many of these are one-hour, multiple-choice tests in a wide variety of fields. You can't fail, as such. Your score (from 200 to 800) earns so many credits, depending on a given college's standards. Many people have taken five of these tests in one day and earned 30 credits—the equivalent of one year in school. You could conceivably get a bachelor's degree in four months.

● **Credit for life experience.** Literally thousands of skills people may take for granted are worth credit, from fluency in French to Army jeep repair.

● **Credit for business experience.** Here you need to demonstrate mastery of skills ranging from finance, marketing and employee relations to typing and computer skills. Many corporate programs (from one-day seminars on up) earn automatic credit on the directory of the American Council on Education. If you developed these skills less formally, however, you may be able to get credit through a life-experience portfolio. Aside from the standard résumé, this will include detailed letters from coworkers or internal reports that confirm your mastery.

● **Credit through interview.** Let's say your area of expertise is marketing in the Middle East. The school invites you in for two to three hours of discus-

There is hope for the future in educational reform. Meantime, there are things that parents can do to help their children.

The Major Problems With Our Schools

First, our schools are set up to teach all kids the same things in the same way.

But people don't all have the same kinds of minds. In fact, our minds are as different as our fingerprints. Each person has a unique mixture of intelligences, or ways of understanding the world—linguistic, logical, mathematical, spatial, musical, physical (the use of the body to solve problems or make things), understanding of others and understanding of self. Also, each person has a different learning style. Some may respond best to visual information, others to language (lectures, reading), and still others must touch, or engage the physical world for things to make sense.

Once we understand this, it becomes malpractice to treat kids as if their minds were all the same.

The "Superficial" Trap

We fail in educating our kids by trying to teach too many things, too superficially.

Problem: Our children learn to imitate actions or memorize facts that have no broad context or relevance to their world. Subject matter is seldom reinforced and expanded upon from year to year. But research shows it takes about 10 years to gain understanding of a field of knowledge—the capacity to apply the skills and concepts learned in school to new situations that occur beyond the classroom.

Even talented memorizers may not be able to use

---

sion with two professors in the field. These experts will then decide how much your knowledge is worth (usually from 5 to 75 credits).

● **Traditional correspondence classes.** These are worth two to six credits each. In some cases you can get full credit merely by passing the final exam.

You can mix credits from several sources to earn your degree. Two particularly flexible schools are Regents College (based in Albany) and Edison State College (Trenton, NJ). They have no campus, faculty, or classes. But they evaluate work done elsewhere, administer exams and interviews, and award fully accredited degrees.

Graduate Work

Advanced degrees aren't much more difficult to obtain. *Major difference:* You must demonstrate the ability to do original work in your field. But this need not be a traditional academic thesis, and some schools allow submission of previously completed pro-

jects. One businessman earned his MBA with a 150-page report on whether his company should build a factory in South America. An author could submit a novel, a psychologist, some case histories.

Some schools require a limited residency. At Syracuse University, MBA students attend three eight-day summer seminars a year apart to plan and monitor their programs. *Other outstanding nonresidential master's programs:* California State University (Dominguez Hills), Bellevue University (Nebraska) and Empire State College (New York). *Helpful:* Make sure a degree from an unaccredited school is acceptable to your company before you enroll.

If you're aiming for a nonresidential Ph.D., it's often possible to skip the master's or to obtain a combined degree. The requirements are similar,

although some schools demand an internship—about 50 hours of real-life experience in a business or agency unrelated to your own.

The best nontraditional Ph.D. programs: Union Institute (Cincinnati) and The Graduate School of America (Minneapolis, Minnesota). *Foreign schools that enroll Americans:* The University of London and the University of South Africa-Pretoria.

Source: *John Bear, author of* Bears' Guide to Earning Degrees Nontraditionally, *Ten Speed Press. Visit his website at* **www.degree.net.**

what they "know" in their daily lives. Instead, they may revert to the simple "scripts" and primitive ideas we all create in our earliest years to help explain the world, and often carry into adulthood. *Example:* People who can recite the complex causes of World War I will explain equally complex current events in terms of "good guys" and "bad guys."

Family Help

To help your children learn better and reach deeper understanding:

● **Get to know your children's learning styles, strengths, interests and preferences.** Observe how your children interact with different materials in a very rich environment, such as a children's museum. *Example:* A child might read explanatory cards, watch a demonstration, listen to a guide, physically handle equipment. *Helpful:* Bring along several kids to have a basis for comparison. *Goal:* To be able to communicate with your child in the manner he or she best grasps.

A child having trouble with arithmetic may suddenly "get it" if allowed to manipulate blocks or marbles rather than being told how to solve a problem.

● **Use the educational opportunities available in your area.** Investigate school-sponsored lessons, clubs and trips, programs at Y's, community centers and camps, childrens' theaters, orchestras, sports teams or other organizations and private instructors.

● **Encourage a variety of activities.** Discuss with your children which activities interest them. Choose several different areas—maybe one art, one sport, something in the sciences, something in the humanities—some things done alone and others requiring a group or team.

● **Encourage your kids to stick with their choices for a number of years**—long enough to gain skill and understanding. There is little benefit from superficial practice of dozens of activities. The tendency to jump from one activity to another is an especially common problem in affluent families.

● **Encourage one-on-one apprenticeships.** One of the best ways to gain mastery is to work with a

teacher who embodies a deep understanding of a discipline. Apprenticeships can range from informal cabinetmaking sessions with Grandpa to a formal work or study agreement with a professional teacher.

● **Choose schools carefully.** Avoid shopping for labels (Montessori, Waldorf). *Better criteria:* Quality of teaching, enthusiasm and success of the kids who attend. Visit classes, talk to teachers and to people you respect whose kids have gone to the schools you're considering.

● **Talk to your children from multiple perspectives** to help them learn to think about things in different ways.

● **Accept responsibility as your kids' most important role models.** You can tell your children to read and write every day, but if you don't read and write regularly yourself, your kids won't read and write productively. They may learn how, but they won't use it. Parents must embody whatever they want for their kids, just as they must find teachers and apprentice-masters who are strong role models.

> "Encourage...apprenticeships. [A great way for a child] to gain mastery is to work with a teacher who [has] a deep understanding of a discipline."

● **Expose your kids to a variety of people to help offset stereotypical thinking.** Travel with your children, entertain families from backgrounds different from your own. *Example:* When the Gulf War broke out, my son Andrew happened to be attending a high school with kids from Kuwait, Jordan, Israel and Iran. It was very educational for him to see how different nations and cultures made sense of the event.

● **Expose kids to thought-provoking environments.** Let your children see where you work. Visit historic houses, museums, zoos, gardens and nature preserves. Try foreign restaurants. Take tours of factories, hospitals and city halls. Attend concerts, puppet shows and festivals.

● **Help kids develop a perspective on their own growth process.** Look at family photos, kids' writings and artworks, videotapes of projects, etc., and talk together about these things—what the kids can do now that they couldn't do then, how things change. It's wonderful to be able to see one's growth as a human being, from preschool onward. And this is a gift that parents can give their children.

Solutions that Schools Should Be Looking At

Fortunately, we already have many teaching tools (software, media, etc.) to help reach kids with varied learning styles. But we must decide what is most important to teach, then reintegrate the material at different age levels and in many ways, so every kid has a chance to master fundamental concepts, such as evolution in biology, or democracy in social studies. And of course we need teachers who themselves have a deep understanding of subject matter, and who are enthusiastic about conveying that understanding to their students.

Source: Howard Gardner, Ph.D., professor at the Harvard Graduate School of Education, and a pioneering researcher and theorist in cognitive science. His book is The Unschooled Mind: How Children Think and How Schools Should Teach, *Basic Books.*

How to Avoid the Big, Troublesome, Costly Mistakes Of College Financial Aid

Most parents need financial help when they are paying for their children's college educations. Unfortunately, many parents are not familiar with the best ways to apply for and receive financial aid.

Here are the most common mistakes people make when applying for financial assistance from a college:

Mistake: **Assuming that you're not eligible for financial aid.** *Reality:* There is no real income cutoff. Sometimes families with incomes in excess of $150,000 receive financial aid.

Mistake: **Failing to do any advance planning for the application process.** Eligibility is determined by taking a snapshot of your family's financial situation. If you are applying for aid for your child's freshman year of college, the year that will be scrutinized is from January 1 of your child's junior year in high school to December 31 of his or her senior year. Any financial or investment transactions you make during that year could help, or hurt, your child's chances of getting aid.

Mistake: **Missing the deadlines.** It's crucial to apply for aid at the same time your child is applying to colleges. Find out about aid-application deadlines from the best place—the schools themselves.

Important: Find out if the material must be post-marked, received or processed by the deadline.

Mistake: **Being unaware of other attractive borrowing options.** *Reality:* Even if they don't qualify for need-based student loans, virtually all students qualify for *unsubsidized* Stafford Loans. The colleges' financial aid offices can tell you how to apply for these loans. *How they work:* Although the child is charged interest while in school, it is at an attractive rate based on the 90-day Treasury bill plus 3.1%. The rate is set each year in July.

Some colleges have their own loan programs, which may have very attractive terms. There is also the federal Parent Loans for Undergraduate Students (PLUS) program, which allows you to borrow the total cost of education less any aid offered.

Mistake: **Assuming that outside scholarships are where the real money is.** These awards represent less than 5% of all financial aid. If your child wins an outside award, try to convince the school to reduce the loan and work-study portions of its aid package rather than the grant money dollar for dollar.

Mistake: **Assuming financial aid packages are set in stone.**

Reality: It's possible to negotiate a better package than the one you are initially offered by the college. The first offer a college makes is often not its best offer. The college is leaving room for bargaining. Your strongest bargaining chip could be a better financial aid package from another school. Be honest; you may have to provide a copy of that package.

Source: Kalman Chany, president of Campus Consultants, Inc., a fee-based firm that counsels families and conducts corporate seminars on maximizing financial aid eligibility, 1202 Lexington Ave., New York, NY 10028. He is the author of Paying for College Without Going Broke, *Princeton Review/Random House.*

More Strategies for Winning The College-Aid Game

Here are more strategies to ensure that your child receives the best possible financial aid package.

Do Your Taxes Early

Colleges determine how much financial aid you should receive based partly on your previous year's income. So aid for the 1999/2000 academic year will be based on your 1998 tax information.

Early deadlines: Because the deadlines for

many colleges come so early in the year, most parents will probably have to estimate their figures on the aid forms. It's better to estimate now and revise your figures later than to miss a deadline while waiting for your tax returns to be completed. When your tax returns are complete, send copies to those colleges that require them. At many colleges, you will not get your final financial aid package until the financial aid office receives copies of your returns, so try to get taxes done as soon as possible.

Get the Right Forms

● **The Free Application for Federal Student Aid (FAFSA).** Since there is no income cutoff for federal aid, any family that thinks it will need aid should fill out a FAFSA for each student.

The FAFSA is also required to determine your eligibility for a Stafford Loan or Parent Loan for Undergraduate Students (PLUS). The FAFSA can be obtained from your child's high school guidance counselor. Make sure you get the proper version for the year for which you are seeking aid.

● **The College Scholarship Service Financial Aid PROFILE Application** may also be required, especially by private colleges. This form is more detailed than the FAFSA.

The PROFILE can only be obtained by registering with the College Scholarship Service, a private needs-analysis company. High school guidance counselors can provide information on how to register.

Meet Your Deadlines

Missing a financial aid deadline is worse than missing a mortgage payment. Your bank will likely give you another chance, but colleges probably will not.

Review the admissions and financial aid materials for each college under consideration to determine the financial aid deadlines and which forms must be completed.

Important: Don't wait to be accepted by a college to apply for financial aid. At some schools,

10 SURPRISE EXPENSES FOR COLLEGE STUDENTS

● **Books and supplies.** Costs of $700 to $800 a year are common.

● **Health insurance.** If your child isn't covered by your policy, the college may require you to buy a policy.

● **Furniture/ appliance rental.** It can cost $75 to $100 a year to rent a refrigerator for a dorm room. Students living in off-campus housing may need to rent furniture. *Annual cost:* At least a few hundred dollars.

● **Damage assessments.** Even if your child didn't do anything to damage school property, he or she may be liable for a share of the fix-up costs. Such charges are most common in freshman dorms.

● **Activity and lab fees.** Many schools assess students a per-semester activity fee. Some science courses may impose lab fees.

● **Sports** can be an important part of campus life for which you'll have to pay. Student admission to ball games is seldom free these days. Students who play on *club* teams may have to pay for uniforms and equipment.

● **Parking.** Semester fees can range from $10 to several hundred dollars.

● **Administrative fees.** The cost of changing courses after the semester begins can add up. Many schools assess drop/add charges of $20 to $30.

● **Noshing.** Regular college meal service is included in the room and board charges. Between-meal munching on pizza and other snacks is not. College students are notorious snackers and partyers, for which you can expect to pay.

Source: Kalman Chany, president of Campus Consultants, Inc., a fee-based firm that counsels families and conducts corporate seminars on maximizing financial aid eligibility, 1202 Lexington Ave., New York, NY 10028. He is the author of Paying for College Without Going Broke, *Princeton Review/Random House.*

you may even need to complete financial aid applications before the admissions deadline. Be sure to sign the forms, make copies, then send the documents by registered mail, return receipt requested, to the appropriate address.

Note Any Special Circumstances

In some cases, your previous year's finances are not an accurate representation of your family's current financial situation. *Examples:* if a parent has lost a job, or received an unusually large bonus, or there were large nonrecurring capital gains, such as from the sale of real estate.

Explain such circumstances in a separate letter to each school's financial aid office. Be brief and to the point. Remember, these schools must deal with thousands of aid applications in a very short time.

Compare Packages

The tough work begins when the acceptance letters and financial aid awards start to arrive in April.

Once you've compared the relative merits of the schools that have accepted your child, you may want to go back to some of the colleges to try to improve your financial aid packages.

Important: Negotiate while you still have leverage. Don't accept any college's offer of admission until your financial aid package is set. Otherwise the college won't have much incentive to sweeten the deal. However, you must accept or reject the admission offer by May 1.

Many colleges—especially selective ones—have become more flexible about their initial financial aid offers.

What to do: Be cordial and frank. Because time is of the essence, you should first call the college's financial aid officer to briefly explain your situation. Most likely you will have to mail or fax a letter outlining your reasons for appealing the aid package. Before you call, know the precise amount of increased aid you're seeking. If you have unusual circumstances, or your situation has changed, try to provide supporting documentation.

Source: *Kalman Chany, president of Campus Consultants, Inc., a fee-based firm that counsels families and conducts corporate seminars on maximizing financial aid eligibility, 1202 Lexington Ave., New York, NY 10028. He is the author of* **Paying for College Without Going Broke,** *Princeton Review/Random House.*

Better than Summer Jobs… Summer Businesses

With college costs rising and the summer job market tightening, many students turn to their own resources to earn a buck. In the process, a number of the traditional avenues for self-employment— baby-sitting, tutoring, teaching a sport or a musical instrument, trimming shrubs, mowing lawns—are widening into much more imaginative and lucrative small enterprises.

How to Get an Enterprise Started

● **Think about services that are missing in your community.** The first step is to consider what people in your town need. Students have been very successful with catering hors d'oeuvres and supplying bartenders and cleanup crews for parties in many areas. Organizing interesting field trips for young children to local museums, parks or historic landmarks is a more lucrative variation on baby-sitting. Putting together food, games and entertainment for children's birthday parties is a similar project that succeeds in some towns. Student cleaning services that include washing windows and scrubbing floors and student house-painting teams are often profitable with a minimum of investment. Shopping services can work in a community with a large population of older people without cars.

● **Get professional help.** Some communities have an executive volunteer corps manned by retired businesspeople who can help youngsters work out proper business plans and accounting procedures.

● **Work from strengths.** A music nut with good equipment and a thorough knowledge of the latest music can hire himself out as a disc jockey for parties, tailoring the music to the hosts' preferences. Youngsters who are particularly good with animals could organize a pet-care service for vacationers or a dog-training service for working couples.

Student summer entrepreneurs often find hidden talents for business that can help them make money during the school year. Or they may discover some talents or personality traits that will help in career choices. A successful summer enterprise earns a student special self-confidence as well as money.

Retirement Planning

9

Formulas to Use in Retirement Planning

A big problem in America today is most people's lack of adequate retirement planning. Out of every 100 people who retire, three are financially independent, 27 must continue to work to maintain their standard of living, and 70 remain dependent on family and social welfare to survive. In addition, the Social Security system reports that 85% of all Americans reaching age 65 do not have as much as $250 in personal savings.

The main reason for this problem is simple—lack of planning. People often forget that their prime earning years, between 30 and 60, should be spent not only earning enough income to support themselves and their families, but also accumulating enough funds to live from age 60 to 90.

My first and most important piece of advice: Don't wait until you're 65 to start thinking about what you will realistically need for retirement.

The first planning step is to determine the three major factors for your future retirement—present resources, income needs at retirement, and income resources from investment assets and other sources when you have retired. The goal of any retirement plan is to accumulate as large a fund of investment dollars as possible, with the ultimate goal of reallocating those funds into a mix of assets that will provide you with a steady income and some growth potential. In all scenarios, inflation will be your worst enemy. (At 5% inflation, prices double every 10 years.) To protect yourself against inflation, invest a portion of your retirement funds in growth assets. The majority of your funds, however, should be invested in secure income assets to provide a reliable income base. Expect your retirement needs to be approximately 85% of your present working gross income.

The following formulas and examples illustrate how to determine what you should set aside each year to maintain a satisfactory lifestyle during retirement.

ARITHMETIC TO DO BEFORE YOU RETIRE

How to size up your financial situation:

1. List your assets. Include income-producing assets (stocks, bonds, annuity-generating insurance policies, real estate, company profit-sharing plans), plus nonincome-producing assets (paid-up life insurance, furniture, and household goods), and assets that require expenditures for maintenance (houses, cars, etc.). Estimate total dollar value, factoring in appreciation.

2. Figure out postretirement income. Add up income from assets, pensions, and Social Security.

3. Calculate postretirement expenses, then deduct costs stemming from work (commutation, clothes). Next add on the cost of benefits (health insurance) that will no longer be covered by an employer. Estimate an annual dollar figure. Factor in the inflation rate.

4. If postretirement expenses outstrip postretirement income, develop a plan for liquidating assets. *Rule of thumb:* The percentage of total capital that a retired person may spend annually begins at 5% at age 65 and increases by 1% every five years. At age 80, it is 10%.

Retirement Worksheet

The following formulas and examples illustrate how to determine what you should set aside each year to maintain a satisfactory lifestyle during retirement.

Note: You will need access to a business or scientific calculator, a personal computer or present value of annuity tables in order to complete this worksheet.

Assumptions: You will retire 10 years from now. You will require $100,000 per year for 22 years after retirement. You now earn $200,000 gross pretax income.

Step 1

Gather all financial data. Establish balance sheet, cash-flow needs and rough tax analysis (use the current year).

Step 2

Determine assets available:

a)	Cash/cash equivalents	$ 50,000
	Invested assets at fair market value:	
	Certificates of deposit	$ 60,000
	Treasury notes	$ 20,000
	Stocks	$ 70,000
	Real estate	$ 300,000
	Total (a)	$ 500,000
b)	Investment debt	$ 0
	Bequests	$ 200,000
	Other	$ 0
	Total (b)	$ 200,000
c)	**Total available assets (2a–2b)**	$ 300,000

Step 3

Determine the future value of available assets:
(What your assets will be worth at retirement)

a)	Total from Step 2(c)	$ 300,000
b)	Future Value (FV) Calculation	
	Number (n) periods (years) until retirement	10
	Rate of return (i) after tax	6%
	Future value factor $(1 + i\%/100)_n$	

$(1+.06)^{10} = 1.791$

c) Multiply 3(a) by future value factor to determine value of available assets at retirement.
Future value of assets at retirement—
FV: **(300,000 x 1.791) =** $ 537,300

Step 4

Estimate retirement income fund:

a)	Annual income needs during retirement	$ 100,000
b)	Expected Social Security and other retirement benefits and income from other resources	$ 60,000
c)	Net income needs during retirement— subtract 4(b) from 4(a)	$ 40,000
d)	Income adjustment for inflation	
	Number (n) periods (years) until retirement	10
	Rate of return (i) after tax	5%
	Future value factor $(1 + r\%/100)_n$	

$(1.05)^{10} = 1.629$

Multiply 4(c) by future value factor to determine annual income needs during retirement adjusted for inflation.

(40,000 x 1.629) = $ 65,160

e)	Retirement fund needed:	
	Number (n) of periods (years) of retirement assumed	22
	Rate of return (i) after tax	6%
	Rate of inflation (r)	5%
	Annual income after retirement— Payment (PMT)	$ 65,160

Calculate the lump sum needed at retirement to provide PMT over (n) years.

Adjusted interest factor— $\dfrac{(1 + i\%/100)}{[(1 + r\%/100) - 1]}$

$\left[\dfrac{1.06}{1.05} - 1\right]$ f =   0.00952

Lump sum = **PMT x (1+ f)**   x $\left[\dfrac{-(1 + f)\text{-}n}{f}\right]$

Lump sum =
$65{,}160 \times (1.00952) \times \left[\dfrac{1-(1.00952)^{-22}}{.00952}\right] =$

$1,300,100
(rounded)

Amount needed for emergency fund at retirement:

a) Emergency fund needed in
today's dollars   **$ 20,000**

b) Future value calculation
Number (n) of periods (years)
until retirement   **10**
Rate of inflation (r)   **5%**
Future value factor $(1+ r\%/100)^n$
$(1.05)^{10} = 1.629$
Multiply 5(a) by future value factor to
  determine future value of emergency fund
  needed at date of retirement.
Future value of emergency fund—
FV: **(20,000 x 1.629)** =   **$ 32,580**

Determine additional savings at retirement:

a) Resources needed
From Step 4(e)   **$1,300,100**
From Step 5(b)   **$ 32,580**
Total resources needed   **$1,332,680**

b) Resources available
From Step 3(c)   **$ 537,300**

c) Subtract 6(b) from 6(a) total
Additional savings needed
at retirement: **$ 795,380**

d) Deflation calculations
Number (n) of periods (years)
until retirement   **10**
Rate of inflation (r)   **5%**

Present value factor— $\dfrac{1}{(\frac{1+r\%}{100})}$

$\dfrac{1}{1.05^{10}} = 0.614$

Multiply additional savings needed at retirement by present value factor to determine
  the savings needed at retirement in today's
  dollars. Present value of additional savings
  needed at retirement.
(795,380 x 0.614) =   **$ 488,360**

Determine the amount of money (after tax) that needs to be saved annually:

a) Savings (S) needed at retirement
from Step 6(d)   **$ 488,360**

b) Serial savings calculations
Number (n) of periods (years)
until retirement   **10**
Rate of return (i) after tax   **6%**
Rate of inflation (r)   **5%**
Calculate the first serial payment to be
  invested at the end of the current year.
Adjusted interest factor— $\dfrac{(1 + i\%/100)}{[(1 + r\%/100) - 1]}$

$\left[\dfrac{1.06}{1.05} -1\right]$ f = **0.00952**

First serial payment— **PMT** $= \dfrac{S}{\left[\frac{(1 + f)_n - 1}{f}\right]}$

$\dfrac{488,360}{\dfrac{(1 + 0.00952)^{10} -1}{0.00952}}$ **$ 46,780**

c) Inflation adjustment
Annual savings required
from Step 7(b)   **$ 46,780**
Rate of inflation (r)   **5%**
Multiply annual savings by inflation rate
  (written as 1 + r%/100).
Adjusted serial payment
(46,780 x 1.05) =   **$ 49,120**

d) Percent of income needed to be saved
Annual adjusted savings   **$ 49,120**
Gross income (pretax)   **$ 200,000**
Divide annual adjusted savings by gross
  income to determine percent of income
  to be saved.
(49,120 ÷ 200,000) =   **24.6%**

Source: Paul E. Ferraresi, president of Founders Group, 11 Greenway Plaza, Suite 3030, Houston, TX 77046. Mr. Ferraresi advises individuals and corporations on investment, tax and estate planning. He is also an instructor and lecturer, as well as the publisher of a national newsletter, Personal Money Management.

A Threat to Retirement

Baby boomers have to secure their retirement future now, or they'll be forced to continue working "forever." Companies are offering decreasingly generous pension plans; many people no longer stay at one job long enough to accumulate significant pension benefits; Social Security—burdened by the growing elderly population—is being pared down; Medicare benefits are likely to be trimmed back.

Self-defense: Establish a savings and investment plan now to meet current and future needs.

Source: *Anna Rappaport of William M. Mercer-Meidinger Hansen, Inc., financial consultants, Chicago, IL.*

More Income

Becoming a partner in her husband's business could boost a woman's ultimate Social Security retirement benefits. As a partner, the woman will have self-employment income. When she reaches retirement, her benefits will be based on that income. This could far exceed the $37\frac{1}{2}$% to 50% of her husband's retirement benefits that she would get if she had no earnings of her own on which to compute her Social Security entitlement.

Source: *Dr. Robert S. Holzman, professor emeritus of taxation at New York University and author of* The Encyclopedia of Estate Planning, *Boardroom Books.*

Break on IRA Withdrawals

At age $70\frac{1}{2}$ you must begin making withdrawals from your Individual Retirement Accounts—but not from Roth IRAs, which do not have a mandatory age by which you must begin your withdrawals. In the past you had to make at least a minimum with-drawal (figured from IRS life-expectancy tables) from each of your IRA accounts.

Now you can figure the total required withdrawal and take it out of any account or any combination of accounts. (This allows you to withdraw from lower-yielding IRAs and let higher-yielding IRAs continue to grow.)

Checking up on the SSA

The Social Security payments you receive monthly upon retirement will depend on both the age at which you retire and the dollar amount of earnings credited to your account by the Social Security Administration.

Problem: The SSA's records may reflect less than your earnings.

Social Security records should be checked every two years to ensure that the right amounts have been credited. If you find any errors, locate supporting documents—such as tax returns and W-2 forms—for the periods in question, and take them to your local Social Security office.

How to do it. Ask for a Personal Earnings and Benefits Statement from your local Social Security office, or by calling 800-772-1213. You can also download the form via computer at **www.ssa.gov.** A report of your account will be sent to you about five weeks after you mail the form. The service is free. Don't be taken in by companies that offer to obtain your savings records for a fee.

Source: *Social Security Administration, 6401 Security Blvd., Baltimore, MD 21207.*

ROTH IRAs: New Ways to Save for Retirement and Build up Your Estate

On January 1, 1998, Roth IRAs became the third type of IRA, along with traditional deductible and nondeductible IRAs. Contributions to Roth IRAs are not deductible and must be based on earned income. However, Roth IRAs offer many advantages over traditional IRAs:

Contributions can be made at any age as long as you have earned income (the age $70\frac{1}{2}$ limit for making contributions to traditional IRAs does not apply to Roth IRAs). Participation in a qualified retirement plan does not affect your ability to make Roth IRA contributions.

Distributions from Roth IRAs are entirely tax-free if taken at least five years after the year in which the contributions were made, and you are at least $59\frac{1}{2}$, disabled, or you use the funds to pay first-time home-buying expenses (up to $10,000 in a lifetime). There are no mandatory withdrawals during your lifetime (compared to required minimum distributions from conventional IRAs commencing no later than April 1 of the year after turning age $70\frac{1}{2}$).

You can contribute up to $2,000 annually to a Roth IRA if your Adjusted Gross Income (AGI) is below a set limit: $95,000 for single taxpayers and $150,000 on a joint return. The contribution limit phases out for singles with an AGI between $95,000 and $110,000 and for married couples filing jointly with an AGI between $150,000 and $160,000. Married persons cannot avoid these AGI limits by filing separately, since there is a zero limit for those filing separate returns.

You can convert your existing IRAs to Roth IRAs, provided your AGI is no more than $100,000. The converted amounts taken into income are not counted toward this AGI limit. Married couples must file joint returns to make the conversion. SEP-IRAs and SIMPLE-IRAs cannot be converted into Roth IRAs (you'll need to roll them over to a regular IRA, and then convert to a Roth IRA).

Drawback: When the conversion is made, all the income that would have been reported if a distribu-

PENSION BENEFITS TRAPS

The bottom line in retirement planning today: Don't count on anticipated pension benefits being available when you need them. With general restructuring and cost-cutting efforts, many companies have been finding ways to terminate or reduce their pension obligations. *Changes to watch out for:*

Terminating a Pension Plan

It has become very popular for companies to terminate their pension plan and recapture any excess funds to help pay off the debt in a leveraged buyout. Although the law says that employers must replace that coverage with paid-up annuities, you still come out behind.

Deducting Social Security Benefits

Companies often take workers' Social Security payments into account when figuring pension benefits. They reason that since they paid half of those premiums, they're entitled to reduce their share of your defined benefits by half of whatever you'll be receiving from Social Security.

Problem: Most employees think of their pension benefits as separate from Social Security. *Somewhat helpful:* The Tax Act of 1986 specified that in most cases employers can't subtract more than 50% of your pension benefits, regardless of how much you receive from Social Security.

Protection: Ask your employer annually for a benefits statement showing how much you would receive at retirement if you left the company now or at various points in the future. Ask for the figures with and without salary increases, since those are not guaranteed. Never assume that pension benefit projections will hold up 100%. Often they turn out to have been too optimistic. *Goal:* To replace at least 50%–70% of your final salary. That's considered a minimum for living in relative comfort during retirement.

tion from the IRA had been taken must be included in income. You need to have the income (outside of your IRA) to pay this additional tax. If you use your IRA funds to pay the tax, it is also subject to an early-distribution penalty if you are under age 59½ .

Source: Barbara Weltman is a tax attorney and the author of several books on business, including The Complete Idiot's Guide to Making Money After You Retire, *Alpha Books, and* J.K. Lasser's Tax Deduction for Your Small Business, *Macmillan.*

Spotting Trouble in Your Pension Plan

Many people take their company's pension plan for granted. Although most pension funds are sound, there are some that bear watching, and it is in your interest to know if yours is one of them.

First, you need to understand the kind of plan or plans your company offers. There are two basic types: defined benefit plans and defined contribution plans. Your company may have one or the other or, possibly, both.

Defined Benefit Plans

Defined benefit plans are the more traditional kind. Under such plans, at retirement you receive a set yearly income—your defined benefit—from the pension fund. The payments continue for the rest of your life. How much you are paid annually is based on such factors as the number of years you worked for the company and your salary level.

Contributions to the pension fund under a

Changing Vesting Requirements

Companies must vest employees after five years or start vesting them after three years and work up to full vesting in five years.

Implications: Before making a job change, take into account these vesting requirements and the relative pension benefits. Even if a new job looks attractive, you may lose earned pension benefits by moving now.

Self-Protection

The responsibility (and the risk) for retirement planning is being shifted away from companies and onto the shoulders of individual employees.

In a survey of 1,000 companies, we found that 93% of them now offer 401(k) plans, compared with only 23% in 1983. The 401(k) allows you to save $10,000 a year (in 1998) tax-deferred (the amount is indexed annually for inflation), with many companies matching 50¢ on each dollar you put in.

Our advice:

If possible, contribute the maximum to your 401(k) plan, even if this means taking money out of the bank. If the combined contributions earn, say,10% a year, you will be using your 50¢ to accumulate 60¢ tax-free over the years. That's a terrific deal.

If you are self-employed or are not covered under a company pension plan, the law allows you other alternatives for retirement saving:

● **IRAs (Individual Retirement Accounts)** give you the right to put away up to $2,000 per year, tax-deferred. You can start withdrawing funds without penalty when you are 59½. You must start to withdraw funds when you reach 70½.

For the Roth IRA, there is no required date by which you must begin withdrawals.

Taxpayers who participate in a company retirement plan face income restrictions on their eligibility to make deductible IRA contributions. For joint returns the range in 1999 is $51,000–

$61,000; for single filers $31,000–$41,000. These limits will increase each year until 2005 for singles and 2007 for married persons filing jointly. If you are unable to make a deductible contribution, you can add after-tax dollars to these funds, and the earnings won't be taxable until withdrawal.

● **Keogh plans** let you set aside as much as $30,000 from self-employment income or noncompany income such as outside director's fees. Here again, if you are eligible, it's well worth saving as much as possible in this tax-deferral plan.

SEPs (Simplified Employee Pension Plans) let you put aside 15% of what you earn, with a cap of $24,000 (in 1998.) You can change the amount of your contribution each year, skipping poor years and putting away the maximum in good ones.

Source: Kenneth P. Shapiro, president, Hay/Huggins Co., Inc., the benefits and actuarial consulting subsidiary of HayGroup, Wanamaker Bldg., 100 Penn Square East, Philadelphia, PA 19107-3388.

defined benefit plan are made annually, usually by the company alone. The fund is invested by its trustees, who are appointed by the company and often include company officers. If the pension fund makes higher earnings than expected, the company can contribute less in future years. Conversely, if the fund underperforms, the company will be obliged to contribute more.

If you believe that your company's defined benefit plan is underfunded, there isn't much you can do about it. There is, however, government insurance to protect most of your benefits.

> **"Federal law requires that a yearly overview of the finances of any fund managed by a large company or a union be sent to all its members."**

Defined Contribution Plans

Defined contribution plans don't have a predictable payout. Your benefit depends on how much money is contributed to your account in the fund and how well it is invested. When you retire, you will receive only the amount that has accumulated in your name, usually in a lump sum.

Profit-sharing and money-purchase plans are examples of defined contribution plans in which the company usually makes all the contributions. Savings plans, such as 401(k) and 403(b), are funded primarily by employees, although companies often match some part of the employee's contribution.

Defined contribution plans are not insured, and the size of your pension is dependent on the investment judgment of the plan's trustees.

Checking the Financial Statements

Federal law requires that a yearly overview of the finances of any fund managed by a large company or a union be sent to all its members. This Summary Annual Report (SAR) tells you how much money is in the plan, how much money the plan made (or lost) in investments, and what the administrative costs were for that year.

Learn to read your plan's SAR. Heavy investment losses and high administrative costs are signals that you should look further into the performance of the fund. Along with general financial informa-

tion on the fund, the SAR will tell you how to get a copy of the more detailed financial statement—Form 5500—that the plan is required to file with the federal government.

Form 5500 will give you more specific information on the fund's investments, such as how much is in stocks, bonds, real estate or other investment vehicles. For larger funds, you are likely to also receive a detailed list of all the investments held by the fund, the amounts paid to people providing services to the fund, and a report by a certified public accountant that the figures are reliably reported.

Blowing the Whistle

If you discover any questionable information in Form 5500, such as excessive fees paid to fund managers or transactions made with company or union officials, their relatives or those with close connections to the plan, you can get a reading on the matter from the Department of Labor's Pension and Welfare Benefits Administration (PWBA). If the fund is involved in illegal practices, this is the agency that can take action.

Look for a field office of the agency under the U.S. government listings in your local phone book. If there is no local listing, contact the national office of the Pension and Welfare Benefits Administration in Washington at 202-219-8776.

The PBWA also publishes a booklet, called "Protecting Your Pension—A Quick Reference Guide," that may help you understand Form 5500, 800-998-7542 plus show you other ways to safeguard your financial future. Call to request a free copy.

To obtain all this information and more online, visit the Department of Labor website at: www.dol.gov.

Source: Karen W. Ferguson is director of the Pension Rights Center, a nonprofit consumer advocacy group at 918 16th St. NW, Washington, DC 20006.

WHY 401(K) PLANS ARE BETTER THAN IRAS

If your employer has a 401(k) plan, take full advantage of it, even if participating in the plan makes you ineligible for deductible IRA contributions. 401(k) plans are better than IRAs. *Here's why:*

● **You can put in more money.** The limit is $10,000 per year in 1998. For an IRA, the limit is $2,000 a year or 100% of your pay, whichever is lower.

● **Many employers make matching contributions to the plans,** the most common being one dollar for every two from the employee up to a prescribed level.

● **The plans are managed by professionals,** saving you the trouble of handling your own account.

● **Contributions to the plan are by payroll deduction,** a nearly painless way of saving.

● **You can borrow from your account tax-free, if the plan permits.** By contrast, borrowing from an IRA is considered a withdrawal, subject to tax.

Editor's note: Starting in 2000, five-year averaging is repealed. Ten-year averaging is still available to those born before 1936.

● **Contributions to a 401(k) plan reduce your Adjusted Gross Income (AGI).** This can result in bigger medical, casualty and miscellaneous deductions, all of which are based on a percentage of your AGI. *More:* If your 1999 AGI is reduced to below $51,000 (joint filers) or $31,000 (single), you can participate in the 401(k) and also make fully deductible IRA contributions.

Editor's note: The AGI limits for active participants to make fully deductible IRA contributions will rise to $80,000 on a joint return by 2007 and to $50,000 for singles by 2005.

Source: Frederick W. Rumack, national director of tax and legal consulting, Buck Consultants, a leading pension and employee benefits consulting firm, One Pennsylvania Plaza, New York, NY 10119.

Keogh Plans: for the Self-Employed

Keogh plans—retirement plans for people with self-employment income—allow you to make yearly tax-deductible contributions of up to 20% of net earnings from self-employment (as reduced by one-half of the self-employment tax imposed for the year) or $30,000 (whichever is less) to certain defined contribution plans.

If you're nearing retirement age, you may be able to contribute even more using a defined benefit plan, which basically allows you to contribute as much as necessary—even if it is virtually all of your self-employment income—to ensure a set income from the plan in retirement. (Check with your tax adviser.)

Complication: If you set up a Keogh plan for yourself, you must also set one up for your employees. Your employees either must be 100% vested after five years or must gradually vest over seven years, starting after the third year, at 20% annually.

You don't have to be a full-time business owner to qualify for a Keogh. You may contribute up to the deductible limit if you have any self-employment income, including revenue from sideline businesses and freelance and consulting work—just about any income that you report on Schedule C.

Source: Peter I. Elinsky, partner, KPMG Peat Marwick, 2001 M St. NW, Washington, DC 20036.

What to Expect From Your IRA

For years, everyone has been aware of the tax advantages of reducing current income by investing pretax dollars in IRAs. But not everyone appreciates the impact of compounding, a factor that makes IRAs safe vehicles for accumulating wealth.

Even if your IRA contribution is not deductible, the effect of compounding will be impressive. Of course, if your employer doesn't have a pension plan, you may still fund your IRA with pretax dollars, subject to the annual limit of $2,000 for an individual; one-earner couples can contribute up to $4,000 a year. But if you and your spouse are each covered by a pension plan at work, the full $4,000 contribution is deductible only if your combined Adjusted Gross Income (AGI) is $51,000 or less in 1999. A phased-out IRA deduction is permitted for AGIs between $51,000 and $61,000. Once your AGI hits $160,000, any IRA contribution you make is nondeductible, but the earnings will grow tax-deferred. The following chart illustrates the dramatic effect of compounding on IRAs.

FULL ANNUAL CONTRIBUTION: $2,000				
NUMBER OF YEARS	RATE OF RETURN			
	8%	10%	12%	14%
5	$ 11,733	$ 12,210	$ 12,705	$ 13,220
10	28,973	31,874	35,097	38,675
15	54,304	63,544	74,599	87,685
20	91,524	114,550	144,104	182,050
25	146,212	196,694	266,667	363,742
30	226,566	328,988	482,665	713,574

Source: *Geraldine Parrott, certified financial manager, Stifel, Nicolaus & Co., 615 E. Michigan Ave., Suite 400, Milwaukee, WI 53202.*

When Are IRA Contributions Deductible?

Who can make fully deductible contributions:

● **All taxpayers** not covered by a company pension plan at any time during the year. *(Editor's note:* If a spouse is covered, the nonparticipant spouse can make a fully deductible IRA contribution only if the couple's AGI is under $150,000. A partial deductible is allowed for those with an AGI between $150,000 and $160,000.)

● **Single taxpayers** who are covered by a company pension plan but whose AGI is less than $31,000 in 1999.

● **Married taxpayers** who are covered by a company pension plan but whose combined AGI is less than $51,000 in 1999.

Who can make partially deductible contributions:

● **Single taxpayers** who are covered by a company pension plan but whose AGI is $31,000–$41,000.

● **Married taxpayers** who are covered by a company pension plan but whose combined AGI is $51,000–$61,000.

Who can't make any deductible contributions:

● **Single taxpayers** who are covered by a company pension plan and whose AGI is over $41,000.

● **Married couples** whose AGI exceeds $61,000, if both spouses are covered by a company pension.

Editor's note: These figures are for 1999, and will be adjusted annually for the next several years.

Source: *Sheri Robinson, CPA and CFP with The Welch Group, 3940 Montclair Road, Birmingham, AL.*

The Deductibility Loophole

Say you are covered by a company profit-sharing plan, but the company won't make any contribution to the plan this year because it won't make a profit. Can you make a deductible IRA contribution? *Yes.* An individual is not deemed a participant in a profit-sharing plan during a year in which no employer contributions or forfeitures are credited to the individual's account. Thus, if you are not a participant in any other qualified plan, you will be able to make a deductible IRA contribution this year, regardless of the restrictions imposed under tax law.

IRA Strategies After Tax Reform

You cannot make deductible IRA contributions if your Adjusted Gross Income (AGI) is more than $61,000 ($41,000 if you're single) and either you or your spouse are covered by a retirement plan.

If your AGI is between $51,000 and $61,000 (between $31,000 and $41,000 for single taxpayers), you may make partially deductible contributions. If your income is less or if you and your spouse aren't covered by any retirement plan, you may make fully deductible contributions as before.

Nondeductible Contributions

Regardless of your income or plan participation, you may make nondeductible contributions, which grow tax-deferred until withdrawal. The contributions themselves may be withdrawn tax-free, but all earnings taken out are taxed.

Caution: You can't just designate a withdrawal as being made from nondeductible contributions. The law provides a formula for determining which portion of a withdrawal is taxable and which part is nontaxable:

$$\text{Nontaxable percentage of a withdrawal} = \frac{\text{Total nondeductible contributions}}{\text{Total value of all your IRAs}}$$

Example: Your IRAs are worth $48,000, all taxable. You then make a nondeductible contribution of $2,000. Suppose you then decide to withdraw $1,000. The nontaxable percentage of the withdrawal will be $2,000/$50,000, or only 4% ($40). The remaining 96% ($960) will be taxable.

Whether to Make Nondeductible Contributions

The only advantage of a nondeductible IRA is tax-deferred growth. The decision to contribute will depend on your complete financial picture and retirement plan, so it's wise to consult with your financial adviser. *Two points to take into account:*

For younger taxpayers: Nondeductible IRA contributions can be a good investment because the money will have many years to grow free from taxation. But be cautious if you expect to need cash in the near future. Taxable IRA withdrawals made before age 59½ are taxed as ordinary income and

Correcting a Mistake

If you claim an IRA contribution as a deduction on your tax return, then realize that you forgot to actually make the contribution to your IRA, what should you do? File an amended tax return, Form 1040X, for the applicable year, correcting the mistake by omitting the deduction and paying the tax due on the contribution.

You should do this right away, not only to cut off the interest that's running on the underpayment, but also to minimize the risk of incurring tax penalties. If you report the mistake yourself, you will be more likely to avoid penalties for negligence (or fraud) than you will be if the IRS discovers the error on its own. And it probably will discover the mistake eventually, since IRA contributions are reported to the IRS via computer tape by the institutions that receive them.

penalized 10%. Because the nontaxable percentage of early withdrawals is taxed according to the same formula as regular withdrawals, if accumulated earnings and deductible contributions are substantial, an early withdrawal can be expensive. *Exceptions:* The 10% penalty will not apply in certain situations such as distributions from IRAs of up to $10,000 for first-time home buyers and distributions to pay qualified higher-education expenses for taxpayers and dependents. (Income tax will apply, where appropriate.)

For taxpayers closer to retirement: Tax-deferred growth is less valuable. If you already have a sizable IRA, the taxable percentage of any withdrawals is likely to be high. Other investments may be more suitable for retirement funds than nondeductible IRAs. *(Editor's note:* No more than a total of $2,000 can be contributed annually to all IRAs. So, for example, if you are eligible, you may contribute $1,000 to a deductible IRA and another $1,000 to a Roth IRA in the same year.)

New IRA Investments

Certain investments that previously were unappealing or illegal for IRAs are now worth considering, thanks to the new tax law.

● **Gold and silver.** IRAs have been prohibited from investing in precious metals for years. But the law permits investment in some U.S.-issued gold, silver and platinum coins and bullion. Taxpayers who want to hedge against inflation may consider this option.

Source: *Deborah Bourne Allen, senior manager, KPMG Peat Marwick LLP, 2001 M St. NW, Washington, DC 20036.*

Consider a Roth IRA

Regardless of whether you're an active participant in a qualified plan, you may make nondeductible contributions to a Roth IRA as long as your AGI is under $95,000 if you're single, or $150,000 on a joint return. Partial contributions are allowed for singles with an AGI between $95,000 and $110,000, or

THE BEST WAYS TO MAKE YOUR IRA GROW

Don't worry about the taxability of the earnings in your traditional IRA. All growth inside your IRA is tax-deferred, whether or not your original IRA contribution was deductible when you made it. Choose investments that have the best solid long-term growth; tax status is secondary. *(Editor's note: Keep in mind that all income from your deductible IRA is taxed as ordinary income, even if the underlying investment produced capital gains for your account.)*

Decide how much risk you want to take. Choose investments that are very safe or at most have only modest risk. *Not recommended:* High-risk investments of any kind.

The Best Investment Choices

● **Mutual funds.** These are set up by managers who pool many investors' contributions and invest in 50–150 different stocks or bonds. You share proportionately in the income and gains or losses. *Advantages:* You reduce the risk of taking a large loss that could result from putting your entire contribution into one stock or only a few different stocks. You can invest in a mutual fund that has a higher risk/higher growth potential or in one that invests in conservative common stocks with less risk potential. Or you can choose a combination of the two.

Duration of investment: Plan on leaving your IRA in a common-stock mutual fund for at least four years to get the advantage of the long-term growth trend and to reduce the effect of short-term market fluctuations.

What to expect: On the average, common-stock investments have grown at a rate 6% better than the rate of inflation when measured over a period of many years.

● **Self-directed IRAs.** With a self-directed IRA you manage your own investments rather than pooling with others and relying on a professional manager.

Caution: Self-directed IRAs are appropriate only for very experienced and knowledgeable investors. Don't even consider a self-directed IRA unless you know how to choose investments or know how to work

with a broker—and you or your broker has had a successful track record over a long period of time. But if you fit into this category and believe in risk taking, the growth potential may be worth it.

● **Bank money-market accounts and money-market funds.** These are the safest kinds of investments for an IRA and are best for people who don't want to take risks because they are near retirement. You earn interest on the money, and your principal is completely protected.

Bank certificates of deposit are longer-term and usually give you a higher interest rate. However, if interest rates go higher than the rate you are earning, and you take the money out of the certificate before maturity, you will probably be penalized.

Source: *Arnold Corrigan, economist and investment adviser and coauthor (with Phyllis C. Kaufman) of* The No-Nonsense Financial Guide to Understanding IRA, *Longmeadow Press, and author of* How Your IRA Can Make You a Millionaire, *Harmony Books.*

$150,000 and $160,000 on a joint return.

The main advantage of a Roth IRA over traditional IRAs is that funds can remain in the account past age 70½ and continue to build up on a tax-deferred basis. Eventually your heirs will pay income taxes on the funds but can spread out withdrawals over their own life expectancies, thereby adding to tax-deferred buildup of earnings.

If you want to take distributions, you can take your contributions at any time, income-tax- and penalty-free. Earnings from your contributions can also be taken tax-free if they remain in the account for at least five years and you're over age 59½, become disabled or use the funds to pay first-time home-buying expenses (up to $10,000 in a lifetime).

Source: *Barbara Weltman is a tax attorney and the author of several books on business, including* The Complete Idiot's Guide to Making Money After You Retire, *Alpha Books, and* J.K. Lasser's Tax Deduction for Your Small Business, *Macmillan.*

IRA Investments and Capital Gains Rates

With the maximum tax rate on long-term capital gains pegged at 20% (10% for those in the 15% tax bracket on other income), some investment advisers suggest that income-type investments (bonds, money-market funds, CDs) be held inside the IRA and equity-type investments (stocks and stock mutual funds) be held outside the IRA. This will allow your equity investments to be taxed at favorable capital gains rates while earnings in IRAs are taxed as ordinary income when withdrawals are taken. *Note:* For assets acquired after 2000 outside the IRA and held more than five years, an 18% rate applies to gains (8% for those in the 15% bracket on other income).

Caution: Congress is continually adjusting tax brackets and capital gains rates. It may be better to invest for return than plan for tax savings.

Source: *Barbara Weltman is a tax attorney and the author of several books on business, including* The Complete Idiot's Guide to Making Money After You Retire, *Alpha Books, and* J.K. Lasser's Tax Deduction for Your Small Business, *Macmillan.*

Picking the Right Stocks for A Retirement Account

Most IRA investors can make the best use of their retirement funds by putting them into stocks, particularly a family of no-load mutual funds. But the volatility of the stock market means that there are still times when an IRA owner should get out of the market to reduce risk.

How do you determine those times? There is a technique for keeping your eye on only two simple indicators—both of which have to be positive to enter or remain in the stock market.

Follow the Prime Rate

The market's major direction depends in large part on the trend in interest rates and in Federal Reserve Board policy.

The prime rate is especially convenient to use as an indicator because it generally doesn't change frequently (less than once a month, on average). And changes in the prime are hard to miss because they always make headline news. *When to take action:* If the prime is below 8%, a sell signal occurs on the second of two increases in the prime or on an advance of a full percentage point in the rate.

Tracking the prime in the future:

● **If the prime has been climbing but hasn't yet reached 8%,** move into stocks at the first drop in the rate.

● **If the prime is climbing and is 8% or higher**, move into stocks only after two consecutive drops in the rate or a full percentage point drop.

● **If the prime is dropping but is still 8% or higher,** move out of stocks whenever the rate starts to rise again.

Pay Attention to Price Trends
Guidelines:

● **Keep a record** of each weekly close of the *Value Line Composite Index.* You'll usually find the figure in the weekend financial pages of most major newspapers and in *Barron's.*

● **Check to see if the index climbs 4%.** A 4% change, not simply a four percentage point change, on a weekly closing basis indicates a move to stocks.

● **Maintain that position as long as the weekly index doesn't drop 4% or more.**

The price trend indicator is right only about half the time, but stock profits made from the times that it's right are substantial.

If you prefer to switch investments less often than this indicator might provoke, simply increase the "4% rule" to 5% or 6%.

These indicators can be used by the most conservative IRA investors to minimize risk.

How to do it:

● **Wait until both** the prime rate indicator and the price trend indicator signal "buy," choosing stocks over money-market instruments.

This conservative system will occasionally miss an up market, but you'll be able to sleep at night, and you'll be playing the stock market only when the odds are greatly in your favor.

Source: *Martin Zweig, chairman of the Zweig Fund ($370 million under management) and author of* **Martin Zweig's Winning With New IRAs,** *Warner Books.*

IRA Setup and Transfer Fees In Mutual Funds

Most mutual funds charge an annual fee for custodial duties in addition to a fee for setting up an individual retirement account. The custodial fee is a pass-along because of charges by the bank's trust department, which provides the accounting services required by the IRS.

Frequently the largest expense for IRA investors is the transfer fee incurred if they wish to change their IRA from one brokerage or fund to another, from a broker to a mutual fund, etc.

Problem: This entails a change in trusteeship (the bank providing the custodial service). And that can be costly as well as time-consuming. Believe it or not, it often takes three to six months. *Reason:* Those trusteeships were set up with the belief that the accounts would be held there until retirement. The trustees never expected to give up the accounts quickly. To discourage transfers, they require all kinds of information and material from the investor and they charge heavily for making the transfer.

Borrowing From Your IRA

Borrow from an IRA legally by making a short-term loan. Generally, IRA borrowings are prohibited. But it is possible to move funds from one IRA to another, as long as the transfer is completed in a 60-day period. *Benefit:* You have use of the funds for 59 days. *Warning:* The exact amount you take out of the first IRA must be placed in the second one within the 60 days. And you can use this device only once in a 12-month period.

Better transfer method: Roll over your IRA account instead of transferring it directly. In a rollover, you close your account and take personal possession of your IRA money for up to 60 days. You are allowed one rollover per year. All funds, brokers and trustees are set up to do this easily. Rollovers are faster than transfers, and at most firms they are less expensive.

Another way to avoid transfer fees: Use a no-load family of mutual funds. Then, when you are unhappy with the stock market, you can switch into another type of investment fund free of charge, and switch, and switch.

Banking alternative: Banks don't charge fees for setting up IRAs, since they are trustees for themselves. There is, however, a hidden fee. Banks give a lower rate of return on your money. The differential between what an investor can expect to earn in bank certificates of deposit and a growth-stock mutual fund over a 10- to 20-year period is very large. *Estimate:* Banks will average 10%, while growth-stock mutual funds can average 20%.

Source: *William E. Donoghue, publisher of* **Donoghue's On-Line** *(800-982-2455), an electronic mutual-fund performance service.*

Tax Penalties Can Be Avoided

The 10% penalty tax is imposed on early withdrawals (before age 59½) from qualified retirement plans and IRAs. *The penalty does not apply if:*

- **You become permanently disabled.**
- **You withdraw the money as an annuity.**
- **You have reached age 55** and take distributions under an early-retirement provision of the plan (this does not apply to IRAs).
- **You use the funds to pay qualified higher-education expenses.** (This applies only to IRAs).
- **You use the funds to pay health insurance if you are unemployed for at least 12 consecutive weeks.**
- **You use the funds to pay medical expenses in excess of 7.5% of your AGI.**
- **You use the funds to pay first-time home-buying expenses** up to $10,000 in a lifetime. This applies only to IRAs.
- **Distributions are made under a domestic-relations order** (alimony, child support, etc. (This does not apply to IRAs).
- **You take certain types of distributions** from an employee stock ownership plan (ESOP).

Note: The only exception for early withdrawals from a Roth IRA are disability and first-time home-buying expenses.

HOW INFLATION CAN RAVAGE AN IRA

When looking for an investment vehicle for your retirement funds, always remember the disastrous effect inflation can have on those funds. Even low levels of inflation can easily negate the benefits of compounding.

For example, an average inflation rate of just 5% over 35 years will reduce the purchasing power of $1,387,145 to the paltry sum of $344,634. The farther away you are from retirement—or the longer your retirement—the greater the impact.

To avoid this consequence, keep an eye toward growth. Consider using mutual funds as the vehicle for your IRA investment. *Helpful:* Split your $2,000 annual contribution into two parts, with one half invested in a high-quality bond fund and the other half invested in a growth mutual fund.

In alternate years, substitute one of your investments with an investment in a real-estate income program. Your returns should still be relatively high, your risk minimal, and your investment will be hedged against the possible onset of high inflation.

As you approach retirement, begin reducing the amount devoted to the growth portion of your funds—but don't do away with it altogether. Even retired people need protection from the danger of inflation.

Source: Geraldine Parrott, certified financial manager for Stifel, Nicolaus & Co., 615 E. Michigan Ave., Suite 400, Milwaukee, WI 53202.

All About Rollovers

Sometimes the best thing to do with a lump-sum distribution from a qualified pension, profit-sharing or Keogh plan is to roll it over into an IRA, where the funds can grow tax-deferred until they are withdrawn. You have 60 days from the time of the distribution to shelter the money in an IRA rollover. After that, the lump sum is subject to tax as ordinary income (although a five-year forward-averaging option may be available through 1999, or a 10-year averaging for those born before 1936) and the chance for tax-deferred growth is forfeited.

Caution: To avoid income-tax withholding, transfer the lump sum directly from the company plan to the trustee of the IRA.

You can begin withdrawing penalty-free from your IRA at age 59½ and are required to begin distribution by age 70½. Your payout will be calculated on the basis of your life expectancy and can be recalculated each year (or on joint life expectancy

285

if you name a beneficiary such as your spouse). The advantage of this system is that you can draw out money over a longer period of time and have the opportunity to leave a substantial amount of your IRA rollover to your heirs.

Your age, financial requirements, and tax status are important considerations when deciding whether to roll over a lump-sum distribution into an IRA. If you are uncertain of your future financial situation, you may want to roll over only a portion of the funds. You determine how much of the distribution to place in an IRA. The portion not rolled over is immediately taxed.

Unless you specify otherwise, your employer is required to withhold tax on lump-sum distributions at the rate of 20%. If you take the distribution and tax is withheld, you still have two options. First, you can roll over only the cash you receive, but this means you will have to pay ordinary income tax on the amount withheld. Your second option is to roll over the full lump-sum distribution by making up the amount of the withholding tax from other assets. The withheld tax is not lost—it can be either credited against taxes you owe or claimed as a refund on your next income tax return.

Editor's note: You cannot roll over retirement plan distributions directly into a Roth IRA. You must first make a rollover to a traditional IRA. Then, if you are eligible, you may convert the account to a Roth IRA. But you'll have to pay tax on the converted amount (income may be spread over four years if the conversion takes place in 1998).

Source: *Nancy Weinberg, assistant vice president of E. F. Hutton & Company, Inc., 31 W. 54 St., New York, NY 10004.*

Creditors and Retirement Accounts

A pension-plan account may be safe from creditors, but money in an individual retirement account may not be (it depends on state law protection). When Jack Innis declared personal bankruptcy, the court ruled that his creditors could press claims against the money in his IRA. ***Key:*** IRA rules allow the owner of an IRA account to withdraw from it at any time. And since the owner can take money out of the IRA, creditors can too.

Editor's note: After 1999, IRS levies on IRAs to pay taxes will not be subject to the 10% early-withdrawal penalty where the IRA owner is under age $59\frac{1}{2}$.

Source: *Jack Innis, Bank. SD CA., No. 86-01837-LM7*

Double-Rollover Loophole

A woman rolled over a pension distribution into an IRA. Then she withdrew part of this IRA and rolled it over into another IRA. *IRS ruling:* She did not violate the rule against more than one rollover in a year. The once-a-year rule applies only to rollovers from one IRA to another. It does not apply to rollovers of pension distributions. So the taxpayer had made only one rollover subject to the rule.

Source: *IRS Letter Ruling 8651085.*

IRS Rulings on Inheritances and IRAs

● **Beneficiaries can split an inherited IRA.** Three sons inherited their mother's IRA. Each son had different financial circumstances and investment philosophies. The IRS said they could separate the IRA into subaccounts and then have them transferred to different financial institutions. This allows each son to make investment decisions for his share of the mother's IRA. However, each must take disibutions according to the terms of the mother's original IRA.

Source: *IRS Letter Ruling 9810031.*

● **Revocable trust ignored for IRA beneficiary.** A husband set up a revocable trust for his wife's benefit. She named the trust as beneficiary of her IRA and then died. The husband, who was beneficiary of the trust, wanted to roll the funds to his own IRA (to obtain greater tax deferral). The IRS ruled that he could revoke the trust since he created it. However, he had to roll the funds from the trust to an IRA within 60 days of the trust's receipt of funds.

Source: *IRS Letter Ruling 9811008.*

● **Beneficiary loses deferral option because of bank's failure to notify him or her.** A beneficiary (other than a spouse) cannot roll over an inherited IRA to his or her own IRA but can elect to have the inherited IRA taxed to the beneficiary over his or her life expectancy. This election must be made within one year after the death of the IRA owner. When a bank did not notify the IRA owner's brother of the existence of the inherited IRA until four years after the owner's death, the IRS ruled it was too late to make the election.

Source: *IRS Letter Ruling 9812034.*

Winning Retirement Spots

Many of us hope that snow shovels, galoshes and earmuffs will be things of the past when we reach our "golden" years. And unless you're one of those hearty individuals who can't wait for the first nip of frost, a white Christmas and sweet sap running from the maples, you're probably dreaming that your magic retirement address will be somewhere in the Sunbelt. But instead of following the crowd, you may be hoping to find a more private haven.

Using a combination of standards—including cost of living, crime rate, temperature and humidity, air quality, housing, medical facilities and cultural and recreational activities—we arrived at the leading candidates.

North Carolina

Tryon: This little city is called Shangri-la by some of its residents. It's in the western end of the state, in the Appalachian Highlands. But don't assume it's in the sticks just because it's off the beaten track. About half its residents are retired, sophisticated people from all parts of the U.S. and the world, representing both business and the arts. Its Fine Arts Center is home to theater, art, music, and films.

One feature that attracts people to Tryon is its weather. It's in a thermal belt that makes its weather uniquely comfortable year-round. With mountains to the north and east, it's sheltered from the cold. But since it's exposed to the south, warm air swaddles the area in a temperature inversion that keeps the temperature relatively stable from summer to winter. Sun is plentiful, making it a gardener's delight, with the growing season lasting about 200 days. That creates an abundance of fresh farm and orchard produce.

Sports facilities are abundant, too: Well-lighted tennis courts, a year-round swim club, two golf courses, horseback riding, hiking, and even special "enrichment centers" that provide game and craft activities for retired residents. Housing is more than adequate. Medical facilities are also good, and comparatively inexpensive.

Georgia

Jekyll Island: This community is one of the three so-called "Golden Isles" off the Georgia coast. It used to be a retreat where the Rockefellers, Morgans, Goulds and Vanderbilts built "cottages." Although the island has been converted into a public park, private homes are available under an unusual arrangement: You can buy a house, but the land upon which it sits must be rented (on a 99-year lease) from the state.

The weather is moderate. And although the island occasionally has snow, it's not unusual to be able to have Christmas dinner outdoors in shirtsleeves.

Medical facilities are superior. Living costs are moderate. If you fish for your supper, which many do, and frequent the local farm stands, grocery bills will be even lower.

Florida

Mount Dora: This community lies right in the so-called "Retirement Belt," near Orlando (which is close to Disney World and the Space Center). Yet it's thousands of miles away in other respects. Mount Dora is the New England of the South, nestled among hills and lakes on a bluff overlooking Lake Dora. It boasts huge oak trees and lantern lampposts (one reason that it's also called the Antique Center of central Florida).

The weather is splendid, averaging 61°F in the winter, 70° in April and October, and 82° in July. Health-care facilities are excellent.

Housing is attractive and not expensive. Rentals are modest.

Culture is not ignored. There are regular theater and musical programs, and sports activities are varied.

The population is about 50% retired, many coming from New England and the Midwest.

Alabama

Fairhope: This town is on the Gulf coast, built on high bluffs overlooking Mobile Bay. It's noted for its magnificent waterfront, breathtaking views and thriving artists' colony. Although the weather is mild, Fairhope is one of the southernmost points in the U.S. that still have four distinct seasons (July's temperature average is only 82°F, while January's is 54°). Because it's a coastal town, humidity is high (average, 70%), but refreshing winds travel up from the Gulf of Mexico. As a result, it is a gardener's paradise.

Living costs are low. Housing is abundant and modest. Some of the building lots can be rented (with a 99-year lease), which keeps building costs down.

Fairhope is a cultural center. It has a well-stocked library, a summer theater, and an active art association where art classes are conducted.

Medical facilities are exceptional. About 15 doctors live in town.

Louisiana

Covington: This lovely town is only a half-hour ride from New Orleans and right in the middle of the so-called "Ozone Belt" (a pine-covered section north of Lake Pontchartrain, considered by many to be one of the world's most healthful regions). The land is above sea level and remains cooler than New Orleans in the summer. Although winters are mild, there are occasional cold snaps with snow. The mean temperature in January is 55°F, in July, 80°. Autumn days have the crispness of New England, and the leaves turn orange and gold.

Home prices range widely.

Medical facilities here are exceptionally good.

The area has a well-rounded cultural program, independent of nearby New Orleans.

Texas

Kerrville: Kerrville is in the Texas hill country, site of the late President Johnson's LBJ Ranch. The area is high (elevation, 1,650 feet) and surrounded by cedar and oak. The weather is on the cool side, averaging 63°F in the summer and 47° in the winter.

One-third of the residents are retired, and they initiate most of the area's cultural activities.

The medical facilities are modern.

The nearest big city is San Antonio, which, despite the presence of skyscrapers, has a small-town atmosphere.

New Mexico

Roswell: Roswell is in the middle of the state's retirement center. Summer temperatures average 77°F, with low humidity (30% in the midafternoon). Nighttime temperatures often drop to freezing, but since the sun shines 70% of the time, the days warm up quickly. In this wide-open country you can drive for hours without seeing a house. Roswell is the largest town in the area, an urban oasis in the desert.

Although the town has the best medical facilities in

> **"Unless you...can't wait for the first nip of frost, a white Christmas and delicious, sweet sap running from the maples, you're probably dreaming that your magic retirement address will be somewhere in the Sunbelt."**

the area, they are not quite as good as those of the other areas mentioned in this article.

Housing is inexpensive. The many cultural activities include a symphony orchestra and a little theater.

Arizona

Prescott: In the middle of the state—about an hour's drive from metropolitan Phoenix—Prescott is in excellent skiing country. Many wealthy people have "cabins" in the area.

A major attraction of the city is its healthful air. With an elevation of 5,354 feet, Prescott is a haven for people with respiratory problems.

But beware: Living in an area a mile high takes some getting used to, even if you're young. A couple of beers can leave you feeling pretty tipsy because of the altitude.

The weather is just about perfect. Summers average about 70°F, with a high of 87°. At night it dips to the 50s. In winter, the temperature swings from nearly 60° to freezing. Humidity hovers near 50%, so cold or hot, Prescott is comfortable.

Prescott has a reputation as a health center, since its medical facilities are unusually good.

Living costs in general are not cheap, because nearly everything must be shipped from Phoenix. A state income tax runs about 10% of the federal tax. Housing is abundant, with most people living in cabin-type homes in the woods. Some rentals are available.

About 25% of the area's residents are retired. The sports facilities are varied and abundant because the climate is so invigorating. The area is big on arts and crafts, and a junior college offers extension courses.

California

Hemet: Midway between Los Angeles and San Diego (about a 90-minute drive to either), it's distant enough to avoid the smog and the congestion of L.A., yet close enough for a day trip. With year-round sun, it specializes in growing avocados (you can raise them in your backyard) and in housing retirees escaping the big-city life. Because it's warm and dry, many people with rheumatism and respiratory ailments come to Hemet.

Summers are warm, with an average high of 95°F, but the low humidity makes it comfortable. April, the coldest month, posts an average high of 65°.

Living costs are lower than in other areas of Southern California. Local foods sell at roadside stands for a fraction of supermarket prices.

Medical facilities are quite adequate.

The well-planned town has many civic boosters. As a result, despite its recent growth, there's no congestion or serious suburban problems. Because the area is flat, it's perfect for bicycling. Although Hemet is not a high-culture center, adult education is popular.

The Benefits of Early Retirement

Collecting Social Security early can pay off. Even though benefits are reduced, they'll usually add up to more in the long run. *Example:* If full benefits are $750 per month for retiring at age 65, you can get reduced benefits of $600 a month by retiring at age 62. You'd have to collect full benefits for 12 years to make up the $21,600 you'd receive during the three years of early payments.

Source: Changing Times, *Washington, DC.*

The Overview

Large metropolitan areas with the best retirement ratings are in Southern California—the Anaheim-Santa Ana-Garden Grove and San Diego areas.

For medium-sized metropolitan areas there are Austin (Texas) and Santa Barbara (California).

For small metropolitan areas, two Texas towns, Midland and Tyler, get excellent ratings.

That's not to say other areas should be avoided. But generally they have one or more drawbacks that keep them out of the top groupings—and out of the mainstream of those hurrying to find a retirement home.

Still, some people's blemishes are other people's beauty spots. Not everybody agrees that Southern California and Texas are the Edens of Retirementville.

Source: Peter A. Dickinson, author of Sunbelt Retirement, *a survey of the best cities in the Sunbelt to consider for retirement. He is also the author of two related books,* Travel and Retirement Edens Abroad *and* Retirement Edens Outside the Sunbelt. *(All three books are out of print.)*

WORKING AFTER RETIREMENT

Many retirees would like to keep working after retirement, at least part-time. But those who want to work for financial reasons should be aware of these drawbacks:

● **You can work and still collect Social Security benefits,** but if you are 65–69 or older, for every $3 earned above a government-determined ceiling, you lose $1 in benefits ($15,500 in 1999). Lower limits apply to those under 65. There's no limit for those 70 and older. When you add your commuting costs, job-related expenses, and payroll deductions, you may find part-time work doesn't pay off.

● **If you continue working part-time for the same company,** you may not be eligible to collect your pension. One way around this, if the company will go along, is to retire as an employee and return as a freelancer. Since you're now self-employed, your pension won't be affected.

Editor's note: If you work full-time or part-time, you may be able to make Roth IRA contributions. There's no age limit for making these nondeductible contributions based on your earnings. The annual limit: $2,000. However, your AGI must be below a set amount to qualify for making contributions.

Source: William W. Parrott, a chartered financial consultant, Creative Retirement Planning, 1 Hollow Lane, Suite 306-B, Lake Success, NY 11042.

Safeguards When Retiring Abroad

● **Protect your dollar assets.** Maintain assets in U.S. institutions and forward the funds as needed. High inflation, even in comparatively cheap countries, can destroy a nest egg with horrible speed.

● **Wills can be especially tricky for overseas retirees.**

Best move: Have two wills—one for U.S. assets, the other for foreign assets. This strategy will avoid the possibility of international cross-claims that could complicate disposal of the estate.

● **Plan for health insurance.** Blue Cross and Blue Shield protect travelers but not expatriates. But there are several types of international health-insurance policies, and many countries have local insurance plans similar to those of Blue Cross and Blue Shield.

● **Medicaid and Medicare don't extend coverage beyond the United States.**

● **Many countries let foreign residents take advantage** of their government-run health plans, which offer medical care at little or no cost. (*Countries with first-class medical care:* Australia, Barbados, Canada, Costa Rica, Israel, and most European countries.)

Delayed Bonus

An executive retired knowing that he had earned a $20,000 bonus under a company incentive plan. But under the plan's terms, the bonus wouldn't be paid until January of the year following his retirement. *IRS ruling:* The bonus will be treated as earned income in the year the executive receives it, even though he'll be retired in that year. Thus, the executive can use the bonus to make an IRA contribution for that year, even if he doesn't work at all during the year.

Source: IRS Letter Ruling 8707051.

Putting Money Into an IRA After Age 70½

You have to start your withdrawals from your traditional IRA no later than April 1 of the calendar year following the year in which you reach age 70½. *(Exception:* the Roth IRA does not require minimum distributions to begin at age 70½.) The minimum withdrawal depends on your life expectancy or the combined life expectancy of you and your beneficiary. (The IRS has actuarial tables that determine the life expectancy you must figure on.) However, you might be able to put more funds into the IRA at the same time you make your withdrawals. *Example:* A retiring executive expects to receive a lump-sum distribution from his firm's profit-sharing plan when he reaches age 72 or 73. He asked the IRS if he could roll it over into an IRA. *IRS ruling:* Yes. He can put the full amount in (and thereby defer taxes on it). But he must immediately take part of it back out.

Source: Revenue Ruling 85-153.

Forced Retirement: Know Your Rights

Accepting early retirement may not bar an employee from subsequently suing a company and alleging that he or she was a victim of age discrimination. *Recent case:* A 54-year-old assistant vice president at an insurance company was told that if he did not accept the company's early-retirement offer, he faced being terminated. *Court:* Such a "Hobson's choice" can be tantamount to firing, opening the way for a substantial damage award.

Source: Smith v. World Insurance Co., *USCA Eighth, 10/17.*

All Retirement Plans Are Not Necessarily the Same

A retirement plan for disabled employees does *not* have to provide the same benefits as a conventional length-of-service retirement plan sponsored by the same employer. The difference in benefit levels between the two plans is not a violation of the Americans with Disabilities Act (ADA), says the EEOC. In fact, the only ADA requirement is that a length-of-service plan not discriminate against disabled employees.

Source: Robert A. Maroldo, editor in chief, Disability Compliance Bulletin, *747 Dresher Rd., Box 980, Horsham, PA 19044.*

Retirement-Savings Mistake

Many employees over age 40 who leave their companies use their lump-sum 401(k) distribution checks to pay bills.

Problems: If you're under age 59½, the lump sum will be taxed as much as 50%—and you will have spent your retirement savings. *Better:* Always move the lump sum into a rollover IRA or a new 401(k) plan. If you need money, take out a home-equity loan or a 401(k) loan, or explore taking monthly distributions from your IRA—without tax penalty.

Source: Anthony Gallea, senior portfolio manager at Smith Barney in Pittsford, NY, and author of The Lump Sum Handbook, *Prentice Hall.*

> "[When leaving your company], always move your lump-sum 401(k) distribution check into a rollover IRA or a new 401(k) plan [to avoid tax penalties]."

Insurance Tactics
& Strategies

10

How to Pick an Insurance Company

Your number one consideration as you're selecting an insurance company should be its financial strength. Buying insurance (especially life and health insurance) is—we all hope—a long-term proposition. You want to be sure that the company you are buying it from will be healthy for many years.

Nevertheless, most people fail to verify the strength and stability of the company they are choosing. It has taken the failure of several firms to drive home the point that not all insurance companies are created equal. But analyzing a company on your own is virtually impossible. Their statements are inscrutable, even to accountants without special training. Leave the analysis up to the professionals.

The Rating Firms

Five rating firms evaluate the strength of life-health insurance companies and publish ratings: A.M. Best (908-439-2200), Duff & Phelps (312-629-3833), Moody's (212-553-0300), Standard & Poor's (212-208-8000) and Weiss Ratings (800-289-9222). Consumers should be aware that ratings can change (either up or down) in a short time, so it's best to get current updates by phone.

A rating is an expression of the rating firm's opinion about the strength of a company. The higher the rating, the greater the likelihood the company will fail.

The opinions of rating firms about a company's strength are often similar, but opinions sometimes differ. For that reason, you should check all the available ratings of a company that interests you. *Helpful:* You should also read the rating firms' reports about a company. A report may consist of only a few pages, but often it provides useful insight into the company's strength.

Helpful Guidance

To understand what a rating means, you need to know where it fits among a rating firm's categories. *Example:* A+ looks like a top rating, and it is Weiss' highest category. However, it is Best's second category, Duff & Phelp's fifth category, and Standard & Poor's fifth category. Similarly, A1 looks like a top rating, but it is Moody's fifth category.

Quality of Service

Financial stability is not necessarily an indicator of how fast or well a company pays claims. The best way to gauge the service of an insurance company is to find out how satisfied its current customers are. Unfortunately, there is no comprehensive nationwide ranking.

The best alternative: A few state insurance commissions publish "complaint ratios" for companies licensed to operate within their borders. These give consumers some indication of the kind of service a company will provide. *Example:* Each year, the Illinois Department of Insurance issues pamphlets that compare the number of complaints made against each insurance company with the dollar value of the premiums the company has written in the state. Each figure is listed separately. The companies are then ranked, from the best to the worst, in terms of complaint ratios.

The Illinois Department of Insurance offers four complaint-ratio pamphlets: Automobile, Homeowner's, Life and Accident & Health. They are available from the Illinois Department of Insurance, 320 W. Washington St., Springfield, IL 62767.

If you do not live in a state that publishes complaint ratios, you can use another state's listing as a guide. A company that offers poor service in one state is unlikely to do much better in another. Some states list all calls to their insurance departments as "complaints," however. Check to be certain lists are for complaints only, and don't include consumer questions as well, which could be misleading.

> " You should...read the rating firms' reports about a company. [It] may... only [be] a few pages, but...it gives... insight into the company's strength. "

Source: Joseph M. Belth, publisher of "The Insurance Forum," a newsletter for the insurance industry. He is professor emeritus of insurance at Indiana University and author of Life Insurance: A Consumer's Handbook, *Indiana University Press.*

PROTECTION FROM UNREALISTIC EXPECTATIONS AND SALES ILLUSTRATION GAMES

Cash-value life insurance remains one of the few investments whose earnings can build up tax-free and that can protect your family from the financial consequences of your untimely death.

But be wary. In the scramble to persuade you to buy their products, some life insurance companies and their agents are using misleading sales techniques and aggressive investment practices that have turned once boring (but usually safe) policies into high-risk gambles. *How to measure risks:* The first thing to understand is that sales illustrations are not projections or guarantees.

● **Using "unguaranteed" rates of return that are higher than current market rates.** The government bond market may be paying 7½%, but the insurance agent shows you an illustration using an unguaranteed rate of 10%–11%. Or the agent uses illustrations based on "past experience," for example, choosing interest rates from years ago, when rates were much higher, without showing what is currently being credited.

Protection: Find out if the company pays a guaranteed rate and what it is. Ask the salesperson to rework the illustration using current market rates.

● **Illustrating nonguaranteed results for unreasonable lengths of time.** Salespeople who guess at future interest rates may add to the deception by extending the illustration to periods as long as 40 years. *Result:* Expected earnings will be greatly exaggerated. The difference between 7% and 10% annual rates of return compounded over 40 years can be enormous.

Protection: Ask for demonstrations using realistic rates for shorter periods of time—say, 10 years and 15 years.

● **Offering high first-year interest rates.** Some companies entice buyers by inflating the first year's interest rate, then reducing the rate in following years. Because of high expenses in the first year, during that time there is usually little cash in the policy to earn the tantalizing interest.

Protection: Find out exactly how much of your first-year premium will be eaten up by expenses and commissions and how much will be left to earn interest. Ask how the company is crediting rates on older policies.

Dangerous Investment Strategies

With competition so intense, some companies are wooing buyers by offering high rates of return on even their most conservative fixed-rate products.

Danger: They may have turned to increasingly risky investment practices to sustain these rates:

● **Investing in low-quality, high-yield bonds.** In the old days, insurance companies invested in conservative government and top-rated corporate securities. In the 1980s, some companies turned to higher-risk, higher-yield bonds. That trend has reversed, but conservative rates mean lower returns.

Protection: Request a copy of the company's investment portfolio to see what percentage is devoted to bonds rated BB or lower. There is reason for caution if junk bonds comprise over 10%–15% of the company's portfolio.

● **Investing in longer-term securities—such as 30-year bonds.** *Better:* less volatile short-term securities, such as five- to 10-year bonds. Although long-term bonds pay higher rates than short-term bonds, the value of a long-term bond declines much more rapidly than the value of a short-term bond if interest rates increase, causing returns to diminish. If they fall significantly, dissatisfied policyholders might surrender their policies to take advantage of higher rates elsewhere. *Likely consequence:* The insurance company would be forced to raise cash quickly by selling its investments at depressed prices—which would further reduce its returns and threaten its financial security.

Protection: Find out the average maturity of the company's investment portfolio. Any term that is longer than seven to 10 years is cause for concern.

Source: Charles Rohm, senior vice president, The Principal Financial Group, Des Moines, IA. The firm provides a wide range of financial services, including insurance for individuals and corporations, pensions, 401(k) plans and residential mortgages.

Answers to Challenging Insurance Questions

Despite everything you have read about insurance, buying any type of policy need not be complicated or expensive. Shrewd consumers only have to remember two rules:

● **Seek protection against catastrophes**—not inconveniences.

● **The more completely your needs are covered**—instead of having partial coverage through various policies—the better the deal.

Answers to today's big insurance questions:

When does it make sense to drop a cash-value life insurance policy and buy term instead? Cash-value policies have two parts—a savings account and life insurance protection that can last until you're 100 years old. As a result, these policies—sometimes known as whole-life policies—cost a lot more than term insurance, which only provides insurance coverage for a set period of time. They are also more confusing.

What to do: If your cash-value policy doesn't pay dividends, you might want to drop it and buy a term policy. Call your insurer or agent to find out if it pays dividends on your policy.

If your cash-value policy pays dividends, the answer becomes complicated. If you've held the policy for two or three years, there may not be much cash value to withdraw from the policy. Typically, much of your premium in each of the first few years goes toward the agent's commission and other charges. There will also likely be a surrender fee, even if you change policies with the same insurer.

You have to assess how much you'll be losing and what you'll be saving to see if it's worth the switch. *Rule of thumb:* For a one-income family with two children, insurance would have to cover five to seven times annual earnings.

Do I really need disability protection if my company already provides me with coverage? It's quite likely that you need additional coverage. Very few employers provide enough long-term disability coverage.

Corporate disability policies often don't start until six months after you are disabled—and pay a percentage of your salary. While the amount is certainly better than nothing, it's too often not enough. If you have a company-provided disability policy, you need to supplement it.

Drawback: Disability coverage can be expensive. A policy that provides replacement for $50,000 in annual income can cost $600 or $700 a year. You can cut this in half by increasing the *elimination period*—the waiting time before benefits start—to six months rather than 30 or 60 days. This is the point at which you should tie in your starting date of coverage to what your employer offers.

Don't try to cut costs by buying a policy that won't pay benefits if you can perform "any job" rather than your own occupation. In such cases, if you are a doctor, for example, and can perform menial work, you won't qualify for benefits.

> "Do [you] really need disability protection if [your] company already provides [it]? It's quite likely.... Very few employers provide enough long-term disability coverage."

Warning: Disability coverage is one of the areas in which insurance companies tend to sell you too little insurance.

Policies are to replace the income you have lost because of disability—not to make you rich. Insurers worry that some policyholders may not hurry back to work if they have excessive coverage.

How do I know if I have enough homeowner's insurance? Most homeowner's insurance companies automatically increase your premium—and coverage—each year to keep pace with rising real estate values and construction costs. They say the increases protect policyholders against inflation should the need to rebuild arise.

Problem: Most policy increases reflect *average estimated costs* in a region. Real estate values and construction costs can vary between neighborhoods.

Solution: Every three years, determine the current repair value of your house (excluding land value), and compare it with your insurance coverage. If you're insuring for a high home value, ask your insurer not to

INSURANCE YOU SHOULDN'T WASTE YOUR MONEY ON

The best rule when purchasing insurance: Buy only comprehensive policies that will protect you against all catastrophic economic eventualities in a particular category.

Piecemeal policies leave gaps in coverage. After years of paying premiums, you get absolutely nothing if your accident or illness falls between the policies' provisions. In addition, piecemeal coverage is always more expensive than comprehensive coverage.

Policies to avoid:

● **Cancer insurance.** If you wind up in a hospital or bedridden at home, you'll want to collect for *any* disease.

● **Air-travel life insurance.** Fear of flying aside, this is a terrible deal statistically. If you have a dependent, you need good life insurance to cover any cause of death. Besides, your survivors can sue an airline.

● **Accident life insurance.** Will your survivors need more money if you die in an accident rather than from natural causes?

● **Automobile medical insurance.** Your comprehensive health plan will cover your medical expenses, while auto liability coverage will take care of your passengers.

● **Rental-car insurance.** When you had to assume only a $500 deductible, this was easy to ignore. Now that the deductible is commonly $3,000, it's a tougher call. But before you fork over an exorbitant $17 a day (to cover liability and physical damage to the car), call your agent. Your current auto policy may already cover cars you rent.

● **Credit insurance.** This policy pays off loans in the event of your death—for a usurious fee.

Example:

A three-year policy on a $5,000 loan costs $144 in annual premiums, for average coverage of only $2,500. (Coverage decreases as the loan is repaid.) But a 40-year-old man can buy $250,000 in annual renewable term life insurance for $350 a year—100 times the coverage for less than triple the premium.

● **Mortgage insurance.** Again, annual renewable term is a superior deal. With mortgage policies, your coverage slides as your debt declines. With term life insurance, your coverage is constant—unless you choose to reduce it to cut your premiums.

Source: *J. Robert Hunter, director of insurance, Consumer Federation of America, 1424 16 St. NW, Washington, DC 22207.*

raise the premium. If the cost to rebuild exceeds your current protection, raise your coverage.

Source: *Robert Hunter, director of insurance, Consumer Federation of America, 1424 16 St. NW, Washington, DC 20036.*

Life Insurance Savvy

If you find that you need more life insurance, don't replace your current policy with a bigger new one. Instead, keep your current policy and supplement it with a small second policy.

An insurance agent may try to sell you an all-inclusive new policy to replace your existing one, claiming that you will get a greater rate of return, among other benefits.

Trap: A bigger new policy actually benefits the agent, not you. The bigger the policy, the bigger the agent's commission. You will have to pay for that as well as new administrative costs before you get any return. In addition, the new policy may have higher premiums and exclude some causes of death covered in the old policy.

Source: *Robert Hunter, director of insurance, Consumer Federation of America, 1424 16 St. NW, Washington, DC 20036.*

Insurance You May Not Know You Own

● **A homeowner's policy usually covers** stolen purses and wallets, lost luggage, and property taken in a car break-in. It also may cover many offbeat accidents, such as damage to a power mower borrowed from a neighbor; trees, shrubs, fences or tombstones;

damages by vandals or motor vehicles; and property lost or damaged while moving.

- **$25,000 in travel life insurance is provided if** a ticket is bought on an American Express, Diners Club or Carte Blanche card.
- **American Automobile Association** (AAA) members have automatic hospital and death benefits if hurt in a car accident.
- **Many clubs and fraternal organizations** have life and health benefits.
- **It's possible to collect twice on car accident injuries,** once through health insurance and again through the medical payments provision of auto insurance.
- **Family health policies usually cover children away at college.** Check before buying separate policies for them.

The Secrets of Avoiding— or Fighting—Bad Ratings

The discovery that an insurance company is charging you extra for an individual health, life or disability insurance policy can be infuriating—especially when you're not told why. Almost 10% of all health, life and disability insurance applicants are hit with extra charges (ratings, in insurance jargon) for medical or moral reasons.

What They Can Pin on You

- **Health problems,** such as high blood pressure or obesity—which you may have had years ago and since resolved.
- **Drug or alcohol abuse.** Occasional use is easily exaggerated by malicious colleagues or neighbors.
- **Psychiatric conditions.** Even light therapy may make extracautious underwriters nervous about your mental stability.
- **Criminal associations.** If a relative or close friend is a known member of organized crime, you're considered a greater risk.
- **Homosexuality.** Not just because of AIDS, but merely for moral reasons.

In-Depth Investigation

When you sign an insurance application, you give an insurance company permission to undertake a thorough investigation of your medical, social and financial history. When they delve into your past, insurance companies look for consistency—a straight story. They ask the same questions of several sources and ask each source the same question three or four times

TROUBLE WITH A CLAIM?

Before a Claim

Before you have a claim, it is a good idea to read your insurance policy closely. Write a letter to the company informing it of what you think the policy covers. If you are right, it will tell you. If you are wrong, it should say so—you can then ask the company to change the situation, or choose to go to another company.

If there is ultimately a problem with a claim, the courts should hold any ambiguous language in the policy in your favor, since the insurance company wrote it and you were stuck with the language. Further, the courts look to the "reasonable expectation" of the insured when a claim occurs. State your expectations in writing up front when you first purchase coverage, and they will more than likely be binding later.

Also, know what you are insuring before a claim: Keep detailed records of what you own and their condition. For example, make records of the condition in which you keep your car. Then, if an accident occurs, you will be able to prove that the car was in excellent shape. Make an inventory of your home. It's surprising how many important items people are not able to recall after a fire. Document ownership with photos to give the claims adjuster sufficient evidence. All valuables should also be documented with sales slips or periodic appraisals. Be sure to keep these records in a safe-deposit box or at work—records are not much good if they're destroyed along with the contents of your home.

After a Claim

- **Do not sign any insurance company releases without careful consideration.** *Document everything that happens first:* When did the insured event occur? What were the circumstances? Who are the witnesses? When did you inform the agent or company? Whom did you talk to? What did that person tell you?

from different angles. The more inconsistency they find, the more they dig. *Sources:*

● **You.** When filling out applications or answering questions at medical examinations, keep it simple. Make yourself as small a target as possible.

Important: If you hide a condition that later forces you to make a claim within the so-called "contestability period"—usually one to two years—an insurance company will cancel your policy because you have misrepresented yourself. For example, if you hide a known heart condition and die of cardiac arrest six months later, your life insurance policy will be canceled and your family will collect only a half year of returned premiums.

● **Your doctor.** Ask your physician to examine your medical file to see if it conveys an accurate picture of your current physical condition. If an item could be misconstrued, ask the doctor to attach an explanatory note.

● **References.** Insurance companies usually ask for an accountant, a friend, and a business associate. Pick carefully.

● **Your agent** must file a report on you but is unlikely to be a problem, since an agent is always interested in making the sale.

● **Information-gathering services** investigate you, looking for both medical and moral problems.

(Most companies now use Equifax.)

● **The Medical Information Bureau** (MIB) compiles information on previous insurance applications and claims in search of special health situations.

Knowing You're Rated

All your careful efforts notwithstanding, you've been rated if:

● **You are rejected outright for coverage.**

● **The premium charged is higher**—or the benefits less—than your agent originally quoted. With disability insurance, terms may be less favorable.

● **Your policy arrives with the words *rating* or *modified benefit* printed on the page where your name appears.**

● **You are required to sign a rider or an amendment.**

Fighting Back

You must refute the existing underwriting records. An insurance company's information may be completely mistaken or, more likely, out of perspective —old, exaggerated or misinterpreted. Unfortunately, the nature of the negative information will not always be volunteered. The law requires, however, that an insurance company surrender the rea-

● **Keep a complete record of each contact with the insurance company.** Your ability to have a claim paid will be directly proportional to the quality of your record keeping. If the company tries to delay or reduce the size of the claim, you will be able to document what is happening and will have the evidence you need to appeal higher up in the company or to the state insurance department or, if need be, to court.

If you go to a lawyer, you will not only have a better chance in court with good evidence, but if the insurance company gives you an abusive runaround, you may also be entitled to sue for punitive damages in some states. Before you sue, though, which could take a long time and be costly, consider other help. Call the National Insurance Consumer Helpline (800-942-4242). It will refer you to sources of help, answer basic questions and contact company consumer divisions on your behalf.

Complaints should be directed first to the company (write to the president). Be reasonable, but don't believe everything the insurance company tells you. If that avenue of relief fails, appeal to the state insurance department. Be brief and factual. Clearly state the relief you want. If you do not get a satisfactory response from the state and the money is significant, you may have to be prepared to go to an attorney.

Source: J. Robert Hunter, director of insurance, Consumer Federation of America, 1424 16 St. NW, Washington, DC 22207.

son for a rating to you—
or your doctor, if medically
oriented—upon written
request.

A good agent can
make your case to the
company. *Advantage:* If
the agents are respected,
their arguments will carry
more weight.

● **Medical situations.**
Generally, you or your agent will
have to present a letter and test
results from a doctor to the company's medical director. Suppose
you had high blood pressure
when you first applied for insurance, but that was because of
stress on your old job. If a physician can show that you no longer
have this condition, the company
may reconsider.

Trap: The insurance company
may have received information
from your physician with a
request that it be kept from you.
You won't get that information
from the insurance company. You
will be told, however, that the
rating is based on confidential
information from your doctor.

● **Moral ratings.** These are
even harder to fight. Often, you will not be told the
exact source of a bad reference. You will just get a
very general statement. Such sources may be vindic-
tive or mentally unbalanced.

While you won't have an opportunity to answer
these charges directly, the Fair Credit Reporting Act
does give you the right to make the insurance company and its sources recheck their facts. This
shouldn't take more than two or three weeks.

If the charge is proven wrong, the insurance company will probably correct its files. If the charges are
based on opinion rather than fact, have your own
response placed along with the allegations in your
file. Ask the company to talk with other sources.
Give the company personal references.

Mistakes in Filing Property Claims

● **Failure to accurately calculate losses.** It's hard to believe,
but many people can't accurately determine their losses—whether by
damage or theft. They fail to maintain effective accounting and record-
retention procedures to document the losses. It's not uncommon to
hear of a situation where a theft loss amounted to $250,000, but the
claimant could only substantiate $100,000 of the loss. It's important to
plan ahead with your accountant to determine the best procedures for
demonstrating what you own, should you have to make a claim.

● **Overstating the loss.** This is a subtle problem. If a claimant
purposely overstates the loss to the point where the insurance
company could question his or her integrity, the company will take a
hard line. Generally, if the claimant takes a fair position, the insurer will
still bargain over the loss claim but will be more reasonable.

● **Underestimating the loss.** This sounds like a contradiction of
the above, but it's not. Immediately after losses are claimed, an adjuster
will ask the claimant for an estimate of the damage, not an accurate,
justified number. The insurer requires such a rough estimate, but be wary
of providing a number before taking time to get a reliable estimate. If the
adjuster reports a number that's too low and then must go back later to
the insurer and restate it much higher, his or her credibility and yours
are hurt, making future loss negotiations tricky. So tell the adjuster
about any problems in coming up with a number.

Battling an insurance company requires patience
and dedication. However, if you make enough noise,
and with good reason, your chances of erasing a
costly insurance rating are very good.

Source: *Leonard B. Stern, president, Leonard B. Stern & Co., an
insurance and consulting firm, 305 Madison Ave., New York, NY 10165.*

You Can Avoid a Physical Exam

Insurance medical exams are being abandoned by
some insurance companies, even for $100,000–
$200,000 term insurance sales, according to a major
insurance broker. The reasons are the high cost of the
exams and the poor reliability of the information

given by those seeking insurance. Even the best exams, say the insurers, protect them for only about six months anyway. They often rely on a medical history taken by the insurance broker. They may also request an electrocardiogram and a chest X ray.

Finding a Lost Insurance Policy

Hundreds of life insurance policyholders die each year and their named beneficiaries either don't know they are beneficiaries or can't find the policies. If you suspect that you are the beneficiary of a lost policy, don't expect a life insurance company to volunteer the information. The search is up to you.

Check the obvious places first: the box with the tax records, the desk with the cubbyholes full of papers and the safe-deposit box. Talking to family lawyers and insurance agents helps, too. If you don't find what you're looking for, try these other sources of leads:

● **Checkbooks.** Check stubs often tell the tale. Keep alert for checks made out not only to insurance companies but also to trusts, trade associations, alumni organizations and individual agents.

● **Employers.** Company personnel offices can provide information on benefit plans, including voluntary programs, life insurance and severance benefits. Their computers or files can quickly determine who the employee chose as a beneficiary if they know of a policy.

● **Supplemental life insurance agents.** They may have had contact with your loved one in or out of the workplace. They usually remember their prospective clients well.

● **Money orders.** Try the company credit union, the local bank or even the drugstore to find out if a money order was purchased to pay for an insurance policy.

● **Insurance agents.** Anyone in the insurance business—friends, acquaintances from religious organizations, relatives or neighbors of the deceased—can be a source of facts.

● **Old policy applications.** These are always a good place to look because they contain a list of previously owned insurance.

● **Veterans Administration.** Check for National Service Life Insurance.

● **Relatives.** Older members of the family may recall a policy taken out as a present.

● **Loan documentation.** Frequently, this will reveal insurance policies used as collateral.

● **Possible former beneficiaries.** These can include a former spouse or lover or anyone else who may have been a beneficiary at one time.

● **The funeral register**. Former insurance agents, unknown associates and acquaintances may have the information you're looking for.

● **The Medical Information Bureau.** This clearinghouse for medical and lifestyle information has computerized facts about many who have applied for insurance, but does not readily provide information—you may have to hire a lawyer or go to court to find out anything. The address is Box 105, Essex Station, Boston, Massachusetts 02112.

If you uncover a company name through this search, the next step is to write to ask about policies that might have been in effect when your loved one died. Provide the company with the deceased's full name, any other names the person might have used, date and place of birth, and Social Security number. If you still find nothing, you can contact all insurance companies in states where the deceased lived. The names of these companies are available at state insurance departments, although the lists won't include companies no longer in business or mail-order companies.

● **If all else fails,** there is the American Council of Life Insurance. This trade organization will forward your inquiry to about 100 member companies. Their address is 1001 Pennsylvania Ave. NW, Washington, DC 20004-2559. Attention: Policy Search Department.

Source: Benjamin Lipson, president, Benjamin Lipson Associates Insurance Agency, Inc., 7 Bulfinch Pl., Boston 02114. Mr. Lipson is an independent insurance broker specializing in insurance for people with medical problems. He is also the author of How to Collect More on Your Insurance Claims *and writes a weekly newspaper column.*

A Canceled Check Is Not Enough

Fire and casualty policies should be in hand (on file) before the full premium is paid. One firm, after finding its plant burned to the ground, didn't have the policy it had paid for. Although it produced the canceled check to the broker, its claim was disallowed. The wise course is to buy insurance as you would an automobile: Give the broker a small deposit, but don't pay up until the policy is delivered.

When a Lawful Claim Is Refused

When you buy an insurance policy, you are purchasing protection for yourself, your family, and your possessions. If your car is totaled or you're disabled by a fall or your home is burglarized, you submit your claim and wait a reasonable time for your check. It's a simple enough transaction in theory.

But now, in too many cases, the check never gets there. The insurance company balks and refuses your claim or it offers a sum far lower than your actual loss. What do you do then? In nine of 10 cases, people do nothing. They figure there is no use in fighting this $200 billion industry. And that's a shame, because policyholders have strong legal rights under both statute law and case law. You can take on an insurance company and win. *The right tactics:*

- **Never inflate your claim.** This will annoy the claims adjuster and make payment more difficult. At worst, it can make you vulnerable to a criminal charge of fraud. An honest claim lays the foundation for further action, should the company refuse to settle.

- **Request a written explanation of why your claim was denied.** An explanation is required by law in most states. If the explanation cites some technicality, such as failure to file on time, the company is probably out of line. Even if you are months late in filing, your claim is still valid unless the company can show that its investigation was harmed by the delay.

- **Keep in mind that the company's interpretation is not gospel.** Insurance firms are no friendlier than other corporations—the fewer claims they pay, the larger their profit. They can be very subjective, and even ridiculous, in interpreting a policy's language. *Example:* One company refused to pay a claim for a patient on a respirator in an intensive-care ward. The company insisted the patient had received "custodial" care, which was excluded in the policy. Even in an honest disagreement, courts have often ruled for the policyholder whenever a policy's language was deemed unclear.

Bottom line: If you think your interpretation is reasonable, stick to your guns.

- **Don't be bullied by the fine print.** If your claim was denied because of a fine-print "exclusion," take heart. Most courts have ruled that the company must prove that such exclusions were phrased clearly, plainly and conspicuously.

- **Ask your agent to go to bat for you.** Insurance agents want to see valid claims paid, if only to keep their customers happy. A nudge to the home office may help grease the wheels. But the most honest agent in the world may have little influence over a distant adjuster.

- **If you're still not satisfied, take your case to higher-echelon people in the insurance company**—first by telephone, then by mail. The company may decide to pay your claim after hearing your side of the story. But if it fails to respond to two letters, write a third letter that says you will commence legal action within 30 days. Given the size of some recent court awards, this can work wonders. While you wait, keep a log and a copy of all communications.

> "Never inflate your claim; an honest claim lays a foundation for further action, should the [insurance] company refuse to settle."

- **Contact your state's department of insurance.** In some states these departments are helpful consumer advocates. In others, they are understaffed or are heavily influenced by insurance-industry interests. Even at best, however, a state agency does not have the authority to force a company to settle.

- **Take the company to small claims court.** You can represent yourself, and you will get quick results.

One major drawback: Most of these courts have a jurisdiction limit of $1,500 or less.

- **If all else fails, see a lawyer.** To find someone experienced in this particular area of the law, contact your state or local trial lawyer's association or consumer advocate group. Many attorneys will take insurance-claims cases on a contingency basis. If you win your case, the lawyer keeps a portion of the award, usually one-third. However, if you lose, you pay nothing.

About 95% of insurance suits are eventually settled out of court. But cases in which a policyholder's attorney can demonstrate "bad faith" by the insurance company can result in huge punitive awards.

Source: William M. Shernoff, partner, Shernoff, Bidart & Darras, a law firm that specializes in consumer claims against insurance companies, Claremont, CA. He is the author of How to Make Insurance Companies Pay Your Claims, Hastings House.

The Most Common Mistakes In Buying Life Insurance

In addition to offering protection for your family, life insurance can be a good investment. But life insurance policies are complicated, and without facts and comparisons, it's easy to spend a lot of money for the wrong coverage. Here's a list of the most common mistakes to avoid and recommendations on what you should buy.

Mistake: **To buy life insurance when you have no dependents.** Agents tend to create needs where none really exist in order to sell policies. If you are single, you don't need life insurance.

Mistake: **To buy mail-order insurance.** It's a bad bargain for most people.

Mistake: **To buy life insurance for your children.** Unless there's some extraordinary reason, there are better ways to save money.

Mistake: **To put money into a cash-value life insurance policy,** unless you have fully funded any 401(k), Roth IRA, or tax-deductible IRA for yourself and your spouse. (Cash-value policies are whole life, universal life, variable life, or any form of life insurance that contains a savings element.)

Be cautious about variable life, which tends to have high built-in expenses and must (like any cash-value policy) be held until death to maximize tax advantages. Traditional whole life policies bought from mutual life insurers generally offer better value than universal life or interest-sensitive whole life. Any policy bought from an agent must be held at least 20 years to amortize heavy up-front charges. Term insurance is safer.

Mistake: **To buy a cash-value policy from a high-pressure salesperson.** Keep in mind that agents make five to 10 times as much commission selling you a $100,000 cash-value policy as they would on a term policy for the same amount. So you should always be alert to the hard sell for such policies.

Mistake: **To buy life insurance and not disability insurance.** People may automatically buy life insurance without realizing that a long-term disability can be an even worse financial event for their families than dying. If you're disabled, you not only lose your income, but you are still around, incurring expenses.

A majority of workers lack the proper amount of disability insurance. Everyone is covered by Social Security disability, but it's very restrictive, especially for white-collar workers.

Mistake: **To buy riders on your policy,** such as the accidental death benefit or the additional-purchase option. These should be treated like options on a car—high-profit items that are best avoided. *Example:* Double indemnity—contrary to popular belief, you're not worth more dead in an accident than dead otherwise.

Controversial rider: The waiver of premiums in case of disability. You don't need it if you're covered for disability. If you become disabled, you'll have enough money to keep up your life insurance premium.

Smart Buying

For young buyers, annual renewable term is probably the best choice in term life insurance. *Rule of thumb:* Buy five to seven times your annual gross income—choose the lower multiple if you have group life insurance at work. For those 45 and up, level premium term is a good choice. Pick the period of coverage that suits your needs. *Helpful:* Compare any cash value or term quotations to the "low-load" policies offered by USAA Life (800-531-8000) or Ameritas (800-552-3553). These insurers deal directly with the public, allowing consumers to bypass agents' commissions. Also check with the rate-of-return service (particularly valuable for cash-value policies you already own) that is run through the nonprofit Consumer Federation of America, 1424 16th St. NW, No. 604, Washington, DC 20036, 202-387-0087.

Some policies are so complicated that it's impossible to figure out exactly what you're getting without a special computer program. *Example:* If a universal life policy says it pays 6.5%, that may be figured on whatever is left after a lot of expenses. You have to compare it with what you would have earned if you had bought term and invested the difference. Assuming you hold the policy 20 years, 6.5% may turn out to be more like 5.5%.

Reevaluate your older policies. If your old policy is a term policy, you should assume you can replace it with a lower-priced policy, at least if you're a non-smoker. If your old cash-value policy doesn't pay dividends, it probably should be replaced. If it does pay dividends, you'll be better off keeping it, especially if it has a low policy-loan interest rate that allows you to borrow on it and reinvest elsewhere.

Source: *James H. Hunt, a life insurance actuary with the Consumer Federation of America, and former commissioner of banking and insurance for the state of Vermont.*

More Life Insurance Mistakes That People Make

Mistake: **Buying life insurance without keeping other financial goals in mind.** Providing for loved ones is important but so is buying disability insurance and so is saving for your children's college educations and your own retirement.

Every dollar you spend on life insurance is one dollar less for retirement—and most people are not likely to die before they retire.

Important: Buy life insurance—and every other financial product—as part of a well-conceived plan, not as a reaction to a sales pitch.

Mistake: **Failing to take advantage of level-premium term products.** In today's marketplace, healthy people can get terrific term policies with low premiums that are guaranteed to remain at those levels for 15 to 20 years. *Example:* Recently I worked with a 46-year-old man who wanted insurance coverage of $1.5 million for 20 years. At that point in his life, he would be retired and his children would be out of school. One of the best term policies I found would cost $4,275 a year for 20 years—guaranteed—and the company was financially sound.

I compared this policy with a competitive annual renewable term policy offered by another sound company. In present dollars, that policy cost $2,565 for the first year—increasing annually to $4,560 by the eighth year and to $21,690 by the 20th year.

The first policy was far better. The present value of premiums calculated at a 4% discount rate would be $60,400 over 20 years, while the other policy would cost $102,100.

Important: The equation changes if you think that your insurance needs will change. *Example:* If you bought the first policy and dropped it in the 12th year—when you would have spent $41,700 in present dollars on premiums—you would have been better off with the increasing-premium pol-

icy, for which you would have spent $40,700.

In addition, if the level-premium policy expires after 20 years and you find that you still need insurance, you will have a problem getting life insurance if you're in poor health.

Mistake: **Failing to shop around for insurance.** Premiums vary widely. By making a few phone calls, you can get a good sense of what the product you want might cost.

● **For instant term life quotes,** I contact Quotesmith (800-556-9393), which will scan the rates and coverages of 150 companies and mail a price-comparison report in one day for free. The list includes policies that are available through any agent or broker.

Mistake: **Replacing existing cash-value policies.** In most cases, it is a mistake to replace a policy after you have paid the heavy up-front costs. Even if the policy is a poor one and merits replacement, evaluate what you stand to lose. *Example:* A woman with a poor-quality, $400,000 universal life policy was unable to keep up with the premiums. She wanted to drop the policy but would have been charged $3,000 to do so. I suggested that she obtain less-expensive coverage elsewhere and leave just enough money in the old policy to keep a reduced policy in force for a few years until the surrender charge disappeared. The effective rate of return on her small "investment" will exceed 20% a year, with almost no risk.

Mistake: **Failing to make optimal use of existing policies.** Cash-value policies that have flexible premiums, such as universal policies, allow you to pay less—or more—than the required annual premium and may be a good place to put additional tax-deferred savings. You can pay more, and the money will grow tax-deferred at 6% or more until you take it out. In many cases, no taxes are due when you withdraw. That beats CDs, which are earning about 3% to 4% interest in 1998.

If you are requesting that dividends be paid directly to you in cash, one of the best bargains in insurance is what the industry calls *paid-up additions*. Policy dividends are used to buy tiny single-premium policies. Then the death benefits and cash values of these tiny policies are combined with your major policy. You'll be getting more insurance without paying additional commissions.

Finally, ask your agent if your insurance company has any *update programs*. With these, you get a higher dividend rate in exchange for agreeing to pay a higher rate if you borrow money against the policy.

Mistake: **Dropping a policy when you no longer need life insurance.** This occurs when your children have grown up, eliminating the need to pay higher premiums for a cash-value policy that was purchased to protect them. But rather than drop a policy in which you've invested, ask to convert it to a *reduced paid-up policy*. This means that you use your accumulated cash value to buy a policy that charges a single premium.

In effect, it converts your whole life policy into a single-premium policy that still carries a death benefit that is lower than your original policy. It also will provide a relatively safe investment that is competitive with a short-term bond fund.

Mistake: **Paying premiums semiannually, quarterly or monthly rather than annually.** Opt to pay once a year. If you decide to pay more frequently, the policy will cost you more. The interest charge for "fractional" premiums is often 8% or higher.

Mistake: **Not paying enough attention to early cash values.** The cash value of your policy is money that is available to you to withdraw or borrow against. A sizable cash value reduces the risk of losing money if you want to drop the policy for any reason.

Compare the first year's cash value with the annual premium. The higher the cash value, the better.

Source: *Glenn S. Daily, a fee-only insurance consultant, 234 E. 84 St., New York, NY 10028. He is the author of* **The Individual Investor's Guide to Low-Load Insurance Products,** *International Publishing Corp.*

How Much Life Insurance Do You Really Need?

The function of life insurance is to replace the economic value of a family member and to provide liquidity to meet the surviving family's cash needs as the estate is settled. The amount of insurance you *need* is not necessarily the amount you can *afford*. Before you visit with a life insurance agent, take a few minutes to understand the logic involved in determining your life insurance needs.

● **Talk with your spouse or "significant other."** What would he or she do if you were not around? The answer dramatically affects the amount of life insurance you need. He or she could decide to stay at home and care for the family or return to work. Returning to work may require paying for some additional education. Alternatively, relocating the family may reduce the amount of income needed to maintain a similar lifestyle.

● **Determine your family's income needs.** Most people underestimate the amount of money it takes to live from month to month without a change in lifestyle. Try working from a cash-flow page to estimate what costs would change if you were no longer in the picture. *Cash flows will differ as the family ages:* **(1)** while children live at home, **(2)** after the children leave home, **(3)** while your spouse is in retirement.

● **Determine what will generate the required amount of income.** Remember that funds can be invested in a number of ways, each of which will generate a different amount of income. Also keep in mind the effects of taxes and inflation on your family's income stream.

● **Evaluate your liabilities.** Some liabilities should be paid off immediately at your death. Others, like a 7% home mortgage, may not be difficult for your surviving spouse to meet.

● **Estimate a college education fund.** Determine the amount of money that you would have to invest today to meet the expense of college for your children when they turn 18.

● **Estimate readjustment-emergency funds.** Most people go through a period of grieving, when it may be impossible to earn income and start a new life simultaneously. Funds will be needed for ordinary and unanticipated expenses during this time.

● **Calculate last expenses.** In addition to funeral costs, there is the expense of getting your estate passed to your heirs. Assume that 7%–9% of the total value of your estate will be needed for administrative expenses.

> **"[When buying insurance] determine your family's income needs. Most people underestimate the amount of money it takes to live from month to month."**

● **List your assets.** Know what is already available to your survivors.

Once you've done some thinking, make the following calculations to determine your insurance needs. And don't forget to reevaluate these calculations at least once a year.

Add	
Lump sum necessary to provide income:	
while children are at home	
after children leave home	
for spouse in retirement	
Debts that should be paid off	
College education fund	
Readjustment/emergency funds	
Last expenses	
Amount of estate required	

Subtract	
Available assets	
Existing insurance payable to survivors	
Amount of insurance needed	

Source: Karen P. Schaeffer, president, Schaeffer Financial, 7855 Walker Dr., Greenbelt, MD 20770, a financial-planning firm affiliated with Hibbard Brown & Co.

A Quick Way to Estimate Coverage

The multiples-of-salary chart was developed to permit a breadwinner to estimate life insurance requirements in the event of premature death. While many factors besides these multiples should be accounted for when arriving at a final figure, the chart will give you an idea of what to expect.

The calculation is based on your current income and on the assumption that your family will receive Social Security benefits in addition to insurance proceeds. It also accounts for your spouse's age. For example, if your gross income is $30,000, your spouse is 45 years old, and your goal is 75% net income replacement, you will need a policy worth 8.5 times your gross income, or $255,000.

MULTIPLES-OF-SALARY CHART

YOUR PRESENT GROSS EARNINGS	25 yrs. 75%	25 yrs. 60%	35 yrs. 75%	35 yrs. 60%	45 yrs. 75%	45 yrs. 60%	50 yrs. 75%	50 yrs. 60%
$15,000	4.5	3.0	6.5	4.5	8.0	6.0	7.0	5.5
23,500	6.5	4.5	8.0	5.5	8.5	6.5	7.5	5.5
30,000	7.5	5.0	8.0	6.0	8.5	6.5	7.0	5.5
40,000	7.5	5.0	8.0	6.0	8.0	6.0	7.0	5.5
65,000	7.5	5.5	7.5	6.0	7.5	6.0	6.5	5.0

Source: Morton Tolchin, chartered life underwriter with HL Financial Services of New York, Inc., 780 Third Ave., New York, NY 10017, is a member of the American Society of Chartered Life Underwriters and the Association for Advanced Life Underwriting.

Inflation Calls for More Insurance

The classic solution to the problem of how to increase one's estate when income and the stock market aren't enough is to take out additional life insurance. For example, our businessman is now middle-aged. The cost of additional insurance starting at his present age would be great. He even may be uninsurable. His business success may also have accustomed him to a standard of living that he doesn't want to lower too drastically.

Life insurance without the necessity of taking a physical examination is the best possibility. If it is group insurance, the costs are appreciably less than they would be if the employee took out his own individual policy. If the coverage is group term life, there is the important advantage of not having to report as income the premiums paid by his employer on the cost of providing up to $50,000 in coverage, provided the plan doesn't discriminate.

The solution, then, is to locate an employer that has a liberal group term-life insurance program for its employees. The best possibility for an aging executive who wants to move is to sign up with an executive search agency, the sizable fees of which are tax-deductible in most instances. If, in your preliminary interview, you ascertain that this agency hasn't done its homework about analyzing compensation packages well enough to know of the group insurance plans available from various employers, seek help elsewhere.

Source: Encyclopedia of Estate Planning by Robert S. Holzman, Boardroom Books.

Where There's Smoke...

More and more insurance companies are using a test to detect smokers who say they don't smoke so they can get lower premiums on new life insurance policies. How the test works: When you visit your doctor for the required physical, insurance forms instruct the doctor to send your urine sample to the insurance company's lab for testing (the form usually doesn't say what kind of testing). The test looks for traces of nicotine and has never given a false-positive reading.

Although the test supposedly shows whether you've ingested nicotine within the 36 hours prior to giving the sample, it's really effective for only 24 hours. The test isn't sensitive enough to pick up nicotine traces in those who live or work with heavy smokers. *Note:* Insurance companies need not volunteer that applicants are subject to the test unless asked.

Alternatives to Whole Life Policies

If you're interested in permanent life insurance, what kind should you buy? Here's a primer on some alternatives to whole life policies illustrating their strong and weak points.

"Economatic" Policies

If you need more permanent protection than you can immediately afford with whole life, you may be interested in an "economatic" product. This policy combines whole life and term insurance, with dividends used over time to convert the term to permanent protection. The advantage of this policy is that you can buy permanent protection at a cost lower than that of ordinary whole life. The policy builds a cash value, and you can borrow from it at any time.

A limited number of life insurance companies now offer a new type of flexible life insurance that extends the limits of earlier economatic products. The new product is a flexible combination of the three basic life insurance types—whole life, term, and paid-up insurance. Generally, the insurance is backed by a company's entire investment portfolio, which softens the impact of dramatically changing interest rates.

This type of policy allows you to custom-design your insurance at time of issue. You decide the premium you can afford and, depending on the protection you need, direct the proportion of your premium into permanent insurance, term insurance, and paid-up additions. You can also use a lump sum—a single premium—at issue and buy a chunk of single-premium insurance to obtain tax advantages and to increase cash-value buildup.

Universal Life

In the late 1970s, in response to high interest rates, some insurance companies began offering universal life insurance—a flexible premium insurance plan that combines term insurance with a separate investment fund often tied to short-term interest rates. A prime feature of universal policies is that premium payments are optional. Like whole life policies, earnings on the cash reserve portion of a policy are tax-deferred until withdrawn.

Although policy owners may find the flexibility of universal life insurance convenient, there can be problems. The ability to reduce or even stop premiums may be too tempting and may override your commitment to your insurance program's future. Another potential problem is that the short-term investments that back many universal life products make them vulnerable to major investment or interest rate changes.

Some universal life policy owners have received notices from their insurance companies stating that their "permanent" insurance will not last as long as expected unless they increase their premiums. And the notices have announced that death benefits and cash values, as projected just a few years or even months earlier, also will drop unless premiums are increased.

How do you compare whole life, economatic, and universal life products? The flexibility available with an economatic policy may make it more attractive than whole life insurance. Because of its emphasis on long-term investments, the economatic policy also may be a better choice than universal life. However, for careful policy owners, universal life may be preferable because it permits skipping a premium or paying a lower premium than originally planned.

Variable Life

For policy owners who want to control how their cash values are invested, a number of companies now offer variable life insurance. Like traditional

ARE YOU SPECIAL?

People with chronic physical ailments or who enjoy risky hobbies must take special measures to obtain adequate life insurance coverage. Insurance companies make their money by selling insurance to the "right" people—people in good health who lead "low-risk" lives. Special-risk people—such as those who suffer from cancer, diabetes, nervous disorders, alcohol problems, or hypertension, those who have had bypass surgery, are older, or are scuba divers or pilots—are not the kind of clients insurance companies favor.

If you have any reason to believe that you are a person with special risks, don't be afraid to "sell" yourself to the insurance company. It's legal and moral, and you owe it to yourself and your family to be properly protected.

Passing the Physical

● **Go early.** People who have physicals early in the morning are most likely to pass. Your weight is lower in the morning, you are usually under less stress, and you haven't eaten, so you are prepared for a blood test.

● **Control your vices.** Don't eat, smoke or drink before your physical. Alcohol, salt and coffee can produce an undesirable effect on your blood pressure or blood analysis.

● **Try to provide a urine specimen before your blood pressure is taken.** Urination reduces blood pressure. If you jog or exercise heavily, be sure to tell the doctor. Oftentimes, heavy exercise will cause urine specimens to turn up "abnormal."

● **Don't withhold information about your smoking habits.** If you smoke, admit it. Chances are the physician will find out anyway, and you could be rejected for withholding information.

● **Consult your own doctor** *before* **the insurance physical.** The doctor should know precisely what your condition is—in order to help answer possible questions by the insurance company. Be sure to ask about stress and/or other special tests you might be given. Some of these may not be safe for you, and your own doctor can recommend suitable equivalents.

● **Don't change your medical routine just before the insurance examination.** Your system may react badly or unusually. Always provide a record of any medication you're currently taking.

● **Preparation counts.** Try to find out what questions you'll be asked. Plan your answers and obtain records to back up your statements. Try not to forget anything—if the insurance company thinks you're withholding information, you may be rejected.

● **If you've just gotten over a cold or are feeling tired,** you won't test well, so it's smart to reschedule the exam. Once you've been turned down for a medical reason, an insurance company will rarely reconsider.

Beyond the Physical

Apart from passing the insurance physical, there are other things you can do to get coverage. Undergo regular physicals and keep records of the results. Underwriters can be swayed by evidence that you've controlled a chronic condition such as hypertension or diabetes.

Shop around. High-risk insurance candidates frequently fail to shop enough.

If you've already been rated and assigned to an expensive, high-risk premium category, don't give up. Ratings can be reversed. For example, three years after a cancer operation, you could legitimately receive a removal of a rating that imposes a surcharge of $15 per $1,000 of coverage. New information, actuarial studies, and correcting simple errors may make it possible to reduce your premiums over time.

Remember, if you face special risks, don't apply for insurance in the usual manner. Know what your options are, keep records, be patient, and never take no for an answer.

Source: *Benjamin Lipson, president of Benjamin Lipson Associates Insurance Agency, Inc., 7 Bulfinch Pl., Boston, MA 02114. Mr. Lipson is an independent insurance broker specializing in insurance for people with medical problems. He is also the author of* **How to Collect More on Your Insurance Claims** *and writes a weekly newspaper column.*

whole life, variable life has a fixed annual premium, and you can borrow against a policy.

The unique feature of variable life is that part of your premium is invested in an investment pool of your choice. The pool can be a money-market fund, a stock fund, a bond fund, or a managed combination of the three. Some companies will let you invest part of your premium in each, and switch among funds.

If your investment pool fares well, the cash value and pure insurance value of your policy will increase. If your investments don't fare well, however, neither will your cash value, although your insurance benefit will never drop below its initial value.

Source: Mark J. Lucius, advertising and corporate information officer for Northwestern Mutual Life Insurance Company, 720 E. Wisconsin Ave., Milwaukee, WI 53202.

Understanding Term Insurance

Term insurance is usually the least expensive form of insurance to get for a maximum of five years. *The choices:*

● **Yearly renewable term.** The rates start low and rise annually as your age (which increases the risk) goes up. Choose this policy if you're in a short-term venture (for example, a construction project or a short-term contract).

● **Five- and 10-year term insurance.** Appropriate for a person starting a high-risk or highly leveraged business, when the bank may insist that the entrepreneur's life be covered by a large policy for a specified period of time. The premium is averaged out on an annual basis over the life of the policy.

● **Yearly renewable term policy with a reversion to lower premiums on evidence of insurability.** This is a recent development. At a specified time (usually after four or five years), if you pass a medical exam, the premiums can be reduced by perhaps 35% of what they might have been. *Example:* If your insurance premium starts at $1,000 a year and climbs $200 annually, you must pass an exam during the fifth year to get the premium lowered to $1,200.

Potential problem: Bad health at the time of the examination will negate the possibility of lowering the premium.

● **Avoid term insurance even for the short haul if you are almost 70 years old.** Since the risk at that age is so high, the point at which the term and straight-premium rates would cross would be attained within five years. At that point, a permanent (or straight) life policy is best.

● **If you need life insurance for more than five years, permanent insurance is usually best.** The reason for this is that the total acquisition price usually evens out over a period of 10 years. If you are relatively young, say in your thirties, the cash value of the policy may increase at a greater rate than the premium after the third year. The straight-life policyholder may borrow on the cash value at a low rate of interest.

Alternative: Some creative insurance agents combine the two types of coverage, thus lowering premium costs and ensuring cash value at a specific time.

Source: Leon Sicular, president, Leon H. Sicular Associates, New York, NY.

News About Life Insurance Replacement

People who hold old cash-value life insurance policies (most of which carry interest rates as low as 5%) are being urged to replace them with new policies with higher returns. Although such substitutions make financial sense in some situations, in other cases the client stands to lose.

Best-case scenario: The client who changes saves up to 25% on premium costs.

Drawback: Since the client's buying a new policy, he or she has to pay the acquisition cost—which often amounts to as much as one year's premium.

People buy cash-value life insurance for two reasons, one of which usually takes precedence:

● **Permanent insurance protection.** If this is your primary reason for owning a policy, you may come out ahead by switching. Even though you're buying insurance at an older age (which carries a higher premium base), new actuarial tables could lower your actual premium layout. (*Note:* People who need short-term protection are often better off with term insurance. Cash-value life insurance is best for people who want long-term protection.)

● **Accumulation of capital.** If this is your primary reason for owning coverage, you may lose in a replacement. Usually you do better by negotiating a conversion of your existing policy to a higher rate of return than by paying a second set of acquisition costs. *Example:* Most insurers will raise your interest to the current T-bill rate if you agree to pay them the market rate for loans.

Important: Your math must be correct, and so must your reason for buying the insurance.

What to Do

Without a detailed financial and actuarial analysis, it's impossible to predict whether a replacement is prudent. There's no rule of thumb, since companies have reacted to the rash of replacements with incentives (such as higher dividends on old policies, premium discounts on new insurance, and even free insurance for up to 10 years) for customers who keep their original policies and agree to pay the market rate on loans.

Consumer laws forbid insurance brokers to make a replacement without first conducting a full analysis, submitting substantiating evidence to the insurance company, and having the client sign a statement verifying that he or she saw all the data before making the decision. This regulation has been difficult to enforce, however.

If, without making an analysis, your broker categorically tells you a replacement is good for you, he or she is acting in his or her best interest, not yours. On the other hand, if your broker suggests doing the analysis to find out whether you can gain, he or she is acting on your behalf.

Source: Arthur Schechner, chairman, Schechner Lifson Corp., insurance agents and brokers, Millburn, NJ.

BORROWING FROM YOUR LIFE INSURANCE POLICY

Is your life insurance policy a good source of readily available funds? When should you borrow from it?

The rate at which you can borrow from your life insurance policy depends primarily on when you bought it. If your policy dates back to the 1970s or earlier, you may be able to borrow at 5% or 6%. Newer policies generally have 8% loan provisions. If you've purchased a policy in the early 1980s, your policy may have either an 8% loan provision or a "variable loan rate." The latter means that the rate at which you can borrow varies and is pegged to an index such as Moody's Corporate Bond Index.

One certainty is that, regardless of the rate at which you can borrow, policy loans are somewhat more expensive than they used to be. Since the Tax Reform Act of 1986, policy-loan interest is no longer tax-deductible.

Despite this revision, borrowing from a life insurance policy is still less complicated than most other borrowing. You can borrow from your policy without delay—and without the approval of a bank officer.

However, because the cash accumulation inside a life insurance policy is tax-deferred, and depending on your tax bracket, you may find that you are better off borrowing from a bank than borrowing from your policy, particularly when interest rates are low. Borrowing from a life insurance policy at 8% is convenient, but may prove more costly in the long run.

Why? You may find that borrowing from your policy affects the dividends you receive from your life insurance company. If you have a "participating" life insurance policy— one that pays dividends—talk to your agent or life insurance company before borrowing. If dividends are calculated by a technique called "direct recognition," you may get higher dividends and greater tax-deferred cash accumulation if you don't borrow from your policy.

Source: Mark J. Lucius, advertising and corporate information officer for Northwestern Mutual Life Insurance Company, 720 E. Wisconsin Ave., Milwaukee, WI 53202.

The Darlings of Tax Reform

The insurance industry's deferred annuities have been one of the most attractive investment products around. But the Taxpayer Relief Act of 1997, with its lowered capital gains rates, has lessened their appeal. Nevertheless, if you have at least 20 years for investing, and have fully funded other retirement plans, such as 401(k)s and IRAs, annuities may still have a place in your portfolio. Although contributions to a deferred annuity are not tax-deductible, earnings do accumulate tax-deferred. Advantage over an IRA: There is no limit to the amount of money you can invest in an annuity.

How Annuities Work

An individual buys an annuity from an insurance company, paying a lump sum or a series of payments over time. In return, the insurance company guarantees that the funds will grow at a certain tax-free rate. Then, beginning on a specified date, the individual receives regular income payments for life.

Payments depend on the amount of money contributed to the account, the length of time the funds are left in it, and the rate of return earned on the funds. Also a factor in determining the size of the payments is whether you include your spouse and other heirs as beneficiaries. Different options enable you to have payments continue to your spouse, or to your children, or for a minimum of, say, 20 years, regardless of who is there to receive them after you die.

Deferred annuities therefore can be considered part insurance and part investment. If you are willing to part with at least $5,000 (the minimum amount can differ from company to company) for five years or longer, you can be guaranteed a competitive, tax-free return on your funds. Because the earned income is not taxed until you begin withdrawing the money (presumably at a lower tax rate), your funds accumulate much faster than they would if they were taxed. The insurance component, of course, is guaranteed regular monthly income payments for the rest of your life. Also, should you die before you begin receiving payments, your heirs are guaranteed to receive the full amount of your original principal.

Fixed Rate Versus Variable

There are two basic types of deferred annuity—fixed and variable.

Fixed annuity: The insurance company guarantees that your funds will grow at a specified rate for a specified period of time. Most companies guarantee a specific rate of return for at least the first year. Thereafter, the rate usually fluctuates at least once a year, according to the then-prevailing interest rates. Although the rates of return for fixed annuities may vary, your principal always remains intact.

Variable annuity: The rate of return is determined by the performance of investments you select from a range of mutual funds offered by the insurance company. Investing in a variable annuity is almost identical to investing in a family of mutual funds. You have the same exchange privileges and the choice of putting all your money into one fund or a blend of different funds, or even of dividing your money between a fixed annuity and a variable annuity. You can earn a larger return than you might with a fixed annuity. However, if your investments perform poorly, your original principal may diminish. Most annuity companies will return to your beneficiary your original investment or current market value of your holdings, whichever is higher, if you die before you annuitize.

The minimum investment for a deferred annuity is usually $5,000, although some single-premium annuities can require a one-time lump-sum investment of as little as $2,500. A flexible-premium annuity, paid over time, may have an initial minimum of $1,000 and require small monthly payments. Most companies levy an annual management charge of 0.5%–1.5% of total assets. If you invest in a variable annuity, you will pay a percentage of your total assets to cover management costs for the mutual fund.

Insurance companies typically charge a declining surrender fee of 5%–6% (which usually falls to zero after five or six years) if you liquidate the principal of your annuity. And if you withdraw your money before age 59½, the IRS will charge you a penalty.

Source: Alexandra Armstrong, CFP, president of the independent financial-planning firm Armstrong, Welch and MacIntyre, Inc., 1155 Connecticut Ave. NW, Washington, DC 20036.

Profit From Life Insurance

It's possible to come out ahead by donating a paid-up life insurance policy to charity.

Key: Your contribution will not be valued at the policy's cash value, but rather at its replacement value, which may be much greater than its cash value. You can then obtain additional coverage for yourself by buying inexpensive term insurance.

Source: Joseph T. Ryerson, 312 US 260.

How to Collect Claims From Insurance Companies

In many situations, you can negotiate successfully with an insurance company without retaining a lawyer. It is important to know when to negotiate yourself and how to negotiate effectively.

Where to start:

● **Your insurance agent,** if he or she is not an employee of the insurer, should be the first line of inquiry. An independent agent is better able to assist in obtaining the full amount to which you are entitled. A good relationship with clients is what keeps an agent in business.

He or she will often present your claim, negotiate it and obtain a satisfactory settlement for you without charge. An agent is especially valuable on smaller claims. Also, if you negotiate yourself, he or she can be a major source of information and advice.

Should you hire a lawyer?

● **The major deciding factor is economic.** On small claims, a lawyer's fee might be prohibitive, but on larger claims you could lose money by negotiating with an insurance company yourself.

In some cases, you might simply pay a flat fee for the attorney's review of your claim. Initial consultation will usually provide you with helpful information and assist the attorney in deciding whether or not it will pay for him or her to take your case.

Other considerations:

● **Subjective factors.** If you don't feel comfortable retaining a lawyer, go it alone.

● **No-fault versus at-fault states.** Negotiating your own claim makes a lot more sense in a no-fault state, where the insurance company is bound by law to reimburse you for your losses. But even in a no-fault state, or if you don't apply in time for all of the benefits to which you were entitled, your claim may not be honored if the forms are presented incorrectly.

● **Language.** Understanding the convoluted terminology used in insurance policies and law is a major stumbling block for the layperson. To negotiate successfully, you must be comfortable with the language.

● **Reputation.** Some insurance companies deal fairly and quickly. Others are notoriously difficult and slow. Ask your insurance agent or a negligence attorney about the company you are dealing with. You may need legal help to negotiate a favorable settlement with a difficult company.

> " [Before negotiating a claim] find out what [it] is worth. Ask your insurance agent or a negligence lawyer what a reasonable offer would be. "

● **Pain and suffering.** When multiples of out-of-pocket expenses are involved due to pain and suffering, it is best to hire a lawyer. Lawyers can point out losses you have not even thought of. Also, the insurance company will take into account what you are saving by not hiring a lawyer and offer you less.

If you go it alone:

● **Read the policy very carefully.** Pay special attention to exclusions and coverages. Before presenting your claim, take a close look at the policy. Make sure you're presenting it in a way that makes it evident that your claim is covered. (If you can't find your policy, the insurer is obligated to give you a copy.)

● **Document everything completely.** It is the most important part of an insurance claim. Support every aspect of your claim, including doctor bills, receipts for medicines, transportation for medical reasons, and a letter from your employer stating lost wages. Think of everything. Witnessing an injury to a loved one may cause compensable emotional trauma. A husband or wife may recover for the lost services and companionship of his or her injured spouse.

● **Find out what your claim is worth.** Ask your insurance agent or a negligence lawyer what a reasonable offer would be in your situation.

● **Be prepared to take a discount.** There has to

be a motivation for the insurer to settle a claim. One advantage of negotiating without a lawyer is that a quick settlement may be offered to avoid legal expenses. So decide what amount you are willing to settle for. The settlement offer will depend on various factors, including clarity, proof of coverage, damages, documentation, how likely you are to prevail at trial and the caseload of the court in which you would have to sue. (Some insurers offer nothing until the trial date.)

Bodily injury:

Claims for bodily injury can be the most complicated and negotiable, especially when based upon pain and suffering.

● **In a no-fault state,** you are limited to out-of-pocket expenses in a nonserious injury. This includes lost wages. In a fault-governed state, you can negotiate for more.

● **Don't miss damages.** Start at the top of your head and go down to your toes, to include every part that's been hurt.

● **Photograph your injury.** In addition to medical reports, photos are the best documentation of suffering.

● **Consider every aspect of your life affected by your injury.** Include your career, sports, hobbies, future interests, and family relationships.

● **Ask what a lawyer would ask**—at least twice the actual expenses when there has been no permanent disability. Where liability is clear, the insurance company will be likely to give you what you ask, if they believe that you really had difficulties and were out of work for a few weeks. However, where there has been permanent disability, multiples of expenses do not apply. *Example:* Your medical bills for a lost eye might have been only $3,000, but a jury might award you 50 times that amount.

If you cannot reach a settlement: An insurance company has a fiduciary duty (a relationship based on trust, like that with your lawyer or stockbroker) to deal fairly and in good faith with its insured.

What to do if you are not treated well:

● **If you feel that the company is either unreasonably delaying your claim or acting in bad faith,** make a complaint to your state insurance regulatory agency. In most cases, the agency will write a letter to the company.

● **If your time is being wasted by the insurance company's bureaucracy,** the small claims court may

be appropriate. Such action will pressure the company to settle with you more quickly on your terms.

Many states have laws penalizing an insurer for bad faith. If you feel the company has been acting in bad faith, you can initiate a lawsuit and possibly collect a multiple of your claim in punitive damages.

Source: *Dan Brecher, a New York attorney.*

What Insurance Companies Don't Tell You

Consider two houses, side by side, both destroyed in a disaster. One home owner gets an $18,000 check from his insurance company to rent temporary housing. The other gets just $500 a month—and must haggle each month to get even that.

Sound unlikely? As an insurance company disaster supervisor, I saw this happen after the 1989 San Francisco earthquake. People who were savvy about their insurance received bigger settlements than those who trusted their insurers to look out for them.

What you don't know about your homeowner's policy could permanently reduce your standard of living after a calamity. It could even cost you your home.

Rules for Insurance Self-Protection

● **Don't rely on fluffy language.** Regardless of how a policy is advertised, read the fine print of a homeowner's policy before you buy. Don't depend solely on your insurance agent. To wrap up the sale quickly, he or she has an incentive to sell you something basic and cheap.

● **Read your policy now.** If you aren't sure what your policy covers, if something isn't absolutely clear, have your insurer or agent explain it and confirm the conversation in writing.

● **Don't expect the insurer to put you first if disaster strikes.** If the company had known you were going to have a loss, it would never have written a policy on you.

How to Buy the Protection You Need

● **Buy coverage to restore your home** exactly as it was before the disaster. This is the "face value" of the policy. Coverage for other possessions, such as furnishings and landscaping, are usually expressed as a percentage of the replacement cost.

The cost of restoration has nothing to do with the price you paid for the home.

Key question: What would it cost to exactly reproduce this dwelling on this property?

Answer: Only an expert contractor can tell you. Invest $150 or so to get an estimate.

● **Tailor the insurance to your own home.** Insurance companies like to base their payments on the cost of modern, tract-house-style construction. Your home—especially if it is older—could have more costly features, like lathe-and-plaster instead of sheetrock walls. *Strategy:* Buy a policy that provides "Guaranteed Replacement Cost" (GRC) coverage. This will pay the cost to replace your dwelling regardless of the "face value." *Helpful:* Some policies that claim to be "Guaranteed Replacement Cost" have a limit usually expressed as a percentage of the face value. Even if the policy has GRC on the dwelling, the other coverages that are expressed as a percentage are usually a percentage of the face amount, not the actual replacement cost.

● **Don't neglect "code and ordinance or law" coverage.** After Hurricane Andrew, many homes had to be elevated 13 feet—or they couldn't be rebuilt. After the San Francisco quake, new homes in the area had to have much stronger foundations.

Home owners without this additional protection had to pay those extra costs themselves. The cost of code protection is about 10% of the annual premium.

● **Know what replacement cost means.** While your coverage may say "full replacement cost," you must complete the replacement to collect.

If you can't—because you can't afford to elevate the home or build that new foundation—you might collect only the "actual cash value" of the lost home, which might be one-third less.

● **Your possessions.** Make sure your furnishings and possessions are covered for replacement cost, not current value. A used sofa is worth half its replacement cost, at best—but you won't replace it with used merchandise.

Most policies cover the contents of a home only up to 50% or so of the face amount. If your possessions are worth more than that, pay around $1.50 per each $1,000 of coverage per year.

● **Your valuables.** If you have artwork, collections, antiques or other valuable personal property, study the "limits of coverage" section of your policy to see how much of the value of lost or destroyed valuables the insurer will pay.

Consider a "floater" to provide supplemental coverage. It will cost about $0.25 to $2.50 for each $100 of coverage.

● **Know about "other structures."** Structures separated from your dwelling are covered separately in your homeowner's policy—usually for 10% of the "face value" amount. But what about attached decks and patios? Are they considered other structures, or are they included in the face amount?

Any kind of structure that is "attached" to the dwelling should be included in the face value, but be sure to clear this up at the time of purchase.

● **Take inflation into account.** Construction costs rise every year. So do the costs of replacing your furniture, snowblower, kitchen appliances, etc. Unless you have replacement value coverage, make sure the policies covering contents—as well as the dwelling itself—are protected with a rider that raises coverage periodically to reflect rising costs.

● **Buy all the liability coverage you need.** Standard policies provide some protection in the event your neighbor trips over your sprinkler and breaks his leg. But consider "umbrella" coverage, which unifies liability under all your policies—cars and boats as well as the house.

Umbrella policies often cover hazards that homeowner's insurance does not, such as a claim of slander when your neighbor doesn't like what you said about him or her. You would pay about $300 a year for $1 million of umbrella coverage.

● **Protect yourself in case of disaster.** Make sure the policy will pay all expenses necessary to maintain your standard of living for as long as necessary while your home is being restored.

Important: Avoid coverage of "actual incurred costs." That will skimp on paying for temporary quarters and force you to argue with your insurer over every receipt.

● **Don't be penny-wise/pound-foolish.** The best coverage doesn't necessarily cost more. In fact, insurance companies price their best policies very competitively because "better" customers are good prospects for the companies' other products.

● **Don't just buy a policy and forget it.** Every

few years review your coverage to make sure it still meets your needs. And then shop around to make sure you're still getting the best price. *Helpful:* Start with your current agent. He or she may be willing to improve your coverage—and trim the price—if he or she fears losing the annual commission.

Source: *Ina De Long, executive director of United Policyholders, a non-profit group devoted to consumer education on insurance. Box 2071, Merced, CA 95344.*

Guarding Your Life Insurance From the IRS

The cash surrender value of a life insurance policy is subject to an IRS lien for unpaid taxes. Even if you have given the policy away, it's vulnerable if you have retained any right in it whatsoever (e.g., the right to borrow against the policy or to change the beneficiary).

To protect the beneficiary fully, it's necessary to write to the insurance company and renounce totally any and all rights in the policy. *Another way:* Buy only term insurance, which has no cash surrender value for the IRS to levy against.

INSURANCE TRAPS: BUYERS, BEWARE

Don't buy life insurance from television or mail-order advertisements. No matter how much you trust their paid shills, it is a rip-off.

Serious drawbacks: These companies accept anyone who applies—no matter how high the risk—and charge a monthly fee about twice what other insurers charge per $1,000 of life insurance coverage.

Major trap: You don't receive any coverage until you've made at least two years of monthly payments. If you die before that, your estate receives only the premiums you've paid—without interest. *Much ado about very little:* One of the policies we reviewed paid out only $1,900 after two years. After age 55, the payout dropped annually. *Example:* If the insured dies between the ages of 75 and 80, the estate receives only $200. *Exception:* Some university alumni insurance programs are less expensive and are legitimate.

Source: *Robert Hunter, head, Consumer Federation of America, 1424 16 St. NW, Washington, DC 22207.*

What to Do When Your Insurance Company Says No

Americans spend billions of dollars on health and life insurance every year to protect against financial ruin in case of a serious illness in the family or the death of a family breadwinner.

But when we file insurance claims at times of crisis, it can feel like a betrayal of life-threatening proportions when an insurer is slow to respond, refuses to pay a claim or digs in its heels when challenged. Here are the best ways to ensure your claims are paid the first time through—and what to do if your claim is denied.

Before You Make a Claim

● **Tell the truth on all insurance applications.** Many health-insurance policies have a contestability clause, which allows the company to rescind the policy at any time if it discovers a "material misstatement" on the application. *Examples:* Omitting an existing medical condition, understating the severity of a condition.

The insurer may not review your application until after you file a claim, even if you have been paying premiums for years. If a misstatement is discovered, you could lose benefits at the very time you need them the most.

Self-defense: Don't leave out information you consider unimportant or perhaps fear will result in your application being turned down. *Examples:* High blood pressure, allergies. Your position is far stronger if the insurer sees evidence of your truthfulness.

● **Ask which percentile your health insurance company uses** to determine "reasonable and customary charges." Most health insurance policies agree to pay a percentage of the "reasonable and customary" fees for medical services. Insurers calculate what is reasonable and customary in each area of the country, sometimes even by ZIP code, by sampling doctors' and hospitals' fees, then limiting their coverage to the 70th, 80th or 90th percentile. *Result:* The same procedure in the same hospital may be covered for a different amount, depending on your carrier. But the fees the insurer has decided are reasonable and customary may not be representative of *your* doctor's.

● **Have medical procedures and fees preapproved.** Whenever possible, ask your doctor for a preoperative report, have the procedure preapproved by the insurer—and ask how much it will pay.

● **Negotiate with your doctor.** Often, physicians will agree to perform services for the amount your insurer will cover. It is also not unusual for insurers to "negotiate" with doctors on fees. Here your agent could be very helpful.

If Your Claim Is Refused

● **Don't panic—your first round with an insurance company need not be final.** Here are the major reasons an insurer may deny a claim and what you can do about it. *If the insurer says:*

"This procedure/condition isn't covered."

● **Read your policy and/or descriptive booklet carefully.** Enlist the help of the agent who sold you the policy or your company-benefits manager if necessary.

● **Get a letter from your doctor** explaining what he or she did and why it should be covered. If the doctor feels the procedure is covered based on your policy booklet, often a letter is sufficient.

"This procedure/condition isn't covered because it is considered experimental."

● **More and more insurers are willing to negotiate on this point,** with the result that many procedures once considered experimental are now fully or partially covered. *Examples:* Bone-marrow transplants, liver transplants, some fertilization procedures.

● **If your problem is chronic,** let the insurer know of the future claims for medication and treatment for which it will be liable for the rest of your life if it doesn't pay for the procedure. Show the insurer it is in its long-term interest to try something new, even if it is a long shot.

"We'll only pay a portion of your doctor's fees."

● **Ask your doctor to clarify which procedure was done.** It is possible the code for the procedure that was performed does not accurately describe your case. *Example:* A procedure that should have taken 20 minutes took seven hours because complications set in.

● **Ask your doctor to write the insurer as to why the fee is reasonable and customary.**

● **Have your doctor submit the appropriate medical reports to your local medical society for peer review.** If he or she refuses, you know that the fee is out of line.

Virtually every insurer will accept the verdict of a peer review committee. Often, the finding is that the doctor has overcharged. In the unlikely event a committee says the insurer should pay less than it agreed to, insurers will generally stick to the amount originally promised.

If Your Claim Is Contested

Most life insurance claims are paid automatically. But insurance companies occasionally investigate some claims. Reasons:

● **Suicide.** In the event there is a question, insurers will generally rely on police reports.

● **Misrepresentation of age.** If the deceased has claimed to be younger in order to qualify for lower insurance rates, insurers will prorate the claim.

● **Misrepresentation of smoking.** The insurer must have evidence to suspect a policyholder was a smoker at the time of application. If you are a smoker, you should tell the insurance company at the time of the application. If you don't provide this information, the insurance company can generally rescind the policy at any time—even after death.

● **Accidental death.** If the policyholder was insured for an accidental death benefit, or double indemnity, the insurer may investigate an ambiguous cause of death. *Example:* Did the deceased have a heart attack, then drive into a tree—in which case the heart attack was the cause of death and the insurer is not liable for the double benefit—or did the crash cause the heart attack, in which case the insurer must pay up? In this case, the family will have to depend on medical reports to support their claim.

Source: Sam E. Beller, CLU, ChFC, president of Diversified Programs, Inc., an insurance sales organization based in New York City. He is the author of The Great Insurance Secret, *William Morrow & Co.*

The Best Buys in Health Insurance

Finding the absolutely best deal in health insurance would probably require a company-by-company and policy-by-policy search. To avoid spending most of your free time for the next several months doing that kind of research, try following a few general rules to help keep costs down without sacrificing coverage.

The first rule: You can usually obtain the most cost-effective insurance by purchasing major-medical instead of basic health coverage. This allows you to assume the small risks of everyday bumps and scratches and to pay for routine medical care while insuring yourself against the risk of potentially devastating major illnesses and injuries.

● **The second way to contain costs is through group insurance.** Most employers offer some form of group insurance at a cost that may be 20%–40% less than individual coverage. You usually don't have to take a physical, and coverage stays in force until you leave the company.

The number of employees in the group will determine the most inexpensive type of coverage. If more than 100 employees are involved, self-insuring may provide substantial savings. The one problem with this type of approach is the risk of a large claim during the first few years of the plan, before a sufficient reserve has accumulated. However, the company may be willing to assume this risk or to obtain regular group coverage during the accumulation period.

● **Group underwriting offers another way of cost cutting through shared funding.** The employer, employee and insurance company share in the losses up to a predetermined limit, say $10,000 per individual. After the limit is reached, the insurance company assumes full responsibility up to the limits of the policy. The split among the three parties is determined on an actuarial basis, according to the group census. Under either a self-insurance plan or a shared-funding plan, you must calculate in advance whether there are true cash-flow gains or whether the payments have simply been deferred to the end of the contract year.

● **Another cost-containment strategy for group health plans is precertification.** Under a precertification contract, employees must obtain authorization for prospective hospital coverage or operations in order to be reimbursed. Prior to any operation, the employee submits a detailed plan from the doctor to the company outlining the procedures to be undertaken and the estimated costs. Any expenses incurred without approval, except emergency room visits, are not covered by the policy.

Editor's note: Yet another cost-containment strategy for group health plans of small employers and self-employed individuals is using high deductible plans. These plans can then be supplemented on a tax-favored basis with medical savings accounts (MSAs).

● **Some insurance companies seek to reduce costs and lower premiums** by requiring second opinions before any surgery. Although the second doctor's appointment increases the up-front costs, the reduction in unnecessary surgery more than offsets it. These savings may be in the form of reduced premiums for individual as well as group plans.

● **A final trend toward lower costs in group health insurance** is restricted access for employee dependents. Many companies are offering insurance only to their employees, requiring substantial if not total contribution for any benefits to the employees' families. The result is a reduction in premiums for the company, but the plan may not be the best one for you, depending upon your family's needs.

> "[To reduce premiums] Many companies are offering insurance only to their employees, requiring substantial... contribution for any benefits to the employees' families."

Source: *Karen P. Schaeffer, president, Schaeffer Financial, 7855 Walker Dr., Greenbelt, MD 20770, a financial-planning firm affiliated with Hibbard Brown & Co.*

Collecting More on Your Company Health Policy

Health insurance policies are not etched in stone. There are contractual provisions in the insurance policy that are negotiable. Most companies give health insurance to engender goodwill among employees. Many problems in collecting the maximum due you are a result of incompetence or of negligence on the part of the administrators in your company who handle insurance benefits. They may be too busy or unaware of how to get more for you. *Three ways to improve your ability to collect:*

● **Know the insurance contract and all its provisions.** Be aware that everything is negotiable. *Example:* Home health care by someone other than a registered nurse or practical nurse is not covered in the policy. Contractually nothing needs to be said, but administratively an alternate source of home health care could be covered. It is really a question of negotiation.

● **Have the company's insurance broker help negotiate with the insurer.** The broker is the one who is making the money from selling your company the policy. He or she also has more leverage than you do with the insurance company. If he or she is unwilling to help, encourage your company to switch to a more cooperative broker.

● **Set up a liaison.** The individual in your company in charge of claims should have a good working relationship with the insurance company. If a settlement is too low or doesn't fully cover your needs, the claims person at your firm can make a better settlement. After all, the insurance company is selling policies.

If your claims person is uncertain whether you can get more compensation for a treatment, ask to contact the broker. The broker should know the terms of your contract and be familiar with the people at the insurance company. He or she should have an idea of how to get the claim paid.

Unallowable Treatments

Trying to make specifically unallowable treatments allowable: This is between the doctor and you. *Example:* If you want to claim an experimental procedure that could prolong your life or improve its quality, convince your doctor to go to bat for you. If he or she won't go along with it, you are not going to get anywhere with the insurance broker, the personnel at your office or the insurance company.

If you're stuck with a flawed company policy and have huge deductibles and other uncovered expenses, take out a personal policy that coordinates with the company's.

Source: Leonard Stern, president, Leonard B. Stern & Co., an insurance consulting and brokerage firm, 305 Madison Avenue, New York, NY 10165.

Buy the Right Protection

If you are among the 37 million Americans who do not receive health coverage at work, it is still possible to find a great health insurance policy. There are even options for people who are dissatisfied with the coverage they receive from their employers. *Here are the most important questions people are asking me now:*

● **What are the least-expensive health-coverage options available?** For individuals and their families, there are actually just two—Health Maintenance Organizations (HMOs) and Preferred Provider Organizations (PPOs).

● **HMO plans are usually the most affordable for individuals or families,** and they provide medical care through networks of physicians. *Benefits:* Unlike traditional health insurers, if you sign up for an HMO, you won't have to fill out forms after each doctor's visit. You also won't have to worry about meeting a deductible requirement. You probably will pay $5 to $10 per doctor visit.

How HMO coverage works: When you are ill, you first consult your primary care physician, who is also known as the gatekeeper. He or she will then refer you to a specialist, if necessary. *Exception:* Most plans permit women to visit a gynecologist without a gatekeeper referral.

If you choose an out-of-network doctor or hospital, you are generally not covered. You also must first obtain permission from your primary care physician to see an in-network specialist. In most situations out-of-network specialists are not covered at all.

● **PPO plans are slightly more expensive than HMOs.** They too provide medical care through a network of doctors.

Big difference: There are no gatekeepers—you can consult a specialist without first getting a referral from your primary care physician. Your co-payment—or fee—for each doctor's visit is comparable to HMO rates. *Remember:* Out-of-network doctors and hospitals are not covered.

● **How do monthly costs of HMOs and PPOs compare?** A family of four with HMO coverage in any major U.S. city could expect to pay about $700 and up per month. For PPO coverage, that could run about 10% higher.

● **What if you don't like the idea of network care?** Many insurance carriers have stopped selling traditional or indemnity plans to individuals. Insurers that still sell them usually make it tough to qualify because of strict underwriting standards. If you are opposed to network care, see if you can apply for indemnity coverage through an organization to which you belong.

Drawback: While you have complete freedom to use the doctor of your choice, such plans are very expensive. A family of four that chooses a plan with a $200 deductible and a reimbursement rate starting at 80% of the first $5,000—and 100% of all expenditures above that—would pay about $1,000 monthly.

● **Can you combine the flexibility of an indemnity plan with the cost savings of an HMO or a PPO?** Yes, with a Point-of-Service (POS) plan. It allows you to decide whether to consult a network doctor or an out-of-network doctor any time you need medical care.

Members' costs vary: When you stay within the network, the charge is $5 to $15 per visit. If you choose to go out of network for care, your costs will be higher, since insurers will reimburse only 70% to 80% of the cost of a doctor's visit once you meet the plan deductible.

Monthly cost comparison: POS plans cost more than HMOs or PPOs, but less than traditional indemnity plans. *Example:* A family of four in a major city would pay about $800 per month for an HMO/POS plan and about $900 per month for a PPO/POS plan.

Drawback: In today's insurance market, individuals and their families may find it difficult to purchase POS coverage. It's primarily sold to businesses, which offer it to employees. *Helpful:* If you're self-employed—or own the company—you can apply for POS health-care coverage as a business, rather than as an individual.

How to Find a Great HMO or PPO

Because there are many different types of plans, and consumer options keep changing rapidly, it makes sense to consult a licensed insurance agent who works with a range of insurers and can help you compare your choices.

Selection priorities: While low cost is important, it should not be your top consideration.

More important: Evaluate the quality of the insurer and its network by contacting present and former policyholders, the Better Business Bureau and your state department of insurance.

Over time, you'll tend to use doctors in the network more and more, so it pays to shop for a plan whose network physicians are conveniently located—*and who are well qualified*—to meet your family's needs. Networks are growing rapidly as more doctors join them. While your physician may not be a member now, that may change in the near future.

If you don't love the choices your agent has suggested or are concerned that they're too costly, sign up for the best plan that's available now. Then, in three to four months, ask your insurance agent to survey the marketplace to see if better products have become available.

Health-care policies are changing so rapidly these days that it is possible something better will come along soon.

When Employees Need More Insurance

In some cases, people who already receive health-care coverage from their employers need additional protection. To decide whether you need more coverage, ask yourself—*does my policy only provide hospitalization coverage?* If so, it makes sense to buy an HMO or a PPO plan to cover other medical costs. Choose a plan with the best physicians, but don't worry about its hospitalization feature, since you're already covered.

Important: If your decision to seek additional coverage is due to your unhappiness with the doctors who belong to your plan's network, don't despair. Many states have passed *"any willing provider"* laws. These laws require HMO and PPO networks to accept any willing physician who meets their licensing, training and other standards.

That means your physician choices may soon improve within your existing plan. So it makes sense to wait, rather than spend money for supplementary coverage.

Coverage for Retirees

Increasingly, the biggest decision for retirees is whether to remain in the traditional Medicare program—and purchase a Medigap policy to cover any expenses that Medicare fails to reimburse—or switch to one of the newer Medicare HMOs. *How it works:* If retirees sign up and commit themselves to visiting network physicians, they won't need to buy Medigap coverage. Instead, they'll pay only $10 to $20 per doctor's visit— depending on the geographic area—and Medicare will reimburse other expenses. It's an option worth considering.

Editor's note: In 1999 there are new Medicare options, such as Medicare MSAs.

Source: Sam Beller, CLU, ChFC, president of Diversified Programs, Inc., an insurance sales organization, and Diversified Advisory Services, Inc., a financial services organization, 450 Seventh Ave., New York, NY 10123. He is the author of **The Great Insurance Secret***, William Morrow.*

Health Insurance if You Are Not in a Group Plan

Most people have their health insurance needs taken care of by their employers. For those who are not covered by an employer, the task of obtaining adequate medical coverage can be difficult as well as expensive. Good coverage costs a great deal, and even then the policy may have large deductibles that require you to pay some portion (often 20%) of the remaining expenses.

If you must buy health insurance on your own, consider a health maintenance organization (HMO). For a set fee, you will receive all of the coverage you need but without deductibles and co-insurance. This goes for people on Medicare as well. If you cannot find anyone in your area qualified to provide information on HMOs, contact the American Association of Health Plans, 1129 20th St. NW, Washington, DC 20036, 202-778-3200.

If you decide not to join an HMO, then Blue Cross/Blue Shield is probably your next best buy. These policies usually return 85%–90% of the premiums paid in claims, although in some instances

Something to Tide You Over

Temporary health insurance is available for periods when you're between jobs, starting a new business, etc. Policies are sold for specific periods of 30 to 180 days and are generally renewable only once. Most don't cover pregnancy or preexisting disabilities. Rates are low.

people have had difficulty getting their claims paid. Major-medical policies from life insurance companies return about 60¢ per $1 in premiums. For younger people and those willing to take a fairly large deductible, these policies may be the best choice.

If you are under 65 and have a health impairment, there may not be a suitable program for you. Some individuals may be able to get coverage from Blue Cross/Blue Shield (although most plans can reject you for health reasons); a few people may be able to obtain coverage through the use of riders or extra premiums.

If you are thinking about leaving a job that covers you with a group policy, take the time to learn about the policy's privileges regarding conversion into an individual policy after you leave the job. Oftentimes, conversion privileges provide you with an expensive individual policy with only limited coverage.

If you can't afford any of these alternatives, you may qualify for Medicaid. Check with the local social services agency in your state. For those 65 and over, Parts A and B of Medicare should be purchased. Your local Social Security office can provide you with information.

Source: J. Robert Hunter, head, Consumer Federation of America, 1424 16 St., NW, Washington, DC 22207.

Medicare: What It Doesn't Cover

Don't fool yourself that all your old-age medical needs will be taken care of by Medicare. This program is riddled with coverage gaps. Be aware of what not to expect from Medicare.

What Is Medicare?

Medicare must be distinguished from Medicaid. Medicaid is the federal program providing medical coverage for the indigent of all ages. Many elderly people wind up on Medicaid when their assets are exhausted paying for what Medicare doesn't cover. This can be a tragedy for people who had hoped to leave something to their children.

Medicare is an insurance program for people over 65. It is subsidized by the federal government through the Social Security Administration. Each month, elderly people pay premiums whereby private insurance companies (like Blue Cross/Blue Shield) act as fiscal intermediaries for Medicare. The program is overseen by a watchdog agency, the Health Care Financing Administration (HCFA), which makes sure hospitals are used properly.

Drawbacks: Private insurance companies, acting in their own best interests, tend to deny benefits whenever possible. HCFAs interpret Medicare regulations restrictively, in order to save Medicare Trust Fund monies.

Major problems with Medicare:

● **Congress passed much of the Medicare legislation with the intention of helping the elderly by keeping them out of institutions.** However, the local agencies administer Medicare restrictively in a misguided attempt to save money. Actually, money is being wasted by forcing the elderly into nursing homes unnecessarily.

● **Medicare does not deal with custodial care.** It is geared toward rehabilitation, which is hardly realistic for the population it serves.

● **Medicare is part of an overall supply-and-demand problem.** There are more and more old people every year, as modern medicine enables us to live longer. Because of this, nursing homes are filled to capacity and have long waiting lists, and Social Security benefits and services to the elderly are being cut back.

● **Hospital cutoffs are the biggest problem with Medicare today.** *Example:* An elderly woman goes into the hospital with a broken hip. After surgery, she cannot go home because she can't take care of herself. She needs nursing-home rehabilita-tion or an around-the-clock companion at home. Because of the shortage of these long-term-care alternatives, she has to remain in the hospital, although everyone agrees she is ready to leave. But Medicare cuts off hospitalization benefits, claiming that she no longer needs hospitalization. The family gets a threatening letter from the hospital—if she isn't out in 24 hours, the family will have to pay privately. At the present rates for a hospital bed, the family's assets will be wiped out very quickly.

The Appeal Process

The only way to deal with such unfair (and inhumane) bureaucratic decisions is to appeal them aggressively. *Chances on appeal:* Very good. At the highest level, federal court, the reversal rate on Medicare cases is extremely high. *There are four levels of appeal:*

● **Reconsideration is a paper review by a bureaucrat.** You can request this when Medicare is first denied. Some 95% of reconsiderations confirm the original denial of benefits.

● **An administrative law judge will review the case after the reconsideration is denied.** You present evidence at this hearing, and a lawyer is recommended. Some of these judges are competent and sympathetic. However, many judges fail to understand the issue.

● **The Appeals Council in Washington is the next step.** It will usually rubber-stamp the decision of the administrative law judge.

● **Federal court is your final crack.** You stand a good chance of winning, because judges at this level are not employees of the Social Security Administration. They tend to be less sympathetic to the agency's viewpoint. You will need a lawyer at this.

Important: No new evidence can be presented in federal court, so be sure all your facts are presented to the administrative law judge.

EXPLANATION of AMENDED MEDICARE BENEFITS

Medicare and Nursing Homes

Under the law, up to 100 days of skilled nursing care in a nursing home are to be paid for by Medicare. In fact, Medicare pays for an average of only five days, claiming that nursing homes do not provide skilled care. This is another patently unfair decision that must be appealed on an individual basis.

Beyond 100 days, you're on your own as far as nursing-home care is concerned. Medicaid will take over only after your assets are totally exhausted. At an average cost of $40,000 to $100,000 per year, depending on the state of residence, few families can afford long-term nursing-home care.

Important: Plan ahead for this possibility well before a nursing home becomes necessary. Transfer your assets to your children, or set up a trust fund that the government can't invade.

Beware: You may be liable for payment if your assets have been transferred within less than three or five years if a trust fund was established. *Helpful:* Consultation with a specialist in elder law. Ask your lawyer or a social worker in a local hospital or nursing home to recommend one. There is also now a National Academy of Elder Law Attorneys, with a directory of Elder Law attorneys in every state: 1604 North Country Road, Tuscon, AZ 85716.

Home Care

The home-care situation under Medicare is also dismal. Medicare will pay for a skilled person to come into the home occasionally on a doctor's orders to perform tasks such as giving injections or physical therapy.

There is virtually no coverage for the kind of help most elderly people need—a housekeeper/companion to help with personal and household tasks. Many senior citizens groups are currently lobbying for this type of home custodial care to be provided by Medicare.

Assignment Rate

As far as general health is concerned, Medicare supposedly pays 80% of the "reasonable rate" for medical care as determined by a board of doctors in the community. In reality, the "reasonable rate" is usually set so low that most doctors will not accept it. So instead of paying 20% of their doctor bills, the elderly frequently wind up paying 50% or even more.

Suggestions

● **Don't drop your major-medical insurance when you retire.** If you keep it up, it will cover the gaps in your Medicare insurance. It is extremely difficult to buy such coverage after you reach 65.

● **Be wary of insurance company policies that supplement Medicare.** You must be extremely careful when you buy one. Be sure it complements rather than duplicates Medicare coverage.

● **Get together with other senior citizens to create consumer leverage.** If a group of 50 seniors goes to a doctor and all promise to patronize him or her provided he or she accepts the Medicare assigned rate, it might be worth the doctor's while.

● **Purchase long-term-care insurance.** In 1997 Congress enacted legislation to encourage the purchase of long-term-care insurance to pay for nursing homes. For the first time, there are federal standards to protect the consumer. If a senior citizen can afford long-term-care insurance, this eliminates the need for "Medicaid planning." These policies provide for custodial care and pick up where Medicare ends with nursing-home coverage.

● **Convert life insurance to long-term-care insurance.** Some insurance companies are beginning to offer the right to convert the cash value of life insurance policies to long-term-care policies. Since children are no longer dependents at this time, the need for life insurance is diminished at the very time that the need for long-term-care insurance has increased.

Source: *Charles Robert, partner, Robert, Lerner & Robert, 100 Merrick Rd., West Bldg., Suite 508, Rockville Centre, NY 11570.*

Supplemental Health Insurance If You Are on Medicare

Although Medicare provides national health insurance for the elderly, the program actually covers less than half of health expenses. The gaps in coverage are difficult to understand and are constantly changing—as a result, many elderly people end up buying supplementary insurance that is inadequate.

Those whose coverage at work is not extended upon retirement to supplement Medicare should consider the best Blue Cross/Blue Shield Medicare supplement policy available and the Prudential policies offered through the American Association of

DISABILITY INSURANCE: WHAT YOU NEED, WHAT TO LOOK FOR

Too many people overestimate their ability to withstand the financial impact of a disability lasting more than 90 days. *Their most common misconceptions:*

● **Their employers "will take care of them,"** either through a formal income-replacement program or by simply keeping them on the payroll.

● **Their family's standard of living can be lowered** to accommodate the loss of income.

● **A spouse who has not worked outside of the home for a number of years** can attain a relatively high-paying job in a short period of time.

● **A growing net worth,** which may be invested in illiquid assets or assets that could only be sold at a substantial discount, can cover their loss of income. Don't underestimate your needs for adequate disability protection. If you aren't in a position to self-insure against the risk of a disabling accident or illness, you need some insurance to help fill the gap.

Maximizing Value

Whether you are seeking employer-provided or individually purchased coverage, the objectives and criteria for selection are essentially the same. The key in both cases is to maximize the value of the premium dollar by budgeting for smaller losses and insuring against the catastrophic occurrences that could ruin your personal financial plan.

A major point to consider when choosing a plan is the need to keep your "waiting or elimination period" (the period during a disability when the insurer is not responsible for paying you benefits) between three and six months. These are usually financially acceptable waiting periods. Purchasing the traditional 30-day elimination period can be as much as 40% more expensive and often provides unnecessary coverage.

The "benefit period"—the length of time you can expect to receive disability income—should extend to at least age 65 for each separate incident of disability. For extra safety and where the family unit is relatively young, pay a higher premium in exchange for a lifetime benefit period.

As you get older, you can reduce your coverage and save money by increasing your policy's elimination period and/or reducing the benefit amount. In most cases, a family's financial burdens decline over the years and its ability to meet those burdens improves. As children move out and investment assets are accumulated, the necessity for maintaining disability insurance declines, although it may not be eliminated. However, you should generally avoid cutting costs by reducing your benefit period. If you were struck by a catastrophic disability, you would want benefits for as long a period as possible.

Another major concern is the manner in which the condition of disability is defined in an insurance contract. Some policies use the "pure residual" approach, with the reduction in the level of earnings as the sole criterion. Since this approach is relatively objective, such contracts are frequently less expensive than those using the alternative approach: evaluating your ability to perform the duties of an occupation or profession. This approach has many variations, ranging from "ability to perform any duties of any occupation or profession" to "ability to perform the material duties of your profession until age 65." Since the approach is more subjective, premium rates are generally higher.

Normally, the policy with the broadest definition of disability is best, unless you can claim true "specialist" status and justify the added cost. Therefore, the residual approach is suitable for occupations offering the flexibility of reduced hours and duties, while the "ability to perform" approach is best for professions that lack that flexibility—for example, the medical profession. Some policies do feature characteristics of both approaches.

Source: *Andrew E. Gross, treasurer and shareholder of Dennis M. Gurtz and Associates, Inc., 4910 Massachusetts Ave. NW, Suite 112, Washington, DC 20016, a financial-planning and consulting firm. The author has an extensive academic and professional background in accounting, risk management and other financial-planning matters.*

Retired Persons. In some states, anyone 65 or over can become a subscriber to Blue Cross/ Blue Shield, without evidence of insurability, during the annual "open enrollment" periods.

Buying more than one supplemental policy will not necessarily increase your coverage. Most policies have provisions that require claims payments to be coordinated with other policies so that one policy won't pay if another does, or both policies will pay only half. Medicare supplemental policies almost never cover nursing homes or extended care. Some insurers have begun to offer such coverage, but a congressional study has criticized many of these policies.

Source: J. Robert Hunter, head of the insurance group at Consumer Federation of America, 1424 16 St. NW, Washington, DC 22207.

What to Consider Before Choosing a Nursing Home

Cost of nursing homes in your locale; whether the policy requires hospitalization before entering a home; the amount of the deductible; coverage for custodial care as well as for skilled care; the duration of coverage; inflation coverage; whether mental illnesses are included or excluded. A policy that excludes mental illness only if there is no organic cause still protects you in the event of Alzheimer's disease. The younger the insured, the lower the premiums.

Important: The 1997 Taxpayer Relief Act enables taxpayers to include with medical expenses the payments for *qualified* long-term-care insurance premiums (with limits); payments you receive from such plans are tax-free. Be sure any plan you consider meets the standards set in the tax law.

Companies to consider: Travelers, CNA, GE Capital, John Hancock and Time Fortis.

Source: Norma Severns, former nurse practitioner and fee-based financial planner with Armstrong, Welch, and MacIntyre, 155 Connecticut Ave. NW, Washington, DC 20036.

More About Disability Insurance

Most people shy away from buying disability insurance because they think they'll never become disabled. Statistics show, however, that at age 37, you're three and

a half times more likely to become disabled than to die, and that disability remains more likely than death until you're 68. Many people suffer injury or illness severe enough to make them unable to work, but insufficiently serious to kill them.

Disability policies are among the most confusing to decipher. *Look for:*

● **Noncancelable by the company**—only by you.

● **Guaranteed continuable** until age 65–70 (75 is even better).

● **Restrictive riders** shouldn't be added by the company when the policy is issued. Look for the broadest coverage you can find.

● **Premium cost should be guaranteed not to rise before you reach 65.** *Trade-off:* Your coverage will remain flat, regardless of inflation. You can pay extra for a cost-of-living adjustment rider to pick up the slack.

● **Prompt processing of claims**—within 10 business days, unless the claim is complicated. (One otherwise good company processes claims through its zone managers. If a manager has a bad quarter with a lot of claims, your claim might be held back and not processed until the following quarter.)

How Disability Is Defined

A useful definition of disability is "your inability to perform the material and substantial duties of your occupation." Under this definition, for example, an anesthesiologist who contracted hepatitis and could no longer practice had to change his profession to hospital administrator, and he was covered. He received $4,000 a month from the insurance company in addition to his regular salary.

Bad definition: One that deals with your inability to work—period. A policy like this won't protect you at all. (The definition used by Social Security is the inability to perform any occupation.)

Injury versus sickness. Insurance companies handle injury claims differently from claims due to illness. Illness-related claims almost always pay fewer benefits than accident claims. Sometimes the company will simply change the classification to its own advantage. *Example:* In a policy, the wording "After a stated period of time after your accident, we'll pay you as though you were sick" will reduce both the amount of money you'll receive and the length of time that you'll receive it—sometimes from a lifetime (the longest possible length of payments for an accident claim) down to as little as five years. *Much better:* that payments for injuries due to an accident remain in the injury-claim classification, regardless of how much time elapses.

● **Disability insurers also use tricky language to define exactly when you get sick.** Since getting a claim approved hinges on when you became ill, using the wording "when the illness first manifests itself" permits the company to deny the claim on the grounds that the illness predated the policy but wasn't diagnosed until after the policy was signed.

Typical: An insurer denies a claim for cancer because the policyholder had the disease for years before the problem became apparent.

● **Occupational classes.** Disability benefits are highly dependent on your occupation at the time of the accident or illness. How long you'll receive benefits depends on the complexity of your training for your current job and the ease with which you might be trained for a new one. *Examples:* Surgeons are covered for life; managers, 10 years; salespeople, five years; barbers, two years. Good insurance agents help find the company with the most favorable length of occupational coverage and will help you get into the best category.

● **Specialties within a profession.** Some insurance companies don't recognize specialties, and, for example, lump together all their insured lawyers. Avoid these companies. Look for an insurer that differentiates between a litigator and a patent attorney and differentiates in payments for, say, a broken leg, which obviously incapacitates the litigator much more than the patent attorney.

● **Residual (partial) disability.** This desirable rider—available at extra cost—will pay you if, after an illness, you can work only one or two days a week. Usually, if you lose 20% or more of your earned income, you are considered to be residually disabled.

Exclusionary Period

You can choose from exclusionary periods (also known as elimination or deductible periods) of seven, 14, 30, 60, 90 and 180 days—the number of days after the onset of illness or injury it will take for payments to begin. The longer the period, the lower the cost of the policy. Your choice should depend on what other insurance benefits you have.

Recommended: 60–90 days.

● **Amount of coverage.** Most companies won't insure you for more than 50%–60% of your earned income. Payments are tax-free if you—not your employer—have paid for the policy. You often can end up with as much as 85% of your after-tax income.

● **Best package.** If your funds to buy insurance are limited and you're a professional or an executive, buy lifetime accident coverage, sickness to 65 (lifetime, if you can afford it) and residual disability, with a 60- or 90-day exclusionary period. Cost-of-living adjustment riders can be added or dropped each year.

Traps

Here are some serious drawbacks to group disability plans that can leave you high and dry in the event of an accident or illness:

● **The issuer can cancel the policy.**

● **Premiums aren't guaranteed**—the issuer can raise them dramatically.

● **Coverage and claims practices favor the company, not the insured.**

Source: Leonard B. Stern, president, Leonard B. Stern & Co., a financial services and consulting firm, 305 Madison Ave., New York, NY 10165.

How Much Disability Insurance Is Enough?

Before buying disability insurance, it is important to assess what resources you already have that would enable you and your family to manage in the event of an accident or illness. Compare these resources with your expenditures. Then, make up any gap with disability insurance.

Key questions:

● **Would you get partial pay from your employer?** How much? For how long?

● **Do you have a benevolent family member** you could count on to keep you going or at least to help?

● **What assets do you have that could be converted quickly?**

● **Are you already covered by disability insurance policies?** (Don't forget to check what's provided by credit cards and association memberships.)

● **What could you expect from Social Security?**

You should always reassess your disability coverage whenever:

● **Income changes.** Almost everyone increases lifestyle and financial needs when income increases.

● **Financial responsibilities increase.** *Examples:* You have a new child, a new mortgage, or build a new house.

There is a Social Security trap to watch out for in planning your insurance needs. To get disability payments from Social Security, you must have paid into the system for 40 quarters. But there are errors in the Social Security records, and you may find out too late that records are wrong and you're not covered.

Safeguard: File form 7004 with your local Social Security office every three years for a copy of your account. If there's a mistake, immediately notify your local SSA office. It does not matter how long ago the mistake was made.

Homeowner's or Renter's Insurance

Homeowner's insurance provides protection for risks such as fire, lightning, wind, hail and theft. It does not cover some catastrophic events such as flood, earthquake and nuclear accident. Policies also include liability coverage in case someone sues you for an accident other than an auto claim, such as a dog bite or a fall on your property.

Renter's insurance, which is usually inexpensive, covers your own personal property (furniture, etc.) and most liabilities you may incur when renting a property. Similar coverage is available for owners of condominiums, cooperatives, or mobile homes.

Buying Suggestions

To decide how much homeowner's coverage you need, get an appraisal of the cost to rebuild your home if a disaster happens. *Don't* insure to market value. An appraisal calculates the cost per square foot by builders in your area. Real estate values fluctuate. You don't want to insure the land or basement. Your insurance agent usually appraises homes free. Or you can get a professional appraisal for around $200 and up, depending on your area.

For example, if it would cost $50,000 to replace your home, only insure to $50,000, not more. But don't insure for *less* than 80% of its value, because you'll forfeit the right to collect full replacement, at

today's costs, of your home and possessions. Instead, you'll only get its *actual cash value.* That's what it costs, less depreciation.

Note: If you qualify, the federal government will sell you flood insurance (call the National Flood Insurance Program, 800-638-6620). The government does this because not all areas of the country are flood-prone.

Communities in flood-prone areas get government insurance if they promise to take steps to protect against flooding (dikes, levees, stricter building costs). It would be unfair for companies to charge for flood protection in, say, Kansas, so flood protection is not standard in homeowner's policies.

When shopping for a homeowner's policy, keep in mind that you can usually save money by buying from a direct-writing insurer (one that doesn't use so-called "independent agents").

Source: J. Robert Hunter, head of the insurance group, at Consumer Federation of America, 1424 16 St. NW, Washington, DC 22207.

Easily Overlooked Discounts

Homeowner's policy discounts are offered by many insurers for sprinkler and alarm systems (15%–20%); burglar alarms and fire department inspections (2%–5%); deadbolt locks and smoke alarms (2%–5%). *Other discount possibilities:* No smokers in the household. Homeowners who are 55 or older.

Source: Medical Economics.

Coverage for College Students

A college student's valuables may be best insured by personal articles "floaters." These extend standard homeowners policies. *Most reasonable rates:* CD players, cameras and musical instruments.

Bonus: Floaters provide coverage for loss or accidental damage as well as for theft.

Source: Sylvia Porter's Personal Finance.

How to Avoid Homeowner's Insurance Pitfalls

Most people buy their homeowner's insurance from the company that gives them the best price. And for many buyers, that's the smart way to go. But if the insured's property—home and belongings—is valued at more than $200,000 or if they also have a vacation house and some jewelry, silver and fine art, they may be inadequately covered or may be wasting money on overlapping coverage.

Insurance companies usually aim for one segment of the marketplace. Most go after the big middle market—homes valued at under $200,000 and owners who have few or no valuables such as fine art, jewelry, furs or silver. And for those people, the homeowner's policies issued by these firms are indeed adequate. In fact, the cost of that type of coverage is usually quite competitive because so many firms are fighting for a share of that large pie.

But when the value of property starts to climb, the owner should look at insurance in a fundamentally different way. Are the changing values of possessions being tracked? Prices for fine art and jewelry don't remain static. They may rise or fall, depending on market conditions. Some fine art posts dramatic swings, especially the moderns.

With mass-market insurance policies, upper dollar limits are usually built into the coverage of some items. These limits vary for different parts of the country.

Of course, you can consider buying additional coverage for items that exceed the upper dollar limit. This extra coverage is called a personal articles floater (known as a PAF in the trade). However, in order to get higher-value PAF coverage, you will have to prove the value of those items, either by providing a bill of sale or by getting an appraisal from an expert in the field.

Insurance firms that aim for the middle market may discourage such special coverage for valuable items because they don't really have a ready-made policy to offer. Their prices for special items are usually not competitive. And, before offering coverage, they may require an appraisal (inconvenient and not that inexpensive) on an item valued as low as $1,000.

Some people who started out adequately covered by the midrange homeowner's policy when they were young find after several years that they are starting to grow beyond the protection of their coverage. Many people buy "inflation guard," coverage that increases protection automatically, about 1% every four months. This increases the premium, but not significantly.

BETTER HOME INSURANCE BUYING

Many people spend far too much money for home insurance and then end up with the wrong coverage.

Key: Don't waste money protecting yourself against small losses.

What you should look for:

● **Home replacement coverage:** Protect yourself against the total destruction of your house. Urban and suburban homeowners may need to buy coverage for only 80% of the replacement value of a home because local fire services in the city are quicker to respond than those in rural areas. If your insurance is for a dollar amount, check annually to see if it will still pay for a replacement home.

● **High deductibles:** A $1,000 deductible can cut insurance premiums by 15%. The savings will normally more than make up for the cost of repairing minor damage such as a broken window.

● **Extra coverage of high-value items:** Most policies limit payment for certain valuable items. *Typical:* Jewelry losses can't exceed $1,000–$2,000 (depending on the company you use), silverware, $1,000. To insure these for their true value, purchase a personal articles floater that spells out how much the company will pay in the event of a loss.

Adequate liability protection: Most policies provide only $100,000 for personal liability. That's not enough coverage if you have above-average income and assets.

Better: An umbrella policy that picks up where your homeowner's and automobile insurance policies leave off (a particularly good idea for pool owners, for example).

....

Source: Rodale's Practical Homeowner, *Emmaus, PA.*

What to Do

Just as some insurance firms specialize in the middle market and thus offer the best prices for that one, other insurance firms specialize in the narrower, higher-bracket markets. Once the value of your home and belongings exceeds $200,000, you should investigate what coverage is available from these firms. They may offer not only a better price, but also policies that are tailored to your special needs. If your current agent represents only middle-market firms, ask him or her to recommend an agent or broker that can service you. Other routes: Contact your local insurance association, or call the National Association of Casualty and Surety Agents.

Second Home

If you own a vacation house in addition to your main residence, be aware of the gap trap or the overlap trap. Often a vacation-home owner buys coverage from a broker or agent in the vicinity of the dwelling on the theory that if anything should happen, the representative is here. That is logical—up to a point.

Problems:

● **The agent at the vacation spot** may assume that, say, a small boat is covered by the insured's main policy. So he or she omits it from the vacation-home policy. Or the insured may have the boat covered under both policies. With two uncoordinated policies, the insured may be paying for too much liability coverage.

● **There is no discount for coverage on two houses,** as there is for coverage on two or more cars.

Other Considerations

Important basic: What formula does the homeowner's policy use to settle claims? Many midrange policies guarantee to pay actual cash value (known as ACV in the trade). That certainly sounds good—until you discover (perhaps belatedly) that the insurance company subtracts from the actual cash value the damaged article's depreciation.

To see how ACV works, let's use as an example a damaged sofa that cost $5,000 new and has a useful life of 10 years. It has depreciated by $500 a year. If

> **"Homeowner's insurance trap: Letting friends use your home when you're not in residence may invalidate your insurance."**

the sofa is eight years old when damaged, the owner will wind up with a settlement check of $1,000 (minus, probably, a $250 deductible).

Some policies have a four-times-ACV clause for settlement, which means the owner of the sofa will get a check for $4,000 (minus the deductible). And still other policies call for payment of full replacement cost of the damaged item. Considering inflation, that could put the settlement check at something like $7,500.

A conscientious agent will point out these and other differences that could have an impact on the settlement you receive as a result of a loss.

Source: Robert Fergusson, assistant vice president and personal client services marketing manager, Marsh & McLennan Companies, Inc., New York, NY.

You're Covered—or Are You?

An "all-risk" homeowner's policy isn't necessarily what its name implies. Some policies may not give you protection against heavy damage caused by a flood, hurricane or other natural disaster.

For adequate protection, insure your house for at least 80% of replacement value—the cost of rebuilding it with the same materials, at today's labor rates. Also, pay the added premium for a "replacement cost endorsement" on your home's contents. Otherwise, the insurer will pay you only a depreciated amount on items that suffer wear and tear.

Source: Benjamin Lipson, Benjamin Lipson Associates Insurance Agency, author of How to Collect More on Your Insurance Claims, *Simon & Schuster.*

While You Were Gone...

Homeowner's insurance trap: Letting friends use your home when you're not in residence may invalidate your insurance. Insurance companies assume that the owner will take better precautions to protect the property than a renter will. If you rent out your vacation home, for example, purchase either "all-risk" or "special multiperil" insurance. These policies cost more, but they'll cover both theft and liability losses.

Source: Profit Building Strategies for Business Owners, Scarsdale, NY.

Protection for Renters

Only one renter in five has property or liability insurance.

Problem: The landlord's policy covers only the building, not tenants' possessions. *Guidelines:*

● **For adequate property protection,** buy a policy with full replacement coverage. This will cost 15%–40% more than the same policy at actual-cash-value coverage (replacement less depreciation), but is well worth it.

● **The standard policy sets a liability limit of $25,000,** inadequate for most people. For $10 or so extra, you can raise the limit to $100,000.

● **Expensive jewelry, watches and furs are best protected by a personal articles floater,** a policy amendment that insures each item individually.

● **You can save 10% by raising your deductible** from $100 to $250, and another 10% by increasing it to $500.

Source: Money, New York, NY.

How to Save on Auto Insurance

There are four major areas of coverage in a typical auto insurance policy:

● **Bodily injury liability** (including personal injury protection in "no-fault" states), in case you injure someone.

● **Property damage liability,** in case you damage someone else's property.

● **Collision,** in case you damage your own car.

● **Comprehensive,** in case your car is stolen, vandalized or otherwise damaged.

Each of these areas is subject to cost cutting.

● **Don't buy unnecessary coverage.** As a rule, every $1 of auto insurance premiums returns approximately 60¢ in claims—the rest is overhead. By self-insuring for the small risks you can afford, you can save up to 40%.

● **Avoid collision insurance on older cars.** Collision insurance is generally expensive relative to other types of coverage and is not economical if your car is not very valuable. Comprehensive insurance is a less expensive alternative and, given the chance of total loss due to theft, should probably be purchased anyway.

● **Increase your deductibles.** Increasing your deductible $200–$500 could reduce your collision cost by 15%–30%. The trade-off is that you are required to

pay for more small claims. Over time the savings in premiums should, however, more than pay for your claims if you are an average or better driver. And because small claims increase your premiums, filing fewer claims will reduce the chance that your premiums will rise in the future.

● **Avoid incidental coverages.** Buy good medical insurance and skip auto medical payments. (In no-fault states, use medical insurance in lieu of personal injury protection if you are able to legally.) Avoid coverage for substitute transportation, which pays for rental cars when your car is being repaired, for towing coverage and for memberships in insurance-company auto clubs, which are not good values.

● **Shop around.** Some companies charge two or three times what others charge for identical coverage.

Trouble Finding Coverage?

If you can't find coverage, call insurers that specialize in "nonstandard" risks, those for drivers with higher than average risk. Most agents can recommend one or two. Or call your state insurance department for referrals. You'll have to pay more for the coverage. In many states, however, claims or other items such as where you live, or how you live, or even the whim of the insurance company, may cause inexpensive insurers to reject your application. As a result, you may be forced to seek insurance from high-rate companies that specialize in selling insurance to people who have difficulty finding coverage. In some cases, you may be better off going to the state-guaranteed assigned-risk plan than paying the rates of some of these high-risk insurers. These state-required mechanisms must sell auto insurance to licensed drivers who have the money to pay their premiums.

Source: J. Robert Hunter, head of the insurance group at Consumer Federation of America, 1424 16 St. NW, Washington, DC 22207.

Children's Car Insurance Costs

You can cut car insurance costs when children who still live with you start driving.

● **List them as occasional drivers,** not principal drivers. That alone will cut the premium by up to one-third for boys and by one-fourth for girls.

● **Allow your child to drive only one of your cars** (if you have more than one), preferably the least expensive one. If more than one child has a driver's license, cover girls for driving the more expensive car.

● **Make sure the youngsters take driver's education.** Insurance discounts of 10% are available for those who pass.

● **Look into "good student" discounts.** For the minimum discount, your child must maintain at least a B average; maintaining a higher average increases the size of the discount. Good-student discounts commonly cut the premium by one-fourth.

● **If your child is going to a college more than 100 miles** from home and does not have a car on campus, try to get a college student discount of 10% to 15%.

● **If your child has a car,** have it put on your policy. Multicar discounts can be anywhere from 10% to 25% depending on the insurance company.

Guarding Against The Uninsured

An accident with an uninsured or underinsured motorist can be financially ruinous. As part of your own policy, underinsured (in some states) and uninsured motorists coverage is obtainable to deal with such accidents.

Uninsured Coverage

Most states have statutory requirements that automobile liability insurance policies include uninsured motorist's coverage.

● **Financial responsibility limits.** The law requires that uninsured motorist's coverage be provided in an amount mandated by the state. These financial responsibility limits vary.

● **Getting more coverage.** Usually you can buy coverage up to your liability limits. *Example:* If you carry $300,000 in liability, you can get the same amount in uninsured coverage.

● **Proof of fault.** Under uninsured coverage, your company has to pay you only what the other party is legally liable for. So, the other party must be proved at fault.

● **Comparative negligence provisions.** In some states, if the other driver is proved somewhat at fault, you can recover proportional damages from your own insurance company.

● **Making a claim.** You are placed in an adversarial position with your own insurance company. You must prove the extent of the injury, establish its value, and negotiate with your own carrier to settle. If you can't reach a settlement, most claims will go to arbitration, not to court.

● **Limits.** Most mandatory uninsured motorist's protection covers only bodily injury. Property damage is covered under your collision insurance, after the deductible. (As with any collision claim, your rates may go up after filing.)

Underinsured Coverage

This type of coverage is becoming more and more popular. Some states require that underinsured coverage be offered. In others, it is optional. With underinsured coverage:

● **You must first recover the maximum amount** from the other party's liability policy before you can collect on your own policy.

● **As with uninsured coverage, you are in an adversarial position with your carrier** and must prove that the value of your injury has exceeded the liability limits of the other party's policy.

Important: Uninsured motorist's coverage will not pay you if the other driver has any insurance at all, no matter how inadequate.

Pedestrian Accidents

You will be covered by your uninsured motorist's coverage just as if you were in a car at the time. If you don't own a car, you might be able to get coverage under the policy of a family member in your immediate household who does own one. If neither you nor anyone in your family has coverage, you can apply to a fund that some states maintain to cover such accidents, or pursue a court action directly against the responsible party.

Source: Richard P. Oatman, assistant claim counsel for Aetna Life & Casualty, Hartford, CT.

Hold on to Your Title Insurance

Keep your owner's title insurance policy even if you sell your home. The insurance is permanent protection for your interests in the property. *Example:* If a previously unknown title problem arises against the house you sell, even if it was against a previous owner, your buyer can sue you for resulting financial loss. Owner's title insurance will pay valid claims, and will pay for defending against an attack on title as insured.

Most home purchases are covered by lender's title insurance required by the mortgage lending institution as protection for its interest in the real estate. Lender's title insurance is usually paid for by the home buyer. Remember that owner's, not lender's, title insurance is needed to fully protect the buyer.

In some locales, owner's title insurance is provided and paid for by the seller of a home. In others, the buyer who wishes to have protection must request and pay for owner's coverage. It's a matter of local custom.

In buyer pay locations, owner's title insurance often can be obtained at the same time lender coverage is ordered—for a relatively modest additional charge.

Source: US News & World Report.

HOW TO BUY AN UMBRELLA INSURANCE POLICY

Anyone who owns a home or significant assets needs an umbrella insurance policy.

An umbrella policy protects your family's assets in the unlikely—but possible—event of your being sued for damages in a lawsuit. It also covers you against suits filed as a result of accidents beyond those that occur in your home or car, as well as legal fees to defend against such a suit. *Examples:* if you're golfing and injure another golfer with a ball or your dog runs off and bites a pedestrian.

What a Policy Costs
Most umbrella policies are inexpensive. For $150 to $300 a year, you can buy up to $1 million in coverage. *Strategy:* If you don't want to increase your total insurance costs by adding umbrella coverage, increase the deductibles on your auto and homeowner's policies.

Shopping Strategies When shopping for a policy, ask your insurer for a comprehensive breakdown of what is—and what is not—covered.

Important: Don't leave risky gaps between your umbrella policy and your auto and home-owner's policies. Reason: Most umbrella policies are structured to provide $1 million of coverage—after your first $300,000 in liability losses, which are covered by your auto and home owners policies.

Self-defense: Check your existing policies, and eliminate any gaps. If necessary, raise your auto or homeowner deductibles to balance out the added cost of higher liability protection.

Shopping for a Policy
Start by contacting the insurers that have sold your family its policies. If their rates are reasonable and their coverage levels comprehensive, you'll reduce complications by keeping your coverage under the same roof. Ask your insurer if you can qualify for a dis-

count by adding an umbrella policy to your coverage.

Special Needs
● **Operating a home-based business.** You may need a separate, commercially oriented umbrella policy to protect you against related liability risks. A total of $1 million worth of protection may not be sufficient. Ask your insurance agent for recommendations.

● **Owning more than one home.** If you own primary and vacation residences, a good policy should cover both. But it pays to investigate, particularly if one or more properties provide significant rental income.

● **Serving on a nonprofit board.** Some umbrella policies include Directors and Officers (D&O) liability protection, but others do not. If you are asked to serve on a board, ask if the board is covered by the nonprofit's insurance.

If it is not, check your own coverage before joining the board of your child's nursery school, your co-op building or any other nonprofit group. *Note:* As a rule, for-profit companies buy D&O coverage for their boards.

Source: Robert Hunter, head of the insurance group at the Consumer Federation of America (CFA), a consumer advocate organization, 1424 16 St. NW, Suite. 604, Washington, DC 20036. He is the author of Buyer's Guide to Insurance, *available from the CFA.*

Estate Planning

11

What Gets Taxed and How the Tax Is Calculated

To achieve your estate-planning goals, the first step you should take is to understand the size of your estate and the manner in which it (not your beneficiaries) will be taxed. The following guidelines should enable you to make estimates for federal tax purposes.

The Gross Estate

The gross estate includes all property you own, some property you may not realize you own and property you no longer own. Property you own includes cash, stocks and bonds, real estate (including your home) and other personal property—car, furniture, jewelry, etc.

Property you may not realize you own often comprises the largest assets in an estate. Among these are life insurance proceeds that are either payable to your estate or payable to others (if you own the policy). Pension and profit-sharing plans, once eligible for certain exclusions, are now also included.

Other property you may overlook includes joint tenancy property. Only half the value of joint tenancy property held by a husband and a wife is included in the gross estate of the spouse who dies first—regardless of who actually provided the funds for its purchase. Other joint tenancy property, however, is fully included in the gross estate unless the estate can show that some or all of the funds used to purchase it came from another joint tenant.

Property you no longer own that is included in your gross estate is generally property you've transferred to others, but over which you still retain certain rights. For example, if you made a gift of stock to your children but retained the right to the dividends, the entire value of that stock would be included in your gross estate.

Deductions From the Gross Estate

The gross estate is reduced by deductions for debts (including home mortgages), funeral expenses, expenses of administering the estate, amounts trans-

> "Property you no longer own that is included in your gross estate is generally property you've transferred to others, but over which you still retain certain rights."

ferred to charity and, perhaps most significant, amounts passing to your surviving spouse.

Oftentimes, the primary objective of estate planning is to give as much property to the spouse as possible without paying taxes. The "marital" deduction is available for property passing outright and for amounts left in trust, assuming you meet certain conditions. Of course, an estate tax will ultimately be payable by your spouse's estate.

Calculating the Tax

After reducing your gross estate by allowable deductions, the remaining amount is your taxable estate. Normally, this is the figure on which the tax is based, although there is a further adjustment for gifts in excess of an annual gift tax exclusion (currently $10,000 per donee, or $20,000 if your spouse consents to the gift). For every taxpayer, the federal government grants a credit against the estate tax, computed so that estates of $650,000 or less in 1999 are not subject to the tax. (This figure increases gradually each year until it reaches $1 million in 2006 and thereafter.) In excess of this amount, estates pay tax at a minimum rate of 37% and at a maximum rate of 55%.

Source: Gary Hart, president of Gary Hart & Associates, Ltd., 333 West Wacker Drive, Suite 700, Chicago, IL 60606, a certified public accounting firm providing tax, financial planning, and accounting services to individuals and closely held businesses. He is also a frequent speaker on personal financial planning and estate planning.

Tough-Minded Estate Planning

It may seem callous to even think about taxes when a loved one faces a life-threatening illness. But if tax planning is ignored at that point, assets carefully accumulated over a lifetime may be squandered unnecessarily. For many facing a final illness, dealing with these matters provides a life-oriented focus that helps them combat depression and achieve a sense of completion in seeing that their affairs are well ordered. *Some things to consider:*

● **Gifts by the patient.** In many cases, estate taxes can be saved by making gifts to family members and other intended beneficiaries. An unlimited amount may be transferred gift-tax-free provided no one person receives more than $10,000. The maximum tax-free gift per recipient can increase to $20,000 if the patient's spouse is still alive and consents to treat each gift as having been jointly made. *(Editor's note:* Transfers of life insurance and certain other interests made within three years of death are still part of the patient's estate.)

● **Gifts to the patient.** This tactic may seem useful when the patient doesn't have enough property to take full advantage of the applicable estate tax exclusion amount ($650,000 in 1999, increasing to $1 million in 2006). *Reason:* Property that passes through the decedent's estate gets what's known as a "stepped-up basis." That is, the person who inherits it is treated for income tax purposes as though he or she bought it and paid what it is worth on the date of death (or what it was worth six months after the date of death if the executor chooses this alternative date to set the value of the taxable estate). *Example:* Mr. Jones, a cancer patient, has $150,000 worth of assets. His wife has a large estate, including $75,000 worth of stock that has a tax basis of $10,000. That means there's $65,000 worth of taxable gain built into the stock. She gives the stock to her husband. (There's no tax on gifts between spouses.) Mr. Jones leaves the stock to the children. The children inherit the stock with the basis stepped up to $75,000. So if they turn right around and sell it for $75,000, there's no taxable gain. With these shares, Mr. Jones's estate is still only $225,000—under the applicable exclusion amount. So the stepped-up basis is achieved without paying federal estate tax. And the property is taken out of Mrs. Jones's estate, where it might be taxed.

In most cases, it doesn't pay to use this tactic with property that will be bequeathed back to a spouse who gave it to the patient. *Reason:* Unless the gift was made more than a year before the date of death, stepped-up basis will be denied. But when the patient is expected to survive for substantially more than a year, this tactic can be quite useful. *Example:* Mr. Smith owns a $150,000 rental property with a $25,000 tax basis. Mrs. Smith has a disease that will be fatal within two to five years. She has few assets of her own. So Mr. Smith gives her the building and inherits it back from her a few years later with the basis stepped up to $150,000. This substantially increases his depreciation deductions if he keeps the building and eliminates any taxable gain if he sells it.

● **Loss property.** In general there is a tax disadvantage in inheriting property that is worth less than its original cost. *Reason:* Its tax basis is stepped down to its date-of-death value and the potential loss deduction is forfeited. If the patient has substantial income, it might pay to sell the property and deduct the losses. But it doesn't pay to generate losses that are more than $3,000 in excess of the patient's capital gains. *Reason:* These excess losses can't be deducted currently, and there's likely to be no future years' income on which to deduct them.

Alternative: Sell the loss property at its current value to a close family member. *Result:* The patient's loss on the sale is nondeductible, because the purchaser is a family member. But any future gains the family member realizes will be nontaxable to the extent of the previously disallowed loss.

● **Charitable gifts.** In some cases, bequests to charitable organizations should be made before death. *Benefit:* current income tax deductions. But it's important not to give too much away. This tactic may generate more deductions than the patient can use.

Income Tax Planning

A number of income tax moves should be considered:

● **Income timing.** If the patient is in a low tax bracket, it may pay to accelerate income. The key here is to compare the patient's tax bracket with the bracket in which his or her estate is likely to be. In some cases it will pay to accelerate income to make full use of deductions that would otherwise yield little or no tax benefit. Medical deductions, in particular, may be very high.

● **Choosing gift property.** In making gifts to save estate taxes, it does not pay from an income tax standpoint to give away property that has gone up in value. *Reason:* The tax basis of gift property is not stepped up. So the recipient will have a potential income tax liability built into the gift. This potential is eliminated if the property is kept in the estate and passes by inheritance. For similar reasons, the patient should not give away business property that has been subject to depreciation. (There's a built-in tax liability for recapture of the depreciation deductions. This is eliminated if the property passes through the estate.)

● **Other moves.** For owners of stock in an S corporation, it may pay to accelerate distribution of income, particularly if the ill shareholder has previously taxed income that wasn't distributed.

Where death is expected, but not clearly imminent, a private annuity may be a useful way of disposing of property. *Reason:* IRS regulations will key the required annuity payments to a healthy person's life expectancy.

An experienced estate planner can help you explore all aspects of these moves and other possibilities.

Source: G. William Clapp, CPA, financial planning consultant and former partner, Bessemer Trust Co., N.A., New York, NY.

Avoiding Probate by Becoming Your Own Beneficiary

Three good reasons for keeping your property out of probate court if you can possibly do so:

● **Cost:** Probate involves fees to the court, executors, attorneys and possibly others (such as appraisers and accountants).

● **Time:** In some states, it can take years to settle an estate. Meanwhile, the heirs can't get their inheritance.

● **Publicity:** Probate proceedings are public records, open to inspection.

Some assets automatically go to the beneficiaries without probate when the owner dies. Insurance proceeds are paid to the named beneficiaries, as are many pensions, IRAs, annuities and company benefits. Jointly held property goes directly to the survivor, bypassing probate.

Editor's note: And property held in trust passes to a beneficiary under the terms of the trust. Almost everything else, however, must be probated—and it makes no difference whether there's a will or not.

Create a Living Trust

An individual can avoid probate by putting property into one or more revocable trusts, naming himself or herself the income beneficiary for life. Upon death, either the trust assets can be paid out to designated beneficiaries or the trust can continue. *A common provision:* After the taxpayer's death, income goes to his or her spouse for life. The remaining assets then go to the children on the spouse's death.

A single trust or separate trusts can be created for different types of property or different beneficiaries.

Since the trust is revocable, it can be added to, property can be taken out, the beneficiaries can be changed or the trust can be ended altogether. In short, the person who sets up the trust retains complete control, but the property escapes the probate court.

Estate tax impact: Avoiding probate doesn't mean avoiding estate tax. The only way to do that is to give everything away before death—but then a gift tax must be paid, unless the gift is to your spouse.

Setting Up the Trust

Appoint yourself as trustee and appoint a co-trustee. One advantage in naming a bank or other financial institution as co-trustee is that, unlike an individual, an institution can't die or become incapacitated. If an individual co-trustee is appointed, be sure to name one or more alternatives to serve in case the first named is unable to do the job. It is possible to give the co-trustee the power to appoint others.

Trap to avoid: If a sole trustee dies or becomes incapacitated, court proceedings will be required to administer the trust.

If the trust is not intended to continue after death, the designated beneficiary of the trust can be named trustee, with the sole duty of transferring the property to himself or herself after your death.

Transferring property to the trust: It's not enough just to draw up a trust agreement. There must be an actual transfer of property to the trust.

Stocks and bonds must be sent to the transfer agents to be put in the trust's name. Bank accounts must be transferred and placed in the trust's name. Real estate must be deeded to the trust and the deeds properly recorded. Cover everything.

Trusts vs. Joint Property

Probate can also be avoided by placing property in joint ownership with a beneficiary. But this means loss of control over the property. Joint ownership is not revocable. If the original sole owner has a change of heart, there's nothing he or she can do except ask the beneficiary to give the property back. *Note:* If the transfer into joint names is to anyone but a spouse, there may be a gift tax to pay.

Tax advantage to trusts: If the property increases in value, there's an advantage to a trust. When the person who created the trust dies, the tax basis of the trust property is stepped up to its fair market value on the date of his or her death. If the property is later sold, the profit is figured on the stepped-up value, not the lower original cost. For joint property, the step-up applies only to the decedent's half. *Example:* A trust owns property purchased in 1985 for $100,000 but now worth $300,000. At the taxpayer's death, the basis of the property becomes $300,000. If it is then sold for that figure, there is no taxable gain.

SPRINKLING TRUSTS

With trusts often lasting 10 years or more, it's difficult for a settlor to predict what long-term tax and management benefits his or her beneficiaries will need. Many trusts in which income is uniformly distributed are too inflexible to adapt to beneficiaries' changing circumstances.

Classic problem: Income from a trust is equally distributed among beneficiaries in different tax brackets. The result is that income is eaten up by the taxes of the wealthy beneficiary, while too little income is directed to the beneficiary in a more favorable tax situation.

The flexibility to solve this problem can be built into a trust with an income "sprinkling" (or "spray") clause. This arrangement gives the trustee discretionary power to disburse or accumulate income and principal during the life of the trust.

Income-sprinkling trusts can create two types of tax benefits. First, by favoring lower-tax-bracket beneficiaries, a sprinkling feature can produce family income tax savings. Second, a sprinkling trust can yield estate tax savings by restricting the disposition of unnecessary income to wealthy beneficiaries, thus avoiding buildup of their estates.

Here are factors to consider when establishing a sprinkling trust.

1. You must provide detailed and comprehensive guidelines for the trustee regarding the purpose and priorities of the trust.

2. Try to create a trust in which sprinkling is established between a beneficiary and his or her descendants, rather than among beneficiaries. By doing this you may eliminate potential conflicts over unequal distribution of trust income.

3. If the beneficiary is to be your surviving spouse, he or she should be provided with a set minimum amount of income that is excluded from the discretionary powers of the sprinkling clause.

4. If you retain benefits from or control over a sprinkling trust, you will be taxed on the trust's income.

5. Careful consideration must be given to the trustee of a sprinkling trust. If one of your beneficiaries serves as sole trustee, income will be taxable to the beneficiary. If you give him or her sprinkling power over the trust, the trust's property will, for tax purposes, be included in his or her estate. This is also true even if the beneficiary is only a co-trustee. To provide the fullest tax advantages, it is best not to have a beneficiary serve in this capacity.

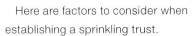

Sources: Israel A. Press, CPA, tax partner and Tom Spiesman, J.D., tax associate with Grant Thornton, 7 Hanover Square, New York, NY 10004. Mr. Press is the author of numerous tax articles.

Estate Planning

Now, suppose the same property is owned jointly by the taxpayer and his or her spouse. After the taxpayer's death, the basis is only $200,000. (The taxpayer's half goes from $50,000 to $150,000, but the spouse's half remains at $50,000.) If the property is then sold for $300,000, the surviving spouse will face a taxable capital gain of $100,000.

Source: *Isaac W. Zisselman, partner with the law firm of Young, Kaplan, Ziegler & Zisselman, New York.*

Be Careful of Leaving Everything to Your Spouse

Husbands and wives often leave everything to their spouses to escape death taxes. Transfers in any amount between spouses, during life or at death, are not taxable, but you should nevertheless avoid making such transfers to excess.

If you and your spouse don't take full advantage of your lifetime transfer credits, the survivor's estate could pay more tax than necessary. The credit allows every estate to leave a certain amount tax-free; the figure is $650,000 in 1999, rising every year until it reaches $1 million in 2006 and thereafter. ***Example:*** A husband dies before his wife and leaves an estate valued at $1.3 million to her. Because of the marital deduction, no tax is payable from his estate. However, the husband forfeits his unified credit by overusing the marital deduction. The spouse has only one $650,000 lifetime exemption to offset estate taxes, meaning that the remaining $650,000 will be taxed heavily.

A better alternative: Instead of leaving the entire $1.3 million to his wife, the husband should leave her only $650,000 and put the balance in a trust for her benefit. The trust preserves the use of the credit in his estate and prevents the property from being taxed in hers. Both estates utilize their $650,000 applicable exclusion amounts; neither one pays transfer taxes, and the entire $1.3 million, although benefiting the wife for her lifetime, passes to the children tax-free.

Source: *Archie M. Richards, Jr., CFP, president, Archie Richards Associates, Inc., 10 Mall Rd., Burlington, MA 01803. He has been admitted to the Registry of Financial Practitioners and is a member of the International Association for Financial Planning and the Institute of Certified Financial Planners. He is also a weekly newspaper columnist.*

QTIP Trusts: Estate-Planning Opportunity

There is an unlimited marital deduction for federal estate tax purposes. No matter how big your estate is, if you're married and you leave everything to your surviving spouse, not a penny of federal estate tax will have to be paid on your death. Tax will be postponed until your spouse's death.

Planning Problems?

One way to take advantage of the marital deduction is to leave property outright to your spouse, with no strings attached. But that creates problems.

Problem 1: When you leave assets to your spouse outright, you relinquish the right to control who gets the remainder of the estate after your spouse's death. The widow (assuming the husband has the assets and dies first) can do whatever she wants with the property she inherits. She could remarry and leave everything to her second husband—leaving nothing to the first husband's children.

Problem 2: An estate left outright to a spouse who has no knowledge of the money market or investments can easily be frittered away.

The QTIP Solution

You can solve these estate-planning problems by putting some of your estate into a Qualified Terminable Interest Property Trust, or *QTIP trust.*

A QTIP lets you provide for your spouse for his or her lifetime, get an estate tax marital deduction and control how the property is disposed of when your spouse dies. *To qualify as QTIP property:*

● **All the income from the trust assets must go to your spouse,** payable at least annually, for life.

● **Your executor must elect** to have the property qualify for the marital deduction in your estate.

● **There can be no restrictions** on the spouse's right to receive income. For example, he or she must continue to get income even if she remarries. *Angle:* None of the money in the QTIP can be paid out directly to other family members while a widow or widower is alive. For example, you can't have the trust pay for your children's college education. However, money for this purpose can be distributed to your spouse from principal at the discretion of the trustee, and he or she can spend it on the tuition.

Taxes and QTIPS

The QTIP property will be taxed when your spouse dies. When setting up the trust, you must consider the taxes your spouse's estate will have to pay.

Trap: Putting too much of your estate into the QTIP. This could cause taxes on the combined estates of you and your spouse to be higher than they would be if only a limited amount had gone into the trust. Put into the QTIP only an amount that exceeds your applicable exclusion amount—$650,000 in 1999 rising to $1 million by 2006. This is the amount that can be left to your heirs tax-free, apart from amounts that qualify for the marital deduction. If you have an estate of $2 million in 2006 (and "plan" to die that year), $1 million can go into the QTIP. *The balance:* It can be put into a "nonmarital trust." This is a trust that will not qualify for the marital deduction and will not be taxed in your estate as long as the value is below your exemption equivalent. *Example of a nonmarital trust:* Income to widow or widower and/or children as the trustee sees fit. Balance on her death or remarriage, or at stated intervals, to children. *Another reason for not putting the whole estate into the QTIP:* If your widow or widower lives to be 100, your children could be 75 or so before they inherit. That may be too long for them to wait.

Source: Edward Mendlowitz, partner, Mendlowitz Weitsen, LLP, CPAs, 2 Pennsylvania Plaza, Suite 1500, New York, NY 10121.

SMARTER THAN LEAVING IT ALL TO A SPOUSE

New York attorney Marvin W. Weinstein, who specializes in taxes and estate planning, suggests using dual trusts in some cases, with one qualified and the other not qualified for the marital deduction. This is important when the objective is to provide liberally for the surviving spouse, but reduce estate taxes on transfers to the next generation.

A marital trust is eligible for the marital deduction from the estate tax, but it has the disadvantage that the assets will be taxed in the spouse's estate when he or she dies.

By contrast, a nonmarital trust isn't eligible for the marital deduction from the estate tax. The assets are moved to the next generation without being taxed in the widow's or widower's estate when she or he dies. A typical non-marital trust would be one in which the widow or widower gets all of the income as long as she or he lives, but on the widow or widower's death the principal passes to the children.

The two types of trust differ in the degree of control over the assets that the widow or widower has. And there are legal requirements that a trust lawyer should handle. But this

is unnecessary if the estate is less than the applicable exclusion amount ($650,000 in 1999, increasing to $1 million in 2006) because there's no estate tax below that.

Tax-Free Gifts to Family Save Taxes

Annual gifts of up to $10,000 a year per recipient are not subject to gift tax. Married couples can give twice as much. Every year for the rest of your life, you and your spouse can jointly give $20,000 tax-free to each heir and reduce your taxable estate by the same amount. *(Editor's note:* The annual gift tax exclusion may be indexed for inflation.) Tax savings are impressive even if you're widowed or divorced. An individual with four married children and 10 grandchildren can give the children, spouses and grandchildren $180,000 a year with no tax.

Avoiding tax on gifts over $10,000: Give a part interest each year. Or transfer property through an installment sale, taking back notes that are payable at annual intervals, canceling these notes as they fall due.

Gifts to reduce family's total income tax: Transfer income-producing assets to low-bracket members. Children under age 14 can receive up to $1,400 of income from the asset before the parent has to pay income tax in his or her higher tax bracket. (There's no gift tax if the $10,000 limit is observed.)

Reducing heir's income tax: Give assets to a minor child by putting them into a trust that accumulates up to $1,400 per year in income. Income can be paid to a custodian or can be taxable to the trust so as not to propel the heir into a higher bracket.

Lifetime Giving in Financial Planning

Gifts made during your lifetime should satisfy two primary objectives: the personal needs and desires of you and your beneficiaries and your tax-saving needs. Personally, you will want to provide as much financial support to both children and adult beneficiaries. As for tax savings, there are two basic motivations. The first is to achieve income tax savings through transfer of income-producing property to lower-tax-bracket recipients. Another way of thinking about it is that if you have to provide financial support to members of your family anyway, gift giving enables you to save tax dollars while in the process. The second tax motivation is to transfer your wealth and its potential for future appreciation at the lowest possible transfer tax (gift and estate) cost.

To accomplish these goals requires a sound understanding of the available gift tax exclusions and exemption, gift and estate tax rates as well as income tax rates for you and your beneficiaries.

Ideally, the property you transfer should satisfy the dual objective of being able to generate current income that is available to your beneficiary (and

Avoid Tax on Debts

Suppose your son owes you $10,000. Your will provides for cancellation of that debt upon your death. *Tax result:* Even though your estate does not collect it, the value of that debt is considered an asset of the estate that is subject to federal estate tax. *Better way:* When the debt is first established, spell out that the payment obligation will cease at your death. *Result:* When you die, there is no repayment right for your estate to succeed to and there is no asset to be taxed.

Caution: The transaction establishing the debt should reflect the cancellation feature. *Example:* Your son is buying some stock from you. The stock is worth $100,000. If he gives you a note with a cancellation-at-death clause, the purchase price should probably be higher than $100,000. Otherwise, the IRS can argue that your son got more than he paid for and treat the transaction as partly a sale as well as partly a taxable gift.

Source: Estate of Moss, 74 T.C. No. 91.

removed from your tax bracket) as well as removing any potential appreciation in the property's value from your estate. The form of the transfer will be equally critical. You have the choice of outright transfer or a custodianship or trust arrangement that allows for more management and control over the transferred property.

Tax Considerations

Any property over a certain amount that is transferred during your lifetime is subject to gift tax. Transfers that occur at death are subject to estate tax. Since the U.S. transfer system is "unified," estate and gift tax rates are the same, and the amount of taxable gifts an individual makes during his or her lifetime is included in the final computation of his or her estate tax.

In essence, gift tax is nothing more than a prepayment of estate taxes. But it should be noted that gift taxes paid are removed from the transfer tax system and are never subject to gift or estate tax.

Most important tax-free gifts: The annual exclusion allows a tax-free transfer of $10,000 per year to each donee on the condition that the transferred property is available currently for use by that donee—the donee receives the current income or has current enjoyment from the property. If your spouse joins in the taxable gift or the property is jointly owned or owned in community title, then the annual exclusion can be doubled to $20,000 per donee. *(Editor's note:* The annual gift tax exclusion may be indexed for inflation.)* Over a long-term period, this transfer technique can result in a substantial overall tax savings. For example, a husband and wife with three children can give $60,000 to their children every year tax-free. *Benefit:* Gifts that are excluded from tax under the annual exclusion also are not counted in computing estate taxes.

A problem with using the annual gift exclusion is that you must give up entire control over the property to your beneficiaries to qualify for the tax exclusion. In theory, an individual could avoid all estate taxes by planning to give all his or her property to children throughout his or her lifetime. But in the case of children, this usually is not desirable —and you will want to exercise care in giving up too much financial independence too soon.

Tax benefits: All income tax on gift property that is transferred outright or in a trust (with the income being distributed to the beneficiaries) is based on the donee's tax bracket, not on your income tax bracket, provided the donee (recipient), if a child, is over age 13. Otherwise, if a minor child under 14 receives the income over a limited amount ($1,400), it is taxed at the parent's top bracket. *Even trickier:* For property that is transferred through a trust but where the income is not currently distributable to the beneficiary, the trust itself is subject to income tax. In these cases, the income from the trust is taxed upon distribution to the donee under a complex "throwback" rule, which looks upon the distribution as being made in the year in which the income was accumulated. Also, it is subject to a compressed—i.e., higher—tax bracket than if distributed in many cases.

For all gifts to be considered a tax-free transfer it is essential that you relinquish all rights of control over the transferred property.

Taxpayers should be cautioned about making gifts

to family members more than one generation younger than the donor (i.e., grandchildren). These gifts are subject to a generation-skipping transfer tax of 55% in addition to gift tax. There are broad exemptions, so this tax applies only to large gifts. Since this tax, when added to gift taxes, is confiscatory in nature, individuals planning gifts to younger generations should be careful to meet one of the exemption rules.

Source: Byrle M. Abbin, managing director, Office of Federal Tax Services, Arthur Andersen & Co., 1666 K St. NW, Washington, DC 20006.

What Types of Property Should Be Transferred in Trust

The major objective of most major gift giving is to transfer income to other family members and thereby lower the taxes paid on the income. Since you want to shift income and potential future appreciation, you must choose property that produces the desired amount of income and is likely to generate significant appreciation. In most cases, you will have to make a compromise between the two objectives. For instance, a transfer of cash invested in high-yield bonds would shift income for income tax purposes but perhaps only result in a moderate ability to shift any appreciation. On the other hand, assets with high appreciation are not likely candidates for transfer because they throw off little or no current income and produce minimal income tax advantages for the family overall.

Special situation for business owners: Stock interest in a closely-held family business is frequently used as lifetime gifts even though there are little or no current earnings to be derived. In these cases, the goal of removing future appreciation from the donor's estate outweighs income tax planning motivation.

Warning: If there is too much control by the donor, it is possible for income from the transferred property to be reallocated to the donor regardless of the legal transfer of title. The IRS may also attempt to include the property in the donor's estate.

Avoid making gifts of property that have depreciated significantly. *Reason:* The depreciable basis of the property the donee receives will be equal to the lesser of fair market value at the date of the gift, or donor's basis. A better approach would be to sell property with a current value less than your basis so that you may claim the benefit of the loss. The proceeds of the sale then should be given to the donee.

Of course, a better gift would be property that has appreciated in value. *Result:* Any gift taxes that have to be paid on the property will increase its basis. Also, the gain on the sale will be taxed in the donee's lower tax bracket.

Long-term trusts: For individuals with significant assets who want to exercise more control over their distribution, a longer-term trust can provide for a term of 20, 30 or 40 or more years with distributions tailored to the desire of the donor. To qualify for the $10,000 annual exclusion, income from the trust must be distributed as it is generated, or the donee must be given the privilege of taking distributions from the trust ("drawing down"). All of these types of transfers are irrevocable. Once the gift is made, it cannot be modified without eliminating the tax benefits of the trust.

For the sophisticated "giver" there are a number of deferred gift techniques that allow you as the donor to retain income interests (or an annuity) for a set period of time or your life. *Effect:* to reduce the gift tax value of the remainder interest, since the benefit of ownership to the donee is delayed. For the charitably minded, a charitable lead trust provides

GIFTS TO MINOR CHILDREN

For adults, an outright gift of property is usually the most efficient and practical way for you to distribute assets to your beneficiaries—the title is simply transferred from you to the beneficiary. This is not usually the case with young children. You may want to make a gift for tax purposes or other personal reasons but do not want to give up complete control of the property to your children.

The simplest solution is to establish a custodianship under the Uniform Gift to Minors Act (UGMA) or the Uniform Transfers to Minors Act (UTMA). The UGMA and UTMA enable you to transfer ownership of property to a custodian who has broad management powers over the property until the child reaches a specific age, generally 18 or 21, when ownership reverts fully to the child. While the property is in custodianship, the income and property may be used only for the benefit of the minor for whom the UGMA or UTMA account is established. In this case, you as the donor should not

be the custodian; otherwise, the assets will not be removed from your estate. The only drawback with UGMAs is that there are limits on the type of assets that may be placed in the account; UTMA is more liberal.

Common mistake: A strategy sometimes used, but improperly, is one in which assets are transferred to a joint or trusteed bank account for a minor's benefit.

Problem: In most of these cases the income from the property is at least partially taxable to the donor and the property may be included in the donor's estate at death.

The 2503, or "Children's," trust gives control of the assets to a third party until the minor donee becomes an adult. Income and/or principal of the trust may be withheld until the child reaches the age of majority.

Because of the special rules pertaining to trusts of this type, gifts to the trust will qualify for the $10,000-per-donee annual gift exclusion, even though the donee cannot have immediate access to the property. To qualify for the full set of tax benefits of the trust, it is preferable for a nonparent to be the custodian or trustee to hold title of the property.

Source: Byrle M. Abbin, managing director, Office of Federal Tax Services, Arthur Andersen & Co., 1666 K St. NW, Washington, DC 20006.

income to charity for a period of time, after which the property goes to designated family members (outright or in trust). This form of delayed family gift also reduces the gift tax value.

Source: Byrle M. Abbin, managing director, Office of Federal Tax Services, Arthur Andersen & Co., 1666 K St. NW, Washington, DC 20006.

Estate-Planning Mistakes

Without an executor, even the best estate plans can't be put into effect. But, incredibly, many otherwise smart businesspeople bungle the process of naming an executor.

Problem: Family members can usually be trusted as executors, but they're not always capable, especially if they're distraught after a death. Lawyers are usually capable, but may not be privy to important details—such as location of assets, records or debts that are owed to the estate. *Solution:* Name co-executors—a family member to administer the estate and a professional to handle the paperwork.

Essential: State in your will who is responsible for which functions—and say who will have the deciding vote in case of a disagreement.

It's also important to list backup executors in your will. If only one executor is named and that person dies or declines the responsibility, the courts will appoint an administrator as though an executor were never named. If you choose a banker or a lawyer, it makes sense to name the firm, not the individual. That way, if something happens to the person chosen, another member of the company can step in.

Other Frequent Mistakes

● **Out-of-date will.** Whenever tax laws change, you should go over your will to ensure it's consistent with

Head Off Trouble

If you own a tax shelter, or any investment that might involve you in a dispute with the IRS, think twice before leaving it to your spouse or children unless they share your financial sophistication—and your willingness to battle the government.

Alternative: Leave it to someone with a lot of financial savvy, or put it in trust and appoint a smart trustee.

the law. This is especially important when your estate passes the federal tax-free level ($650,000 in 1999, increasing to $1 million in 2006). Even if tax laws don't change, it pays to review your will carefully every five years.

● **Not informing the person you've named as executor.** If you haven't talked with the executor ahead of time, there's a chance that the person will refuse to do the job.

● **Not writing a new will when you move to another state.** States have different laws on what is required for a will to be valid. Virginia, for example, requires that one of the executors of a will be a state resident. And only two witnesses are necessary in most states, but in New Hampshire, South Carolina, and Vermont, three are required. If your will fails to meet all of your new state's requirements, it might end up being tossed out by the courts.

● **Listing bequests in dollars.** If the size of the estate is reduced after a will is written, it's possible that specific dollar amounts will deplete all assets before all inheritors are provided for. *Better:* Make bequests as a percentage of the entire estate.

● **Storing your will in your own safe-deposit box.** In many states, boxes are sealed upon the death of the owner. It can sometimes take months to have it opened. *Better:* Leave the will with your attorney or have your spouse keep it in a separate safe-deposit box.

● **Listing assets in the will.** A will isn't rewritten often enough to keep up with frequent changes in assets. Instead, write a letter of instruction that notes your assets and their locations, and file it separately. Do the same with your burial instructions.

● **Keeping old wills.** When you write a new will, destroy the old one. That way there's no chance it will be used to contest the most recent one.

Source: Alexandra Armstrong, CFP, president of the independent financial-planning firm Armstrong, Welch & MacIntyre, Inc., 1155 Connecticut Ave. NW, Washington, DC 20036.

Why You Need a Common Disaster Clause in Your Will

Include a "common disaster clause" in your will to cover the possibility that you and your spouse (or other beneficiary) may die together in an accident. Otherwise, your state's "simultaneous death statute" will govern all questions of inheritance, taxation, the marital deduction, the disposition of jointly held property, who gets insurance proceeds and all other questions of who gets your property.

The provisions of the law may not be to your liking. The only way to be sure your wishes are carried out is to put a provision in your will.

Do-It-Yourself Wills

Writing your own will is very dangerous. The requirements that must be met for a will to be valid vary in almost every state. *Example:* A will written in New York may be unacceptable in Vermont because there weren't enough witnesses.

If the courts rule a will to be invalid, the estate will be divided up according to state law, which may be very different from the way that you want it done.

Source: *Alexandra Armstrong, CFP, president of the independent financial-planning firm Armstrong, Welch and MacIntyre, Inc., 1155 Connecticut Ave. NW, Washington, DC 20036.*

Keeping Peace Among Your Beneficiaries

A man's will provided that his daughter could choose "any three items in my estate," with the remainder distributed to others. His estate included 19 Thoroughbred horses, and the daughter selected all 19 as a single item. The other beneficiaries sued—one horse, one item, they claimed. The judge disagreed—all 19 counted as one.

Although extreme, this example demonstrates the family discord that can arise over vaguely worded instructions regarding the disposition of property. The market value—not to mention the high emotional value—of furniture, jewelry and other tangible property makes it imperative to avoid carelessly planned dispositions that ultimately may have to be handled in court.

The Problem of Equal Shares

Suppose you own securities, tangibles of moderate value and a magnificent $300,000 desk. Everything is to go to your children in equal shares. With the desk indivisible, how can your children apportion

Protecting a Valuable Collection

If breaking up your collection would greatly reduce its value, consider forming a corporation to inherit the collection under your will. It can then be sold as an entirety and the proceeds distributed to your heirs and beneficiaries (to whom you would will specify numbers of shares in the corporation). If the collection is willed to various individuals, it may make the sale more difficult and less lucrative.

all the tangibles and still maintain equality? *Solution:* Add a codicil to your will that allows for the disproportionate allocation of your securities to adjust for inequality in the tangibles.

Avoid catchall phrases in your will. References such as "the contents of my safe-deposit box" simply invite conflict. Allow for moderate inequality by permitting the tangibles to be divided in *substantially* equal shares. Making gifts during your lifetime also helps reduce friction when you are no longer around.

You don't have to amend your will every time the plans for your tangibles are changed—the will can refer to a nonbinding memorandum to be rewritten by you from time to time. However, if the executor of the will is empowered to make allocations, make sure he or she is not one of the beneficiaries.

Placing tangible property intended for one family member temporarily in the hands of another can also result in inequalities. A mother left a painting to her minor daughter. The father was allowed to take temporary possession of the painting, which he later sold. The daughter had legal recourse, but decided not to sue her own father. The mother could have avoided this by providing that the painting be left in storage to await her daughter's possession.

Be wary of the impact of estate taxes. If an estate contains shares of stock, for example, a number of them may be sold to provide tax money. The same cannot be done with a valuable chair—chipping off a leg to raise taxes is impossible. Conflict is guaranteed if one beneficiary receives the chair and another pays the taxes derived from it.

Source: *Archie M. Richards, Jr., CFP, president, Archie Richards Associates, Inc., Ten Mall Rd. Burlington, MA 01803.*

Who Is the Spendthrift?

A grantor may not be concerned so much that his or her son or daughter has spendthrift tendencies, but that this person's spouse is the one who is likely to be wildly extravagant or gullible. The grantor may provide that anything he or she gives or leaves to a son or daughter is to be in the form of a life income from a trust, so that the principal cannot get into the hands of the spouse. The remainderman or remaindermen will be specified as the grantor sees fit—often the grandchildren are named, rather than the prodigal spouse.

Use of Mutual Wills Can Forfeit Marital Deduction

A husband might want to leave a big chunk of property to his wife when he dies, but he may fear that she will make no provision to bequeath any of this property to his relatives or friends. She may feel the same way about leaving property to him. One solution to this dilemma is to have the spouses make mutual wills, in which each party agrees to leave inherited property to the survivor, who after death will leave specified property to designated relatives or friends of both parties.

Problem: The solution may create tax problems involving marital deductions on the estate tax return.

WRITING A WILL THAT WORKS

● **Include a simultaneous-death clause** that dictates how property will be disposed of in the event both you and your spouse die simultaneously in a common disaster. This prevents acrimony among the beneficiaries as well as potential litigation.

● **Consider a no-contest clause** to prevent a disappointed beneficiary from suing to have your will overturned. Such a clause says that any beneficiary who challenges the will must forfeit his or her share under the will.

● **Tailor bequests to the beneficiary.** Leave property to each beneficiary in the form that he or she can best handle. This may mean outright transfers. But depending on the beneficiary's age, experience, financial sophistication and personal inclinations, a trust or a custodianship, or some other form of management, may be more appropriate.

● **Avoid giving complicated or risky investments,** such as tax shelters, to financially unsophisticated beneficiaries who may not have your desire to fight the IRS.

● **Don't leave property in joint ownership** when one of the co-owners is likely to be dominated by the other.

● **Don't give undivided fractional interests in property** to beneficiaries who have very different ideas about the management or selling price of the property. Instead,

transfer the property to a corporation and give the beneficiaries voting shares.

● **Consider percentage bequests to favored beneficiaries,** rather than absolute dollar amounts. In inflationary times, an estate can turn out to be worth far more than anticipated. A bequest of a dollar amount, no matter how generous it seemed at the time you made it, may be embarrassingly small in relation to the size of the inflated estate.

Source: *Dr. Robert S. Holzman, professor emeritus of taxation at New York University and author of* Estate Planning: The New Golden Opportunities, *Boardroom Books. This book is no longer in print.*

If the wife, for example, was contractually bound by a mutual will to bequeath whatever remains of her late husband's property to, say, the children, his property has not passed on to her without strings attached. This deduction only applies if the property passes outright.

State law is important here to determine whether the property passing to her under her husband's will was really contractually subject to a condition. In one decision on this frequent issue, the court held that under New York law, a state resident is bound by such a restriction and hence the property earmarked for the children upon the death didn't qualify for the marital deduction because she didn't receive this property outright and without strings. *Indicated action:* Check with tax counsel for the precedent in your state.

Source: *David A. Siegel Estate, 67 T.C., No. 50.*

Who Gets Your Money If You Don't Leave a Valid Will

Most Americans don't have a will. And they probably have no clear idea what will happen to their property when they die.

State laws vary, but the provisions of most are very similar when someone dies without leaving a will.

● **Surviving spouse:** A surviving spouse is always entitled to a substantial part of the estate, sometimes all of it. If there are also surviving children, the spouse's share is usually one-half or one-third, depending on state law and on the number of children.

If there are no children or grandchildren, the spouse often takes the entire estate. Some states, however, give a share to parents or brothers and sisters. The spouse usually takes a specified amount plus a fraction of the balance.

It doesn't matter if the parties have been separated. Only a legal dissolution of the marriage (by divorce or annulment) will cut off the spouse's right to inherit.

● **Descendants:** Subject to the rights of the spouse, descendants usually have first claim on the estate. Each child takes an equal share, and the children of deceased children take the share their parent would have received. If all children are deceased, the grandchildren inherit. If great-grandchildren enter the picture, the same rules apply.

The rules on adopted children vary from state to state. The trend is to treat them exactly the same as non-adopted children. Illegitimate children inherit from their mother. But the laws on inheriting from the father vary widely.

● **Ancestors:** In practice, this means parents. In rare cases, a grandparent may survive even though both parents are dead. If the deceased left any descendants, parents generally take nothing. If a spouse survives, but no descendants, parents take a share in some states. If there are no surviving descendants or spouse, the surviving parents or parent usually takes the entire estate. Some states divide it among parents, brothers and sisters.

● **Collateral relatives:** If there is no surviving spouse, descendant or ancestor, the estate goes to those with the closest degree of blood relationship to the deceased. Some states bar remote relatives by limiting inheritance to a specified degree of relationship.

If there is no relative who can inherit and no will, the property goes to the state.

One misconception: Lack of a will won't keep your estate out of the courts. Even holding property jointly won't necessarily do that. Most assets such as stocks, bonds and savings accounts above a certain amount cannot be transferred without court administration.

> **Misconception: Lack of a will won't keep your estate out of the courts. Even holding property jointly [may not] do that.**

● **Administration:** The court will appoint an administrator, usually one of the heirs. The administrator normally has to post bond, with the cost paid by the estate. If there's more than one heir, any unreasonable disputes among them (including who is to be administrator) must be settled by the court. Such family quarrels can be highly destructive, especially if the estate includes an ongoing business or any other assets that require management.

Once appointed, the duties of an administrator are the same as those of an executor: to collect and manage the assets and distribute them to the proper persons.

● **Minor children:** If any of the heirs are minors, the court must appoint a guardian or trustee of the property. The trustee's job is to conserve the inheritance until the minor grows up. Income from the property can be used for the child's benefit or saved, but the principal can't be touched without a court order. This can mean a great deal of trouble and expense if money is needed to cover items such as educational costs or medical bills for the minor.

Here's how to avoid problems: The cost of a simple will (without trusts) drawn up by a competent attorney should be modest. A will can avoid many of the possible costs and problems of administration as well as making sure that your estate goes to persons you really want to have it.

Source: Edward D. Moldover, senior partner, Moldover, Hertz, Presnick & Gidaly, New York.

Naming the Right Executor

It's a touching gesture to name a spouse or grown child an executor. And he or she will also get to keep the estate's administration fee (which can run to 4%

or more of the gross estate). The fee would otherwise go to an outsider.

True, the relative (most often the widow) may not have any specialized knowledge of estate administration matters, but so what? An experienced lawyer and accountant can be hired to see things through. You might even supply a few recommended professionals to help when the time comes.

Life—and death—aren't that simple, however. *Point:* The executor is personally responsible for estate-tax liabilities and late filings, as well as for making sure that the estate is distributed in accord with the will. He or she is not relieved of this responsibility by delegating to a lawyer the task of "doing whatever is necessary." *Exception:* In a very few cases, courts have waived personal penalties when an executor with no business or tax experience, and with scant formal education, had relied upon a seasoned lawyer to take care of the matter. *Warning:* The great weight of court authority is to the contrary.

An executor also may have to pick up the bill personally if he or she distributes estate assets to beneficiaries so that there isn't enough left to pay federal taxes. That would happen if there was any reason to suspect that the IRS would still be owed money. *Example:* An IRS agent warns the executor that the value of shares in a closely held corporation as shown on the federal estate tax return probably will be jacked up.

The executor may also be held personally responsible for unpaid taxes if the IRS has not put him or her on notice that more taxes might be payable.

One case: An executor spoke to an officer of the bank where the decedent hadn't paid any federal tax on his considerable earnings for years. This should have alerted her to the fact that estate assets couldn't all be distributed to heirs without leaving enough for what Uncle Sam would demand. The IRS was paid out of her own funds.

Old-Will Traps

"My mother recently passed away. She left a will, but it was 30 years old and all the witnesses have died. Can I still submit the will or can I file intestate? And how will it affect the tax bill?"

If your mother left a legally drawn up will, you have no choice. You must submit it. It makes no difference that the witnesses have died.

The applicable estate tax exclusion amount ($650,000 in 1999, increasing to $1 million in 2006) applies whether the estate passes through the will or not. Even if the estate is larger than the exclusion amount, the will should make little estate tax difference, unless it contains tax-planning provisions or other provisions affected by the tax code.

Of course, the tax law has changed a great deal in the last 30 years, so any tax-planning provisions contained in the will are likely to be obsolete. This is the reason wills and estate plans should be reviewed periodically, while the planner is still alive.

Another liability: An heir can hold the executor personally responsible for the amount the heir may have lost through mismanagement of the estate's assets.

Other problems for a spouse: A spouse, in particular, may be too emotionally upset to do a competent job as executor. That has happened even when the spouse was an attorney with vast estate tax experience.

A spouse or other really close relative is also at a disadvantage when gathering all of the estate assets as required by law. Relatives and friends may insist that money or property that the decedent had lent to them really had been intended as gifts, with an alleged "understanding" that the advance would be forgotten when the decedent died. A widow would have the unpleasant task of trying to collect from her husband's relatives—or of having to sue them. *A common occurrence in such cases:* The widow instead fails to report assets of that type on the estate tax return, then gets caught by the IRS.

Another danger: An executor might regard her husband's will and its property dispositions as sacrosanct, to be honored at all costs—including the cost to herself. *Example:* State laws generally allow a widow a certain percentage of her husband's estate, such as 35%, as dower rights. If he leaves her a lesser amount, she can "take against the will" and get this 35% at the expense of other beneficiaries. But, to preserve family sensitivities, the executor might refuse to tamper with her husband's instructions and hence would be short-changing herself.

The saving on administrative fees is not large enough to make that the basis for selecting a family member. An individual is not subject to federal tax on what he or she inherits. But if the widow is executor, the IRS may claim that part of what she inherited actually had been intended to be payment for administering the estate, and she will be assessed income tax on it.

The other side: Consider the potential expense and other consequences of being an executor. That should help to shape your response if a relative or friend flatters you by inviting you to serve as his or her executor. Even if he or she offers you a fee, it may not be worth it.

The Scariest Tax Audit Is the One Right After You Die

It is standard operating procedure for the Internal Revenue Service to examine the federal income tax returns of a decedent for the three years prior to his or her death.

Unless clear and well-documented work papers can be shown and explained to the IRS by a knowledgeable person familiar with the facts, there are apt to be disallowances because of lack of substantiation.

Can your returns be explained satisfactorily by someone else when you are not available?

Information as to where records are located should not be in the will. Rather, include it in a separate communication to the executor in advance, or leave it among personal possessions.

Source: Dr. Robert S. Holzman, professor emeritus of taxation at New York University and author of Estate Planning: The New Golden Opportunities, *Boardroom Books. This book is no longer in print.*

Cash Found in Decedent's Safe-Deposit Box

What was the source of any cash in a safe-deposit box or in your home or office? In the absence of proof to the contrary, the Internal Revenue Service will consider any unexplained cash to represent previously untaxed income. This presumption can be refuted if there is credible evidence. For example, there may be a letter to your executor stating that Social Security checks or horse track winnings (reported) will be converted into cash, to be kept in the box as an emergency fund. Correspondence can identify cash as having been found money, which had been turned over to the police department and given back to the finder when no claimant appeared.

Source: Encyclopedia of Estate Planning *by Dr. Robert S. Holzman, Boardroom Books.*

● Don't stash cash without a note explaining its source. A man died, and when his safe-deposit box was opened in the presence of tax officials, a large amount of cash was found. There was no evidence showing where this money had come from. The IRS wanted the money allocated as unreported income for the years that he rented the box. And the Tax Court agreed.

Source: Aggie L. Mizell, TC Memo, 1984-254.

How to Choose a Guardian For Your Children

Whom do you want to take care of your children in the event you and your spouse die in the same accident?

This important estate-planning question exasperates most parents. But if you don't appoint a guardian, a probate judge will. And you are likely to make a better choice than the judge is. *To do the job right, follow these guidelines:*

● **Prepare a list of possible guardians.** Rate each individual or couple according to their degree of responsibility, accessibility, lifestyle, moral tenets, opin-

---

WHAT YOUR EXECUTOR NEEDS TO KNOW

You choose your executor with great care and expect him or her to do a good job. But he or she can't be effective unless you provide some essential information. *Questions:*

● **How can an executor collect all of the estate's assets** if he or she doesn't know precisely what or where they are or the extent of your interest in them?

● **How can he or she prevent co-owners of bank or brokerage accounts** from drawing out funds if he or she doesn't know that the accounts exist? How can he or she put a stop payment on the accounts? How can he or she prevent safe-deposit boxes from being invaded by co-owners and those in possession of keys or combination numbers? *Solution:* Write your executor a letter listing all the facts he or she must have in order to effectively administer your estate. *Include:*

● **A complete list of what you own and where it is,** plus any identify-

ing serial numbers (such as those on stock certificates, bank accounts and insurance policies). If there are co-owners or persons holding power of attorney over any of your property, supply the details.

● **The location of all documents the executor will need immediately**—your most recent will, cemetery-plot deed or number, marriage license, divorce decree.

● **A description of the rights you have, or may have,** under the retirement plans of all employers you have ever worked for. You may have vested rights under the plan of a company you worked for many years ago. If you were in the armed forces or with a government agency, identify which one and give your serial number. Are you a member of a fraternal organization or lodge that may provide death benefits or survivor rights?

● **The name of the person who prepared your federal income tax returns,** at least for the past three years. Who has the work papers? Who understands them?

● **The names of your insurance broker and stockbrokers.** Where are brokers' confirmation slips of all purchases you have made at any time?

● **A list of all money, jewelry or other property you've lent.** Are you the co-owner of any property that may not be in your possession? Does anyone, including the IRS, owe you money?

● **A list of all your debts,** including insurance policy loans and tax assessments.

● **The whereabouts of copies of all the federal gift tax returns you ever filed.** Your executor may need these returns to prove that gifted property isn't part of your estate. Similarly, where are the deeds of gift or transfer of other property that might be erroneously included in your taxable estate?

● **A list of all documents that could establish the value of property** you own or the price that your executor could get for it. *Include:* Financial statements of closely held corporations in which you own stock, partnership agreements, buy-sell agreements between a corporation and its shareholders or between the shareholders themselves, real estate or jewelry appraisals, special markets where estate assets such as collectibles might be sold at a good price.

Put the letter in a well-sealed envelope with your executor's name on it. Attach the envelope to your will or put it in your safe-deposit box.

Source: *Dr. Robert S. Holzman, professor emeritus of taxation at New York University and author of* Estate Planning: The New Golden Opportunities, *Boardroom Books. This book is no longer in print.*

ions on child raising, and personal compatibility with your children. *Other factors:* The candidates' ages, whether they have children and their children's ages.

- **Have meetings with the candidates.** From these meetings you should learn each individual's willingness to become your children's guardian, the individual's short- and long-range plans and his or her viewpoints on issues that are crucial to you as parents.

- **Select only individuals who satisfy all your criteria.** And remember to provide for a succession of guardians. Choose alternates in case your first choices become unable or unwilling to carry out their duties of caring for your children.

- **Keep in touch with the guardians you have appointed.** Meet with them from time to time to fill them in on the current needs and plans for your children. These meetings will also give the guardians a chance to voice changes in their own lifestyles that might have a dramatic impact on your children. You may decide to change guardians because of impressions you pick up. You might also use these sessions to let your children and their guardians get to know each other.

- **Prepare a memorandum of instructions for the guardians, and keep it up-to-date.** Include a list of things important to your children's well-being, such as their allergies, medical requirements, family medical history, personality traits and behavior responses. State your personal opinions about allowances, dating, schooling, driving, drinking and other areas of parental discretion.

- **Provide direction about spending funds to achieve short-range and long-range goals.** Indicate which goals have priority. For instance, are short-range goals such as a car or a vacation in Europe more important than long-range goals such as college or a nest egg for going into business?

- **Set a minimum monthly allowance** to be paid to the guardians for the children's day-to-day spending needs. This monthly amount should be reviewed from time to time for reasonableness. Give your trustee the power to increase the allowance to meet your specified spending goals or to adjust for inflation.

- **Project your estate's future cash flow.** How much will be available after taxes are paid on the income earned? You need this figure to set a realistic monthly allowance. What will the earning power be

How to Avoid the Naming of an Administrator

To ensure that an executor of your selection will serve, this is what you should do:

✓ Sound out your designated executor to see whether he or she will actually serve if named in your will. Do this periodically. Is his or her health still satisfactory? Has he or she taken on full-time responsibilities elsewhere? Is he or she still interested in you and your beneficiaries? If not, replace him or her.

✓ Seek to ensure your designated executor's agreement to serve by recommending to him or her knowledgeable and able attorneys, accountants, and (where appropriate) appraisers and brokers who can help your executor to carry out his or her responsibilities without excessive detailed work with which he or she isn't familiar.

✓ Name one or more successor or contingent executors so that if the person of your choice doesn't serve, at least it will be your second or third choice, rather than an administrator whom you would never have engaged.

✓ Name a trust company as co-executor. This virtually assures the permanence and continuity of an executor you have seen fit to name.

✓ Make certain that your will is valid so that the executor chosen by you will qualify. Have an attorney familiar with state law check such requirements as the minimum number of witnesses required. State laws vary as to the technicalities to be met.

✓ Be sure that your will can be found when the time comes to have it probated. A perfectly executed and technically correct will is useless if nobody knows where it is. Have your will in your attorney's office, or with your federal income tax work papers.

Source: Encyclopedia of Estate Planning, *Boardroom Books.*

Estate Planning

after money is spent on a long-range goal, such as a college education for one of the children? Much care must be used in projecting both future cash flow and future budget requirements.

Personal Risk Protection

If you're well-off and travel a lot, have health problems or engage in a high-risk business, consider providing a trusted friend or adviser with an *evergreen power of attorney* over your financial affairs. Unlike ordinary powers, evergreen powers remain effective even if you're in a coma or are otherwise unable to act.

By giving the holder the legal right to manage your affairs, evergreen powers ensure that your estate won't become paralyzed should you be disabled or detained in a foreign land. Of course, you can revoke an evergreen power of attorney at any time.

Prepaid Funeral Plans

Trap: Consumers who buy them may lose out if the company selling the plan misappropriates the money or if the funeral home goes out of business. Before investing in a prepaid plan, call your state attorney general's office and/or the Better Business Bureau to see if there are any problems with the company. Then, check out its track record, and review the contract with an attorney.

Safer alternatives: Set up your own trust fund or savings account, or add to your insurance policy to cover funeral expenses.

Pay-before-you-go funeral programs allow you to make all arrangements in advance, sparing your family difficult decisions. Payment can be made in installments through an insurance plan that covers all costs even if you die before all the premiums are paid.

Who Pays the Legal Fees When a Will Is Contested?

Helen Safran's will was contested by her relatives. The contestation dragged on for several years. When it was settled, the estate tried to deduct more than $100,000 in legal fees that it had run up as an administration expense. *Court:* Too late. More than three years had passed since the estate had filed its tax return, so the statute of limitations had run out. No refund was possible. *Better way:* The estate could have made a protective refund claim when the contest started. That would have kept a deduction available for expenses incurred in the future.

Source: Joseph I. Swietlik, CA-7, No. 85-1887.

Unexpected Liability For Estate Taxes

If an executor distributes an estate without leaving enough to pay the federal estate tax, the government can assert transferee liability against any or all beneficiaries to the extent of the property each has received.

IF YOU OWN A FAMILY BUSINESS

Harry Lee owned 100% of the stock of a family business, and transferred it to his son, Robert. Harry continued to receive a large amount of income from the corporation under an oral agreement with Robert. Then Harry died. *Court:* The stock was taxable to Harry's estate because he had really kept an interest in the stock after nominally giving it away to his son. That was the only way to construe the continuing payments. *Better way:* Harry could have gotten the stock out of his estate and kept a healthy income by entering into a formal agreement with the company that would have provided him with compensation payments independent of stock ownership.

Source: Robert A. Lee, WD Ky., No. C 84-0139-L(B).

Moreover, the government doesn't have to apportion the tax among the beneficiaries—it can collect the entire amount from any one of them, if that person has received enough from the estate to cover it.

The beneficiary can then try to recover a proportion of the tax from the executor or the other beneficiaries, but that means a great deal of trouble at the least, and possibly a protracted lawsuit. *What to do:* If you're the beneficiary of an estate, check to make sure all taxes are being paid. If you're naming an executor in your own will, be sure to pick someone who understands the duties of the position and knows how to carry them out.

Estate Borrowing Trap

A person borrowed against his real estate shortly before he died. The loan terms did not allow early repayment. After the borrower died, the estate tried to deduct the interest payments that it still owed. *IRS ruling:* No deduction. An estate cannot deduct interest payments owed on borrowings, unless the borrowings were essential for the administration of the estate.

Source: *IRS Letter Ruling 8444003.*

Estate Tax Loophole

A person died while jointly owning bank accounts and savings certificates with his wife and children. Within nine months of his death, his children filed valid disclaimers of their interest in accounts and certificates. *IRS ruling:* The money now all goes to the wife. *Tax benefit:* Property that passes to a spouse is protected by the marital deduction, so it escapes estate tax. If the money had gone to the children, it would have been subject to tax.

Source: *IRS Letter Ruling 8625001.*

How to Protect Significant Overlooked Assets in Your Estate

Most people have only a rough idea of the true value of their estate for tax purposes. They often overlook significant assets, ones that can make a costly difference between a taxable estate and an estate that escapes tax. *Frequently overlooked items:*

● **Insurance.** Naming a person as beneficiary of your insurance policies doesn't keep the proceeds out of your estate, even though the proceeds don't pass under your will. Life insurance proceeds are part of your estate if you possess what are called "incidents of ownership" in the policy. The "incidents" include the right to borrow from it and the right to change beneficiaries. Naming your spouse as beneficiary of the policies is not enough. It will avoid tax in your estate, but the policies' proceeds will be taxed in your spouse's estate when he or she dies.

● **Pensions.** Survivor payments from company pensions, 401(k)s, Keogh plans, and IRAs are subject to both estate tax and income tax. However, you get an income tax deduction for the estate taxes paid attributable to the property. *(Note:* Roth IRAs are not subject to income tax.)

Pensions are taxable even though you can't collect on them without penalty before you're 591/2. Like insurance, if you name your spouse as the beneficiary of a pension plan, you won't pay estate tax on your death, but anything left will be subject to estate tax on your spouse's death.

● **Joint property.** If you own the property jointly with your spouse, one-half the value is included in your estate. Your half escapes taxation—it passes to your spouse tax-free. The problem with jointly held property is that you can't dispose of your half by your will. It passes to your surviving spouse by operation of law outside of your will.

● **Living trusts.** Assets that you've put into a revocable, or living, trust avoid probate, which can save fees in certain states. But they don't avoid estate tax. The assets of the trust are fully taxed in your estate.

● **Growth.** Assets are taxed in your estate at their full market value on the date of your death. Appreciation both past and future should be included in your calculation of what your estate will be worth. Include appreciation on collections, your home, your business, and marketable securities.

Even though you don't have a taxable estate now, you might in the future. If assets grow at the rate of 10% a year, your net worth will double in just over seven years. In another seven years it will double again.

● **Anticipated inheritances.** While you might not want to count on an inheritance until it materializes, it should be included in figuring out your potential taxable estate. Expected inheritances are something you must tell your estate planner about.

Tax Savings

To avoid federal estate tax entirely you need to get your estate down to the exempt amount (see chart that follows). *Here are some of the things you can do:*

● **Remove life insurance from your taxable estate and your spouse's.** Set up an irrevocable life insurance trust. Make your children the beneficiaries of the trust—your spouse could get income during his or her life. Transfer your life insurance policies and all control over them to the trust (and live at least three years beyond the transfer). This will take the insurance proceeds from the policies out of both your estate and your spouse's.

Editor's Note: Make annual gifts to the trust to pay the premiums and make sure the trust contains a Crummey power that allows beneficiaries the right to demand distributions of additions to the trust within a set time period. Without this Crummey power, gifts to the trust to cover premiums do not qualify for the annual gift tax exclusion.

Note: Payment of the premiums are also gifts that have to be included in your annual total.

● **Reduce the size of your taxable estate.** Set up a lifetime giving program. Reduce your estate by giving assets away during your lifetime. Every year you can give to each of any number of recipients up to $10,000 without running into gift tax. The tax-free amount is $20,000 if your spouse joins you in making the gift.

If your estate is large enough, it may pay to make big taxable gifts during your lifetime, ones that are beyond the $10,000/$20,000 limit. The reason for making such gifts is to remove from your estate future appreciation and income on the assets you give away.

Problem: Making taxable gifts during your lifetime reduces the amount of property you can give away tax-free at your death.

But the property you gave is out of your estate.

Another way to remove assets and future appreciation on them from your taxable estate is to set up one of the breed of trusts called GRITs, GRATs and GRUTs. These are Grantor Retained Income Trusts, Grantor Retained Annuity Trusts and Grantor Retained Unitrusts.

The great benefit of these trusts is that you retain an annuity from the assets for a period of time, while the assets are removed from your estate at a low gift-tax cost. *Catch:* You must outlive the trust term to keep the property out of your estate.

● **Avoid having inheritances flow into your estate.** Talk the person who's making the bequest into setting up a trust for your children instead.

Caution: Watch out for the generation-skipping tax if, for example, the person who sets up the trust is your parent and the beneficiaries are your kids. This is the 55% tax that hits gifts that bypass a generation of heirs. But as much as $1 million can still be transferred free of this tax.

Note: The trust can be set up in such a way that you get income from the assets during your lifetime and it still won't be taxed in your estate.

Personal Estate Tax Exemption

YEAR OF DEATH	INDIVIDUAL EXEMPTION (OR SPOUSE IF MARRIED)
1999	$ 650,000
2000	$ 675,000
2001	$ 700,000
2003	$ 700,000
2004	$ 850,000
2005	$ 950,000
2006	$ 1,000,000
and after	$ 1,000,000

Source: David S. Rhine, partner, BDO Seidman, 330 Madison Ave., New York 10017.

Investing to Win

12

- Portfolio Strategies

- Guide to Stock Market Indicators

- Bull Market Trap

- If the Stock Market Makes You Nervous

- Time to Crisis-Proof Your Investments

- Selecting Superstocks

- Secrets of Playing It Very Safe

- Foreign Investing Risks

- The New Inflation-Proof Bonds

- A New Look at Savings Bonds

- Mutual-Fund Selection Secrets

- CD Savvy

- Ten Golden Rules of Investing

Setting Your Investment Objectives

In setting investment objectives, few investors effectively unify their understanding of their personal financial circumstances, risk preference and knowledge of the financial markets. Instead, a close inspection of most investors' objectives indicates a foundation of wishful thinking.

This lack of perspective and realism is exemplified in the financial press all of the time: returns of 9%–10% are put down in favor of highly risky "opportunities" for 20+% returns. It may be true that 20+% returns would multiply an investment almost a hundredfold in 25 years—but how many people have enjoyed that kind of success?

Remember, too, that 10% is close to the long-term average return to common-stock investors, who have accepted considerable risk to achieve it. Identifying resources, including future earnings, carefully calibrating future needs, understanding personal risk tolerance and allowing low-risk investment returns to compound have worked magic for many investors.

Failure to diversify is another product of many investors' wishful thinking. Putting all of your eggs into one high-flying basket can be exciting and, if you are right, ultimately can lead to the greatest potential returns.

But if you have a lot to lose (such as your life savings), then disaster may be waiting just around the corner if you don't diversify. On the other side of the coin, hedging every potential development is probably only appropriate for the extremely wealthy. If you fall somewhere in the middle, always employ reasonable diversification, both in terms of types of investments and within the selected types. This will temper the risk and opportunity reflected in your investment objectives.

Source: *M. David Testa, vice chairman and director, T. Rowe Price Associates, Inc., 100 East Pratt St., Baltimore, MD 21202. As chief investment officer, he oversees $140 billion in mutual funds and separate accounts.*

Investment Strategies for High-Net-Worth Individuals

While only an in-depth analysis of an individual's risk tolerance and financial condition will produce an intelligent investment strategy, general strategies can be devised for the high-net-worth individual based on assumptions of changes in risk tolerance and in earning power that reflect the investor's age. *Four such strategies:*

EARNING POWER	AGE	INVESTMENTS
High	30–40	30% high-quality growth stocks
		30% aggressive growth stocks
		40% real estate (investments, not personal residences)
High	40–50	25% high-quality growth stocks
		25% municipal bonds
		25% income stocks
		25% real estate
High	50–60	50% high-quality bonds
		25% income stocks
		25% high-quality growth stocks
None	Retirement	75% high-quality bonds
		25% income stocks

Source: *Jeffrey J. Miller, CFA, executive vice president, Provident Investment Counsel, 225 South Lake Ave., Pasadena, CA 91101. Mr. Miller's responsibilities include portfolio management of over $400 million in assets, research and marketing. He serves on the board of directors of the Association of Investment Management Sales Executives and the board of governors of the Investment Counsel Association of America.*

The Real Impact of High-Risk Investments

Some investors go for the quick kill. They select investments, not for reliable growth, but to attain riches they don't feel they can acquire through their own earnings. Some do this by investing in speculative stocks on margin; some purchase futures or puts and calls.

Success with high-leverage, high-risk investments requires tremendous attention and skill. It usually requires buying when most others are selling and selling when others are buying. Investing against the grain is no easy task.

The danger of high-flying investment strategies is that when you lose, you usually lose big. And, when you suffer an investment loss, your funds must work extra hard to make up for the loss.

For example, if you invest $100 in the stock market, suffer a 10% loss in the first year and realize a 10% increase the next year, your investment is worth $99, not $100. Even worse, if your $100 investment declines by 50% in the first year and increases by 50% in the second, it is worth only $75— far short of the original amount, despite a spectacular turnaround.

When an investment incurs a loss in the initial stages, it must work much harder thereafter to attain the initial objectives.

Let's say you expect an investment to appreciate at 10% a year for five years. But in the first year, its value drops by 10% instead. Your investment must now compound at a rate of 15.7% annually to catch up with your initial five-year expectations—such a high rate is usually attained only by buying common stocks at the depth of a recession and holding for a market recovery.

Source: *Archie M. Richards, Jr., CFP, president, Archie Richards Associates, Inc., Ten Mall Road, Burlington, MA 01803. Mr. Richards is a member of the Institute of Certified Financial Planners and has been admitted to the Registry of Financial Planning Practitioners. He is also a weekly newspaper columnist.*

An Investment Strategy For All Seasons

There is no investment for all seasons, but there is a season for each investment. The primary factor determining that season is inflation. During periods of decelerating or stable inflation, financial assets— stocks and bonds—are the superstars. During periods of accelerating inflation, real assets—real estate, precious metals and commodities—are winners.

The problem for investors is trying to determine whether inflation is going to remain stable, accelerate or decelerate. Inflation is primarily caused by government monetary and fiscal policy, so the most important economic indicator for investors to keep track of is what government policy makers are actually doing (as opposed to what they *say* they are doing).

The following guidelines should help you determine when inflation is beginning to speed up and when the best time is to change the character of

Portfolio Strategies

● **Conservative:** Invest 27% in domestic and 8% in international growth funds and 65% in cash equivalents.

● **Venturesome:** Invest 45% in domestic and 15% in international growth funds, 5% in international bond funds and 35% in cash equivalents.

Source: *William E. Donoghue, publisher of Donoghue On-line, an electronic mutual-fund performance service, Seattle, WA.*

your portfolio to take advantage of changes in the inflation rate.

Changes in Money Supply

The main ingredient for accelerating inflation is excessive growth in the country's money supply. If the percentage change in the money supply, measured on a year-to-year basis, begins to rise sharply, you can reasonably expect an increase in the inflation rate.

The lag between an acceleration in the money supply and an acceleration in the inflation rate is approximately two years. That gives the astute investor ample time to restructure his or her investment portfolio accordingly. On the other side of the coin, when the monetary growth rate begins to decline as measured by the year-to-year percentage change in the money supply, it is probable that inflation will also decline in approximately two years.

Acceleration

When the monetary growth rate accelerates for more than six months and rises by more than three percentage points from its low, it's time to prepare for an acceleration in the inflation rate. Since the trend may change slowly, it's best to first liquidate only half of your long-term financial assets.

Sell the remainder of your assets when bond and stock prices fall below their respective 39-week moving averages. *Helpful:* Initially invest the funds generated by the sales in short-term financial instruments such as certificates of deposit and/or Treasury bills or money-market funds.

Investments in inflation hedges should be made only after the monetary growth rate has accelerated for more than six months and the year-to-year monetary growth rate is more than three percentage points from its recent low. Additionally, the economy should be expanding and an index of inflation-sensitive commodity prices should be above its 20-week moving average. The best equity investments in an inflationary environment can typically be made in

MORE INVESTMENT STRATEGIES FOR THESE TRICKY TIMES

Last year was good for stocks. But whether the stock market will rise further depends on how fast profits grow and whether interest rates and inflation remain low.

During this time, the stock market will remain highly overvalued, making it harder to find stocks that will appreciate at the same rates as last year.

Slow and Steady

The most important force fueling the stock market is the economy, which is growing, although at a slower rate than in recent years. *Reason:* The growth rate has slowed because many consumers are carrying large amounts of debt, making them incapable of sustaining the recent rapid rate of growth in personal consumption spending.

Yet there is still more than enough cash available to finance slow economic growth. Indeed, the ample money supply will continue to help stock and bond prices.

The other forces driving the stock market are low rates of inflation and interest. These positive trends should continue, but are at their peak despite the economy's slow growth. *Result:*

Foreign economies will likely benefit from similar economic developments. In Japan, where a major stimulus package has been unveiled, interest rates are already near zero. European countries have begun an expansion cycle.

Clouds on the Horizon

There are, however, some negative factors on the horizon that could upset the present equilibrium. First, because we're in a slow-growth economy, many industries are experiencing more frenzied competition for market share. *Possible results:*

- **Cuts in consumer prices**—and reduced earnings expectations.
- **The big productivity gains** that many companies have enjoyed will be much more difficult to sustain from here on. So much has already been achieved from such moves to restructure management and operations.

Result: We could see corporate earnings disappointments and shortfalls over the next few quarters. This trend would cause Wall Street to slash its earnings estimates, which in turn could cause some people to sell investments or hold off investing altogether.

Second, even though high levels of corporate and consumer cash are a positive force for the U.S. market,

stock prices are extraordinarily high, no matter what measure you use.

Now and in the future, investors *must* choose stocks and stock mutual funds carefully. I think that portfolios that copy the major indexes will go nowhere and that now is probably a good time for individual investors to go for sector funds.

We're in very tricky times. If the economy looks like it's about to overheat and the Federal Reserve boosts interest rates too quickly, economic growth would slow and the stock market could grind to a halt.

On the other hand, if the economy slows more than expected, earnings could slump and the market could retreat.

My Favorite Sectors

I think the great story of the next six months—and the next few years—will be the impact that rising growth in emerging markets will have on the world's economies. In particular, demand and prices for industrial commodities—metals, paper and chemicals—will rise. I also believe that restructuring to maximize corporate values is a critical play for investors who should keep an eye on those companies or industries that have not restructured already.

Finally, I believe that certain drug manufacturers with good product mixes and promising biotech products in the test pipeline could exhibit strong growth in earnings and market value during the coming years.

Source: *Michael Metz, managing director at Oppenheimer & Co., 1 World Financial Center, New York, NY 10281. He also manages an investment partnership for wealthy clients.*

Investing to Win

mutual funds containing stocks of gold-and-silver-mining companies. Holding a portfolio of short-term money-market instruments is a conservative way to keep pace with inflation, since short-term interest rates rise sharply once inflation takes hold. Also, when inflation is accelerating in the United States, the dollar usually declines in value. To take advantage of a weakening in the dollar, try investing in foreign stocks or mutual funds with portfolios of foreign stocks.

Deceleration

Use a similar process to anticipate decelerating inflation. Wait for the monetary growth rate to decline for at least six months and to fall at least three percentage points from its recent high. The economy should show signs of weakness, and an index of inflation-sensitive commodity prices should decline below its 20-week moving average. At that point, liquidate inflation-hedge investments and invest the proceeds in money-market instruments or money-market mutual funds.

Source: *Dr. Roger Klein, president, The Interest Rate Futures Research Corporation, Princeton Junction, NJ, and money manager and consultant to financial institutions. Dr. Klein is editor of The Klein-Wolman Investment Letter and coauthor, with William Wolman, of* The Beat Inflation Strategy.

Securities and Commodities Fraud

To reduce the chances of becoming a victim of an investment swindler, send for the free pamphlet "15 Questions to Turn Off an Investment Swindler," National Futures Association, 200 W. Madison St., Chicago, IL 60606.

All About Hiring an Investment Counselor

The trick in hiring an investment counselor is to demystify the position. Put it in a realistic context—you are hiring an employee who works outside of your home or office. The longer he or she has been doing the job effectively, the more likely it is that he or she will continue to do so.

Until the early 1970s, the services of investment counselors were available only to the very, very rich. Computers have made it easier and more profitable

for counselors to take on smaller accounts. Today, individuals with $200,000 to invest can find counselors willing to manage their accounts. (Until you have accumulated that kind of capital, your best bet is mutual funds.) *Three groups to avoid:*

● *One-man firms.* These are limited to the ideas of the founder, and the accounts can't be supervised when he or she is out of the office.

● *Bank trust departments.* They are generally disadvantaged by low salary levels and too many committees. Talented money managers cannot afford to stay at most banks.

● *Brokerage firms.* Their money managers are often limited to using research generated inside the firm. They also channel most of their clients' investments through their own firm.

Myths Debunked

Several misconceptions surround the investments-management business:

● *You will have a custom-designed portfolio. Reality:* At almost all firms, all accounts are managed essentially the same way.

● *You will receive personal attention. Reality:* Good portfolio managers do not have time to speak with their clients often. Most will talk to you once a quarter and meet you face to face annually.

● *Your existing portfolio will be scrutinized closely. Reality:* When you turn your portfolio over to the firm, the manager will scan the list to see if he or she actively follows any of the stocks. If not, the manager will sell them. If you do not want the stock to be sold, you should not have the issue managed.

What to Look For

Ask to see the performance record for the entire time the firm has been in business. Beware of 20-year-old companies that show you only five-year results...what happened in the previous 15 years?

Compare performance for each quarter of the last eight years with the Standard & Poor's 500 Index. The company should have outperformed the index, especially in down markets.

Look for a firm that is registered as an investment adviser with the Securities & Exchange Commission. And ask the firm for its disclosure form ADV-II to make sure that the people responsible for whatever success the firm has had still work there.

Meet the portfolio manager who will handle your account. Find out how the firm is organized, so you know who will make your investment decisions.

Get client references that go back through periods of stock market adversity such as 1973–74, 1977, 1981–82 and 1987.

What It Costs

Annual fees usually range from .5% to 3% of the amount of the account. Accounts over $1 million are able to negotiate fees at a number of good firms.

It is, of course, important to monitor your investment counselor. A reasonable rate of return on your money over several years is 1.2 times the 90-day Treasury bill rate. A 12%–15% compounded rate or a rate that beats inflation is a very good performance. If after a full market cycle (usually three to five years) the account has a gross return of less than 25%, you should look for a new investment counselor.

Source: *Michael Stolper, president, Stolper & Co., a consulting and performance-measurement firm, 525 B St., San Diego, CA 92101.*

How to Evaluate a Money Manager

Selecting a money manager takes more than just looking at recent performance numbers and picking the firm that ranks at the top. If it were that simple, you could pick a money manager using a computer. The four basic criteria to be considered before you place your money in someone else's hands are: (1) philosophy, (2) process, (3) personnel and (4) performance.

Philosophy

A prospective money manager's philosophy is his or her beliefs about how to successfully make money in the market and do better than the major stock averages. Does the manager focus on growth stocks or high-yield stocks? Or is he or she a contrarian, always investing in out-of-favor stocks? Investment philosophy can also include a manager's belief about his or her market-timing ability; that is, being 100% invested in equities in an anticipated bull market and then moving to cash-equivalent securities when the market is expected to be bearish.

Your main objective in determining a manager's investment philosophy or style is to see if the manager has been consistent over time, and whether his or her style goes along with your basic investment instincts. If a prospective manager's style has been continually changing, be cautious—a successful style should be able to stand the test of time. Also, knowing a manager's style helps you to evaluate performance. For example, a high-yield manager should do well when interest rates are falling, but might not be at the top of the pack when interest rates are rising.

Process

Be familiar with the way a manager chooses specific securities for his or her portfolios. One typical process is the "top-down" approach, whereby the investor begins with projections for the economy followed by a determination of the industries that should do well in the forecasted economic environment. Within the favored industries, specific stocks are selected that should benefit most from the industries' growth. Another process is the "bottom-up" approach, in which stocks are picked on their own individual merits and only secondarily on the basis of their industry and its relationship to the economy. Make it your objective to find a manager whose process makes sense to you.

Personnel

What is the manager's experience in the business and what kind of backup support does he or she have? How long has the individual been in the business? Has he or she been through the good and bad times? Is the manager a Chartered Financial Analyst? Who manages the portfolios while he or she is out of the office? Are there other individuals who will be familiar enough with your account to handle it when the manager is on vacation?

Performance

The last consideration should be performance. What kind of long-term track record does the manager have? These figures may be difficult to get from the manager, but it's worth pushing a little to find out. When reviewing a prospective manager's track record, be sure to compare performance to the market (Standard & Poor's 500) or to a universe of professional money managers (this information is available from various consulting services). The minimum time period to consider is one market cycle, which will show how a manager performed in both up and down markets. If he or she hasn't done better than the market or the average manager, it's probably a good idea to consider someone else.

Source: David C. O'Donovan, vice president, SEI Corporation, Funds Evaluation Services, 2 N. Riverside Plaza, Chicago, IL 60606.

Finding the Right Stockbroker

The risky and expensive way to find the right stockbroker is by experimentation—switching from one account to another. Instead, minimize the cost of your search for the right broker by considering the following points.

● *A broker's livelihood depends solely on commissions generated by transactions.* The pressures of the securities industry can cause some brokers to unnecessarily buy and sell securities in an account for the sake of generating commissions ("churning"). To resolve this issue, ask a prospective broker what his or her philosophy is regarding holding periods for stocks. If the broker is a short-term trader—one who usually holds stocks for a year or less—look elsewhere unless this matches your investment strategy. You may be in for heavy commissions.

● *How well do you communicate with the broker?* Will he or she be readily available? Does the broker answer your questions directly, or evade issues? The question of communication is most important for accounts in which you do not plan to give the broker discretionary power over buying and selling. Does the broker try to find out about your investment objectives and risk tolerance? How will the broker communicate with you on a regular basis—by newsletter, research reports, monthly calls, quarterly meetings? What will your responsibilities be as a client? Will you be expected to monitor your own account, or wait for the broker to make recommendations? It is essential that you clarify each person's responsibilities at the outset.

● *What is the average rate of return you should expect as a client?* Is the response you receive to this question realistic? Does the broker promise guaranteed

> "Once you've signed on with a broker, review the broker's performance regularly. Is he or she really making money for you after you deduct commissions?"

returns? Beware if he or she claims to have a surefire way to beat the market.

● *Does the broker invest his or her own money in the market?* If the broker does not, why is he or she recommending that you do so? Ask to see the broker's own account record for the past several years. This will tell you what his or her past results were and the types of securities the broker buys and sells. Remember, however, that brokers sometimes buy riskier stocks for their own accounts.

● *Find out about the broker's clients, to determine if they are similar to you.* What is the average client like? Older? Younger? High-income? Are they high-risk investors? Are they more interested in investment vehicles such as limited partnerships, load mutual funds, and insurance products? Be sure to ask the broker for references—and call them. Since you will only be referred to the broker's most satisfied clients, always ask the clients how long they have been with the broker. This will tell you whether they have gone through several market cycles with the broker.

● *What is the broker's experience?* How long has he or she been in the industry? Be wary of new brokers—in general, they rely on others to tell them what to recommend. This can be a problem if the firm is pushing its brokers to sell certain stocks, such as new issues. New brokers also have not had the invaluable chance to learn from their mistakes.

● *How does the broker pick stocks?* Does he or she have a system? If so, does it make sense? What does the broker read and whom does he or she listen to for advice? Does the broker talk directly to corporate officers and analysts?

● *What is the broker's firm like?* Are the rates charged in line with the services provided? Has there been a major change in the account executives recently? If so, are there problems at the branch office?

● *Once you've signed on with a broker, review the broker's performance regularly.* Is he or she really making money for you after you deduct commissions? Set regular periods for review of your account results with your broker. If the broker consistently reduces the value of your account in both up and down markets, it's time to apply these search ideas to the next candidate.

Source: Laura Waller, president, Laura Waller Advisors, Inc., 201 East Kennedy Boulevard, Suite 1109, Tampa, FL 33602. She is a certified financial planner, a registered principal of NASD, a registered representative of Investment Management & Research, Inc., and a licensed insurance agent. Southern regional director on the national board of the Institute of Certified Financial Planners, Ms. Waller is a frequent speaker and has been quoted in many financial publications.

What to Expect of a Full-Service Broker

If you like to map out your own investment strategy, do your own research and closely monitor all of your stock transactions, then you probably won't want a full-service broker. Why pay full commission when you won't utilize a broker's advice and services? However, if you're like many people and don't have the time to devote to watching over your stock portfolio, then a full-service broker can be well worth the extra money you will pay in heftier commissions.

What You Pay For

The process of choosing a full-service broker should be handled with care, since the quality of his or her advice will largely determine how well you do with your investments. The following list will tell you what you should expect from a good full-service broker.

● *Advice.* A full-service broker is full of investment ideas. If he or she is good, those ideas will be tailored to fit your financial requirements and investing style. If the broker is very good, he or she will help develop your financial plans in the same way an accountant might handle your taxes or a lawyer might draw up your estate. *But remember:* A stockbroker only makes money when you make a trade. You must ask yourself if that type of incentive system bothers you.

● *Monitor your stocks.* A good broker can watch over your stocks and help you trade more effectively. An experienced broker will know trading techniques that might not be familiar to the average investor. You can decide the extent to which a broker monitors your portfolio—whether the broker calls you before each transaction or takes full control.

● *Research products.* Large brokerage houses spend millions of dollars each year on providing research products. Reports published by these firms can be of great value to the investor who wants to stay up-to-date on industries, specific companies, the overall stock market and new investment areas. Check to see that your broker's firm offers a high-quality research product. It should be meaningful, comprehensive and timely. (Each year, *Institutional Investor* ranks Wall Street's research departments according to their ability to provide the soundest investment advice.)

● *Other investment products.* A full-service broker will also provide you with a wide range of alternative investment vehicles, including municipal bonds, zero-coupon bonds, tax shelters, mutual funds, real estate investments, and insurance. Other extras include free checking, money-market accounts and borrowing facilities. Alternative investment products can become increasingly important during changing economic times, when you have entered a new stage in life, or when you have simply changed your investment strategy.

Choosing a Broker

Referrals from friends may not always be the best way to make your selection. A broker may have performed exceptionally well for your neighbor, for instance, but because of a different style or different financial profile, he or she may not be appropriate for you and your needs.

Before choosing a broker, always try to accurately establish your investment goals: Are you looking for safety, or are you primarily a speculator? Do you have need of immediate income, or will you need income in the future? How much risk are you willing to assume? What rate of return would adequately compensate you for assuming that amount of risk?

When you've decided what your investment goals are, take the time to meet and interview all prospective registered "reps." The primary trait to look for in a broker is compatibility. You want your broker's investment style and trading technique to be suited to your investment goals. For example, if you are looking for long-term capital gains, then stay away from brokers who are more interested in making short-term gains in the options market.

Always test a broker for personal professionalism, and examine his or her firm, noting the level of seriousness you find there. Is it a noisy office, with loud talk about sports, movies, etc.? A lack of adequate secretarial help is also a dangerous sign. (A firm building a relationship with the public relies on clerical help.) Are the employees doing their work? Remember, the seriousness of any investment company may be measured in direct proportion to the level of "horsing around" prevalent in its branch offices.

If a broker meets the compatibility test and the professionalism test, then it's time to ask for at least two references. Make sure that you ask for references from people whose goals are similar to your own. If their recommendations are strong, open an account and watch it carefully to check on the quality of your decision.

Source: Louis Ehrenkrantz, president of Ehrenkrantz King Nussbaum, investment advisers, 635 Madison Ave., New York, NY 10022.

HOW TO CHOOSE A FULL-SERVICE BROKER

In today's increasingly complex financial world, it is almost mandatory for the busy individual to have a full-service broker at his or her disposal. And that doesn't just mean a stock picker. In fact, the term *broker* itself is no longer appropriate. The title *financial consultant* much more accurately describes the position. A full-service broker must belong to a firm that can provide superior investment advice, tax planning, estate planning and a menu of investment vehicles such as money-market funds, checking and borrowing capabilities, zero-coupon bonds, certificates of deposit, municipal bonds, commodities and options.

Referrals from friends are a good way to start. But remember, your investment style might not be the same. Find a broker who meets your needs, not someone else's.

If you have to start the search cold, it's a good idea to pick several large brokerage houses in your area that you think will be in business in the future. Be sure that the brokerage firms are members of all major stock exchanges and that you are able to select from a wide variety of investment vehicles in addition to stocks and straight debt securities. Find out if the brokerage firms are properly insured. Also determine whether they have the necessary communications and computer equipment to execute transactions quickly and effectively.

When you've narrowed down your prospects to one brokerage house, go to the firm's largest office in your area. Speak to the senior manager of the office. (The trick is to start at the top and work your way down.) Carefully review with the senior manager your investment objectives as well as the kind of investments that appeal to you. Discuss the type of broker you are looking for. Finally, arrange a face-to-face interview with several prospective brokers recommended by the manager.

Questions to ask:
- **How long have you been a broker?**
- **How long have you been in the securities industry?**
- **How long have you been associated with this firm?**
- **What type of clients do you have?** Are they income, speculative, or tax-shelter oriented?
- **Do you specialize in any one area?**
- **What is your attitude toward risk?**
- **Do you advise any of the senior officers of this firm?**
- **Do you have any clients whom I could speak to regarding your performance?**

The last question is the most important. Referrals are the best test of a broker's quality. Equally important as a broker's performance record is his or her ability to communicate. Good rapport with your broker is critical.

Source: Stanley P. Heilbronn, first vice president, Merrill Lynch. Mr. Heilbronn advises clients—including individuals in the fields of entertainment and medicine—on their investments. In addition, he is a contributor to Medical Economics *magazine.*

FULL SERVICE BROKERAGE SELECTION
HUTZ PARTNERS
DENEY, BEATEM & HOWE
NEEDEM, GOTEM & GETUM
STOCKET HOLDING

Investing to Win

363

How to Make a Deal With Your Broker

Many companies charge a range of prices for the same goods and services. This means some people are paying less than you for the identical item—a hotel room, car rental—anything that can't be warehoused and sold later. That's why, although they'll never brag about it, most sellers actually need to negotiate.

So-called "standard rates" are almost always negotiable. Suppose you like your stockbroker but want to pay lower commissions and interest rates. Check the ads in *Barron's* or call a couple of discount brokers for their rate structures. Once you have the facts, visit your broker and explain that other brokers charge much less than he or she does, and that you'd like to discuss a new, fairer arrangement.

Show your proof (ads or notes you took while calling discounters). Expect the usual responses about excellent service, discounts that depend on volume, your account is too small, etc. *Your response:* "My account doesn't require much servicing, I don't use your research or other expensive facilities and I'm not asking for the moon. I just don't think it's fair that I have to pay the top rate."

If the broker says that he or she can't help you, find out who can. *Inside information:* The broker probably has more discretion than he or she is willing to disclose. He or she should be able to arrange a 20%–30% discount off the top rate. *That accomplished, ask for one last favor:* You're paying the firm's highest interest rate on your debit balance, and you'd like a one-percentage-point discount. Since brokers usually charge one-half to two percentage points above prime, a one-point reduction off the high end of this gravy isn't unreasonable—even for a small account. If you're told that rates are based on the size of the debit balance, explain that you know rates are negotiable, that others pay less and that you'd like the same treatment as those paying less. *Later:* Negotiate for your share of free stock guides and charts, access to the broker's financial library and occasional shares of "hot" issues.

You have a right to these, but they won't be handed to you on a silver platter. You have to ask for them.

Source: *Ralph Charell, former CEO of his own Wall Street securities firm, 242 E. 72 St., New York, NY 10021.*

When Not to Listen To Your Broker

The few words the average investor finds hardest to say to his or her broker are, "Thanks for calling, but no thanks." There are times when it is in your own best interest to be able to reject the broker's blandishments.

● *When the broker's hot tip* (or your barber's or tennis partner's) is that a certain stock is supposed to go up because of impending good news. *Ask yourself:* If the "news" is so superspecial, how come you (and/or your broker) have been able to learn about it in the nick of time?

Chances are by the time you hear the story, plenty of other people have, too. Often you can spot this because the stock has already been moving. That means that insiders have been buying long before you got the hot tip. After you buy, when the news does become "public," who'll be left to buy?

● *When the market is sliding.* When your broker asks, "How much lower can it go?" the temptation can be very great to try to snag a bargain. *But before you do, consider:* If the stock, at that price, is such a bargain, wouldn't some big mutual funds or pension funds be trying to buy up all they could? If that's the case, how come the stock has been going down?

It's wildly speculative to buy a stock because it looks as if it has fallen "far enough." Don't try to guess the bottom. After all, the market is actually saying that the stock is weak. That is the fact, the knowable item.

● *Don't fall for the notion that a stock is "averaging down."* It's a mistake for the broker (or investor) to calculate that if he or she buys more "way down there," he or she can get out even. The flaws are obvious. The person who averages down is busy thinking of buying more just when he or she should be selling. And if a little rally does come along, the broker waits for the target price "to get out even"—so if the rally fades, the broker is stuck with the mathematical target.

Stock market professionals average up, not down. They buy stocks that are proving themselves strong, not ones that are clearly weak.

If Your Broker Goes Broke

Your money may be tied up for months if your brokerage house fails. Although brokerages are insured by the Securities Investor Protection Corp., assets are frozen during the bankruptcy period. You will receive any gains, but market losses are not covered.

Alternative: Ask your broker to send your stock and bond certificates to you for keeping in your safe-deposit box.

Source: Sylvia Porter's Personal Finance.

WHEN TO USE A DISCOUNT BROKER

If you are an independent thinker and like to make your own investment decisions, then a discount broker is probably for you.

Discount brokerage firms (independent or bank-affiliated) offer no advice, a limited number of products and services, salaried brokers to take your orders and much lower commissions. Generally, commission rates for discount brokers are 50%–70% lower than the published rates of full-service brokers. Of course, if you are a substantial investor, you can usually bargain for a discount from your full-service broker, but the commissions still won't be as low as a discounter's. (A substantial investor can always bargain with a discount broker as well.)

Discount brokers don't make sense when you invest infrequently and/or when your transactions are $2,000 or less. That's because most discounters charge minimum commissions of $30–$45. So, if you are only going to save $5 once in a while, you might as well use a full-service broker. At least then you'll get research reports and other services.

Discount brokers do offer some services. Some will give you copies of Standard & Poor's or *Value Line* research reports, sell you mutual funds or unit investment trusts and pay interest on your cash balance. Discounters affiliated with a bank will automatically switch your funds between your brokerage and bank accounts.

If you are nervous about relying solely on a discount broker, consider using both a discounter and a full-service broker. *Many substantial investors have two or more brokers:* a full-service broker for ideas research and for watching certain investments and a discount broker when the investor knows what he or she wants or when commissions cut too deeply into profit margins.

Source: J. Bud Feuchtwanger, president, Feuchtwanger Group, 161 E. 91 St., New York, NY 10128. He is a consultant to commercial banks, savings and loans, insurance companies, and securities firms on marketing, product development and distribution.

What to Watch Besides the Dow

Too many investors rely exclusively on the Dow Jones Industrial Average for a quick view of what the market is doing. But the Dow reflects only stock price changes of 30 large, mature companies. Their performance does not necessarily reflect the market as a whole. *The Dow should be supplemented with these indexes:*

● *The Over-the-Counter Composite Index* gauges the cumulative performance of over-the-counter issues. It points to a bull market when it outpaces the Dow Jones Industrial Average and to a bear market when it is weaker.

● *TRIN, an acronym for the trading index,* measures the relative volume of rising and declining issues. The market is bullish when the TRIN falls from a reading of above 1.20 to below .70 during one day of trading. It is bearish when the TRIN goes from below .70 to 1.20. A reading of 1.00 shows an even relationship between advancing and declining stocks.

● *The Quotron change,* named for the company that developed it, measures the daily percentage change for all issues on the New York Stock Exchange (the QCHA index) and the American Stock Exchange (QACH). It gives an excellent picture of what the market is doing in broad terms. Mutual funds track more closely with the Quotron change than the Dow Jones Industrial Average.

● *The Dow Jones Transportation Average* is a generally reliable lead indicator of intermediate trends. The Dow Jones Utilities Average reflects income- and interest-sensitive stocks. It's a good long-term lead indicator.

● *In a bull market*, the total number of shares traded expands on days when advances outpace declines. The opposite occurs in a bear market. A sign of market reversal is a high-volume day when the market moves in one direction all morning, then turns around.

To Find Out Which Way The Market's Going

A quick, easy technique to determine the market's general direction: The outlook is bullish if the discount rate is greater than the three-month Treasury bill rate, the federal funds rate is lower than a year ago, the three-month T-bill rate is below 7% and lower than a year ago, and rates on seven-year Treasury notes and 30-year Treasury bonds are lower than a year ago but higher than rates on three- and six-month T-bills. The outlook is bearish if the opposite is true for all of the above. (All rates are listed in your daily newspaper.)

Source: Elaine Garzarelli, chief quantitative analyst, Shearson Lehman Brothers.

How to Recognize a Stock Market Rally Before It Gets Going

Stock market rallies don't begin without some kind of warning. In most cases, market advances and rallies have been signaled long before their arrival. Most of the data required to track these indicators are available weekly in newspapers that provide

GUIDE TO STOCK MARKET INDICATORS

● **Speculation index:** Divide the weekly trading volume on the American Stock Exchange (in thousands) by the number of issues traded. Calculate the same ratio for New York Stock Exchange trading. Divide the AMEX ratio by the NYSE ratio to calculate the speculation index.

To read the index: Strategists believe the market is bearish when the index is more than .38 (and especially so if it rises to .38 and then falls back). Less than .20 is bullish.

● **Member short selling:** Divide the number of shares NYSE members sell short each week by total NYSE short selling.

To read the index: It is bearish when readings of .87 are reached. A reading below .75 is very bullish, particularly if it lasts several weeks.

● **New highs, new lows:** The market is usually approaching an intermediate bottom when the number of new lows reaches 600. The probable sign of an intermediate top is 600 new highs in one week, followed by a decline in number the next week.

● **NYSE short interest ratio:** The total number of outstanding shares sold short each month divided by the average daily trading volume for that month. A strong rally generally comes after the ratio reaches 1.75.

● **Ten-week moving NYSE average:** Compute the average NYSE index for the previous 10 weeks. Then mea-

sure the difference between last week's close and the average. *How to read it:* When the gap between the last weekly close and the 10-week average remains at 4.00 or below for two to three weeks, investors can expect an intermediate advance. Market tops are usually near when the last week's index is 4.00 or more above the previous 10-week average.

● **Reading the indicators together:** Only once or twice a year will as many as four of the five indicators signal an intermediate bottom, but when four do, it is highly reliable. The same is true for intermediate tops.

Source: All indicators are available weekly in Barron's. The Speculation Index was developed by Indicator Digest.

extensive financial coverage. Here are some especially accurate indicators that can help you predict when the market is likely to stage a major advance or rally.

● *Declining member short sales ratio.* Members of the New York Stock Exchange (NYSE) are usually very astute traders. When they cut back their short selling, it's likely that the stock market is ready for an advance.

● *Favorable Federal Reserve action.* The market loves to watch the Federal Reserve for indications of changes in monetary policy. Falling interest rates are usually very bullish for the stock market. A really strong signal is a drop in the discount rate (the rate the Fed charges for loans to banks) two times in succession without an intervening rise. This action implies a bull market that could last for months rather than weeks or days.

● *NYSE "new lows" reach a high level and then turn down.* Long market declines are usually concluded when the number of weekly new lows rises over 300 and then declines to under 150. Major bull markets often follow this signal.

● *The advance/decline line shows strength after an intermediate low point. Expect a sharp market advance if the following conditions are met:* (1) the NYSE Index falls to a four- to five-week low, then (2) the market stages a strong daily rally—850 more stocks advance than decline. Odds are good that the market advance will be strengthened if volume increases sharply.

● *Newspapers and magazines become overly bearish.* The public media always follow rather than lead the investment markets. You can tell a bear market has bottomed out when front-page articles recall the crash of 1929 and unfavorable articles are written about major corporations such as IBM or General Motors. You can usually invest safely when such articles become commonplace.

● *Brokerage stocks start to show strength.* Brokerage stocks, such as Merrill Lynch, often lead the list in a bull market rally and can be very reliable in calling market turns.

Source: Gerald Appel, president, Signalert Corporation, 150 Great Neck Road, Great Neck, NY 11021. In addition to being an investment adviser, he is the author of several books, a regular contributor to investment periodicals and a frequent lecturer.

Bull Market Trap

When the market is in an up cycle, prices of many stocks with a weak earnings potential are pushed up by the market's overall momentum. Inevitably these issues will drop in value before the market as a whole declines.

Safeguard: If insider sellers greatly outnumber buyers, it's a clear signal to stay away.

Source: The Insiders.

Bullish Indicator

Stock mutual fund liquidity. Historically, mutual funds' holding a big portion of their assets in cash is a sign of an imminent stock market rally. *Reason:* Cash represents buying power, and once it's poured back into the stock market, a new spurt in prices is fueled.

Source: Norman G. Fosback, editor, Income & Safety.

Downturn Warning

Investors must watch market signs closely and react quickly when indicators change.

A key indicator that the market is about to turn bearish is a shortening of money-market fund maturities.

Traditional average: 30–45 days. Once these maturities drop down to 37–38 days, it's time to reassess your entire stock position—individual issues *and* mutual funds. When money-fund maturities shorten significantly, a stock market downturn will follow almost immediately.

Source: William E. Donoghue, publisher of Seattle-based Donoghue On-line (800-982-2455), an electronic mutual-fund performance service, updated daily.

When to Get Out of the Stock Market

Be ready to sell stocks as soon as a major market top starts to form. *Definition of a major top:* The beginning of a market decline that lasts from six months to several years. A typical long-term stock market cycle is about four years—from one major bottom to the next. To spot a top you must follow two different kinds of market barometers:

● **Fundamental indicators,** which warn when stocks are getting overpriced.

● **Technical indicators,** which provide early clues to market behavior.

When to Sell

● **Scenario 1.** The blue-chip stock averages keep hitting new highs, but the indexes of smaller, secondary stocks (the NASDAQ Composite and *Value Line*) stall. The rally won't have long to go.

Check the newspaper each week for the number of stocks making new 12-month highs on the New York Stock Exchange. If that number is falling while the Dow Jones Industrial Average (DJIA) is rising, a major market correction will probably hit within a few months—at the latest.

● **Scenario 2.** The DJIA stops rising, and market action begins to focus on the secondary stocks and stocks concentrated in a few select groups.

Trap: A speculative binge would be under way—and the smart money would have already begun to leave the table.

Whether the action starts to narrow in blue-chip stocks or in secondary issues, any sign that fewer investment sectors are participating in the rally should prompt defensive action.

Readying Your Defenses

● **Lighten holdings as soon as a major top starts forming.** You probably have two to eight months to act, so don't panic—but pay off any margin debts and accumulate cash.

● **Identify stocks you own that have stopped rising.** Either sell them or place protective stop orders with your broker. (A stop order is an order given to a broker to sell a security at a specific price below the rent market price, if the security falls to that price.) If a market slide begins, those stocks will be sold automatically at the price you've specified.

● **Get out of any mutual fund whose net asset**

> " **When speculation is at its highest, the market is usually overpriced. That's the time to get ready for a correction [and the] time to get out.** "

value suddenly drops 5% or more. Be very cautious with aggressive growth funds.

● **Buy only cash equivalents** (money-market funds and Treasury bills) unless you're a very nimble seller. If you have a lot of cash and a recession comes along, you'll be in a position to buy up assets cheaply at the next market bottom.

Source: *Gerald Appel, president, Signalert Corp., money managers, 150 Great Neck Road, Great Neck, NY 11021.*

How to Tell When Stocks Will Tumble

It is unfortunately the case that the American public usually enters the stock market after prices have risen, rather than before. The obvious result is that the market soon reverses itself, and investors get caught in the downswing.

This doesn't have to be the case. The stock market tips its hand, so to speak, often far in advance of a general decline. Here are some guideposts to alert you to a coming downturn.

● **The Federal Reserve increases interest rates.** Stocks are extremely sensitive to actions taken by the Federal Reserve, especially with regard to interest rates. The market usually declines when it appears that the Fed is going to pursue a restrictive policy (i.e., increase interest rates). The time to be cautious is when the Fed has raised the discount rate (the rate charged by the Fed for loans to banks) three times in a row with no intervening reductions.

● **Heavy stock churning.** Market peaks are often marked by churning—volume is heavy, but prices go nowhere. The way to recognize churning is to check the number of issues advancing on the NYSE and the number declining. Expect a market downturn when advancing and declining issues remain in relative balance over a period of five weeks. A second method is to compare the number of the week's issues that reach 52-week highs versus the number that reach 52-week lows. The outlook is very bearish if 150 issues reach new highs *and* 150 or more reach new lows during the same week.

● **Excessively bullish sentiment.** When specula-

HOW BEAR MARKET RALLIES CAN FOOL YOU

Bear market rallies are often sharp. They're fueled, in part, by short sellers rushing to cover shares. However, advances in issues sold short often lack durability once short covering is completed.

Details:

- **Bear market rallies** tend to last for no more than five or six weeks.

- **Bear market advances often end rapidly**—with relatively little advance warning. If you are trading during a bear market, you must be ready to sell at the first sign of weakness.

- **The first strong advance** during a bear market frequently lulls many analysts into a false sense of security, leading them to conclude that a new bull market is under way. The majority of the bear markets don't end until pessimism is wide-

spread and until the vast majority is convinced that prices are going to continue to decline indefinitely.

- **Although the stock market can remain "overbought"** for considerable periods of time during bull markets, bear market rallies generally end fairly rapidly, as the market enters into "overbought" conditions. An "overbought" condition occurs when prices advance for a short time at a rate that can't be sustained.

One way to predict a decline—using the advance-decline line as a guide: Each day, compute the net difference between the number of issues that rise on the Big Board and the number that decline. A 10-day total of the daily nets is then maintained. During bear markets, be careful when the 10-day net differential rises to +2,500 or more, and be ready to sell immediately once this figure is reached and starts to decline. The decline will usually indicate that the advance is beginning to weaken.

- *Sharp price rises in speculative stocks.*

- *A flood of "hot" new issues.*

- *A high level of secondary stock offerings.*

- *Friends on the golf course boasting about profits* they've made in the stock market.

- *Secondary markets fail to keep pace with the major market averages.* Be cautious when gains in the stock market are limited to blue-chip issues. Check the percentage gain each week in the NASDAQ Composite Index. Be prepared to sell if, after several weeks, these gains do not match gains in the Dow Jones Industrial Average.

Source: Gerald Appel, president, Signalert Corporation, 150 Great Neck Road, Great Neck, NY 11021.

Sources of Information On Stocks

You don't have time to read every newspaper and financial publication or listen to all the investment advice available. Still, take your investment homework seriously. Informed investors—those who base investment decisions on careful analysis of a stock, the company's industry and general stock market conditions—are more likely to be successful investors.

A vast array of investment vehicles merit your attention: stocks, bonds, Treasury bills, money-market funds, mutual funds, commodities, etc. Similar resources provide important investment information regarding each of these vehicles.

- *Daily newspapers, financial publications.* Tracking stocks on a daily, weekly or even month-to-month basis can help you get a clear picture of what is happening to a company or an entire industry. *The*

tion is at its highest, the market is usually overpriced. That's the time to get ready for a correction. In other words, when everyone has fallen in love with the stock market, it's time to get out. Look for the following signs:

- *Frequent newspaper and magazine articles* that feature discussions of a rising stock market.

- *A plethora of bullish investment advisory advertisements.*

Wall Street Journal and the business section of *The New York Times* provide extensive daily coverage of markets, industries and individual companies. You can expect that most pertinent business news will be printed in one or both of these publications.

● ***Market guides and newsletters.*** An exceedingly broad variety of publications provide detailed reports on individual stocks, industry trends, where pension and mutual-fund managers are investing and emerging growth companies. The list of subjects for market guides and newsletters is virtually endless. You can find publications devoted to one particular industry, a specific region of the world, leveraged buy-outs, insider trading, specific investment vehicles, such as options or futures, or just plain old technical market analysis. The range in the quality of these publications is equally broad. Many have been very successful in forecasting trends in the economy or particular stocks, while others have not called a market turn in the history of their existence.

Although often worth the investment, subscription costs of market guides and newsletters can be high—$300 a year and more. Before you subscribe, visit a local library or call a stockbroker. Check the accuracy of the newsletter's past predictions. Make sure the newsletter bases its advice on substantial research. It helps if the publication employs a variety of market analysis techniques. Many investment firms will provide certain guides and newsletters to clients at little or no cost. In today's high-tech home environment, you can even gain access to research services on your home computer screen via database services.

● ***Corporate publications.*** If you have been tracking a stock in the press and had your optimism reinforced by a market advisory report, the corporation is the next place to turn. Public corporations are required by the Securities & Exchange Commission to publish documents describing almost every aspect of their current and historical operations. Annual and quarterly reports, proxy statements, and certain financial filings are available to potential investors either through stockbrokers or directly from the corporation.

Note: No matter what a stockbroker or a friend may tell you about a "hot tip," always look at the company's financial statements before investing in it.

● ***Personal knowledge.*** Investors, and in particular novice investors, often overlook personal knowledge of a company or industry when making investment decisions. Some of the most successful investments may be sitting in your own backyard. If a local company has just concluded favorable labor negotiations, applied for a patent on a revolutionary new design, made a major sale to an international client or recently signed a long-term contract, take a closer look at the company. Think about the products you and your friends use. Try to avoid investing in companies and industries you know nothing about, have not carefully researched and whose business does not interest you.

Outside Help

You don't have to wade through this ocean of research by yourself. Your stockbroker can help, although you should make it your business to develop at least a general understanding of how to pick and follow an investment.

Large investment firms employ full-time staffs devoted to studying individual investments and market trends. In fact, the advice your stockbroker gives is largely based on the opinions of these experts—industry specialists, technical analysts who track and study market data, experts in particular types of investments and economic research teams who follow the health of the overall economy and certain segments of it.

Any securities analyst's job is to use the available resources to determine which stocks are most valuable. He or she then makes buy, sell or hold recommendations accordingly. To analyze your own investments, do your homework—evaluate what you've learned and consider all the alternatives. Then, take advantage of your investment firm's research services. If its advice matches your own opinions, you can invest with added confidence. If there is a mismatch, find out why—you may want to rethink your choice to ensure that your final decision is one you feel comfortable with.

Source: *Stanley P. Heilbronn, first vice president, Merrill Lynch, Pierce. Mr. Heilbronn advises clients—including individuals in the fields of entertainment and medicine—on their investments. In addition, he is a contributor to* Medical Economics *magazine.*

INVESTING WITH THE INVESTMENT NEWSLETTERS

Investment advisory newsletters are there to help you choose individual stocks and bonds, put together investment portfolios and even time your moves in and out of the markets.

Some are highly focused, providing advice exclusively on small over-the-counter stocks, or on mutual funds or on more esoteric investments such as options and commodities. Others inform you of investment opportunities in a wide variety of markets.

Think Twice About...

● **Newsletters that make near-impossible claims.** Virtually all investment newsletters are bought through the mail. To attract subscribers, many of them display outlandish quotes such as "I made 1,000% in one year with no risk." Be very cautious. Take the time to determine whether the claims are truly within the realm of possibility. *Preferable:* A newsletter that claims it made 20% a year during the last 10 years over one that claims 500% in just one year. Twenty percent annually over 10 years is a very respectable return. At least it doesn't insult your intelligence.

● **Newsletters that quote performance results out of context.** Since *Hulbert Financial Digest* is the only publication that ranks the performance of newsletters, many stretch the truth to advertise that they were listed among the best.

Problem: They may have been ranked in the top 10 for one month—

but their overall performance may be horrible. Look for newsletters with consistent performance through good and bad markets over at least five years.

● **Unfamiliar newsletters that don't offer a trial subscription.** Most newsletters offer an inexpensive trial subscription for two weeks to three months. Such offers are an ideal way for you to study the newsletter's style, methodology and performance—and to see if it is truthful about its record.

Once You've Subscribed, Be Wary of...

● **Newsletters that quote selectively from previous issues.** Many newsletters provide both the bearish case and the bullish case. Then, two months later, they quote whichever case most closely corresponds to actual market events.

● **Newsletters whose recommended issues disappear** or fall through the cracks when their performance turns out to be poor. A bad newsletter makes lots of recommendations and then neglects to report on their later performance—especially when the performance turns out to be bad.

● **Newsletters that cover up or make excuses for their mistakes.** A newsletter that admits its mistakes and is objective about the future is preferable to one that spends most of

its time making excuses and explaining why the market didn't do what it was supposed to do. A newsletter is supposed to predict the turn of events—not explain why the market didn't move in its favor.

● **Newsletters that do not make specific recommendations.** Some offer strict portfolio recommendations, telling you exactly what and when to buy and sell. Others are general and vague. If you're going to pay $150–$300 a year for a subscription, you should get concrete, worthwhile suggestions. You don't want to have to read between the lines, as you are forced to do with the more general newsletters. Remember, you don't have to follow advice just because it *is* specific.

● **Highly aggressive newsletters** (unless the potential returns are large enough to justify the risk). Many newsletters take incredible risks in an attempt to win a high-performance ranking to use in their advertising. But high-risk strategies don't always provide the best opportunity for high returns. *Irony:* In recent years the more conservative newsletters have actually performed better than the most aggressive newsletters on a risk-adjusted basis.

Source: *Mark Hulbert, editor of* Hulbert Financial Digest, *316 Commerce St., Alexandria, VA 22314. It ranks 160 of the best-known investment newsletters on a monthly basis.*

Economic Indicators For Profit and Safety

We hear these terms on the news all the time—*Gross Domestic Product, Consumer Price Index, Consumer Confidence Index*, etc.—yet most of us have no idea what these indicators are or how they affect the financial markets. Here are six of the most important economic indicators, when they are released and how to invest based on their results.

Federal Reserve Board's Policy

The Federal Reserve Board directs monetary policy, which is largely influenced by the chairman, currently Alan Greenspan. He has the power to control the markets by tightening the money supply or pumping more into the system. This affects the value of money directly. *What to do:*

● *Whenever the chairman makes a public statement,* read the key sections and study the commentary of the professional Fed watchers. The chairman's viewpoint usually takes a while to work its way through the system—but eventually it has a considerable impact.

Interest Rates

Focus on long-term bond rates and the discount rate, which is the rate the Fed charges banks to borrow money. Long-term rates change continually. The discount rate only changes when the Fed wants to make a shift in monetary policy. *What to do:*

● *Don't dive into the market—or bail out—at the first change in the discount rate.* That alone will not alter the overall direction of the market. You can lose money by reacting too early either way.

● *Two or three moves in the discount rate*—in either direction—constitute an unmistakable trend, and the markets will react dramatically. Know in advance how you'll respond if that second move occurs. If you're going to act at all, act fast.

● *If the interest rate trend is up,* rethink the asset allocation in your portfolio. Cash will likely outperform stocks and bonds. In this environment, choose a fixed-rate mortgage over an adjustable-rate mortgage, since you'll want to lock in at the low rate.

● *When the trend is down,* you should be buying stocks and bonds.

Gross Domestic Product (GDP)

The GDP is the dollar value of all goods and services produced in the United States. It is announced at the end of March, June, September and December, and provides a snapshot of how fast the economy is expanding or contracting. The markets typically interpret GDP growth of between 0% and 3% as anemic…3% to 5% as robust and healthy…and more than 5% as frothy and probably unsustainable. When the GDP drops for two consecutive quarters, the economy is officially in a recession. A total of three consecutive quarters in which the GDP increases is considered a growth trend. *What to do:*

● *If the GDP is growing at a slow pace* following a steep decline, it's a good time to buy stock or real estate. The values of both will rise as the economy strengthens.

● *If the GDP is growing at a fast pace,* quality growth stocks are good investments. Remember that with expansion comes contraction and the growth environment won't last forever.

> "Whenever the chairman [of the Federal Reserve Board] makes a public statement, read the key sections and study the commentary of the… Fed watchers."

Warning sign: If growth is 5% or more for two consecutive quarters, the Federal Reserve, which regulates the flow of money into the economy, will probably raise short-term interest rates to slow borrowing and combat inflation. Consider selling some stocks and shifting the profits into long-term bonds.

● *If the GDP growth rate is declining,* review your stock portfolio. *My strategy:* Hold those blue chip issues that are solid, long-term investments—and sell the rest.

Producer Price Index (PPI)

Released around the 15th of the month, the PPI measures the rate of change in wholesale prices according to commodity, industry sector and production stage—or what it costs to manufacture goods. the PPI helps show the direction of inflation—I consider three consecutive months of movement up or down a trend. *What to do:*

● **When the PPI is rising slowly**—0.3% or less per month—inflation is under control. Combine that with a slowly rising GDP and investors have the best of all possible worlds. Be wary of a one-time jump in the PPI—either up or down. It won't move the markets significantly. Pay careful attention to how the PPI is interpreted by the media and analysts—not just what the number is.

● **If the PPI advances sharply for two consecutive months** at the equivalent of a 6% annual rate (about 0.5% per month), it's costing companies a great deal to make goods. *My strategy:* Sell your stocks and bonds before the market overheats. Also, purchase big-ticket items before those wholesale prices are passed along to consumers.

● **If inflation is rising and the PPI rate of change starts to slow or declines,** buy stocks and bonds. Companies will be earning higher profits, as it costs them less to make goods, but they can still charge consumers higher prices.

Consumer Price Index (CPI)

Often referred to as the cost of living, the CPI measures the change in consumer prices for goods and services bought by households. It is released in the middle of every month—always one day after the PPI. *What to do:*

● **If the economy is expanding moderately** (a GDP of 4% or under) and the CPI is also rising at a modest rate (annual rate of about 3%), consider buying stocks or real estate—and avoid bonds because interest rates are likely to rise.

● **If the CPI moves up sharply for two months** and the cause of the rise is not easily explained by the economists, avoid bonds. *Attractive:* Stocks that will either profit from inflation or not get clobbered in the recession that may be looming.

● **If the CPI falls by 1% or more for two months,** I like stocks that pay dividends. To lock in yields before they fall, add quality corporate bonds and Treasury bonds to your portfolio.

● **If the CPI rises by 4% or more over four consecutive months,** expect interest rates to rise. Buy short-term CDs.

Consumer Confidence Index (CCI)

The CCI reflects consumers' attitudes toward the economy, the job market, their own financial situations and the future. The government releases the CCI during the first 10 days of each month.

When assessing the CCI, remember that consumers account for two-thirds of all U.S. economic activity. So how we're all feeling matters. *What to do:*

● **Don't react to the month-to-month** ups and downs of the CCI. Rather, value it as a big-picture forecaster.

● **If inflation is high and consumer confidence falls below 80**—20% lower than the index's benchmark of 100—prepare for a recession.

● **If inflation is low and the CCI shows signs of reviving**—lower unemployment and rising auto or home sales, for example—bet on a stronger economy. Big-ticket durable goods, such as autos and appliances, may soon do very well.

Source: Jay J. Pack, vice president of Burnham Securities, Inc., 1345 Avenue of the Americas, New York, NY 10105. He is coauthor, with Nancy Dunnan, of Market Movers: A Complete Guide to Economic Statistics, Trends, Forces, and News Events—and What They Mean to Your Investments, *Warner Books.*

Hidden Balance Sheet Values

Most top Wall Street research analysts base their stock recommendations on a set of sophisticated earnings estimates. It's difficult for amateurs to develop comparable estimates because they lack professional investors' combination of experience, access to information source and ties to industry. *But there is a way for amateurs to beat the pros:* by looking for hidden value in a company's balance sheet.

The best tools for finding value are the annual report and the company's 10K. Both can be acquired from the company itself or the Securities & Exchange Commission (SEC).

Read the Fine Print

Begin your search with the footnotes. If taken seriously, a reading of the footnotes can reveal an abundance of information that many investors are simply too lazy to track down. The following list will point you on your way.

● **Company pension fund.** Until the 1980s, the pension obligations of American industry were dramatically underfunded. Since then, pension assets have built up more rapidly than obligations. The result has been a vast net overfunding. Thus, what appears to be a liability—a pension obligation—is often a net asset that can be easily tapped by management as a source of ready cash. Exceptions to this overfunded situation are primarily companies in industries characterized by years of strong union domination.

● **Inventories.** A company that uses what is referred to as the LIFO (last-in, first-out) system of accounting for inventories may have a huge cushion of extra value hidden in its inventory account. That's because the LIFO method values inventory at historic costs rather than at the cost of the inventory if a company had to purchase it today.

To gauge hidden value, the investor must distinguish between raw materials and finished products. The closer inventory is to the raw materials stage, the more likely it is that the LIFO values in inventories can be ultimately realized.

● **Natural resources.** These assets may be well above their carrying value in the balance sheet. Thus the investor has to distinguish between raw materials that have declined in value in recent years and those that have risen. For example, even with the price of petroleum far below its peak levels, oil reserves are often carried at conservative valuations if their discovery cost was low. As a cross-check, use the calculation required by the SEC of the present value of its oil reserves.

● **Business segments.** Probably the most important way to locate hidden value is through a careful analysis of a company's different business segments. The footnotes in a 10K and annual report provide fairly detailed information regarding a company's lines of business, separating them in terms of investment, capital spending, earnings and other important variables.

What investors should look for is a company's "crown jewel"—a highly profitable or potentially profitable segment—which may be masked by poor financial results in the company's other operations. The stock market's overall appraisal of the company may not reflect the potential of the profitable division. The payoff comes if you can find a diversified company with a top-performing division that may become the target for a potential acquisition.

Acquirers of diversified businesses often look for one profitable segment, calculating that they will be able to dispose of the losers.

● **Company property.** The value of the company's property could be grossly understated. The 10K normally indicates how much square footage the company leases and owns. Most important is office and commercial space. Unless you are familiar with the particular real estate market in which the company's property is located, it may be difficult to estimate the property's value. However, by examining the company's plant account, with a close eye to location, you may find a clue to the value of company-owned real estate. Similarly, even though they are labeled as liabilities on the balance sheet, assignable leaseholds at below-market rates can be enormous assets.

● **Intangible assets.** Large hidden assets that have no place on the balance sheet include brand recognition, technology, distribution and marketing networks, franchises, etc. Intangibles such as these may have taken years to build up and could very well be a company's most important assets. They are usually of enormous value to potential acquirers.

> "[Value in a company] can be found in hidden assets that [aren't] on the balance sheet, [such as] brand recognition...[and] technology."

Note: Beware of capitalized expenses for R&D costs. These expenses are treated as assets on the balance sheet. If the product to which the R&D is devoted does pay off, there may be an eventual write-off. Also beware of deferred marketing expenses.

Source: *Michael Metz, chief strategist, Oppenheimer & Co., Inc., One Oppenheimer Tower, World Financial Center, New York, NY 10281.*

Spotting the Traps in Earnings Figures

Figures on company earnings are deceptive. They are useful guides only to investors who interpret them correctly.

● **Retained earnings** for some American companies can be overstated by significant amounts. *Example:* $1 in after-tax profit shrinks to just 60¢ after 40% is subtracted to adjust for the effect of inflation on depreciation and costs. Another 40% might then be deducted in order to pay out a dividend.

● **The real corporate tax rate is elusive.** *Reason:* Inflation boosts costs, resulting in inventory profits and underdepreciation of plant and equipment.

Advice: Have more confidence in the earnings reports of companies that use last-in, first-out (LIFO) inventory accounting methods that make adjustments for inflation.

● **Return on equity** is often one-fourth of the reported percentage. *Reason:* Profits are nearly halved by inflation. But the book value might be almost doubled when current prices are used to calculate.

In most cases, it is not worth trying to make a quick trade based on a quarterly report. *Reason:* There is almost always a correction that brings the stock price back to where it was before the report. *When to trade:* After the price settles back. *What to focus on*:

● **Deviation in the long-term trend** of a company's earnings.

● **Changes in net margin.** If sales move ahead but income is level, watch for a trend toward lower profits. And vice versa.

● **Underlying changes,** such as currency fluctuations, tax rate and number of shares outstanding. They all affect earnings per share. Translating the earnings figures into the price/earnings ratio (p/e ratio) is even trickier because the price of a stock is based on anticipated earnings, but the ratio is calculated on earnings in the previous 12 months.

Brokers are quite shameless about recommending one stock to a client as a good value (because the p/e ratio is low) and another as an excellent growth stock (because company prospects are so exciting that the p/e ratio is meaningless).

Rationale for buying low-multiple stocks: There is less downside risk in a declining market. And they have higher upgrade potential in an advancing market.

Rationale for buying high-multiple stocks: If the company really grows by 40% a year for the next

MAKING PROFITS ON A STOCK SPLIT

When a stock splits, the average profit to an investor is 20%. But the greatest profits are generally made in the three to six months before the split is announced. The general pattern is that the price stays high for two days after the split announcement and then declines. *To spot a candidate for a split, look for:*

● **A company that needs to attract** more stockholders, diversify or attract additional financing.

● **A takeover candidate** (heavy in cash and liquid assets) whose management holds only a small percentage of the outstanding shares. (Companies with concentrated ownership rarely split stock unless there are problems with taxes, acquisitions or diversification.)

● **A stock priced above $75.** A split moves it into the more attractive $25–$50 range.

● **A stock that was split previously** and whose price has climbed steadily since then.

● **Earnings prospects so strong** that the company will be able to increase dividends after the split.

Likely prospects are over-the-counter companies with current earnings of $2.5 million, at least $2 million annually in preceding years and less than 1 million shares outstanding (or under 2,000 shareholders). A stock split is necessary if management wants to list on a major exchange.

Source: C. Colburn Hardy, Your Money and Your Life: Planning Your Financial Future, *Books on Demand.*

Investing to Win

375

10 years, paying 40 times earnings is acceptable. Current earnings of $1 compounded for 10 years at a 40% rate amounts to nearly $30 of earnings 10 years from now. Even if the p/e ratio falls to 10 by then, the stock will have gone up more than seven times in value (from 40 to 290).

Bottom line: Keep a clear head when earnings, earnings forecasts and p/e ratios are being loosely presented as reasons to buy now.

Source: Peter De Haas, portfolio strategist, L.F. Rothschild, Unterberg, Towbin, New York, NY.

The Truth About Stock Buybacks

Offers by companies to buy back shares at premium prices usually are worth accepting. In fact, these buyback offers are often 10% or more above market levels. If you hold your shares, chances are they won't go up more than 2%–3% in the months following the buyback because the market will already have discounted the impact of the offer. In addition, buybacks divert large amounts of company cash from other productive investments, lowering the potential for future share price increases.

Source: Changing Times.

Wisdom From a Wise Source

Smart investors avoid the following big mistakes:

● **Assuming that a stock that's moving in a certain direction** will continue to move in that direction forever. When a stock is heading for the moon, take profits—and when a stock is headed for zero, be a buyer. *Veteran's insight:* Very few stocks get to zero, and none reach the moon.

● **Worrying about whether the stock market is too high.** The stock market isn't a single entity—it's a universe of individual stocks. *Smart investor's goal:* To buy value whenever it's reasonably priced. Even when the market as a whole is too high, there are always a few undervalued stocks around.

● **Believing every stock story you hear.** *Wise rules:* Never follow the crowd, avoid fads and investigate thoroughly every story that seems plausible.

● **Buying stocks for dividends.** This has recently become popular thanks to tax reform's lower tax rates and the elimination of tax-favored treatment of capital gains. Dividend income has become more attractive relative to capital appreciation.

Risk: Common stock dividends *aren't* guaranteed. If the going gets rough, many companies will cut their dividends.

Only source of guaranteed income: Top-quality bonds—but even these aren't risk-free. If interest rates rise, the market value of bonds falls. And if you have to sell the bonds before maturity, that can be a problem.

● **Paying too much attention to market gurus.** No one person has ever been able to predict consistently what's going to happen in the stock market.

Problem: Unpredictable events that affect the overall market, such as wars, assassinations, OPEC decisions, etc. *Safer:* Predicting that an individual stock will rise if the company's earnings are growing 20% a year and it's a leader in its industry. Whether or not somebody shoots the President, its value will continue to go up.

● **Not being patient enough.** Patience is the key to making money in stocks. Unfortunately, 90% of investors—including institutions—lack it. Nowadays everybody thinks short term; what used to take six months to happen in the market now takes six days. *To beat the market:* Keep your eyes fixed on the long-term horizon. Do your homework, and then give your stock selections time to perform. Often it takes years for an investment scenario to play itself out.

● **Acting too quickly.** There's always time to buy a stock. If it's now at $22 a share and it's rising to $50,

Dividend Reinvestment

Dividend-reinvestment plans permit shareholders to buy additional stock by automatically reinvesting dividends. A list of firms offering reinvestment plans is available from Standard and Poor's Corp., 25 Broadway, New York, NY 10004.

Source: How to Invest $50–$5,000 by financial analyst Nancy Dunnan, Harper & Row.

does it really matter if you pay $22 or $24.50?

Never take action until you understand why a stock is moving. *When to suspend judgment:* Triple Witching Hour—the third Friday in March, June, September and December—when stock index futures, stock index options and individual stock options all expire and the market often makes wild swings up or down. Wait at least a day to confirm the trend.

With the sophistication of computerized program trading, this extreme volatility has started to pop up on other days. Whatever happens, don't be panicked into making a move that you might regret later.

Source: Louis Ehrenkrantz, president of Ehrenkrantz King Nussbaum, investment advisers, 635 Madison Ave., New York, NY 10022.

Those Great Old Investment Strategies

Ever since the stock market's inception, investors have been searching for strategies and rules of thumb to help them decide whether, how and when to invest in a particular stock. The strategies that have evolved range from the very complex (detailed calculations of risk, economics and financial analysis) to the very simple (tracking newspaper headlines or even gauging the strength of the tides). *Here is an analysis of today's most popular investment strategies:*

Strategies That Work

● *Small-firm strategy.* This is a tested, investment strategy. *How it works:* Small stocks (issued by companies with a market capitalization between $20 million and $100 million) have provided consistently higher returns over time than large stocks—even when adjusted for risk. *Probable reason:* The large institutions avoid many small yet high-quality stocks, leaving opportunities for individual investors. If the stock continues to do well, the institutions eventually jump in, bidding up the price of the stock significantly. *Results:* Since the Depression, small stocks have provided returns that, on average, are annually 2% higher than returns from large stocks. Over time that kind of spread can significantly boost the total return of a portfolio.

Risk: Small stocks are much more volatile than large stocks—when the market goes up, small stocks increase in value very rapidly, but when the market goes down, they fall fast, too.

● *Contrarian-investing strategy.* Stocks that are out of favor (neglected by the big institutions, research analysts and the press) have provided higher returns than stocks considered "hot." *Best ways to identify out-of-favor stocks:*

● *Low price/earnings multiples* (low price to book-value ratios.)

● *High dividend yield.*

● *Low institutional ownership.* If more than 10 to 12 institutions own a stock, it is probably too popular. Monthly institutional ownership figures can be found in the *Standard & Poor's Stock Guide.*

Approach: When the market heats up, find the stocks investors are ignoring. Then do a thorough job of fundamental research to determine whether there is a strong chance for future gains.

● *Calendar-effect strategy.* Although this one defies all logic, certain days do provide consistently higher returns than other days.

Best: Don't trade solely on the basis of calendar effects. *But keep these points in mind:*

● *The first half of the month* usually outperforms the second half. The difference between these two periods is significant—as much as 1% for the first half of the month. Over a year, that can really add up.

● *Preholiday trading days are very positive.* The day immediately preceding a major holiday tends to be bullish. The biggest preholiday day is December 31.

● *January is the best month of the year*—especially for small stocks. This period includes the last trading days of December to the last days of January.

● *Dollar-cost-averaging strategy.* This is one of the most profitable ways to invest and to minimize risk. *How it works:* Invest a set amount of money in one particular stock at regular intervals over an extended period of time (usually one full market cycle)—regardless of whether the stock is up or down. *Rationale:* If you invest the same amount each time, you end up buying less of the stock when the price is high and more when it is down. Over time, the strategy irons out the wrinkles of a volatile market.

● *High-relative-price strategy.* A stock selling for a price that's high relative to its average historical price tends to do better than other stocks. You may not believe in technical analysis, but this simple stock-picker's rule has turned out to be a notable exception.

Strategies That Don't Work

● *Market-timing strategy.* Trying to move in and out of the market on the basis of short-term movements has never worked as well as buying and holding a stock for an extended time. *Attraction:* Some investors can call market twists and turns for short periods. But no one can keep this up indefinitely.

Risk: If you lose, chances are you'll lose big. Also, the more trading oriented your investment strategy becomes, the greater your transaction costs.

● *Penny-stocks strategy.* "Small is beautiful" goes only so far. Although a high-quality small stock can do very well over time, an extremely cheap stock (issued by a company not listed on the NY, AMEX or NASDAQ exchange—a "pink sheet" stock) can be highly risky. Many investors think that a low-priced stock, such as a 50-cent stock, will offer a huge upside potential and little downside risk. Wrong. Studies have shown that portfolios of very low-priced stocks have performed far worse over the years than other portfolios.

TRADING STOCKS BY THE CLOCK AND THE CALENDAR

Investors can increase their odds of successful stock trading by planning purchases and sales around certain times and dates. The following observations should be of help.

Best Times of the Day

● **Stocks usually reach low points each day** at around 10:45 A.M., 1:25 P.M. and again at around 2:50 P.M. If you plan to take a position in a rising market, try to purchase around these times.

● **Keep track of market action between 3 P.M. and 4 P.M. (closing);** pay special attention to activity during the final few minutes of the day. A strong final hour and/or a strong final five minutes usually means a strong opening the next day. If the market closes with a very powerful burst of trading, the odds are high that the next day's opening will be strong, but that stocks will sell off later that day.

● **High points during market rallies** tend to occur at 10:30 A.M., 2:30 P.M. and, if it is a strong day, at the close.

Best Days of the Week

● **Fridays tend to be weak days** for the stock market. If prices show little change for Friday, but edge up near the close, expect Monday, a stronger day of the week, to show a gain.

● **Mondays tend to be favorable days** for stocks. Most Mondays are good days for selling. You will notice that this is a reversal from the best selling days several years ago.

Best Days of the Month

● **The market is usually strongest** the final two to three trading days of one month and the first two to three trading days of the next month. This is a well-documented pattern—traders make extensive use of it. Price gains during these five-day periods often exceed gains shown in all the rest of the two months' trading days combined.

Best Months of the Year

● **Buy** in November and **sell** in April.

Holiday Buying

● **The stock market tends to be strong** one or two days before a holiday. A really good time is a preholiday period that coincides with turn-of-the-month strength.

● **Expect excellent performance** during the period prior to July 4 and between Christmas and New Year's.

The Political Cycle

● **Stocks tend to rise** during the two years prior to a presidential election, and have historically been weaker during the two years following an election.

A Special Coincidence

● **For no explainable reason,** years ending in "5" have proven to be extremely strong for the stock market.

Source: Gerald Appel, president, Signalert Corporation, 150 Great Neck Road, Great Neck, NY 11021.

● **Initial public offering strategy.** Buying stocks that are going public, particularly just after the initial offering, is a losing strategy. Plus, if you can get the stock at the offering price, you probably don't want it. All the really good IPOs are available only to the institutional investors.

● **Technical-analysis strategy.** Except for the high-relative-price strategy mentioned above, virtually all forms of technical analysis—stock-price runs, charting, moving average and so forth—have proved almost worthless as investment strategies.

Source: *John Markese, Ph.D., president, American Association of Individual Investors, 625 N. Michigan Ave., Chicago, IL 60611.*

How Stan Weinstein Beats the Stock Cycles

By tracking the price cycles of stocks, investors have a good chance of timing for maximum appreciation.

To plot the cycles, chart the 30-week moving average for stocks that you hold or may want to trade. The chart can be plotted from the closing Friday prices available in financial journals or most daily papers. Then compare this moving average with the latest price in the daily papers.

From the chart, you'll be able to recognize the four stages of each cycle:

● **Stage 1: The base.** The first sign of this stage is that daily prices start to nudge above the 30-week average. This typically occurs immediately following a major price decline. At first glance, it might appear that this is the time to buy—but don't buy stock at this stage. It's impossible to tell how long the price will remain flat, and you could have your money tied up for a long time with no movement.

● **Stage 2: The advance.** As this phase begins, prices surge ahead of the 30-week average. This is the ideal time to buy the stock—the major advance is first getting under way.

● **Stage 3: The top.** The surest sign of a top is that daily prices are no longer consistently above the 30-week average. Instead, they move within a narrow range above and below the average. At the same time, trading volume steadily increases. This is the time to consider selling the stock.

● **Stage 4: The decline.** Now the stock trades increasingly below its moving average. Stay away from the stock throughout this period.

Source: *Stan Weinstein, publisher,* The Professional Tape Reader.

Chart Patterns to Help You Time the Purchase and Sale of Stocks

Graphic representations of stock market trends are readily available to all investors. Each day, newspapers such as *The Wall Street Journal* and *The New York Times* print charts of the movement of the stock market for recent time intervals. Other financial newspapers and investment newsletters provide longer-term, sometimes weekly or monthly, charts of the same movements. Investors with home computers can even purchase moderately priced software that receives data and generates stock and stock market charts.

By themselves, charts cannot guarantee successful stock market trading. However, they can serve as useful tools for general market timing. The following tips should help you know when movements in the market are going to take place.

● **Congestion areas.** A congestion area is a price area in which a large amount of trading takes place without much price movement.

Prices tend to stall just under previously developed congestion areas (areas of resistance). The market is bullish if prices penetrate and rise above a previously formed congestion area. Conversely, price declines tend to stop just above previously formed congestion areas (areas of support). The market is bearish if prices penetrate downward through such an area.

● **Uptrends and downtrends.** Uptrends in price may be considered intact as long as prices continue to reach new high levels on each upswing and continue to find support at progressively higher levels. Downtrends may be considered intact as long as each decline carries the market lower and each rally fails to reach the highs of the previous rally. Remain in the market during uptrends—stay out during downtrends.

● **Double bottom formation.** A double bottom occurs when the stock market declines to a certain level, rises, declines back to the area of the first low, and then starts back up again. The entire formation looks like a "W" on a chart. When the "W" is complete, the market usually continues to advance. Patterns that take only a few trading sessions to develop indicate short-term rallies. Patterns developing over a period of several weeks suggest longer advances.

The reverse pattern appears as an "M" on a chart. It indicates a future market decline.

● **Volume patterns.** Most charts carry volume data in addition to price movement data. The following are bullish volume patterns.

● **Stock prices rise broadly off a low,** on sharply increasing volume. It is especially bullish if prices rise on strong volume at the same time a "W" formation is completed.

● **Prices pull back** after a few days of a strong advance on sharply reduced volume. Pullbacks during uptrends usually last for a week to 10 days. Expect prices to retrace about 40% of the gains recorded on the previous advance. This is a good time to accumulate positions if you missed the initial leg up.

● **It is usually bullish for the intermediate trend** (lasting for several weeks to a few months), if the Dow Transportation Average performs at least as well as the Dow Industrial Average. It is bullish for the major trend (lasting for months to years) if the Dow Utility Average performs at least as well as the Dow Industrial Average.

● **Time cycles and stock purchases.** Chart patterns often reveal time cycles that underlie stock price movements. Low points for stocks tend to occur at fairly regular intervals. Once you recognize those intervals, you can often anticipate when low points are likely to develop, sometimes weeks in advance. The following are regularly repeating cycles for the stock market.

● **Stocks tend to reach their bottom** in a minor price swing at 13- to 15-day intervals. Market lows tend to be spaced about three weeks apart.

● **A more important market cycle** is the six- to eight-week market cycle. Low points tend to occur at intervals of approximately seven weeks. Once the market turns up at the seven-week low point, expect the advances to last for about two to three weeks.

● **Important low points** tend to be spaced at approximate intervals of between 16 and 18 weeks. This very important cycle provides the most significant intermediate market movement.

● **It is very bullish** when a 16- to 18-week low point coincides with a seven-week low point. The nesting of these two cycles indicates a strong market advance for the future.

● **Very few market swings**—upward or downward—last for longer than five to six weeks before a price reversal takes place. If the market has already risen for five to six weeks, wait to buy—you usually will be able to get a better price later. If, on the other hand, the market has been falling for five to six weeks without an intervening rally, then your gains are likely to be greater if you wait to sell.

Source: *Gerald Appel, president, Signalert Corporation, 150 Great Neck Road, Great Neck, NY 11021.*

How Jonathan Pond Reads Barron's

The average investor can benefit greatly by reading *Barron's*, the weekly financial newspaper. I read *The Wall Street Journal* and other daily newspapers, but they can often be more distracting than helpful. *Reason:* Daily newspapers explain why the Dow Jones Industrial Average (DJIA) went up or down the day before. They study the daily fluctuations so closely that the average investor may overlook a more important week-long or month-long trend.

My Ritual

I pick up a copy of *Barron's* every Saturday morning when it first hits the newsstands. Then—as my family knows only too well—I disappear for a few hours to study the data listed. *Here are the things I look for:*

● **Stock market trends.** First, I look at the data in the section called *Market Laboratory.* I focus on the relative performances of the DJIA, the S&P 500 Index, the NASDAQ composite index and the Russell 2000 Index, which comprises the best-known small-cap companies.

Although I don't believe in market timing, I do think it's possible to spot some market trends early. So when one index suddenly begins to outperform the others, I pay close attention. *Example:* During the past 12 months, the S&P 500 Index has been beating most of the other averages and outpacing almost every mutual fund in sight. As a result, I have increased the S&P 500 Index fund weighting of some clients' accounts. *Added benefit:* Index stock mutual funds have relatively small capital gains distributions, which makes them attractive for taxable accounts.

● *Mutual fund track records.* The Lipper Mutual Fund Performance Averages pages in *Barron's* are especially helpful to me. They track performance by mutual fund type for several different periods. *Example:* The Lipper table shows you how 40 different categories of funds have performed over the past week, month, quarter and 12 months.

Looking at the mutual-fund tables, an investor can quickly gauge how his or her funds are performing relative to their peers and to funds in other categories.

I look for *fund types* that may show promise for the coming year, such as science and technology funds, as well as those that should be avoided, such as extremely volatile emerging-markets funds.

● *Money-market-fund yields.* This table helps me see how the funds I own compare with industry averages. I can see how the rate of the average tax-exempt fund compares with the after-tax yield of the average taxable fund.

● *Insights and analysis.* Columns on the stock market, bonds, international markets and real estate help give me the big picture. I get a sense of what long-term trends may be unfolding. *Example:* Recently, the real estate column, The Ground Floor, did a wonderful statistical analysis of the performance of Real Estate Investment Trusts (REITs). *Two points were clear:*

● *Long-term performance*— greater than 10 years—of REITs is superior.

● *Buying a newly public REIT* is a sucker's game. *Strategy:* Consider making REITs permanently part of your portfolio, but do so through professionally managed real estate mutual funds.

● *Opinions of great minds in interviews.* *Barron's* has access to the best investors around, and I want to know what they're thinking. If two great investors—such as Fidelity's Peter Lynch and Michael Price of Mutual Series Fund—suddenly begin seeing the same emerging theme, readers should start tracking the trend.

Source: *Jonathan Pond, president of Financial Planning Information Inc., Watertown, MA. He is the author of* 4 Easy Steps to Successful Investing, *Dell. He also appears regularly as a commentator on PBS-TV's* Nightly Business Report.

Bear-Proofing Your Portfolio

With the major stock market indexes up more than 20% since the end of the year, your investment portfolio has probably produced amazing returns.

But if you're like most investors, you're probably nervous about where the stock market is headed over the next 12 months—and whether the Dow Jones Industrial Average can climb much further.

Here are strategies to consider for preserving the value of your portfolio—no matter what happens to the market during the coming months. By taking action now, you will be able to relax, no matter what occurs.

● *Sell half your position in stocks that have had big gains this year.* This is one way to have your cake *and* eat it. *Example:* Last year, you bought 1,000 shares of a company at $10 a share. Now the stock's price is $50. Even if you believe, for sound reasons, that the stock could go higher, you could protect your profits by selling 500 shares. That way, you would pocket $20,000 in gains (before commission and taxes) and still profit from the company's future growth.

● *Set stop-loss orders to protect yourself* in case a stock fails to perform as you had hoped. Stop-loss orders authorize your stockbroker to automatically sell a stock once it reaches a price determined by you. This does not mean it will be sold at your price but at the available market price. *Example:* Let's say you buy 1,000 shares of a company at $10 a share on the expectation that its earnings will grow at 20% a year. But the company suddenly encounters supply problems and those expectations are dashed.

Investing to Win

381

Subsequently, the stock drops to $7 a share while you're away on a fishing trip. Had you placed a stop-loss order to sell your stake at $9 a share, your position might have been liquidated before the stock lost another two points.

A good rule of thumb is to sell automatically when a stock drops 20% below its highest price since you've owned it.

● *When buying stocks now,* only invest if there is little downside risk. Don't be dazzled by the prospect of big gains—without considering the possibility of big losses.

I hold on to a stock if it has the potential to increase its value by at least one-third over the next 12 months. But I won't buy a promising stock unless I also think its downside potential—its negative risk for investors—is *half that amount.* To put it another way, I look for a risk/reward ratio of at least two to one. *Example:* If we think a stock is likely to go up by 40% over the next year, it might be a potential purchase as long as we also think that it is unlikely to lose more than 20% of its value over the same period.

● *When in doubt, hold on to the stock.* The best approach to investing in stocks is to take a long-term view and to measure the success of your portfolio's performance over the next five to 10 years, not the next quarter.

This strategy allows you to filter out the temporary surges and dips in stock prices and focus instead on what hopefully will be the steady increase in their market value.

For this reason, there's something to be said for the advice of some successful older investors who say their secret was to buy stocks decades ago and stick them in a box. This strategy prevented the investors from selling when things got shaky or overheated. And because their stocks were generating dividends for them year after year, these investors got maximum mileage out of the enormous power of compounding—or the phenomenon of earnings producing more earnings.

● *Diversify by buying bonds.* Bonds generate a flow of income, which can be reinvested in stocks when a buying opportunity arises. There's no magic number for allocating a percentage of your portfolio to bonds or bond funds. Buy as much as you need to feel comfortable. *Good news:* Bond yields will continue to fall because of low inflation, making bonds an ideal investment.

All-Weather Stocks

● *Allstate.* Allstate announced a two-for-one stock split in June 1998 and is buying back a significant amount of its stock. This company has costs under control and has reduced its exposure to earthquakes in California and hurricanes in Florida. It's also using the strong Allstate brand name to build its life insurance and annuity business.

● *Chase Mountain Bank.* This high-quality international banking franchise continues to increase its productivity by substituting computing power for brick, mortar and additional personnel—yet it trades at only 10 times 1999 earnings. Its stock split two for one in July 1998 after a 16% dividend increase earlier that year.

● *Maytag.* This company has revitalized investor interest by a management change and a new focus on traditional premium-brand strengths. Improved marketing and manufacturing efficiencies in the home-appliance division have significantly strengthened Maytag's financial position. Sales, earnings per share and returns on assets have doubled since 1993. Dividends were increased at the end of 1995, again at the end of 1996, and a 10.8 million stock repurchase plan is under way. Consistent, improved operating results suggest a much higher market multiple as new management carries out its business plan.

Source: *Douglas Raborn, chairman of Raborn & Co., an independent advisory investment firm for individuals and retirement plans located in Delray Beach, FL, 800-798-1124.*

If the Stock Market Makes You Nervous...

In recent years, the stock market has rewarded the optimists and penalized the pessimists.

What should you do with your money now if you feel strongly that the bull market may be cooling? *Here are our strategies for stock investors who are uneasy:*

● *Don't change your strategy.* If you're a long-term investor with a time horizon of 10 years or more—

and you're happy with the stocks and mutual funds you own—leave them alone. Presumably you have an investment strategy that is designed to work for you over the long haul, so stick with it.

Responding to every anticipated move in the stock market makes you a market timer. Even the great professionals have trouble timing the market consistently. *Better:* A long-term strategy that ignores temporary ups and downs in the stock market should give you a higher return over time. *Exception:* If you own stocks that have large profits and you're not comfortable with the market's future, sell some of your stocks. Remember the Wall Street adage that no one ever lost money taking profits. You'll pay long-term capital gains taxes of no more than 20%—and about 80% or more of the profit will wind up in your pocket.

Important: If you're five years away from retirement—or will need the money soon to buy a home or pay tuition—you shouldn't be too heavily invested in the stock market. You're better off in more conservative investments.

● ***Put the money you were going to invest in stocks into safer places instead.*** If the stock market frightens you, shift cash to money-market accounts where it will be safe and readily available when the market quiets down. *Another alternative:* U.S. Treasury bills. They pay higher returns than bank accounts or money markets—and they have the absolute backing of the government, making them completely safe. They are also free of state income taxes. You can buy them from a bank or broker, paying a commission to do so.

You can also buy Treasury securities at the nearest branch of the Federal Reserve through the Treasury Direct program and pay no commission.

Anyone above the 28% tax bracket should investigate tax-exempt money-market and short-term bond funds. In most cases, they will offer higher after-tax returns with no additional risk.

● ***Rethink your asset allocation.*** The key to successful investing is having the right mix of stocks, bonds and cash. The right mix depends on your own personal financial situation and current economic conditions. *Strategy:* Depending on your goals, you might want to examine your allocation annually—or at least every time there is a shift in the investment markets—to see if the mix still makes sense for you.

If the market makes you nervous, change the allocation by adding new money to bonds and cash.

Pay particular attention to your allocation after a long rally in the stock market. Maybe you started with 50% of your assets in stocks. Now, after a long market run-up, rising prices have pushed that stock allocation to 65% of assets. Take profits to restore your allocation to the way you want it to be.

● ***Invest in foreign markets now.*** Economies around the world move at different paces—and so do international stock markets. *Example:* The Japanese economy and the Japanese stock market stayed weak when the U.S. economy and the U.S. stock market were booming. *Strategy:* If you believe the U.S. stock market is turning sluggish, shift money to foreign stock markets that are doing better. Most investors will be better off buying shares in a foreign stock mutual fund.

Important: Pick *foreign* mutual funds, which only invest overseas. *Global* funds invest internationally *and* in the United States—the market you want to avoid.

If you are a more sophisticated investor, you can invest directly in foreign stocks through American Depositary Receipts (ADRs). They represent shares of foreign companies but trade on U.S. stock exchanges. Any stockbroker can sell them to you.

● ***Use investment money to pay off debts.*** This offers a better return on your money than investing in a stagnant stock market. It is also better than putting the money in a low-return bank account. The higher the interest rate on the debt, the better the payoff to you.

● ***Invest the money in your home.*** Studies show that money spent on a new kitchen, master bathroom or extra room can add to the value of your house on a dollar-for-dollar basis.

● ***Invest in yourself.*** Use money that might have gone into stocks to take courses that will improve your skills and learning potential. Adding to your education could help you find a new, better job. You could also use the money to launch a part-time or sideline business, which could grow into a full-time venture someday.

● ***Give away the money.*** Anyone can give $10,000 to anyone else each year and not incur a federal gift tax. Once the money is given away, it is out of your estate and your income taxes forever.

Strategy: Use the money to create custodial accounts for college-bound youngsters age 14 and older. At age 14 and beyond, income from the custodial account is taxed at the child's lower tax rate. If you hold appreciated stock and sell it, you'll be hit with a capital gains tax at a rate as high as 20%. If you give it to a child in a low tax bracket, the child can sell it and pay taxes at a 15% tax rate.

Warning: Never give away money you might need for your own security. Examine your finances—with the help of a financial adviser—before giving any money away, to make certain you can spare it.

Source: *Laurence I. Foster and Thomas J. Hakala, partners in the personal financial planning practice of KPMG Peat Marwick, LLP, the accounting and consulting firm, 345 Park Ave., New York, NY 10154.*

When You Invest Abroad

When you invest abroad, you invest not just in the foreign stocks or bonds you purchase—but also in the foreign currency. If the currency drops in value, so will your investment. When selling a currency that will keep its value, remember that over the long run, countries with high savings and productivity rates together with low interest rates have the strongest currencies. When selecting foreign investments, examine the fundamentals of the country you invest in as well as those of the business.

Source: *Getting Rich Outside the Dollar by Christopher Weber, investment consultant, Ormond by the Sea, FL, Warner Books.*

Quick Securities Analysis

You don't need an MBA to judge the financial health of a business in which you might invest. First get its latest financial statement. Then figure its *quick ratio*—cash and marketable securities divided by current liabilities. If this is more than 1.0, the company can pay its debts.

Insider Buying Vs. Insider Selling

Insider selling is less meaningful than insider buying as an indicator of a company's prospects. Since sales may be made for a variety of reasons (diversification, shortage of cash, etc.), sales by two insiders in a company should be accorded roughly the same importance as one purchase by an insider.

Source: *Norman Fosback, editor,* Income & Safety.

If not, don't invest. Also figure its debt-to-capital ratio—total long-term debt divided by total capital, which consists of long-term debt plus the total value of all outstanding common stock. Long-term debt is part of the company's capital, so it is counted on both sides of the equation. Typical debt ratios vary by industry, but a ratio of more than 25% may be risky.

Source: *Barron's Guide to Making Investment Decisions by John Prestbo, markets editor,* The Wall Street Journal, *Prentice Hall.*

Signal That a Large Block of Stock Is About to Be Dumped on the Market

Very frequently, knowledge that a large block of shares of a particular stock is up for sale can influence the decision of whether to buy or to sell those securities. For example, you might postpone or permanently avoid purchasing shares about to come under institutional liquidation. Or you might choose to sell before a competing large sell order becomes operative.

While mutual funds and other institutions don't "advertise" that they plan a liquidation prior to actual sale, such information not infrequently manages to "leak out," and this often puts a sizable dent in the stock's price. There usually are hints available to the alert investor that a liquidation of the block is imminent.

The major indication that a block is coming up for sale lies in a sudden shrinkage of the trading range of the issue in question. For example, a stock might usually demonstrate an average trading range of perhaps a full point or point and one-half between its daily high and low in a typical trading day. If, for two or three days, this trading range shrinks to, say, one-tenth to three-eighths of a point, you might anticipate a block is coming up for sale at near current market levels or below.

HOW TO FIND TAKEOVER TARGETS

Short of consulting a crystal ball, the best way to tell if a company's a possible takeover target is by watching the buying patterns of investors with top track records. You can do this by tracking SEC 13D filings.* They're required within 10 days of a purchase that brings an investor's holdings to 5% or more of a company's outstanding stock. That's not to say you should blindly follow. You must also analyze the company's balance sheet and market position.

When calculating a company's book value to compare it with its market value, research its adjusted book value—including assets that don't show up on the balance sheet (find them in annual report footnotes)—often, an overfunded pension plan or last-in, first-out (LIFO) inventory reserves. *Reasons:* Spectacular rises in the stock and bond markets boost the funds held in pension plans—and if a company uses LIFO accounting procedures, its inventory is usually worth more than stated on the books.

Insight can also be gained from looking at the company's securities portfolio, also listed in annual report footnotes. *Question:* Is the portfolio's market value higher than its stated book value? When the Dow Jones averages are as high, almost any company with a securities portfolio has these high off-balance-sheet assets.

Also take a look at the market value of a company's real estate holdings. *Where to find them:* the company's Form 10K, filed annually with the SEC and available from the company's investor relations department.

You'll have to research land values in the area—and will often find that the value of the property is higher than stated on the company's books. Find out from its annual report whether the company has a tax-loss carryforward that might benefit another party.

In addition to hidden balance-sheet assets, you need to know how the company is faring within its own industry. *How:* by comparing its price/earnings ratio with p/e's in the rest of the industry and with the general market. That gives an idea of whether it's fairly, over- or undervalued. *Best:* Undervalued.

Next area to investigate: The company's market share. Is it a major player or an also-ran? Always go for the major players.

How to get 13Ds: They're available from the SEC in Washington on the day they're filed and in Chicago, Los Angeles and New York two days later. Other sources: SEC Today *and* Street Smart Investing.

Source: *William Wood, senior vice president, Street Smart, Inc., publisher of* Street Smart Investing *and* 13D Opportunities Report.

The shrinkage probably represents awareness on the part of knowledgeable floor and other traders that a large sell order exists and an unwillingness to bid up for the stock until the overhead supply, which is immediately forthcoming, is fully liquidated.

When to Sell a Stock

Buying stocks is easy. It's selling them that's hard. Many otherwise intelligent investors sabotage their stocks' performances by not recognizing the signs to bail out of positions. Greed and ego are the two major enemies. *But they can be controlled with these criteria:*

● *Sell when you reach your target price.* Planning an exit strategy in advance can help counteract your emotions. We always set a target sale price—based on a reasonable multiple of the company's expected future earnings. *Formula:* This target can be calculated by multiplying the company's expected growth rate by its earnings estimate for the next year. These numbers can be found in any broker's analyst report on the company.

● *Sell if the fundamentals worsen.* If a key executive departs, or if same-store sales worsen or if margins start eroding seriously, it's usually smart to sell a stock—even if the price doesn't yet suggest that you should.

● *Sell when the reason you bought the stock is no longer valid. Example:* You bought the stock because the company was the industry's dominant player, but now a competitor is doing better and is more efficient.

● **Sell when a stock is technically weak.** Watch out if your stock's price is declining while the volume—the number of shares traded—is large. A stock's volume is listed in the stock tables. For greater comparison, check with your broker.

● **Sell if a moving stop-loss is reached.** Think of a decline as an indication that something is probably wrong with the company. We *always* sell if a stock drops 20% from its high during the time we own it. This not only limits losses but locks in profits. Using a 20% drop removes the emotion from a difficult decision. *Example:* If a stock that hit a high of 40 six months ago sags to 32, we unload it.

Source: *Douglas K. Raborn, J.D., chairman, Raborn & Co., an investment management firm, 777 E. Atlantic Ave., Delray Beach, FL 33483.*

> **"Blunder: Buying second-rate stocks because they pay high dividends. Dividends are not as important as increasing earnings per share."**

The Biggest Stock-Picking Blunders

When the stock market begins to rise significantly, many people who have been sitting on the sidelines with cash will likely rush to invest. But as we have learned from the correction, it's better to look—and then look again—before you part with your money. *Here are the biggest mistakes people make when investing in stocks:*

Blunder: Not using critical stock-selection criteria. Most investors are unaware of the fundamentals that make up a successful stock. Instead, they buy fourth-rate stocks that are not market leaders.

A common method touted by experts is to choose stocks with low price/earnings ratios (p/e ratios). This strategy is a mistake. It's like saying you want to hire lousy players for your football team because they won't cost as much as great ones. *Reality:* The better stocks almost always have p/e ratios that are higher than the market average. As a result, these stocks look expensive.

I have studied the stocks that have done best during the past 40 years over all different types of market cycles. Because of their superior earnings records, most of them had p/e ratios that were higher than the market average at the time.

To differentiate between the great stocks with high p/e ratios and the lousy ones with high p/e ratios—read on.

Blunder: Buying a stock whose price is declining. We are a nation of bargain hunters. Individual investors are always looking for stock bargains and shopping for stocks that have reached new lows for the year. *Reality:* This is a good way to ensure miserable returns. A declining stock seems like a true bargain because it is cheaper than it was a few months ago. But the company may also be headed for an extended period of poor performance or even bankruptcy. Institutional investors occasionally buy these stocks because they have lots of money invested elsewhere to minimize the risk—and can make up any loss somewhere else. An individual with a handful of stocks in his or her portfolio cannot afford to bet that a stock has hit its absolute bottom.

Blunder: Using the dollar-cost-averaging method to buy shares of a stock whose price is declining. Dollar-cost-averaging involves investing the same sum of money at consistent intervals, such as once a month, regardless of the stock's price. The logic here is that you will be buying more shares as the stock price declines. *Reality:* Investors who follow a stock down can lose big. If you buy a stock at $50 and buy more at $40, your average price per share is $45. If it continues downward, you are throwing good money after bad. *Exception:* Using dollar-cost-averaging to buy shares of a growth mutual fund whose price is declining is a good strategy. *Reason:* A mutual fund's portfolio is diversified and will *almost always* come out of decline when the general market recovers.

Blunder: Buying second-rate stocks because they pay high dividends. Dividends are not as important as increasing earnings per share. In fact, the more the company pays in dividends, the weaker it may be. That's because the company may have to pay high interest rates to replenish the money that was paid out to shareholders. Realistically, you can lose the amount of a dividend in one or two days' fluctuation in the stock's price.

Blunder: Continuing to hold on to declining stocks because the losses are small. It's human nature to become emotionally involved with stocks and to keep hoping for a turnaround. *Reality:* In most cases, your loss will get much bigger.

The only way to prevent a huge loss is to take a small loss. The best way to do that is to set a loss limit. We sell when the stock has declined 8% from our purchase price. If you're indecisive, have your broker put in a stop-loss order at 8% below the purchase price. The stock will then be sold automatically. *Example:* If you buy a stock at $40 and it drops to $36¾, sell it.

This strategy is like taking out a little insurance policy. Otherwise, if you take a big loss, another stock will have to produce an even bigger return to make up for it. Conversely, you should also avoid cashing in small, easy-to-take profits while holding on to losers. Many investors sell stocks with profits before they sell those with losses. The move helps them feel like winners rather than confirming that they've made a mistake. *Reality:* This is a bad strategy. If you're going to sell a stock, you should think of the process as if you were weeding a garden. You want to get rid of the poor performers.

Blunder: Worrying too much about taxes and commissions. Your key objective should be to make an overall net profit on your stock portfolio. Focusing on taxes often leads to…

● **Making unsound investments** in the hope of finding a tax shelter or a way to limit your overall tax burden.

● **Losing out on a good profit** because you wanted to hold the investment for more than 12 months. By doing this, you only incur the 20% long-term capital gains tax—rather than being taxed at your higher income bracket for short-term gains. (After the year 2000, the top tax rate for long-term capital gains will be 18% if a five-year holding period is met. The 18% rate will apply only if the holding period for the assets begins after the year 2000.)

If you hold a stock that can be sold at a gain to avoid taxes, the gain may disappear and you will miss an opportunity.

Commissions shouldn't be a key factor either. The cost of buying or selling stocks, especially through a discount broker, are minor compared with making the right decisions and taking action when needed.

Blunder: Being influenced by events that are not really crucial to the stock's outlook. Many investors focus on stock splits, dividend increases, news announcements and brokerage firm recommendations. None of these significantly contribute to a stock's advance. Instead, read the major daily and weekly business publications, take a look at the companies in which you have invested and develop selection criteria. There are always plenty of opportunities in the stock market. *Strategy:* Consider companies whose stocks showed large and improving percentage increases in their quarterly earnings per share.

Source: *William J. O'Neil, trader and stock analyst, founder and chairman of* Investor's Business Daily, *a national business and financial newspaper.*

Stock-Churning Alert

Beware if your brokerage firm sends you a letter that thanks you for doing business with it, mentions your account has been reviewed, expresses the hope that you are happy and asks if there is any way it can improve its service. This is not junk mail or a customer solicitation. It is a warning that an unusually high volume of trading has occurred in your account.

Trap: If you ignore the letter, then later discover improper trading and complain or sue, the firm can respond that it asked if you were happy with how your account was being managed and you requested no changes.

Defense: Review statements immediately after receiving such a letter, and respond in writing if you have any complaints.

Source: *Dan Brecher, attorney of counsel, Fishbein, Badillo, Wagner, Itzler, 909 Third Ave., New York, NY 10022.*

About New Issues

Investors will always have a hard time solving the two big problems of initial public offerings (IPOs):

● **How to choose companies** that haven't been analyzed extensively by professional investors.

● **Where to find a broker** who will sell the newly issued stock, which is often grabbed up by a few of the underwriter's favorite clients.

Profits and Safety

Conducting a shrewd analysis of companies that go public is the only way to minimize the enormous risk of investing in IPOs. As a group, IPOs have risen in price an average 64% in the first year of being publicly traded. Some of them double in value after even minutes of being traded. *The downside:* About 40% of all IPOs lose half their value in the first year, and a substantial number go bankrupt.

The document to ask your broker for is the final prospectus of the IPO. *What to look for:*

● *How money raised from the initial stock sale will be used.* Proceeds from the offering should be used to improve or expand what the company is currently doing. *Examples:* Increase production or pay for a major marketing plan. *Be wary when:* proceeds of an IPO go toward retiring debt or entering new fields.

● *What the IPO's past performance has been.* Even if the company has been operating for only a short time (less than three years), there's usually evidence in the prospectus of management's ability to find a market niche and make a profit. It there's no track record of this ability, avoid the stock.

● *How the original owners profit from the IPO.* When a company goes public, owners occasionally take out big cash profits for themselves. That's bad because big profits at an early IPO stage mean the owners are more interested in making quick profits than in keeping an equity stake while they run the company.

Evidence of this shows up in the prospectus under the heading Beneficial Ownership After Offering. It's usual for an officer to take a small profit, but the prospectus also lists the number of each owner's shares that are being converted into cash. Be cautious about an IPO if all the officers as a group are selling more than 15% of their shares.

● *Who the underwriter is.* Brokerage houses have cycles of success and failure in taking companies public. For that reason it's usually safe to buy an IPO whose underwriter has had a good track record for the previous six months to a year. But don't expect an underwriter that had great success two years ago necessarily to maintain its pace today. (The success/failure record of underwriters is regularly reported in publications that specialize in new offerings and occasionally in the general financial journals.)

● *If warrants were issued to the underwriters.* Check the final prospectus to see whether the underwriter is receiving part of its fee in warrants that give it the right to buy the stock at a fixed price in the future. Willingness to accept warrants means the underwriter has more than average confidence in the IPO. Historically, these stocks have a better chance of appreciating in value than others.

● *Who the venture-capital investors are.* It's also a sign of confidence when prominent venture-capital firms are listed as shareholders, or if they put up capital earlier when the company started up. Participation of these firms is also assurance that new management talent can be brought in if the existing team falters. (Most brokers can tell you if a venture-capital firm has a good track record of backing start-up companies.)

Finding the Impossible

If demand for a new issue is high, it's usually impossible for any but the broker's favored clients to get shares at the initial price.

The first step is to get advance information on which IPOs are coming up.

Best sources: SEC filings (available at the commission's regional offices) and publications that specialize in new issues.

Next, tell your broker as far in advance as possible which upcoming offering you're interested in. Because prices of new issues aren't decided until the last minute, give your broker a top limit on what you're willing to pay for the stock.

Caution: If your limit is $16 per share, for example, and the price is set at $18, you can cancel the deal. But don't expect your broker to put out an extra effort the next time around.

Even if the broker's own firm is participating in the underwriting, he or she may have trouble getting shares when demand is high. In that case only clients with large trading accounts can expect access to shares.

If your broker can't promise you the shares, it often pays to try a smaller, regional broker that is participating in the underwriting. If that fails, it pays to open an account with the brokerage firm that's managing the underwriting. The managing underwriter is usually allotted more shares than the others and may be willing to arrange a sale, especially for someone opening an account.

Don't take no for an answer, even if this ploy fails. As a last-ditch maneuver, call one of the directors of the new company directly. The director may be willing to ask the underwriters to reserve shares for you. This is especially likely if it's a local firm interested in signing up local investors.

If it's impossible to get shares in the initial offering, consider buying them in the first trading session after the initial offering. Usually the price won't have climbed too high, and some investors are quick to sell and take an immediate profit. Profits may be smaller by buying in this secondary market, but they can still be substantial. *Example:* Home Shopping Network shares sold in the initial offering for $18.

BIG OPPORTUNITIES IN SMALL COMPANY STOCKS

Though investing in less-well-known businesses can lead to big payoffs, investors must be prepared to do more homework to find them than they'd do if they wanted to invest in better-known companies. Some data can be found in annual reports and filings with the Securities & Exchange Commission. *Look for:*

● **A 15% annual revenue growth.** If a company's increase in sales is below that level, high dividends and stock appreciation are unlikely. Also look for companies in industry segments that are growing.

● **Large market share.** This is especially important because small companies are very vulnerable to economic slowdowns. Market share is about the only cushion that can carry them through rough times. The safest businesses for investors are those with at least a 20% share of their market.

Caution: Avoid investing in small companies that are competing against giants. They may do well in good times but be squeezed if the economy falters.

● **Good management.** This factor is the toughest to judge. Solid management is much more important to the success of a small company than to that of a big one, whose momentum can drive it for years. Look through the company's annual reports of several years—then look at its current 10K and 10Q SEC filings to see whether performance has lived up to management expectations. (These filings are available from local SEC offices.) The 8K also reveals extraordinary changes in a company's situation, such as key management moves and litigation. If possible, talk with the company's executives, customers and suppliers. And, of course, obtain copies of research reports by the major brokerages.

● **Good value.** The lower the price/earnings ratio, the better.

Useful guideline: Invest in companies that have a price/earnings ratio well below the company's expected annual growth rate. A company with a price/earnings ratio of 12 and annual sales growth of 18%, for instance, is one that you would usually move into.

Also watch the relationship between the company's capitalization (total value of outstanding shares) and its sales. We look for companies whose market capitalization is attractive in relationship to their revenues. Avoid stocks of companies whose sales are very high in relation to their capitalization.

Avoiding the Pitfalls

Prices of secondary stocks are very volatile. And, there's danger that the company will issue new shares, which lowers the value of shares that are already in investors' hands. If there are rumors of a new issue, wait until all the new shares have been absorbed in the market. Then the price will almost certainly be depressed.

One of the biggest mistakes investors make is buying stock in industries with which they're not familiar.

Source: *Richard F. Aster, president, Aster Investment Management Co., which manages the Meridian Fund, a no-load mutual fund specializing in secondary growth stocks, 60 E. Sir Francis Drake Blvd., Larkspur, CA 94939.*

Within minutes after trading began, shares were going for $38. Three months later, each of these shares was worth more than $130.

In fact, if there's little demand for the IPO, it may make sense to wait to buy it until trading begins. *Reason:* There's sometimes a 10%–20% decline from the IPO's price in early sales.

Besides screening new issues carefully, the best protection is to diversify your IPO investments into different companies and industry groups. When the market as a whole is high, there won't be many long-term values in IPOs because their prices will be high too. These shares may be more attractive for short-term profits though, because prices may double or triple during the first few months.

If the market is generally weak and there's not much speculative excitement, it's time to look for long-term returns from IPOs. What to look for: As with other types of investments, look for young growth companies that can be bought for well below their value.

Source: *Norman G. Fosback, editor,* Income & Safety.

How to Recognize Undervalued Industrial Stocks

A favorite investment approach is to look at unpopular stocks of good companies, particularly companies with small market capitalizations. Ignore the big names and the Wall Street "whiz stocks." They've already been touted and bid up way too far.

There are many small- to medium-sized companies that merit your attention because of their potential long-term appreciation. Sifting through them can seem like an overwhelming task, but there are two good techniques any investor can use for finding undervalued companies.

Price/Sales Ratio (PSR)

The PSR is computed by dividing the total market value of a company by the company's total sales. PSRs provide a useful valuation technique for comparing large numbers of potential investment candidates.

Oftentimes, good companies will have reduced earnings and temporary losses, but their sales will remain stable. Because of the decline in their earn-

ings, Wall Street assigns a lower value to the stocks. However, since sales have remained the same, there is a good chance that earnings will return to prior levels and that the stock prices will rise along with earnings.

Debt Adjustment Factor (DAF)

Using the PSR you can sift out a large number of potentially strong, undervalued companies. The next step is to find the companies with strong balance sheets by using the DAF to determine whether a company has too much debt on its books.

To perform this calculation, divide the current assets by the current liabilities. This will give you the current ratio. Divide the current ratio by 4. Then divide shareholders' equity by total assets. Add the equity/assets and the current ratio/4. If the total is 1.00 or greater, the balance sheet is strong. If the total is less than 0.80, the company has too much debt.

Using only PSRs and DAFs, you can consistently pick stocks that outperform market expectations. You can further improve your chances of picking an undervalued stock by utilizing other tools of fundamental analysis (evaluating the quality of management and competition, insider trading, etc.), but the key to winning with undervalued stocks is to buy unpopular stocks of good companies and to hold them long enough for their quality to be reflected in the stock prices.

Source: *Kenneth L. Fisher, chief executive of Fisher Investments, Woodside, CA 94062, an investment management firm.*

Contrarian Investment Strategies

A contrarian investment strategy involves buying financial instruments that are "out of favor," that are in industries that are shunned as boring or whose prices have fallen sharply. Contrarians invest "against the grain" of conventional thought. A contrarian assumes that the market frequently overreacts to both good and bad news, and invests counter to the consensus.

The history of the market is full of examples of low-expectation stocks whose results have exceeded those expectations. At the start of World War II, John Templeton instructed his broker to purchase 100 shares of every stock on the New York and

American Exchanges with a price below $1.

Important: Templeton did not exclude those with the worst possible expected future—a third of the companies were in bankruptcy proceedings. Four years later his portfolio had quadrupled, significantly outperforming the market.

Conversely, there are also numerous examples of the demise of so-called "glamour stocks" whose future seemed particularly bright. Xerox, once dominant in duplicating office equipment, sold as high as $170/share in 1972 with earnings of only $3.16. In 1985, earnings per share were only $3.46, and the stock sold at about $60.

HOW TO RECOGNIZE AN OVERVALUED STOCK

How many times has your broker sent you a glowing report about a great company whose stock price is bound to skyrocket? How many times has he or she been right? Probably few or none. Investors need to take the upper hand and be able to identify quickly whether a company is overvalued in the stock market.

One of the best tools for determining whether a stock is overvalued is the price/sales ratio (PSR)—the price per share/sales per share. If the PSR is greater than 0.75, the stock is too expensive—investors are paying a premium for future growth, so the upside potential in the stock's price is dwarfed. *Example:* IBM reported revenues per share of $74.98 for its 1984 fiscal year. At the time, the price of the stock was $127.50. IBM's PSR was equal to $127.50 divided by $74.98, or 1.70. This was too high. While IBM is a great company, investors had already incorporated their expectations for growth in the current stock price. If you had bought the stock in 1983 at a price of $123.75, held it for a year and then sold it for $127.50, your total annual gain would have

been only 3%. You would have been better off with an almost risk-free money-market fund.

It's important to know that initial public offerings (IPOs) are generally overvalued stocks. The purpose of a stock offering is to raise cash for a company, whether it's to open a new plant, pay off old debt or accomplish some other business purpose. Unless it is desperate, company management will wait to make the deal until it can receive the maximum amount of cash possible. As a result, the offering price of the stock will be at or near the highest price level to be expected—there is a very strong chance that the price of the stock will decline when it starts trading in the open market. How can you profit from this? Let the stock price drop after the offering, then buy the stock when the PSR is at a more reasonable level. (Of course, do not buy the stock from any offering without first checking the PSR.)

Insider selling is another good indicator of overvalued stocks. If management does not want to own its own company's stock, then why should you? Vicker's Stock Research of New Jersey publishes the *Weekly Insider Report,* which allows investors to see exactly who is selling how much of what stock. Often, insiders sell stock of companies with high PSRs.

High-PSR stocks are frequently high-price/ book-value stocks as well. Book value is the company's assets minus *all* liabilities. In other words, it is the company's net worth on the books. You have a much better chance of making money with stocks selling at less than book value than those selling for more than book value. *Example:* 53 companies with high PSRs were featured in the *PSR Stockwatch* investment newsletter. During one year, 37 stock prices tumbled, compared to gains in only 16 companies. Many of the values were halved or worse, because the stocks had been too popular. If you don't beat everyone else to the investment, you can't hope to beat them to the profits.

Source: *Margaret Brill, a former stockbroker at L.F. Rothschild, Unterberg, Towbin, in San Francisco, and editor of a newsletter on undervalued stocks,* **PSR Prophet.**

Techniques Used by Contrarians

Contrarians look at many signals of overly low or overly high market expectations. *These include:*

● *Low p/e investment strategies.* The classic contrarian investment strategy may be buying low p/e stocks. Given an earnings level, low p/e stocks tend to be stocks whose prices are depressed or at least are not lofty. Often, low p/e stocks have low expected earnings or are simply perceived as stodgy investments. *The key to the strategy is this:* If the low expectations pan out, there will be no negative surprises to cause selling of the stock. If, however, earnings exceed expectations, the surprise is positive and the stock will rise.

● *New highs, new lows.* Stocks that approach new highs are presumably more vulnerable to price drops on bad news. Stocks that reach new lows are more likely to have most or all of the bad news reflected in the low price.

● *Market newsletters/research reports.* A uniformly bearish consensus of market newsletters and brokerage house research reports is perceived as a bullish sign for the market. It is thought by some that investors who follow the advice of these newsletters would have sold all their stock in the face of bearish recommendations, making further selling pressure unlikely. As the opinions of the reports change to a bullish tone, these investors will buy back in, raising stock prices. *Conversely, a bullish consensus is considered a bearish sign for the market:* Market tops occur when all the bulls are fully invested, and market bottoms occur when all the bears have sold.

● *Institutional cash positions.* This is a frequently used measure of market sentiment. If institutions are fully invested—i.e., cash positions are low—new buying of stocks will be unlikely. On the other hand, high institutional cash positions (greater than 15%, for example) suggest untapped buying power.

● *Cash flow analysis.* Inasmuch as a primary tool for valuation is a p/e ratio, investors often focus on reported earnings. However, substantial depreciation and amortization (non-cash) charges to reported earnings may mask a company's operating stability. For

example, in 1985, Chevron generated funds from operations of $6,521 million. However, net income was only $1,547 million. Depreciation depletion and amortization charges (well in excess of capital expenditures) accounted for the bulk of the difference, but required no cash outlay. Accordingly, the cash flow (earnings plus non-cash charges) measure of profitability reflects a much more stable and healthy operating picture.

While some allowance must be made for future capital expenditures and working capital needs, it is useful to look at cash flow. Often, companies with weak earnings figures may have relatively stable cash flows. Accordingly, a contrarian may see greater than perceived stability and value in a company with negative earnings but positive cash flow.

● *Asset values.* Companies that sell at a discount to asset value may be undervalued. A contrarian may buy companies with temporarily depressed earnings and stock prices if the assets of the company are perceived to be worth more than the current market price. Obviously, determining so-called "asset value" is an imprecise task. If these assets are worth more to another company, a takeover could yield significant profits to investors. Such would be the case of significant tax-loss carryforwards. Assets may also have a liquidation value in excess of current market prices (which may reflect only short-term earnings potential). While book value is not synonymous with asset value, companies with prices below book value are more likely to fall in this category.

Contrarian investment strategies often require patience because success requires a change in the market sentiment that initially created an overvalued or undervalued security. Moreover, contrarian investing is a more difficult investment strategy to follow because it involves investing against the tide of conventional wisdom. However, investors who bet against the prevailing short-term market sentiment may realize significant profits.

> " **Contrarian investing is a more difficult...strategy to follow because it involves investing against the tide of conventional wisdom. However, [you] ...may realize significant profits.** "

Source : *Bruce H. Monrad, analyst, mergers/acquisitions & leveraged buyout department, Prudential-Bache Securities, Inc., Prudential-Bache Building, One Seaport Plaza, New York, NY 10292.*

How to Find Values in The Market Now

We are value investors, which means we look for stocks whose prices are cheap compared with corporate assets. Instead of basing investment decisions on a company's earnings-growth potential, we look hard at companies that most investors ignore—searching for unrecognized value. With the Dow Jones Industrial Average reaching all-time highs, it is harder to find stocks whose prices will rise much further in the foreseeable future. But there are some left. *Here's how we pick value stocks:*

The Secret of Value Investing

We buy stocks that are selling at a deep discount to the company's value. To determine a stock's discount, we look at a company's current cash flows and earnings, the cash on its balance sheet and the values of comparable businesses. We try to determine what another company would pay for parts of the business.

By contrast, growth investors try to predict a company's future earnings in order to determine its current worth. We think the odds of getting this right are lower than using present valuations of a company.

Example of a value stock:

● *General Motors Corp.* (NYSE:GM, Detroit, MI) In addition to substantial cash reserves, GM holds positions in many other companies, which we think alone nearly equal the value of GM's auto business. Also, management continues to divest non-auto operations.

Value investing may have less downside risk than growth investing. If a growth company stumbles and has one quarter of disappointing earnings, the damage to the stock's price can be severe, as investors try to get out while the price is high.

But if a company that is considered a value stock comes out with disappointing earnings, it may not matter as much. Because the stock is selling at a discount to what the company is worth, the investors may be less likely to sell.

We search for bargains in companies that are out of favor—and look carefully at those no one else wants to touch.

Value in Financial Services

Several years ago, we reduced our holdings in banks (other than Chase, which we still own), insurance companies and brokerage firms, which had already appreciated in value.

Recently we revisited these areas and have a significant stake in these stocks—domestic and foreign—in our six funds, one of which is devoted to this sector.

Some current favorites as of June 1, 1998:

● *Chase Manhattan Corp.* (NYSE:CMB, New York) We believe the "new Chase" is one of the best-positioned large U.S. banking companies and should continue to benefit from cost savings resulting from the merger with Chemical Bank.

● *Kansas City Southern Industries, Inc.* (NYSE:KSU, Kansas City, MO) We think KCSI's crown jewel, 83%-owned Janus Capital, a money management firm with $80 billion in assets, is worth much of the share price itself. The company announced in February 1998 that it will separate its financial services business from the railroad business to realize value.

● *Pohjola Insurance Co. Ltd.* (Helsinki Stock Exch.:PHJA, Finland) We purchased this insurer at a deep discount to book value, and are beginning to see market recognition of some of the value inside the company.

● *Western Bancorp* (NASDAQ:WEBC, Newport Beach, CA) This is a medium-sized California banking company that is a consolidator of smaller California banks. It has an outstanding California franchise and is controlled by investors whom we believe know how to create value.

● *Banco Nazionale del Lavoro SpA* (Milan Stock Exch:BNLR, Italy) Lavoro has remained by far the cheapest of the large Italian banks. We expect privatization and a merger with Basodi, Napoli, both of which will have a positive impact on valuation and share price.

● *United Asset Management Corp.* (NYSE: UAM, Boston, MA) UAM manages over $200 billion, primarily for institutional investors. Money management is rapidly consolidating, and we think this is an excellent business.

Value in Transition Companies

As value investors, we are always looking for good companies that are coming out of bankruptcy, being taken over, merging with other companies or selling off their assets. We especially like companies that are spinning off parts of their businesses—setting up divisions as separate, publicly traded companies. The big plus here is that the stock price of the parent company is often less than the sum of its parts.

Restructuring favorites as of June 1, 1998*:

● *Morgan Stanley Dean Witter & Co.* (NYSE:MWD, New York) We are enthusiastic about the merger of Dean Witter, Discover and Morgan Stanley, which, combined, are two powerful franchises that offer compelling synergies.

● *Suez Lyonnaise des Eaux SA* (Paris Stock Exchange:LYOE, France) This company is in the midst of a major restructuring of its four core businesses—water service, waste management, electricity and communications. It has sold a number of non-core assets, and purchased the minority stakes of its major subsidiaries. Stock is trading at a discount to our valuation.

● *Société Elf Aquitaine* (Paris Stock Exchange: ELF, France) This integrated oil company is in the midst of a massive restructuring, which includes significant cost reductions, stock repurchases and divestitures of non-core businesses, which should narrow the gap between the company's stock price and the value of its assets.

*Information and opinions on stocks are as of June 1, 1998 and are subject to change without notice. This information is furnished to illustrate our value-driven investment style, and does not constitute investment advice or a recommendation to purchase or sell any security.

Sources: *Franklin Mutual Series Advisers manages the assets of Franklin Mutual Series Fund, which consists of six funds: Mutual Shares, Qualified, Beacon, Discovery, European and Financial Services. The funds are sold solely by a prospectus that contains more complete information, including sales charges, expenses and investment risks. Investors should read it carefully prior to investing. Franklin Templeton Distributors, Inc., 51 John F. Kennedy Parkway, Short Hills, NJ 07079. Michael Price, one of the country's most respected value investors, has selected and worked for many years with this investment team, which includes Peter Langerman, Larry Sondike, Rob Friedman, Ray Garea, Jeffrey Altman, David Marcus and David Winters.*

Time to Crisis-Proof Your Investments

The volatility of the stock and bond markets has left many investors yearning for an investment strategy that will let them sleep at night.

While dramatic rises in the markets result in profits and excitement, declines often follow, creating fear and anxiety. *Here are some easy steps that will help you invest free from daily worry:*

Determine the Right Mix of Stocks and Bonds

If you are going to reach long-term goals, you must make a commitment to invest at least some of your money in stocks.

But you should also hold some bonds so that you aren't totally at the mercy of the stock market's swings. As a rule, the younger you are, the greater the proportion you can commit to stocks because you can afford to ride out such fluctuations. *Strategies:* If you are a conservative investor, your age can represent the approximate percentage of long-term savings that you should invest in bonds. Invest the remainder in stocks.

> " If you are a conservative investor, your age can represent the approximate percentage of long-term savings that you should invest in bonds. "

If you want to take moderate risk, subtract your age from 110. The result is the minimum percentage of your long-term investment portfolio that should be allocated to stocks. Aggressive investors might use 120 as a factor. *Example:* At age 50, an investor who wants to take conservative risks should adopt a portfolio that includes a 50% stake in bonds and a 50% stake in stocks. If he or she wants to be aggressive, the investor could make at least 70% of his or her portfolio stock purchases and 30% bond purchases. It is best to rebalance with the IRA portion of your portfolio, which is tax-deferred. A discount broker is also advisable, to limit commissions on stock and bond sales.

Important: Short-term income investments—such as money-market funds or bank savings accounts—have no place in long-term investment portfolios. They simply don't provide the returns you

Investing to Win

need to beat inflation over time.

Some people insist on holding large sums—as much as six months' worth of income—in such investments as an emergency reserve. But since most investments can be sold in a matter of days, it doesn't make sense to keep money languishing for years on end in such low-paying investments.

Choose the Right Types of Stocks and Bonds

Studies have shown that long-term investment success is far more dependent upon allocating your money appropriately among the various investment categories than it is on trying to select the best-performing investments.

By far, the best strategy is to divide savings among a range of mutual funds. That way, some of your funds will be working for you even when others are not—and you won't feel left out when one sector is doing particularly well, since chances are you will own a piece of it.

Stocks: I advise my clients who are willing to take moderate risks to divide their portfolio holdings as follows:

- *Growth stocks* /20%.
- *Growth and income stocks* /40%.
- *Small-company stocks* /20%.
- *International stocks* /20%.

If you're an aggressive investor, split your stock holdings equally among those four categories.

Bonds: Divide your holdings equally between long- and either short- or intermediate-term funds that invest in corporate, municipal and U.S. government bonds.

Important: You will need approximately $25,000 to divide among the different stock and bond funds. If you have less, start by investing your stock money in growth and income funds and your bond money in government bond funds.

Beginning investors can start with one single balanced fund—which divides its money between stock and bond investments.

Trap: Many investors start out by committing too much money to a *sector fund*, which invests in stocks of companies in a single industry or related industries. That is a risky approach. If you invest in sector funds at all, limit those investments to 5% to 10% of your long-term portfolio.

Select Great Funds

If you pick funds that are solid long-term performers, you won't have much to worry about.

Some of my favorite no-load stock funds in each category:

- *Growth:* Janus Fund.

Janus Service Corporation, 100 Fillmore St., Denver, CO 80206.

- *Growth and income:* Babson.

Jones & Babson, Inc., 2440 Pershing Road, Kansas City, KS 64108.

- *Equity income:* T. Rowe Price Equity-Income.

T. Rowe Price Associates, 100 E. Pratt St., Baltimore, MD 21202.

- *Global stock:* Janus Worldwide.

Janus Capital Corp., 100 Fillmore St., Denver, CO 80206.

- *Balanced:* Vanguard Wellington.

Vanguard Group, Box 2600, Valley Forge, Pa 19482.

- *Sector:* Vanguard Specialized Health.

Vanguard Group, Box 2600, Valley Forge, PA 19482.

Some of my strong no-load bond funds in each category:

- *Intermediate-term corporate:* Columbia Fixed-Income.

Columbia Funds, Box 1350, Portland, OR 97207.

- *Long-term corporate:* Vanguard Fixed-Income Long-Term Corporate.

Vanguard Group, Box 2600, Valley Forge, PA 19482.

- *Short-/intermediate-term U.S. Treasury:* Dreyfus 100% U.S. Treasury Intermediate-Term.

The Dreyfus Corp., 200 Park Ave., New York, NY 10166.

- *Long-term U.S. Treasury:* Vanguard Fixed-Income Long-Term U.S. Treasury.

Vanguard Group, Box 2600, Valley Forge, PA 19482.

- *Medium-term municipal:* Scudder Medium-Term Tax-Free.

Scudder Stevens & Clark, Inc., 2 International Pl., Boston, MA 02110.

- *Long-term municipal:* Strong Municipal Bond.

Strong Funds, 100 Heritage Reserve, Menomonee Falls, WI 53051.

Periodically Rebalance Investment Allocation

This strategy is very important to the success of your long-term investments. Changes in the financial markets can have a big impact on your portfolio and possibly leave you with the wrong mix of investments.

Example: A sharp run-up in stock prices might increase the value of your stock funds. The result is that they will account for a greater percentage of your overall portfolio than before. After a few years, you may be holding a much riskier portfolio than you realize or intended. *Strategy:* About every six months, return the investment allocation to the original percentages you established. *Example:* Let's say you set up a 60%/40% stock/bond split, but stock prices have climbed to the point that stock funds now account for 67% of your portfolio's total value.

Sell shares in your stock funds so that your stock allocation is 60%, and use the resulting money to add more to bond funds.

Important: If you have to make a major change in your current investments right now to achieve an appropriate allocation of funds, do so gradually. Don't go from 0% in stocks to 50% overnight. You might wind up investing just before a major market decline that will cause you to suffer a heavy loss. Instead, sell and reinvest gradually. *Example:* If you currently have 100% in cash investments and want to get to a 60%/40% stock/bond allocation—here is a sensible schedule:

● *For the first six months,* gradually build up to 20% stocks, 15% bonds and 65% money-market funds.

● *Then for the next six to 12 months,* go to 40% stocks, 25% bonds and 35% money market funds.

After two years, you can redistribute your investments to your desired 60%/40% split.

Source: Jonathan Pond, president of Financial Planning Information, Inc., Watertown, MA. He is the author of 4 Easy Steps to Successful Investing, Avon.

Spotting Low-Priced Stocks Ready to Bounce Back

The key to success in the stock market is knowing how to recognize value, and value has little to do with a good company versus a bad company. A top-quality large company selling at a high price/earnings multiple is less attractive than a lesser-quality company selling at a depressed price in terms of its past and future earning power, working capital, book value and historical prices.

Here is where analysts look for value:

● *Stocks that have just made a new low* for the last 12 months.

● *Companies that are likely to be liquidated.* In the process of liquidation, shareholders may get paid considerably more than the stock is selling for now.

● *Unsuccessful merger candidates.* If one buyer thinks a company's stock is a good value, it's possible that others may also come to the same conclusion.

● *Companies that have just reduced or eliminated their dividends.* The stock is usually hit with a selling wave, which often creates a good buying opportunity.

● *Financially troubled companies* in which another major company has a sizable ownership position. If the financial stake is large enough, you can be sure that the major company will do everything it can to turn the earnings around and get the stock price up so that its investment will work out.

● *Opportunities in stocks that are totally washed out*—that is, situations where all the bad news is out. The stock usually has nowhere to go but up. *How to be sure a stock is truly washed out:*

● *Trading volume slows to practically nothing.* If over-the-counter, few if any dealers making a market.

● *No Wall Street research analysts* are following the company anymore.

● *No financial journalists,* stock market newsletters or advisory services discuss the company.

● *Selling of the stock* by the company's management and directors has stopped. *Signs of a turnabout:*

● *The company plans* to get rid of a losing division or business. If so, be sure to learn whether the company will be able to report a big jump in earnings once the losing operation is sold.

● *The company is selling off* assets to improve its financial situation and/or reduce debt.

● *A new management comes on board* with an established track record of success with turnaround situations.

● *Management begins buying the company's stock* in the open market.

Also, be sure to follow 13D statements filed with the Securities & Exchange Commission (SEC). A company or individual owning 5% or more of a public company must report such holdings to the SEC. If any substantial company is acquiring a major position in a company, it's possible a tender offer at a much higher price is in the wind.

Source: Robert Ravitz, director of research, David J. Greene & Co., an investment management firm, 30 Wall St., New York, NY 10005.

How to Make Big Money In Good Markets and Bad

Set strict rules about when to buy stocks and when to sell them, and never deviate from these rules.

The Ideal Company

● **Dominates its marketplace** as an "unregulated monopoly." *Example:* Paychecks Corp. is similar to Automatic Data Processing, which handles payrolls for firms with 100 or more employees. Paychecks' payroll companies have fewer than 100 employees. It now has an unregulated monopoly in that segment of the market and is thriving.

● **Grows more than 20%** per year in both earnings and sales.

● **Has a high return on equity.** Avoid off-the-wall companies, start-up companies and new issues. Buy only companies with $300–$500 million in sales and a track record of at least five years.

Rules for Buying and Selling

In addition to the above criteria, buy only:

● **Stocks that are undervalued.** *How to measure:* A company that has grown 35% per year over the past five years and has a price/earnings multiple of less than half that rate (17) is attractive. Low p/e multiples are important. It's easier to expand the multiple from 10 to 18 than from 20 to 30.

● **Stocks that you think will meet a specific price objective.** For each stock you buy, set a goal based on its price over the past years. If it reaches your goal, take a hard look to determine whether you should stay with the company. Automatically unload stocks that report a decline in earnings. This decline is for a single quarter, compared with the same quarter the previous year. Never violate this rule. *Reason:* If you find enough good companies, you don't have to risk keeping one in decline. When something bad happens to a company, it takes time for it to turn around.

Source: Eugene G. Martin, executive vice president and portfolio manager, National Investment Service, 815 E. Mason St., Milwaukee, WI 53202.

Investing in Blue Chips

Conservative or blue-chip stocks often pay high dividends and can be owned with very little risk to the

Rules for Picking Common Stocks

✔ **Try to buy the industry leader** or, at the very least, a company that has an important position in its industry.

✔ **Look for an industry** with a limited amount of competition.

✔ **Avoid an industry** that is an essential part of the Gross National Product or the Consumer Price Index, such as autos or steel. *Reason:* Highly visible companies are easy targets for government pressure.

✔ **Stick to stocks** that have price/earnings ratios lower than that of the Standard & Poor's 500 Index.

✔ **The stock should yield** at least 4 ½% to 5%.

✔ **The company should have** a record of significant dividend increases.

✔ **The market price of the stock** should be close to book value per share.

✔ **Both the industry and the company** should have growth rates higher than the median of American business.

One helpful rule of thumb: Sales and earnings ought to have doubled over the past decade. If they haven't, you probably won't be able to keep ahead of inflation in the years ahead.

✔ **Stay away from companies** that are too heavily in debt, especially in relation to industry-wide standards.

✔ **Look for companies** where managers are owners, too. Nepotism can be a danger in such situations. More often, though, owner-management is a big plus. Owner-managers have a real incentive to keep the company growing as well as to boost the stock's value.

Source: Roy Papp, investment counselor, 5631 Echo Canyon Circle, Phoenix, AZ 85018.

investor because their prices fluctuate relatively little. The advantage of conservative stocks is that when the economy goes into a recession and the market takes a turn for the worse, conservative stocks usually are the least affected. For this reason, blue chips can act as a cushion for the rest of your portfolio. The goal is to have about 30% or 40% of your portfolio invested in conservative stocks.

Selling the Successes and Failures

The best way to make money with blue chips is through constant turnover. Since you are not going to double or triple your investment with one stock, you have to be willing to sell your successes and reinvest in other blue chips immediately.

Say you have a portfolio of 100 blue chips. If one of your stocks rises by 20% or 30%, check the stock's fundamentals to see whether something really good is happening. If it is, you may want to add to that stock, but normally the best strategy is to sell it and add to a stock in your portfolio that has a chance of earning 30% for you. If you can make 30% returns six times in a year, you will quadruple your money. A problem is that investors in conservative stocks may make 30% on a stock, but instead of selling it immediately, hold on to it for three more years. The result is that a 30% gain turns into a 7% or 8% gain.

In addition to selling your successes, sell a blue chip whenever the fundamentals go wrong—for instance, when the industry or the product is about to deteriorate. Use the gains from all of your sales to invest in other companies with sound fundamentals whose stocks haven't appreciated.

Source: Peter Lynch, retired manager of Fidelity Investments' Magellan Fund, which soared in value during his tenure and beat the average equity fund every year he was at the helm.

One Way To Spot a Good Investment

Big cash reserves usually mean companies are strong investment prospects. *Reason:* They can use cash to repurchase stock, fund expansion and invest in securities that bolster profitability. *Result:* The stock market favors firms with cash amounting to 15% or more of the market value of their shares, and so share prices perform comparatively well in market downturns.

Source: Merrill Lynch Market Letter, New York.

Selecting Superstocks

Everyone dreams of finding another IBM or Xerox or Hewlett Packard—a "superstock" that appreciates many times in value. The problem faced by all investors is that out of the thousands of stocks available for investment today only a small fraction of them will turn into the "superstocks" of tomorrow. In most markets, careful examination of the superstock successes has revealed each to have the following eight characteristics.

Small to Medium Size

Small- to mid-sized firms with annual sales of $25 million to $100 million usually are neglected on Wall Street, either because they are hard to analyze or, more important, because they do not represent enough liquidity (that is, they do not have enough tradable shares of stock) to interest institutions. Yet smaller firms usually represent outstanding value in terms of growth in earnings per share and assets.

Look for companies with innovative managements that find a niche and fill it with a new product or service. Such managements usually have a dedication to quality rather than price and tend not to diversify. They also avoid building bureaucracies (no overstaffing or private planes).

The most attractive prospects are smaller companies on the threshold of growth. Companies with $25 million–$500 million in sales usually combine management that is reasonably well-seasoned with a sales volume large enough to be generating a meaningful cash flow. The firm (or the market it serves) is generally not quite large enough to attract major competition and is eager to grow.

The bad news is that the smaller company is more vulnerable to industry downturns due to less diversification, is more in need of costly debt financing and has less staying power in a recession. These are the trade-offs investors must consider when attempting to reap the potentially higher rewards.

Rising Unit Sales Volume

Rising sales are essential to any growth company. How fast should sales be rising? As a general rule, growth should not be less than an annual rate of 12%–15% during a strong economic year. The prospects of at least 15%–20% annual growth should not be out of reach.

It is important for investors to realize that a rising sales trend does not necessarily mean a company is enjoying greater prosperity. Sales may be going up, but the cost of producing products or services may be rising even faster. It's possible for a company to survive this squeeze temporarily by cutting expenses or producing more with the same or less labor and equipment, but without sales growth, a company is ultimately doomed as an investment prospect.

A good signal for investors is a three-year total sales increase (in percent) that is higher than the total increase in the Consumer Price Index over the same period. If sales growth is equal to or lower than that index, the company just isn't growing.

Rising Pretax Profit Margin

A company's profit margin can be defined as the relationship of income (profit) before or after taxes to net sales.

Best measure: The pretax margin reflects the efficiency of a company in extracting a profit from each dollar of sales. Also, more than any other ratio or percentage, the pretax margin indicates just how profitable and effective a company has been within its industry. Most experts favor pretax profit margins as an analytical tool, since the profitability of different companies can be compared without having to account for variations in tax rates.

Above-Average and Improving Return on Equity

The profit earned on the stockholders' investment is the indicator of management's efficiency in using the stockholders' funds remaining in the company. In other words, management's productivity of capital. Return on stockholders' equity tells you how successful management has been with the stockholders'

money. This profit, or the percentage return on stockholders' equity, is found by dividing net profit after taxes by stockholders' equity.

What constitutes an above-average return? There is no single answer, but in a superstock search, look for a company whose return is (1) better than the competition's, (2) above the aggregate rates of return of the companies in broad market averages such as Standard & Poor's and the Dow Industrial, and (3) above the prevailing level of interest rates. Any return on equity below 15% is unsatisfactory. Moreover, like pretax margins, the trend is important. As the company matures, its productivity improves and its assets are used to greater advantage.

Above-average returns are essential to growth. If a company earns 20% on stockholders' equity and pays out half in dividends, the remaining 50% will be plowed back into the business to produce a future growth rate of roughly 10% (0.20 x 0.50 = 0.10); if the company pays out only 15% of earnings as dividends, the remaining 85% will sustain a growth rate of about 17% (0.20 x 0.85 = 0.17).

Low but Rising Dividends

Dividend statistics are an important indicator of a company's value in the marketplace and its future growth. *Two dividend ratios can be used:* (1) The dividend yield is expressed as a percentage calculated by dividing the current annual dividend by the market price of the stock; (2) the dividend payout ratio is the percentage of the company's earnings paid out in dividends to the stockholders.

Dividends cut two ways. On one hand, the payment of at least a modest dividend helps stocks gain acceptance in the marketplace among institutional investors, setting the stage for eventual price appreciation. On the other hand, the higher the dividend payout, the less of a company's earnings remain for reinvestment in operations. Plowback of earnings increases the company's future earning power and, eventually, the price of the stock.

Low Debt Ratio

How much debt is too much? The answer depends on the industry and stability of earning power, the company's profitability and, of course, the level of interest rates. For utilities, where the markets are monopolistic (only one company in the area), a debt level of 50% to 60% of total capitalization is acceptable. For cyclical companies such as those in the steel, aluminum and copper industries, debt above 25% of total capitalization is dangerous. As a general rule, for growth companies, debt should not exceed 35% of total capitalization—when interest rates are high, debt should be even lower.

Institutional Holdings

Look for growth stocks that are relatively unknown, but not completely obscure. Since institutional research is intensive and thorough, buying stocks with some ownership by institutions vindicates your own research process and investment decision. The information on institutional ownership is available for most companies from services such as Moody's or Standard & Poor's.

Look for stocks with institutional ownership of less than 10%. When institutions own 20% or more of a stock, the growth company has been "discovered." The probable result is that your stock will become fully priced—no one will be left to bid up its price.

Increasing Price/Earnings Ratio

The price/earnings (p/e) ratio indicates investors' attitudes toward a company's earnings and growth potential. The ratio's significance stems from the fact that price appreciation in a growth stock is achieved not only by steadily increasing earnings per share, but also by the amount, or p/e multiple, the market is willing to pay for each dollar of those earnings.

To use the p/e ratios, first compare the ratios of companies within the same industry. Next, compare the ratio of your prospective growth company with the ratios of the overall market. (The Dow Jones Industrial Average and Standard & Poor's are commonly used indexes.) Also examine trends in p/e ratios to discern how attitudes have changed over time.

Generally, investors pay higher p/e ratios in bull markets than in bear markets, and when interest rates are low. Speculative or "hot" stocks usually carry high ratios. Look at "undiscovered" growth stocks whose p/e's are rising rather than falling. If the earnings potential of two companies is the same, buy the company with the lower p/e (considering the other seven superstock characteristics, of course).

The company with the lower p/e will be cheaper— the market might not know what it's missing.

Source: Frank A. Cappiello, president of the investment counseling firm McCullough, Andrews & Cappiello, Inc., 502 Washington Ave., Suite 240, Baltimore, MD 21204. Mr. Cappiello is also chairman of The Carnegie-Cappiello Growth Fund, Carnegie-Cappiello Total Return Fund, and director of a number of publicly owned financial and industrial companies. He is widely known for his regular appearances on Wall $treet Week with Louis Rukeyser.

Overcome Psychological Stumbling Blocks to Wise Investing

With more investors taking greater risks to achieve higher returns, many are finding that their anxiety levels are rising, too. Parting with money is hard enough, but investments that can erode in value can be nerve-racking.

Although the fear of losing one's money is perfectly healthy—and in many cases prudent—many investors are becoming overly fearful and paralyzed into inaction.

It is possible to overcome these fears. The first step is to recognize the characteristics of your investor type:

The Conflicted Investor

The conflicted investor is unsure of what he or she is doing and often embraces whatever financial opinion is being expressed at the time. He or she often feels relieved after losses and needlessly agonizes about trades. Successful trades even cause anxiety.

Action plan: Carefully analyze your mistakes and determine why they occurred. Were you investing in companies about which you knew little?

Then find a good investing role model by imagining your ideal self and finding a real-life character who best matches your image. This person will patiently explain to you how the markets work and how to find a good investment.

Use a notebook to keep a private record that charts your reasons and emotional reactions, wishes and thoughts. Put these comments alongside entries for your investments. This will help you come to grips with reality rather than allow you to wonder why you made certain investments.

Review this record often so you can see the patterns of conflict. Pay particular attention to the anxiety or agitation you feel. Open up to a friend or your spouse, who can help you develop confidence in your investment decisions.

The Consumed Investor

The consumed or revenging investor can't get enough of the investing scene. Investment talk is exciting. He or she may have suffered some serious losses and feels seduced, abandoned and betrayed by the market as a result. The consumed investor is determined to get even—to triumph over his or her adversary.

Revenging investors cannot bear rejection. They often feel anger at their losses or the financial gains of others and seek to get even by also making a financial killing.

Action plan: *Shift your focus from past problems to new opportunities.* One solution is an automatic investment plan that factors out your emotional input. Another is to find a mentor who can help you keep the right focus and develop a disciplined investment plan. Your mentor should be someone who shares common values, goals and ideals—someone whom you admire and aspire to be like.

The Masked Investor

The masked investor feels inadequate and takes on a bigger-than-life persona in an attempt to project a winning image. A favorite "mask" is that of the swashbuckling competitor. But such people wind up in competition with themselves. Often they are confused as they act against their natural impulses, and their confidence breaks down.

Action plan: *Shed your mask.* Identify your own strengths and talents—not the ones you wish you had—and be honest about your weaknesses as well. Then form an investment action plan that is consistent with your real personality.

Avoid uncomfortable strategies. An impulsive person, for example, will not be happy with a highly technical trading strategy, nor a cautious one with big risks.

The Fussy Investor

The fussy investor is orderly and tidy, checking and double-checking all the details of an order, and he or she often keeps detailed charts and records.

Action plan: *Loosen up.* Experiment by making a small trade based on gut feelings instead of mounds of research. Find friends, mentors or brokers who will push you to make quicker, smarter decisions. Find another outlet for your fussy feelings and talk it over with a friend.

The Paranoid Investor

The paranoid investor feels an intense need for a guru—often a broker or media personality.

But in reality, he or she trusts the judgment of no one and no system.

Paranoid investors look for scapegoats and assign blame when things go wrong, instead of doing a sound analysis of the trade that can lead to wise future decisions.

Overly cautious, they do not even trust themselves and feel embarrassed or disbelieving when complimented, but may risk everything on one roll of the dice.

Action plan: *Try to balance holdings among several low-risk investments.* When things go wrong, find out the real reason, rather than blaming someone else.

The Depressed Investor

The depressed investor is unhappy, discontent and burned out. Everyone is depressed on occasion, particularly over events like a death in the family or the loss of a job. But if you are chronically resigned and apathetic, it's time to take action.

Action plan: *Do not make important investment decisions when you feel depressed.* Successful investors are happy investors, so get together with family members or friends who can help you snap out of it. If there is a family history of depression, there may be a genetic basis, so get medical help.

Tools for a Sound Investor Psyche

Several psychological tools can help you become a happier, more disciplined investor, whatever your psychological type.

● **Keep a mind/money journal.** The journal may be set up separately or alongside your current market or financial charting system. The best size is 8 ½ inches by 11 inches, which is big enough to see and small enough to fit in a briefcase. It is for your eyes only.

Write five categories across the top of a piece of paper: Date, event, emotion, thought and fantasy/dream. *Example:* Under these headings might be: 8/30/95, new contract, hassled, too much work, vacation house.

Then write a succinct paragraph of what is on your mind, as well as trading moves. Jot it down quickly whenever you trade or make an important business move and review it at least weekly. Soon you will see a pattern of your emotions and how they are affecting your actions.

● **A personal money time line.** Make quick notes in five-year segments—zero to five years, five to 10 years, 10 to 15 years, etc., through your present age.

In each segment, write a paragraph of significant family events, particularly as they relate to money.

That snippet shows a background of family conflict over money that can lead to a conflicted investor. And several five-year snippets can help you discover more about attitudes you hadn't recognized.

Sources: *Ira Epstein, founder and president of Ira Epstein and Company, a Chicago-based discount brokerage house, and David Garfield, M.D., an associate professor of psychiatry at the Chicago Medical School. They are the authors of* **The Psychology of Smart Investing**, *John Wiley & Sons, Inc.*

Winning in Insurance Stocks

If you're looking for a sound investment, don't neglect the insurance industry—it's one of the longest-running growth shows in town. The insurance business is unique because it is populated both by 100-year-old companies that continue to grow and by fast-growing newcomers whose first-generation management is still in control.

Diversity and Opportunity

Insurance companies differ in size, operating characteristics, profitability, and stock market price action. This diversity can represent a potential headache for some but an opportunity for those who take their investment homework seriously.

The three broad categories of insurance companies are life insurance, property/casualty and multiline companies. Today, there are very few "pure" life or "pure" property/casualty companies. Most firms specialize in one or the other area, but have subsidiaries involved in a variety of other lines of the business.

Until the 1980s life insurance companies were considered relatively predictable investments. Any life insurer with good products, solid marketing and adequate expense control could be counted on to show healthy, stable returns over both the short and the long run. Property/casualty insurers were usually more cyclical than pure life insurers—their earnings were tied to competitive conditions and catastrophe experience—but over the long haul, property/casualty companies also produced healthy rates of return.

The life insurance industry went through a product revolution in response to high and volatile interest rates. The introduction of new interest-sensitive and investment-type policies caused problems for many traditional companies serving the upscale market, and created exciting opportunities for aggressive competitors. Some companies suffered substantial earnings declines for the first time in their operating histories while others have grown faster than most people believed life insurers could.

On the investment side of the insurance business, rising interest rates tend to boost investment income and operating earnings, but also tend to push down the market value of investments held. The reverse happens when interest rates decline. Reflecting this fact, neither high nor low interest rates can be proven to be best, but relative stability certainly helps management run its company most efficiently. The valuations (p/e ratios) of almost all stocks, including insurers, are benefited by a low inflation and low interest rate environment.

Guidelines for Investment

● **Look beyond the big names.** Size does not necessarily go hand in hand with growth, profitability or quality. The problem with the strategy of most investors, including a large number of professionals, is that they limit their participation in the insurance industry to the biggest, best-known insurers, usually because it's too much trouble to investigate and follow the lesser-known names. That's a mistake. The bigger the insurance company, the more efficiently priced its stock will be and the less chance you will have of making large price gains.

● **Emphasize the differences.** The insurance industry's diversity means that economic and other events can have equally diverse effects. In any typical year, apparently similar firms may experience opposite market price actions and valuations, particularly if they operate in limited geographical areas or specialized market niches. It pays to know the companies—how or why they are unlike their competitors—before you invest, in order to take advantage of low prices resulting from market inefficiencies.

● **Examine management.** The most important investment task is to recognize differences in managements and identify those best equipped for the particular demands of their business. While this is difficult to accomplish without personal contact, much can be learned from annual reports and the trade press. Is management motivated by the same goals as shareholders (i.e., long-term growth in earnings, dividends and market price)? Is management consistent—does it stick to areas that make sense in light of its resources and abilities? Is management willing to change when conditions point to potential problems? Beware, however, of companies that plan to move aggressively into a new or untested area of business. If the market is already filled with a large number of competitors, chances are that a new player will have little chance of making money.

● **Be an investor, not a trader.** A successful insurance operation takes time to develop—when you find a good one, stick with it. Overtrading, trying to catch popularity swings or profit cycles, can produce very poor results. By the same token, don't be afraid to change your mind if your ongoing research suggests a faulty initial premise or an adverse change in long-term conditions.

● **Diversify to reduce risk.** In an industry with hundreds of companies to choose from, it makes sense to invest in more than one or two issues unless you are certain that those are the best to own without any question. If your basic selection process is sound, diversification reduces the risk that an occasional loss will ruin your entire investment program.

● **Average your cost per share.** Since it's virtually impossible to predict the market's short-term direction, investing all of your available funds at one time is bad strategy. The safer alternative is to buy equal dollar amounts at intervals, buying more shares when prices are low, fewer shares when prices rise. The results are a lower average cost for your total holdings as well as an increased number of opportunities to reevaluate the soundness of your investment program.

Source: William W. Dyer, trustee, Century Capital Management Inc., One Liberty Square, Boston, MA 02109, a mutual fund worth more than $200 million concentrated in insurance company stocks. In addition to being an insurance stock analyst for more than 25 years, Mr. Dyer has written articles in a variety of financial journals.

> **"Beware, however, of companies that plan to move aggressively into a new or untested area of business.... Chances are that a new player will have little chance of making money."**

Investors, Beware

Standard & Poor's created a risk rating for investments—an "r" rating indicating there is a significant risk that a security may lose market value.

Even a security with the highest AAA safety rating against risk of issuer default may incur the "r" rating. *How:* usually when it is a derivative whose value is tied to that of underlying assets, such as mortgage pools, currencies or commodities. The "r" rating was adopted because many investors mistakenly took the AAA rating—which applies only to risk of default—to indicate an investment is equally safe against price fluctuations.

Source: Leo O'Neill, president, S&P Ratings Services, New York.

Secrets of Playing It Very Safe

Not everyone wants to risk their money in stocks, bonds or mutual funds. Plenty of investors stay safe in Treasury bills and CDs. But even super-safe investments can be risky if you don't know the rules. *Here's how to use super-safe investments safely:*

● **Know your goals.** Start by deciding your time frame. Don't just park your money because you don't know what else to do with it.

Super-safe investments should not be long-term. If you need a lump sum in six months to a year, you can play it safe. If you are looking toward retirement, you are better off taking some risks.

● **Consider inflation.** The more conservative you are, the greater your inflation risk. A 4% return from an insured bank account is no return at all when inflation is near 4%.

● **Do it yourself.** You won't earn much by keeping your money safe. Therefore, you can't afford to give any of your return away. Bypass brokers and banks when possible. Their fees will eat into your return.

● **Beware of gimmicks.** Avoid anything touted as a "new" way to protect your investment and improve returns. Wait until there's a track record. Derivatives and portfolio insurance are both examples of strategies that promised higher returns, but turned sour. How safe investments stack up today:

● **Certificates of Deposit.** Yields run from about 4% for three-month CDs to about 4½% once you get out to five years.

Important: You may have to shop around for the best rate on a CD because many banks aren't pushing CDs aggressively. They would rather push mutual funds, which, unlike CDs, don't require them to pay for FDIC insurance. Start with the local newspapers, where banks that are in the market will advertise their highest CD rates.

A brokerage house may get you a higher rate on a CD from an out-of-town bank. Remember to subtract the commission on the CD from your return.

● **Money-market mutual funds.** They typically pay more than a CD—with the current average yield more than 5% for money you can retrieve at any time just by writing a check.

HOW TO PICK LEISURE STOCKS

The great advantage of leisure companies—manufacturers of recreational products such as golf clubs, boats, running shoes, etc.—is that you don't need a Wall Street analyst or industry expert to tell you how a product works and/or how successful it might be. With most leisure stocks, your own judgment is good enough to pick out the potential winners from the losers.

For this reason, leisure stocks are perfect for the investor with an eye for changes in the public mood. Trends in sports or exercise or new developments in old products create opportunities for growth almost overnight. For example, a few years ago, there was a strong demand for a boat specifically designed for sports fishermen, one of the largest groups of boat buyers in the country. Several small, innovative companies recognized this need and produced what is now known as the "bass boat." The result was instant success for the companies involved and sizable stock price appreciation for the companies' stockholders.

The second advantage of leisure stocks is that they tend to be much less cyclical than industrial or high-tech stocks. It doesn't seem to matter whether the economy is good or bad, once Americans take an activity to heart, money is no object in acquiring the equipment to pursue it.

Remember, however, that identifying emerging trends in the leisure market or potentially hot new products is only half the battle. You still have to make sure the company fulfills the rest of your investment criteria—strong growth rates; solid, innovative management; a strong balance sheet; etc.

Also, with any industry governed by popular taste, you have to be careful of investing in companies that rely on one particular trend for most of their earnings. If the trend is short-lived or brings with it a great number of competitors, as was the case with running shoes, you may see your company's profits squeezed from all sides.

Source: Scott Miles, president, Miles & West Insurance Agency, Inc., 12221 Merit Drive, Suite 940, Dallas, TX 75251. He is responsible for marketing and finance at the agency.

Unlike CDs, where the rate is fixed, the return on a money fund will rise as interest rates rise. The shorter the average maturity of money fund investments, the quicker its return will rise in line with interest rates.

If you think interest rates will rise, look for a fund with more short-term paper. For this purpose, I like a 30-day average maturity.

Some money funds tried to inflate yields by investing in exotic securities called derivatives. The derivatives lost big when the market slumped in 1994, and several funds had to be bailed out by their managers.

Ask any fund you are interested in whether it invests in derivatives. If it does—or if you don't get a satisfactory answer—don't buy. *Helpful:* If you are in a high tax bracket, consider tax-free money-market funds. The yield is lower than on conventional money funds—around 3% on average today. But your income will be exempt from federal income taxes.

Fund companies typically offer money funds for each higher tax state, with the return exempt from federal, state and local taxes.

● *Short-term Treasury issues.* Treasury bills (issued for one year or less) and notes (one to 10 years) are guaranteed by Uncle Sam. And you pay no state taxes on them in most states.

If interest rates climb, your Treasury issue will lose value. You'd get less than the purchase price if you must sell early. The longer the maturity, the more the price is likely to fall. Two- and five-year notes offer the best combination today of return and short-term maturity.

● *Short-term bond funds.* You can buy short-term issues yourself. Or you can buy a mutual fund that invests in short-term securities. *You get the same advantages of any mutual fund:* Diversification and professional management.

Because bond funds actively trade their portfolios,

RIPs

Investors in dividend reinvestment programs (DRIPs) should be aware of two tax-planning points: Extra shares bought with dividends through a DRIP are taxable income, even though the DRIP does not pay out any cash with which to pay the tax. So you'll have to come up with cash from other sources to pay the tax bill. And if you invest automatically through a DRIP, you'll probably be buying small lots of shares at least quarterly, at different prices. You will have to maintain accurate cost records for each purchase in order to figure out your tax bill when you sell.

Important: If you sell just part of your holdings, pick the particular shares for sale that will produce the best tax results.

Source: Charles B. Carlson, CFA, editor, **Dow Theory Forecasts**, 7412 Calumet Ave., Hammond, IN 46324.

the higher interest rates generally go, the more you'll earn on your fund. As with any bond or bond fund, the higher rates go, the lower prices will go.

Average returns on short-term bond funds today: 5¼% on short-term government funds, 5½% on short-term corporate funds and 4% (but tax-exempt) on municipal bond funds.

Source: Scott Kahan, certified financial planner and president of Financial Asset Management Corp., One West 34th St., New York, NY 10001.

Stock Sales Caution

When you sell part of your stock in a company, the IRS assumes that you're selling the first ones purchased. This can be costly if early purchases were much cheaper than subsequent blocks you bought. *Example:* You purchase 100 shares of a company for $5,000. Six months later you buy another block of 100 shares for $8,000. When the price of the stock drops to $7 per share, you sell 100 shares.

Trap: The IRS will assume there's a capital gain of $2,000 and tax it accordingly, unless you direct your broker in writing to sell the second block. In that case, there's a $1,000 loss with no tax due.

Source: Leon Gold, Phillips Gold & Co., CPAs, 1140 Avenue of the Americas, New York, NY 10036.

How to Make Money in the Stock Market in Tough Times

Short selling is easier than you think—but it's risky. Short selling involves borrowing common stock from another investor and then selling it in the hope that the stock's price will fall and you'll be able to replace it at a lower price. But instead of going down, the stock's price could go up—and there's no limit to how high it could go—losses can be staggeringly large. *Classic example:* In 1901 Northern Pacific Railroad's stock shot up from under $150/share to $1,000 in just a few days—wiping out all short-sellers. Such a big move in a stock's price rarely occurs, but a swing of just 10–20 points can also be devastating to a short-seller.

Lesson: Never stay short when the market turns against you—buy the stock back quickly and get out.

Psychological Factors

Short selling is unpopular, and especially unpopular in bull markets, when people think that stocks will go up forever. Of course, no market goes up forever. *Signs of an overvalued market ripe for decline:*

● *Everyone talking about their market gains.*

● *Magazine covers emblazoned with a rampaging bull.*

● *No one urging caution.*

Even when investors think that the market may be headed for trouble, most either just refrain from buying stock or move to cash. These are solid protective steps. But they don't enable investors to make money in a downturn—as short selling does.

Underrecognized: Investors can actually make money much faster by selling stocks short than by buying them as investments. *Reason:* Stocks go down much more rapidly than they go up. Typically, if it takes a stock a year to go from $20/share to $30, it can fall back from $30 to $20 in as little as two or three days in a bear market.

There's a place for short selling in any kind of market. Investors who have a substantial portfolio ($50,000 or more) should hedge by putting 5%–10% of capital into short sales.

Selecting Shorts

Companies are always eager to talk about good news that they expect, but in order to find out about possible earnings declines or dividend cuts, short-sellers must do their own homework. *Signs that a sector is overvalued:*

● *A sharp run-up in stock prices in that sector.*

● *Stock sector analysts* rationalizing the run-up and claiming that the stocks are still undervalued.

● *Extensive media coverage.*

Signs that a stock is *overvalued:*

● *A rapid price increase* on the promise of a concept that's caught people's imagination but hasn't yet been developed into a marketable product.

● *The company finally coming* out with a new product that was extensively promoted but doesn't measure up to its promise.

● *The stock hitting a new low* in volume after a long increase.

In general, when a sector weakens, it's best to short the companies that have been laggards. They will decline first and furthest.

Source: Louis Ehrenkrantz, president of Ehrenkrantz King Nussbaum, investment advisers, 635 Madison Ave., New York, NY 10022.

Selling Short in a Bull Market

Short-selling opportunities develop even during bull markets. Most such markets are interrupted at least once by a severe decline.

Suggestions for profitable short selling:

● *Sell only heavily capitalized issues* with a low outstanding short interest. They are less likely to be subject to a short squeeze (sharp rallies caused by many short-sellers rushing to cover and too few shares available).

● *Cover short sales during moments of market weakness.* Take advantage of market declines that are stimulated by bad news to cover periods of weakness.

Warning: Do not wait for a rally to cover shorts. *What the pros do:* Cover short sales just before weekends in case favorable news triggers sharp Monday rallies.

● *As an alternative to selling short,* consider the purchase of puts (selling an option contract at a stated price on or before a fixed expiration date).

● *A stock that is sold short* can decline by only so much, but there's no limit on how much it can rise. *Result:* Short selling bucks the odds because the ultimate risk is always greater than the potential reward. Place stop-loss orders to cover when the short sale goes against you by more than 10%–15%.

● *Sell short stocks* that show definite signs of overhead resistance (areas of heavy trading in that stock just above your short-selling level) on their charts. Such areas tend to impede upside progress.

● *Do not sell those short issues* that have just made new highs. Wait for definite signs of weakness before selling short.

Source: Personal Finance, Kephart Communications, Alexandria, VA.

What to Do When a Company You Have Invested in Goes Bankrupt

You basically have two choices when a company you've invested in goes bankrupt: Sell the stock and take a loss—or hold the stock and hope the company and its stock recover.

A bankrupt company will do one of two things. It may reorganize under Chapter 11, in which case it is maintained as a viable public entity and given the chance to reverse its losses and pay back its creditors. Or, the company may be dissolved as a public entity under Chapter 7 or 13, with its assets liquidated to pay back the creditors. Both outcomes are decided by a bankruptcy court on the basis of creditors' needs and the ability of the company to repay its debts.

The worst case for the owner of common stock occurs when the company files under Chapter 7 or 13. After the firm's liquidation, taxes, wages and court costs receive top priority. Debt holders and preferred stockholders are next—common stockholders are last in line. Most often, liquidation barely raises enough cash for the company's debt holders.

The best scenario for stockholders occurs when the company is allowed to reorganize under Chapter

Protection From Short-Selling Risks

Although short selling is often used, the risks are great.

To protect yourself: Leave a buy-stop order with your broker, limiting possible losses, avoid shorting stocks at new highs, since they often continue to climb, don't short thinly traded stocks that you may be forced to replace in the event of a "short squeeze."

Source: Stan Weinstein, publisher, The Professional Tape Reader, Hollywood, FL.

11, is made profitable in a relatively short period of time (a few years), and its creditors are paid back. Then the stock may recover a portion of its value or even return to its original price.

Sell or Hold?
There are several questions you must ask yourself, when deciding what to do with your stock. First and foremost, how likely is it that the company will be allowed to reorganize under Chapter 11? If you think the firm will be liquidated, it's probably better to sell the stock when you can still get a fraction of its original value. However, if the company is allowed to reorganize, what are the chances of the stock recovering even part of what you paid for it? What are the opportunity costs of holding it—that is, what could you do with the money if you sold the stock? What value is the tax loss to you this year? Can you handle the emotional stress involved in holding a bankrupt company?

One of the decision-making problems you face is that you can't know how long bankruptcy proceedings will last: They may end in a couple of months or drag on for years without a satisfactory resolution. Another problem is that the company may come out of reorganization, not make a profit and fizzle back into Chapter 11 later. Your biggest risk is that after the company goes into Chapter 11, it may run into hard times and be liquidated under Chapter 7 or 13.

Risk Reduction Tactics
The best way to minimize your risk is to remain well informed at all times. Try determining what the bankruptcy court will decide before its decision is announced. Unfortunately, once a company goes into bankruptcy proceedings, information becomes scarce, but you can look for indications that the company can pay back even a portion of its debt.

The single most important indicator to look for is

available cash flow. If the company has sufficient cash flow to pay down debts slowly at some modest discount from full value, it's likely the court will allow the company to exist. But beware of dilution. The company may try to issue new shares as a way of raising additional capital. While stock issues are a good sign that the investment community has faith in the company's future, they also mean that the value of your shares will decline.

Profitable divisions of the company can help your chances of recovering your equity. In many cases, bankruptcies are due to one or two unprofitable divisions of a diversified company. If a large part of the company is still profitable, there's a good chance the unprofitable divisions can be sold or shut down.

A strong equity holders' committee can help, too. These committees are established after bankruptcy is announced and serve as the only means for stockholders to influence the outcome of the legal proceedings.

If you are a large stockholder in the company or just want to play an active role in the proceedings, you have a good shot at becoming a member of the equity holders' committee. This will give you access to a great deal of information. The only drawback is that you will be considered an insider by the Securities & Exchange Commission and severely restricted in your buying and/or selling of the company's stock.

Source: *Kenneth L. Fisher, chief executive of Fisher Investments, Woodside, CA 94062, an investment management firm. Mr. Fisher is the author of a regular column in* **Forbes** *and of several books.*

Before Investing in a Foreign Company

If you're unsure about a foreign company being all it claims to be, check to see if it has been put on the Securities & Exchange Commission's "Foreign Restricted List." Call the SEC at 202-942-8088.

Foreign Investing Risks

(1) If you buy stock in a country whose currency falls against the dollar, gains in the share price are reduced by the currency loss. (2) Information about most foreign companies is less detailed than that of U.S. companies. That adds to the risk of buying the shares. (3) Most foreign stock markets are so small that a single large share transaction can swing the entire market.

Source: *Dr. John Rutledge, chairman, Rutledge & Co., a merchant banking and economic advisory firm, One E. Putnam Ave., Greenwich, CT 06830.*

A Safe Way to Invest In Foreign Stocks

Foreign stock investments should be hedged against fluctuations in their countries' currency. Each position in a country's stock should be paired with an opposite forward position in the country's currency. This will eliminate changes in stock value due to changes in currency value and result in a portfolio that can be compared with U.S. equity portfolios.

Source: *Michael Adler, professor, Columbia University, Graduate School of Business.*

Know All About Bonds

While most investors have a good understanding of how the stock market works, too few are even remotely familiar with bonds—or the bond market.

As a result, many individuals invest blindly and are unaware of the risks. That's unfortunate, because bonds deserve a place in every portfolio. Over time, they can produce higher returns than other fixed-income investments—if you understand what you are doing.

Bond basics:

● *The face value of a bond is fixed at the time it is purchased.* It is the amount a bondholder can count on getting in cash on the date the bond matures, which could be anywhere from one year to 100 years, depending on the particular bond.

● *The market value*—the price at which you can sell a bond any time before maturity—is profoundly affected by changes in interest rates. These rates are driven by expectations about the course of inflation. The longer the amount of time until a bond comes due, the more vulnerable it is to these expectations on a day-to-day basis.

● *When interest rates go up, the prices of bonds held by investors go down.* Reason: Newer issues offer higher yields. For example, investors won't pay the

$1,000 you paid for a 7% bond if they can get 8% now.

● **A guess about the probable course of inflation** is built into a bond's interest rate—or "coupon"—at the time it is issued. For example, a bond paying 7% may assume a 4% inflation rate, for a real return of 3%.

But if inflation turns out to be much higher, you will take a beating if you have to sell a bond before it reaches maturity. You can, of course, hold a bond to maturity and collect its face value—but the dollars you will get back may have a lot less purchasing power than they did when you invested them.

How to play interest rates:

● **If you think interest rates will rise**—buy bonds with short or intermediate maturities, generally not more than eight to 10 years. A spurt in interest rates after you buy the short or intermediate bond will not affect its price as much as it would a long-term bond because the substandard return lasts for a much shorter period. In other words, you will get back your principal sooner and be able to reinvest it at the new, higher interest rates.

● **If you think interest rates will fall further**—buy bonds with low coupons and long maturities (more than 10 years) that are selling below their face values.

● **If you have no idea** about which way interest rates are heading—"ladder" your investments. Buy bonds of different maturities—short, intermediate and long—to give you some protection against rate movements in either direction.

Common problems and solutions:

● **Bonds can be difficult to buy at fair prices.** Bonds have always been a game for major players—commercial banks, insurance companies, pension funds and mutual funds—which buy and sell them in huge quantities and pay less for them than you could.

Self-defense:

1. Buy new issues. Initial offerings by governments, agencies and corporations usually sell for set prices. Commissions are generally paid by the seller, not you.

2. Buy U.S. Treasury securities directly from the government. The Treasury "auctions" one-year bills every month. Other bonds and notes are auctioned at various times during the year. (For information on the direct purchase of Treasury securities, check with your local Federal Reserve Bank or write to the Bureau of the Public Debt, Division of Consumer Services, 300 13 St. NW, Washington, DC 20239, 202-874-4000.)

● **Bonds can be hard to sell at fair prices.** Many issues rarely trade in the secondary market. Dealers don't like to handle small numbers of bonds and often cut prices to move them quickly. If you have to sell, the bid price may shock you.

Self-defense:

1. Hold bonds to redemption. This is almost always the best strategy for individuals. Invest in bonds with the intention of holding them to maturity.

2. Buy bonds that are likely to have an active secondary market. If you feel the yield on long-term bonds is too good to pass up, choose those that are part of large offerings from well-known issuers. Find out if they are actively traded by asking your broker.

GOOD WAY TO BUY FOREIGN STOCKS

Foreign stocks need not always be bought on exchanges abroad. *Easier:* Buying shares of a foreign company through American Depositary Receipts (ADRs). These instruments are available for some foreign stocks. They trade on U.S. exchanges and are treated just like U.S. securities. They generally are available in units that represent one to 10 shares of a foreign company's stock. They certify that the shares have been bought and are being held by a custodian outside the United States. *Advantages:* Lower brokerage commissions than on trades of actual foreign shares and dividends paid in U.S. dollars.

Source: Joseph Velli, ADR business manager at the Bank of New York in New York City.

● **Bonds can be retired early**—or "called" — years before their scheduled maturity. Issuers can call bonds when interest rates fall if a call feature is part of the original issue. Just as home owners rush to refinance mortgages, bond issuers reduce interest expenses by replacing old, high-interest bonds with new ones at much lower rates.

Even though the call price is usually slightly above a bond's face value, early redemption is almost always a blow to bondholders. They lose the high returns they've expected to earn for years and must then reinvest the principal at lower market rates. *Even worse:* An investor may have paid a premium for a high-yielding bond and so will lose income when it's called.

Self-defense:

● **Buy bonds that can't be called.** Read the prospectus on a new issue carefully to check for call provisions. If a bond is already trading in the secondary market, ask your broker whether it is callable before you commit. If you decide to buy a callable bond for the increased yield, you should understand the call provisions and how they may affect your investment.

● **Interest and principal may not be paid.** Corporations and municipalities sometimes do go belly-up. When they do, you may lose most of your investment.

Self-defense:

● **Look for quality.** Unless you have good reason to think a company that is facing hard times is due for a comeback, forget it. Invest in conservatively managed companies that are leaders in growing industries.

● **Insist on collateral.** Don't rely on an issuer's revenue stream to service a bond. If the assets pledged to secure the debt are valuable, chances are you'll get most or all of your money back if disaster strikes. Bondholders can force the sale of these assets to pay their claims.

● **Invest in U.S. Treasury securities**—the ultimate security, since our government isn't going out of business.

A case for bond funds:

● **Unless you have large amounts of money to invest in bonds** (more than $100,000 for municipals, $50,000 for corporates), beware of buying individual issues. You are bound to sacrifice diversification—either in terms of issuers or maturities—and it is easy to get lost in the intricacies of some of the markets.

Generally, individuals are probably better off investing in bond funds.

Drawback: Mutual funds don't "mature," so there is no guarantee that you will get back your investment on any specified date.

Be sure to match a fund with your own investment standards and invest in at least two of the following types of bond funds:

● **Longer term**—13 years or more—for the higher yield.

● **Intermediate term**—from two to 12 years to reduce risk.

It's important to know a fund's fee structure before you invest, so read the prospectus carefully. *Look for:*

● **Low expense ratios.** This is critical. An expense ratio of more than 1% is a big drag on your yield. *Example:* A bond fund with a gross return of 7.5% yields a net return of 7.2% if the annual expense ratio is 0.3% of assets, but yields only 6.5% if the ratio is 1.0%.

● **Loads.** Some funds charge a front-end load—or fee—when you invest. Others charge a back-end load when you sell. Back-end loads are generally reduced over time, for example, from 6% of net asset value on shares held less than a year to no fee at all on shares held five years or more. Clearly, it is more costly to sell before the fees phase out.

● **12b-1 fees.** Many bond—and stock—mutual funds charge 12b-1 annual fees to cover their distribution and marketing costs. The amount is small (0.25% to 0.50%), but over the long haul these charges mount up.

Source: *David L. Scott, Ph.D., professor of accounting and finance at Valdosta State University in Valdosta, GA. He is the author of* The Guide to Investing in Bonds, *Globe Pequot Press.*

The New Inflation-Proof Bonds

The inflation-indexed 10-year Treasury notes introduced in 1996 can be a good deal, especially for retirees. Like any other Treasury securities, they pay annual interest. But they also keep pace with inflation, changing every six months by the same rate as the Consumer Price Index (CPI).

Drawback: You'll owe federal income taxes on

the interest paid each year and on the annual inflation adjustment, even though you won't receive inflation gains until the notes mature. *Strategy:* Buy these bonds for tax-sheltered retirement accounts; you defer taxes until you cash in the notes or begin withdrawing money from the retirement account.

The notes have a minimum purchase of $1,000 and are sold by brokers or can be bought from the Federal Reserve.

> "Before buying a convertible bond, check its "call" provisions—the right of the issuer to redeem your security. Call provisions can... have a...substantial effect on the price of a bond over time."

Convertible Bonds

Convertible bonds are hybrid securities that carry a fixed interest rate like a bond, but may be exchanged for a specified amount of the issuing company's common stock. (Usually the issuer will spell out several limitations regarding when and how conversion can take place.)

Convertibles' dual character produces dual advantages. The bonds provide you with interest income that is usually higher than what you would receive from a common stock dividend, but lower than the income from a straight debt security. At the same time, the bonds' convertibility feature gives you the chance to play the stock market.

Convertibles act as a compromise investment for times when you are uncertain about the future of the bond market and uncertain about the future of the stock market. When stock prices climb, convertibles rise. When they fall, convertibles don't fall quite as quickly, and still pay you reasonable current income. As a result, convertibles allow you to smooth out the effects of a volatile stock market.

What to Watch For

Keep an eye on the market for rare opportunities. There are situations in which the market for convertible bonds and the market for the bonds' underlying stocks are not well coordinated. The result is inefficient pricing. In these situations, it is possible that (1) a bond's underlying common stock actually provides a higher yield than the convertible, and/or (2) the convertible bond is selling at or below its conversion value. Both situations would allow you to purchase the underlying common stock at a discount.

Convertibles are fairly complex instruments to understand. The pricing can get tricky, and most individual investors end up paying a fairly large premium for the opportunity to play both the bond and stock markets. Also, by trying to have the best of both worlds, you can severely limit your potential gain from either one. Remember, too, if both the bond and the stock markets drop, the price of a convertible could decline substantially.

Special notes on buying and selling:

● *Before buying a convertible bond,* check its "call" provisions—the right of the issuer to redeem your security. Call provisions can sometimes have a very substantial effect on the price of a bond over time.

● *When you decide to convert a bond into its common stock equivalent,* wait until after the next interest payout. Interest on convertibles is paid semiannually and does not accrue.

● *Unless you are a large investor,* consider using no-load mutual funds, which specialize in convertible bonds.

Source: Jay Goldinger, president and chief investment strategist at Capital Insight, 190 N. Canon Drive, Suite 200, Beverly Hills, CA 90210, and author of Keys to Investing in Government Securities, Barron's.

Zero Coupon, Yes Zero Risk, No

Zero-coupon bonds are often sold as a simple, predictable, risk-free investment. If that sounds almost too good to be true—believe me, it *is* too good to be true.

Zero-coupon bonds are an appropriate investment only for people who are certain they will hold bonds until maturity—and who want to have a specific amount of money at a specific future date—to pay a college tuition, make a down payment on a house or pay off the mortgage at retirement.

For reasons I'll get to, a zero is very risky for anyone who might have to sell before maturity.

Important Differences

● **Traditional bonds** are sold at or near face value and pay periodic interest until maturity, when you get back your principal. You are paid interest every six months—so every six months you have new money to reinvest at whatever rate you can get at that moment.

● **Zero-coupon bonds** are sold for a fraction of their face amount and pay all interest, along with principal, in a lump sum at maturity. Since no interest is paid until maturity, there's no need to keep reinvesting. *Advantage:* Zeros are affordable because they're sold at a deep discount. Say that today's rate is 7½% for long-term U.S. Treasury bonds, you'd pay $1,142.21 for a 30-year zero government bond that will be worth $10,000 at maturity.

Risk: Having an issuer solvent enough to pay off:

● **U.S. Treasury or federal agency** zeros are sure to pay off.

● **Municipal zeros** are also safe—if you buy good credit quality bonds and diversify by buying bonds issued by more than one city.

● **Corporate zeros** are another story—and I recommend against them. *Reason:* A corporation generally issues zero-coupon bonds because it has no money to pay current interest. What does that tell you about its quality?

ZERO-COUPON BONDS

Zero-coupon bonds are simply ordinary U.S. government bonds stripped of their coupon yields and sold at a deep discount from their face value. Like U.S. savings bonds or Treasury bills, they pay no current interest to the investor. Instead, the bonds increase in value until they mature, when they can be redeemed at full face value. Interest that normally would have been paid out to the investor over the life of the bond is used to increase the value of the bond.

For example, buy $10,000 worth of zero-coupon bonds due in the year 2015 and appreciating at a compounded rate of 8.1%, and they will be worth $50,000 when they mature.

Return, Tax and Cost Advantages

Zero-coupon bonds can offer some of the highest overall returns to be found among U.S. government-guaranteed securities. In addition, they provide a fixed rate of return for the reinvestment of your interest income.

The problem with most bonds is that you have to reinvest your interest income. Zero-coupon bonds eliminate the burden of reinvestment, because interest income is reinvested at the rate initially guaranteed to you when you bought the bond.

Zero-coupon bonds are ideal fundings for tax-free or tax-deferred investment vehicles. Their most popular uses are in qualified pension/profit-sharing retirement plans, IRAs, Keoghs, or financing a college education. However, be careful how you fund the last. If the zero bonds are purchased for a custodial account by a parent for a youngster under 14, the first $700 of income in 1998 accruing inside the bonds is completely tax-exempt. The next $700 of investment

income is taxed at the child's own rate (the federal minimum is 15%). Investment income exceeding $1,400 a year is taxed at the parents' rate. If the child is over 14, the income is taxable at his or her rate.

Think twice, also, about investing in zero-coupon bonds if you're not using a tax-advantaged investment vehicle. Even though you don't receive interest payments on a zero-coupon bond, the IRS requires that you pay the annual income tax on interest you would have received. The only exception to this is zero-coupon municipal bonds.

Source: Jay Goldinger, president and chief investment strategist at Capital Insight, 190 N. Canon Drive, Suite 200, Beverly Hills, CA 90210, and author of Keys to Investing in Government Securities, *Barron's.*

Understanding the Risks

If you can't hold to maturity, zeros are a wildly unpredictable investment—much more volatile than traditional bonds. *Here's why:*

● **When interest rates fall,** zeros can be sold at premium prices because of the higher interest rate locked into the bond.

● **When interest rates rise,** the zero-coupon bond's locked-in lower rate sharply reduces what it can be sold for. If the current long-term bond rate should rise from 7½% to 8½%—the zero you bought for $1,142.21 will be worth only $865.18.

Best prospects: Zeros should be bought only by people who feel interest rates won't go much higher, know they won't need this money until the bonds mature and won't lose sleep over price fluctuations in the meantime. For the other 98% of investors, I'm not a big fan of zeros.

Important: You're taxed every year on the interest you earn on a zero-coupon bond, even though you don't receive it until the bond matures. Generally, you should buy zero-coupon bonds only for a nontaxable account, like an Individual Retirement Account or a Keogh. *Exception:* Zero-coupon municipal bonds, since municipals are exempt from federal income tax.

Source: *Lew Altfest, CPA, CFP, president of L.J. Altfest & Co., a financial planning firm, 116 John St., New York, NY 10038. He is the author of* Lew Altfest Answers All Your Questions About Money, *McGraw-Hill.*

Zero-Bond Trap

● **When zero-coupon bonds are called** and you miss notification of the call, unredeemed bonds stop earning interest. The longer the bonds go unredeemed, the greater the loss. Investors who move frequently are most vulnerable, since many zero-coupon-bond issuers send notice of calls through the mail.

Safeguards: (1) Ask the broker who sold you the bonds to check at least twice a year on whether they've been called. (2) If you move, notify the paying agent bank (listed on the bond certificate).

Source: *Ben Weberman, senior editor,* Forbes.

● **When zero-coupon bonds are called early,** the issuer may have no way of notifying the holders other than through an ad in the financial pages. If you don't see the ad, your money will remain with the issuer at zero interest. Some investors have lost years' worth of earnings.

Source: *Kiplinger Washington Letter.*

Junk-Bond Alert

If you're in a so-called "high-yield fund," or holding junk bonds, you should consider getting out.

Concern: The yield advantage between junk bonds and equivalent T-bonds is around 3%, and that's not enough to compensate for the added risk, especially when interest rates will probably rise again and cause bond prices to fall.

Source: *Martin Weiss, editor of the* Safe Money Report, *4176 Burns Road, Palm Beach Gardens, FL 33410.*

Muni-Bond Opportunities

Investors who want municipal bonds should consider buying individual issues instead of bond mutual funds, which took a terrible beating. Studies have shown that the average municipal-bond investor has $50,000 invested.

Such an investor could put $10,000 in each of five different municipals, with different maturities ranging between seven and 12 years. Most bond funds have much longer maturities and are thus vulnerable to price declines as interest rates rise. Many funds contain risky derivatives.

Important: Buy AAA-rated insured municipals that have an ironclad no-call provision. Ladder the maturities so that each $10,000 bond comes due in a different year. Interest rate risk is minimized.

Best bet: Prerefunded bonds originally issued during the 1980s, when interest rates were much higher. These have been refunded (refinanced) as interest rates have come down, with much of the proceeds going into escrow accounts invested in Treasuries and government agency securities. Even if the issuing municipality was wiped out by a natural disaster or a "man-made" disaster, such as the Orange County debacle, bondholders would get paid their interest and principal at maturity.

Source: *Marilyn Cohen, a bond portfolio manager with L&S Advisers, Los Angeles, CA.*

Small-Town Vs. Big-City Municipals

Small-town bonds pay better returns than their big-city counterparts, and because these municipal-bond issues are small—usually less than $10 million—rating companies don't bother to evaluate them. In most cases the issues are just as safe as rated bonds. But because they're unrated, the yield is higher.

Safest: Invest in municipal-bond funds that spread their money around many small issues.

Zero-Coupon Municipal Bonds

Zero-coupon stripped municipals are attractive investments for people who know exactly when they want to use their money and are in a high tax bracket. Municipal zero-coupon bonds compound interest free of federal tax, and, in many cases, free of state taxes as well. Like zero-coupon Treasuries, zero-coupon bonds do not pay interest. They are sold at a deep discount to their face value. Instead of current interest payments, investors receive the face value of the bond when it matures. The gain comes from the difference between the discount price of the bond and its face value. *Example:* A 10-year zero-coupon bond with a face value of $10,000 and paying 5% would sell for $6,102. The bonds are tax-exempt, so investors who bought at the original issued yield—and held them until maturity—would not pay any tax on their investment.

Risks

Zero-coupon bonds can be less marketable than coupon-bearing bonds, especially if they are purchased in small lot size. Investors should be prepared to hold them until maturity. If you must sell before maturity, it's important to know that zero-coupon municipal bonds are more volatile than similarly maturing, coupon-bearing bonds. *Reason:* They don't have the cushion of regular coupon payments,

How Much Is Tax-Free Income Worth?

To find out, divide the yield from a tax-free investment by 1 minus your tax bracket. The result shows how much you would have to earn from a taxable investment to get the same after-tax return as from the tax-free one. *Example:* A tax-free municipal bond pays 4% and you are in the 31% bracket. Divide 4% by 0.69 (which is 1 – 0.31). The result is 5.797%. So a taxable investment must pay more than 5.797% to give you more after-tax income than the tax-free bond.

Source: Jay Schabacker's Winning in Mutual Funds *by Jay Schabacker, Schabacker Investment Management, Gaithersburg, MD, American Management Association.*

which act as a buffer to interest rate changes.

Important: There are also zero-coupon bonds that are callable (bought back by the issuer on demand). This feature can impede the price appreciation of the bond, and affect its reinvestment potential.

Best bet: Those investors looking for maximum price appreciation from declining interest rates, or a guarantee on what their investment will return, should look only at noncallable zeros.

Types

Municipal zeros can be bought in a wide variety of maturities and credit categories. The majority issued in recent years have been insured by one of the major bond insurers such as MBIA (Municipal Bond Insurance Agency) and FGIC (Financial Guaranty Insurance Corporation), and carry an AAA rating from one of the ratings services, such as Standard & Poor's or Moody's. Zeros have been issued for a variety of purposes, such as building schools.

Caution: Credit quality is important, since an investor receives nothing before maturity. That makes zero-coupon municipal bonds more vulnerable to a default. Because of their price volatility, any downgrading in the credit quality of zero-coupon municipal bonds will have a greater effect than it would on a coupon-bearing bond.

Source: *John Mousseau, CFA, director of municipal-bond management, Lord, Abbet & Co., 767 Fifth Ave., New York, NY 10153. He is the portfolio manager for five Lord, Abbet funds, which have more than $3.2 billion in assets.*

Investing to Win

Create Your Own Bond Fund

You can do this by building a portfolio of laddered Treasury bonds. *How:* Invest among bonds with varying maturities, such as one, three, five and seven years. You obtain the benefit of diversification—if rates go down you earn capital gains from the longer-term bonds; if rates go up, you get more income when your short-term securities are re-invested. You also get the complete safety of U.S. Treasury investments. For investors who don't require professional money-management services, this strategy will avoid bond-fund management fees that average about 0.7% annually—or 10% of a 7% bond yield.

Key: You can purchase Treasury bonds through a broker or by buying them directly from the Federal Reserve.

Source: *Bruce Ventimiglia, senior vice president, Quest for Value, retail investment advisory arm of Oppenheimer Capital, New York.*

A New Look at Savings Bonds

The U.S. government made some changes to Series EE and E savings bonds. But the bonds are still good deals for investors. *Reasons:* Series EE and E bonds (series E bonds are no longer available) are an excellent form of forced savings, especially for long-term goals like college education or retirement.

Because the interest rate varies with the market, you are protected against rising interest rates created by inflation. The bonds are guaranteed by the U.S. government.

Key tax benefits: U.S. savings bond interest is free from state and local taxes. *(Editor's note:* For federal income tax purposes, interest can be deferred until the bonds mature or are redeemed. If the bonds are used to pay for higher-education costs and certain conditions are met, the interest may be totally tax-free.) *How they work:* You still buy savings bonds for one-half of their face value and then collect the purchase price interest when you cash in. If you hold to final maturity, the bond can be worth several times face value. *Example:* EE bonds with a face value of $100 can be purchased for $50. When they reach final maturity (30 years), the bonds will be worth more than face value.

Limit: No one can buy more than $15,000 worth of Series EE bonds in one year.

New rule: Older bonds carry a minimum interest rate guarantee, no matter how low market rates fall. There is no guaranteed rate on series EE bonds you purchase now.

How interest is figured: Interest rates are based on when the bonds were purchased. EE bonds will receive an interest rate based on 90% of the average of five-year Treasury yields. The rate, published every May 1 and November 1, is based on the six-month period prior to the date it is published.

New rule. For the first time in the history of savings bonds, you receive a three-month interest penalty if you cash in a bond before it turns five years old. Any bond can be cashed as early as six months after purchase—just be prepared to pay that penalty.

Danger: Most bonds purchased prior to May 1, 1997 increase in value only twice a year. Cash in before the increase date and you forfeit six months of interest. EE bonds purchased since May 1, 1997 will increase in value monthly. *Strategy:* Investors who don't plan to hold older bonds to maturity should make sure to redeem bonds just after interest has been credited.

New rule. Because the interest paid on savings bonds is now variable, not fixed, the bonds no longer mature at a definite time. However, if a bond doesn't reach face value in 17 years, the U.S. government will make a one-time interest payment to bring the bond up to its face value.

Key: The 17-year figure is based on a 4.11% interest rate. So the guarantee really hasn't been eliminated for investors who hold savings bonds for at least 17 years. However, people who redeem bonds early can be hurt by the rule changes.

Source: *Dan Pederson, author of* U.S. Savings Bonds: A Comprehensive Guide, *and president of The Savings Bond Informer, P.O. Box 9249, Detroit, MI 48209; 1-800-927-1901.*

How to Guard Against Losses in the Options and Futures Markets

Most amateur investors lose money with high-leverage investments because they carelessly put most of their trading capital at risk in the hope of making large, quick profits—they invest on the basis of emotions rather than a disciplined trading strategy.

Contrary to popular belief, disciplined trading is the real way to make consistent profits over the long term in either the options or futures markets. The key to successful, disciplined trading is managing your capital, controlling your risks, and watching the markets.

Managing Your Capital

Don't commit funds to leveraged investments that you can't afford to lose. Since you only make big profits in futures and options markets when you assume a correspondingly high level of risk, always limit the capital you commit to an amount you feel comfortable about losing completely. As a general rule, if you can't handle large losses over a short period of time, you probably shouldn't be trading in options or futures.

Once you've determined the amount of capital you can devote to trading, always keep a large portion of capital in reserve. Never risk all or most of it on a single trade, regardless of how successful you've been in the past or how attractive the next trade appears. *Remember:* There will always be losing trades. By compounding your capital after a few profitable trades, you can only expose yourself to potentially dangerous losses. This strategy will give you the staying power to ride out losses and, ultimately, to make a profit.

Controlling Your Risk

Diversify your positions. *The old rule still applies:* Never have all your investment eggs in one futures or options basket.

For futures trading, maintain a minimum of two positions in different futures complexes. (The major futures complexes consist of stock indexes, metals, financial instruments, meats and agricultural commodities.) A long position in gold and a long position in silver does not constitute diversification. Don't just trade on the long side (buying with the hope that prices will rise). Since markets rise and fall, you must learn to trade on the short side as well (profiting from a decline in prices).

For options trading, maintain at least two positions in different underlying instruments. Also try to invest in puts as well as in calls.

TODAY'S U.S. SAVINGS BONDS

U.S. savings bonds were once considered the ugly duckling of personal investments. They paid below-market interest rates and had lengthy maturities, making them uneconomical for most investors. The only time you bought them was when you felt particularly patriotic or when you couldn't think of a better birthday or Christmas present.

That's not true anymore. Today, you can buy EE U.S. savings bonds for any amount between $50 and $15,000, with the purchase price equal to half the bond's face value. You pay no commission charge (one reason you won't hear about these bonds), they are virtually risk-free and they are extremely liquid. Now the interest even accrues monthly and compounds every six months.

Interest and principal on the EE savings bond are paid in a lump sum at the bond's maturity, making it, in effect, a zero-coupon bond. *(Editor's note:* For bonds issued after May 1, 1997, interest is 90% of the average market yield on five-year Treasuries for the preceding six months. Rates change every six months—May 1 and November 1. Bonds redeemed before the end of five years are subject to a three-month interest penalty.)

What is the advantage of a variable interest rate? The bond offers unlimited upside interest. This enables you to stay in step with inflation. *(Editor's*

Protect against major losses by using stop-loss orders. Diversification will help protect you against adverse moves in a particular market, but protective stop-loss orders will close out losing positions before they deteriorate into huge losses. Determine your stop-loss points in advance and stick to them; 50% maximum loss on your original investment is appropriate for most trades.

Watching the Markets

Many futures and options traders are short-term-oriented, and their approach tends to be technical in nature. This means that they analyze past trends in price and volume to predict future market direction. It is also possible to look at markets in terms of fundamentals, such as interest rates, inflation, production, and demand. However, although these will ultimately dictate price movements, it is very difficult to translate them into profitable short-term trading programs.

Closely follow the markets that most interest you. It's the only way to gain a feeling for a market's underlying direction. Don't be afraid to utilize the advice and recommendations of outside advisory and information services. Most good traders rely on a number of excellent information sources beyond just the daily financial press to help determine market movements. Sources include investment advisory services, brokerage reports devoted to futures and options, chart services and computer databases.

Source: Bernard G. Schaeffer, executive director, Investment Research Institute, Inc., 110 Boggs Lane, Suite 365, Cincinnati, OH 45246. He is coeditor of **The Option Advisor** and several other newsletters on short-term trading, as well as coauthor of **The Options Handbook** and **The Trader's Handbook**.

How to Profit With Options: The Basics

The sad truth about options is that most people who invest in them end up losing money. That is primarily because few investors take the time to learn exactly how options work or, more important, how to use them to make money.

Good advice: Always learn the basics well, then proceed with caution. *For serious investors, options can serve three basic functions:*

---

note: There is no guaranteed minimum interest rate (only bonds issued before May 1, 1995, carry a guaranteed minimum rate.)

Best feature: EEs are not only exempt from state and local taxes, but with EE savings bonds you can defer the federal income tax liability until redemption. In effect, then, you are buying a zero-coupon bond with none of the obligations to pay taxes on interest you don't receive until the bonds' maturity. *(Editor's note:* If the bonds were purchased after 1989 and are redeemed to pay for higher-education costs, all of the interest may be tax-free. There are income limits and other requirements for claiming this tax break.)

When your child was born, chances are he or she received savings bonds as gifts. And you might have decided to take advantage of the automatic tax deferral on interest that bonds earn each year. That may not be the wisest decision. Instead, consider electing to have the youngster report the interest on the bond(s) as taxable income each year.

Why? Because your child, who is under 14, is entitled to $700 worth of earned income in 1998, tax-free, and another $700 at a 15% tax rate. Over $1,400, kids under 14 have to pay tax at the same higher rate as their parents. This idea will avoid recognizing the income later, when there may be more tax due. *Exception:* EE savings bonds may be tax-exempt if used for college. This feature depends upon the family income the year the bonds are redeemed.

Remember also, as U.S. savings bonds, EEs are virtually risk-free. And because they have a variable interest rate, your principal is always secure. *Disadvantages:* None, except that the maximum that an individual can invest in EEs is $15,000 per year under one name and Social Security number.

Editor's note: Bonds that have reached their final maturity date (30 years, or 40 years for E bonds issued before December 1965) no longer pay interest.

Source: Lawrence A. Krause, chairman of the board of Lawrence A. Krause & Associates, Inc., 1001 Bayhill Drive, Suite 170, San Bruno, CA 94066, a financial planning firm with a nationwide clientele. He is a certified financial planner.

- *High-risk speculation* on the direction of the market.
- *Supplementing current dividend* and interest income from a portfolio.
- *Hedging* against portfolio risk.

But, again, options only provide these advantages to investors who know what they're doing.

The Basics of Options

An option is nothing more than a contract that gives you the right to buy or sell a security at a set price by a specified date in the future. *There are two types of options:* A *call*, the right to buy a security at a set price in the future; and a *put*, the right to sell a security at a set price in the future. *Example:* Company X's stock sells for $30 a share. You buy a call, which expires in three months, at $35 a share. This means that within three months, you have the right to buy the stock of Company X for $35 a share no matter how high the share price has risen.

The price of the option, or premium, is 50¢. This represents the time value of the option. It is based on the length of time before the option expires and the likelihood of the stock actually reaching the option's exercise price. If investors think there is only a small chance that Company X's stock will reach $35 in three months, then the premium will be low. If, however, investors think there is a large chance that the stock will reach $35, then the price of the option will be higher. At 50¢, investors probably think there is relatively little chance of the stocks reaching $35.

A month later, the price of the stock jumps to $40. The value of the option is now $5, because you could exercise the option, buy the stock at $35 and then sell it for $40 in the open market. Your 50¢ investment is therefore worth 10 times its original value. If the stock did not reach the exercise price of $35 however, the option would expire worthless.

A put operates in the reverse fashion. If you think a stock will go down in price, you buy a put or the

right to sell the stock at a set price in the future. *Example:* Company X is selling for $35 a share. This time, you think the price will go down, so you buy a put to sell the stock for $35. The premium you pay for the option is $1. One month later, the company experiences problems and the price of the stock drops to $30. You can now buy the stock for $30 in the open market and, by exercising your put, sell the stock for $35. Your profit is $4, or a 400% gain on your original investment.

> " If an option's underlying stock or index does not perform according to your expectations, the options contract expires with no value at all and you lose your entire investment. "

Huge Returns—and Risks

With options, a very small investment can rack up huge returns in a very short period of time. To otherwise achieve the same results in the stock market would take massive amounts of capital and a great deal of patience.

The risk is that most options expire worthless. Unlike the stocks themselves, if an option's underlying stock or index does not perform according to your expectations, the options contract expires with no value at all—you lose your entire investment. Also, options are typically short-term investment vehicles—they usually involve a great deal of buying and selling. As a result, total commission costs can be very high.

Source: *Carl A. Futia, investment consultant, 16 Colles Ave., Morristown, NJ 07960.*

Options Investing Strategies

Professional investors have devised a large and impressive array of investing strategies utilizing the options market. Some of these strategies are exceedingly complex and, because of the large amounts of capital involved, are not recommended for use by individual investors. However, a number of basic options strategies can expand your investing capabilities significantly.

Selling Options on a Stock Portfolio

Selling options on a stock portfolio, better known as "writing covered calls," allows you to generate current income over and above the income received by dividends. Instead of buying call options, you actually "write" or sell them on your own portfolio. In return for selling the call option, you receive a premium from the investor who purchases the call. This strategy is used when you don't expect your stocks to move much either up or down. *Example:* You own 200 shares of Company X at $40 a share. Company X pays a regular quarterly dividend of $1 or an annual yield of 10%. This is a respectable dividend, but you want more current income. You believe that the stock of Company X is going to remain relatively stable for the near future, so you decide to write a covered call on your stock of Company X at an exercise price of $45. The investor who buys the call pays you a premium of $1.

As a result of this transaction, you have doubled your quarterly income in no time at all. The risk, though, is that your outlook for Company X is not correct and the stock's price will actually rise above $45. Then, your stock can be called away any time before the option expires. If this happens, you will not participate in the stock's gains beyond $45. And, if it is called away from you before a quarterly dividend date, you won't receive your dividend, either.

Sale of a Naked Call

This is a much riskier version of writing covered calls. The main difference between the two is that when you sell naked calls, you receive a premium without actually owning the underlying securities. Who should use this strategy? Investors who are willing to take on large and sometimes unlimited amounts of risk. Why are naked calls so risky? If you sell a naked call for $45 and the stock rises above that exercise price, you are responsible for purchasing the stock in the open market at the current market price. *Example:* If the naked call is exercisable at $45 a share and the price of Company X's stock rises to $50, you will have to buy the stock at $50 in the open market and sell it to the owner of the call for $45. Your loss will equal $5. In theory, your loss is potentially limitless.

Straddles

Use a "straddle" when you think a stock will move dramatically up or down, but you're not sure which direction it will take. This situation might arise when a company's future earnings will be severely affected, positively or negatively, by a specific event—for instance, a court ruling on a series of new products, the movement of interest rates or a cutoff of supply of natural resources. *Example:* Company X's stock trades for $40 a share. An FDA ruling on a new product will dramatically affect Company X's potential for future earnings. You're not sure which way the stock will move, so you buy a $40 call and a $40 put. The cost of each option is $5—your investment is $10. Now, if Company X's stock goes above $50 or below $30 before the put and call expire, you will make a profit.

Hedging a Broad Stock Portfolio

Options on market indexes can be used to hedge against a portfolio's inherent market risk. Use this strategy when you own a broad portfolio of stocks and are uncertain about the future movement of the stock market as a whole and, hence, of your portfolio. If this is the case, buy a put option on the most comparable market index (Standard & Poor's 500, Value Line, etc.). If the market and presumably your portfolio do in fact decline in value, you will make a profit on your put. If your prediction does not come true, then the rise in the value of your portfolio can offset the premium you paid for the option. Index options (unlike stock options) are settled with cash.

The advantages of hedging a portfolio, rather than liquidating it outright, are that you save a significant amount of money in brokerage commissions, and you are able to hold on to stocks you believe are fundamentally sound long-term investments. However, there are also risks. If your portfolio is not well correlated with a specific market index, you will not be fully protected. You can potentially lose money on your hedge and your portfolio. If the stock market goes up, you do not get the full benefit from the increase in the value of your portfolio.

Limiting Your Losses

Most first-time options investors lose. *So, be careful:* Don't let your losses amount to more than 50% of your initial investment. Options investors are notorious for waiting out a downturn in the market in the hope that their position will become profitable by expiration time. When your loss amounts to 50%, admit you were wrong and liquidate the position to ensure that the option won't turn into a 100% loss by expiration day.

Source: *Carl A. Futia, investment consultant, 16 Colles Ave., Morristown, NJ 07960.*

Investing in No-Load Funds

Beware of investment salesmen who try to convince you that load funds are better than no-load funds. To support their position, they will say that some load funds have outperformed no-load funds.

Then they will tell you not to worry about the load because you'll only have to pay that 3% or 5% or 8% fee *once*. After that, you'll be entitled to switch between funds in the same family, free of charge. *Reality:* Arguments are not convincing. No-load funds are still the only way to go—for individuals and institutions.

Since load funds charge you money up front, they automatically have to work harder than no-load funds to produce real returns for investors. Sure, some load funds outperform no-load funds, but there's no guarantee that they will.

As for free switching—why is it beneficial to be limited to one fund family? No one fund family is ever going to have the strongest funds in every category.

The Power of No-Load Managers

While only 15% of *all* mutual funds beat the Standard & Poor's 500 index over time—that still leaves you with *600 market-beating mutual funds* from which to choose. And some are managed by world-beaters.

What to look for in a no-load-fund manager:

● *Independent thinking.* Invest with someone willing to buck conventional wisdom, who has the courage of his or her convictions but can adjust a portfolio when the markets don't cooperate.

You can gauge this by looking at the manager's portfolio and reading the semiannual letters to shareholders.

● *Long-term track record.* The past is an imperfect guide to the future, but a record of excellence sure beats one of mediocrity.

● *Recent strength.* It's inevitable that top managers will sometimes underperform their peers. But

if this happens for more than a nine-month stretch, I'm not happy, and we vote with our feet.

Important: Be sure you're comparing apples with apples. If *value investing* is out of favor, no *value manager* will beat the market. But if you insist on value investing, at least pick someone who is outperforming his or her value-stock peers.

● *Disciplined approach.* Invest with someone who has a clear view of how the world works and a willingness to stick with that approach.

● *Ownership stake in the fund family.* The fund family can tell you whether the manager owns shares in his or her own fund. That's obviously a positive sign. But there's another benefit to this as well. The more shares a manager owns, the more likely it is that he or she will stay put for a long time.

How to Check the Numbers

We use data from a variety of sources, including *Morningstar,* which any investor can obtain either at the library or by subscribing to the service (800-876-5005, $425/yr.). *Here's what to do with the data once you get it:*

● *Look behind the numbers.* Two similar funds may both have advanced 50% last year. That's tentatively appealing, but you have to see what the numbers mean. Did the manager profit from huge stakes in two or three highly speculative companies? Was the fund strong in the first half of the year but weak in the second half?

Key: Given a choice, we would always invest in the fund that came on strong in the second half of last year rather than in the first half. *Morningstar* has this information.

Investing Strategies

● *Don't just go for the famous fund-family names.* We believe that the most innovative and courageous fund managers are more likely to be found outside the large fund families.

● *Invest in the future.* Put some money where you think the market is *headed*, not where it has been. It's a wonderful way to enhance returns.

● *Consider applying a top-down approach. How we made one recent portfolio shift:* Our macro view is that large U.S. companies are in the best position to compete on a global basis. We also believe the two

Investing to Win

broadest leading sectors will continue to be financial services and technology.

So, when we did our research screening (you can use *Morningstar* for this), we looked for large-cap U.S. stock funds that overweighted technology and financial issues.

● **When a great fund closes to new investors, be careful.** When this happens, don't automatically put your money in a fund with a similar name.

Use careful analysis to try to find a fund with a similar investment philosophy and track record.

● **Paying too much attention to expense ratios can be penny-wise and pound-foolish.** An expense ratio—what a fund charges investors to cover its marketing costs—is crucial when it comes to bond funds but not as important for stock funds. That's because the ratio for bond funds tends to eat into total returns more so than stock funds.

More important: Check the results after expenses.

● **Diversify correctly.** Buying six different growth funds in an attempt to seek diversification is a mistake. Ideally, you want to own funds that will work in tandem. Our growth and real estate funds will often move in opposite directions.

You can only diversify intelligently if you know exactly what's in each of your fund's portfolios. The typical U.S. equity fund now probably has about 10% of its money in foreign stocks.

But some "domestic" funds have enormous foreign holdings.

If you own such funds and also own several international funds, you may be overexposed to foreign markets. If that's a strategic decision, fine. If it's an oversight, adjust your portfolio.

Source: *Robert Markman, president of Markman Capital Management, 6600 France Ave. S, Edina, MN 55435.*

How to Win the Mutual-Fund Race

Consistent—rather than spectacular— returns is the best way to build long-term wealth. *This approach eliminates several problems:*

Trap: Altering your strategy when the market drops. If your funds are highfliers, your portfolio's value will really sink if the market suffers a severe decline. It's hard for many investors to stay the course at such times.

Trap: Underperforming by seeking maximum performance. Losses really drag down a portfolio's return over time—as opposed to *gains* that are below the market indexes. It's very hard to make up for a bad year.

Trap: Sustaining losses. If you start with $10,000 and lose 50% the first year, you're left with $5,000. You need a 100% return the second year to be even. You would need a 142% gain to achieve a 10% annualized gain for those two years.

Strategy

Choose the tortoise, not the hare. When building a fund portfolio, pick consistent winners rather than top-10 performers.

But isn't it wise to buy a fund that has been red-hot lately? *Absolutely not.* Of the top 10 funds in any year, more than five will fall to the bottom half of all funds in performance within one or two years. When a home-run hitter doesn't hit home runs, he strikes out a lot. *Advantage:* Besides giving you relatively consistent returns over time, this approach offers peace of mind. When the market swoons —as it did in 1987 when the S&P 500 lost 30% of its value in six days—your portfolio will do much better. It won't look like the end of the world. *Added benefit:* At such times, this conservative approach will make it more likely that you'll be an opportunistic buyer rather than a rattled seller.

● **Investing shouldn't be exciting.** Most people would be better investors if they considered the process boring. They wouldn't be looking for instant gratification. They wouldn't be concerned about finding a hot fund that will give them bragging rights at their next party.

● **Don't expect too much.** The performance of your fund portfolios will not wow you during runaway bull markets.

● *Allocating your assets*. The average investor should employ a *fixed-mix* approach. Establish an asset-allocation mix at the outset and stick with it. It works. *Strategy:* Review the mix quarterly. If you started with 60% equities, 35% bonds and 5% money-market funds, make adjustments to get back to your original allocation. If the market has been soaring, you may need to lighten up on equities and put more into bonds and money funds. If stocks fall, you'll add to equity holdings. *Advantage:* This imposes some buy low/sell high discipline that can improve your overall returns.

● *Beware of sector funds and international fund risk.* Sector funds are simply too volatile and dangerous. Besides, the temptation is to pick a sector after it has soared, rather than before it begins a good move.

International funds, on the other hand, can add currency risk. Avoid funds that are not allowed to do currency hedging. Find out by reading the prospectus or asking the fund representatives. *Reason:* If the dollar rises, your international investments could be worth much less in dollars. *Better:* Buy global funds instead. They own international and U.S. stocks and usually hedge their currency bets.

● *Objectives.* I think preretirement and retirement portfolios should be different, but not radically so.

A conservative preretirement portfolio might be 50% equities and 50% bonds. After retirement, the objective might shift slightly to the income (bond) side. *Result:* 60% bonds, 40% equities. In each case, you need significant equity holdings to withstand inflation.

● *Choosing specific funds.* I swear by the three P's: *performance, people and process.*

● *Any single year of grossly subpar performance should raise a red flag.* When analyzing a fund's past performance, ignore cumulative returns. Focus instead on year-by-year returns. You want a fund that is consistently profitable. This means you'll buy funds that almost never finish in the top 10 in an up-market year. In general, these tortoise funds tend to perform slightly better than the middle of the pack, year after year.

Studies show that over time, the best pension-fund managers do slightly above average for a long period of time. The same managers should have been running the fund for at least three years.

A fund should have a disciplined, well-defined style. If it calls itself a large-cap value fund, that's what it should be. How can you tell? Call the fund and request semiannual and annual reports for the past five years. See if it has lived up to its designation. If, in the past two years, the fund has been loading up on small-cap growth stocks, this isn't the right place for your money.

Source: *Michael D. Hirsch, chairman of the M.D. Hirsch division of Freedom Capital Management, a firm managing more than $250 million in mutual funds through private accounts and the Fund Manager Trust family of funds. Mr. Hirsch is the author of* The Mutual Fund Wealth Builder: A Mutual Fund Strategy That Won't Let You Down No Matter What the Market Is Doing, *HarperBusiness.*

A Simple Case for Mutual Funds

There are at least 100 variables that may influence the future values of any security. How can the amateur investor balance those variables and decide how each will affect an investment? By following a simplified step-by-step decision-making process that seldom requires dealing with more than two variables at a time.

● *Stocks or bonds?* Historically, the Standard & Poor's 500 Index has outperformed bonds almost three to one. If you are confident you can invest in stocks successfully, this decision is not difficult—go with stocks.

● *Do it yourself or delegate?* Although many investors think they can beat the system, it's smart to delegate stock-investment decisions to professionals. Historical results indicate that professionals have the advantage.

● *Stockbroker or portfolio manager?* It's best to delegate the decision-making process to fee-based portfolio managers. Stockbrokers graduate to fee-based management only if they are successful—when you choose a portfolio manager, you have a better chance of getting someone with a proven record.

● *Private or public portfolio managers?* Most successful portfolio managers have minimum account sizes of $100,000 to $5,000,000. If you are a smaller investor, you have the option of joining forces with other investors, retaining some of the best portfolio managers and investing in publicly owned mutual funds. These funds offer diversification to protect you from stock risk. Also, most funds are members of a family of funds, each with a different investment objective. Once you have invested in a family of funds, switching back and forth between funds usually can be accomplished without a commission or fee.

● **What kind of fund is right for you?** If you are young and have many years to retirement, you may be best served by a growth-oriented mutual fund. If you are nearing retirement, a more conservative growth and income fund may be appropriate. At retirement, many investors seek the extreme safety of bond or income funds.

● **Load or no-load funds?** No-load funds make the most sense for most people. Load funds charge up-front commissions or expensive liquidation fees. No-load funds have no commission at the time of purchase and can be liquidated without penalty. To date, no-load funds have performed as well as load funds, so there is no reason to accept the extra burden of a load fund.

● **Buy and hold or use market timing?** If you make the decision to buy and hold a mutual fund, you are relying on the abilities of a portfolio manager to diversify your investment among stocks that will generally go up in bull markets and not go down in bear markets. Yet diversification will not protect a portfolio from the 25%–50% declines suffered in a major bear market.

The goal of market timing is to be in equity funds during market advances and safely moving to money-market funds during market declines. Market timing of no-load funds can cut the risk of investing by approximately 50%. Most market timers are in equity funds about half of the time, during which they are exposed to whatever risk or volatility factor each fund carries. The other half of the time the funds are in near-zero-risk money-market funds.

● **Do it yourself or professional market timing?** This decision depends on whether you have the ability, time and desire to manage your investments on a daily basis. Although there can be no guarantees of profitability, hiring a professional market timer relieves you of this obligation and allows you to concentrate on evaluating only his or her performance.

● **Newsletter or private management?** The key to market timing is the signal that instructs you either to be in equity funds or safely in money-market funds. Market-timing signals can be purchased from services that contact you through the mail or by telephone. Or,

for those who do not want the responsibility of tracking a newsletter or contacting mutual funds, there are a handful of managers who will perform the switching function without client involvement. A few private management services provide timing for accounts as small as $2,000, but most have minimum account sizes of $25,000 to $100,000.

Source: Paul A. Merriman, registered investment adviser and president of Paul A. Merriman & Associates, 1200 Westlake Ave. N, Suite 507, Seattle, WA 98109. The firm market times over $28 million of no-load mutual funds on a private management basis. Mr. Merriman is publisher and editor of The Fund Exchange *and the author of* Market Timing With No-Load Mutual Funds.

Selecting the Right Mutual Funds for Your Portfolio

Selecting the mutual fund that's best for you hinges on five basic rules:

1. Diversify.
2. Analyze performance over a long period of time.
3. Seek funds with continuity of investment style.
4. Use your money fund wisely.
5. Recognize mistakes.

Diversify

Even with mutual funds, it pays to diversify your portfolio. Select at least three basic types of mutual funds as your foundation. Choose among the broad groups of "growth" and "growth and income" funds for your portfolio's anchor. To satisfy your opportunistic side, add a "sector" fund (which invests exclusively in a particular area, such as technology, health care, finance or energy) or a "small company growth" fund. Maintain a money-market fund as your reserve.

Consider a "fixed-income" fund if you are building your portfolio in a tax-sheltered retirement plan—the high yield will compound your tax-deferred income. You may be able to capitalize on volatility of interest rates or make this fund the longer-term reserve element of your portfolio. But, don't remain in long-term fixed-income investments if inflation begins to reemerge.

Analyze Performance

Evaluate a fund's performance over a long period of time in order to analyze how a fund performs under varying market conditions. Does it rise faster than the general market, but fall faster too? Does it climb steadily and hold its ground well? How do these characteristics mesh with your strategy?

Go to the rating services to evaluate a fund or group of funds. *Rating services generally can be grouped into two types:* Quantitative and qualitative. The quantitative services measure performance results, using total return as their indicator. The other services provide advice on market timing and reveal general attitudes toward funds, particular groups of funds and/or fund managements.

Seek Continuity Of Style

Carefully read the fund's annual and interim reports, the proxy statement and statement of additional information. Call the president or the vice president of marketing of the fund for answers to these questions: Have there been important shifts in strategy? If so, when? How has this affected the fund's tactics? Did it help results? Have there been changes in personnel? Why? Who is the portfolio manager? For how long? If there have been any significant changes in style, strategy or personnel, it will be difficult to evaluate the past as a guide to future success. Be cautious.

> " If you want to pay taxes as you earn your money, then you are the most common investor....You don't worry about the largest investment cost, income taxes. "

Use Your Money Fund Wisely

Separate your cash-management money from your investment reserves. Emphasize convenience and service when selecting a money-market fund. The quality of the assets held in the portfolio is more important than the small difference in yield among money-market mutual funds. Also look for ability to exchange with other funds in a family of funds.

Recognize Mistakes

As with any other investment, cut your losses. Monitor your funds' strategies and their results. Most well-selected mutual funds will remain appropriate as

investments for a long time. However, opportunistic funds are more vulnerable to changes in the economy—monitor these funds very closely.

Sources: *A. Michael Lipper, CFA, president, Lipper Analytical Securities, Inc., 74 Trinity Place, New York, NY 10006, publisher of performance reports on the mutual-fund industry. Maureen J. Busby, CFA, president of Lipper Advisory Services, Inc., 322 East Michigan St., Milwaukee 53202, a registered investment adviser.*

Put Together the Right Mutual-Fund Portfolio for You

Today's sophisticated mutual-fund investment adviser has three basic decisions to make before building a mutual-fund portfolio:

1. When do I want to pay the income taxes on my investment profits each year—when I withdraw my money, or never?

2. Where are we in the investment cycles? Which type of investments should I choose?

3. What is my investment style? Am I a passive or an active investor?

With the answers to those three questions, you can create the right mutual-fund portfolio for you.

When Do I Want to Pay Income Taxes On My Investment Profits?

With most investors today having long-term investment goals (they won't need most of their investment principal for five to 10 years or more) the amount of money after income taxes is a primary concern.

Remember, when you retire, you will face the second half of your adult life. Today, if you survive to age 65, it is likely that you will survive to age 90. Those are sobering thoughts.

If you want to pay taxes as you earn your money, then you are the most typical investor. You worry about your investments day to day and don't worry about the largest investment cost, income taxes. This is the most common and most expensive way to invest.

Many investors have learned to concentrate their retirement investments into tax-deferred accounts:

employer retirement accounts, IRAs and annuities. This only defers the income taxes until they are withdrawn. After retirement there are many confusing restrictions, such as minimum withdrawals and penalties associated with this process. Often administrative accounting and legal costs can eat up part of the advantage of the deferral benefits.

Few investors have discovered and taken advantage of two plans, which provide for 100% income tax-free investment profits (including profits on stock and bond portfolios): the new Roth IRA Account and Variable Universal Life (VUL) Insurance, the hottest investment for the new Millennium. *When choosing among these investments, keep the following in mind:*

● *Variable annuities* are expensive ways to turn long-term capital gains into ordinary income. Very simply, investors pay insurance costs to grow their capital on a tax-deferred basis only to find that they are taxed at the higher ordinary income rate rather than the lower capital gains tax rates. Why pay extra to be taxed at a higher income tax rate?

● *Converting your IRAs and IRA rollovers into Roth IRA accounts makes sense only if you can afford to pay the income taxes required to cash in the IRA accounts.* The advantage to such a conversion is to allow you to increase the amount of tax-free profits you will be able to withdraw from the Roth IRA in five years or at retirement, whichever comes second. Consult your tax adviser before converting.

● *Considering the liquidity of VUL and (after five years and retirement) Roth IRAs, there is no reason for an individual to invest in a taxable account.* If you need money, either invest less each year and use the excess for your current needs, borrow (at zero or low interest rates) from your VUL account or withdraw from your Roth IRA (assuming you have held it five years and are over 59½).

● *All new IRA investment should be in Roth IRAs* rather than in traditional IRAs. Clearly, this will result in greater after-tax cash flow in your retirement.

● *Take full advantage of your employer's matching contributions* in your retirement plan before investing in any IRA. That matching contribution has a value greater than any tax advantage of a Roth IRA. Then invest in the Roth IRA if you can still afford it.

Where Are We in the Investment Cycle?

As I write this, the Dow-Jones Industrials are challenging the 10,000 level. Long-term investors must take note that this is a precarious time. One of two trends could emerge.

The Optimistic Forecast: Over 30% of 401(k) money (employee retirement savings) is being invested in company stock, and considerable additional money is being invested in the S&P 500 large capitalization index funds. That means that the demand for the stocks of larger companies (also the largest employers) is drawing a disproportionately large amount of new investment. When the market rises, this tends to make these stocks lead the market, and when the market declines, the new investment flow to these stocks tends to buoy up these same stocks.

With the Baby Boomers moving through the demographics like a pig through a python, this trend should make large capitalization stocks and S&P 500 index funds the more prudent and profitable investment for the coming decade. Given that unmanaged index funds have outperformed 89% of the managed stock funds over the past year, index funds appear to be excellent investments for buy and hold investors. *Strategy:* Invest in Vanguard 500 Index Fund, the lowest-cost index fund. This could be a volatile investment in the short term, but given the above economic scenario, this could be the best investment in the long term. This strategy might not be for the faint of heart.

The Pessimistic Forecast: The stock market, no matter how attractive it has been, is vulnerable to both economic and non-economic events, which could send it into a tailspin. *Examples:* the India-Pakistan nuclear threat, a government anti-trust victory against Microsoft or the failure of the government to balance its budget with a big tobacco settlement. *Strategy:* Invest in Rydex or Pro-Funds index funds that allow you to invest in funds that are engineered to perform between plus-or-minus-two times the S&P 500. In effect, you could construct a portfolio that could make money in a dramatic market decline or make it back in a dramatic market rally. This can be a risky strategy if your timing is not perfect; however, it may be prudent for part of your portfolio.

What Is My Investment Style?

- **Are you willing to roll with the punches and buy-and-hold?** Then S&P 500 index funds are probably the best choice for you.

- **Are you willing to trade your portfolio actively?** Then a fund family with an assortment of index funds is probably best for you.

- **Are you somewhere in between?** Most investors are. Your best choice is to use asset allocation to spread your risks. *You can build your portfolio from some of the following choices:*

Vanguard 500 Index Fund. Unless your portfolio is managed by a professional, you should consider riding out the market's ups and downs in an unmanaged index fund. *You can reduce the risk of your portfolio by using low-risk, high-return strategies:*

Gateway Fund. This fund is a conservative option income fund that has a reliable track record and a very low volatility record. The more of this fund in your portfolio, the lower the volatility.

A managed portfolio of high-yield bond funds can be a big help to investors. High-yield ("junk") bond funds have historically provided investors with very attractive returns and nowhere near the risk that the junk-bond name implies. If you can find a manager who has the discipline to accept a very narrow band of volatility, there is an excellent chance that you can avoid the few times that these funds have experienced extreme volatility and risk. It's sort of like breaking a wild horse so children can ride it. This can be the best deal in the bond markets.

Money Funds. Sometimes, it can be a very

FOR CONSERVATIVE INVESTORS

The best deals for conservative investors searching for high yields without significant principal risk are managed high-yield bond fund portfolios. First of all, these so-called "junk"-bond portfolios have greatly reduced the risks associated with the "Mike Milkin Bond" period (when more marginal issuers were encouraged to offer junk bonds for marginal purposes) of the early 1990s. Most of those earlier high-yield bonds are no longer considered investment quality. In fact, it can be argued that investing in a high-yield bond fund is much safer than investing in high-yield bonds because the fund can buy a better-quality bond, do better and more selective research among the thousands of offerings and invest larger amounts in the more liquid (at a fair price and narrower spread)

issuances. Investing in a no-load high-yield bond fund makes even more sense. *Advantages:* First, this type of fund can be better diversified among investment styles. Second, the fund managers can have an investment discipline that will tolerate only very limited amounts of volatility. Finally, such portfolios have long-term track records to demonstrate their success.

A new wrinkle in this investment strategy is a *managed high-yield municipal bond fund portfolio.* With most of its dividends exempt from state or federal income taxes (depending on the client's needs), it can allow certain investors the ability to sidestep the $55,000 taxable income limit above

which Social Security payments are taxable without reducing after-tax income significantly. The way to avoid taxable income is to earn income that is not taxable.

Bottom line: Conservative investors should consider increasing after-tax returns and reducing investment risk and volatility by considering managed high-yield bond-fund portfolios. These are among the most imaginative and liquid conservative investment choices in recent years.

Source: William E. Donoghue, publisher of Bill Donoghue's WealthLetter *(free sample issue on request), chairman of W. E. Donoghue & Co., Inc., registered investment advisers, and author of* Donoghue's Mutual Fund Super-Stars, *Elliott & James, Box 360, 100 Medway Road, Suite 401, Milford, MA 01757, 800-982-2455.*

Investing to Win

aggressive strategy to reduce your exposure to a vulnerable stock market simply by investing in virtually risk-free money-market mutual funds. The greater the position in money funds, the lower the risk of the portfolio. No individual has ever lost money investing in a modern money fund. *Additional "common sense" risk-reduction strategies include:*

● *Avoiding funds that charge commissions.* If you invest in a fund with a 5% load or a 5% back-end load (contingent deferred sales charge) and hold it for only six months because the stock market declined and you wanted to reduce your risks, the annual cost would be 10%. The greater the load, the greater the added principal risk.

● *Spreading your risk over several funds.* In the stock market, the index funds are the exception to this rule. When you invest in one unmanaged index fund, you are diversifying better than investing in five or more managed stock funds. Since index funds are beating the pants off of most managed funds, the only reasons to invest in managed funds is to find funds that can beat the index or have a lower downside risk.

● *Invest very selectively in international funds.* Right now European stock funds are performing well and Asian stock funds have been a disaster. The "Asian Contagion" is complicated by Japan's extremely low interest rates, which allow investors to leverage their positions and increase the volatility of the region. Europe is about five years behind the United States in downsizing and has some nice growth potential.

● *Refuse to stick with losers.* If your stock fund is not performing well, shift your money into an index fund.

Source: *William E. Donoghue, publisher of* Bill Donoghue's WealthLetter *(free sample issue on request), chairman of W. E. Donoghue & Co., Inc., registered investment advisers, and author of* Donoghue's Mutual Fund SuperStars, *Elliott & James, Box 360, 100 Medway Road, Suite 401, Milford, MA 01757, 800-982-2455.*

Mutual-Fund Selection Secrets

It's most important when picking mutual funds first to define your investment objective. Investors are interested mostly in preserving capital they already have (and invest for income) or they want primarily to increase their capital (growth). Few people shoot for 100% income or 100% growth, but you should choose a fund with investment objectives that are your own.

● *Identify several top-performing no-load funds that pursue your objective.* Helpful: *Handbook for No-Load Fund Investors,* and *Morningstar Mutual Funds.* Both are available at public libraries.

● *Analyze performance in-depth.* Don't just glance at overall five- or 10-year returns. For stock funds, look for 10 years of annual gains that have consistently beaten the Standard & Poor's 500 stock index in up and down years. If a stock fund did badly in 1973, 1974, 1977, 1981–1982, 1987, 1990 and 1994, it may perform poorly when the next bear market hits. For bond funds, compare performance to an index that matches the maturity of your fund. Generally, it is best to stick with short-term and intermediate-term funds.

● *Opt for consistency.* If two funds have similar returns but one's share price swings widely while the other's is relatively stable, go for the least volatile. *Reason:* If you suddenly have to sell your shares, there's less risk they'll be significantly depressed.

● *Investigate the current portfolio manager.* Is the person managing the fund responsible for the fabulous gains of the past 10 years? Or has the star performer moved on to manage another fund? *Little known:* Many of the top-gun investment advisers who require a prohibitively large personal portfolio ($1 million or more) before they'll accept your business also manage mutual funds. You may be able to tap their brainpower with a tiny fraction of that amount.

● *Think small.* Mutual funds with more than $1 billion in assets have a harder time producing superior results because they must invest in larger, more lethargic companies.

Dangerous pattern: A fund becomes a hot performer and suddenly receives a tidal wave of cash, the manager is forced from small stocks into big ones and the exciting returns evaporate.

● *Don't invest in new funds.* They don't have a track record.

● *Don't accept biased advice.* Brokers and financial planners who recommend funds often receive a commission when you buy in. Take their advice only if the funds they suggest meet the criteria outlined above.

● **Don't jump in and out of funds.** Professional investment advisers know that for growth, they must be in the market at all times—although the percentage of their portfolios kept in the market may vary depending on the outlook. For most people, market timing is a risky business and highly impractical.

Source: Kurt Brouwer, president of Brouwer & Janachowski, Inc., a San Francisco-based investment company managing over $500 million for corporate and private investors. He is the author of Kurt Brouwer's Guide to Mutual Funds, *Wiley. He has written for* Forbes, Barron's *and the* San Francisco Chronicle.

How to See Through Murky Advertising of Mutual Funds

Mutual-fund advertising often confuses investors—whether or not funds intend to do so. Mutual-fund advertising is actually more heavily regulated than advertising in banking, but most consumers are more familiar with personal banking than fund investing and are easily led astray.

Mutual funds and bank accounts are completely different animals. While a bank can promise you a federally insured account with a fixed yield, the stability of principal and rate of return in a mutual fund depend on market factors and can't be guaranteed. All numbers that appear in mutual-fund ads describe only past performance.

Potentially Misleading

● **Track records.** Every fund tells the best story that it has—but all the stories are different. *Example:* One fund claims, "We're up 200% in the last four years," while another says, "We're up 250% in the last five years." Both claims are true, but they can't be compared meaningfully. *To make a significant comparison:* You have to compare funds' performance data for the same periods (available in the prospectuses or by phone from the funds).

Editor's note: Just about all funds today may have glowing track records for two reasons. First, their performance during the crash of 1987 is no longer part of their 10-year record. Second, until the third quarter in 1998, there have been unprecedented returns in bull markets in the past three years.

● **"Current" yields.** The numbers in magazine ads are often two to five weeks old.

Trap: Using old yields to compare bond funds.

● **Load (sales charge) status.** Unfortunately, funds aren't simply "load" (with a sales charge) or "no-load." Some are pure no-load funds and have no initial or deferred sales charge and no redemption fee—but many others carry one or more of the above. Initial sales charges run as high as 8.5%, but are usually 4%–6%.

Deceptive: funds advertised as "no-load" that charge you a fee when you sell your shares. This can be done through a contingent deferred sales charge, which runs as high as 6% if you sell shares within the first year of ownership (it usually declines by one percentage point each year thereafter). The charge is generally explained only in the fine print of the prospectus.

The other back-end charge: a fixed redemption fee—usually 1% to 2%—which applies no matter how long shares are held.

● **12b-1 plans.** The Securities & Exchange Commission allows funds to charge an annual fee to pay for advertising and distribution costs—as high as .25%.

Self-defense: Compare performance *after* the fee has been taken into account.

● **"100% insured" and "government guaranteed."** Many bond funds purchase issues whose principal and interest are guaranteed by a private insurer or federal, state or local governments, but bond funds themselves—unlike bank accounts—are *never insured or government-backed*.

Risk: If interest rates go up, the shares of all bond funds—even those of U.S. Treasury bonds—will fall in value.

● **Phantom income.** Under tax reform, because of the way in which mutual funds are structured, they have to report to the IRS more taxable income than they pay to shareholders. *Sample result:* If you earn 8%, you may have to pay taxes on 8.5%. The fund retains half a percentage point for its expenses—which the IRS considers taxable income paid to you.

Funds aren't required to disclose in ads the percentage of phantom income reported, but this number must appear in the prospectus.

● **Switching costs.** Some fund families charge $5 every time you move money from one fund to another. Others offer a limited number of free switches per year and charge per switch beyond that limit.

IRA trap: Many fund families charge IRA accounts a $10 annual fee for each fund in which the IRA has

HOW TO READ A MUTUAL-FUND PROSPECTUS

Once you've narrowed down the vast number of mutual funds available to a few top performers, send for the prospectus and annual report prepared by each. The prospectus is required to disclose any information that would be needed to make an informed decision regarding investment in the fund. The annual report must contain the financial reports on the fund, but may include other information as well. A fund's "statement of additional information," which you can also request, provides detailed information on the fund and its practices.

Use these reports to determine how well each fund you have tentatively selected compares to your particular investment goals and preferences. The following checklist will guide you in covering a fund's most important characteristics.

● **Date of inception.** A fund that has existed less than one year is difficult to judge since, technically, it doesn't have a performance record. At times, it may be possible to rely on the record of the new fund's manager to gauge performance, but older funds are obviously going to give you more to go on.

● **Investment adviser's performance history.** The big question here is whose performance record is being relied on for the period being measured? Traditionally, a record belongs to the person or persons who are responsible for buying and selling securities during a particular period of time. Occasionally a fund will have an excellent long-term record in spite of

changing advisers. In this case, the record may be credited to the person(s) selecting the advisers.

Information on registered investment advisers is a matter of public record. Each adviser must file a Form ADV with the Securities & Exchange Commission. A fund may be willing to provide this information if requested.

● **External advisers.** Since advisory fees tend to be among the largest of a fund's expenses, any fund that hires outside advisers tends to have a higher expense ratio than those depending on in-house staff. However, if performance indicates that the fund has benefited from external advisers, the expense may be justified.

● **Expense ratio.** The average mutual-fund expense ratio will be 1% or less. If the ratio is greater than 1%, try to determine the cause in order to make a judgment about whether the expense results in any added value. A good place to check for the cause is the management or advisory fee, since generally this is a mutual fund's largest expense.

● **Turnover ratio.** This figure indicates the level of trading in a fund's security holdings. If the ratio is greater than 75% to 100%, the fund's expense ratio and, ultimately, shareholder's return may be adversely affected by high transaction expenses.

A high turnover ratio may be acceptable in one situation—specifically, a change in advisers. A new adviser will often sell many of the securities pur-

chased before his or her appointment. This may be beneficial to a fund particularly if poor performance was the reason for the change in advisers.

● **Fund's portfolio.** The prospectus will reveal what kinds of securities are being invested in and how diversified the portfolio is. Diversification usually reduces risk. So a sector fund, investing in securities in a single industry, will be riskier than a general stock fund.

● **Total assets under management.** Large fund groups can take advantage of certain economies of scale by spreading their costs over a larger asset base. On the other side of the coin, smaller funds—with about $100 million in total assets—often find it easier to locate and purchase high-quality investments. Smaller funds can also change direction more quickly than the large funds if circumstances warrant it.

● **Other fees.** Many funds charge fees for processing certain kinds of shareholder transactions. This is especially true for IRAs. All charges should be explained in the fund's prospectus.

● **Shareholder services.** These vary considerably among funds. Some funds, particularly those that are part of a large fund group, offer almost every conceivable service from check writing to telephone transactions. Other funds are strictly invest-by-mail organizations.

Source: Elizabeth A. Watson, formerly assistant to the chairman and assistant treasurer, the Ivy Fund.

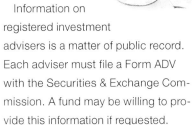

Investing to Win

invested during the year. So just three switches could cost $40 in IRA fees. And if your money isn't in a tax-deferred account, remember that when you switch out of a fund in which you have made a capital gain, you must pay income tax on that gain (up to 20%).

Source: *William E. Donoghue, publisher of* Bill Donoghue's WealthLet-ter *(free sample issue on request), chairman of W. E. Donoghue & Co., Inc., registered investment advisers, and author of* Donoghue's Mutual Fund SuperStars, *Elliott & James, Box 360, 100 Medway Road, Suite 401, Milford, MA 01757, 800-982-2455.*

How to Get Money Out of A Mutual Fund...Quickly

Most mutual-fund investors don't think about getting their money out of a fund when they put it in. Too often, when financial markets dip and they want to redeem their shares, they find that getting their money back is time-consuming, frustrating and sometimes costly. *Reasons:*

● **The phones are tied up.** Mutual-fund offices can be so inundated with orders to buy and sell shares that their switchboards may be busy at critical times. When you call requesting information about how to redeem shares, you may have to let the telephone ring for a few minutes before someone answers.

● **The procedures for redeeming shares are bureaucratic.** With most funds, you must not only write a redemption letter requesting a check for the value of your investment, but you must also have your signature guaranteed by a commercial bank or by your broker. That can be time-consuming, especially if you bought your shares directly from the fund instead of through a broker, and you don't happen to have an account with a commercial bank. Notarized signatures aren't acceptable and most funds will refuse to accept guarantees from savings and loan institutions. If your personal bank is an S&L, you'll have to go to a commercial bank with which your bank has established a relationship to have your signature guaranteed.

To avoid these obstacles:

● ***Make a copy of the section of the fund prospectus that refers to redemption procedures*** —and keep it handy. That way you won't have to make a phone call to get information on redemption procedures.

● ***Prepare a redemption letter in advance.*** Have your signature guaranteed by your broker or commercial bank so you can simply date the letter whenever

Mutual-Fund Sales Charges

Beware of funds that charge redemption fees. They're not the same as deferred sales charges. *Reason:* A redemption fee is a percentage of the value of your investment at the time of redemption. A deferred sales charge is a percentage of the initial investment but paid upon redemption. *Result:* Funds that charge deferred sales fees leave you with more money. *Example:* A $10,000 investment that doubles in value will be redeemed at $19,400 if the fund charges a 3% redemption fee (3% of $20,000 = $600). But a fund that has a 3% deferred sales charge will reduce the value of the $20,000 investment by only $300 upon redemption.

Source: *Norman G. Fosback, editor,* Income & Safety.

you decide to pull out of the fund. Follow prospectus instructions for writing a redemption letter (usually, all you need to do is request that a check be sent to your home address, and give the number of shares owned, and your account number). Send the letter by fax, or send a day letter using overnight mail.

● ***Consider buying shares only in stock or bond funds*** managed by firms that also have money-market funds to which you can switch part of or all of your account by telephone. That way you have access to the money via money-market-account checks, usually within two days.

Caution: It's always a good idea to call in a switch as early in the day as possible, because after 3 P.M. on heavy-volume days, many fund offices can be especially busy. *Helpful:* Many funds now allow investors to transfer their money via computer. Check with your fund to see if you can register online for this service.

● ***When you fill out the forms to purchase fund***

shares, complete the section for authorizing wire transfers of redemptions to your bank. That service allows you to have shares redeemed and the proceeds deposited directly in your checking or savings account, usually on the same day you make the request. If you need the money fast and you have trouble getting through by phone, you can request a bank transfer in a redemption letter sent by overnight mail.

Source: Sheldon Jacobs, editor, publisher, **The No-Load Fund Investor,** *and president of the BJ Group, a money management company.*

How to Buy a Money Fund

Money funds offer instant liquidity, full market rates of interest, check writing and a high degree of safety. Nevertheless, there are differences among money funds, and investors need to know those differences before buying.

Yield

Money funds are mutual funds that invest their shareholders' assets in high-quality government and corporate securities, and in bank deposits. Their operating expenses are relatively low—all it takes to run a money fund is a portfolio manager, a computer, and a staff of telephone operators. As a result, money funds are usually able to pass through to shareholders upwards of 99% of their gross investment income.

Money funds can have the upper hand over banks. Banks have hefty overhead expenses, capital construction costs for buildings and stockholders who demand profits. Larger, efficient money funds therefore can afford superior managers, attract more shareholders and offer yields consistently superior to yields on consumer money-market accounts at banks and thrifts.

Most newspapers report money-fund yields on a weekly basis, but be careful when judging the results: Various funds compute their yields differently. Merrill Lynch, for example, uses a computation method that results in volatile yields that can be extremely high one week and very low the next. The best policy is to ask money funds for their average yields over the last several months.

If you're a high-tax-bracket investor, put your money in a fund that specializes in short-term municipal securities. The returns are fully exempt from federal taxation.

Unlike money-market accounts in a major bank, money mutual funds are not entirely risk-free. Still, the money fund industry's record for safety has been relatively solid. In the late 1970s a few large funds such as First Multifund for Daily Income and Dreyfus Liquid Assets took a bath and investors in the former took a loss. To avoid disaster, pay close attention to the phases of the economic cycle and to the following three factors.

● ***The quality of a fund's portfolio.*** Some funds own exclusively U.S. Treasury bills, the safest investment. Most other funds buy high-quality bank deposits and corporate securities. The highest-risk funds attempt to boost their yields by purchasing low-quality securities, such as low-grade or unrated commercial paper and certificates of deposit of small banks. Pay careful attention to the percentage of a fund's assets made up of these high-risk investments.

● ***Average portfolio maturity.*** The maturity of investments in a typical taxable money fund is between 25 and 60 days. The average maturity of tax-free money-fund investments is normally about twice that. Watch out for funds that extend their portfolio maturity significantly beyond the industry average. These funds are probably trying to lock in higher yields from longer-maturing investments. If interest rates rise sharply, the value of longer-maturing securities can decline, resulting in losses to money-fund investors.

● ***Portfolio disclosure.*** Money funds are required to publish details of their portfolios only twice a year. Since typical fund investments mature in just a couple of months, much can happen in a six-month period that goes unreported. Before buying any money fund, ask for a current or very recent portfolio. Avoid funds that refuse to comply.

Service

Money funds offer a broad range of shareholder services. Be sure to check them thoroughly before investing. Minimum initial investments are usually quite low, typically about $1,000. Most funds offer nearly unlimited and free check-writing privileges, subject only to a minimum check amount of $250 or $500. Some funds don't have any minimum at all. Most funds can also establish special accounts for IRAs, Keoghs and other retirement plans.

Liquidity is the greatest service. Investors can get their money back from a fund at any time without penalty. Interest is fully credited to accounts right up to the day of withdrawal.

It is actually easier to open a money-fund account than it is to open a bank account. Investors can call most money funds from their home or office on toll-free telephone numbers to obtain an account form, a prospectus and a current portfolio. Many money funds are also set up to handle wire transfers.

For investors who like to play the market, most money funds have relationships with other mutual funds that invest in stocks, bonds and other securities. A phone call can usually switch an investment from a money fund to another type of fund or vice versa.

Source: Norman G. Fosback, editor, Income & Safety.

Money-Market and Mutual Funds

A complete list for individual investors (there are more than 6,000 funds) is available for $8.50 from The Investment Company Institute, 1401 H St. NW, Washington, DC 20005.

Safer Than Banks

Investors suffering from high anxiety are turning more and more to the safest investment there is: U.S. Treasury securities.

Treasury bills (maturing within one year), notes (maturing in two to 10 years) and bonds (maturing after 10 years) are actually safer than government-insured bank accounts.

Trap: There's only 1¢ in government insurance for every dollar of insured bank accounts. *Even worse:* Some of the insurance funds aren't in cash, but in illiquid receivables accepted from troubled banks.

By contrast, every penny of a T-bill is guaranteed

by the full faith and credit of the federal government. And the government has *never* failed to pay its obligations.

Bonus: Liquidity, especially if they're purchased through a mutual fund that offers check-writing privileges. *Special tax status:* T-bills, notes and bonds bought by individuals aren't subject to state income taxes. When these securities are purchased through a mutual fund, 25 of the 40 income tax states levy a tax.

Source: James M. Benham, chairman, Benham Capital Management Group, 755 Page Mill Rd., Palo Alto, CA 94304.

Ginnie Maes Vs. Treasury Bonds

When interest rates are likely to drop, you're better off investing in Treasury securities than in higher-coupon Ginnie Mae bonds. *Reason:* As rates move down, the mortgages backing the Ginnie Mae bonds will be paid off, thereby reducing the return to Ginnie Mae investors. But Treasury bonds can't be paid off early, so buying bonds will produce capital appreciation as lower rates make bonds more valuable.

Source: John Rutledge, chairman, Claremont Economics Institute, writing in his Main Street Journal.

CD Savvy

● **Customers who deposit more than $50,000** into a certificate of deposit (CD) can usually negotiate their own maturity date and when and how interest will be paid. *Not negotiable:* minimum penalty for early withdrawal. That is mandated by federal law.

● **Buy several CDs in small denominations** instead of one large one. *Reason:* If you need only part of the money, you won't have to withdraw it all and pay an early-withdrawal penalty on the full amount.

Source: William E. Donoghue, publisher of Bill Donoghue's WealthLetter *(free sample issue on request)*, chairman of W. E. Donoghue & Co., Inc., registered investment advisers, and author of Donoghue's Mutual Fund SuperStars, *Elliott & James, Box 360, 100 Medway Road, Suite 401, Milford, MA 01757, 800-982-2455.*

Investing in Mortgage-Backed Securities

Pass-through securities based on pools of mortgages are attracting investors interested in higher yields than those from comparable fixed-maturity securities. The size of the yields is the trade-off for variable cash flows and maturities and for the accounting problems associated with holding these securities.

Mortgage-backed securities reflect the underlying

cash flows of their respective pools of mortgages. The mortgages produce monthly payments of principal and interest, but monthly prepayments can vary. This unknown factor is largely a product of fluctuations in interest rates.

When interest rates are declining, mortgage holders generally speed up prepayments, effectively shortening the maturity of the pass-through security. For the investor, this means reinvesting the capital sooner—at the current lower rate. Conversely, as interest rates increase, prepayments decrease. The maturity of the security is lengthened just at the time the investor wants to shorten it to protect his or her capital.

> **" As an agency of the U.S. government, Ginnie Mae guarantees the timely payment of principal and interest for FHA and VA mortgages submitted to it by mortgage originators. "**

The accounting problems attached to mortgage-backed securities stem from the need to keep track of monthly cash flows. For example, the investor must reduce his or her cost basis by the return of principal, calculate whether there is a profit or loss and whether it is short-term or long-term. Also, the amount of the monthly interest—as opposed to principal—payment must be accurately recorded. Nevertheless, the yield spread on these pass-throughs makes them very attractive.

Government-Sponsored Securities

While any institution may pool mortgages and sell interests in those pools, the three best-known sources of mortgage-backed pass-throughs are the *Government National Mortgage Association*, also known as GNMA or Ginnie Mae; *the Federal Home Loan Mortgage Corporation*, FHLMC or Freddie Mac; and the *Federal National Mortgage Association*, FNMA or Fannie Mae.

As an agency of the U.S. government, Ginnie Mae guarantees the timely payment of principal and interest for FHA and VA mortgages submitted to it

by mortgage originators. The mortgages are pooled by Ginnie Mae and sold to investors. Freddie Mac, a corporation owned by the Federal Home Loan banks, provides its guarantee to those mortgages submitted to it for pooling. Fannie Mae is a federally sponsored, publicly owned corporation that also guarantees the cash flow of the mortgages behind its pass-through securities. Thus, while all of the mortgage pools are guaranteed by each entity, only Ginnie Mae is backed by the full faith and credit of the U.S. government.

The three government-sponsored securities provide investors several advantages: Mortgage quality is standardized, there is geographic distribution within pools and the size of origination is conducive to an active and liquid secondary market in mortgage-backed securities.

Mutual Funds

Mutual funds of mortgage-backed pass-throughs have made it possible for more investors to enjoy the benefits of these securities. The $25,000 minimum investments for government-sponsored securities close the primary market to the small investor, but also prevent even the large investor from plowing back cash flows as they are received, thus reducing total return. Mutual funds have lower minimums for both initial and subsequent investments.

They also simplify the accounting process, provide professional management, offer diversification and, by pooling the funds of many investors, reduce the markups entailed in buying and selling the securities. For a fee, the mutual funds turn a complicated investment into a relatively simple—and profitable—one for all types of investors.

Source: Jack H. Lemein, vice president and portfolio manager, Franklin Resources, Inc., Box 5994, San Mateo, CA 94402.

Gold vs. Inflation— Gold vs. Deflation

Gold is an investor's best insurance against the changing value of money. It's common knowledge that gold tends to appreciate in value during inflationary periods, just like other tangibles such as collectibles, precious gems and real estate. *Little known:* The price of gold also rises in deflationary times.

Deflation usually occurs when people get themselves so deeply in debt that they must produce and sell increasing quantities of goods and services to raise the money to meet their interest payments. As more and more goods and services get dumped on the market, their prices fall and the real value of cash rises.

At first glance, it would seem that in this scenario the price of gold would go down. *Reason:* People with gold would sell it to raise cash to make interest payments. But this logic doesn't take into account the complexity of the financial system. The price of gold would actually rise. *How:* In a severe deflation, widespread default on bank debt would cause a rapid erosion of confidence in the bank system. Panicked investors would convert cash into gold, boosting the price of the metal. This buying would counter the selling of gold to raise cash to pay down debt.

To restore confidence in the financial system, as a last resort, central banks would have to raise the price of gold to such a high level that gold holders

SHOULD YOU INVEST IN ART?

Art should be purchased because it provides pleasure, not because it may appreciate. Historically, the art market has been unstable and, generally, unpredictable. *It progresses in cycles:* What is desirable today may be undesirable tomorrow. Due to the number of variables involved in these cycles, it is best not to classify art as a sound financial investment.

Investment-Quality Art
For any work of art to become a good investment, it must be able to stand the test of time. The value of an item rarely appreciates overnight. Instead its value develops over a period of time, often after decades have elapsed.

Art that does appreciate is usually an outstanding example of a specific type of art. It becomes investment-quality because of its uniqueness and because it exemplifies the artist's style and period.

Trying to find these examples on today's art market is difficult. When they do appear, they are generally sought by museums, major institutions and established collectors. Most contemporary art available for purchase has not met the test of time or uniqueness.

Be especially careful of purchasing prints as an investment. In general, contemporary art that is mass-produced does not appreciate. Most prints, whether they are designated lithographs, serigraphs, etchings, mezzotints or something else, are simply prints on pieces of paper containing an artist's signature.

There may be thousands of these prints available from a given work. Only a minute percentage of them will ever appreciate. Remember that an original is always more valuable than a mass-produced duplicate.

The Best Reasons for Acquisition
Art is an expression of a given artist. It is something that conveys a message, a thought or a feeling. If you are interested in acquiring a work of art that may appreciate, ask yourself not only whether it has stood the test of time and is unique, but also whether it conveys anything to you.

Do not allow your judgment to be clouded because an item appears to be increasing in value. Disregard advice that says it is a good investment. Some dealers will tell you, "This is a great investment." Do not let them persuade you. If it is such a great investment, why is it still on the market, or why hasn't the dealer added it to his or her private collection?

Buy a work of art because it appeals to you and you feel that it will bring you pleasure. These should be your primary reasons for acquisition.

Source: Richard Friedman, president, auctioneer and appraiser, Chicago Art Galleries, Inc., 5039 Oakton Street, Skokie, IL 60077. He is a member of the Appraisers Association of America, the International Society of Appraisers and the American Arbitration Association, Panel of Arbitrators.

would finally be willing to sell it in exchange for paper money. This occurred in the deflation of the 1930s, when the government had to boost the price of gold by about 70%—to $35 an ounce—to stabilize the financial system.

How to Buy Gold

● *Gold coins are the most convenient way for most people to buy gold.*

Best: The Mexican Gold Peso and Austrian Gold Crown, whose prices closely reflect their gold content. Collectors' coins, such as the American Eagle, carry a significant numismatic premium.

● *Gold-mining stock mutual funds.*

● *Gold-mining stocks.* On the surface, the best value are the blue-chip South African shares. But given South Africa's political troubles, they're high-risk.

Source: John Hathaway, principal, Hudson Capital Advisers, 3 E. 54 St., New York, NY 10022. The firm advises wealthy individuals and corporate pension funds.

Why Rubies, Emeralds and Sapphires Are a Safer Investment Than Diamonds

When prices of investment-grade diamonds plunged as much as 30%, colored gemstones magically held on to heady price gains. *Reason:* Scarcity. Only some $200 million in rubies, emeralds, and sapphires were sold in the United States in a recent year, a fraction of the amount of diamonds sold.

The areas where the finest stones come from: Cambodia, Thailand, Sri Lanka, Burma and parts of Africa. *Scarcity factor:* These areas are politically unstable and, therefore, are not reliable sources.

● *Grading.* Although techniques in grading colored stones are less advanced than those for diamonds, tests under microscopes and refractometers allow gemologists to distinguish synthetic stones from real ones. They can often tell you the origin of the stone. Certain countries of origin command higher prices. *Example:* Burma rubies.

● *Flaws.* Although all stones have flaws, gross flaws ruin the stone.

● *Setting.* Determine whether the setting does justice to the stone. Does it overwhelm the stone?

● *Color.* It is the most important determinant of price once the stone is adjudged authentic. Never view a single stone. Compare it with several others. *Reason:* The clarity of the redness of a ruby, and the absence of orange, pink, purple or brown, is what makes it most valuable. The variation is best seen by looking at several stones.

A family-owned jewelry retailer with an excellent reputation is the best place to buy. It is willing to risk its own money investing in fine gems from around the world. Larger chains of jewelers can't afford to invest. They custom-order.

In small towns without direct access to a large selection of colored gemstones, go to reputable jewelers and commission them to find the kind of stone you like and can afford. Many fine jewelers have connections with the American Gem Society, which will send them a selection of stones for conditional purchase. The jewelers receive a commission for their advice and service.

The best gems to buy are stones over one carat that are free of externally visible flaws. Buy one that will look good mounted in jewelry. That way, if the investment does not gain in value, at least you will have a remarkable piece of jewelry, not just a stone in a glass case.

Expect to keep a colored gem for at least five years, when buying for investment. Then evaluate what the stone would go for on the dealers' (wholesale) market. *Alternative:* Put stones up for auction at Sotheby's or Christie's. Although you cannot be sure of a definite sales price, you can put a minimum price on your item.

Bronze and Marble Sculpture

If you plan to buy a bronze sculpture strictly for decoration or sentiment, don't hesitate. If you plan to buy it as an investment—think twice. The bronze market is flooded with reproductions and prices have begun to fall, because the reproductions are so good that they are almost indistinguishable from the originals.

On the other hand, if you plan to buy a bronze sculpture because you wish to own an original by a famous artist or artisan, make certain that you go to a reputable dealer or auction house. If you are not knowledgeable, always seek expert advice.

Old and New Bronze

An original will be accompanied by a history, or provenance. It will have been authenticated as an original work of the artist. *Be prepared:* Since old original bronze castings have all but disappeared from art market inventories, an original reproduction will probably also have a high price.

Because of the flood of reproductions into the marketplace, many serious collectors have turned away from the eighteenth-, nineteenth- and early-twentieth-century masters. They are now more interested in modern and contemporary masters. As a result, these works are bringing record auction prices.

To acquire the work of a modern master, watch the auction market carefully for artists' works that rise in value. Good sources of information are magazines such as *Art & Auction* and *Art & Antiques. Art News, ADEC Art Price Annual* and Mayer's *International Auction Records* are also valuable sources.

Marble and Alabaster

Unlike bronze sculptures, marble and alabaster sculptures are difficult to reproduce and relatively few copies have been made. Consequently, sculptures in these materials that appear on the market have increased in value.

Some marble and alabaster pieces of fine quality are available at less than exorbitant prices. Many late-nineteenth- and early-twentieth-century works—good examples of the work of French, German, American and Italian artisans—can be obtained at estate sales.

Source: *Richard Friedman, president, auctioneer and appraiser, Chicago Art Galleries, Inc., 5039 Oakton Street, Skokie, IL 60077. He is a member of the Appraisers Association of America, the International Society of Appraisers and the American Arbitration Association, Panel of Arbitrators.*

Finding Good Sources And Honest Dealers for Collectibles

How do you locate the best dealer or source for collectibles? Whether you are interested in paintings, sculpture, silver or antique furniture, most major cities have a range of sources, including auction houses, dealers specializing in particular items, art galleries and wholesale/retail stores.

To find out which of these are good sources and honest dealers:

● ***Make inquiries of persons*** who have dealt with businesses in your area of interest.

● ***Ask opinions of dealers in the trade.***

● ***Check with the local Better Business Bureau*** for information about local business practices.

● ***Study publications,*** such as *Dun & Bradstreet,* which provide specific information on corporate conditions and credit ratings of individual firms.

Buying at Auction

Auction houses are excellent sources for collectibles, antiques and works of art. They usually have their own experts who can answer questions and advise you. Their auction catalogs give valuable information on the history, provenance and condition of the items that are for sale. *Note:* The conditions of sale will be published in the catalog. Read them carefully—each auction house has its own set of conditions.

Trust officers of banks can be one of the best sources of information on the reliability of auction houses. Why? They are often called upon to liquidate estates through auction. Also, a variety of magazines and newspapers publish information on auctions. Among the more widely read magazines are *Art & Auction, Art & Antiques, Connoisseur* and *Antique Monthly.* Some newspapers that publish information about auctions are *The New York Times, The Boston Globe, The San Francisco Examiner, The Washington Post, The Chicago Tribune, Antique Week* and *Maine Antiques Digest.*

Buying from a Dealer

If you don't have connections with the art world, magazines and newspapers are a good place to start when searching for a reputable dealer. The more prestigious magazines are selective in their choice of advertisers. You can expect that the dealers who are accepted as advertisers have been checked out and are generally reliable. Still, it is prudent to investigate them. Make inquiries to publishers, editors and critics of these publications.

Seek the opinions of those in the trade. Ask dealers

their opinions about the reliability of other dealers. Look for dealers with connections to public and private institutions such as museums and banking establishments. Ask the curators of these institutions who they use for the acquisition of works of art for collections.

In addition to helping you locate the item you want, a reputable dealer will always try to answer questions. If an answer is not readily available, he or she will assist you in finding it.

Dealers sometimes allow you to purchase an item on approval. If, within a designated period of time, the item is not what you want, you may return it at no charge. Reputable dealers usually issue a certificate of authenticity for an item they sell. Some dealers also offer guarantees—others offer exchange privileges that hold for a particular period of time. Find out about the dealer's policy in these areas before making a purchase.

> " **Opportunity: Not everything in your closet today will be worth big bucks in a few years. But chances are that you do have some things stashed away that will be worth money.** "

Source: *Richard Friedman, president, auctioneer and appraiser, Chicago Art Galleries, Inc., 5039 Oakton Street, Skokie, IL 60077. He is a member of the Appraisers Association of America, the International Society of Appraisers and the American Arbitration Association, Panel of Arbitrators.*

The New Rules On Hot Collectibles

It used to be that something had to be old to have collector value. That's still true for genuine antiques, of course. But these days collectors will pay hundreds of dollars for items less than two decades old. *Reason:* Many people got burned in the art boom of the 1980s. They spent a lot of money for things that shot up in value—and then lost it all when the market crashed.

Cheap collectibles may be perfect for the more cautious 1990s. In a tight economy it doesn't cost much to get into as a hobby and the possibilities are endless.

Opportunity: Not everything in your closet today will be worth big bucks in a few years. But chances are that you do have some things stashed away that will be worth money.

Picks for the Future

Here are our guidelines for sorting through what you own—and finding items for which collectors will someday pay big. Generally, only consider things that can meet these five standards:

● *Possible to find,* but not so plentiful that it turns up at every rummage sale.

● *Well-known enough* that it will attract a number of collectors.

● *Priced low enough* that it will be affordable even to novice collectors.

● *Useful,* historic or visually or emotionally appealing.

● *In the best possible condition.*

Our best bets for fairly common household items likely to increase in value—whose prices in some cases already are gaining:

● *Italian designers.* They are very hot right now and some pieces were made in limited quantities. *Example:* Gufram of Italy produced some plastic statues and six-foot-tall cacti. In 1975, those cacti sold for $250 each. Today, prices for those 25-year-old cacti can range from $2,000 to $3,000.

● *1980s high-tech.* There is a lot of interest today in old handheld electronic games, teapots and actual usable high-tech items from the 1980s. *Also:* things like first-of-a-kind phones, answering machines and computers.

● *Almost anything with a "smiley" face on it.* Those smiley faces showed up everywhere in the early 1970s—on cups, T-shirts, mugs. We're just waiting for the first mug collectors to show up. We figure they'll pay $20 for them.

● *Kid stuff.* Good bet—children's dishes—done in plastic with cartoony drawings on the cup, saucer and plate. Some of the better designers of the 1980s also did doll dishes (the little bitsy size) that already are showing signs of popularity. Disney items of any kind are going to stay good.

● *Hard plastic bubble bath and shampoo bottles*—those shaped like popular Disney or other cartoon characters. These already are all over the antique stores. A Yogi Bear Bubble Club container with removable head from 1961 goes for about $75 today.

● **Political memorabilia.** It always has a following. A Reagan-Bush thimble from the 1984 election now fetches $4.

● **Cheap—often free—collectibles.** This category would include such things as sports programs, souvenirs, matchbook covers, swizzle sticks and Cracker Jack prizes. These are all enjoying a revival.

● **Sports stuff.** Anything from the days when the Dallas Cowboys were "America's Team" and winning all those championships is popular with collectors—especially those in Texas and Oklahoma.

Since the Cowboys won the Super Bowl two years in a row, we figure anything connected with this team will eventually become hot collectibles. *Example:* The Cowboys had been featured on Wheaties boxes for a second straight year. If you have such a Wheaties box, a good bet would be to empty the cereal, wrap the box in plastic to keep it in mint condition and let it sit for a few years.

Olympic stars are good bets down the road.

● **Costume jewelry.** It is fun to buy and wear, relatively inexpensive, and almost any piece that has a designer's mark is collectible. There is an especially active market for jewelry made by Marcel Boucher, Hattie Carnegie, Chanel, Eisenberg, Kenneth Jay Lane and Trifari.

It does take time for things like toys, games and other collectibles from a particular era to gain a big following. *Example:* People in their 40s are buying all the stuff they remember from when they were kids in the 1950s. A set of 1959 Fleer bubblegum cards in mint condition goes for $1,000.

For your items from the 1980s to have value, you may have to hold them into the 21st century—when people who were kids in the 1980s can afford to buy back their childhoods. The above rule is not absolute. Fairly new items may already have value to someone who, for whatever reason, has decided to collect it.

Opportunity: Somewhere, there is someone collecting almost anything. In 1995, one of our newsletter readers wrote to us looking for a buyer for a collection of more than 3,500 key chains from 60 different countries. We didn't know of one back then, but by 1998 key-chain collecting had become a huge fad among teenagers.

You can also find collectors through newspapers, magazines, books and more recently via the Internet; especially the online shopping malls and auctions. Authors of books about a particular field are often collectors or dealers themselves.

Flea markets and collector shows are great places to meet people who share your particular interest—and maybe pick up some bargains.

Warning: Beware of items that are in demand because of something in the news. Fame is fleeting. A hot collectible today can lose its value once the news event is past. *Example:* Everyone was hunting madly for an O.J. Simpson doll that was put out a couple of years ago. But the same thing happened to it that happened to a Pee Wee Herman doll that went way up when he was first caught in trouble—but then quickly went way down in value.

Source: *Ralph and Terry Kovel, editors of the newsletter* Kovels on Antiques and Collectibles. *They are also authors of* Kovels' Antiques & Collectibles Price List 1999, *Crown Publishing, and 75 other books.*

More on the Hot Collectibles Now

Many of the most popular items that seemed silly in the 1960s are worth big money today—if they survived years of housecleaning, rough handling and neglect.

Whether you're looking to sell what you own or want to recognize a bargain when you see one, here are the hottest collectibles of that decade:

Toys

● **Hot Wheels** are one of the most popular collectible toys from the era. The little metal cars introduced by Mattel in 1968—and still sold today—were designed to race on plastic tracks set up to take maximum advantage of gravity.

Hottest Hot Wheels: 1969 Volkswagen Beach Bomb, which had a surfboard sticking out through the rear window, was produced in small numbers and is hard to find today ($1,500), pink 1967 Custom Mustang ($200), which was the first car produced in the series and is the most popular, 1968 Custom Camaro ($250), Hot Heap ($55).

● **Barbie dolls.** Among the most valuable Barbies

are a mint-condition doll from 1959 that's still in its original box ($5,000), Bubble Cut Barbie—without the ponytail—from the early 1960s ($175 with its box/$100 without the box).

Note: The years are indicated on the dolls' bodies. *Also valuable*: Barbie's friends Ken ($400 in the box) and Skipper ($300 in the box) and accessories such as Barbie's 1964 Lavender Austin Healey ($450) and her Sophisticated Lady Outfit ($150 to $300).

● *Cartoon and TV characters.* These are in big demand right now—in particular, anything from the 1960s that depicts Rocky and Bullwinkle. *Reason:* Few items exist because the duo was never heavily marketed. *Examples:* Bullwinkle wristwatch ($800), Bullwinkle target game ($250), Rocky and Friends coin bank ($250), and Bullwinkle coloring books ($15 to $40, if never used).

● *Flintstones* battery-operated Dino the Dinosaur, with Fred, Wilma, Barney and Betty riding on top ($500 and up), and 1960 Flintstones bowling-pin figures ($75 each).

● *Batman* board game ($165).

● *Addams Family's* "Thing" hand bank ($50 to $75).

● *Monkees*—for collectors, the second most popular rock group after the Beatles. The Monkees were extremely likable and had widespread TV exposure at the time. *Example:* Monkeemobile—a vehicle with the four group members riding inside ($500).

● *Soakies*—plastic figures that were filled with shampoo or bubble bath. They can be worth as much as $100 each.

Hottest Soakies: Superman ($100), Touché Turtle Bubble Club ($75), Yogi Bear ($72) and Casper ($37 at a recent auction, although the price will rise now that the movie was a hit).

Furniture

● *Heywood Wakefield Danish Modern pieces*—blond with rounded corners—command good prices. All post–World War II examples have a wood-burned stamp of the maker's name on the underside. *Examples:* A 34" x 44" sliding door cabinet with interior drawers ($1,100), a four-drawer dresser ($495).

● *Vinyl beanbag chairs*—labeled Sacco, which is the original by Gatti, Paolini & Teodoro—might be worth $500 to $1,000 each, if you can prove they are old.

● *Rigid, colorful plastic furniture* from the period is hot and will likely get hotter because it's so useful and so brightly representative of the 1960s. Look for items such as dressers with curved sliding drawers.

● *Plastic stack-of-cans storage units* made in the 1960s for kids are also rising in value. The cans stack up and have curved doors. They're great for storing toys, and their loud colors—usually bright orange, red and yellow—can add life to a room ($30 to $40 per unit). *Large:* 8½" high, 12½" diameter; *Small:* 9¼" high, 16½" diameter.

● *Nauga,* the pointy-headed creature that looks like an alien teddy bear was the spokescharacter for Naugahyde furniture ($100). These stuffed animals were given away as promotional items but never sold.

The Beatles

One of the most popular items is a set of four six- to eight-inch-high Beatles dolls whose heads were attached to springs and bobbed up and down ($425 to $920 apiece). *Other hot collectibles:*

● *Set of four Yellow Submarine clothing hangers,* each depicting one of the Fab Four ($400).

● *Piece of Beatles wallpaper*—the size of a card table—depicting the Mop Tops playing instruments ($200).

Other Beatles collectibles: Guitar toys ($650), wigs ($100), clothing such as sweatshirts ($150), Halloween costumes ($50 to $125), lunch boxes ($350).

Beatles records usually fetch fairly low prices because collectors value good sound reproduction above everything else. *Exception:* Plastic 45-rpm records with the group's image on the vinyl. Collectors usually frame them as works of art. *Examples:* "All You Need Is Love" ($60 to $125), "A Hard Day's Night" ($100).

Clothing

● *Dresses made by Emilio Pucci* were—and still are—wildly colorful, psychedelic ($400 to $1,000). His fancy evening gowns command the best prices. Dresses should have labels reading *Emilio Pucci, Florence, Italy.* Most Pucci items have his signature on the front. Without the label or signature, you probably have a knockoff.

- *Any paper dress,* a quintessential 1960s fad ($75 to $100), if it is in decent condition.
- *Pierre Cardin's* navy blue wool dress, which has paddle-shaped flaps ($3,600).
- *Plastic mesh dress* by Paco Rabanne ($725).

Pez Dispensers

These three-inch-high plastic candy dispensers were designed in Germany and introduced in the United States in 1952. They depict characters whose heads tilt back to eject tiny, brick-shaped candies.

The ones from the 1960s and early 1970s are in demand because of their nostalgic value.

Hottest dispensers: The Pineapple, from the Crazy Fruit collection ($700 to $900). The Pear ($650) and the Orange ($100) are also valuable.

Other hot dispensers: The baseball glove and ball ($299), Bullwinkle ($200), Green Hornet ($155 to $200).

Soon to Be Hot

- *The 1964 New York World's Fair* is not big yet—but it will be. Today, most collectors remain more concerned with the 1939 New York fair, which attracts Art Deco collectors. Others are nostalgic about the fair because it was their most pleasant memory before World War II.
- *Any item in vivid color.* For the collectible to be important, it has to virtually shout that it is originally from the 1960s.
- *Science-fiction crossover items.* While *Star Trek* is still popular with collectors, other space-related shows are gaining strength, in part because the shows are being aired on TV again. Valuable collectibles are toys and lunch boxes depicting characters from *Lost in Space, The Jetsons* and *My Favorite Martian.*
- *Georges Briard glassware* is not hot yet, but it will be. Briard's set of eight highball glasses was a classic 1960s wedding gift. The distinctive glasses have gold geometric designs near the rim, and each piece is signed "Georges Briard." Briard's pebble-finished glass trays and chip-and-dip sets were also popular.

Not Worth Much

Not all 1960s icons have great value. *Examples:*

- *Original lava lamps* are not very valuable—in any condition. They were never great works of art, and there have been so many new ones produced recently that there is no longer any novelty to the old ones. An old one in good condition fetches $50 to $100. New ones go for around $50. *Exceptions:* Early examples such as prints on scarves ($100 or more), clocks ($200) and psychedelic tennis shoes ($400 to $500).
- *Pottery* without the maker's name.
- *Ashtrays* of any kind.

Source: Ralph and Terry Kovel, among the nation's top collecting experts. They are publishers of the newsletter Kovels on Antiques and Collectibles, *and authors of* Kovels' Antiques & Collectibles Price List 1999, *Crown Publishing, and 75 other books.*

How an Insider Buys At an Auction

Here's how you can bid like an insider at an auction.

- *Obtain an auction catalog.* Read the descriptions of the items for sale, noting their estimated selling prices (prices may not be included in the catalog). Also read the conditions of sale printed in the front of the catalog—these vary from auction house to auction house.
- *Research the terminology* that will be used in the auction. A glossary is usually part of the catalog.
- *Attend the pre-auction exhibition* to scrutinize the items that most interest you. Leave no unsettled questions. (Once they are sold, items are the responsibility of the purchaser, so examine carefully for any chips, cracks, touch-ups, etc.)
- *Ask for estimates* if you do not know them. Decide what you are willing to spend and set your limits.
- *Arrive at the auction early* and select a location accessible to the vision and hearing of the auctioneer. Dealers generally sit or stand at the rear of the

audience to gain an overview of the proceedings. They are interested in seeing who is bidding and how the bidding is progressing.

- **Take note of your competition.** Insiders, particularly dealers, are customarily discreet in their bidding. Occasionally, they will use a prearranged signal to alert the auctioneer. Most bidding is indicated by a wave of a hand, a catalog or a paddle.
- **To minimize the chance of error,** verbalize your bid if it varies from the increment established by the auctioneer.
- **Do not exceed your preset limit** unless the item is rare and may not come on the market again. Do not be carried away by emotion. Only novices do that.
- **You may bid against a known dealer.** If you bid after a dealer has stopped bidding, realize that you may buy the item and will probably pay far less for it than you would in the dealer's shop.

Intangibles Are Important

Act with assurance. Assume command of a situation when it is to your advantage and remain silent when it is not. Address people by their first names, especially the auctioneer. If you can, chat with the auctioneer before, during or after the auction. Conversely, you may choose to remain inconspicuous, sitting quietly, waiting for what you came to bid upon.

Insiders are astute and concise. They know when, where, how and how much to bid. Most important, they know when to stop bidding.

Source: Richard Friedman, president, auctioneer and appraiser, Chicago Art Galleries, Inc., 5039 Oakton Street, Skokie, IL 60077. He is a member of the Appraisers Association of America, the International Society of Appraisers and the American Arbitration Association, Panel of Arbitrators.

What You Should Know About Appraisals

When you need an appraisal for any type of collectible, certain information should always be included: the qualifications of the appraiser, the purpose(s) of the appraisal, a description of the object being appraised, its history or the provenance, the economic factors at the time of the appraisal, the date and the appraiser's signature.

CHOOSING AN APPRAISER

The qualifications of an appraiser are critically important to an appraisal's value. When you choose one, seek a professional rather than a local antique dealer who may have just opened last week and hung a sign in the window professing to be an appraiser.

Recommendations from people familiar with an appraiser's work are invaluable—attorneys, accountants and bank officers frequently utilize the services of appraisers. The local Chamber of Commerce and the local Better Business Bureau also may provide information regarding the business practices of appraisers. In certain instances, the opinions of other appraisers can be helpful as well.

Since the appraisal industry is not regulated, it is important that an appraiser belong to a recognized appraisal organization. These have developed strict requirements for membership and ensure that anyone carrying its credentials will know what he or she is doing. Some of the more highly esteemed organizations are the American Society of Appraisers, the Appraisers Association of America and the International Society of Appraisers. Most qualified appraisers belong to one of these organizations, and some belong to two or more.

Experience is important, too. An appraiser's years of experience give some indication of his or her knowledge and expertise. Do not expect to find an appraiser who knows everything. As in other professions, appraisers specialize in specific areas. Ask if the appraiser is qualified to appraise the items you have. Find out his or her areas of specialty.

Finally, check on the appraiser's fee in advance. It is a fairly accepted practice among appraisers to base their fees on the time they spend executing the appraisal, rather than on a percentage of the value of the appraisal.

Source: Richard Friedman, president, auctioneer and appraiser, Chicago Art Galleries, Inc., 5039 Oakton Street, Skokie, IL 60077. He is a member of the Appraisers Association of America, the International Society of Appraisers and the American Arbitration Association, Panel of Arbitrators.

Sometimes a photograph of the object is included.

The qualifications of the appraiser are of primary importance and should always be stated on the appraisal. They should encompass the appraiser's professional affiliations, his or her particular area of expertise, and the length of time he or she has been appraising.

Appraisals may be done for several reasons: for insurance purposes (retail replacement value), tax purposes, donation purposes and "fair market value" purposes.

Note: Appraisals for tax purposes should be executed by members of recognized appraisal organizations. To be accepted by the Internal Revenue Service, the appraisal must fulfill the requirements outlined in IRS regulation number 20.2031-6, paragraph 6407.25. Most appraisal societies have established criteria for doing appraisals similar to those of the IRS.

The description of the object should be well detailed. It should state what the object is, the material of which it is composed, its size, color, clarity, subject, rarity, age, uniqueness and any other information the appraiser feels is important.

The item's history, or provenance, tells where the item originated, which galleries or dealers have sold it and for what prices, and gives an evaluation of its quality relative to others of its kind.

Since the art market fluctuates continually, the appraisal should state the pertinent economic factors prevailing at the time of the appraisal. What is important today may not be important tomorrow. For example, a silver spoon currently valued at $50 may be valued at $6 tomorrow because of a drop in the price of raw silver.

Source: *Richard Friedman, president, auctioneer and appraiser, Chicago Art Galleries, Inc., 5039 Oakton Street, Skokie, IL 60077. He is a member of the Appraisers Association of America, the International Society of Appraisers and the American Arbitration Association, Panel of Arbitrators.*

The Investment Mistakes That Too Many People Make

As an investment counselor who has been practicing for decades, I've probably witnessed just about every possible investor mistake.

Here are the most common mistakes that investors tend to make on their own, before they finally seek professional advice:

● ***Mistake: Chasing yield.*** Many investors are particularly vulnerable to such behavior these days, with bank CDs only paying about 3.5%. In their quest for higher rates, these investors are stretching out their maturities longer and longer.

Trap: When interest rates start to rise, the market value of these long-term investments will plummet. And their total return (rate of return plus appreciation—or depreciation) will fall as a result. Instead of focusing on current yield, you should structure your entire portfolio—which includes cash, plus stocks, bonds and mutual funds—so that it produces the total return you need.

● ***Mistake: Failing to diversify your portfolio.*** It's important to divide up your portfolio into different asset classes that move in opposite directions from each other. That way, if one or two of the asset classes in your portfolio move down, the chances are that the others are moving up.

In our firm, we work with 22 different asset classes, but the individual investor can diversify with just five or 10.

The most common asset classes are cash and cash-equivalents, such as money funds, bank CDs and Treasury bills, domestic and international stocks, domestic and international bonds, real estate and gold and foreign currency. You can further diversify in the stock area by dividing investments into large-capitalization, medium-cap and small-cap stocks. In the fixed-income area, you can divide investments into different maturities, ranging from short- to long-term, and along the quality spectrum ranging from government bonds to AAA-rated corporate bonds to junk bonds.

● ***Mistake: Not understanding the trade-off between risk and return.*** People now—as always—want to get something for nothing. But to get bigger returns on your investments, you have to be willing to assume more risk.

Problem: Most people don't quantify how much risk they're willing to accept. You should select a tolerable range of returns. ***Example:*** In nine out of every 10 years, your rate of return on stocks—based on past performance of the Standard & Poor's index of 500 stocks—would have ranged from minus 15%/yr. to plus 37%/yr. If the performance of an individual stock falls within your allowable range, it's okay. Otherwise, bail out. Select a mutual fund or—better yet—buy an index fund. A properly diversified portfolio might be expected to earn between 5% per year and 14% per year in nine out of 10 years. The performance of your overall portfolio, and whether it falls within your allowable range of return, is far, far more important than the performance of the individual securities or asset classes.

● *Mistake: Not using dollar-cost or value-averaging.* About 80% of individual investors are in cash or cash equivalents. And when they decide to venture into stocks, they either want to do it all at once, or to go much too slowly.

A much better approach is to dollar-cost average—invest a set amount of money on a regular basis, say once a month. This way, you smooth out market fluctuations and usually wind up purchasing at a lower cost per share than if you bought all at once.

Value-averaging is a variation in which you invest whatever amount is needed to make the value of your investments increase by some preset amount each period. If you've decided to try the stock market, I usually suggest averaging into the market over a period of six to 12 months, with a two-year investment period the outside maximum. *Example:* If your goal is to invest 24% of your entire $1 million portfolio in large-cap domestic stocks—that's $240,000. Buy $20,000/ month over 12 months, or $10,000/month over 24 months.

● *Mistake: Letting the tax tail wag the dog.* All too often, doting grandparents want to minimize hefty estate taxes by setting up a generation-skipping trust naming their grandchildren as beneficiaries.

Problem: Young people who inherit enormous amounts of money very often tend to be enfeebled—rather than empowered—by their wealth. Oftentimes, they suffer from low self-esteem and are unable to support themselves through regular employment.

A healthier route is to provide your children (or grandchildren) with sufficient funds for college and graduate school, and then give them enough to purchase a first house or start up a business. After that, they should be on their own. And if you're still wor-

ried about estate taxes, then bequeath the rest of your assets to charity.

● *Mistake: Giving too much to children through custodial accounts.* Gifts made to children under the Uniform Gifts to Minors Act (UGMA) or its newer relative, the Uniform Transfers to Minors Act (UTMA) are all right—up to a point.

That point is where the income produced by the assets transferred to a child equals the amount of unearned income that the child can have before he or she becomes subject to the "Kiddie Tax."

At current interest rates, that means you should only put between $10,000 and $15,000 into a custodial account. Any gifts above that level should be transferred to a "minor's trust."

With UGMA or UTMA accounts, the assets in the account automatically become your child's property when he or she reaches the age of majority, which is 18 or 21—depending upon state laws.

If, at that point, the child wants to take the money and give it to a cult group or buy a Ferrari instead of going to college, the parents are powerless. But with a trust, the parents remain in control.

When establishing the trust, parents can specify how and when to distribute interest and principal from the trust. Also, if a parent dies before the child reaches the age of majority, the assets in a properly drafted trust do not become part of the parent's taxable estate the way that they would with a custodial account. Nor can trust assets be attached by creditors, or by a spouse in the event of divorce.

● *Mistake: Poor record keeping.* It always amazes me how often people will come into my office with their financial affairs in a state of total chaos.

I've had first-time clients who came in with huge portfolios—but were totally befuddled when I asked them how much they paid for each of their holdings. They didn't know the basis (tax cost) of the securities in their portfolios. This information is vital because it determines the profit (or loss) and, thus, the amount of capital gains tax you must pay to the IRS if you sell.

If you're in this predicament, you may have to hire an accountant to unravel the truth. Then resolve that you or your investment counselor will keep good records from here on out, especially if you are reinvesting dividends from stocks or mutual funds.

● *Mistake: Looking for the guru.* By concentrating on short-term performance results, you wind up choosing yesterday's guru. The probability is that that guru will wind up being tomorrow's average performer or—even worse—tomorrow's loser.

A much better approach, particularly with mutual funds, is to purchase index funds, which mirror a broad segment of the market. They are the lowest-expense, lowest-risk way to represent a particular asset class in your portfolio.

Source: *Gary Greenbaum, fee-only financial and investment counselor with Greenbaum and Associates, Inc., 496 Kinderkamack Road., Oradell, NJ 07649. The company's high-tech asset-allocation investment strategy is designed to help clients meet financial objectives with reduced risk and lower cost.*

TEN GOLDEN RULES OF INVESTING

1. Don't be intimidated by the professionals.
Small investors have been intimidated by the media into believing that they don't stand a chance of beating the market because it is dominated by professionals. *Reality:* The amateur investor actually has a better shot than ever of succeeding today. *Reason:* The professionals act like a mob. They all act the same and think the same, because they all went to the same few schools. How many are very wealthy? Very few.

The individual investor has the advantage of being able to think independently of the herd.

2. Look in your own backyard.
My favorite source of investment ideas is a mall near my home. It provides a delightful atmosphere in which to study great stocks. As an investment strategy, hanging out at the mall is far superior to taking a stockbroker's advice on faith or combing the financial press for the latest tips. Many of the biggest investment gainers of all time come from the places that millions of consumers visit all the time.

An investment of $40,000 in 1986 divided equally among four popular retail stocks—Home Depot, The Limited, The Gap and Wal-Mart—and held for five years was worth more than $500,000 at the end of 1991.

Note: Your own backyard can often include the business or industry you work in.

3. Don't buy something you can't illustrate with a crayon.
Buying stock in companies that make things you understand is a sophisticated strategy that many professionals have neglected. It would have kept you from losing a bundle in mysterious biotechnology and memory-module stocks.

On the other hand, you would have made out very well if you had bought stock in such easy-to-illustrate well-known companies as Walt Disney, Coca-Cola, McDonald's and Nike a while back.

4. Make sure you have the stomach for stocks.
Market declines are as predictable as snow in Minnesota in January. Over the last 70 years, stocks have had average gains of 11% a year, while Treasury bills, bonds and CDs have returned less than half that amount.

But during this same 70 years, there have been 40 scary declines of 10% or more in the stock market. Of these declines, 13 have been drops of 25% or more, which puts them into the "terrifying decline" category.

A successful stock picker must be prepared to ride out these declines and seize them as opportunities to jump in and buy more of a favorite stock when its price goes down along with the rest. If you are susceptible to selling everything in a panic, you should avoid stocks and stock mutual funds altogether.

5. Avoid hot stocks in hot industries.
A great industry that's growing fast, such as computers or medical technology, attracts too much attention and too many competitors.

When an industry gets too popular, nobody makes money there anymore. But great companies in cold, non-growth industries are consistent winners. In a lousy industry, the weak drop out and the survivors get a bigger share of the market. A company that can capture an ever-increasing share of a stagnant market is a lot better off than one that has to struggle to protect a dwindling share of an exciting market. *Example:* Shaw Industries, a Dalton, Georgia, carpet manufacturer. There hasn't been a worse industry in contemporary America, but Shaw has thrived as a low-cost producer. Since 1980, Shaw has managed to maintain its 20% annual

Should You Attend an Investment Seminar?

Missed the greatest bull market on Wall Street in memory? Worried that your retirement savings will fall short of your retirement needs? Just trying to make sense out of the financial markets? Many choose to attend one or more investment seminars to hear the opinions of experts.

growth rate. The stock price has followed dutifully and risen 50-fold.

6. Owning stocks is like having children. Don't get involved with more than you can handle. The individual investor probably has enough time to follow eight to 12 companies. Your portfolio doesn't need to contain more than five companies at any one time. If you can't find any companies that are attractive, put your money in

the bank until you discover some.

7. Don't even try to predict the future. Nobody can predict interest rates, the future of the economy or the direction of the stock market, so dismiss all the forecasts. Instead, concentrate on what's actually happening to the companies in which you're invested. Their individual per-

formance is what's important—not the performance of the economy or the market or any of the indexes.

8. Avoid weekend worrying.

Beware: The weekends are prime time for dwelling on bad news and the consequences this news may have on stocks. Catching up on the news can be dangerous. It's no accident that Mondays historically are the biggest down days in stocks, and that Decembers (when tax-loss selling is combined with extended holidays during which people have extra time to consider the fate of the world) are the biggest down months. The key to making money in stocks is not to get scared out of them.

9. Never invest in a company without first understanding its finances. The biggest losses in stocks come from companies with poor balance sheets. *Example:* The S&L industry, once an untouchable among equities. A while ago, there were two kinds of S&Ls—ones that

were losing money but had a good financial position—and ones that were losing money and had a bad financial position. The stock prices of the second type dropped to nothing, while the stock prices of the first type increased five- or 10-fold.

10. Don't expect too much, too soon. My greatest stocks have turned in their best performances in the second, third and fourth years I've owned them, not the first week, the first month or the first year. The stock market is totally random over one or two years. If your horizon is that short and you need the money you're investing for something fairly immediate, like sending your kid to college next year, investing in the stock market is a bad idea. You should be in a money-market fund instead. But over five, 10 or 20 years, the stock market will deliver fairly good results.

Remember, time is on your side. If you had waited 10 years after Wal-Mart went public, you could still have bought its shares for 90 cents. A share of Wal-Mart today is worth $55.

Source: *Peter Lynch, the retired manager of Fidelity Investments' Magellan Fund, which soared in value during his tenure and beat the average equity fund every year he was at the helm. He is the author of* Beating the Street, *Simon & Schuster.*

Caution: Remember, their recommendations are aimed at a general audience and may or may not be suitable for your needs at that time. *Advantage:* These investment seminars allow you to identify people whom you feel you can trust and with whom you can schedule later consultation sessions.

Who Conducts Investment Seminars?

Investment seminars come in four basic flavors: (1) major exhibitions and national tours, (2) regional trade shows and local seminars, (3) investment advisers and (4) stock and insurance brokers. Most are free of charge if you ask for tickets from an exhibitor or publisher.

The largest national exhibition by far is the Inter-Show Money Shows in Las Vegas, Chicago, Seattle, Orlando and San Francisco and features many speakers, newsletter writers and advisers who operate on a national scale. For example, I appear at all five national shows because I can speak to as many as 50,000 people a year, I get to meet a lot of people and then I or my staff can give them a free telephone consultation soon afterwards. *Advantage:* National seminars provide many contrasting opinions rather than the single sales pitch typical of local seminars.

Regional trade shows tend to be run by newspapers or local entrepreneurs and often attract as exhibitors local offices of stockbrokers, mutual-fund families, banks and financial planners.

Local seminars are much smaller and conducted mainly by registered investment advisers (most are paid by managing your portfolio, often in no-load mutual funds) and brokers and financial planners (most are selling commissioned financial products and services). Knowing how the seminar hosts make their money will help you understand the motivation behind their recommendations.

Caution: A good adviser teaches customers how to buy his or her services; a good broker knows how to sell his or her services. An adviser can choose from hundreds of investment choices; a broker is limited to those products his or her boss requires to be sold or on which the greatest commissions can be made. An adviser provides continuous management, but a broker often provides only one-time advice.

How to Get the Most Out of The Seminar

● *Get information in advance.* This allows you to decide which speakers will likely be of the greatest interest to you

● *Find out if the experts publish a newsletter or have written a book.* This way you can visit the library and review their book or books to see if their advice suits you. Call them directly and get a free sample of their newsletter, which most offer (see number below for free sample copy of my newsletter).

● *Prepare a schedule of the speakers you want to hear in advance.* That way you can prepare questions you want to ask them.

● *Narrow the list of investments you want to learn about.* For example, focus on no-load (no-commission) mutual funds or small company stocks. Be wary of options, penny stocks and get-rich-quick schemes.

● *Take a notepad or pocket tape recorder and take notes on the best ideas.* You may also want to pick up brochures and audiotapes of the presentations.

● *Attend the workshops of lesser-known speakers on your favorite subjects.* The contrasting opinions will help you put the best ideas in perspective and challenge superficial ideas.

● *Talk to as many people as possible.* Sometimes the best ideas—about speakers and investments—come from fellow attendees. Ask people their best and worst investing experiences.

● *Call some of your favorite advisers' offices* and talk with them about managing your money.

Caution: These investment seminars are designed to assist the advisers in selling their services. Even the most "educational" speakers are selling something. Remember that their presentations offer general advice for the masses. If you want to get a specific evaluation of your portfolio and your investment goals, call them after the seminar with a list of questions.

If an adviser does not ask you what your investment needs are before making a recommendation, and launches into a sales pitch, hang up. Ethical advisers are required to recommend only what is suitable to your needs.

Source: *William E. Donoghue, publisher of* Bill Donoghue's WealthLetter *(free sample issue on request). Chairman of W. E. Donoghue & Co., Inc., registered investment advisers, and author of* Donoghue's Mutual Fund SuperStars, *Elliott & James, Box 360, 100 Medway Road, Suite 401, Milford, MA 01757, 800-982-2455.*

Investment Clubs

The average investment club doubles the value of its portfolio every five years. Few mutual funds can claim such a prestigious record. *The little clubs beat out big mutual funds for several reasons:*

● *Funds* have to pay their managers.

● *Clubs can invest in small,* fast-growing stocks while the funds, because they are so large, must favor large companies.

● *Quarterly reporting requirements* force funds to do a lot of costly trading.

● *When the market is low and stocks are cheap,* funds are constrained by their unsophisticated individual investors, who tend to pull their money out just when it's time to buy.

Club Investing

Philosophy: Invest small amounts (on average $25–$40/month per member) on a regular basis—in up and down markets. Doing this reduces the average price paid per share of stock. *Example:* When a stock is trading at $4/share, $24 buys six shares—but if the stock rises to $6, the same sum will buy only four shares. You purchase more shares when a stock is cheaper—fewer when it's more expensive.

Clubs usually reinvest all dividends and select only stocks that they think have a good chance of doubling in value within five years. They also try to diversify their holdings, maintaining a portfolio of 12–20 different issues.

No matter how thorough a club's research, not all its picks will double—a few will even go down. But in most clubs' experience, there are always several big winners that pull up overall results.

Tried and true: If stocks are researched and selected carefully and a club invests on a regular basis, it will make money—often a lot—over the long term.

Trap: Going into an investment club to get rich quick—it won't happen. But within three to five years most clubs begin to realize a handsome payoff on their investment.

Forming a Club

The best way to get into an investment club is to form one yourself. Clubs have prearranged member limits, so unless you have a friend in a club, chances of getting in are slim. *Optimal number of members:* 10–15—a group that can meet at members' homes.

Look for prospective members in social or business groups that you belong to. Ask each interested person to bring a friend. Try to assemble a group that's not too homogeneous—in which each member contributes something different. *Example:* One member may be a computer whiz, another, someone with good intuition about trends, another, a very sharp stock picker, etc.

Schedule monthly meetings on the same night each month—for example, the third Monday—so that everyone can plan ahead.

Big mistake: Starting out with substantial lump-sum investments of, say, $500 or $1,000. If the market happens to be topping when this first investment is made, losses and disappointment will ensue. *Better:* Set a regular sum of $25–$30—more if everyone is willing—and start investing those small amounts regularly. Later, members will be able to increase their participation, if desired.

Investment decisions should be made by vote at each meeting. If some members have invested more money than others, votes should be weighted proportionately.

Structure a Partnership

A partnership is a more favorable structure than a corporation because, unlike shareholders, partners don't pay tax on profits twice. Corporations pay corporate income tax, and then individual shareholders are liable for tax on dividends. But in a partnership untaxed earnings flow through to the partners directly and are taxed only once at the individual's level. *Extra tax benefit:* Potential losses are also passed through to partners, who can use them to offset gains for tax purposes.

In most states, partnerships are exempt from the onerous registration requirements and regulations that govern corporations. But even as a partnership, a club must register its name with the county clerk and pay a small fee. *Helpful:* Check your state's registration requirements with an attorney.

You'll also need a lawyer to draw up a partnership agreement. This spells out the purpose of the club, its organizational structure, how accounts and bookkeeping will be handled, and what happens if a member dies or wishes to withdraw funds. It should be signed by every member of the club.

Because money is involved, the agreement should also state what partners may *not* do. *Examples:* Obligate the partnership to any extent whatever—or use the partnership's name or property without proper authority.

At the first meeting the club members should elect a presiding partner to run meetings, a recording partner to keep minutes and a financial partner to keep records of receipts and disbursements, place buy and sell orders with the club's broker and prepare a statement of the liquidating value of the club's portfolio before each meeting is held.

The Broker

When the club's funds are still small, you may have trouble finding a broker willing to take your account.

Helpful: Explain that you will add to the club's portfolio monthly. To facilitate relations, call your broker early or late in the day and keep the conversation short. It's least confusing to have only one member deal with the broker.

Before each meeting, check with the broker for any comments on your holdings and any new ideas or recommendations on the two or three stocks that the club will be discussing that evening. (It's impossible for a broker to attend every meeting, but invite him or her at least once a year.)

Encourage your broker to provide annual and quarterly reports—and analysts' research. The relationship with the broker should be governed by a signed document in which both sides agree to their responsibilities. Securities can be kept in a "street name" with the broker, in the club's name or in the

THE PRACTICAL VIRTUES OF JOINING AN INVESTMENT CLUB

The hard truth about investing is that you only learn when you risk actual money, and when you invest via an investment club, you risk little and learn a lot.

The 37,000 clubs that belong to the National Association of Investors Corporation (NAIC) have an average number of 17 members. Rarely do more than one or two of the 17 members have any investment experience when they join. After five years in the club, however, 13 or 14 of those people will have individual investment accounts, investing three times as much as

they do in the club—typically about $40 a month.

Inside a Club

Each club runs like a business. There are regular meetings with agendas and officers.

The learning process starts when members are assigned individual stocks to research. They use practical guidelines from the NAIC, as well as from independent sources, to help them conduct their research. They are expected to write actual reports on the financial basics and the business outlook for the companies they research. Once completed, these reports become the basis for

detailed, in-depth discussions during club meetings.

After every member is satisfied that the stock has been discussed fully, a vote on whether or not to invest in the company is taken. No stock is purchased without majority approval.

Through the camaraderie of a club, members get the learning experience of studying the fundamentals of companies and discussing the pros and cons of a long-term investment.

More Learning Material

In addition to the research materials, the NAIC provides the names of stocks that have done well for other investment clubs.

It also provides a list of 150 U.S. companies offering dividend-reinvestment plans. Through these plans, the NAIC is able to purchase for the club one share of a desired company, which qualifies the club to continue to add to its position in the company without paying the brokerage commissions that have so dis-

name of one or more nominated members.

Easiest: Keeping stocks in a "street name" at the broker's office.

But some clubs prefer to actually hold the stock certificates and receive dividend checks directly. If stocks are in the name of the club or club members, company mailings such as quarterly reports and proxies also will arrive directly.

Caution: If stock certificates are held by the club or members, keep them in a very safe place. It's very difficult and expensive to replace lost certificates.

Broadening Horizons

The main function of membership is to learn about investments and how the economy works. *Best*

training: Researching an individual company. *Great resource:* The broker's office, where you will find abundant research information that's available to the firm's customers.

Some clubs name one member their "economist." *Duties:* To follow economic indicators that could affect the club's holdings and report to the group on a regular basis.

To learn more about investing and the stock market, you can also plan joint meetings with other clubs, dinner meetings with speakers or field trips to local stock exchanges.

Source: Thomas E. O'Hara, chairman, National Association of Investors Corporation, (NAIC), 711 W. Thirteenth Mile Rd. Madison Heights, MI 48071.

couraged individual investors in recent years.

In addition to the educational benefits of investment clubs, this advantage of inexpensive stock purchasing is a valuable aspect to being a club member.

Generally, the club has a bank and/or brokerage account and it receives monthly statements that are analyzed by the members to decide when to buy and sell stock positions. Again, all of this is very useful experience.

I belong to the Mutual Investment Club of Detroit, which has been in existence for 52 years. The 18 members have put in $450,000—less than $25,000 apiece. We make monthly investments of between $10 and $100 per member. Over the years, we've taken more than $2 million out (to buy homes, finance college, etc.), and the club still has a net worth of more than $4.5 million. That's an average annual compounded rate of return of 12%.

Our association's goal is to buy companies that can give a club a total return of 15% a year, including stock price appreciation and dividends. When that's achieved by a club's total portfolio (always some stocks will be losers), it will double its money in five years—not bad for any investor.

Lessons Learned

In these exciting years, club membership has given me many, many valuable insights into investing. If I had one piece of advice to investors, it would be to *start early.*

Most people don't even think of investing until they hit their 45th birthday. By starting earlier, you can take better advantage of the magic of compounding—that is, earning interest on your principal plus interest.

Once you accept this, the following three invaluable investment lessons will always serve you well:

● *Invest regularly.* One of the best lessons we've learned is that

market swings can't be predicted. Members who survive a market downturn and keep on buying in bear markets learn to become lifetime investors. Despite sometimes violent ups and downs, the long-term trend of the stock market is up. The U.S. economy doubles roughly every 23 years.

● *Reinvest earnings.* Insofar as possible, use dividend-reinvestment programs. When you sell a stock, quickly reinvest that money in another stock. The longer you compound your earnings, the better off you will be financially.

● *Pick value companies.* That means companies that can outperform the market over time. You can find them because their growth is better or, when lucky, you can find them at a bargain price because they're out of market favor for some reason unrelated to fundamentals.

Source: Kenneth S. Janke, president, National Association of Investors Corp., 711 W. Thirteenth Mile Road, Madison Heights, MI 48071.

Investing to Win

Real Estate Strategies

13

Property Ownership That's Right for You

Property can be held in a variety of forms—as an individual, a corporation, a partnership, a trust or a syndicate, pool or joint venture. Within each general category there are further variations that affect your tax treatment and legal liability. The primary factors to consider when choosing among the different forms of ownership are the degree of economic protection and the tax incidence factor. Use the following list of general guidelines when deciding on the most appropriate form of ownership for you.

● **Individual ownership.** This is the simplest form of ownership, and the economic profits and tax benefits of property flow directly to you. Yet it does have disadvantages. It exposes you to the greatest risk—your liability is unlimited. This form of ownership should therefore only be undertaken if the property in question does not unduly expose you to potentially excessive losses or legal claims from third parties. Also, for taxpayers in a high personal tax bracket, property held in this form that starts to produce operating profits may result in needlessly high taxation. Finally, individually owned property often becomes the center of disagreement during marital discord and divorce. (A spouse usually does have rights in such property.)

● **Corporate ownership**. To limit your liability and gain the ability to effectively transfer ownership interests without triggering local real estate transfer taxes, consider corporate ownership. The two kinds of corporations are the so-called "C corporation" (whose income and losses are generally taxed separately from those of its shareholders) and the "S corporation" (whose income and losses are generally passed through and taxed to its shareholders proportionately).

C corporations insulate owners from the profits and losses of the property (both economically and taxwise). However, profits are subject to double

taxation—first when earned by the corporation and again when dividends are distributed. A solution to this problem is to extract the profits from the corporation through tax-deductible owner-employee compensation arrangements. However, C corporations also subject the latent gain in corporate assets to double taxation—when such assets are sold and/or the corporation is liquidated. And this double taxation of gain may generally only be avoided by electing "S corporation" status considerably in advance of the sale.

S corporations allow profits to pass through and be taxed (only once) to the shareholders at their normal personal tax rates. Shareholders' deductions for losses generally are limited to the extent of their loans and capital contributions made directly to the corporation. With limited exceptions, corporations are compelled to utilize the calendar year as their tax year. Use great care when employing the S corporation. The tax laws regarding its operation can be tricky:

S corporations may have no more than 75 qualifying shareholders (a husband and wife are treated as one). Generally, only individuals, estates, tax-exempt organizations and special trusts can qualify.

There can only be one class of corporate stock, but voting differences are permitted.

Election of S corporation tax status requires the consent of all the shareholders. Election must have been made during the preceding tax year of the corporation or by the fifteenth day of the third month of its current year.

Editor's note: S corporations that have converted from C status may be taxed on certain gains and/or passive income. The tax is on the corporate level, not on the shareholders.

● **Partnership ownership.** Most frequently used for multiparty ownership, a partnership is not treated as a separate taxable entity—it merely acts as a conduit for gains and losses to pass to its members.

> "To limit your liability and gain the ability to effectively transfer ownership interests without triggering local real estate transfer taxes, consider corporate ownership. The two kinds of corporations are the C…and the S corporations."

A partnership facilitates the maximum use of tax-shelter deductions. As a partner, you can personally deduct losses to the extent of your capital contributions and loans to the partnership (although passive-loss rules may limit losses). In the case of real estate, you can also deduct losses to the extent of third-party nonrecourse loans to the partnership. A limited partnership, which has both general and limited partners, provides limited liability for the limited partners, while exposing the general partners to the greatest legal and economic risk.

● **Limited liability company ownership.** All states now allow the creation of a limited liability company, which can provide its owners with the limited liability protection of corporate ownership and the favorable pass-through tax features of partnership ownership. This new type of entity is becoming the structure of choice for multiparty real-estate and commercial ventures.

● **Trust ownership.** Several states allow the creation of a "land trust," which operates solely as a title-holding vehicle—the trustee has no actual power over the property. Trust ownership of this type is treated not as a taxable entity, but merely as a conduit to the owners. It is important that the trustee not have "real" powers over the trust, or it will be considered a "business trust." In this event, unless very carefully structured and operated, the trust will be taxed as a corporation.

● **Real estate investment trusts (REITs)** are a special kind of trust whose treatment under the tax law is similar to that of mutual funds. To qualify as a REIT, the trust must meet strict ownership, income and asset tests and must actually distribute 95% of its taxable income (excluding net capital gains). This kind of distributed income is taxed to the beneficiaries upon receipt rather than to the trust, and the remaining 5% is taxed to the trust at regular corporate rates. Because REITs can only be effectively utilized for large, specialized ventures with numerous participants, this form of ownership has limited application.

● **Syndicate, pool or joint venture.** These are business labels for a group of individuals, partnerships, trusts or corporations that have joined together to acquire, hold and/or develop an interest in property.

PASSIVE-LOSS RULES

All rental real estate activity (with two exceptions noted below) is categorized as a "passive" activity. General rule: Losses from passive activities can be used to offset passive-activity income only. They can't be used to offset portfolio income (interest, dividends, capital gains, etc.) or other income (salary and wages).

A passive activity is one that the investors don't materially participate in managing. Someone else takes care of the day-to-day business decisions, supervision, and operations for the investors. The investors' main contribution to the business is cash.

Special exceptions: Taxpayers can offset some rental real estate losses against their salary and portfolio income. Taxpayers who actively manage rental real estate and whose Adjusted Gross Income is under $100,000 are allowed to offset up to $25,000 a year in losses against their nonpassive income. This deduction is gradually phased out for taxpayers whose AGI is $100,000–$150,000. The deduction is unavailable to those whose AGI exceeds $150,000

Editor's note: Individuals can deduct all of their passive losses from real estate activities if they are considered real estate professionals. To meet this requirement, they must work a certain number of hours each year in real estate businesses.

Source: *Arthur I. Gordon, tax partner, Ernst & Young, 787 Seventh Ave., New York, NY 10019.*

The distinction among the terms is not well defined, although for tax purposes each is generally treated as a partnership. Broadly defined, "joint venture" denotes a team effort on a single transaction; "syndicate" denotes the sharing of financial responsibilities; and "pool" emphasizes the joining of the participants' financial and management resources.

Source: Richard J. Flaster, Esq., president, Flaster, Greenberg, Wallenstein, Roderick, Spigel, Zuckerman, Skinner & Kirchner, 5 Greentree Centre, Suite 200, Marlton, NJ 08053. In addition to working as a tax attorney, he has written several books and lectured widely on a range of tax subjects, including real estate taxation, divorce taxation and personal tax planning.

For the Income-Oriented Investor

Unleveraged equity investment programs and participating mortgage loan funds can produce real rates of return regardless of an inflationary environment. Programs such as these are appealing to income-oriented investors because they feature low-risk, high current return and capital growth potential.

Equity Programs

Unleveraged equity programs (usually executed through limited partnerships) purchase properties with cash and assume all operating risk associated with the properties. Many sellers will negotiate a significantly discounted price for a property in exchange for an all-cash payment. As a result, buyers are able to acquire high-quality, debt-free real estate at very attractive terms. The discounted price creates a "built-in" level of appreciation that pays off in later years when the property is sold.

The major benefit of equity programs to the investor is that income from the real estate operations flows directly to the partnership and then to the limited partners. Since there is no debt service, the bulk of the cash flow can be distributed in a steady and predictable income stream. For rental properties, it is possible to maintain a positive cash flow even in times of low occupancy, and there is little risk of losing the properties.

Results of equity programs depend for the most part on the income-producing potential of the under-

lying real estate. Other factors are the sponsor's ability to acquire quality properties at the best price, manage them efficiently, and sell them at the right time.

In general, all-cash purchases are a very conservative way to invest in real estate. They offer investors greater income potential and stability—and, hence, less risk—than most other traditional investments.

Participating Mortgage Loan Funds

Mortgage loan funds lend investors' capital to other real estate investors. In return, investors in participating mortgage loans earn a fixed rate of interest plus a share of any future increase in cash flow and property appreciation. The mortgage terms secure both types of payments, and each mortgage is secured by the property it is financing.

The major benefit to investors comes from participation in the increases in current income and appreciation. As tenant leases in a property expire, new leases are written. Typically, new leases call for a rent increase, which in turn produces a growing stream of revenue to the property's owner. In a participating mortgage, the lender begins to share in the increased revenue once a prenegotiated level is reached. Increased revenue from the property also produces appreciation of the property's value. The investor shares in this growth at the time of sale or refinancing.

Investment results depend largely on the expertise of the mortgage loan fund's sponsor or general partner to finance properties with high income potential. His or her ability to negotiate the highest percentage participation and loan interest rate for the investor relative to the amount financed is also an important consideration.

In deflationary periods, when interest rates are likely to drop, the fixed-income component of a mortgage loan provides a high current return. In the reverse scenario—an inflationary period with rising interest rates—investors benefit through participation in rent and equity increases.

Source: Arthur H. Goldberg, president and chief operating officer, Integrated Resources, Inc., 666 Third Ave., New York, NY 10017, a diversified financial services company offering a variety of limited partnerships and mutual funds, as well as insurance products and annuities to individual, corporate and institutional clients.

Real Estate Partnerships For Economic Returns

Real estate partnership investments should be made on the basis of true economic potential, which generally translates to a competitive cash-on-cash return. The following is a "back to basics" approach for analyzing the economic potential of a real estate syndication.

Review the underlying properties of the investment. In most cases you will be looking at improved real estate, such as an apartment complex. For substantial investments, use someone with expertise to inspect the property for you. *Many factors affect the value of a property:*

● **Acquisition cost of the property,** including land and buildings, on a square-foot basis and capitalization-rate basis. Compare the cost with recent transactions on similar properties.

● **Type and quality of construction**—wood frame, brick, etc.; amenities—pool, fireplaces, landscaping; and the quality of heating, air conditioning, plumbing, wiring and insulation.

● **Age**—quality of the structure.

● **Occupancy** (present and projected).

● **Projected cost** for proposed improvements to the property, whether for maintenance, upgrade or rehabilitation.

● **Financing**—avoid short-term balloon payments (less than 10 years in most cases). Except in isolated instances, assume that you will hold a property for at least 10 years. Carefully examine interest rates and amortization periods, and conflicts, such as loans and fees payable to the general partner or to the related parties.

● **Take into account all expenses,** i.e., fees, commissions and participation in sale and income proceeds.

Learn as much as you can about the sponsor. A partnership's sponsor can make or break the investment. *The first thing to look for:* Depth of real estate management and experience with the type of property and the area of your investment. You want a good, well-financed manager as general partner. If the investment is substantial, arrange

Swapping Property

Case: Garcia had real estate that, for tax purposes, he wanted to exchange rather than sell. But the person who wanted the property had nothing that Garcia wanted. Other parties were contacted, and after a series of deals involving three properties, four parties, and several escrow arrangements, the taxpayer managed to exchange his property for another rental property. The IRS held that the transaction was a sale because cash had been involved in the escrow arrangements. But the Tax Court disagreed with the IRS. *Reason:* The final result was that the taxpayer had in fact exchanged one property for another.

Editor's note: Deferred exchanges involving several parties must meet certain time limits for identifying the properties to be exchanged and for completing the exchange.

to meet the general partner and key staff members in person. Look for hands-on long-term real estate acquisitions and in-house property-management experience.

● **Carefully analyze the sponsor's track record.** Remember, because of high appreciation rates, real estate investments covering the period of the late 1970s almost always look good, regardless of the sponsor's ability.

● **Find out if the sponsor plans to invest cash.** If so, is it really his or her own? Cash invested by the sponsor that has been taken out of the up-front fees charged by the sponsor is not a signal of good faith in the partnership.

Study estimated returns and objectives. Accurate projections are crucial to the success of a real estate investment. Therefore, make sure that the assumptions used in the sponsor's projections are conservative. Look closely at assumptions regarding rent increases, operating budgets, refinancing terms and interest rates, inflation projections, sale price and terms, any other factors that affect the projected return. The projected increases in expenses should go up at the same rate as projected increases in rents. Don't be afraid to ask the sponsor to provide you with more conservative projections if you don't agree with them.

Look closely at the effect that projected tax losses (income), credits, tax preference items, investment interest expense and cash flow as a percentage of investment to date, will have on you. Make sure you can use projected tax losses in light of current tax laws.

> **[Property purchasing tip]: Before buying, hire a professional inspector to evaluate the condition of major items such as structural damage, the roof, plumbing, the furnace, termites, etc. If problems are discovered, use them to negotiate a better price with the owner.**

Compute the payback period (the time it takes to get your investment back through all projected benefits). Carefully consider the number of years in absolute dollars and the number of years in discounted present-value dollars.

Examine major tax-deductible items you can claim over the pay-in period. *Items to consider:*

- **Passive-loss limitations.**
- **"At risk" issues.**
- **Valuation issues. (Is there any appraisal to support the valuation?)**
- **Unusual tax structures.**
- **Accrual issues.**
- **Allocation issues.**

Find out whether a respected tax firm states unequivocally in its tax opinion that the tax treatments to be claimed by the partnership are correct. Also make sure a reputable CPA firm is associated with the estimates of future operations and investor benefits.

Source: *Arnold G. Rudoff, J.D., CPA, former director, partnership analysis, Price Waterhouse, 555 California St., San Francisco, CA 94104. He assists clients in analyzing, structuring, and financing real estate partnerships and direct investments.*

Investing in Rental Properties...the Right Way

With mortgage rates hovering near all-time lows, many investors are buying houses or apartments to rent out for extra income. While investing in rental property can be highly profitable, it's easy to make mistakes. *Here are the general rules:*

- **Consider properties that do not look good.** Few real estate properties are truly beyond repair. A building that looks as if it's in bad shape may only need a fresh coat of paint and some light cleaning to get it back to fair market value and a potentially handsome immediate gain. *Strategy:* Before buying, hire a professional inspector to evaluate the condition of major items such as structural damage, the roof, plumbing, the furnace, termites, etc.

If problems are discovered, use them to negotiate a better price with the owner. Cosmetically distressed properties often have distressed owners, a potentially good combination for you, the buyer. *Rule:* If you can cover the cost of repairs and still make money, the property is a good investment. If you can't, it isn't.

- **The date of the closing is important.** When you buy *occupied* rental property, always arrange to take ownership on the third or fourth day of the month. Most rents are due on the first, paid in advance.

So if ownership transfers a few days after the rents are collected, you, the new owner, are entitled to receive a prorated share. And that prorated share can be applied against the down payment.

The same principle applies if you're buying a business. Some research on payables and receivables may reveal ways to generate more cash for the down payment.

- **You may not need to call in a company or professional to make every repair.** Contract with individuals rather than businesses to do any work you can't do yourself. A handyperson can replace washers in faucets a lot cheaper than a licensed plumber. He or she may also be able to do the bulk of your maintenance, too.

If you use a painting contractor, you will also be paying for the company's overhead and profit. Instead, find two or three people who can handle paintbrushes and put them to work.

● **Look for hidden costs and anticipate service needs.** For example, leaky faucets run up your water bill, and ill-fitting windows increase heating and cooling costs. Check with local governments or the utility company about the availability of grants to pay for any energy-conservation improvements.

Think about the basic services that your tenants will need, and try to accurately meet those needs. *Example:* If you provide a dumpster for trash collection, make sure the size is appropriate—not too small but also not too large—since an oversized one is costly.

● **Use as much of the space as possible to generate revenue.** Always try to create a *higher and better use* for the property. Look to turn unused space into a revenue source. Then maximize that revenue by upgrading the property cosmetically—a new paint job, some simple, attractive landscaping.

● **Don't assume that your taxes are correct.** Get copies of the tax bills for comparable properties in your area. This is public information that is easy to look up at the county courthouse.

If your taxes are higher, file a protest with the tax collector's office. That's your right, and the tax collector's office can tell you how to do it.

● **Run the numbers.** Calculate your anticipated net profit without regard to any tax-shelter benefits for which you may be eligible. This is the money you have left after all of your expenses have been paid. *Formula:* Subtract all of your expenses (taxes, utilities, insurance, maintenance and mortgage payments) from the rent you receive. The result is your *net operating profit. Example:* If you have multiple tenants in a rooming house, you might want to build in a vacancy rate to be on the safe side. Your local realtor can give you data for your area.

Here's an example of how it's done:

Monthly gross rents (4 units at $500 each)	**$ 2,000**
Annual gross rents (12 x $2,000)	**$ 24,000**
Vacancy rate (at 10%, meaning that, on average, 90% of the units in your area are occupied) (0.9 x $24,000)	**$ 21,600**
Annual expenses	**$ 9,600**
Gross annual operating profit (minus annual expenses)	**$ 12,000**
Minus debt service (12 x $590, the monthly mortgage payment)	**$ 7,080**
Total net operating profit	**$ 4,920**

Rule: Never lose money on real estate just to get a tax break. With the right property, you can have positive cash flow and tax benefits. Depending on your tax bracket, you can make additional income by deducting depreciation as well. Not all of your monthly mortgage payment goes toward the interest on the loan. Some principal is also repaid, resulting in a buildup of your equity over time.

● **Make the government a rental partner.** You may be able to lessen the anxiety and keep your units occupied with timely rent-paying, low-income tenants by qualifying for Section 8 rental subsidies.

A government representative inspects your units for verification that health, safety and security standards are met. You retain full screening rights regarding prospective tenants. If you decide to rent to a qualified low-income tenant, a portion of that tenant's rent is paid directly to you by the federal government. Contact your local Department of Housing and Urban Development office for details.

Source: Russ Whitney, real estate and small-business entrepreneur in Cape Coral, FL. He is the author of Building Wealth: How Anyone Can Make a Personal Fortune Without Money, Credit or Luck, Simon & Schuster.

Real Estate Strategies

Five Simple and One Sophisticated Way to Analyze Rental Real Estate Investments

Even with the shrewdest real estate and tax experts at your side, it's essential for you to understand the basic economics of a rental real estate investment. While the combination of variables involved often makes it difficult for investors to compare the merits of different properties, there are five fairly simple formulas that can help.

The first step is to draw up an annual *pro forma* operating statement demonstrating the annual income, expenses, and tax benefits expected from a proposed investment. Next, these figures and further information about the price of the property, type of financing, appreciation rates, etc., are evaluated according to several different criteria. The following definitions and explanations cover five of these criteria, along with the advantages and disadvantages of each, to help buyers make better investment decisions (and help sellers assess a property's worth better).

1. Gross Rent Multiplier (GRM)

GRM = Sale Price/Gross Annual Rent.

The GRM (also known as the Gross Income Multiplier) tells you the number of years of rent you would have to receive to equal the sale price of the property. The lower the GRM, the better.

Ideal for comparing a variety of separate yet similar properties, GRMs can vary widely depending upon the age, location, type of tenant, and state of repair of the structures. The GRMs for very old buildings in poor repair with high tenant turnover may be quite low (sometimes less than 5); for new homes they may be above 12.

The GRM is simple to calculate, but does not make allowances for differences in investor objectives, financial terms, operating costs, changes in the annual income stream, tax considerations, appreciation or the time value of money. It can be misleading.

2. Debt Coverage Ratio (DCR)

DCR = Net Operating Income/(Annual Mortgage Principal Payments + Interest Payments).

The DCR indicates the ability of a project to service its debt obligation without recourse to outside resources. Its most popular use is in comparing the merits of various financing arrangements rather than evaluating a project's profitability. The higher the ratio, the less risk there is of the project not being able to make its mortgage payments.

Lenders generally like a DCR to be at least 1.25. This means that net operating income will be at least 25% larger than the principal and interest payments. A ratio of less than 1.0 means that funds from outside the project will be required to meet annual mortgage payments.

The DCR is easy to use and is a meaningful indication of an investment's cash flow characteristics. However, it does not incorporate estimates of a property's potential for appreciation, the time value of money or the tax ramifications of the investment.

3. Overall Return on Total Capital (OAR)

OAR = Net Operating Income/Total Investment.

The OAR measures the productivity of an investment. It is more reliable than the GRM because it accounts for operating expenses, vacancies and bad debts by using net rather than gross income. Generally, the higher the rate, the better. What is an acceptable minimum rate really depends on your particular investment needs and alternatives.

OAR is a straightforward way of comparing the returns from various rental properties. It does not, however, account for differing financial terms (most important, the degree of leverage involved in the investment), tax factors and the time value of money.

4. Cash-on-Cash Return (COC)

COC = Cash Flow Before Taxes/Initial Investment.

Many investors use the COC ratio as an indication of how productive their equity would be in a given project. Ratios a few percentage points above rates that are available on savings accounts at local banks and thrifts are frequently considered acceptable.

The COC ratio is suitable for investors who are primarily concerned about the cash flow of a project. The ratio assumes that all the benefits derived from an investment are in the form of cash flow—tax considerations and appreciation potential are ignored, as is the time value of money.

The COC is often negative, because many projects in today's market have a negative cash flow before taxes for the first few years. Thus a negative ratio can misrepresent the merits of a property—the investment may be very sound if tax advantages and appreciation factors are considered.

5. Equity Dividend After Taxes (EDAT)

EDAT = Cash Flow After Taxes/Equity Investment.

The EDAT ratio shows how productive your investment would be on an after-tax basis, in contrast to the before-tax analysis of the COC. It is reasonable to expect the EDAT on your real estate investments to be in excess of 15%.

Most investors insist on a return that is at least equal to what they could earn on their best alternative investment, plus additional allowances for risk and the lack of liquidity associated with real estate. Although the EDAT will give you some idea of what the return would be, it fails to consider the time value of money.

6. Present Value (PV) Technique

The Present Value concept is a sophisticated technique for evaluating alternative investments in rental real estate. It has two major advantages over the more simple methods discussed above. *First,* it provides dollar value for a specific property. This is in contrast to other criteria that help an investor choose among projects but do not indicate the precise dollar worth of any particular project. *Second,* the PV recognizes all of the critical investment considerations, since it is based on the time value of money.

The time value of money is critical because a dollar received a year from now is worth less than a dollar received today, even ignoring inflation. The dollar in hand can be invested to earn interest for you—the dollar you haven't received yet cannot be. Therefore,

> "The time value of money is critical because a dollar received a year from now is worth less than a dollar received today, even ignoring inflation."

you can only determine the value of future dollars by discounting them to reflect the interest you have forgone.

In real estate, the Present Value is defined as the current worth of a property's anticipated future costs and benefits, after the costs and benefits are discounted at a specific rate of return. The size of the discount depends on what rate the investor could have earned if the equity had been put to another use.

Example of PVs: The Present Value of a dollar to be earned in the future depends on both the discount rate and the length of time until that dollar is actually received. Thus the PV of a dollar to be received one year from today with a 6% discount is approximately 94¢ ($1.06 is what it would be worth in a year if it could be invested now at 6% interest = $0.9434). If that dollar is not to be received until two years from now, the PV drops to roughly 89¢ ($1/$1.12 = $0.8929). If the discount rate were 10%, the PV of a dollar to be received in one year would be about 91¢ ($1/$1.10 = $0.91).

The basic technique in calculating the PV of an investment property is to add the following three figures:

1. The present value of the property's cash flow after taxes for each year of the holding period.

2. The present value of the net equity reversion, which is the selling price at the end of the holding period minus all the selling expenses and mortgage retirements.

3. The initial amount of the mortgage balance.

The total is the maximum amount an investor can pay for a property and still earn the specified rate of return on the cash investment. (The rate specified will depend on the investor's objectives and constraints.) Of course, the PV estimate will rise if the investor is willing to accept a lower rate of return on the equity (i.e., a lower discount rate).

This technique is far more comprehensive and accurate than other methods of evaluating rental real estate investments. The only limitation is that this technique requires reliable estimates of future revenues and expenses—the results are only as valid as the assumptions used.

Source: Dr. Arthur L. Wright, economist, the Real Estate Center, Texas A&M University, as well as founder and CEO of Wright Properties. He is the author of more than 100 publications on various aspects of real estate and economics and has been active in both the local and the national Apartment Association.

How Real Estate Investors Get Tricked

The urge to invest in real estate, which is still strong in most parts of the country, exposes buyers to sharp practices by sellers.

The most common distortion is a claim of high-paying tenants. If the rent roll of a commercial building shows that nine tenants pay $6–$8 per square foot and three pay $12, find out who the high-paying tenants are. One may be the building owner, and the other may be affiliated with the seller.

Any fudging of current and future income can cost an investor tens of thousands of dollars. In a small building, where the seller reports that 10 tenants pay $400 a month ($48,000 a year), if buildings in the area sell for six times gross, the market price would be $288,000. But suppose the owner had prepared to sell the building by raising the rents from $350 to $400 a month. That increase in the rent roll costs the buyer $36,000 (the difference between six times $48,000 in annual rents and six times $42,000).

Even worse would be the impact on future rent increases. If the rents in the building were close to market before the increase, the owner may well have offered tenants a free month's rent or a delayed increase. A delayed increase means that the buyer will not realize as much income as forecast. A free

> "If the building has not been assessed for several years, the new owner may have a...tax bite on the next reassessment....Ask the local assessment office for a tax card or listing sheet. It will show when [the building] was last assessed."

month's rent means that the actual increase in rents was only $17 an apartment, not $50. If the new owner tries to jump rents well above that, tenants may move.

Other Seller Claims to Investigate

● **Low operating expenses.** Sellers may be operating the building themselves to avoid a management fee. If buyers cannot take care of the building personally, this fee must be added to real operating expenses. And if sellers do not factor it in, the bank will when it calculates the maximum supportable mortgage.

● **Reasonable property tax.** If the building has not been assessed for several years, the new owner may have a substantial tax bite on the next reassessment. Also, the seller may have made an addition to the building that has not yet been recorded with the tax assessor. As a precaution, ask the local assessment office for a tax card or listing sheet. It will show the building's assessment and when it was assessed. If it was assessed a year and a half ago and there has been no significant addition to the building, reassessment may not hurt the buyer. But if it has not been assessed for eight years, there could be a significant tax boost.

While checking the tax card or listing sheet, check the owner's property description against the one listed. If the owner says that 20,000 square feet are being sold but the tax card says 15,000 square feet, there has been some addition to the structure that has not been recorded and, therefore, has not been assessed. Or there may be an assessment error that, when corrected, will raise costs.

● **Low insurance premiums.** Is coverage in line with the structure's current value? What does the policy cover? Ask to see the policy. Ask an insurance adviser, if coverage is insufficient, how much more will proper coverage cost?

● **Energy efficient.** Verify the owner's claim with

KEY REQUIREMENTS FOR REAL ESTATE INVESTMENTS

Most people believe that the three key words in real estate are location, location, location. Wrong. In today's real estate market, the three key words are research, research, research. Only thorough research will enable you to determine if a property meets your economic requirements in the following key areas, whether you are looking at income-producing real estate or a primary residence.

● **Positive economic environment.** The most important factors here include the area's unemployment rate versus the national rate; the level of bank deposits compared with the national average; retail sales per capita; and migration and demographic patterns.

● **Location.** Location is the specific site you choose within a generally defined area. Ingredients that determine a good location include proximity to shopping and employment; convenient access to the property; availability of cultural activities; and minimum levels of noise and distraction.

● **Structural integrity.** In addition to being attractive, a building must be structurally sound. Before purchasing, make sure you have prospective real estate properties inspected by a qualified, unaffiliated structural engineer. Remember, the replacement cost for one roof could wipe out your cash flow for an entire year.

● **Amenities.** The features that are unique to the property, such as recreational facilities, meeting rooms, parking spaces, and architecture, should match your personal or tenant profile. In the case of income-producing property, for example, if 90% of your tenants are married and over 65, a weight-lifting room may not be as attractive as a card room.

● **Capitalization ratio.** Your capitalization ratio—net operating income (operating revenues minus operating expenses) divided by the purchase price—is the purest form of analysis of your potential cash return from a real estate investment. Tax benefits and the availability of mortgage money are excluded from the analysis, giving you a better understanding of the actual amount of cash that will be generated by a project.

● **Mortgage.** Determining your capitalization ratio will enable you to design the most appropriate debt service schedule for your needs. (All too often, investors do this in reverse—they figure out their mortgage first.) The most important issues when considering a mortgage are the term of the mortgage and the interest charged.

● **Leverage.** Leverage is the crucial link in a profitable real estate program. When used with discretion, borrowing can significantly expand your purchasing power.

Source: Allen Cymrot, president and CEO, Woodmont Realty Advisers, 1050 Ralston Ave., Belmont, CA 94002.

Real Estate Strategies

the local utility to determine actual energy costs. Also check with regulatory commissions to see whether utility companies are scheduled to increase their tariffs.

● **A good buy.** Check the income statement with those of comparable buildings in the area. Consult the annual income and expense analysis by geographical area and building type with the Institute of Real Estate Management (104 S. Michigan Ave., Chicago, IL 60603).

Source: *Thomas L. O'Dea, O'Dea & Co., Inc., 2150 Country Club Rd., Winston-Salem, NC 27103.*

How to Successfully Manage Rental Housing

Do you really have the time and/or dedication to manage a rental property, maintain its physical structure and provide good service to your tenants? The problem with rental real estate as an investment is that once you own a property, you have to figure out a way to manage it. For owners of single homes or properties consisting of only a few units, the solution is usually easy—perform all the management activities themselves. For owners of larger units, however, delegating some or all of the manager's responsibilities to others is a much more practical solution.

Whether you manage a property yourself or turn over the responsibility to someone else, learn the essential elements of good rental property management.

● **Marketing.** Renting apartments requires you to match the services of a unit (i.e., location, lifestyle, amenities and cost) to the needs of your prospective tenants. The first step is to develop and maintain a current rate schedule for the property by keeping abreast of market conditions for comparable rental units. Additionally, pay attention to the number of vacant units nearby and the concessions being granted by your competition.

The purpose of the market survey is to estimate the demand for particular types of rental units. Beyond knowing what your competition is up to, sound estimates of rental demand allow you to project the number of units that could be rented and the number left vacant at each of a series of different rental rates.

● **The value of vacancies.** Remember that "vacancy" is not a bad word. Apartments are like any other commodity—there are trade-offs between increasing rental rates and decreasing the occupancy rate. To achieve the greatest economic returns may mean less than 100% occupancy. Any property manager with 100% occupancy is probably charging too little for the apartments.

Rent reviews should coincide with changes in your area's economic activity and housing conditions. For example, to maximize profits in a rapidly growing economy with a shortage of housing, you should shorten the period between rent reviews. On the other hand, when supply and demand for housing change relatively infrequently, 12 months or more may be a sufficient interval between reviews.

● **Advertising.** You may want to maintain a certain degree of similarity among tenants in your rental units, e.g., single adults, young couples with children, retired couples, white-collar workers or students. The best advertising is usually geared to the individual traits of the group you've targeted. The three best forms of advertising are classified newspaper ads, word-of-mouth referrals and a sign in front of the property. As a general rule, if you have trouble renting a unit to at least one out of five eligible prospects, there is probably something wrong with the rental rate, advertising technique or condition of the property.

● **Leasing.** A successful marketing and advertising program will usually attract several prospective tenants. The next step is to carefully screen each applicant by using a lease application form and a required deposit. These have a double advantage: You should be able to screen out most of the nonserious prospects, and you will have additional information with which to evaluate your prospective tenant.

The four major criteria to use in evaluating a tenant:

● **Income level.** The household's monthly income should be approximately three times as large as the rent.

● **Employment record.** This indicates a tenant's employment stability, responsibility and willingness to cooperate with other people.

● **Credit references.**

● **References** from the tenant's previous landlords.

On the lease, directly state the attributes required of tenants living in the property. Be careful: As an owner, you must guard against any violation of a tenant's civil rights. It is fair to evaluate tenants on the basis of income level and household size. It's illegal to judge on the basis of race, color, religion, national origin or sex. There are also some

Real Estate Strategies

state and/or local laws relating to facts such as age, handicap or sexual preference.

Don't try to rent an apartment without a written lease. Comprehensive leases address issues not specifically covered by the general body of law. The most important of these issues are delinquent rents, eviction procedures, property damage and repairs and abandoned personal property.

● **Repair and collection policies.** To protect your property against damages, use a "Move-in, Move-out Condition Form." New tenants should note all the major defects in an apartment (such as damaged or broken mirrors, appliances, etc.) on the form when they first move in. Use the same form, when the tenant moves out, to assess the condition of the unit and to determine who should bear the cost of repair. As an owner, expect to bear the cost of normal wear and tear—your tenants are liable for damages in excess of that amount.

A fair but firm collection policy reduces payment problems. For late rent payments, you may want to institute a progressive "late fee" for each delinquent day. Talk to the tenant immediately, send statements of overdue rent two days after the rental due date and follow the statement by a "final" notice shortly thereafter. If you don't get satisfactory payment, then begin eviction proceedings after more than two weeks.

● **Tenant relations.** Sound tenant relations are crucial to the successful operation of a rental property. Poor communication between tenants and management can result in false expectations, misunderstandings and conflict.

One study found that more than 70% of the lawsuits initiated by management were related to delinquent or nonpayment of rents; 14% were due to destruction of property; and 11% were due to tenants moving out before the leases expired. Of ten-

ant-initiated lawsuits, 62% concerned security deposit refunds; 33% were due to conflicts over maintenance and repair problems; and 5% involved charges of discrimination.

● **Personnel/Management.** If you have a large operation you can't manage by yourself, hire employees who have adequate technical skills and, almost as important, an ability to get along with you and the tenants. Before you hire, make sure that employees clearly understand their assigned duties and responsibilities, conditions of employment, working hours, vacation days and sick leave.

● **Physical care of the property.** Taking proper care of the premises prolongs its economic life and provides tenants with clean and secure facilities. The manager's responsibility is to authorize the amount, timing and type of operating and repair expenditures.

The best maintenance and repair arrangements will depend on the size of your operation. For large complexes, an on-site maintenance person is preferred. If there are fewer than 80 to 100 units, agreements with repair and maintenance firms should suffice.

● **Record keeping.** Any good record-keeping system includes a detailed account of all operating income and expenses relating to each property, as well as maintenance and repair records, employee activities and tenant information. Most small rental operations (fewer than 15 to 20 units) can use a simple journal of receipts and expenditures. Beyond that size, a simple-entry "pegboard" system works well. Computerized systems usually are not economically feasible until several dozen units are under management.

> " Poor communication between tenants and management can result in false expectations, misunderstandings and conflict. One study found that more than 70% of the lawsuits initiated by management were related to delinquent or nonpayment of rents; ... of tenant-initiated lawsuits, 62% concerned security deposit refunds. "

Source: Dr. Arthur L. Wright, economist, the Real Estate Center, Texas A&M University, as well as founder and CEO of Wright Properties. He is the author of more than 100 publications on various aspects of real estate and economics and has been active in both the local and the national Apartment Association.

Real Estate Strategies

463

Real Estate Appraisers: Making the Right Choice

Today's prudent real estate owner can no longer rely on information from traditional sources such as friends or neighbors to determine the value of a piece of property. Brokers, while helpful, are still concerned with the marketing of real estate (finding buyers), rather than tracking the sale of every single property in every single marketplace.

The best way to determine the value of a property is by using a professional appraiser. For a flat fee that ranges widely, depending on the type of real

HOW TO PROTECT YOURSELF FROM YOUR BROKER

People who invest in real estate directly will find that a good relationship with a broker is probably the most important link to a potentially rewarding investment. For most busy investors, an experienced broker will serve as the primary source of leads and insights into a particular real estate market.

Here are a few general guidelines to follow to ensure a successful relationship with your broker:

● **Make sure that the communication** with the broker goes both ways. He or she should have a clear picture of your needs and objectives.

● **Be straight about your financial situation**—a good broker will always keep it in confidence. If a broker is misled about your investment ability, he or she will probably not be as willing to work for you.

● **Always be ready** to inspect a property at a moment's notice. In real estate, timing is often everything. Failure to investigate an opportunity when it presents itself can mean lost income for you and lead a broker to think you aren't serious about investing.

● **After you inspect a property,** communicate your reaction clearly—both positives and negatives. By the second inspection, everyone concerned with the buying decision should have seen the property and voiced their opinions.

● **Don't be afraid** to rely on the broker to guide you when making an offer. An initial offer that is too low can give owners a bad picture of your intentions and may cause them to dismiss you as a potential buyer. It's always wise to have a second offer ready, should the first one be rejected.

Remember: Try to keep the negotiations from stalling. Alternatively, if your price is accepted, be ready to move quickly to consummate the deal.

A knowledgeable broker will keep you up-to-date on market conditions and suggest the best times to sell a property for the greatest gain. He can also put you in touch with other investors who might be interested in structuring a partnership. Brokers should be able to help you get financing for additional purchases and provide guidance in such areas as tax considerations, property maintenance and zoning restrictions or variances.

How to Spot a Bad Broker

Tip-offs that indicate you're dealing with a bad broker:

● **The broker does not reveal** major defects or impediments of a property.

● **The broker does not bring to your attention** changes in price or terms.

● **The broker is slow** in conveying a seller's response to your offer. (You may lose the sale in the meantime.)

● **The broker wastes your time** by calling about properties he or she should know you have no interest in or are out of your price range.

● **The broker misleads you** by indicating there are other offers for a property—in effect pressuring you to make an offer when there is really no other immediate interest.

Source: Austin K. Haldenstein, formerly a consultant to Douglas Elliman Gibbons & Ives, one of Manhattan's oldest and largest residential real estate firms.

Real Estate Strategies

estate being appraised, an appraiser will compute the "fair market value" of a piece of property. Fees can range from $250 for a single-family home, condominium or townhouse to as much as $10,000 for commercial or industrial properties. Most appraisers rely on a study of comparable transactions in your particular geographic region to arrive at that value.

Finding an Appraiser

Financial institutions are a good place to start your search for an appraiser, since most standard real estate loan applications require a property's appraisal. This category of institutions includes commercial banks, savings and loans and mortgage brokers. Attorneys and real estate brokers are also excellent sources.

Like other service occupations, the range in expertise among appraisers varies enormously. Be careful in your selection—thousands of dollars can hinge on an appraiser's opinion of value. *The following should aid you in your choice:*

● **The type of property being appraised.** The first questions you ask a prospective appraiser should regard his or her experience, expertise, and reputation for appraising the type of property in which you are interested. To check an appraiser's experience, begin with references. *Don't be satisfied with a list of names:* Call the references, find out the types of property appraised and the ultimate accuracy of the appraisals.

● **The appraiser's credentials.** Appraisers with the Member of the Appraisal Institute or MAI designation generally have a very high level of training that includes economics, product knowledge, financial matters and demographics. Another prestigious designation is the SRA, from the Society of Residential Appraisers. Ask the appraiser what he or she had to do to earn these designations.

● **The appraiser's database.** When interviewing

Figures to Check Before a Real Estate Closing

● **Monthly payments.**

● **Per diem figures** for utilities, taxes and/or interest.

● **The broker's commission.**

● **The rent, security deposits** and/or interest on deposits that have not as yet been transferred.

● **A charge for utility bills already paid.**

● **A charge for loan fees already paid.**

● **A contractor, attorney, appraiser** or some other party to the contract who has not been paid.

an appraiser, find out about methodology: Where does he or she get sales information regarding comparable property? How does the appraiser make use of information regarding comparable transactions? What are the dates of the sales? What was the market climate during the time the comparable properties were available? What are the current trends in your particular marketplace? Is it a buyer's or a seller's market?

In today's real estate market, the difference between making a killing and taking a bath can depend on knowing what your real estate property is actually worth at the time you buy it and at the time you sell. Getting the right appraiser will help ensure that you don't make an expensive mistake.

Sources: *Sheldon F. Good, president, and Steven L. Good, vice president/general counsel, Sheldon F. Good & Company, 333 W. Wacker Dr., Chicago, IL 60606. One of Chicago's largest commercial, industrial, and investment real estate brokerage firms, the company also has subsidiaries throughout North America, including in New York, Denver and Toronto.*

Reducing Real Estate Tax by Challenging Assessments

Effective real estate tax is tax rate multiplied by assessed value. There is not much an individual can do about tax rate, but assessment can often be challenged successfully. *Requirements:* The owner must show either that property is overvalued or that the assessment is higher than on comparable property in the same area.

● **Just before making necessary repairs** of damages or deterioration that has lowered the value of the property.

● **Local tax records err** in description by overstating the size or income.

● **Net income drops** due to factors beyond the owner's control.

● **When the price paid** for the building in an arm's-length transaction is lower than the assessed value.

What to do:

● **Determine the ratio** of the assessed value to the present market value. Compare against the average ratios of similar properties recently sold in the same area.

Sources: Ratios are available to the public in tax districts. Real estate brokers and professional assessors can also be consulted.

● **Check tax records** for a description of the property and income.

● **Consult a lawyer** on the strength of the case, find out whether it can be handled by informal talk with an assessor, how much it will cost if a formal proceeding or if an appeal is necessary.

Read This 2X in Real Estate Contracts

● **"Mother Hubbard" clause.** It is important to have a true description of the property being conveyed. Sometimes there is more than one description of the property because it consists of several tracts of land. There may also be rights to travel over and use adjoining property. To cover the situation, a clause may be added to the effect that the seller is conveying any and all property rights owned at a particular location.

● **Certificate of occupancy.** The buyer may ask for a current certificate of occupancy to be sure that the buildings are in compliance with local laws.

● **Flood areas.** If there is any doubt—have the seller warrant that the property is not located in a flood-prone area. (If it is in a flood-prone area, don't buy the property.)

● **Brokerage fees.** It is not cast in stone that either party to a sale must pay the cost of brokerage. This sum can be a wide-open topic for negotiation, and the contract can specify any division of responsibility for payment.

● **Inspection clause.** The purchaser may obtain the right to inspect the property at specified times. Often, the purchaser will negotiate the right to inspect 48 (or fewer) hours before closing, to be sure all is in proper order as indicated in the contract of sale.

● **Condition precedent.** The purchaser or seller may want a specific event to occur before the obligation becomes fixed. For example, a purchaser may want the town to approve a building of a new road before the contract binds him to the purchase. Likewise, a seller may require that before the purchaser's rights become fixed, there must be a third-party guarantee of the purchaser's payments under the contract.

● **Authorization.** If the purchaser is a corporation, partnership or a representative, the seller may want proof of his or her authority to close the transaction. The form of such proof should be determined by counsel.

● **Survey.** An accurate survey can be very expensive, and either party can be forced to absorb this expense. It is a point of negotiation.

● **Building permits.** The seller may be asked to make the sale conditional on the purchaser's obtaining necessary building permits within a specified period of time. The buyer may also pay a set sum to have the seller put the sale at risk during that period.

● **Guarantee.** The seller may ask the purchaser to obtain a guarantee of payment by a financially sound and acceptable third party.

● **Risk of loss.** Damage to the property after signing of the contract but prior to the closing can be borne by either party. The seller can be obligated to restore the property or may be able to subtract its loss of value from the purchase price.

● **Title report.** Who pays for the title report is another item that is open for negotiation. The name of the title company that performs the work is also a matter for discussion.

● **Assignment.** A buyer may want the contract of sale to be assignable. The seller will have to agree that such a substitution can be made.

● **"As is" clause.** The seller may allow the purchaser ample time to inspect the property to determine whether it meets his or her investment needs. At that point, the seller may wish an "as is" clause, stating that he or she is not making any representations or warranties of any kind.

● **Zoning.** The seller may be asked to warrant the zoning applicable to the property. Proof of zoning may be in the form of a letter from the local zoning board showing the present zoning classification.

● **Encumbrances.** The title report will examine all the encumbrances on the property, such as mortgages, leases, easements and restrictions of use. How these items affect value is a matter for negotiation.

● **Title insurance.** The cost of title insurance is often a major cash expense at closing. Who pays for this insurance is an appropriate item for bargaining.

● **Time of essence.** Unless the contract states

that time is of the essence, delays of the closing date by the buyer or the seller may be excused. This clause removes all doubt that the closing must be held on a specified date.

● **Purchaser or seller action.** Where either party allows the contract to be contingent on something the seller or purchaser must perform, there should be a clause to ensure compliance. Such a clause appears where zoning must be changed, plans must be drawn, tests must be made, inspections must be done or some other matter affecting the property needs to be taken care of before both parties are satisfied. Sometimes such actions can be on a "best efforts" basis.

Real Estate Binders Explained

Real estate binders are not necessary to hold deals together and can cause confusion. If they are detailed enough, they can be interpreted as contracts rather than agreements to try to reach a contract. If you feel you must sign a binder, be sure it includes a statement that it is only a binder and is not binding until the parties and their attorneys have agreed to a definitive contract. This rule may vary from state to state. Check with your attorney.

Source: Lawrence Kobrin, real estate attorney, New York.

● **Mortgage assumption.** If the purchaser is assuming an assignable mortgage on the property, the specifics should be detailed. The seller may want more money because the purchaser is obtaining financing below the rates currently available in the marketplace.

Source: How to Make Money in Real Estate, *Steven James Lee, Boardroom Books. This book is no longer in print.*

Buying & Selling a House, Condo or Co-Op

14

Taxes and Home Ownership

In a low-inflation environment, buying or building a home for investment purposes is especially attractive. But the tax advantages of home ownership still remain. Here are the pros and cons, from a tax standpoint, of owning a home.

Points

If you finance your new home via a mortgage, you're likely to pay "points" to the lender. (One point is equivalent to 1% of the amount borrowed; if you borrow $50,000 and pay two points, you will pay $1,000.) If these points are a charge "for the use of money," you can probably itemize them as a deduction on your tax return for the year in which the interest is paid. The IRS will allow you to take the deduction if (1) the loan is secured by your principal residence; (2) the charging of points is an established business practice in your area; and (3) the points charged do not exceed the points generally charged in your area. Avoid financing the points through the mortgage, or you won't be entitled to the deduction. Rather, obtain the full amount of the loan, and pay the points to the lender by a separate check.

Interest and Property Taxes

Mortgage interest and real estate tax payments are both deductible on your federal tax return. This deduction results in significant tax savings and effectively lowers the rate of borrowing. *Example:* If you have an 8% mortgage and are in a 28% marginal tax bracket, the effective rate of your loan is about 5.8%. *Note:* Mortgage interest is deductible on your principal residence and other residences to the extent the mortgage does not exceed $1 million in acquisition debt (to buy, build or improve the residence) plus $100,000 in home equity debt (for any purpose). *Note:* The dollar limits don't apply to mortgages taken out before October 14, 1987. However, under any circumstances, the loan can't exceed the fair market value of the residence.

> " Remember to keep adequate records of all improvements you make, including canceled checks and invoices. If you sell your home, you may be asked to furnish them to the IRS. "

Refinancing

Many home owners buy a home, make all the payments over a period of years and never tap the potential cash value, or equity, a home has built up. Yet as a large asset, a home can serve as a substantial borrowing base.

By refinancing your mortgage, you can realize the cash value of your home without selling it and paying capital gains tax. *Example:* You built a home for $85,000 in 1976. Your present mortgage balance is $22,000, and your home is worth $195,000. Your borrowing base is approximately 80% of your $173,000 in equity, or $138,400.

There are several reasons for refinancing: Payment for college education, starting a new business, major improvements to your home, or an investment that might yield more than the interest expense associated with the loan. *However, there is also a disadvantage:* steeper loan payments. In addition, points paid to the bank on refinancing aren't deductible in the year they're paid, but must be spread over the life of the loan.

Home Improvements

Once you own your home, any permanent improvements are added to the original cost, with the result that they help lower your future taxable gain. Only improvements can be counted, not maintenance and repair costs. (Remodeling your kitchen is a permanent improvement—fixing a leaky pipe in the kitchen is not.)

Remember to keep adequate records of all improvements you make, including canceled checks and invoices. If you sell your home, you may be asked to furnish them to the IRS.

Tax Deferral

You can exclude from income any gain on the sale of a principal residence up to $500,000 on a single return. But you must have owned and lived in the house for two out of five years before selling your home. You can use this exclusion every time you sell your own home, as long as you meet these requirements, (even if you've already claimed the old $125,000 exclusion for those age 55 and older). *Editor's note:* If you're forced to relocate before meeting the two-year ownership and use requirement because of a job change, illness or other unforeseen event, the applicable exclusion is prorated. For example, if you are married and relocate because of a job change after one year in your home, you can claim an exclusion of up to $250,000 (one-half of $500,000).

Source: *William J. Roll, CPA, partner in the CPA firm Herring & Roll, PC, 41 South Fifth Street, Sunbury, PA 17801. He is the author of several tax articles.*

Home Ownership as an Investment

If you are buying a home now, you will want to get every bit of appreciation you can from your investment. This certainly won't be as easy as it was in the days when average home inflation hovered between 15% and 20%, but there are some basic points you can cover to ensure that your home gives you the highest possible return over the long run.

● **Economic outlook.** The prospects for the local economy should be strong. Rising employment and income are good signs, since employment gains usually precede increases in land values.

HOW MUCH HOUSE CAN YOU AFFORD?

When buying a house, the critical question always is: How much can you afford? Many people answer this question using simple rules, such as 25% of your income should be spent on housing, but these rules can be confusing and are not applicable to all situations. If you overestimate your ability to pay back a mortgage, you may find yourself living a substantially lower day-to-day lifestyle than you expected.

Ultimately, the amount of house you can afford will depend on your personal needs, desires and financial capabilities. The best approach to take when determining actual amounts is to write up a household budget for the first five years of home ownership. This should give you an honest picture of how much you will have available for housing expenses.

Include a determination of the savings you will have available for a down payment and closing costs. Also, be sure to use a reasonable projection for inflation and to make reasonable allowances for purchases of major consumer durables (automobiles, home furnishings, appliances) and for education— especially if you will have children entering college. If you use consumer credit for some purchases, include an estimated monthly payment in your budget.

If you do not currently own a home or are moving to a new area, get help estimating your housing expenses. Most realtors and home builders can provide you with appropriate esti-

mates, particularly for real estate taxes and utilities. Allowances for property maintenance and repairs should be 1% to 2% of the purchase price of the home, unless you intend to purchase an older unit needing substantial work. To determine your estimated principal and interest payments, you will have to get an initial estimate of mortgage amounts. Most personal computers have built-in software with amortization tables that can help you in this process. If you don't have a computer, you can consult an almanac.

Write up your personal budget in conjunction with a mortgage loan qualification form. (See the accompanying mortgage worksheet for an example.) A realtor or builder can provide you with estimates of closing fees, such as settlement charges and tax escrow, to complete the form.

Source: *Robert J. Sheehan, vice president and a partner of the management and economics consulting firm Regis J. Sheehan and Associates, 1606 Wrightson Drive, McLean, VA 22101. He is also the author of* **How to Acquire Land***, a contributor to professional journals and a management/economics newsletter, and is widely quoted in the media.*

WORKSHEET FOR MORTGAGE LOAN QUALIFICATIONS

Name _____

Cost of property	**$ 125,000**				
Down payment	**25,000**	Down payment is	**20%**	Loan/Value	**80%**
Mortgage loan	**100,000**	Interest rate	**10.5%**	for	**360** months

1. Monthly housing expense to income ratio (Maximum is 25%)

Income	Per month	Housing expense	Per month	Ratio	
Gross normal	**$ 3,600**	Principal & interest	**$ 914.74**	Housing expense	
Co-borrower	**1,450**	Mortgage insurance	**N/A**	÷	
Dividends		Real estate tax	**208.33**	Income	
Interest		Hazard insurance	**30.80**		
Rental (net)		Association fee	**N/A**	1,153.87	**22.8%**
Other		Total housing expense		5,050.00 **=**	**Ratio**
Total	**$ 5,050**	(Ratio purpose)	**$1,153.87**	**QUALIFIES**	

2. Monthly debt repayment to income ratio (Maximum is 33%)

Installment debts (6 months or longer)	Per Month		
Revolving accounts	**$ 60.00**		Total housing expense + total monthly debt
First Nat'l Bank	**150.00**		Total monthly gross income
Auto Loan	**165.00**		1,153.87 + 375.00 = **30.3%**
Total	**$ 375.00**		5,050.00 **QUALIFIES**

3. Cash required for settlement

Liquid assets		Cash needs	
Sales contract present house	**$**	Contract sales price	**$ 125,000**
Less_____% commission		Estimated settlement charges	**+ 3,400**
Less mortgage & liens		R. E. tax escrow & adjustment	**+ 2,500**
Less payoff of debts		Partial association fee	**+ N/A**
Plus savings	**30,000**	Less deposit	**− 5,000**
Plus other		Less this mortgage loan	**− 100,000**
Total liquid assets	**$ 30,000**	Total cash needs	**$ 25,900**
Net surplus/deficit	**$ 4,100**	**QUALIFIES**	

- **Home prices.** Make sure average home prices in the area are not excessively high. If prices have escalated too much, future appreciation gains will be limited.

- **Structure.** Buy the type of structure most favored in the area. For instance, a six-bedroom house in a three-bedroom community is out of place and can be difficult to sell. As a second example, some areas have a high concentration of ranch homes, while others favor colonials.

- **Turnover.** Areas with a high turnover of homes are better than those with a lower turnover. Realtors are comfortable showing these homes, and market prices are easier to estimate.

- **ARM mortgages.** Consider an adjustable rate mortgage (ARM). ARMs are about 150 basis points ($1\frac{1}{2}$ points) less than fixed mortgages, and are usually much better for families who think they will be moving in the near term or for young families who can benefit from lower mortgage payments initially.

- **Renegotiate.** If you prefer a fixed rate mortgage, don't hesitate to renegotiate if market rates decline 250 basis points. This is an especially good idea for retirees, who usually find fixed rate instruments more appropriate for their incomes.

- **Newly developed areas.** Existing homes located near higher-priced new developments of similar structures usually offer quick appreciation. Most older units offer a price advantage over the new homes.

- **Length of mortgage.** Carefully consider the choice between 15- and 30-year mortgages. The total interest savings that comes from shorter maturity is considerable, but carries the cost of lost investment opportunities. However, if you are a disciplined saver/investor, use a long-term mortgage and make alternative investments. (Remember, you can always make additional payments to reduce your mortgage balance.) If you have trouble saving, the shorter-term mortgage may be the better choice.

- **School system.** Look for areas with good school systems, even if you don't have young children. When it comes time to sell, your home will be more attractive to high-income households.

- **Bond issues.** If you have no children, avoid townships that are undergoing a rapid increase in the number of school-age children. Taxes will rise where there is a need for large bond issues for schools or other services.

- **Home equity.** Learn how to use your home as a source for short-term credit or long-term cash needs. Financial institutions have established loan programs that allow qualified individuals to borrow against the equity established in their homes. Another development is using the asset base of a house to provide retirement benefits.

Source: *Richard E. Mount, formerly senior economist, Merrill Lynch Economics, World Financial Center, New York, NY 10281.*

Way to Pay for Your Dream House

Renting out a room or an apartment in your expensive house offsets monthly payments and provides tax breaks for maintenance/ repairs and depreciation. *Result:* More money available for more house.

Source: *Jay G. Baris, New York City attorney.*

Best Time to Go House Hunting

Save your house hunting for the off-season. During an August heat wave or a snowy winter weekend, you may be the only prospect out there. *Result:* An anxious owner may offer a better deal.

Avoid Vacation Time-Sharing Traps

Some owners of time-shares in beach and ski-area condominiums are becoming disenchanted. They find that committing themselves to the same dates at the same resort every year is too restricting, or they find they overpaid. *To avoid problems:*

- **Locate one of the companies** that act as brokers for swapping time-shares for owners of resort properties in different areas.

- **Don't pay more than 10 times** the going rate for a good hotel or apartment rental in the same area at the same time of year.

- **Get in early on a new complex.** Builders can

Inspection Checklist Before Buying a House

Most home buyers know that it's a good idea to have an engineer check out a house for major defects before buying. But the buyer should examine the structure so that he or she can direct the engineer to report on specific details.

✔ **Start in the basement,** where defects are the most obvious. Check walls for inward bulge, cracks or crumbling mortar, fresh patches and high-water marks. Check floor for signs of leaks, seepage or damp odor. Look for a sump pump, indicating frequent flooding.

✔ **Use a pocketknife to probe for termites or decay.** If the knife goes in easily, the wood is rotten. Other danger signs on joists: marks of water seepage from kitchen or bathroom above; pulling away from supporting masonry; notches more than one-third into the joist for pipes. If joists are propped up, find out why.

✔ **Check basement pipes for corrosion.** Hot-water pipes should be copper, preferably insulated. Cold-water lines should be copper or plastic.

✔ **Check fuse box for power adequacy** (16 to 20 circuits with circuit breakers needed for an 8- to 12-room house).

✔ **Study house from outside for sag,** alignment of walls, missing mortar, broken bricks, cracks in walls. One tip-off to trouble: extra-wide mortar joint on the stair steps may show house is shifting.

✔ **Siding: Aluminum is a plus.** If it's wooden, look for peeling that shows walls hold too much moisture. If windowsills are freshly painted and the rest of the house is not, paint may be covering rot.

✔ **Check roof for broken/missing shingles,** tar paper bubbles, broken patches. Check metal sheathing around chimney and ventilators. They should be watertight and made of nonrusting material. Look for leaks or breaks in gutters. If possible, check attic for watermarks on underside of roof.

usually sell the first few apartments for less.

● **Choose a one- or two-bedroom unit.** Smaller or larger ones are harder to swap or sell.

● **Deal with experienced developers** who have already worked out maintenance and management problems.

● **Pick a time in the peak season.** It will be more negotiable.

● **Look for properties** that are protected by zoning or geography.

● **Beware of resorts** that are hard to reach or are too far off the beaten track. Your time-share will be harder to rent, swap or sell.

What to Ask a Seller

● **Is the house built on a landfill?** If it is, it may be settling and may continue to sink, causing cracks in the plaster and creating more serious, recurrent structural problems.

● **Is the foundation's exterior surface waterproofed?**

● **What's the R factor** (the ability to resist heat flow) of the insulation? *Good ratings:* R 22 for ceilings, R 13 for exterior walls. *For colder climates:* R 19 and R 38.

● **Are windows insulated or double-glazed?**

● **Has the house been protected against termites?** Look for written proof from a pest-control firm.

● **What is under the wall-to-wall carpeting?**

● **If the house is in a rural area, ask if the waste system is hooked up to a sewer system?**

● **What is the inside diameter of the water pipes?** *Acceptable:* $\frac{1}{2}$ inch for feeders, $\frac{3}{4}$ inch for main runs.

● **Are major appliances and heating and cooling units on separate electrical circuits?**

The Worst Mistake That People Make When Buying A Home

The biggest mistake people make when buying a house (or any type of real estate) is securing the wrong kind of financing. This puts them in a very risky position and can end up costing thousands of extra dollars over the life of the mortgage.

Fixed vs. Adjustable Rates

Most new mortgages are adjustable-rate mortgages (ARMs). The interest rate on the loan fluctuates with the index rate to which it's tied.

Problem: Interest rates are bound to increase sometime over the life of the mortgage, so interest payments also will rise. An ARM, therefore, puts all of the financial risk on the borrower. (Fixed-rate loans, on the other hand, put the risk on the lender.)

An ARM is fine if you plan to hold the property for four years or less—the interest rate probably will not vary too much in four years. But if you plan to own the home for more than that, you may want to take out a fixed-rate mortgage (FRM). *Reason:* Although the interest rate on an FRM may start out higher, it does not change. You always know what your monthly payment will be.

If you can't get an FRM, make sure that your ARM is convertible. This provision lets you change your ARM to an FRM within five years of the loan's inception. Converting the loan puts the risk back on the lender.

Assumable Mortgages

An even better way to finance your home is to assume the seller's loan. *Benefits:*

● **Low interest rate,** because the loan was obtained years earlier.

● **Small assumption fee** instead of large loan-origination fee (usually 2% of the entire loan).

● **No credit qualification** necessary on most mortgages.

● **Shorter closing time**—only a few days, versus at least 60 to 90 days for conventional mortgages.

● **The loan will be assumable** when you decide to sell, making it more appealing to prospective buyers.

Problem: Most conventional mortgages contain a due-on-sale clause and are non-assumable. Those mortgages that are assumable require a credit check and have additional fees.

Best assumable mortgages: Veteran's Administration (VA) and Federal Housing Administration (FHA) mortgages. Even though one must meet certain qualifications to originate a VA loan, anyone can assume it.

Most of the VA and FHA mortgages that were negotiated before 1987 are fully assumable with no credit check. And FHA mortgages that originated in 1987 and after do require a credit check.

When the New House Is a Lemon

A home buyer may be able to get out of the entire purchase contract if the seller has misrepresented a house with many serious defects. Normally, when defects show up after the buyers move in, they can sue for damages. *Some state courts have ruled that two reasons for suing to void the entire sale are:* (1) Misrepresentation of an important aspect of the house; (2) The presence of many serious defects.

One case: The builder had assured the buyer that there would be no water problem. But the house was flooded soon after the closing. The court said the related damage would be impossible to repair.

Source: Chastain v. Billings, 570S. W. 2d 866.

Drawback: VA and FHA mortgages are usually not available in expensive metropolitan areas. *Reason:* They are limited to $203,000 and $170,362, respectively, and homes in these areas are much more costly.

Source: Andrew James McLean, real estate investor and author of a number of real estate books, including Investing in Real Estate, John Wiley & Sons.

Radon and Selling or Buying a House

Radon pollution has been found to be much more widespread than anyone previously believed. Its presence may affect home values and directly affect the pocketbook of any unwary homeowner. In many parts of the country, a radon inspection—or proof that the house has been checked for radon—has become as commonplace as an ordinary prepurchase structural inspection.

Implications for Sellers

Take the initiative to have your home tested. If you discover unsafe radon concentrations, you can usually remedy the problem easily and cheaply. It is better for you to eliminate the headache before a prospective buyer discovers it during a structural examination—and either refuses to buy or gains a powerful bargaining chip.

The cost for an effective "do-it-yourself" kit is minimal—and is often available from state or local departments of health. In New York, for example, test kits consisting of charcoal canisters cost less than $15 per canister. Two canisters are used. One is placed in a living area, and the other is placed as close as possible to any suspected infiltration point in the lowest level of the structure. The canisters are exposed to the ambient air for a period of days and then forwarded to a laboratory for analysis. The cost of the analysis is included in the cost of the canisters.

There is no need for a professional to conduct the radon monitoring unless you need results immediately. Instant readout equipment is expensive, and you may pay a fairly stiff fee.

Buyers' Caution

Be cautious when buying a home in a high-risk area,

HOW TO BUY A HOUSE WITH NO MONEY DOWN

As real estate prices skyrocket in many areas, the concern of most hopeful buyers is, "How are we going to scrape together the down payment?" As hard as it is to believe, however, it's not only possible to buy property with no money down, it's not even that hard to do—provided you have the right fundamental information.

Note: No money down doesn't mean the seller receives no down payment. It means the down payment doesn't come from your pocket.

● **Paying the real estate agent.** If a seller uses a real estate agent on the sale, he or she is obligated to pay the agent's commission. At the average commission of 6%, that can involve a substantial sum of money. The sale of a $100,000 home, for example, would return to the agent at least $6,000. *Strategy:* You, the buyer, pay the commission, but not up front. You approach the agent and offer a deal. Instead of immediate payment, suggest that the agent lend you part of the commission. In return, you offer a personal note guaranteeing to pay the money at some future date, with interest. If you make it clear that the sale

depends on such an arrangement, the agent will probably go along with the plan. If the agent balks, be flexible. Negotiate a small monthly amount, perhaps with a balloon payment at the end. You then subtract the agent's commission from the expected down payment.

● **Assuming the seller's debts.** Let's say, as so often happens, that the seller is under financial pressure with overwhelming outstanding obligations. *Strategy:* With the seller's cooperation, contact all his or her creditors and explain that you, not the seller, are going to make good on the outstanding debts. In some cases, the relieved creditors will either extend the due dates, or, if you can come up with some cash, they'll likely agree to a discount. Deduct the face amount of the debts you'll be assuming, pocketing any discounts from the down payment.

● **Prepaid rent.** Sometimes you, the buyer, are in no rush to move in and the seller would like more time to find a new place to live—but you'd both like to close as soon as possible. Or, if it's a multi-apartment building and the seller lives there, he or she may want more time in the apartment. *Strategy:* Offer to let the seller remain in the house or

or a home that was once found to have high levels of radon. Remember, the seller had control over the placement of the detectors. Tests using sophisticated equipment would probably be justified. Some warranty from the seller would be in order. Even if the problem was eliminated, it is a good idea to retest every two or three years.

Dealing with Radon

If you discover radon in significant concentrations, the problem is usually easily resolved. Radon is an invisible, odorless radioactive gas that seeps up through the ground and can enter a home through gaps in the walls and foundation slabs, or as a gas dissolved in seeping ground water. In modern, heavily insulated homes, the gas may be trapped and concentrated. Simply sealing the sources of infiltration—cracks in basement floors and walls, gaps around pipes, etc.—and waterproofing the basement may be all that's needed. In extreme cases, it may be necessary to install a ventilation system under the foundation slab to let the gas escape into the outside air.

Source: John G. Rossi, president, John G. Rossi P.E., P.C., an engineering consulting firm specializing in home and building inspection services, Box 147, Canton, NY 13617.

apartment, setting a fixed date for vacating. Then, instead of the seller's paying the buyer a monthly rent, you subtract from the down payment the full amount of the rent for the entire time the seller will be living there.

● **Satisfying the seller's needs.** During conversations with the seller, you learn that he or she must buy some appliances and furniture for a home he or she is moving into. *Strategy:* Offer to buy those things—using credit cards or store credit to delay payment—and deduct the lump sum from the down payment.

● **Using rent and deposits.** If it's a multi-apartment building, you can use the rent from tenants to cover part of the down payment. *Strategy:* Generally, if you close on the first of the month, you are entitled to all rent normally due from tenants for that month. Therefore, you can collect the rent and apply the sum toward the down payment.

● **Using balloon down payments.** Arrange to give part of the down payment immediately and the rest in one or several balloon payments at later, fixed dates. *Strategy:* This technique gives you breathing room to: (1) Search for the rest of the down payment and/or (2) improve the property and put it back on the market for a quick profit.

Caution: This move can be risky if you don't make sure you have a fall-back source of cash in the event that time runs out.

● **Using talent, not cash.** In some cases you may be able to trade some of your personal resources if you are in a business or have a hobby through which you can provide services useful to the seller in lieu of cash. *Strategy:* Trading services for cash is, among other things, very tax-wise. Many working people can provide services in exchange for down payment cash. *Most obvious:* doctors, dentists, lawyers, accountants. *Less obvious:* carpenters, artists, wholesalers, entertainers, gardeners. Note, however, that bartering produces taxable income, and taxes have to be paid on the value of such services.

● **Raising the price, lowering the terms.** Best applied when the seller is more interested in the price than in the terms of the deal. *Strategy:* By playing with the numbers, you might find that you save a considerable sum of money if you agree to a higher price in return for a lower—or even no—down payment.

● **High monthly down payments.** If you have high cash flow, this could be a persuasive tactic to delay immediate payment. *Strategy:* A seller may be more interested in steady cash flow after the sale than in money up front. An anxious seller might bite at this offer because he or she can get the full amount from payments rather than negotiating the price, starting at the down payment. It also offers you the prospect of turning around and quickly selling the property—since you aren't tying up ready cash.

● **Splitting the property.** If the property contains a separate sellable element, plan to sell off that element and apply the proceeds to the down payment. *Strategy:* A portion of the land may be sold separately. Or there may be antiques that are sellable—the proceeds of which can be applied to the down payment.

Source: Robert G. Allen, real estate insider and author of the best-seller, Nothing Down for the 90's. *He's also publisher of the monthly newsletter* The Real Estate Adviser.

Finding the Perfect Mortgage

Getting the perfect mortgage for your home, co-op, condo, second home, ski lodge, etc., can be greatly simplified if you follow a few basic guidelines.

● **First, take the time** to find out about the wide variety of possible financing plans available to you (fixed rate, adjustable, graduated payment, balloon, etc.). Each type of loan is tailored to a specific set of personal needs and expectations. Carefully consider your long-range and short-range goals and your current financial status. It's better to have an idea of which type of mortgage you may be interested in before you start speaking to loan officers.

● **Next, shop the loan thoroughly.** Whether you do this through ads or word of mouth, your goal should be to come up with a list of the most competitive lending institutions. A possible alternative is to let a mortgage broker locate the best lending institution for your particular loan. Mortgage brokers track hundreds of different mortgage products from a variety of lending institutions. Some mortgage brokers charge a fee; others are paid by banks.

● **When shopping for the best loan,** contact each bank's main mortgage department first. Executives at branches are sometimes not as up-to-date on the latest mortgage information. Also, do your research quickly—mortgage components can change often. Ask for a simple statement that clarifies the details of any prospective financing package for both parties. Remember, it is required that all usual closing costs (title insurance, legal fees, points, appraisal fee, credit agency fee, etc.) be clearly spelled out before you receive a mortgage commitment. Your objective at this stage should be to avoid last-minute surprises.

Don't expect many concessions from a bank on your mortgage-financing package. Unless you are a customer who has substantial accounts with the bank, you will probably not be able to negotiate the terms of the loan. On the other hand, if you do have substantial accounts, you may be able to negotiate on points, but probably not on rates.

● **Mortgage processing takes time.** If a full credit package is required by your lender, expect a delay of approximately 30 days to verify all of the information supplied in your application. You can speed up the process by providing the bank with accurate information as quickly as possible.

The problem with processing delays is that the competitive rate that attracted you in the first place to a particular bank may no longer be available. Ensure that your contract with the seller gives you ample time to have your mortgage application approved. Or you could face higher interest rates than you initially anticipated if your commitment for a mortgage expires before you are prepared to close. As a rule, if a full credit package is required, you'll need a minimum of 45 days—60 days is preferable.

Source: *Jane E. Greenstein, founder and president of Mortgage Clearing House, 1510 Jericho Turnpike, New Hyde Park, NY 11040, a division of The Seldin Organization, Inc.*

Nonbanking Sources Of Mortgage Financing

Most of us associate obtaining mortgage financing with savings and loan associations, commercial banks and savings banks. But these don't have to be your only source. There is a wide variety of alternatives you can turn to for help. *Here is a list of the best:*

● **Mortgage banking companies.** Mortgage banking companies originate mortgages and, in turn, sell them to institutional investors. In the past, mortgage bankers specialized in federal government–insured loans. However, as a result of the significant growth in the secondary market for all types of conventional mortgages, mortgage bankers have become very aggressive in the area of non-government-insured loans as well. Many mortgage bankers work directly with real estate agents, so that would probably be your best place to start your search. They are also listed in the Yellow Pages under mortgages or mortgage banking. A significant number of mortgage banking firms are actually subsidiaries of commercial banks.

● **Insurance companies.** Also increasing their involvement in the direct origination of residential mortgage loans, insurance companies were formerly a major force in the origination of single-family mortgages, but opted for secondary mortgage market instruments and other investments. For the time being, only the major insurance companies are likely to be a direct source of financing. Check with your insurance agent for prospects. The one major advantage of insurance companies over traditional bank sources is that they are less likely to rely on the income from points.

Credit unions. Possibly your cheapest source of mortgage financing. There may be a credit union where you work—if not, you can usually join one with little difficulty. Credit unions are becoming more and more popular with a larger cross-section of the population. They have spread beyond private firms and public agencies to include more broadly based social and fraternal organizations.

Home builders. In many cases, home builders are a source of mortgage financing for the homes they are selling. Some of their sources are traditional lenders, such as savings and loan institutions and banks. However, some of the larger builders have their own mortgage banking subsidiaries, while some large, medium and even small builders pool their mortgages and sell them directly into the secondary mortgage markets or through investment houses that have specific financing programs for builders. You can also find realtors that will participate in financing programs through investment houses and organizations that originate, sell and service mortgage loans.

Relatives and private individuals. Relatives may not be able to provide you with the entire amount of the mortgage, but often can help with the down payment or a second mortgage to reduce the amount of your first mortgage. Relatives and people you know may accept lower rates of interest than an institution because the rate of return is still higher than many of the investments they can make otherwise.

Professionals such as doctors and lawyers often seek investment opportunities in mortgage financing, providing below-market interest rates as a way of deferring income. In return, they generally require a portion of the rights to the future appreciation of the home. If you pursue mortgage financing from an individual investor, it's smart to hire a lawyer.

Home sellers. Cheap and readily available financing can be arranged with the seller of a home. Many will have an assumable mortgage with a lower interest rate than is currently available. The major problem with assumable mortgages is that they can require a large down payment if there is a substan-

tial difference between the sales price and the remaining amount of the mortgage. You will also be required to contact the mortgage lender to determine if there are any special requirements or fees associated with assumption of the loan.

Home sellers may be willing to finance a prime mortgage or a second mortgage if you cannot obtain a large enough prime mortgage through a lender. Sellers most often interested in this type of arrangement are people who are anxious to sell; may be moving to a cheaper home and want to spread their profit over a long period of time; or, if they are older, may be seeking a steady stream of retirement income.

> "The major problem with assumable mortgages is that they can require a large down payment if there is a substantial difference between the sale price and the remaining amount of the mortgage."

A seller may also provide a purchase-money mortgage. For example, the seller gives you a short-term mortgage with a term of, say, 10 years. The monthly payments, however, are based on a 25- to 30-year loan. At the end of the loan term, you will be required to negotiate a new loan or find new financing. In most cases, the equity you build up in the home should make it easier to obtain another mortgage.

Source: *Robert J. Sheehan, vice president and partner, Regis J. Sheehan & Associates, management and economic consultants, 1606 Wrightson Dr., McLean, VA 22101. He has had over 25 years' experience in management and market research in construction and housing. He is a former staff vice president of National Association of Homebuilders.*

Hidden Mortgage Hazards

The increasing complexity of mortgages can leave a home buyer frustrated, confused and even angry about negotiations with a lending institution. Yet much of this emotional turmoil can be eliminated if the borrower avoids focusing on interest rates alone and instead looks at the full range of elements in a mortgage program.

Understanding Mortgage Programs

Mortgage insurance premium (MIP). The MIP insures a lender against a potential loss if a borrower defaults on the mortgage and the lender is forced to foreclose on the property. For a down payment less than 20% of the total mortgage, an MIP is mandated by financial regulatory agencies.

● **Points.** A lender's fee, one point is equal to 1% of the mortgage amount. The number of points quoted by a lender is not always an accurate reflection of the total fee.

● **Other Fees.** Lenders may add fees to cover document preparation, tax servicing, appraisal, credit reporting, over-night mailing charges, flood certification, attorney's fees and funding fees. There may also be a fee for locking in the interest rate. However, this fee is often deducted from the "points" being paid at settlement.

Be persistent about points and application fees. *Always ask the follow-up question:* "Do the points and fees that the lender quotes include all the fees of making the loan, including preparation of papers, counsel fees, origination fees and commitment fees?"

● **When the interest rate is set.** Your interest rate can be set at the time of application, at the time of commitment, just prior to settlement or when one of the points is paid as a nonrefundable fee.

● **How long the rate is set.** The interest rate you are quoted during loan negotiations will be available only for a specified period, varying from seven to 120 days. It is important that you keep the period in line with your settlement date. For example, if your settlement is scheduled for 60 days from the application date, an interest rate set for 45 days won't have an effect on the rate you actually receive. If rates suddenly turn up and your rate is not set, you could get stuck with much higher interest payments than first planned. For the same reason, be cautious of the seller's extending the settlement date.

Don't get caught up in processing delays, either. When interest rates are rising, a delay in the processing of a loan can cost you no matter who is at fault. To avoid paying for delays, follow up continuously. Document phone calls, noting the date, time, content of the call, and to whom you spoke. Make sure your employer sends the employee verification, ask the lender if the verification is acceptable, or what else is needed to submit the loan to the underwriter. Your loan processor will probably tell you that everything is fine. Do not accept this answer. Be specific. If everything is fine, ask when it will be submitted for approval.

The following checklist will help you track all the common items the lender will need to complete processing.

1. Employment verification.
2. Bank account balance verification.
3. Loan balance verification.
4. Credit report.
5. Appraisal.
6. Title report.
7. Wood infestation report.
8. Well water test certification.
9. With less than a 20% down payment, approval from a mortgage insurance company.

● **Amortization.** Monthly mortgage payments cover principal and interest—the amount of principal reduction is known as the amortization (positive amortization). A lender may offer a program with a lower than normal monthly payment in the first year or two. This loan may defer interest until a later time, resulting in the smaller monthly payment for the first year. The interest that is deferred is added to the balance of the principal and paid off gradually over the life of the loan. This is known as negative amortization.

Negative amortization can permit a borrower to obtain a loan and house he or she otherwise could not afford. But it is not recommended unless you expect your income to rise to cover the higher monthly payments in the second and subsequent years.

Adjustable Mortgage Loans

The foregoing elements are common to all loans. Adjustable mortgage loans (AMLs), however, require borrowers to look at even more complex factors.

● **The index.** An AML is based on an index that is chosen by the lender—the restrictions on this choice are that the index must be readily verifiable by the borrower and out of the direct control of the lender. Find out the index's exact name and whether it is a monthly or weekly average.

● **The index's performance.** As the index for an AML moves, so does your mortgage interest rate—if the index goes up by 1.25%, your interest rate rises by the same percentage. Every index performs differently, and has a particular bias depending on the financial instrument on which it is based. For example, indexes based on six-month Treasury securities are more volatile than five-year Treasury securities. When market interest rates drop, the six-month Treasury-bill market reflects the change more quickly than the five-year Treasury market.

- **Margins.** Many mortgage interest rates are expressed as a percentage over the index value. For instance, if one-year Treasury securities are yielding 8% and a lender has a margin of 2.5%, then the home buyer will receive a 10.5% interest rate.

- **Teaser rate.** A lender may offer a borrower a below-market (discounted) rate for the first year of a loan. The undiscounted rate is the sum of the current index value plus the margin. Confusion about the teaser rate can arise if the borrower does not understand that the rate is for one year only, and that the rate the second year will be higher even if the index remains at the same level.

Your decision about a loan should be based on the undiscounted rate as well as the teaser. To calculate the actual rate, find out the exact name of the index, whether it is a weekly or monthly average, and its current value. Add the margin. If you are comparing two loan programs that give the same total, but one offers a teaser rate, you may decide to take advantage of the discount even if it is only for one year.

Teaser rates usually do not result in negative amortization (i.e., the interest you avoid paying is not added to the balance of the principal). However, increases in the second year from the teaser rate to the undiscounted rate may or may not be affected by a cap.

QUALIFYING FOR A HOME LOAN WHEN YOU'RE SELF-EMPLOYED

If you are self-employed, qualifying for a home loan may be a little more difficult than if you were a salaried employee. Mortgage lenders generally require much more detailed income verifications, tax returns and company financial data (if you are a business owner). The specific requirements and documentation vary from lender to lender, but there are several basic criteria used by most in determining whether a self-employed individual can qualify for a loan.

The Requirements

Lenders usually require you to have been in business for at least two years. Self-employed individuals with less than two years of business operation do not have a long enough track record to convince lenders of their ability to pay off a mortgage.

Documentation is crucial. All lenders require the following documents: (1) copies of your signed tax returns for the past two years; (2) a year-to-date profit and loss statement signed by you or your accountant, plus a balance sheet;

(3) if the business is a partnership—the partnership agreement and partnership tax returns for the last two years or, if a wholly owned corporation—the last two years' corporate tax returns; and (4) all information regarding your share in the business, major assets and debts.

The most important item to most lenders is your Adjusted Gross Income figure as it appears on your 1040 tax return. But, don't worry if your gross income figure shows a loss. You may still qualify for a loan. Lenders usually allow certain items to be added back to that figure for purposes of evaluating a loan applicant, including IRA/Keogh contributions, pension or annuity, dividends and non-taxable deductions, plus some depletion and depreciation from Schedule C, the non-taxed portion of long-term gains from Schedule D, certain real estate depreciation from Schedule E and certain amortization from Form 4562.

....

Source: *Ted L. Lyon, formerly a branch manager, Merrill Lynch Realty, 3115 W. Parker Rd., Suite 500, Plano, TX 75023. Recipient of the Merrill Lynch Society of Excellence Award and director of the Texas Association of Realtors, he has taught marketing and finance and has been a speaker for the Institute of Financial Education of Realtor/Lender Relations.*

● **Caps.** Many adjustable mortgage loans have "caps" or limits on increases and decreases. These protect borrowers if rates go through the roof. If you pick a program with a teaser rate, you should make sure that the cap applies to both the monthly payment rate (the starting discounted rate) and the note rate (for determining your future rates). Otherwise you could see your monthly payments protected while your note rate goes through the roof, causing huge unanticipated negative amortization.

● **Adjustment period.** AMLs can adjust every three months, six months, yearly, every three years, five years, etc. Generally, the shorter the adjustment period, the lower the rate will be.

● **Convertibility.** In the event that interest rates come down, some AMLs are convertible into fixed-rate mortgages at specified times. This is an attractive option enabling you to lock in a future rate without extensive refinancing costs. (Most convertibility options require some restrictions and additional fees.)

> "**Fixed-rate mortgages are more expensive than AMLs (adjustable mortgage loans), because the lender takes on the risk of a possible increase in interest rates in the future.**"

Source: Charles A. Breinig, formerly a mortgage analyst, Mortgage Reporting Service, Inc., and now an associate broker with Weichert Realtors in Jenkintown, PA. He is the author of, and lectures on, How to Comparison Shop for a Mortgage.

Adjustable-Rate Mortgage vs. Fixed-Rate Mortgage

Choosing between an adjustable mortgage loan (AML) and a fixed-rate mortgage requires a risk/benefit decision by the individual borrower. Since the many elements involved affect each home buyer differently, how well they are evaluated can make the difference between substantial savings and an expensive gamble.

Affordability

Fixed-rate mortgages are more expensive than AMLs, because the lender takes on the risk of a possible increase in interest rates in the future. With an AML, on the other hand, the borrower assumes that risk in exchange for a lower initial interest rate.

By choosing a 5½% AML over a 7½% fixed-rate

mortgage, for example, you can increase your purchasing power by almost 20%. Assuming interest rates don't rise (making your AML more expensive over the long run), that could mean buying a $130,800 house versus a $110,000 house for the same monthly mortgage payments.

Alternatively, the advantage of a fixed-rate mortgage is that you know exactly how much you will have to pay over a long period of time. This can be very valuable for people living on a fixed income or who don't expect a major increase in their future earnings. In this case, the security of having a fixed monthly payment outweighs the benefit of the potential savings of an AML. However, the extra cost of a fixed-rate mortgage may force a buyer to settle for a smaller house or less desirable neighborhood.

Looking Forward

As a rule, a $100,000 adjustable mortgage (30-year term) at 5.5% interest requires your minimum earnings to be approximately $30,300* (combined family income). How would you handle an increase in interest rates? Assuming the AML had a cap of 2% per year and a 5% maximum lifetime cap, and that the mortgage

*Calculation:

(Allow 28% of income to pay for mortgage)

$30,300 ÷ 12 = $2,528	Monthly income	
x 28%	Allowance	
$ 708.00		
$ 568.00	*Principal & interest*	
120.00	*Real estate taxes*	
+ 20.00	*Insurance*	
$ 708.00	*Monthly payment*	

increased at the maximum rate permissible, your combined family income would have to grow about 3% for the first two years to cover the increase. (Most AMLs today do have caps or limits on increases in your monthly payments.)

Fixed-rate mortgages also require you to think about the future. Before you take on the mortgage, consider the costs involved in refinancing should interest rates drop and you want to get out of a mortgage that has become very expensive.

Do you plan on living in your home for a long or short period of time? Lenders charge a premium for fixed-rate mortgages because of the risk of increases in interest rates; the longer the term of the mortgage, the more difficult it is to predict interest rate fluctuations—and the greater the risk that interest rates will rise to the point where the loan is not producing an adequate return for the lender.

Don't pay a premium for the ability to keep a fixed-rate loan for 30 years if you plan to sell your home in 3 to 5 years, either because of a job transfer or because the home is a "starter home."

The Best Deal

After you've decided which type of loan is best for you, always shop around for the best rate. Rates between different lenders and different geographical areas can vary widely. Rates on the same type of mortgage loan can differ by as much as 2%. Remember that even a small interest rate savings can mean a significant savings on your overall mortgage payments. For example, a $3/4$% reduction in the interest rate on a 30-year, $100,000 mortgage would save you $21,000.

Don't rely solely on your real estate agent for advice on the best rates. Real estate agents work

QUESTIONS TO ASK BEFORE SIGNING MORTGAGE PAPERS

Because it is such a long-term contract, conditions that may seem minor when signing a mortgage loan contract can end up costing a lot of money during the life of the agreement. *Some typical mortgage clauses to negotiate before signing:*

● **Payment of "points":** Percentage of the amount of the loan paid to the lender at the start of the loan. Banks and thrift institutions have no statutory right to charge points. Their presence may reflect competitive local market conditions. And when interest rates are high, points are common. They're inevitable when rate ceilings exist.

Helpful: Try to negotiate on points.

● **Prepayment penalties:** Sometimes as much as six months' interest or a percentage of the balance due on the principal at the time the loan is paid off. With mortgages running for 25 or 30 years, the chances of paying them off early are relatively high.

● **"Due on encumbrance" clause:** Makes the first mortgage immediately due in full if property is pledged as security on any other loan, including second mortgages. Not legal in some places and usually not enforced when it is legal. Request its deletion.

● **"Due on sale"** clauses: Require full payment of loan when the property is sold.

● **Escrow payment:** The popular practice of requiring a prorated share of local taxes and insurance premiums with each monthly mortgage payment.

The bank earns interest on the escrow funds throughout the year and only pays it out when taxes and premiums are due. Amounts to forced savings with no interest.

Have your lawyer check the state's law to see if interest on escrow-account money is due to you. (It is, in several states.) If not, try to eliminate escrow—pay taxes and insurance on your own.

Other alternatives to escrow:

● **Capitalization plan,** in which monthly tax and insurance payments are credited against outstanding mortgage principal until they are paid out to the government or insurer, thus lowering amount of mortgage interest.

● **Lender may agree to waive escrow** if borrower opens an interest-bearing savings account in the amount of the annual tax bill.

● **Option of closing out the withheld escrow payments** when the borrower's equity reaches 40%. At that point, the bank figures, equity interest will be a powerful incentive to keep up tax payments.

Source: The Consumer's Guide to Banks by Gordon L. Weil, Stein & Day.

with only a handful of mortgage solicitors who provide them with rate quotations on a weekly basis. You may be able to find a better bargain elsewhere. The real estate agent has been hired by the seller to sell a house and cannot be expected to spend his or her time finding you the best deal.

Source: *Charles A. Breinig, formerly a mortgage analyst, Mortgage Reporting Service, Inc., and now an associate broker with Weichert Realtors in Jenkintown, PA. He is the author of, and lectures on,* How to Comparison Shop for a Mortgage.

When It Pays to Remortgage

If you bought your home in the past few years, you may now be able to save a bundle by refinancing your mortgage. *Rule of thumb:* Subtract the mortgage rate now available from the rate you now pay. If the difference is equal to or greater than the points you will be charged to refinance, you should remortgage.

How Refinancing Works

If you have a $100,000 25-year mortgage at 15%, your monthly payment is $1,280.84. If you refinance during the first year at 9 ½%, your payment will plummet to $873.70. *Monthly saving:* $407.14. Points (say, $3,000) and other fees (perhaps $750) would be paid off, together with $850 of principal, in less than 10 months.

Even if the drop in interest rates is smaller, you can still benefit. *Example:* If the same $100,000 loan dropped from 14% to 11%, you would still save $223 per month, and you would pay off the cost of remortgaging, plus $1,250 of principal, in less than 17 months.

What to Choose

Best deal: Shorter mortgages. Many banks offer loans that can be paid off in as few as 15 years. Don't let the sound of that scare you. Monthly payments are not that much higher.

Installments on a $100,000 mortgage at 11% would look like this:

Mortgage length	Monthly payment
15 years	$1,136.60
20 years	$1,032.19
25 years	$980.12
30 years	$952.33

Bottom line: The difference between payments on a 15-year and a 30-year mortgage is just

$184.27/month, and you save nearly $140,000 over the life of the loan.

Adjustable-rate mortgages got a bad reputation when rates were high and they were the only type of financing many people could afford. But they bear looking into today.

Source: *David Schechner, real estate lawyer, Schechner and Targan, 80 Main St., West Orange, NJ 07052.*

New Opportunities (and Traps) in Second Mortgages

Second mortgages, often called home-equity loans, are an increasingly flexible and attractive means of raising fairly large amounts of money.

One of the most convenient wrinkles in the second-mortgage business is the ability to write checks against a line of credit secured by the borrower's equity interest in his home. An individual can get a large loan for almost any purpose merely by writing a check.

Moreover, the interest rate on the loan probably will be lower, possibly considerably lower, than it would be if the borrower had obtained an ordinary personal loan. Generally, the interest rate on a second mortgage (because it is secured by residential real estate) is one to two percentage points lower than the interest rate on a personal loan.

Second-Mortgage Risks

A borrower should be aware, however, of some of the dangers inherent in second mortgages. First of all, the borrower is using his or her home to collateralize the loan. If for some reason the loan cannot be repaid as originally planned, there is the possibility that the house will be lost.

Considering this risk, a potential second-mortgage borrower should think carefully about what he or she plans to use the loan for. Is it prudent to put a lien on a home to take a vacation paid for by writing a check against a second-mortgage credit line?

When They Make Sense

Second mortgages have a very legitimate role to play and should be carefully considered, especially when large amounts of money are needed—paying for a child's education or an addition to a home, for example, or dealing with a large medical bill.

Potential second-mortgage borrowers should shop carefully. Different institutions offer substantially different kinds of second mortgages and a wide range of interest rates.

A critical element is the amount of money needed. Some lenders set relatively low limits, such as $50,000 or $60,000, while some will go several times higher.

Of course, the amount an individual can borrow under a second mortgage is limited by the equity he or she holds in the home. That is the appraised value of the property minus the amount owed under the first mortgage. The second mortgage allows the borrower to obtain cash for the increased value of his or her property and for the amount of principal already paid on the first mortgage. He or she thus can "unlock" the frozen cash equity in the home.

> "In almost every market, it's possible to find a two- to three-percentage-point difference between the lowest and highest rates you'll be offered."

Key Consideration

Is the loan fixed rate or variable rate? Usually, the initial interest rate on a fixed-rate second mortgage is higher than it is on a variable-rate loan. *Reason:* On a fixed-rate loan, the lender is assuming the risk of a rise in interest rates. Even if rates were to rise dramatically, the interest paid by a fixed-rate borrower remains unchanged. On a variable-rate mortgage, however, the borrower assumes this risk, or at least a substantial part of it.

Therefore, an individual should consider the purpose of the loan in deciding whether to opt for a rate that is fixed or variable. If the loan is for a long-term purpose, such as adding an extension to a home, it might be wise to take a fixed-rate loan, viewing the initial higher interest rate as a form of insurance against a sharp rise in interest rates in the future. If interest rates were to drop sharply, the fixed-rate loan could be refinanced.

Warning: Check for prepayment penalties, and shop to see which lender's offer is least onerous.

Variable rates usually are better suited for loans that the borrower expects to pay off in a relatively short period. Loans used for investments could be expected to generate enough cash flow to at least keep up with sharply rising interest rates.

Beware of Balloons

Borrowers should also be careful about so-called "balloons." These are second mortgages that fall due within a few years, usually three to five. But the repayment schedule might have been calculated on a basis of up to 20 years. Thus, at the end of, say, five years, although very little might have been paid on the principal, the lender could demand immediate and full repayment. If that were to happen and the borrower could not raise the money, he or she might lose his or her home.

It is therefore essential that the contract have a clause requiring the borrower to renew the loan. *Note:* It is critical that you borrow from a reputable lender. The last thing most well-established financial institutions want to do is take over your home. They will always try to work things out if the going gets tough. That is not always the case with unknown lenders.

If your needs are special, many second-mortgage lenders will try to devise a program that is tailored to your requirements. For example, they might agree to postpone payments for a specified period of time.

Refinancing

An alternative to a second mortgage is refinancing a home. Conceivably, the holder of the first mortgage would be willing to write a new and bigger first mortgage on the home. The interest rate probably would be higher than that on the original mortgage, but the net cost might be lower.

In considering second mortgages or refinancing an existing mortgage, look at all costs. These include taxes and "points" (up-front fees).

Home-Equity Loan Traps

Home-equity loans are dangerous propositions—and can be more expensive than other types of credit.

Consumer drawbacks:

● **Not doing enough shopping *before* you apply.** In almost every market, it's possible to find a two- to three-percentage-point difference between the lowest and highest rates you'll be offered. *Why:* Most lenders put these in their own "portfolio" of loans, and don't sell them, so they're free to charge what they think the market will bear.

● **Prepayment penalties can hit you in the pocketbook.** To keep you from jumping from cheap credit line to cheap credit line, like many savvy credit card hoppers do, lenders are increasingly adding in "early termination fees" that range from several hundred to as much as a thousand dollars if you close the line within a given period of time, usually three years.

● **Annual fees and "non-usage fees" are creeping in to more contracts** to discourage "convenience users" who establish a line of credit as a security blanket but don't actively use it. Lenders make no interest charges if you don't spend, so they'll charge you a fee for not actively using your line, or if you only tap a small amount each year.

New kinds of home-equity loans can be a dangerous proposition, prompting people to borrow way above their heads. ***Trouble spots:***

● **Debt-consolidation loans that lend you well in excess of the value of your home**—as much as 150% of the value. A "zero balance" on a credit card statement may be too much temptation for profligate spenders, who may bury themselves in debt with new purchases.

● **You may not be able to refinance at today's lowest rates**—if at all—when you borrow above the value of your home. In fact, borrowing just 125% of the value may take you as long as 10 years to get back to owing nothing! Without some equity in the home, you can't get today's lowest rates, and lenders may refuse to refinance your mortgage at all. You may be stuck with a fairly high-interest-rate mortgage and home equity loan for a long time.

● **It could cost you thousands out-of-pocket to sell your home,** since not only will you owe more on your mortgage than the home is worth, you'll also have to pay a sales commission to the broker—up to 5% of the home's value.

Source: *Keith T. Gumbinger, HSH Associates, Butler, NJ 07405; www.hsh.com.*

Mortgage Scam

Fraud is increasing through phony notices of mortgage sales. Beware of notices from an unfamiliar bank or finance company saying that your bank has sold its mortgage—and requesting payments be sent to a new address. Send payments only if (1) your original bank also sends you a letter giving notice of the sale, the name of the new mortgage company, your outstanding balance and your account number; and (2) the new mortgage company confirms this information by sending you a book of payment slips with the same account number and the proper balance. *Helpful:* Call your old bank to double-check.

Source: *Real Estate Investment Digest.*

Renovations That Increase Value

Kitchens

Whether you plan a major kitchen renovation (incorporating an entirely new design) or a minor one (mostly cosmetic—refinishing cabinets, new countertops, and a new appliance or two), the emphasis today is the same—new products and sophisticated design concepts. Energy-saving appliances and contemporary European styling are at the top of today's trend list. The following are other trends you may want to adopt in your renovation project.

● **Designer-look laminates** are very popular in many renovated kitchens, but wood is still holding its own as an accent element on counter edging, beams and trim treatments.

● **Colors** are an important selling factor. White, grays and light wood tones are the most popular. Dark woods and intense colors are losing favor.

● **Pay attention to lighting.** This is becoming an

increasingly important factor in the overall appearance of a kitchen. Options range from high-tech fixtures that illuminate work areas to dimmer switches that provide a more subdued dining or entertaining atmosphere.

● **In great demand:** Open kitchens that are integrated into living areas. Some home owners are taking walls out between kitchens and dining areas to achieve an open atmosphere.

In addition to providing energy savings, added convenience, style and enjoyment value, renovation can boost the resale value of your home. By completely remodeling the kitchen at a cost in the $6,700 to $22,000 range (with a typical cost of $15,000), you can expect to recover 50% to 80% of that expenditure in added value to your home if you sell it within five years.

Bathrooms

Most people have two choices when it comes to bathroom renovation—remodel an existing bathroom or add a new one. Additions often make the most economic sense, because houses with only a single bathroom are usually less salable. Adding a second bathroom at a cost of $4,400 to $10,000 (typically $6,000) can yield a cost recovery of 100% to 130% if you sell your home within five years.

If you decide to remodel an existing bathroom, use care. Total renovation is usually less costly than piecemeal replacement and repairs. But don't go overboard renovating a small or average bathroom—if you plan to sell your home shortly, it's probably not worth your while to spend a great deal of money. On the other hand, expanding an existing bathroom can add considerably to your home's market appeal, as can adding custom features. If your prime concern is resale, try using lighter, neutral colors and easy-care finishes when renovating.

In any case, don't compromise on quality. Brand names may be more expensive initially, but you are guaranteed that replacement parts will be available. Also, try to avoid major shifts in the location of the fixtures (sink, tub, toilet). This only adds unnecessarily large costs to your plumbing bill.

Windows, Doors and Skylights

Replace windows and doors that are not energy-efficient with ones that are. If you plan to keep your home awhile or want to sell at a higher price, make sure that your window and door replacements are attractive, too.

Important features to look for when replacing doors are richly carved wood doors with double locking devices, dead bolts, and peepholes; windows should be double-glazed. Adding storm windows and doors are also a good investment.

Skylights are an increasingly popular source of natural lighting that can offer improved ventilation and a feeling of spaciousness. South-facing skylights are potential sources of passive solar heating. Almost any room with a roof directly over it is a candidate for at least one skylight. The one weakness of most skylights—leakage—has been eliminated through better design.

Whether you plan to stay or sell, skylights are a great investment. Their short-term recovery rate is between 60% and 75%, and they are a strong selling point in both cold and warm climates. This is a household addition you shouldn't cut corners on, however. Top-quality units are easier to assemble and provide savings on installation and maintenance costs.

Fireplaces

Energy-efficient fireplaces are the remodeling project with the highest payback—sometimes offering home owners up to a 130% return on their investment at the time they sell their home. The main reason for this is the low initial cost of fireplace renovation (normally less than $4,000) compared to other improvements. Another is the increased savings a home owner enjoys with an energy-efficient unit compared to an open hearth.

Prefabricated units are attractive because of their space-saving features. The most popular models are only 36 inches wide and can be installed in corners to conserve on wall space. The current trend is toward top-quality models finished with floor-to-ceiling stonework, a mantel and a raised hearth. When you decide to buy, look at three or more different brands and types. And, of course, be sure to have whatever model you select properly installed.

Source: Henry F. Broesche, founder and president, Brighton Homes, Inc., 5450 NW Central Dr., Suite 250, Houston 77092. He is a member and former president of the Home Owners Warranty Corp. and of the Greater Houston Builders Association. In addition, he has served on the executive committee of the Texas Association of Builders.

Buying & Selling a House, Condo or Co-op

Home Improvements That Save Taxes When You Sell

Although the 1997 Taxpayer Relief Act eliminated the need for most people to be concerned about owing capital gains tax on the sale of a home, some home sellers may still need to reckon with the issue. For those whose homes have a gain above the limit of $500,000 for married tax filers and $250,000 for singles—or who live in states that impose their own, lower capital gains limits—keeping good records on home improvements remains essential. You can reduce the capital gains tax on any profit from the sale of your home by adding the documented cost of improvements to the original price you paid. The following improvements can qualify for this tax benefit.

Improvements to the House
- **Additions and finishing:** New rooms, porches, closets, laundry chutes, dumbwaiters, attic and basement improvements.
- **Built-in furnishings:** Permanently placed units such as chests, cabinets, shelving; installation of permanent floor covering.
- **Electrical wiring:** Installation of new power lines, outlets, switches, lighting fixtures.
- **Equipment:** Built-in stereo systems, intercoms, fire alarms, garbage disposal units, dishwashers, stoves, refrigerators, washing machines, dryers, elevators.

Plumbing, Heating, Air-Conditioning
- **Installation** of new or additional plumbing fixtures, sinks, laundry tubs, water softeners; piping, tanks, pumps, wells.
- **Upgrading** of heating system, air-conditioning units, attic fans, humidifiers, dehumidifiers.
- **Insulation,** solar heating or other energy-conserving devices (less the amount of energy tax credit claimed).

Structural Work
- **Installation** of louvers and screen vents in attic.
- **Replacement** of roofing, gutters or exterior covering of the house with better materials.
- **Installation** of awnings, sunshades, shutters, blinds, storm doors, storm windows, screens.
- **Upgrading** of interiors with major brick, stone, cement or plastering work.
- **New doors or windows**; acoustical ceilings;

strengthening of structure with steel girders, reinforcing rods, floor jacks.
- **Work done** on the foundation to eliminate water seepage and settling.

Improvements to the Grounds
- **Equipment:** Outdoor sound systems, floodlighting, lampposts, barbecue pits, incinerators, mailboxes, underground sprinkler systems.
- **Landscaping:** Enlargement of lawn area, addition of trees or shrubbery, resurfacing of land areas or installation of drain tiles and other equipment to eliminate drainage problems, addition or redesigning of decorative pools and arbors.
- **Paving and surfaces:** Blacktopping or other improvements to driveway, laying or extension of walks and curbs, addition or enlargement of patios.
- **Recreational facilities:** Installation of swimming pool and related facilities, tennis court, children's playground equipment.
- **Structures:** Addition, improvement or removal of fences, walls, trellises, garages, carports, toolsheds, stables, greenhouses or other outbuildings.

> "You can reduce the capital gains tax on any profit from the sale of your home by adding the documented cost of improvements to the original price you paid."

Source: *William J. Roll, CPA, partner in the CPA firm Herring & Roll, PC, 41 South Fifth St., Sunbury, PA 17801.*

Home-Improvement Mistakes to Avoid

Winter is a good time to turn dreams of adding a bedroom, kitchen or bath into reality. But that calls for shopping around, simple research and hard thinking before you convert your dream project into a contract to build.

The first rule in planning a home improvement is to make sure that you and your family will realize value from the project in convenience and pleasure right now—and that you can afford it right now.

First, shop around for the financing you might need. Tell your banker what you're thinking of doing, and ask for the rates and payment terms on second mortgages, home-equity loans or special home-renovation packages. And if you have a healthy business or personal account at the bank, see what kind of a rate you can get on a straight personal loan. Then, when you start talking with a contractor, you'll be able to compare any financing rates and terms he or she offers with those from other sources. Sometimes the contractor may do enough business with a bank to get lower rates than you can.

Follow the Rules

Once you and the contractor are in serious discussions, don't try to take shortcuts around local regulations. A qualified contractor will know local code standards and can obtain a building permit without delay and without hassle to you.

More and more local communities are licensing contractors. That gives you an opportunity to check them out. Call the local building inspector and ask whether he knows the contractor you're thinking of hiring and whether any complaints are pending. Chances are good that you'll get frank advice to look around further if the contractor has a record of faulty work.

Ask the contractor exactly how he plans to do the work. It's important that you have specific information on how long you will be without a working kitchen, or know how the contractor plans to protect your home if he or she has to open an outside wall. Let the contractor take you step by step through the method he or she will use so you'll know what preparations you will have to make—moving and storing furniture, making alternative living arrangements and the like.

Special precaution: When you're putting an addition on the house, be particularly careful about how the new plumbing lines are installed and protected. Contractors often fail to protect the lines from freezing temperatures. Once the walls and moldings are in place, leaks in these lines will be expensive to repair.

Make clear to the contractor that you expect the work site to be kept clean. Tell him or her that you expect workers to eat their meals in their cars or on trucks. *Reason:* Many home owners find their homes infested with bugs and rodents after a major renovation because the workers dumped their leftover food in the wall spaces.

Good-Neighbor Policy

It usually pays to check your plans for a major renovation with your nearest neighbors before work starts. Put your project in the most positive light, but be alert to signs of opposition, and try to negotiate any differences. A compromise is very likely to be much cheaper than litigation.

Don't rush blindly into even simple projects such as widening a driveway or paving part of the backyard for a basketball court. Many communities restrict the number of cars that can be parked in the front yard, and most zoning codes have restrictions on covering more than a certain portion of the land, which includes the blacktop.

Be careful, too, about when you schedule the work. Most localities have rules about how early in the morning workers can start to use noisy equipment. Many resort communities prohibit major construction during the summer months.

Source: David Schechner, attorney and village counsel for South Orange, NJ, 80 Main St., West Orange, NJ 07052.

How to Hire the Best Home Contractor for You

Over the past 20 years, I have heard some horrible stories about unscrupulous contractors doing terrible things to home owners.

As the number of home-improvement projects in the United States increases, some contractors find it easy to rip off people who have not had enough experience to know better.

A contractor is responsible for hiring others to install a new kitchen, add a new room or make major design changes. Here's how to hire the right one—and to make sure your interests are protected:

Sizing Up the Talent

● **Ask friends for recommendations.** Then get two to three references from each contractor.

Best: Visit at least one completed project as well as one project in progress. *Strategy:* Ask each contractor's former clients specific questions about his or her work and work style. *Key questions to ask:*

- **Was the job started on time?**
- **Did workers show up on time?**
- **Did they complete the job on time?**
- **Was the contractor always available?**
- **Did you get what you wanted?**
- **Were there any surprises?**
- **Was the contractor responsive** to problems after the job was completed?
- **What would you do differently** if you were hiring a contractor again?

Each of these questions is designed to yield critical information. Negative answers shouldn't necessarily rule out a contractor, but instead raise issues to discuss with him or her. *Example:* You may discover that the contractor you like best isn't prompt about returning phone calls. By knowing this in advance, you can stress how important callbacks are to you and insist on a daily or weekly time to speak with him or her.

- **Interview the candidates you like in person.** Face-to-face meetings are always best, since you will be able to determine whether you are comfortable with the contractor. You don't want someone who looks impatient or seems reluctant to answer detailed questions.

Important: Before an interview with a contractor, put together a list of your general expected working rules. Give the list to the contractor so that he or she knows up front what you expect. *Example:* If you want to avoid having dirt tracked through your home, insist that the contractor bring his or her own portable toilet.

- **Ask each of the contractors you like for a bid on the project.** They should provide free job estimates that are typed, easy to understand and specific.

A good bid includes *start* and *completion* dates and pro-consumer clauses like daily working hours and promises to protect existing surfaces.

Important: Make sure there's no clause authorizing the substitution of materials without your written permission.

Making the Choice

If you find that all the contractors are great and all their bids are similarly priced, the answers to these questions may help you decide among them:

- **Does the contractor have a clean complaint record?** Call your local Better Business Bureau, which will provide a verbal or written report. Also, call your state's Attorney General's office, Building Department and Licensing Bureau to find out about complaints. More than one recent complaint is a red flag.

- **How many projects is the contractor working on right now?** If he or she is working on more than two or three projects at once, he or she may be hard to locate and is unlikely to spend much time at your job site.

- **Will the contractor give a warranty for the work for one year?** A written warranty should be part of the contract. All legitimate contractors will include one. A warranty is important because if something falls apart, it will usually happen within the first year. The warranty should state that the contractor will fix the problem within 10 days.

Before Signing the Contract

- **Ask for copies of all professional licenses and insurance documents**—including the contractor's driver's license, which confirms his identity. Without it, you can't be sure that the other licenses you request actually belong to that contractor.

Important: Make sure the contractor purchases a performance bond. It is bought through a surety company for about $100. A surety company provides a bond to the contractor for one year and pays the homeowner if the contractor skips out on the job. The performance bond covers the cost to complete the job if the contractor cannot for any reason.

Other important documents:

- **The contractor should have legible copies** of the occupational license from the city, a county license and—in most states—a state license. Ask your state's Attorney General's office for a list of what is required.

- **A subcontractor** needs to have a county license and sometimes a city license.

- **The contractor should have** workers' compensation and liability insurance. Request a certificate of insurance. If the contractor is a sole proprietor with no employees, confirm that he has personal insurance or workers' compensation.

If your contractor or the people he or she hires aren't properly insured, you're liable for any mishaps. Request a copy of the insurance documents, and call the agent to confirm coverage.

- **Set up a payment schedule.** A contractor is a

businessperson; he or she will want as much in the form of a down payment as possible.

Ideal: You provide 10% of the project's total cost on the day work starts, not when the contract is signed. ***Strategy:*** Create a payment schedule pegged to specific work milestones. Be fair. But write the contract so that you withhold the final 10% to 15% until 20 days after the job is completed. That will give you time to see if everything was really done as you requested. Also, it will give the contractor an incentive to finish promptly. It's a bad sign if the contractor balks at this.

● **Make sure you're getting what you pay for.** Have the contract state that you'll have an opportunity to inspect all materials before they are used. ***Example:*** Consumers often get gouged on insulation jobs. Contractors frequently shortchange people on the amount of insulation that is required. ***Solution:*** Home-repair books or insulation packages can tell you how much you'll need based on the square footage involved.

Important: Count the bags before the insulation is installed. Some contractors bring empty bags to fool people who count this way. If in doubt, ask the company to provide a density test.

Source: *Steve Gonzalez, a professional contractor in Fort Lauderdale, FL. He is the author of* Before You Hire a Contractor: A Construction Guidebook for Consumers, *Consumer Press.*

PROTECTING YOURSELF IN HOME-IMPROVEMENT CONTRACTS

Improving a home has become more attractive than buying a new one for many people.

The key to protecting yourself when hiring a contractor for a major alteration is thoughtful contract negotiation. Even contractors with good reputations sometimes get in over their heads.

● **Try to do your own financing.** While some contractors get better rates from banks they deal with frequently, research the details. They may give the lender a second mortgage on your house—sometimes without your realizing it. That can leave you without leverage to force correction of bad workmanship.

● **Review the document from the contractor's insurance company** covering workers' compensation. A standard homeowners policy does not cover workers (except, in some states, an occasional baby-sitter).

● **Fix responsibility for repairing wind,** rain or fire damage, as well as possible vandalism at the work site.

● **Include a payment schedule in the contract.** Typically, a contractor gets 10% of the negotiated fee upon signing a contract, then partial payments at completion of each stage of succeeding work. You should withhold any payment until the contractor actually begins work. Then hold down succeeding payments as much as possible so that the contractor does not earn a profit until the work is completed.

● **Make sure the final payment** is contingent upon approval of the work by municipal inspectors.

● **Make the contractor responsible** for abiding by local building codes.

If you assume this responsibility, make the contract contingent on your ability to get all necessary building permits.

Be specific about what work you want done, how and with what materials.

● **Don't settle for normal contract language** about the project's being done in "a workmanlike manner," because homeowners' standards for work they want done is often higher than common trade practice.

● **To avoid misunderstandings,** refer in the contract to architect's drawings, where possible, and actual specifications.

● **Include a schedule** against which to measure the work's progress. Use calendar dates—for example, foundation and framing to be completed by March 1; roughing-in by April 1; sheetrock by May 1; woodwork and finish work by June 1.

● **Push for a penalty clause** if the work is completed unreasonably late—for example, all work to be completed by June 1. If, however, work is not completed by June 1, the contractor will pay the home owner $100 a day thereafter.

How Utility Meters Work

Both electric and gas meters operate on the same principle. Each has several dials with pointers that tell you how much of the utility you are using.

Electric meter:

● **It has five numbered dials.** The pointers on three of the dials turn clockwise, while the two others go counterclockwise.

● **It is read from left to right.** The pointer always registers the number it has just passed. *Example:* If the pointer rests between three and four, read the number as three. This holds true even if the pointer is touching the four but has not gone past it.

● **The numbers** taken off each of the dials gives you the reading of the meter at that moment. When it is read again (usually in a month), you know how many kilowatt-hours of electricity have been consumed.

● **Meters can be wrong.** Electric meters can wear out or be damaged during an electrical storm. A dramatic increase in your electric bill should signal a call to the utility company.

Gas meter:

● **It is read** exactly the same way as the electric meter. *Difference:* It has four dials. The pointers of two turn clockwise, while the two others go counterclockwise.

What You Should Know About Real Estate Agents

Knowing your legal rights and responsibilities when selling your home yourself or through a real estate broker can save you thousands of dollars—and a lot of worry and frustration over the possible wrong moves that you might make.

Selling your own home is not an easy task. You need to be able to provide buyers with information about zoning laws, community services and the condition of your home. Also, you have no security against intrusions by unqualified house hunters—curiosity seekers, potential thieves and the like.

If you decide to sell with a broker, shop around to find one who is knowledgeable about your community and with whom you feel comfortable.

The failure of sellers to read the legal documents pertaining to brokers' contracts is the cause of most misunderstandings.

Special points:

● **Commissions paid by the seller to the broker** are not established by any state or federal law agency or by any private trade association. The individual brokerages set their own fees. Some will negotiate a commission rate, others will not. The law does not require them to, however.

● **The listing agreement** is a legal document that outlines the understanding between you and the broker about how your home will be listed for sale. It includes your name, the broker's name, the address of the property, the asking price and other details about the home, as well as the amount of time you are giving the broker to find a buyer (30, 60, or 90 days is usual). This is a legal document, binding you to its provisions.

● **Exclusive right to sell** is the most common type of listing. The seller pays full commission to the listing broker, regardless of which real estate office brings in the buyer—even if the seller brings in the buyer.

● **In an exclusive agency agreement,** the listing broker is authorized to market your property during the agreed-upon time period. However, you owe no commission to the broker if you sell the property yourself. Some agencies will not accept such a listing.

● **Buyers' cries of misrepresentation or fraud** are often heard these days. The seller has a duty to tell the broker about defects in the house that are known to the seller and that might affect a buyer's willingness to purchase the property. Knowing about such defects and not mentioning them invites a suit for misrepresentation or fraud. Honesty will save you fears and problems in the future.

● **Lawsuits against sellers and brokers** about other problems relating to a house and neighborhood are cropping up. Are you required or is your broker required to disclose that the land beneath the home was once a chemical waste dump, or that you were aware of plans for a sewage-treatment plant down the street? Those kinds of questions are still to be resolved by the courts, but the importance of full disclosure of what you do know is clear.

● **Signing a contract** and accepting a buyer's "earnest" money commit you to the sale—unless the buyer reneges and therefore forfeits the money, or some contingency to the sale negates the contract. If you've signed a contract and then refuse to follow through, you could face a lawsuit should the buyer want to initiate

Ways to List Your House

✔ **Open listing:** The owner reserves the right to sell the property him- or herself or to retain brokers.

✔ **Exclusive agency:** No other broker will be hired as long as the original broker is retained (usually for a specified period), but this doesn't prevent the owner from selling the property him- or herself.

✔ **Exclusive right to sell:** The broker gets a commission when the property is sold, whether by the broker, the owner or anyone else.

✔ **Multiple listing:** Brokers combine to sell properties listed with any member of the brokers' pool. The listing broker offers to pay a portion of the commission to the selling broker.

If a time is specified, the agreement will end as stipulated. It would continue only if the owner has waived the time limit by accepting the services of the broker, or if the owner has acted in bad faith (as by postponing agreement with a buyer until after the time limit). In some states, if the listing is for a specified time, the owner can revoke only up until the time the broker puts money and effort into the listing contract.

If the state does not require a specific time period, the owner may revoke the listing before the broker has earned the commission, provided the owner acts in good faith and doesn't revoke when negotiations have been substantially completed. "Good faith" is subject to interpretation, so act on this privilege carefully.

If nothing is said, the broker will earn a commission on finding a buyer ready, willing and able to buy on the terms specified.

The owner, in order to protect him- or herself, should be sure to ask for a provision under which payment of the commission will depend on closing the deal and full payment.

one. In any event, you may still be responsible for the broker's commission.

Source: *John R. Linton, former vice president, legal affairs, National Association of Realtors, and Laurie Janik, current general counsel for the NAR, 430 N. Michigan Ave., Chicago, IL 60611.*

Getting More for an Old House

An old house (built from 1920 to 1950) can be sold as easily as a new one. The right selling strategy and a few improvements may raise the selling price significantly. *Suggestions:*

● **Invest in a complete** cleaning, repainting or wallpapering. Recarpet or have the rugs and carpets professionally cleaned. *Approximate cost for a four-bedroom, three-bath house:* $2,500 to $3,000.

● **Get rid of cat and dog odors** that you may be used to but potential buyers will notice.

● **With the trend toward smaller families** and working wives, it may be desirable to convert and advertise a four-bedroom house as two bedrooms, library, and den.

● **The exterior of the house** is crucial. It's the first thing the buyer sees. Paint or replace shutters if necessary. Clean and repair the porch, and remove clutter. Repaint porch furniture.

● **Landscaping** makes a great difference and can sell (or un-sell) a house. Get expert advice on improving it. *Approximate cost:* Anywhere from $100 to $1,000.

● **Good real estate agents** are vital to a quick sale. There are one or two top people in every agency who will work hard to show houses and even arrange financing. Multiple listing lets these super salespeople from different agencies work for the seller.

Best Color to Paint a House

Yellow houses have the most "curb appeal" and sell faster than those of any other color. Most people associate yellow with optimism and warmth.

Source: Leatrice Eiseman, color consultant and educator in Tarzana, CA

Selling Your House in a Hot Real Estate Market

In a competitive real estate market, homeowners can get an edge over other home sellers with offers to finance the sale themselves. By offering financing, sellers may make their house so marketable that outside financing will be unnecessary. And the commission saving is substantial.

However, although financing the sale of a house is simple in principle, sellers should have the advice of a lawyer who specializes in real estate.

Four Basic Methods

● **First mortgage.** If you are trying to sell a $100,000 house that has no mortgage (a rarity), and the purchaser can afford only $40,000 cash down, then the purchaser simply gives you a first mortgage for $60,000, which is paid out over an agreed-upon period, at an agreed-upon interest rate. In case of default, you keep the cash and foreclose on the house.

● **Second mortgage.** If you are trying to sell the same $100,000 house with an existing $50,000 first mortgage, a second mortgage reduces the cash that a buyer would need. The purchaser assumes the first mortgage and gives you a $20,000 down payment. The purchaser then gives you a second mortgage for $30,000. Interest rate and maturity date are negotiable. But many existing first mortgages held by institutional lenders contain a due-on-sale clause, which prohibits the sale of the house without the consent of the lender. Typically, such consent is given only if the interest rate is substantially increased.

● **Wrap-around.** Similar to second mortgages. Using the same numbers as in the second-mortgage example, you get a $20,000 down payment, but instead of taking back a $30,000 second mortgage, you take back an $80,000 wrap-around mortgage (the amount of the first mortgage plus the remaining $30,000 of the sales price). One advantage is that defaults are quick to catch because the buyer makes all payments directly to you, and you pay the first-

Buyers Who Back Out at the Last Minute

Selling a house can be a problem when the potential buyer makes the deal contingent on the sale of his or her own house. After months of waiting, your deal may fall through. *Solution:* Include a kick-out clause in the sales agreement. This enables the seller to keep the house on the market until the sale is completed. If another buyer makes an offer, the original buyer has 48 hours to decide whether he or she wants to buy the house or not.

mortgage portion to that lender. Another advantage is that the interest rate on the wrap-around is calculated on the entire $80,000, even though the $50,000 first-mortgage portion may be at a lower interest rate. Therefore, you receive the interest average, giving you a higher yield on your $30,000 portion.

● **Leasing with purchase option.** Lease payments may be applied to the purchase price, an amount agreed on when the deal is made. The best approach is to make the term as short as possible. Should another prospective buyer come along with ready cash, you won't be hindered by a long-term contract. And since you are still the owner, you can depreciate the house as a rental unit.

Source: C. Gray Bethea, Jr., is a real estate lawyer in Atlanta, GA.

If the Seller Has a Change of Heart

The seller of a house said he was canceling his contract to sell, and refunded the down payment. The buyer insisted the seller had no right to cancel. The seller argued that the buyer, by accepting and cashing the check, had agreed to cancellation of the sale. The court ruled for the buyer, and ordered the seller to perform the contract. The return of the down payment, the court said, had no legal effect. It was not a sum of money accepted in settlement of a dispute. It was nothing but the return of the buyer's money, which the seller had no right to keep while refusing to complete the sale.

Source: Merrill Lynch Realty *v.* Skinner, Ct. App., *NY, 473 N.E. (2d) 229.*

Condos and Co-ops Defined

The terms *condominium* and *cooperative* are definitions of types of ownership.

● **In a condominium,** you actually own your unit—

just as you do when you buy a house.

● **In a co-op,** you own stock in the building's corporation, which entitles you to the use of your unit.

In both types of residences, you share common areas such as lawns, gardens and pools with other residents.

Co-ops tend to be a bit more difficult to sell because of strong co-op boards that carefully scrutinize new buyers.

Condos and co-ops rarely compete for the same buyers in the same market. When they occasionally do, price differentials are most often determined by location, rather than by type of housing.

Source: *Robert Irwin, a Danville, CA, real estate broker for more than 25 years. He is the author of more than 20 books about real estate, including* Tips & Traps When Buying a Home *and* Tips & Traps When Mortgage Hunting, *McGraw-Hill.*

Condos vs. Co-ops

When you purchase a condominium, you own real property, just as when you buy a house. You arrange for your own mortgage with the bank, pay real estate taxes directly to the local government, pay water bills individually and have an individual deed.

When you buy a cooperative apartment, you are participating in a syndication. A corporation is formed, shares are issued and people subscribe to the shares. The corporation raises money, takes out a mortgage and owns the building.

Maintenance charges for a condominium are likely to cost 50% of a cooperative's charges for an equivalent building. *Reason:* The maintenance on a condominium covers only the common area upkeep. *That includes:* labor, heating oil, repairs and maintenance of the playground, swimming pool and other community areas. Co-op maintenance fees cover those same items plus mortgage payments, local real estate taxes utility and water bills.

Capital improvements: If an extensive, major repair needs to be made (such as the replacement of a roof or boiler), the board of managers of a condo cannot borrow funds from a bank unless it receives the unanimous consent of the condo owners. *Problem:* If a dozen owners are content to live in a dilapidated building, improvements must be funded through maintenance cash flow, which may be very

expensive. In a co-op, the board of directors can take out a second mortgage to fix a roof, plumbing or other major problem. Individual co-op shareholders cannot easily obstruct the board.

Delinquency in paying maintenance fees can be handled more expediently in a co-op than in a condo. In a co-op, an owner who doesn't pay maintenance fees can be evicted almost immediately. The person is served with a dispossess and can be evicted within days. In a condominium, a lien must be placed on the apartment and then a foreclosure proceeding is brought. It can take two years to get the money, and it is a difficult legal proceeding.

Exclusionary rights: Since a co-op is considered personal property, not real property, prospective tenants may be rejected by the co-op's board of directors for any reason whatsoever except race, creed, color, or national origin. *Reality:* As long as the co-op board members don't state the reason, anyone can be excluded for any cause. *Problem:* A tenant may have trouble subletting a co-op if the co-op board members don't approve of the new tenant. In a condominium, each owner has the right to sell or sublet to anyone the person wants, subject only to the condo's right of first refusal, which is rarely exercised.

From the entrepreneur's point of view, a co-op can be more advantageous if the building at the time of the conversion date has a low-interest mortgage. *Reason:* When a building is converted into a condominium, it must be free and clear of all liens. In a co-op, the former financing can be kept intact.

Source: *David Goldstick, former partner, Goldstick Weinberger, Feldman & Grossman, 261 Madison Ave., New York, NY 10016.*

When Buying a New Condominium

Before signing any contract for a *new* condominium, which is harder to check out than an *established* condominium, buyers should study the prospectus for any of these pitfalls:

● **The prospectus includes** a plan of the unit you are buying, showing rooms of specific dimensions. But the plan omits closet space. *Result:* The living space you are buying is probably smaller than you think.

● **The prospectus includes this clause:** The interior design shall be substantially similar. *Result:* The developer is able to alter the size and the design of your unit.

● **The common charges** set forth in the prospectus are unrealistically low. Buyers should never rely on a developer's estimate of common charges. *Instead:* They should find out the charges at similarly functioning condominiums.

Common charges include: electricity for hallways and outside areas, water, cleaning, garbage disposal, insurance for common areas, pool maintenance, groundskeeping, legal and accounting fees, reserves for future repairs.

● **Variation on the common-charge trap:** The developer is paying common charges on unsold units. But these charges are unrealistically low. *Reason:* The developer has either underinsured, underestimated the taxes due, omitted security expenses or failed to set up a reserve fund.

● **The prospectus includes this clause:** The seller will not be obligated to pay monthly charges for unsold units. *Result:* The owners of a partially occupied condominium have to pay for all operating expenses.

● **The prospectus warns** about the seller's limited liability. But an unsuspecting buyer may still purchase a condominium unit on which back monthly charges are due, or even on which there's a lien for failure to pay back carrying charges.

● **The prospectus makes no mention** of parking spaces. *Result:* You must lease from the developer.

● **The prospectus is imprecise** about the total number of units to be built. *Result:* Facilities are inadequate for the number of residents.

● **The prospectus includes this clause:** Transfer of ownership (of the common property from the developer to the home owners' association) will take place 60 days after the last unit is sold.

Trap: The developer deliberately does not sell one unit, continues to manage the condominium and awards sweetheart maintenance and operating contracts to his or her subcontractors.

● **The prospectus specifies** that the developer will become the property manager of the functioning condominium. But the language spelling out monthly common charges and management fees is imprecise. *Result:* The condo owners cannot control monthly charges and fees.

Source: *Dorothy Tymon, author,* The Condominium: A Guide for the Alert Buyer, *Golden-Lee Books.*

Your Financial Liability When You Sit on a Co-op Or Condo Board

It's generally believed that you have "arrived" when you are asked to sit on a board of directors. This applies whether it is a corporation board, bank board, school board or condo or co-op board. However, along with the prestige goes a high level of responsibility and liability.

Whether you are on the board of directors for a profit-making corporation or a nonprofit organization, never underestimate your obligations. Many people who sit on nonprofit boards and who receive no compensation for their services have little understanding that their legal position is similar to that of someone on a corporate board. In fact, a nonprofit board member may even incur a higher degree of responsibility in the eyes of a court, because he or she is seen as holding a position of public trust.

The principles of corporate law are applied to most nonprofit boards. The would-be director of any nonprofit organization is therefore wise to check on the state law—which varies greatly—as to the category of directorship and the legal duties that accompany it.

The primary obligations of an individual on a co-op or condominium board are (1) to act within his or her authority, (2) to exercise "due care" and (3) to fulfill all fiduciary duties. A breach of any of these will result in the following kinds of liability of responsible directors, unless state law specifically exempts nonprofit corporations from statutory proceedings to enforce that liability.

1. If the directors of a co-op or condo do not act within the scope of their authority, a dissenting co-op member may be able to bring suit against the directors to enjoin them or set their action aside, or to render them liable for mismanagement.

2. By law, directors owe their co-op/condo associations a "duty of care." The legislative and judicial definition of this term is not clear as it applies to nonprofit boards. The definition for business corporations, however, is that directors "discharge the duties of their respective positions in good faith and that degree of diligence and care and skill which ordinarily prudent men would exercise under similar circumstances in like positions." A duty of reasonable inquiry and reliance on information provided by others (corporate officers) is also encompassed by the corporate duty of care. The director is liable for dollar-for-dollar damages.

3. Failure to exercise one's fiduciary responsibilities can lead to suits in which a guilty director is liable for dollar-for-dollar damages.

As a fiduciary, a director may not disclose confidential information or use it for personal gain. If a director is ever in doubt about actions taken by management or the authenticity/ accuracy of any or all information furnished, including financial, it is the director's obligation to make known his concern and receive appropriate documentation.

Apart from knowing the applicable law and performing well, what can co-op or condo board members do to protect themselves? Insist on coverage by directors and officers liability insurance.

Source: John M. Nash, president emeritus, National Association of Corporate Directors, and chairman of the Center for Board Leadership in Washington, D.C.

How to Save Money When Building Your Own Home

Much can be said for doing things right the first time, especially when it comes to building your own home. It may be financially helpful to cut corners, but make sure you cut the *right* corners. The last thing you want is a shoddily constructed or designed home.

My advice is to treat the building of your home like any other business project. The two most important things you should do before building are to (1) hire a qualified general contractor, and (2) carefully plan your location, design and budget.

Using a General Contractor

Few people understand the actual number of day-to-day decisions that go into building a house—much less understand the local building rules and regulations. A good general contractor will procure the lowest-priced services, the desired quality, and guar-

The Most Valuable Vacation Homes

For maximum resale value of a vacation home, purchase property on the water, with as much frontage as you can afford, a house that faces northwest (for best afternoon sunlight), mildly rolling terrain, a rustic exterior or a modern kitchen and bath.

Source: Money.

antee the timely completion of your home. *Criteria to use when selecting a general contractor:*

- **Reputation and honesty.**
- **Financial capabilities.**
- **Communication skills.**
- **Business knowledge.**
- **Provision of a written warranty.**

Planning and Budgeting

The best way to ensure that your initial investment at least retains its value, but—more importantly—appreciates with time, is by selecting a good location and marketable design.

Location should always be the first and foremost decision. *The main factors to consider:*

- **Travel time.**
- **Costs.**
- **Schools.**
- **Availability and accessibility of shopping.**
- **Personal preference.**
- **Social and economic status of the neighborhood.**

The second most important decision is the design and the determination of the specific building requirements of that design. Carefully analyzing each room's size and utilization should help you eliminate or scale down little-used rooms or areas in the house, saving significant building and maintenance costs (e.g., heating and cooling).

Be sure to select a design that is marketable in the area you have chosen. In other words, avoid building a California home in Vermont. And remember, the design will have a large impact on the total cost of the house. *The major factors to consider:*

- **Two-story designs are the least expensive per square foot.**

WHEN IT'S TIME TO MOVE

Hiring a moving company should be approached the same way you would buy any other product or service—by becoming informed. A good way to start is by asking your friends which movers they've used. Contact the local Better Business Bureau and review all the literature provided to you by prospective moving companies. If the move will be to another state, the Federal Highway Administration requires your mover to give you a copy of the booklet "Your Rights and Responsibilities When You Move."

If possible, try to select a mover six to eight weeks in advance of your ideal moving date to ensure availability. The peak season for movers is June, July, August and September. During these months, vans may be scarce and costs, higher. You can usually save money by moving between October 1 and April 30, when many movers offer lower, off-season prices.

It's a good idea to obtain estimates from at least two reputable movers. Determine all of their charges and the types of services they offer. Compare to see which mover best suits your needs and budget. Before reaching a final decision, pay a visit to the mover's place of business to get an indication of how professional the company is. Look for (1) professional and business-like personnel, (2) clean and well-organized offices and warehouse and (3) equipment in good condition.

Getting Accurate Estimates

Unless you get binding estimates, most moving estimates are just educated guesses to help you anticipate your approximate moving expense. The final bill could be very different. To help movers calculate the most accurate estimate, show them every item to be moved. Try to reach a clear under-

standing about the amount of packing and other services you'll require—services that are not included in the estimate will be added on to the final cost.

Moving costs are usually determined by the actual weight of your possessions or the amount of space they take up in the mover's van. Factored into this total is the distance your possessions are transported and the optional services provided.

Liability Options

Pay particular attention to the liability options. Moving companies usually offer a variety of liability plans:

● **Released value plan.** You can seek recovery on an item at the rate of 60 cents per pound. The protection is minimal, but it costs nothing.

● **Declared value.** Under this option, the valuation of your shipment is based on the total weight times $1.25 per pound, and any damage or loss claim is settled based on depreciated value. The cost is $7 for each $1,000 of liability.

● **Lump sum value.** This option permits you to declare a specific dollar value for your shipment, but it must exceed $1.25 per pound times the weight of the shipment. The cost is the same as "Declared Value" and claims are based on depreciation.

If any of your possessions are damaged or lost, you have nine months to file a claim. It's always to your advantage to file promptly. The mover is required to acknowledge receipt of your claim within 30 days and within 120 days must make an offer to settle the claim.

Try to plan your packing day one or two days before the actual loading of the van. To save on charges, you may want to pack part of your belongings yourself. Ask the moving company about its policy on liability for customer-packed cartons.

Source: Joseph M. Harrison, president, American Moving and Storage Association, 1611 Duke St., Alexandria, VA 22314, the trade association for the professional household-goods moving industry.

● **Houses with one and a half stories are gaining in popularity,** especially those with first-floor master suites.

● **Ranches** (one-floor plans) are the most expensive per square foot, because the area between the foundation and the roof system is not maximized. It is always cheaper to build up than out.

● **Higher-pitched roofs are more expensive and more eye-appealing.**

● **Vaulted and cathedral ceilings are more expensive than flat ceilings.**

Construction Financing

As a property owner, it's better to obtain the construction loan yourself than to have the builder do it, since you avoid paying double closing costs and construction interest can be written off on your current year's income taxes. When your builder obtains the construction loan, you pay the interest costs and construction loan closing costs in the price of the property, but will have to treat the interest expenses as a capital gain when the property is sold.

Materials

Careful selection and specification of materials can save money without sacrificing quality. But be cautious—sometimes name brand choices can drive up costs and add only limited value. *Examples:* Name-brand plumbing fixtures are more expensive than contractor brands but usually no more effective. High-fashion designs and colors increase costs and possibly date the home's appearance. Nationally advertised windows will add 25% to 30% more to window costs.

Pay attention to areas where short-term savings should be weighed against long-term operating and maintenance costs. *In particular, note:*

● **Energy-related items,** i.e., extra insulation, high-efficiency furnaces with less than a five-year payback, energy-efficient water-heating systems, add-on electric heat pumps for gas and oil heating systems.

● **Exterior siding selection:**

Material	Initial cost	Maintenance cost
brick	high	low
stone	high	low
wood	high	high
aluminum	low	low
stucco	low	low
hardboard	low	high

Lot Selection and Landscaping

A wooded lot can be very appealing as a place to live, but there are problems when it comes to building. The initial cost of a wooded lot is generally higher than for non-wooded lots. Caution must be used to be sure that all of the trees on a wooded lot are not located where the house will be built. Clearing costs can run as high as several thousand dollars, and you can expect that construction equipment will lose some efficiency when operating in wooded lots, thereby adding more costs.

Landscaping expenses can be reduced by selecting small plants and trees that will grow rather than landscaping with fully grown stock, and by negotiating with the landscaping company on eliminating expensive guarantees for growth. This can reduce your total landscaping bill by as much as 25%–35%. Also, if it is summer or early fall, seeding a lawn rather than sodding will reduce your lawn costs by 40% or more.

Source: Jim Sutliff, president and the owner of Sutliff Builders, Inc., 3675 Africa Rd., Galena, OH 43201, a residential building company with $5 million in annual sales.